Politics Russia

First Edition

Politics Russia

Catherine Danks

Senior Lecturer in the Department of
History, Manchester Metropolitan University

Routledge
Taylor & Francis Group

LONDON AND NEW YORK

First published 2009 by Pearson Education Limited

Published 2013 by Routledge
2 Park Square, Milton Park, Abingdon, Oxon OX14 4RN
711 Third Avenue, New York, NY 10017, USA

Routledge is an imprint of the Taylor & Francis Group, an informa business

ISBN 13: 978-0-582-89433-4 (pbk)

British Library Cataloguing-in-Publication Data
A catalogue record for this book is available from the British Library

Library of Congress Cataloging-in-Publication Data
Danks, Catherine J., 1956–
   Politics Russia / Catherine Danks. — 1st ed.
      p. cm.
   Includes bibliographical references and index.
   ISBN 978-0-582-89433-4 (pbk. : alk. paper)   1. Russia (Federation)—Politics and
government—1991–   I. Title.
   DK510.763
   947.086—dc22
                                                                        2008048398

Typeset in 10/12.5pt Sabon by 35

Contents

For Audrey V. J. Danks

Preface

In 2000 I finished writing *Russian Politics and Society: An Introduction* for Longman-Pearson and was able to end on a cautiously optimistic note. At that time Vladimir Putin had just become president, there had been a peaceful hand-over of power and Russia looked set to continue its democratisation. Eight years on Russia now has its third post-soviet president, but while I am still optimistic about Russia's future that optimism is now a little muted. Great strides have been made under Putin and there have been some notable achievements, not least ensuring that all legislation conforms to the Constitution, the rising levels of economic growth and living standards. After the poverty and disorder of the 1990s Russians can once again have a sense of pride in their country and its achievements. On the debit side Putin's ideas such as sovereign democracy, managing democracy and strengthening the power vertical have concentrated power in the executive. President Dmitry Medvedev is Putin's hand-picked successor, chosen as a safe pair of hands to work in tandem with Putin and to continue his agenda. Agendas evolve, however, and both men are aware that there are issues that urgently need to be addressed – not least the fight against corruption, reform of the judiciary, the civil service, healthcare, education, agriculture and the diversification of the economy. It remains to be seen whether further democratisation will form part of that agenda.

This book assumes no prior knowledge of Russia and I have taken the conscious decision to avoid using jargon and social science terms as far as possible. Each chapter is self-contained but I have indicated where there are relevant links to other chapters. Suggested further reading and useful websites are indicated at the end of each chapter. The text is divided into five parts. Part 1 examines the end of the USSR and the creation of the Russian Federation; Part 2 looks at the executive and the legislature; Part 3 focuses on political ideas, parties and the representative process; Part 4 examines the policy process and reforming Russia; and Part 5 is the conclusion, looking at Russia from Yeltsin and Putin to Medvedev.

Transliteration

The transliteration system followed in the book is a modified version of the Library of Congress System. In cases where a particular spelling of a Russian name or word has come into general English usage, this spelling is used rather than the direct transliteration. So Yeltsin is used rather than El'tsin, Fyodorov rather than Federov, and the newspaper *Izvestiia* is rendered as *Izvestia*; the first names Yury, Gennady and Grigory are used rather than Yurii, Gennadii and Grigorii. Surnames ending with ii and aiai are transliterated by the more common y and aya, so Zhirinovsky rather than Zhirinovskii. Names beginning with 'Iu' or 'Ia' have been transliterated by the more common 'Yu' and 'Ya', so Iavlinskii is transliterated as Yavlinsky. Within the text soft signs have not been transliterated although they do appear in the references and transliterated words in brackets in the text. So Lebed is used rather than Lebed', Belarus rather than Belarus', *glasnost* rather than *glasnost'* and *oblast* rather than *oblast'*. As the spelling of Russian names varies in English langauge publications, the spelling employed by the text being cited is always employed, so for example Alexander Solzhenitsyn also appears as Aleksandr Solzhenitsyn.

Acknowledgements

Author's acknowledgements

This book could not have been written without the financial support of the Department of History at Manchester Metropolitan University. Thanks also go to colleagues at MMU for their support and encouragement, particularly Clive Archer, Frank Carr, Geraldine Lievesley, Philip Lloyd, Melanie Tebbutt and Louise Willmot and also to John Dumbrell of the University of Durham.

Publisher's acknowledgements

We are grateful to the following for permission to reproduce copyright material:

Chapter 1, Map of Soviet Union Administrative Divisions 1989; Courtesty of the University Libraries, University of Texas at Austin; Chapter 2, Box 2.2 from Lewin, M. *The Gorbachev Phenomenon: A Historical Interpretation* (1988) University of California Press, Berkeley, CA, 80; Chapter 3, Box 3.6 from Vladimir Putin's 'Annual Address to the Federal Assembly of the Russian Federation' 10 May 2006, Chapter 10, Box 10.3, Transcript of the Press Conference for the Russian and Foreign Media, 31 January 2006, Chapter 14, Box 14.5 Putin's 6 fundamental principles to deal with Russia's economic crisis, and Box 16.9 Vladimir Putin 'Replies to Journalists' Questions Following the Hot Line' Kremlin website 18 October 2007; www.kremlin.ru; Chapter 7, Box 7.3, Map 7.1 Administrative divisions, www.lib.utexas.edu/mapcommonwealth/russiaaddivisions.jpg also used by the author (C. Danks) in her book *Russian Politics: An Introduction* published by Pearson Education in 2001; Chapter 7, Map 7.2 from Fuller, L. (2006) 'Analysis: Are Ingushetia, North Ossetia on the verge of New Hostilities?' Radio Free Europe/Radio Liberty feature article, Chapter 8, Box 8.1 from Jeremy Bransten 'East: Postcommunist Ombudsmen Persevere Despite Obstacles' 29 November 2005, and Chapter 10, Box 10.5 from Claire Bigg (2005) 'Russia: NGOs denounce proposed status changes as move to curb their activities, 11 November. Feature article. RFE/rl Radio Liberty/Radio Free Europe; RFERL website http://www.rferl.org/. Both excerpts from http://origin.rferl.org/info/policies/146.html. Copyright © 2008. RFE/RL, Inc. Reprinted with the permission of Radio Free Europe/Radio Liberty, 1201 Connecticut Ave., N.W. Washington DC 20036; Chapter 10, Box 10.1 from www.lse.ac.uk/ccs, LSE Centre for Civil Society, The London School of Economics; Chapter 10, Box 10.2 Trust in Russia's Institutions Levada-Tsentr (2007) 'Doverie institutam vlasti' 9 April, Levada Centre website, Chapter 16, Box 16.1 from Levada-Tsentr (2007) 'Rol' B. El'stina v otsenkakh rossiian', 1 February, Levada

Centre website; and Box 16.2 from Levada-Tsentr (2007) 'Sil'nye I slabye storony: V Putin, D Medvedeve, S Ivanov Tables 1 and 2, 20 February, Levada Centre website, www.levada.ru; Chapter 10, Box 10.4 from Jamey Gambrell (2004) 'Philanthroy in Russia: New money under pressure' *Carnegie Report* 3(1) Fall, Carnegie Corporation of New York; Box 10.6 from the Washington Post, 2006 © 2006 The Washington Post, All rights reserved. Used by permission and pro- tected by the Copyright Laws of the United States; Chapter 11, Box 11.5 from Andrew Osborn (2007) 'The 20 journalists who have lost their lives in Putin's Russia' *The Independent*, 11 March; Chapter 13, Box 13.1 from CIA World Fact Book website, Central Intelligence Agency; Chapter 14, Box 14.6 from 20 Nation Poll finds strong global consensus: Support for free market system, but also more regulation of large companies', World Opinion website, www.worldpublicopinion.org; Chapter 15, Box 15.1 from UNDP *Human Development Report, 2006*, Human Development Index, Table 1 UNDP website www.undp.org/, with permission of Palgrave Macmillan; Chapter 16, Boxes 16.3 and 16.4 from 'Russia's Weakened Democratic Embrace', Pew Global Attitudes Project, 5 January 2006; Chapter 16, Box 16.6 from Andrew Wilson (2005) *Virtual Democracy: Faking Democracy in the Post Soviet World*. New Haven, CT: Yale University Press.

In some instances we have been unable to trace the owners of copyright material, and we would appreciate any information that would enable us to do so.

Picture Credits

The publisher would like to thank the following for their kind permission to repro- duce their photographs:

(Key: b-bottom; c-centre; l-left; r-right; t-top)

Corbis: Bettmann 41; Dmitry Astakhov/epa 440; Dmitry Astakhov/Ria Novosti/ Kremlin Pool/epa 122; epa 336br; Peter Turnley 151; Reuters 93, 336bl; Robert Maass 4; Sergei Chirikov/epa 238, 274, 368; Shepard Sherbell 121; Yuri Kochetkov/epa 436; Yuri Kotchetkov/epa 307; **DK Images:** 32; **Getty Images:** 210; AFP 234, 405; VLADIMIR RODIONOV/AFP 198; **Kommersant:** 326b, 326c, 327b, 327t, 328, 328t, 329b, 329cr, 329t, 329tr, 393, 393b, 394b, 394t, 395b, 395t, 396,146, 326t.

All other images © Pearson Education

Every effort has been made to trace the copyright holders and we apologise in advance for any unintentional omissions. We would be pleased to insert the appropriate acknowlegement in any subsequent edition of this publication.

List of abbreviations

BERD	European Bank for Reconstruction and Development
CCNS	Chechen Committee of National Salvation
CIS	Commonwealth of Independent States
CMEA	Comecon
COCOM	Coordinating Committee for East-West trade
CPE	centrally planned economy
CPSU	Communist Party of the Soviet Union
DPNI	Movement Against Illegal Immigration
FiGs	financial-industrial groups
FSB	Federal Security Service
FSU	Former Soviet Union
GATT	General Agreement on Tariffs and Trade
ICBM	Intercontinental Ballistic Missile
IMF	International Monetary Fund
KGB	State Security Committee
KPRF	Communist Party of the Russian Federation
NATO	North Atlantic Treaty Organisation
neo-Con	neo-conservative
NGO	Non-Governmental Organisation
NTTM	Youth Centre for Scientific and Technical Creation
OECD	Organisation for Economic Co-operation and Development
OMON	Special Purpose Detachment of Militia
OSCE	The Organisation for Security and Co-operation in Europe
OVR	Fatherland-All Russia
ROC	Russian Orthodox Church
RSFSR	Russian Soviet Federative Socialist Republic
RTSB	Russian Commodities and Raw Materials Exchange
SDI	Strategic Defence Initiative
TNC	Transnational Corporation
US and USA	United States, United States of America
USSR	Union of Soviet Socialist Republics
VTsIOM	All Russian Centre of Political Opinion Studies
WTO	World Trade Organization
WWII	World War II

Part 1

THE END OF THE USSR AND THE CREATION OF THE RUSSIAN FEDERATION

Chapter 1

Gorbachev, *perestroika* and the end of soviet socialism

Gorbachev
National identities
Yeltsin

Learning objectives

- To examine why Mikhail Gorbachev launched *perestroika*.
- To examine Gorbachev's political, economic and foreign policy reforms.
- To examine the role of national identities in the demise of the USSR.
- To examine the August 1991 coup and the end of soviet socialism.

Introduction

In March 1985 Mikhail Gorbachev became general secretary of the Communist Party of the Soviet Union (CPSU), the leader of the USSR. He launched a 'revolution from above' called *perestroika* or reconstruction, designed to revitalise soviet socialism. *Perestroika* entailed radical changes in political, economic, social and foreign policies which were supposed to be mutually complementary. 'Gorbymania' spread throughout the world so that in 1987 he was American *Time* magazine's 'Man of the Year' and in 1990 he was awarded the Nobel Peace Prize. In contrast to this adulation, within the USSR *perestroika* was condemned by ideological hardliners as the abandonment of soviet socialism and by radicals as just tinkering with an economically, politically and morally bankrupt system. The reforms rapidly gained a momentum of their own. Gorbachev lost control over his revolution as the soviet people turned it into a 'revolution from below', making increasingly radical demands that ran far ahead of Gorbachev's more modest reforms. Even some members of the soviet *nomenklatura*, such as Boris Yeltsin, started to renounce soviet socialism in favour of western-style democracy and the market. There was a hopelessly botched hard-line coup attempt in August 1991 but the reform genie could neither be put back into the bottle nor satisfied by Gorbachev's reforms. By December 1991 Gorbachev, who had set out to reform and thereby strengthen the USSR, had unwittingly overseen the demise of the soviet empire in east-central Europe (in 1989), the end of soviet socialism, and the disintegration of the USSR into 15 independent states and was himself out of office.

Box 1.1 Mikhail Gorbachev (1931–)

Gorbachev was born in Privolnoi a village in the Stavropol region of South Russia. The son of a tractor driver he joined the Communist Youth League (Komsomol) in 1945 and the CPSU in 1952. From 1950–55 he studied law at Moscow State University. On graduation Gorbachev returned to Stavropol where he worked for the Komsomol and then the CPSU staff (apparatus). In 1971 he became a full member of the CPSU Central Committee and in 1978 became the CPSU secretary for agriculture. In 1979 he became first a candidate and then in 1980 a full member of the CPSU Politburo. In 1979 Gorbachev was elected to the USSR Supreme Soviet and in 1980 to the RSFSR parliament. He was elected general secretary of the CPSU in March 1985 and was re-elected to the post in July 1990. In 1988 he was elected chair of the Supreme Soviet Presidium and in March 1990 the Congress of People's Deputies elected him the first executive president of the USSR.

Mikhail Gorbachev and Time *magazine cover.*

In August 1991 Gorbachev and his family were held under house arrest at their holiday home in Foros during an attempted coup; they were released by Yeltsin and his allies. On his return to Moscow Gorbachev found the USSR disintegrating and political developments dominated by Yeltsin. He stood in the 1996 Russian presidential elections but received only 0.5 per cent of the vote.

Gorbachev's publications include: *Perestroika,* Nottingham: Spokesman, 2nd edn, 1988; *Memoirs,* London: Bantam Books, 1997; *The August Coup: The Truth and the Lessons,* London: HarperCollins, 1991.

Useful website: Gorbachev Foundation http://www.gorby.ru/en/default.asp

Why did Gorbachev launch *perestroika*?

Gorbachev's explanation

Gorbachev advocated *perestroika* to eradicate the stagnation or *zastoi* that was the legacy of Leonid Brezhnev's long tenure as leader of the USSR from 1964 to 1982. According to Gorbachev, the soviet people had become inert and lacking in initiative, crime rates were rising, corruption was pervasive, labour indiscipline was rife, and drunkenness and alcoholism were endemic. The CPSU was itself culpable as it had lost touch with the people and had not fulfilled its constitutionally prescribed 'leading and guiding role'. Party bureaucrats, who were neither subjected to appropriate party discipline nor democratic oversight by the people and the media, had been able to reduce previous reform attempts to ineffective campaigns and empty slogans. In 1983 two future Gorbachev advisers, the economist Abel Aganbegyan and the sociologist Tatyana Zaslavskaya, produced the 'Novosibirsk Report' (Hanson, 1984) chronicling the precipitous decline of the soviet economy. They argued that the methods used by Stalin to turn the USSR from a backward agricultural country into a great industrial and military power were no longer appropriate. The centrally planned economy (CPE) and the whole soviet command-administrative system needed radical reform.

Gorbachev described *perestroika* as 'a genuine revolution' in all aspects of soviet life and as a 'thorough going renewal' (*Pravda*, 28 January 1987). This did not mean he took office with a clear strategy: although problem areas had been identified, actual solutions were slower to emerge. During 1985–6 there was a lot of discussion about the need for *perestroika* and some new slogans were adopted such as calls for 'acceleration' (*uskorenie*) in the economy, but there were few concrete achievements. Attempts to streamline the bureaucracy through the creation of new super-ministries, such as *Gosagroprom* for agriculture, in reality only added yet another layer of bureaucracy. A new policy of 'openness' or *glasnost* was introduced into the media and the arts in order to expose the scale of the USSR's problems and to persuade the people to support and participate actively in *perestroika*. Gorbachev resurrected his predecessor Andropov's anti-corruption and discipline campaigns, adding an anti-alcohol campaign. Now dubbed the mineral water secretary (*mineral'nyi sekretar'*), Gorbachev seemed to be trying to make the old system work by cleaning and sobering it up. His renewal of party-state bureaucrats or cadres, again a resurrection of Andropov's purge of corrupt and inefficient bureaucrats, also looked like the typical move of a new leader eager to demote opponents and promote allies. In 1987, spurred on by the USSR's escalating problems, Gorbachev launched his radical reforms.

The legitimacy of CPSU rule was supposed to be based upon the ideology of Marxism-Leninism, but Brezhnev had been aware that while ideological exhortations were not unimportant they were not enough to sustain the regime. He had instituted an unwritten social contract between the people and the party, according to which the people had economic security (such as guaranteed work and cheap food) and in return they were expected to be politically pliant. Not all soviet citizens were prepared to abide by this 'contract' and from the 1960s onwards dissident voices challenged the very legitimacy of the soviet system. However, writing in 1980 the dissident soviet historian Roy Medvedev cautioned that, 'The overwhelming majority of the population unquestionably sanction the government's power and show no particular wish to have a run-in with the authorities by voicing their grievances' (Medvedev, 1980: 36). When dissent did emerge the soviet state responded with harassment and force.

Gorbachev was committed to reducing the level of state coercion within the USSR and he also realised that, in the short term at least, economic *perestroika* would lead to unemployment and a fall in real incomes. *Perestroika* simultaneously broke the social contract and weakened the state's ability to put down the resulting growing discontent. Gorbachev had to develop new mechanisms to persuade the soviet people to support the regime and *perestroika*; he had to

Box 1.2 Key terms

Ideology: a set of core principles or ideas.

Marxism-Leninism: the official state ideology of the USSR drawing on the ideas of the German philosopher and economist Karl Marx (1818–1883) and Lenin (1870–1924) the leader of the Bolsheviks, whose real name was Vladimir Ilych Ulyanov. It includes the Marxist ideas that human labour determines economic value; that struggle between classes (such as workers versus the capitalists) is the motor of social change; and that history progresses through stages towards the final stage of communism in which class exploitation no longer exists and so a state is no longer required. Leninism is the application of Marx's ideas to Russian conditions and the policies advocated by Lenin; these include: the communist party as a revolutionary elite, his theory of Imperialism and concept of Peaceful Coexistence.

Useful website: Marxist Writers' Archive http://www.marxists.org/archive/

Soviet socialism: the form of socialism developed in the USSR during the 1920s and 1930s with some later modifications. Its features include a one-party state, Marxism-Leninism as the official ideology, a rejection of political pluralism, state or collective ownership of the means of production, central planning of the economy (CPE) through a series of five-year plans which were disseminated by commands down the administrative system, also known as the 'command administrative system'.

Nomenklatura: often used as shorthand for the soviet elite. The *nomenklatura* were the people occupying the most important posts in the party, state and economic bureaucracies or apparatuses. The CPSU controlled the selection of the *nomenklatura*, whose existence was well-known but its operation was shrouded in secrecy.

overcome the cynicism, suspicion and, for some, fear that the prospect of reform generated. Gorbachev believed that democratisation would foster a sense of responsibility among the people for their own and the leadership's actions, and that the soviet leadership at all levels would be accountable to the people so combating elite inefficiency, ineptitude and corruption. Gorbachev recognised that although he was the CPSU general secretary, supposedly the most powerful man in the USSR, reform entailed confronting vested interests whether in the form of workers or party-state bureaucrats (Zaslavskaya, 1988). In order to reform the economy and maintain a (reformed) soviet socialism, democratisation was imperative.

The systemic and structural problems of the soviet economy

The USSR had a centrally planned economy (CPE) with state or collective ownership of enterprises and farms. In the 1920s and 1930s the USSR was electrified, new coal mines were dug, and dams, railways, new steel mills and gigantic heavy industrial centres were constructed. The CPE proved adept at promoting this extensive economic growth by increasing the inputs of labour, energy and materials directed to these sectors. This economic system achieved growth at tremendous human and ecological costs, and created an economy that was structurally skewed towards heavy industry and mineral extraction. From the 1950s light industry, the consumer sector and agriculture received more investment but still remained hopelessly underdeveloped. By the 1950s the old stress on gigantic factories and the military rhetoric of 'storming the steel front' was no longer appropriate, but reform proved elusive.

Writing in 1966 Alec Nove, an economist at Glasgow University, argued that the USSR was experiencing a slowdown in growth because the soviet system could not cope with a mature economy, but he still anticipated substantial growth. The USSR needed to move away from its overdependence on the old smoke stack industries and to embrace the technological revolution that was sweeping the advanced capitalist economies. The CPE was less adept at promoting this intensive economic growth which required improving the quality, rather than just the quantity, of inputs. The CPE system also suffered from a lack of reliable data, rigid and unresponsive plans, and a general problem of providing incentives. The USSR needed to harness its people's skills by encouraging them to show initiative and by improving their motivation, and it also needed new managerial techniques and new technologies such as computers and electronics. By the 1970s and 1980s most commentators in the west agreed that the Soviet economy was experiencing major problems but few anticipated an economic collapse. A notable exception was the economist Igor Birman (1983, 1989; Birman and Clarke, 1985) who emigrated from the USSR in 1974 and then published extremely gloomy analyses of the soviet economy. According to the British Marxist historian Eric Hobsbawm it was already too late and that, 'Almost certainly the Soviet economy was unreformable by the 1980s. If there were real chances of reforming it in the 1960s they were sabotaged by the self-interests of a *nomenklatura* that was by this time firmly entrenched and uncontrollable. Possibly the last real chance of reform was in the years after Stalin's death' (Hobsbawm, 2005: 21).

Since the 1960s Gorbachev's predecessors had talked about reforming the CPE and restructuring the economy but had achieved little. The logic of reforming a CPE demanded the introduction of some form of decentralisation of decision making away from the State Planning Agency (Gosplan) and the ministries in Moscow. In Czechoslovakia during the 1960s, economic reforms which entailed the devolution of some limited decision-making authority had quickly spread over into popular demands for greater political freedoms. On Brezhnev's orders this 'Prague Spring' was crushed by Warsaw Pact forces in August 1968. According to the new Brezhnev doctrine, soviet states had not only the right but also the duty to intervene in any fellow socialist state in which socialism was in danger. For the Brezhnev leadership in Moscow the message was clear: loss of control over the economy could put communist party rule – and hence soviet socialism – in jeopardy and reform was dangerous. After a rather half-hearted attempt at economic reform in the 1960s, the Brezhnev leadership shelved reform and sought improved relations with the West through a policy known as détente. In the 1970s the USSR was able to

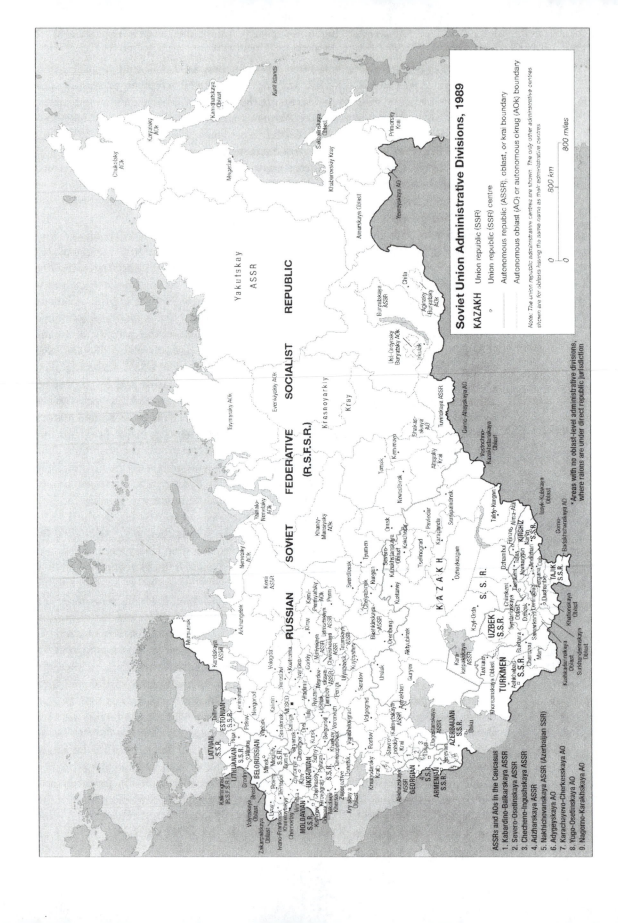

Soviet Union Administrative Divisions, 1989

KAZAKH Union republic (SSR)

○ Union republic (SSR) centre

———— Autonomous republic (ASSR), oblast, or krai boundary

– – – – Autonomous oblast (AO) or autonomous okrug (AOk) boundary

Note: The union republic administrative centres are shown. The only other administrative centres shown are for oblasts having the same name as their administrative centres

0 _____ 800 km

0 _____ 800 miles

ASSRs and AOs in the Caucasus
1. Kabardino-Balkarskaya ASSR
2. Severo-Osetinskaya ASSR
3. Checheno-Ingushskaya ASSR
4. Adzharskaya ASSR
5. Nakhichevanskaya ASSR (Azerbaijan SSR)
6. Adygeyskaya AO
7. Karachayevo-Cherkesskaya AO
8. Yugo-Osetinskaya AO
9. Nagorno-Karakhskaya AO

*Areas with no oblast-level administrative divisions, where raions are under direct republic jurisdiction

take advantage of rising world energy prices to increase their oil and gas exports; at the same time western bankers provided the USSR and its allies with credits. The USSR temporarily had the funds to buy the food, consumer goods and technology from the West that its own economy was unable to provide. The cost, however, included increasing trade dependency upon and financial indebtedness to their ideological enemies, the capitalist countries. Meanwhile the underlying need to restructure the economy and to reform the CPE remained unaddressed. Within the USSR in the 1980s Gorbachev decided that it was now too dangerous not to reform the economy and that the best hope for the success of economic reform was also to pursue simultaneous democratisation.

Soviet modernisation and the development of a civil society

The CPSU argued that its ideology of Marxism-Leninism gave it a scientific understanding of the inevitable course of historical development towards communism. To attain this goal the CPSU demanded a monopoly of political power: no organisation could exist legally without the party's permission and all structures and institutions were dominated by the party. The *nomenklatura* system was employed to ensure that key positions throughout the country were occupied by people loyal to the CPSU. Strict control of education, media censorship, propaganda and agitation campaigns, and the restriction of travel abroad and contacts with foreigners were all used to instil the correctness of the CPSU worldview among the soviet 'masses'. By the 1980s the soviet people had long since ceased to be 'the masses' that the early soviet leaders spoke about after gaining power in 1917. Through party-led modernisation the USSR had undergone major social and educational changes, but political institutions had not changed. As Boris Kagarlitsky (1990: 284) points out, while the Brezhnev period was a time of economic and political stagnation, 'In the 1970s an industrial society was definitely formed in our country, the process of urbanization was completed and a new generation grew up shaped by the conditions of Europeanized city life'.

At 54 Gorbachev was young and healthy for a CPSU general secretary. He was a member of what in the USSR was called the sixties generation. This generation came to political maturity after the death of Stalin and so had not been scarred by the experience of Stalinist repression and terror. They had also benefited from the social mobility and educational opportunities opened up by soviet rule and the somewhat freer political atmosphere of the 1960s. At Moscow University Gorbachev had befriended the Czech communist Zdeněk Mlynář (1930–1997) who was to be one of the leaders of the ill-fated Prague Spring. The 1960s' reform debates within the USSR and the soviet bloc were part of the broader education of a new generation. Throughout the country people were better educated than their parents; they looked around themselves and could see the yawning void between the propaganda images of soviet socialism and reality.

Gorbachev and *perestroika* as a conjuncture of factors

The name of Gorbachev and *perestroika* are inextricably linked, but *perestroika* could not have been the idea or work of one man and he had to have support in the party Politburo to become the CPSU General Secretary. One way of explaining both the rise of Gorbachev and the introduction of *perestroika* is to argue that it was the result of a particular conjuncture of factors in the mid-1980s, including generational change, growing corruption, economic decline and the failure of Andropov's reforms of 1982–84 to reverse the country's decline. Gorbachev was in the right place at the right time, but was he the right man? Archie Brown (1997), who was the first westerner to tip Gorbachev as a possible future leader, and Robert Skidelsky (1995) stress the impact of the 'Gorbachev factor' on both the introduction and the course of the reform process. The need for reform and the arrival of a pro-reform leader, however, did not mean that the reform enjoyed universal or even wide support, or that reform would necessarily be successful at reinvigorating soviet socialism. For adherents of a totalitarian and/or essentialist model of the USSR (see Chapter 2) soviet socialism was fatally flawed and would ultimately fail, whatever reforms were tried. For revisionists (see Chapter 2) who see soviet socialism as enjoying popular support and having an ability to adapt to change, the key to soviet socialism's survival was Gorbachev's ability to devise and implement an appropriate reform programme.

Democratisation and openness

Demokratizatsiia and *glasnost*

Democratisation (*demokratizatsiia*) and *glasnost* involved showing respect for and trust in the people. Previous soviet leaders had proclaimed the unanimity of the soviet people and the CPSU and western sovietologists' suggestions that there was a plurality of opinions in the USSR had been condemned as outrageous slurs. According to a CPSU slogan, 'The party and the people are united'. In a profound move away from this thinking Gorbachev argued that the USSR enjoyed a 'socialist pluralism', and that a plurality of opinions and lively debate under the general leadership of the CPSU would be positive assets. Gorbachev's dilemma was that he believed in the rightness of the CPSU's constitutional monopoly of power and the need for the CPSU to exercise its 'leading and guiding role' as embodied in Article 6 of the 1977 Constitution. At the same time he also recognised that the party had not always provided the USSR with adequate leadership and was responsible for much of the country's stagnation; so it appeared that, without democratisation, elements within the CPSU would continue to obstruct reform. Democratisation entailed encouraging political participation free from direct party control, in order to develop and channel the people's initiative and sense of responsibility towards the reform of soviet socialism, while simultaneously subjecting party officials (or cadres) to greater public scrutiny.

The freer political environment in fact encouraged people to set up their own organisations without CPSU permission. These organisations were called informals (*neformaly*) because they initially had no legal status. Most were not overtly political: they ranged from music-cultural groups, through ecological and religious-philosophical groups, to lobby groups for Afghan war veterans. The informals with overt political platforms included the Club for Social Initiatives set up in the autumn of 1989 with the stated aim of transforming *perestroika* from 'reform from above' into 'practice from below'. Another political informal called Democracy and Humanism opposed soviet socialism, and the Trust group advocated a multi-party system. Nationalist and secessionist sentiments were well-represented among the informals by groups such as the Lithuanian Freedom League and the Karabakh Committee. The rapid development of these informals meant that the authority and legitimacy of the CPSU was now being challenged by would-be political parties. Once the electoral system was reformed and restructured the informals were able to put forward their own candidates and so the CPSU lost its domination over the composition of the USSR's representative bodies, the soviets.

Glasnost saw a widening of the parameters of what could be reported, represented and debated in the media and the arts. Like democratisation *glasnost* was intended to persuade the people to work for *perestroika* while also providing the leadership with additional sources of information and ideas from the people themselves. Before *glasnost* the soviet media had been so censored and bore so little resemblance to the realities of life in the USSR that they had lost credibility. The media were, therefore, failing in their basic function of educating and mobilising the soviet people to support the CPSU's policies and goals. In adopting *glasnost* Gorbachev was attempting to improve the media's credibility, to demonstrate his trust in the soviet people, and to educate and mobilise the soviet people to support and actively work for *perestroika*. *Glasnost* did not mean an end to censorship and anti-reformers continued to dominate the local media and national newspapers such as *Sovetskaia Rossiia*. A new media law in August 1990 enabled the informals to found their own publications and although censorship still existed it became increasingly difficult to enforce. By the end of 1990 the CPSU's domination of the USSR's political life and the media was effectively over.

The institutionalisation of democracy and the separation of powers

Gorbachev believed that a much sharper distinction needed to be made between the functions of the CPSU and the state. The CPSU still oversaw the activities of every institution within the USSR, party membership was a prerequisite of a good career, and through the *nomenklatura* system the CPSU controlled key appointments throughout the country. Gorbachev also believed that the CPSU would be better able to perform its leadership role if it were not embroiled in day-to-day governance. In June 1987 the USSR had its first multi-candidate elections since the 1930s. Only 5 per cent of the local soviet (council) seats up for election that year had more than one candidate, but despite this modest figure the fact that the CPSU could no longer entirely control the outcome of elections was a major change.

At the 19th Party Conference in 1988 Gorbachev announced further radical changes that initiated moves towards a rudimentary separation of executive, legislative and judicial powers. Gorbachev received the Conference's approval for his plan to reform the communist party-dominated and largely powerless soviet parliament. Under the new structure a 2,000 (later 2,250) member Congress of People's Deputies elected 450 (later 542) members to a new two-chamber Supreme Soviet. In formal terms the Congress was the country's highest legislative body, but as it met only once a year its main function was to elect and ratify the actions of the Supreme Soviet. The soviet people had to wait until March 1989 before they had the opportunity to vote for deputies to the Congress of People's Deputies. Most seats in the 1989 Congress elections were contested by more than one candidate; although the CPSU was still the only legal political party at this time, the informals were very active in putting candidates forward.

The new Congress's first session was televised and the soviet people were presented not with the usual carefully scripted speeches but with politicians arguing and Gorbachev being publicly harangued by radicals and conservatives alike. Yegor Ligachev emerged as Gorbachev's leading conservative, communist opponent. Ligachev had initially welcomed reform and did not favour a return to Brezhnevite stagnation and corruption, but he was deeply troubled by the increasing chaos throughout the USSR and the loss of party control. In late 1990 Ligachev joined *Soiuz* (Union), a conservative organisation founded in March 1989 to represent the powerful military-industrial complex and ethnic Russians living outside the Russian republic (RSFSR) of the USSR. Although the majority of the Congress deputies were anti-reform, the Inter-Regional Group co-chaired by Boris Yeltsin and Andrei Sakharov served as an umbrella organisation for pro-reform and radical deputies who ranged from the reforming wing of the CPSU to non-CPSU advocates of western-style democracy and capitalism.

The RSFSR parliament was dominated by the Inter-Regional Group's sister organisation, Democratic Russia. The Inter-Regional Group and Democratic Russia favoured Shatalin and Yavlinsky's '500-Day Programme' of radical economic marketisation against Prime Minister Nikolai Ryzhkov's more cautious approach. They also advocated the transformation of the USSR into a confederation and the abolition of all central administrative and legislative structures including Ryzhkov's government, the Congress of People's Deputies and the USSR Supreme Soviet. Democratisation, far from encouraging a pro-*perestroika* consensus, revealed the ever-increasing plurality of opinion within the USSR which challenged the very legitimacy and authority of the USSR and the CPSU.

A further step towards a separation of powers came in January 1990 with the establishment of the Committee for Constitutional Supervision. For the first time in soviet history there was now an institution that could declare a law unconstitutional. The Committee's powers were limited: for example, it could not annul but only suspend an unconstitutional law for three months. The 15 union republics, fearful that the Committee would be used by Moscow to frustrate the work of republican legislatures (parliaments), managed to restrict the Committee's sphere of competence to all-union legislation. As a result the committee was unable to arbitrate between the rival claims of all-union and republican legislation during the 'Law Wars' of 1990–91. In September 1990 the Committee ruled that President

Gorbachev's April 1990 decree transferring control of demonstrations and public events in Moscow from the city soviet to the USSR Council of Ministers was unconstitutional. This seemingly modest decision established that the soviet head of state was no longer above the law – a major step in soviet democratisation.

The USSR: national versus soviet identities

The USSR: a soviet federation or a Russian empire?

Lenin had described the Imperial Russian Empire as a prison house of nationalities and believed that, after the Bolshevik Revolution, nationality would become irrelevant as proletarian internationalism would provide a firm foundation for the new soviet state. In the 1920s the Bolsheviks wanted to create a soviet identity but feared that the Russians would reassert their role as the imperial people and come to dominate the new state. The Bolsheviks, therefore, chose to recognise the multinational composition of their country by creating a state structure founded on nationality-based administrative areas. The 15 union republics comprising the USSR were named after their dominant nationality but none of the republics were nationally homogeneous. The republics were subdivided into autonomous republics, territories (*krais*), areas (*okrugs*) and provinces (*oblasts*). In order to counter possible Russian domination, the Bolsheviks also adopted a policy of nativisation (*korenizatsiia*) which promoted the development of local elites. As education expanded in the 1920s it was conducted in local languages which helped to foster the USSR's national identities. Before Gorbachev came to office few commentators with notable exceptions such as Hélène Carrère D'Encausse (1979) and Ronald Suny, believed that nationalism posed a danger to the cohesion of the USSR. However, Suny for example argued that 'the erosion of Marxist ideology within the Soviet Union has cleared the way for its replacement by patriotism and nationalism' (1980: 222). Soviet internal passports (identity cards) recorded each person's twin identities: first their citizenship of the USSR (that is, their soviet identity) and second their nationality. As allegiance to soviet socialism and soviet identity weakened during Gorbachev's reforms, it was the second identity – nationality – which provided the mobilising factor and institutional basis for challenging the legitimacy of the soviet state to rule throughout the USSR.

Russians within the USSR

The Gorbachev period also witnessed a rapid development of Russian nationalist sentiments. Many Russians believed that Russian national interests had been damaged within the USSR. Stalin, the commissar (minister) for nationalities in the aftermath of the 1917 revolution, had called the Russians the big brothers and the other nationalities the little brothers. To the little brothers the Russians had rapidly returned as the imperial nationality, dominating key positions throughout the USSR. To the USSR's non-Russians soviet culture, identity and interests were in fact

Russian. For their part, many Russians viewed sovietisation as a loss of their Russian identity and a denial of their true culture and history. While the other republics had their own communist parties, broadcasting services, academies of science and encyclopaedias, the Russians only had the all-union organisations not specifically Russian bodies.

There was a very real sense that Russia was being economically, culturally and socially damaged by remaining in the USSR. The central planning system meant that the RSFSR gave the other republics a net subsidy of nearly 67 million roubles a year. In a bad deal for the RSFSR, it transferred its under-priced energy to the other republics in return for overpriced consumer goods. The republics of Kyrgyzstan, Turkmenistan and Uzbekistan also provided net subsidies to the other republics but these were only worth 0.2, 0.4 and 0.5 billion roubles respectively (Steele, 1992: 19). In 1989 28 Russian nationalist deputies to the Supreme Soviet formed a parliamentary caucus to fight what they called the 'reverse discrimination' by the USSR's other nationalities against the Russians. They opposed the use of Russia's natural resources to subsidise the other republics and deplored the fact that ethnic Russians were now becoming a minority in the Soviet Union because of the higher birth rates in the Islamic republics of central Asia. Yeltsin as leader of the RSFSR called on the Russians to emancipate themselves from the USSR, to pursue a policy of 'Russia first' and to establish their own independent Russian state.

The nationalities issue, the soviet state and Law Wars

The 1977 Constitution described the Union of Soviet Socialist Republics as a unitary federal multinational state, formed as a result of the free self-determination of nations and the voluntary union of equal soviet socialist republics. In reality the 15 union republics were not free to leave the USSR and establish independent nation-states. Within the USSR any manifestation of nationalism was condemned as bourgeois and reactionary. However, in a large multi-ethnic empire in which potentially explosive secessionist sentiments were lying under the surface (Lapidus, 1989) democratisation inevitably led to calls for independence. The period 1989–91 saw the rise of nationalism, separatist movements and ethnic unrest throughout the USSR, which both reflected and contributed to the weakening of the soviet state. The collapse of communist party rule in east-central Europe in 1989 also emboldened some soviet citizens to imagine the end of CPSU rule and the soviet state. In the Baltic republics (Estonia, Latvia and Lithuania) pro-*perestroika* local communist party leaders, such as Algirdas Brazauskas in Lithuania, even joined national fronts in an attempt to harness national aspirations to Gorbachev's reforms and the maintenance of the Soviet Union, but such moves were overtaken by calls for full independence by nationalist politicians. Some nationalist politicians were democrats and others were ambitious power seekers taking advantage of Moscow's weakness by playing a nationalist-populist card. Electoral reform enabled the soviet peoples to elect nationalist deputies to their republican parliaments. These parliaments now had the authority and legitimacy of democratically elected bodies and one by one, led by the Baltic republics, they started to pass their own legislation which was often at variance with all-union legislation and to declare their independence. The 'Law Wars' between the all-union laws passed by Moscow and laws passed by the individual republican parliaments had begun.

Economic *perestroika*

Tackling the systemic problems

Successive CPSU leaders believed that the party's direction of the CPE was vital to their ability to control the country's development. In contrast Gorbachev tried to distance the CPSU from the day-to-day running of the economy. The creation of super-ministries with the danger of even greater centralisation was balanced by the devolution of some decision-making authority to the ministries in each of the 15 union republics. The pervasive problem of poor quality production was similarly addressed by a combination of centralising and decentralising measures. A new state committee called *Gospriemka* was set up to monitor and enforce production quality standards. The 1987 Law on State Enterprises gave enterprises greater autonomy but also subjected them to the USSR's still limited market forces. The law began the move away from central plan directives to a less comprehensive system of state orders (*zakazy*). According to the new principle of self-financing (*khozraschet*), enterprises were to be subjected to the 'discipline' of the market. This entailed an end to automatic state subsidies and enterprises now had to cover their own costs or risk bankruptcy. Such moves scandalised the USSR's ideological hardliners who thought a central plan embodied rational decision making in contrast to the anarchy and irrationality of the market. Terms such as market, profit and bankruptcy, and the idea that unemployment could be necessary to improve efficiency and end overstaffing were alien to soviet economic thinking.

In order to complement increased enterprise decision-making authority, changes were also tentatively introduced into their management. Enterprises were now to operate on the basis of self-management (*samoupravlenie*) with managers elected by the workforce. Soviet workers were generally sceptical about the purpose of these elections and did not show much interest in them. Gorbachev also called upon trade unions to act independently of management and to champion their members' interests, but they did not have the right to prevent the closure of bankrupt enterprises. In 1990 trade unions became supposedly independent organisations rather than bodies controlled by local party committees and they also now enjoyed full financial autonomy. The official trade unions were slow to adapt to this new status and function, and soviet workers began to establish new independent trade unions to protect themselves during this time of rising unemployment and falling real wages. A very basic problem with economic *perestroika* was that it created an incoherent hybrid of a CPE and a market economy. The sequencing of the various components of economic reform was out of kilter. For example, enterprises could not be self-financing if they could not set their own prices, reflecting the true cost of production. However, price reform was constantly delayed because it was feared that price rises would fuel inflation and social discontent so undermining *perestroika*. The result was that certain basic goods such as matches, soap and toothpaste disappeared from the shops because enterprises could not 'afford' to make them.

Co-operatives: private enterprise, popular resentment and crime

The May 1988 Law on Co-operatives gave co-operatives equal rights with state sector enterprises. Prime Minister Ryzhkov denied that the law marked a retreat from socialism and instead stressed co-operatives' potential positive contribution to the soviet economy. Co-operatives were heralded as small and medium-sized enterprises that would be flexible and responsive to the market in contrast to the gigantic state enterprises. Most co-operatives were established in the consumer goods and services sectors (cafes, hairdressing salons, house and car repair services and medical services) rather than in small-scale manufacturing. The co-operatives were not universally popular as their prices were too high for most soviet citizens; their very existence highlighted the poor state provision of goods and services and the ability of the soviet elite to use their personal spending power to bypass the USSR's shortages. The co-operatives were also popularly associated with crime and corruption. Before co-operatives were legalised there had been a thriving illegal 'second' economy in goods and services and this image of illegality stuck. Co-operatives could also make quick profits by buying commodities at fixed state prices and then selling them on with enormous unearned mark-ups. In order to acquire premises, materials and the various licenses and permissions needed to operate, the co-operatives became enmeshed with local bureaucrats in a web of corruption. Co-operatives were also vulnerable to the predation of criminal gangs and protection rackets.

Agriculture: feeding the people

The USSR's inability to feed its people presented Gorbachev with a particularly intractable problem. Previous agricultural reforms had concentrated on bringing more land under cultivation and using fertilisers to increase production, but they did not touch the collectivised ownership and administration of soviet agriculture. The soviet peasants were allowed to work, but crucially not to own, small private plots which were much more productive per hectare than collective land. The peasants could sell the produce from these plots at peasant markets for personal profit and so had a material incentive to produce as much as possible. For Gorbachev the problem was how to provide the peasantry with the same material incentive to produce more without taking the ideologically unacceptable step of introducing the private ownership of land. At the 19th Party Conference Gorbachev talked of 'restoring sovereignty' to the peasantry, of making them the 'real master of the land'. The solution adopted in mid-1988 was to permit peasants to lease land for up to 50 years and then to work the land as independent farmers. This was an ideological sleight of hand which side-stepped land privatisation but which could lead to effective de-collectivisation.

The reform was frustrated by the local agricultural bureaucracies such as the party and soviet bureaucrats, collective and state farm managers and agronomists, who all had a vested interest in maintaining the old system. Peasants were only offered unattractive short-term leases; there were also fertiliser shortages and the farm machinery available was expensive and only suitable for large-scale collective farms rather than small family farms. The poorly developed rural infrastructure was another disincentive to abandon the admittedly minimal security of the collective and state farms. In 1991 soviet food shortages were worse than they had been in 1985, land leasing had not taken off, and most collective and state farms were bankrupt and still dependent on state subsidies to survive.

Opening up to the world economy

An important corollary of domestic economic reform was the further opening up of the soviet economy to the world economy. Historically all foreign trade had been conducted through the USSR Ministry of Foreign Trade but in 1986 the ministry lost this monopoly. Other ministries and some enterprises were empowered to deal directly with foreign companies and they could also keep their hard currency earnings. In 1987 joint venture enterprises between soviet and foreign partners were legalised. It was anticipated that much-needed foreign technology, know-how and investment would come into the USSR through these joint ventures. However, joint ventures were so hemmed in by restrictions on ownership, taxation and the repatriation of profits from the USSR, that they were not terribly attractive to foreign investors. The USSR also began moves to join such capitalist institutions such as the General Agreement on Tariffs and Trade (GATT), the World Bank and the International Monetary Fund (IMF); and discussions about moving towards rouble convertibility were also initiated. Opening the soviet economy to the global capitalist economy was ideologically extremely contentious. For conservatives it was tantamount to throwing away the gains of the 1917 Bolshevik Revolution by letting the capitalists into the USSR and subjecting the USSR to the vagaries of capitalism. For reformist socialists such as Boris Kagarlitsky such moves risked the 'Third Worldization' of the USSR (Kagarlitsky, 1989).

The 'new thinking' on foreign policy

From superpower confrontation to interdependence

Gorbachev's domestic reforms were complemented by a new thinking (*novoe myshlenie*) on foreign and security policies. Since the end of World War II soviet thinking had been dominated by the cold war struggle with their ideological enemy the USA. In contrast the new thinking stressed not this struggle but the concept of interdependence (*vzaimozavimost'*) borrowed from western social science literature. Interdependence means that a country's security is no longer narrowly defined as solely a military issue, but that it also has economic, political and ecological aspects.

Recognition of interdependence stresses countries' shared concerns and interests rather than what divides them. Gorbachev believed that abandoning the cold war adversarial approach to foreign policy would produce dividends not just for the USSR's security but also for domestic reform. Improved relations would mean that the USSR could end the spiralling arms race, reduce its defence spending and transfer precious resources to the rest of the economy. Access to western credits, technology, know-how and increased external trade would also boost economic *perestroika*. In contrast to the muddle of domestic reforms Gorbachev proved adept at international diplomacy and quickly established a good working relationship with President Ronald Reagan.

Box 1.3 Key terms

Brezhnev doctrine: a doctrine of limited sovereignty enunciated by Leonid Brezhnev after the 1968 invasion of Czechoslovakia.

Common European Home: part of Gorbachev's new thinking on foreign policy that stressed the unity of Europe and the need to overcome its artificial division into the pro-American West and the pro-Soviet East, divided by the Iron Curtain.

Gorbachev doctrine: a term coined by the western media for Gorbachev's new foreign policy initiatives.

Sovereignty: the concept that within a defined area (usually a country) the state or government exercises supreme and exclusive political and legal authority, free from external influence or control.

The Common European Home, from Brezhnev to Sinatra doctrines

The division of Europe into two blocs led by the USA and USSR was a key feature of the cold war. The soviet satellite countries of east-central Europe served as a buffer zone between the USSR and capitalist Europe. From 1956 the Warsaw Treaty Organisation coordinated the eastern bloc's military activities and soviet troops were stationed throughout the empire. Economically the soviet bloc was united through the Council for Mutual Economic Assistance (CMEA or Comecon) founded in 1949. The CMEA achieved neither the hoped-for soviet bloc autarchy (self-sufficiency) nor the integration of national economic plans. The empire was subsidised by soviet natural resources, particularly oil, which were supplied at well below world prices; in return these countries exported their best quality goods to the West to earn hard currency and supplied the USSR with their shoddier products. The empire was an enormous financial drain on the USSR, whose own interests lay in increasing their energy export earnings in order to pay for technology imports from the capitalist West.

The new stress on global interdependence led the USSR to move away from its cold war-inspired fixation on relations with the USA and to re-examine its relations with other countries, including Europe as a whole. Gorbachev called for an end to the division of Europe and advocated a Common European Home of all European countries regardless of their political orientation. Gorbachev argued that Europe shared a common cultural heritage and common interests across a range of issues. These issues included developing economic ties, improving communications networks and exchanging information and skills. The Chernobyl nuclear disaster in 1986 highlighted the shared need to combat environmental pollution. Gorbachev also argued that Europeans, East and West, needed to develop a shared military security system. The USA was sceptical of the USSR's motivation, seeing these moves as a device to break the Atlantic alliance between the USA and western Europe and ultimately to destroy the North Atlantic Treaty Organisation (NATO). Nevertheless, the USSR now sought improved relations with the European Community (EC) which it had previously reviled as the economic arm of NATO. This led to a declaration of mutual recognition signed in June 1988 and in 1991 to the exchange of permanent missions between Moscow and Brussels.

In another innovative move Gorbachev abandoned the Brezhnev doctrine in favour of what became known as the Sinatra doctrine. The Brezhnev doctrine had been proclaimed in 1969 to justify the crushing of the Prague Spring, which was depicted as a threat to socialism. Under the Sinatra doctrine countries were now free to declare 'I did it my way', in the words of the song, without fear of outside intervention. Under Gorbachev the USSR was now the leading advocate and exponent of reform within the soviet bloc. Gorbachev made it clear that he would prefer Moscow's allies to reform but that he did not propose to intervene to either force reform or to shore up unpopular anti-reform leaderships. Then in December 1988 Gorbachev announced to the United Nations (UN) General Assembly his plan for the unilateral withdrawal of 500,000 soviet troops and 10,000 tanks from the USSR's east-central European empire. Without the threat of soviet intervention first Hungary then Poland, East Germany, Bulgaria and Czechoslovakia left the soviet bloc. The rapidity and peacefulness of the ending of communist party rule in Europe encouraged nationalists and reformers in the USSR to believe that they too could end Moscow's domination.

Marshall Plan for the USSR?

In the aftermath of World War II the USA had provided the war-damaged countries of western Europe with economic aid known as Marshall Aid, in order to finance economic reconstruction and to counter the feared communist expansionism. Gorbachev believed that western economic aid was vital to soviet economic reform and would be tangible proof that opening up to the West had brought economic and political dividends. In the spring of 1990 the leaders of the seven leading capitalist countries (the G7) began to talk about the need for a new Marshall Plan to encourage democracy and the transition to a market economy in the USSR. In 1991 Yeltsin's economic adviser Grigory Yavlinsky joined a new group based at Harvard University that included the political scientists Graham Allison and Robert Blackwell and the economists Jeffrey Sachs and Jeffrey Fischer (see Allison and Blackwell, 1991; Sachs, 1992). The Harvard group worked on an economic reform programme for the USSR which they believed had to be supported by western economic aid. This was to be the 'grand bargain' between the USSR and the West, which was also called the 'window of opportunity' and in Russian '*shans na soglasie*' or 'opportunity for agreement'. There were however important differences within the Harvard group, particularly about the appropriate level of western economic aid. While Jeffrey Sachs stressed that the West must commit itself to provide annual financial support for reform of around US$30–50 billion for five years, Robert Blackwell and Graham Allison was must more sceptical about the wisdom of the West making such a commitment. The divergence of opinion within the Harvard group typified the diverging and wavering opinions within the G7. The German Chancellor Helmut Kohl and the French President François Mitterrand were inclined to help Gorbachev in order to encourage reform, while the American President George H. W. Bush and the British Prime Minister John Major favoured aid only once reforms had been implemented.

The Harvard group proposed a 'grand bargain' whereby the West would provide US$45–60 billion in aid over three years to strengthen Gorbachev's authority and push through the USSR's transition to a market economy (see Allison and Blackwell, 1991; Sachs, 1992). In return the West was to gain military concessions and influence over soviet foreign and domestic policies. However, western leaders became increasingly alarmed by rumours of an impending hardline coup in the winter of 1990–91 and were troubled by the lack of a consistent approach to economic reform. In July 1990 Gorbachev and Yeltsin had agreed to establish a working group whose task was to elaborate plans for fundamental economic reform. The group was led by Stanislav Shatalin, who was an academician and a member of Gorbachev's Presidential Council, and Grigory Yavlinsky. The group produced a plan for rapid marketisation of the soviet economy which became known as the '500-day plan', after the time period they believed was necessary to implement their radical changes. Gorbachev, however, dropped this Shatalin–Yavlinsky plan in favour of a much less radical reform programme devised by Prime Minister Ryzhkov and his deputy for economic reform, Leonid Abalkin. The 'grand bargain' had been devised to support rapid marketisation; once this was dropped the bargain's foundations looked distinctly shaky. Talk of a grand bargain was, however, overtaken by the August 1991 coup and the demise of soviet socialism.

Authoritarianism versus disintegration, 1990–91

Who governs?

By 1990 the USSR was in turmoil and rapidly fragmenting. The economy was in chaos, there was a huge budgetary deficit, unemployment was rising, workers were on strike, real incomes were falling and the consumer situation was worse than in 1985. Politically, democratisation combined with aspirations for national self-determination led the republics to declare their sovereignty, so that the Union itself seemed on the verge of disintegration. Democratisation and decentralisation of the economy encouraged not only the union republics but also the regions, provinces and cities to lay claim to the ownership of state assets and to make their own policies. Moscow itself was home to two contending power centres: Yeltsin, who had been the chair of the Russian parliament since May 1990, confronted Gorbachev, who was the president of the USSR. Confrontation and rivalry between Gorbachev and Yeltsin would prove to be a key factor in the final collapse of the USSR. In 1986 Gorbachev had brought Yeltsin from Sverdlovsk to Moscow to serve as the city's first party secretary. He was charged with cleaning up the notoriously corrupt capital, but was spectacularly and humiliatingly sacked the following year by Gorbachev. From then on the two men shared a deep and very personal animosity which made it impossible for them to work together or to compromise. Yeltsin campaigned in the RSFSR's first ever presidential elections in 1991 using the slogan 'Russia first', so harnessing Russian nationalism to democratisation and marketisation, and championing greater autonomy from the soviet state for the Russian republic. The Russian republic stood at the very core of the soviet state structure; without Russia it was impossible to conceive of the USSR's continued existence. Whilst Gorbachev was backtracking over reform for the USSR during the winter of 1990–91, the parliaments within the union republics passed ever more radical legislation. Given the increasing turmoil of the time very little was actually implemented but a very basic question for any political system, 'Who governs?' – or more emotively, 'Is anybody governing?' – remained unanswered.

Box 1.4 The results of Russia's first presidential elections, 12 June 1991

Candidate's name	Percentage of votes in favour
Boris Yeltsin	57.3
Nikolai Ryzhkov	16.8
Vladimir Zhirinovsky	7.8
Aman Tuleev	6.8
Albert Makashov	3.7
Vadim Bakatin	3.4
Invalid votes	4.1
Turnout	74.7

Source: The Central Electoral Commission of the Russian Federation, http://www.cikrf.ru/m_menu_i.htm

---

Gorbachev had feared that the CPSU Central Committee might unite to oust him from the post of CPSU general secretary and end his reforms. The logic of democratisation's transfer of power and authority from the CPSU to the soviets and government was an end to the CPSU's constitutional monopoly of power, which was finally announced in February 1990. Gorbachev therefore sought simultaneously to secure his own power base and to continue reform by creating a new post of executive president of the USSR. In a move of supreme irony for a would-be democrat, Gorbachev insisted that he be allowed to stand unopposed and so was duly elected USSR president in March 1990. Although in institutional terms Gorbachev appeared more powerful than even Stalin, in reality he was growing weaker and less effective. His power and authority were being challenged by the union republics and he was increasingly powerless to stop the drift and chaos. At the same time the USSR's new democratic institutions, such as the Congress of People's Deputies, were proving unable to mediate the conflicts that now rent the country; indeed, they seemed to exacerbate them.

Was simultaneous economic and political reform impossible?

The task of designing and implementing a reform programme for a country the size of the USSR in which the state sought to control all political, economic, social and cultural institutions is immense. An important overarching question concerns the relationship between economic reform (marketisation) and democratisation. Democratisation encouraged centrifugal forces such as nationalism, eroded the integrative role of the CPSU, and transformed the dynamics of the USSR's central political institutions in a way that undermined the country's cohesion and the ability to implement reform policies. Gorbachev could have followed the route of the Chinese Communist Party which, in the 1970s and 1980s under Deng Xiao-Ping, introduced gradual marketisation particularly in agriculture, encouraged foreign investment and trade, and maintained some state industries while simultaneously clamping down on any political dissent and resisting all calls for democratisation. In 1989 during Gorbachev's visit to China, pro-democracy demonstrators in

---

Box 1.5 Was simultaneous economic and political reform impossible?

Professor Breslauer considered this question:

It is quite likely that simultaneous democratization and marketization of a Leninist polity and a militarized command economy set within a huge multi-national empire at a time of economic depression, labor unrest, and both eth-nic and ecological militancy is an impossible task. Indeed, even accomplishing the first two elements of this equation without the additional qualifications would be historically unprecedented. If this vision is intrinsically impossible to achieve in the Soviet context, then Gorbachev can hardly be faulted for failing to achieve the impossible. He can, however, perhaps be faulted as quixotic for believing (if he did) that he could, and for trying to do so.

Source: George W. Breslauer (1990) 'Evaluating Gorbachev as Leader', *Soviet Economy*, 5 (4), October–December, 302. Professor Breslauer is a political scientist and chair of the Center for Slavic and East European Studies at the University of California at Berkeley

perestroika

Beijing taunted the Chinese leadership with chants of 'Gorbachev is watching you'. The Chinese communists sent tanks to Tiannanmen Square literally to crush the demonstrators. Gorbachev rejected the Chinese model for the USSR with good reason: although both countries were one-party communist states, the USSR had a much higher level of industrial development and a more urbanised and better educated population than China (see Johnson, 1994). Before Gorbachev became general secretary, the USSR had already attempted economic reform without democratisation, but the reforms did not deliver economic dividends. Gorbachev also rejected the Chinese model because he wanted to reduce rather than increase coercion and because he believed that democratisation was a desirable goal.

Calls for a state of emergency: to either halt or secure reform?

During the winter of 1990–91 Gorbachev came under increasing pressure from CPSU conservatives to declare a state of emergency and to halt reform. In July 1991 the conservative newspaper *Sovetskaia Rossiia* printed a letter from 12 leading figures, including two of the eventual August coup conspirators, Alexander Tizyakov and Vasily Starodubtsev. The letter, entitled 'A Word to the People', called for the declaration of a state of emergency. Even political analysts such as Andranik Migranyan, who favoured market reforms and democratisation, thought that Gorbachev had made a fateful error in trying to pursue simultaneous marketisation and democratisation. In 1990 Migranyan called on Gorbachev to declare martial law in order to push through radical economic reform and suppress the inevitable ensuing labour unrest. According to Migranyan only once the economy had been reformed and stabilised would it be safe to attempt democratisation (Migranyan, 1990).

Gorbachev was now stranded in the rapidly emptying middle ground of soviet politics: too conservative for the radicals and too radical for the conservatives. In June 1990 at the founding of the Russian Communist Party (KPRF) Gorbachev was accused of weakening the USSR through the loss of its east-central European empire, subservience to the West and the introduction of capitalism. In December 1990 Gorbachev's long-time ally Eduard Shevardnadze resigned as foreign minister, warning of the danger of a hardline coup. Abandoned by the radicals, Gorbachev made concessions to the conservatives in appointments and policies. The radical '500-day plan' for the economy was abandoned in favour of the Ryzhkov-Abalkin plan. The conservative Leonid Kravchenko was appointed head of the central television network, which led to the cancellation and postponement of investigative programmes such as *Vzgliad* (View) and *TSN*. In January 1991 the independent news agency Interfax was closed and its assets seized by the state. Gorbachev made these concessions to the conservatives but he did resist demands for a state of emergency. Crucially, this meant that the first direct elections for the presidency of Russia went ahead on 13 June 1991, so securing Yeltsin's power base (Kaiser, 1991). It also meant that in April 1991 Gorbachev went ahead with the 'nine-plus-one' meetings with the union republics to negotiate a new union treaty rather than trying to maintain the USSR by force.

The armed forces and the security services: for or against reform?

At a time of turmoil the allegiance of the armed forces and security forces (the KGB) can be decisive. Gorbachev was commander-in-chief of the armed forces, but as political authority was fragmenting where should – and did – the allegiance of the armed forces and the KGB lie? During *perestroika* the armed forces and the KGB had seen dramatic changes in their status and role. For decades their strength and loyalty to the CPSU were seen as vital to the survival of the USSR and to world communism. Now the reformers within the CPSU seemed to be destroying what they had worked so hard to preserve. Gorbachev had thrown away the USSR's buffer zone in Europe, withdrawn troops from Afghanistan, introduced arms control and troop reductions, and cut defence spending. Under *glasnost* the media subjected the armed forces to unprecedented scrutiny, revealing an unflattering picture of corruption, crime, ethnic strife, drug and alcohol abuse and bullying (*dedovshchina*). On the rising tide of nationalism politicians, particularly in the Baltic republics, supported young men's refusal to answer their call-up. Army officers, used to a high standard of living and status, were returning home from the former Warsaw Pact countries to live with their families in army barracks and even tents.

The political spectrum within the USSR was also reflected within the armed forces and the KGB. Support for *perestroika* came from the Shield (*Shchit*) informal, founded in 1989 by a reformist parliamentary deputy and retired army officer Major Vladimir Lopatin, and in the 1990 elections 22 military officers stood for the Democratic Platform. In April 1989 hardliners took the opportunity of Gorbachev's absence abroad to use troops against demonstrators in the Georgian capital of Tbilisi. During the 1990–91 drift to authoritarianism OMON riot police and KGB commandos were deployed against the Lithuanian Television Centre and the Latvian Interior Ministry. Elements from the republican communist parties and the armed forces in Latvia and Lithuania formed National Salvation Committees which threatened to wrest control of these republics away from their democratically elected nationalist leaderships. Gorbachev claimed that these committees were established and these attacks carried out with his permission. Factions within the soviet armed forces and the KGB saw themselves as the guarantor of the integrity and security of the USSR and believed that they had a duty to frustrate Gorbachev's reforms. When in 1990 Gorbachev signed the Conventional Armed Forces in Europe (CFE) Treaty, the soviet General Staff evaded the agreement by secretly moving armoured vehicles, guns and tanks beyond the Urals. This paralysed the soviet rail system during the winter of 1990–91, severely disrupting food distribution and contributing to the chaos in the country.

For the KGB, the USSR's enemies were now more difficult to define. Former political dissidents had been released from prison and exile and were now free to promote their views. The former dissident Andrei Sakharov had even been elected to the new Congress of People's Deputies in 1989 and challenged Gorbachev on live TV. The KGB now portrayed themselves as the champion of law and order in the face of growing crime, corruption and western subversion. After 1989 the KGB lost its links with fellow security services in east-central Europe and proved unable to subvert the nationalist independence movements within the USSR. As union republics declared their sovereignty, republican KGB organisations transferred their allegiance from the all-union institutions in Moscow to the leadership within their own republic. In the name of Russian state-building an RSFSR KGB was created for the first time in September 1989 by the Yeltsin-led RSFSR Supreme Soviet.

The draft union treaty: maintaining the union?

Gorbachev denounced the union republics' declarations of sovereignty as unconstitutional, but the new reality was that he could either try to impose the union by force or negotiate. Force was likely to be unsuccessful and would terminally damage *perestroika* and the USSR's relations with the West. Against a backdrop of mounting chaos and disintegration, Gorbachev tried to negotiate a new distribution of power and authority between the union republics and the all-union centre in Moscow. The result was a draft union treaty which did not even mention socialism and instead spoke of 'human rights and freedoms', of 'the commitment to develop civil society, law-based societies and democracies' with a free choice over the type of their economy. The union was to be a 'sovereign federative state' (Sheehy, 1990: 2). On 17 March 1991 an all-union referendum was held on the future of the soviet state. The question posed was: 'Do you consider it necessary to preserve the USSR as a renewed federation of equal sovereign republics in which the human rights and freedoms of any nationality will be fully guaranteed?'. Six republics (Estonia, Latvia, Lithuania, Moldova, Georgia and Armenia) did not hold the referendum. The overall turnout was 80 per cent with a 76.4 per cent 'yes' vote, but given the abstention of six republics and the loaded nature of the question, this was not a convincing mandate for the continuation of the USSR. Discussions continued and a new draft treaty was published on 16 August 1991. According to the new draft, membership of the union was to be voluntary, republican law would take precedence over all-union law and taxation was to be devolved to the republics. In effect this would mean that the republics could define central government's 'competencies and capabilities' (Galeotti, 1997: 114). The USSR Supreme Soviet was to be disbanded and the all-union ministries were either dissolved or reduced to coordinating bodies between the republics. For CPSU conservatives the treaty was going from bad to worse and the death knell for the USSR and soviet socialism was sounding.

The August 1991 coup and the collapse of the USSR

The August 1991 coup

To preserve the USSR action had to be taken before the Union Treaty was signed by Russia, Kazakhstan and Uzbekistan on 20 August. The coup conspirators were an amalgam of party conservatives, military-security personnel and representatives of economic bodies alarmed by the impact of reforms. The conspirators did not seem to have a very clear idea of what they wanted to achieve beyond a declaration

Box 1.6 The August 1991 coup conspirators

The State Committee for the State of Emergency

Gennady Yanaev	Soviet Vice-President 1990–91
Valentin Pavlov	Prime Minister 1990–91
Vladimir Kryuchkov	Former head of the KGB's First Chief Directorate, Chair of the KGB 1988–91
Dmitri Yazov	Soviet Defence Minister 1987–91
Boris Pugo	Interior Minister 1990–91
Oleg Baklanov	First Vice-Chair of the Defence Council
Vasily Starodubtsev	President of the Peasants' Union
Aleksandr Tizyakov	President of the Association of State Enterprises

The main figures in the 18 August delegation to Gorbachev's villa at Foros

Valery Boldin	Gorbachev's chief of staff
Gen. Yury Plekhanov	Head of the KGB's Ninth Directorate (bodyguards) Gorbachev's chief of security
Gen. Valentin Varennikov	Commander-in-Chief of Ground Forces 1989–91
Oleg Baklanov	First Vice-Chair of the Defence Council
Anatoly Lukyanov	Chair of the USSR Supreme Soviet 1990–91, a former close ally of Gorbachev he gave the coup tacit rather than overt support

of martial law. They believed that Gorbachev could be persuaded to declare martial law, so making their coup 'constitutional'. On 18 August a delegation went to Gorbachev's holiday villa in Foros to persuade him to declare martial law, but he refused. On Monday 19 August the soviet people were told that President Gorbachev was ill and that a State Committee for the State of Emergency was running the country. Gorbachev and his family were effectively under house arrest, cut off from the outside world until they discovered that one of the telephones in the servants' quarters had not been cut off. Gorbachev was able to telephone out and let his allies know he was not ill and that an unconstitutional coup had taken place.

The conspirators also wrongly assumed that the country's armed and security forces would back them. The soviet armed and security forces were as riven by internal divisions as any other institution in the USSR. Decisive opponents of the coup were air force commander Col. Gen. Yevgeny Shaposhnikov and Col. Gen. Pavel Grachev commander of the airborne forces (paratroopers) and generals Chechevatov, Samsonov and Novozhilov of the Kiev, Leningrad and the Far Eastern military districts. General Aleksandr Lebed refused to storm the Russian Parliament – the White House. The conspirators did have some forces at their disposal and three Yeltsin supporters were killed in a clash with a tank, but on the whole the conspirators were indecisive about how to use their forces. Yeltsin was able to come out of the White House, climb on a T-72 tank of the Taman Guards division and denounce the coup as unconstitutional. The State Committee had not acted decisively to arrest potential opponents; this meant that Gorbachev was their only prize and others were free to oppose the coup.

The conspirators' final error was to underestimate the potential opposition to the coup and not to understand that six years of *perestroika* had changed the USSR. Power and authority were much more diffuse than before and there were now other institutions, such as the Russian Parliament, which could claim legitimacy and serve as the focus of opposition to the coup. Most citizens did take a wait and see approach but there were instances of vital resistance which snowballed. The radio stations *Eko Moskvy* (*Moscow Echo*) and *Maiak* (*Lighthouse*) continued to broadcast in opposition to the coup; the editorial staff of some of the banned print media produced emergency editions and the new newspaper *Obshchaia gazeta* appeared. Foreign broadcasters such as CNN and the BBC provided continuous coverage. As the opposition stood firm and the State Committee dithered, resistance grew. To the union republics the message was clear: Moscow was defeated.

The end of the USSR: the Minsk and the Alma Ata Agreements

In the wake of the coup Gorbachev still believed that the USSR could be saved but no longer believed that the CPSU could be reformed and turned into a modern, democratic party and so resigned as its general secretary (Gorbachev, 1991: 46–7). Drawing lessons from the coup he believed that it was vital to create a reliable system of constitutional and public control over the armed forces and organs of law and order, but the main lesson was the need to speed up democratic reform and remove obstacles to the development of a market economy (Gorbachev, 1991: 44). In an emergency session of the Supreme Soviet of the USSR (parliament) which opened on 26 August 1991, Gorbachev blamed the coup for boosting the centrifugal forces within the country and called for the revival of the union treaty process to save the USSR. Gorbachev was, however, already yesterday's man and the initiative was grasped by other politicians. Soviet socialism was already effectively at an end and this was followed just over three months later by the formal dissolution of the USSR. On 8 December 1991 at Belovezha near Minsk in Belarus, Boris Yeltsin for Russia, Leonid Kravchuk for Ukraine and Stanislas Shushkevich for Belarus signed an agreement dissolving the USSR and establishing the Commonwealth of Independent States (CIS). This move was specifically designed to take the initiative from Gorbachev and to quash any idea that the USSR could survive in any form. Gorbachev was only told about the Minsk Agreement after Yeltsin had informed the US president, George H. W. Bush. On 21 December 1991 the CIS was further strengthened by the Alma Ata Agreement, with 11 former soviet republics agreeing to join the CIS. President Gorbachev resigned as president of the USSR on 25 December and handed over his functions to Boris Yeltsin; the soviet parliament was disbanded. The Soviet Union was formally dissolved on 31 December 1991.

Chapter summary

What had begun as reforms to reinvigorate and strengthen soviet socialism and the USSR had resulted in their collapse. Gorbachev did not cause the USSR's problems but he did not solve them either and, increasingly, control of the reform process and the country slipped from Gorbachev's grasp. By 1989–91 opposition to soviet socialism was spearheaded by nationalists who wanted independence for their republics, and by pro-democracy and market forces. Within this democratic opposition many doubted that reform could be achieved in a country as diverse and geographically vast as the USSR and that its dismemberment was both inevitable and desirable. Elements within the soviet *nomenklatura*, convinced that the soviet command-administrative system was outmoded and often simultaneously seeking personal material gain, also joined the opposition. Meanwhile other elements within the *nomenklatura* sought to save soviet socialism and the USSR by staging the August 1991 coup. However, had the conspirators held on to power they too would have had to address the reform imperative.

The course and fate of *perestroika* highlights the difficulty of formulating and implementing a reform programme, a difficulty compounded by the absence of a pro-reform elite and popular consensus. The ultimate goals of *perestroika* remained poorly defined. This meant that it was difficult to identify the necessary components of the reform programme and how they should work together. The result was a series of inconsistent, confused and at times contradictory half measures. The task of formulating a coherent reform programme to transform the RSFSR from a slightly modified one-party state with a centrally planned economy into a capitalist, liberal democracy now fell to Boris Yeltsin. The new Russian Federation inherited much of the chaos and the centrifugal forces unleashed by *perestroika* and in these inauspicious conditions President Yeltsin launched his reforms in 1992.

Discussion points

- Did Gorbachev cause the collapse of the USSR and soviet socialism or did he just fail to prevent it?
- Was soviet socialism destroyed by the success of its social and educational modernisation policies?
- Was soviet socialism destroyed by the failure of its economic modernisation policies?
- Why did the August 1991 coup fail?

Further reading

There are several good general books on Gorbachev and *perestroika* including Archie Brown (1997) *The Gorbachev Factor*, Oxford: Oxford University Press; Zhores Medvedev (1986) *Gorbachev*, Oxford: Blackwell; Richard Sakwa (1991) *Gorbachev and his reforms,*

1985–1990, New York: Prentice Hall; Rachel Walker (1993) *Six Years That Shook the World*, Manchester: Manchester University Press; David M. Kotz and Fred Weir (1997) *Revolution From Above: The Demise of the Soviet System*, London: Routledge; and finally Jack Matlock (1995) *Autopsy on an Empire*, New York: Random House. For Yeltsin's account of the *perestroika* period read his (1990) *Against the Grain. An Autobiography*, London: Jonathan Cape (trans: Michael Glenny). A comparison of Gorbachev and Yeltsin is provided by George Breslauer (2002) *Gorbachev and Yeltsin as Leaders*, Cambridge: Cambridge University Press.

For accessible analyses of the economic aspects of *perestroika* try Anders Åslund (1989) *Gorbachev's Struggle for Economic Reform*, London: Pinter, and Michael Ellman and Vladimir Kontorovich (eds) (1992) *The Disintegration of the Soviet Economic System*, London: Routledge. Marshall Goldman (1991) *What Went Wrong with Perestroika?*, London: W.W. Norton provides an overview of *perestroika* and raises important questions about the sequencing of the various components of the reform programme. Mark Kramer's three-part article, 'The Collapse of East European Communism and the Repercussions within the Soviet Union', *Journal of Cold War Studies*, Part 1, 5 (4) Fall 2003, 178–256; Part 2, 6 (4) Fall 2004, 3–64 and Part 3, 7 (1) Winter 2005, 3–96, provides a thorough discussion of the interplay of the collapse of socialism in the USSR and in the Soviet bloc.

References

Allison, G. and Blackwell, R. (1991) 'America's stake in the Soviet Future', *Foreign Affairs*, 70 (3), Summer, 77–97

Birman, I. (1983) *Ekonomika Nedostach* (The Economy of Shortages), New York, Chalidze Publications

Birman, I. and Clarke, R. (1985) 'Inflation and the Money Supply in the Soviet Economy', *Soviet Studies*, 37 (4), October, 494–504

Birman, I. (interviewed by P. Lubin and R. Novak) (1989) 'How to dismantle communism – interview with economist Igor Birman', *National Review*, 8 December

Breslauer, G. W. (1990) 'Evaluating Gorbachev as Leader', *Soviet Economy*, 5 (4), October–December, 302

Brown, A. (1997) *The Gorbachev Factor*, Oxford: Oxford University Press

Carrère d'Encausse, H. (1979) *Decline of an Empire: Soviet Socialist Republics in Revolt*, New York: Newsweek Books

Galeotti, M. (1997) *Gorbachev and his Revolution*, London: Macmillan

Gorbachev, M. (1991) *The August Coup. The Truth and the Lessons*, London: HarperCollins

Hanson, P. (1984) 'The Novosibirsk Report', *Survey*, 28 (120), Spring, 83–108

Hobsbawm, E. (2005) 'The last of the utopian projects', *The Guardian*, 9 March 2005, 21

Johnson, J. (1994) 'Should Russia Adopt the Chinese Model of Economic Reform?', *Communist and Post-Communist Studies*, 27 (1), 59–75

Kagarlitsky, B. (1989) 'The market instead of democracy?', *International Socialism*, (45), Winter, 93–104

Kagarlitsky, B. (1990) *The Dialectic of Change*, London: Verso

Kaiser, R. G. (1991) *Why Gorbachev happened: His triumphs and his failures*, New York: Simon & Schuster

Lapidus, G. W. (1989) 'Gorbachev and the National Question: Restructuring the Soviet Federation', *Soviet Economy*, 5 (3), 201–50

Medvedev, R. A. (in conversation with Piero Ostellino) (1980) *On Soviet Dissent*, New York: Columbia University Press (trans: George Saunders)

Migranyan, A. (1990) 'Gorbachev's Leadership: A Soviet View', *Soviet Economy*, 6 (2), April–June, 155–9

Nove, A. (1966) *The Soviet Economy*, London: Allen and Unwin

Sachs, J. (1992) 'The Grand Bargain', in A. Åslund (ed.) *The Post-Soviet Economy: Soviet and Western Perspectives*, London: Pinter

Sheehy, A. (1990) 'The Draft Union Treaty: A Preliminary Assessment', *Radio Liberty Report on the USSR*, 2 (51), December 21, 1–6

Skidelsky, R. (1995) *The World After Communism: A Polemic for our Times*, London: Macmillan

Steele, J. (1992) 'Fear and folly in Moscow', *The Guardian*, 21 February, 19

Suny, R. (1980) 'Georgia and the Soviet Nationality Policy', in Stephen F. Cohen et al. (eds) *The Soviet Union Since Stalin*, London: Macmillan, 200–26

Zaslavskaya, T. I. (1988) 'Friends or Foes? Social Forces Working For and Against Perestroika', in A. Aganbegyan (ed.) *Perestroika Annual*, London: Futura, 255–78

Chapter 2

Explaining the end of soviet socialism: the USSR and the cold war

Learning objectives

- To introduce essentialist-totalitarian, revisionist and Marxist analyses of the USSR.
- To examine the impact of President Reagan and USA policy on *perestroika* and the end of the cold war.
- To introduce neo-conservatism, neo-realism and constructivism.
- To examine the impact of the world economy and globalisation on the USSR.

Introduction

In 1969 the soviet dissident, Andrei Amalrik, wrote his most famous essay entitled, *Will the Soviet Union Survive until 1984?* At the time this seemed an incredible question, the USSR was one of the world's two superpowers, it had rebuilt itself following the Nazi onslaught (1941–45) and held the USA in a nuclear stalemate for over twenty years. In contrast to this image of a mighty USSR, Amalrik (1970) described a decrepit soviet regime and predicted that it would be brought down by ethnic tensions and conflict with China. Amalrik's analysis was in parts uncannily accurate, although by the 1980s the war with China had not broken out, soviet socialism was in crisis and nationalist aspirations were a factor in the USSR's ultimate disintegration. However, the USSR did survive for 74 years and its final collapse was both sudden and largely unexpected by kremlinologists and sovietologists. To outside observers while it was increasingly evident that the USSR had some problems, notably in the economy, these did not appear to threaten its survival. In 1986 the American sovietologist Severyn Bialer (1986: 19) argued, 'it is unlikely that the [Soviet] state is now, or will be in the late 1980s, in danger of social or political disintegration.' International relations theorists were also caught napping by the sudden end of the cold war. They had tended to focus on the maintenance and endurance of the 'long peace' marked by Soviet–American rivalry, rather than on transformation or the peaceful resolution of the cold war. In the 1980s therefore, whether looking at the situation within the USSR or the international system, the stress was on stability rather than on radical change and certainly not on the implosion of one of the world's two superpowers.

Box 2.1 Key terms

Kremlinology: originally the study (by a kremlinologist) of soviet politics and government taking its name from the Kremlin, the seat of the Soviet and now Russian government. As information about the USSR was heavily censored and unreliable, Kremlinology often relied on reading between the lines of what was visible (such as the order in which individuals

The Kremlin, Moscow.

appeared at the May Day parade or at state funerals, the removal of portraits and the size of photographs in the media) to detect what was happening in the USSR's ruling circles. Kremlinology tended to assume that soviet civil society either did not exist or was unimportant and that all change in the USSR was generated from the top down. Kremlinology therefore concentrated on the activities of the Politburo and Secretariat, and to a lesser extent the Central Committee of the CPSU. The term is now used for the study of Russian politics.

Sovietology: the study (by a sovietologist) of the USSR. It included Kremlinology as well as approaches from subjects such as history, politics, economics and sociology. It also incorporated new developments and approaches from these subjects (such as social history or gender issues) into the study of the USSR.

The nature of the USSR

Essentialism, totalitarianism and the USSR

As their name suggests essentialist analyses make certain basic claims about the essential nature of the USSR and soviet socialism. Ronald Reagan, the Republican US president (1981–89), expressed essentialist ideas when in 1983 he described the USSR as an 'evil empire' that must be confronted and ultimately destroyed. For essentialists soviet socialism was fatally flawed from its very beginning in 1917. The Bolshevik Revolution was really a coup carried out by a small, disciplined and highly organised party, which took advantage of the turmoil of the time. Not only was the party unrepresentative of the Russian peoples in 1917, it never then submitted itself to meaningful elections or scrutiny and ruthlessly destroyed real, suspected or even imagined opponents. A range of evidence is used to support these claims: in 1917 the foundation and then growing role of the Secret Police; in 1918 the Red Terror and the ban on right-wing and liberal political parties; in 1921 the ban on rival left-wing parties and the ban on factionalism within the Communist Party itself; and finally the purges, show trials, terror and rapid growth of the Gulag (prison camp) population under Stalin in the 1930s. The soviet regime therefore lacked popular legitimacy and only maintained control and achieved a measure of stability through repression and coercion (see Schapiro, 1972).

Such ideas have formed the basis of a totalitarian model of the soviet regime. The USSR and Nazi Germany, despite their ideological differences, have both been described as totalitarian regimes; regimes in which the state sought total control over all aspects of life in the country. The proponents of the totalitarian model have included prominent academic-political figures such as Zbigniew K. Brzezinski (1962, 1989) who was President Jimmy Carter's National Security Advisor (1977–81) and Jeane Kirkpatrick (1992) who was Ronald Reagan's foreign policy adviser during his 1980 presidential campaign. According to Friedrich and Brzezinski (1956) the USSR had all the characteristics of a totalitarian regime: society was dominated by the CPSU which was a small, centralised, self-styled elite, vanguard party; there was one official ideology namely Marxism-Leninism; and the party strove for monopolistic control of all forms of mass communication, which were used for propaganda purposes to manipulate the people into supporting the party. Although coercion was reduced after Stalin's death in 1953, a civil society that might challenge the CPSU was not allowed to develop. The essentialist-totalitarian approach examines the USSR from the 'top down' – stressing the primacy of the political elite, ideology and politics and seeing the soviet people as the coerced, manipulated and/or passive victims of the elite.

Among those who have an essentialist understanding of the USSR and employ a totalitarian model, there are important differences. Richard Pipes (1977) stresses the continuity between Imperial Russia and the USSR, tracing the beginnings of Russian authoritarianism to the creation of a patrimonial regime during the reign of Ivan III (1462–1505). While Pipes and Leonard Schapiro stress the Bolsheviks' lust for power, the American historian Martin Malia (1924–2004) argues instead that the Bolsheviks were driven by ideological conviction and traces the European lineage of Marxism-Leninism back through Marx and Hegel to Rousseau. Malia describes the USSR as an ideocracy (ruled by ideology), a term also used by the Russian Nationalist commentator Viktor Aksiuchits (1995). According to Malia (1994) as 1917 was an anarchic time it was easy for the Bolsheviks to stage their coup and then their ideology provided a framework, or more accurately a straitjacket, for their actions. For Malia soviet modernisation was driven by ideology and the CPSU simply could not conceive socialism as anything other than what they had created in the 1920s and 1930s. This meant that the USSR lacked the capacity to innovate and any reforms, including *perestroika*, were bound to be insignificant. Writing under the pseudonym 'Z' in 1990, Malia published an article entitled 'To the Stalin Mausoleum', in which he predicted the failure of *perestroika*.

The soviet military historian Dmitri Volkogonov (1928–95), who was an adviser to Boris Yeltsin before the August 1991 coup, also provides an essentialist analysis of the USSR. He notes Gorbachev's personality and policy failings and also accuses him of being slow to shake off the Bolshevik mentality, a step that was necessary in order to deal effectively with the flawed state structure created by Lenin in the early 1920s. Volkogonov (1998: 434) argues that, 'He [Gorbachev] wanted to restructure "everything" without touching the socialist foundations of state ownership, the Party's "leading role", and the regime's Communist goals. It is not hard to see that these goals were not attainable. To restructure everything, and yet to leave intact the foundations laid by Lenin, was a logical impossibility. The Communist system was not reformable. Either it exists, or it does not'.

Revisionist analyses of the USSR

Revisionist historians such as Sheila Fitzpatrick (1982, 1999), Stephen F. Cohen (1985) and Moshe Lewin (1988) stress the primacy of social forces, in contrast to the 'top-down' analysis of the essentialist-totalitarian approach. Revisionists do not deny the existence of coercion, manipulation and terror but argue that it should not be overemphasised. The Bolsheviks could not have triumphed in 1917 and the soviet regime could not have been maintained, if they had not enjoyed a measure of popular support and legitimacy. Stephen White's (1979) study of soviet political culture, for example, notes that while the people rejected the role of the secret police and terror, they nonetheless expected the state to be interventionist and both expected and respected strong leadership. He argues that the party and the people shared many beliefs. Looking at the USSR from the bottom up there were many things that the people valued and took pride in: electrification, rapid industrialisation, literacy campaigns and the expansion of educational opportunities, rising living standards, improvements in public health, the development of cultural and leisure facilities, the achievements of soviet science and victory in the Great Patriotic War (1941–45) to name but a few. According to Lewin the regime viewed upwards from soviet society was both flexible and responsive to social realities. An example of this is the 'social contract' between the people and the party, whereby political conformity was bought by rising standards of living. This flexibility and responsiveness helps to explain why the CPSU did not have to rely on mass coercion to stay in power and so the durability of the soviet regime.

Revisionists do not view the USSR as having been caught in amber under Lenin or Stalin, but instead see it as modernising. Socio-economic development or modernisation created an increasingly complex and differentiated society; this pluralism sat uneasily with the one-party state. However, in the 1960s sovietologists such as H. Gordon Skilling (1966) and Joel Schwartz and William Keech (1968) challenged the totalitarian model of the USSR with an interest group or pluralism analysis. Jerry Hough (1969, 1977 and 1979) found evidence that the soviet political process provided opportunities for group participation. A form of institutional pluralism or corporatism also developed as soviet professional groups, such as the armed forces and economic managers, became adept at using their positions and specialist know-how to promote their professional interests (Merridale, 1991: 16). These analyses suggest that while the CPSU did place limits on what could be expressed, as is witnessed by the treatment of dissidents, for the majority of soviet citizens with concerns or grievances there were ways to get these heard.

For advocates of an essentialist-totalitarian analysis of the USSR, the revisionists' claims that the soviet regime was flexible and stable mean that they cannot explain its collapse. However, the revisionists' focus on society meant that they identified social developments that were eating away at the foundations of the soviet regime. Ronald Suny's (1980) identification of the erosion of Marxist ideology and the growth in nationalism (see Chapter 1) when combined with *glasnost* and democratisation, becomes a potent factor in undermining the soviet state. Similarly, Moshe Lewin argues that due to modernisation by the Brezhnev period there was already an emerging civil society. This meant that when Gorbachev launched his 'revolution from above', seeking to mobilise the soviet people through *glasnost* and democratisation, sections of the soviet people were quick to take these new opportunities to formulate their own agendas, to pursue their own sectional interests and, in some cases, to push for further democratisation. Revisionists see the introduction of *perestroika* as the result of a conjuncture of such developments and events in the 1980s (see Chapter 1).

Box 2.2 A civil society in the very fortress of statism?

Moshe Lewin wrote:

By 'civil society,' we refer to the aggregate of networks and institutions that either exist and act independently of the state or are official organizations capable of developing their own, spontaneous views on national or local issues and then impressing these views on their members, on small groups and, finally on the authorities. . . . The concept of a civil society operating in the very fortress of statism – among broad layers of officials, politicians and opinion makers, and the party apparatus – challenges the conventional thinking about the Soviet state.

Source: Moshe Lewin (1988) *The Gorbachev Phenomenon: A Historical Interpretation*, Berkeley CA, University of California Press. Moshe Lewin was born in Poland and served in the soviet Red Army during World War II. An historian, he teaches at the University of Pennsylvania, USA

Marxist analyses of the USSR

Marxist critiques of the USSR typically pose the question when and why soviet socialism 'went wrong'. Within the USSR there were members of the CPSU who believed that nothing had gone wrong and that what had been created in the 1920s and 1930s, largely under Stalin, was real socialism. During the *perestroika* period these ideas were expressed by hardliners such as the Leningrad chemistry teacher Nina Andreyeva, who wrote a letter entitled 'I Cannot Forego My Principles', which was published in the conservative newspaper *Sovetskaia Rossiia* on 13 March 1988. She accused Gorbachev of betraying socialism, appealed for a 'balanced' assessment of Stalinism and condemned *perestroika* for abandoning a true Marxist class-approach. While recognising that the USSR had some current difficulties, these could be resolved within the existing, well-proven system, which she believed Gorbachev was destroying. In contrast Gorbachev argued that Stalin cast a long shadow over soviet socialism and that *perestroika* was needed to eradicate all trace of Stalinism. For Gorbachev the aim of October 1917 had been 'a genuine people's revolution' but what had actually happened were 'the results of the forcible imposition of the Stalinist model of society' (Gorbachev, 1991: 47–8). Other Russian Marxists such as the economist Professor Aleksandr Buzgalin and Andrei Kolganov (2003), who are admirers of neither Gorbachev nor Yeltsin, argue that despite attempts at reform soviet socialism remained in essence Stalinist. As the USSR 'went wrong' under Stalin, socialism both as an ideal and as a reality can be rescued by going back to the ideas of Marx and Lenin. This in essence was what Gorbachev was arguing when he became general secretary in March 1985.

Box 2.3 Leon Trotsky (real name Lev Bronstein) (1879–1940)

Trotsky was a close ally of Lenin and a leading Bolshevik, who organised and led the Red Army following the Bolshevik Revolution in October–November 1917. During the civil war he clashed with Stalin and the two men became bitter enemies and rivals. While Stalin advocated 'Socialism in One Country', Trotsky championed 'permanent revolution'. Trotsky believed that socialism could not be built in isolation in an economically and socially backward country such as Russia and that it was vital to spread revolution to other countries. During the 1920s Trotsky was outmanoeuvred by Stalin and was eventually exiled from the USSR in 1929, and his ideas and publications were banned in the USSR. In 1938 Trotsky founded the Fourth International to oppose Stalin and in 1940 he was murdered by Ramon del Rio, a Stalinist agent, in Mexico. Trotsky's followers such as Ernest Mandel (1923–95) are known as Trotskyites.

Useful website: The Marxist Archive – Trotsky collection http://www.marxists.org/archive/trotsky/works/index.htm

---

One of the earliest Marxist critiques of soviet socialism was produced by Leon Trotsky. In his *The Revolution Betrayed: What is the Soviet Union and Where is it Going?*, Trotsky (1937) argued that the Soviet Union was halfway between capitalism and socialism. The October Revolution had made the positive steps of eliminating capitalism and instituting a workers' state, but the country's isolation and backwardness meant that under Stalin the USSR had deteriorated into a 'degenerate workers' state'. The communist party had betrayed the Revolution and instead of creating a genuine workers' democracy the bureaucracy were a privileged stratum or caste, which misruled the country. These ideas were developed by the economist and political analyst Ernest Mandel who was a member of the Fourth International. In the late 1940s the former Trotskyite Tony Cliff (1917–2000) abandoned Trotsky's degenerate workers' state analysis of the USSR and in 1950 was excluded from the Fourth International. Cliff (1974) and his followers Duncan Hallas, Chris Harman and Alex Callinicos developed a 'bureaucratic capitalist state' analysis of the USSR, which argued that the soviet state owned and planned the economy like the bourgeoisie under capitalism. The soviet state did this in the name of the working class but in reality the Stalinist bureaucracy retained power.

Callinicos (1991) argues that Stalinism was a counter revolution to October 1917 and a distortion of Leninism that wrongly equated socialism with a one-party state and a command economy. According to Alex Callinicos (1991: 48) the USSR's authoritarian modernisation, that had transformed the country after 1928, had run up against its limits by the Brezhnev era. The soviet people were well-educated and they were encouraged to have rising material expectations, but these were increasingly not being met. Intellectuals and workers were frustrated by the constraints imposed on them by the bureaucracies and resented the *nomenklatura's* privileges. By the time Brezhnev died in 1982, according to Callinicos, 'The state ideology had been hollowed out' and during the 1980s the USSR entered 'a profound crisis of hegemony', that is of rule or leadership (Callinicos, 1991: 48). In a similar vein Boris Kagarlitsky, who co-founded the Socialist Party of the USSR in 1990, argues that the USSR was a 'statocracy' (ruled by the state) or 'state socialist' regime and that under Stalin Marxism had been reduced to ideological dogmas, which lacked any critical or emancipatory qualities (1988: 95). For these writers Gorbachev's reforms were a 'top-down' attempt to respond to the crisis in USSR's Stalinist system. The fate of the reforms was in part decided by the behaviour of the bureaucracies but, crucially, the members of the bureaucracies had different interests. Gorbachev's economic reforms were sabotaged by conservative bureaucrats in the economic ministries, but according to Mandel and Kagarlitsky some elements within the *nomenklatura* saw greater opportunities for self-enrichment – by replacing soviet socialism with capitalism. For Trotsky, Mandel, Cliff, Hallas, Harman, Callinicos, Buzgalin, Kolganov and Kagarlitsky, the USSR needed another revolution in which rule in the name of the working class by the bureaucracy, state or *nomenklatura* would be replaced by rule by the working people and true socialism. What they got was Boris Yeltsin and capitalism.

The Reagan factor: *perestroika*, the end of the cold war and the USSR

The cold war: from containment to the end of the cold war

Throughout the cold war, which lasted from just after the end of World War II until 1990, the USA and its allies grappled with the question of how to deal with the USSR. The cold war never developed into a 'hot' or fighting war directly between the USA and the USSR. Instead the Cold War was characterised by ideological conflict between soviet communism and American capitalism-democracy, the division of Europe into two blocs, a conventional and more especially a nuclear arms race, and the extension of superpower rivalry around the globe. In 1947 US President Harry S. Truman announced a policy of containing communism, which became known as the 'Truman doctrine' or 'containment'. Containment was based on the American diplomat George Kennan's 'Long Telegram' (1946) in which he depicted the USSR as a powerful, expansionist and ideologically motivated regime. Containment remained at the core of US policy towards the USSR until Ronald

Reagan became president in 1981. Reagan rejected President Nixon's 1970s policy of détente towards the USSR, which used diplomacy, negotiation, arms control and increased trade to ease tensions. For Reagan détente had not prevented soviet adventurism in Africa or its invasion of Afghanistan in 1979. During détente the USSR had benefited economically from cheap grain, increased access to western technology and markets for soviet oil and gas, but had not modified their ideologically motivated, expansionist behaviour in return; rather the USSR had indulged in a massive military buildup. For Reagan soviet socialism needed not only to be contained but to be destroyed.

Reagan's approach to the USSR

Reagan had both neo-conservative (neo-Con) and neo-realist advisers, who believed that the USSR was ideologically motivated, expansionist, a source of unrest throughout the world and the prime threat to US security. Reagan held essentialist views of the USSR as a totalitarian state, relying on police terror at home and nuclear intimidation abroad, views shared by his Secretary of Defense Caspar Weinberger and Assistant Secretary of Defense Richard Perle. During his first term (1981–85) Reagan was particularly influenced by the historian and Team B chair Richard Pipes (1984, 1986). Both men often distinguished between the USSR's totalitarian leadership and the downtrodden soviet people, yearning for freedom and democracy. Reagan also agreed with Pipes's essentialist views which held that the USSR was in economic and political crisis and had no alternative but dramatic domestic reform. These ideas were included in Reagan's 1983 National Security Decision Directive 75. Pipes argued that the USA should 'squeeze' the USSR and precipitate the collapse of its economy, so provoking economic and political reform.

The squeeze entailed a twin strategy of sanctions denying the USSR western technology imports and engaging it in an arms race, exemplified by the Star Wars Project (SDI) (Pipes, 1986: 272). In 1949 western governments had established COCOM (the Coordinating Committee for East–West trade) to prevent the transfer of military and dual-use (civilian and military use) technology to the USSR and its allies; Reagan moved to strengthen COCOM and extend the list of embargoed technologies. Reagan announced that he opposed the ratification of the Strategic Arms Limitation Treaty (SALT II), which the Senate had refused to pass after the soviet invasion of Afghanistan in December 1979. While not ruling out further negotiations Reagan said that he was prepared to enter into discussions leading to negotiations, only if the negotiations would lead to real reductions in the number of nuclear weapons. Although Reagan was talking tough, secret negotiations with the USSR were begun on the number of medium-range nuclear missiles both superpowers could deploy in Europe. The real racheting up of the cold war was the US decision to launch the Strategic Defence Initiative (SDI or Star Wars). Although the SDI technology was unproven, it was a threat to the approximate nuclear parity that the USSR had achieved in the 1970s.

The USA also put further pressure on the USSR by channelling funding to anti-soviet groups. The USA provided intelligence, funds and materials to those fighting

Box 2.4 American foreign policy and the USSR

Wilsonian Liberalism (Idealism): takes its name from the American democratic president, Woodrow Wilson (1913–21) who believed that American domestic political, economic and cultural ideals – such as democracy and national self-determination – should form the basis of US foreign policy goals. Wilson believed that diplomacy, international law, treaties and international organisations should be used to spread these ideals.

Team B: has its origins in the belief by influential members on the right-wing of the US Republican party in the mid-1970s that the Central Intelligence Agency (CIA) was consistently underestimating the soviet threat (see Hessing Cahn, 1998). In 1976 three panels were set up to evaluate the USSR. The first to examine the threat posed by soviet missile accuracy and the second to examine the effects of soviet air defences on US strategic bombers. The third, which became known as Team B, was charged with identifying the USSR's strategic objectives. Team B brought together members of the US national security establishment to provide alternative analyses of the USSR to those provided by the CIA. Team B was established with the backing of Richard Perle, Donald Rumsfeld and Dick Cheney; it was chaired by Richard Pipes and its members included his son Daniel Pipes, Paul Wolfowitz, Paul Nitze and Seymour Weiss. In October 1976 Team B reported that the CIA underestimated the soviet threat, that the USSR was inherently aggressive rather than defensive and that détente should be abandoned. In the same vein Richard Pipes also wrote the policy statement 'What is the Soviet Union Up To?' for the second Committee on the Present Danger (CPD). In 1979 Ronald Reagan joined the executive committee of the CPD.

Neo-conservatism: has its intellectual origins in ideas ranging from pre-WWII American Trotskyism to Leo Strauss's elitism and neo-Platonic ideas. The two main founders of neo-conservative thinking are Irving Kristol and Norman Podhoretz. Leading neo-Cons include: Jeane Kirkpatrick, Richard Perle, Paul Wolfowitz, Eliot Cohen, Charles Krauthammer, Richard Pipes and Daniel Pipes. Francis Fukuyama was a neo-Con but broke with their ideas in 2005. Many neo-Cons started out on the anti-Stalinist left or were anti-communist liberals before moving to the right. They all share a militant anti-communism and their foreign policy is strongly influenced by the Wilsonian belief in the universality of democracy and the need to spread American ideals. Unlike Wilson, the neo-Cons believe that a reliance on diplomacy and international law may lead American ideals to be compromised. They therefore believe that it may be necessary for the USA to take interventionist, unilateral action – including the use of force – to achieve their goals. In the 1980s neo-Cons believed that communism should not just be contained but rolled back. Neo-Cons have influenced the foreign policy of Ronald Reagan (1981–89) and George W. Bush (2001–09), particularly in these presidents' commitment to regime change.

Neo-realism: also known as 'new' or 'structural realism', this is a theoretical perspective associated with Kenneth N. Waltz (1979, 1990). It shares traditional realism's belief that states are unitary actors primarily concerned with power and security in an anarchic world, that states have different levels of power depending on their

Box 2.4 (*Continued*)

military and economic capabilities and that there is no authority above states that can regulate their interactions. For (neo-)realists states are the primary actors in international affairs and TNCs, IGOs and NGOs are of only secondary importance. Neo-realists also emphasise the structural characteristics of the international system that states inhabit. Neo-realists do not share the neo-Cons' belief in the importance of spreading the American ideals of democracy and a free market economy; rather believing that the USA should be pragmatic about promoting American interests. During the 1970s neo-realists, such as President Nixon and his national security advisor Henry Kissinger, argued that détente with the USSR was in America's interests. In contrast Zbigniew Brzezinski who also had a neo-realist approach to foreign policy believed that US interests would be promoted by abandoning détente.

Constructivism: shares many of the basic realist and neo-realist assumptions about the importance of states and the anarchy of the international system. However, for Alexander Wendt, the leading advocate of constructivism (1992 and 1999 in response to Waltz, 1979), the anarchic international system could be marked by violent conflict or cooperation. For constructivists, ideas, norms, culture and language are vital to the production, operation, reproduction, modification or fundamental change of all domestic and international systems. They believe people through their beliefs and actions can make a difference; they therefore analyse the impact of the 'Reagan factor' and the 'Gorbachev factor' on the introduction and course of *perestroika*.

Reagan doctrine: is the term used to describe the foreign policy of the Reagan Administration from 1980–88. The doctrine was influenced by right-wing Republicans and think tanks such as Team B, the Heritage Foundation and the Committee on the Present Danger. It is encapsulated in the National Security Council, National Security Decision Directive 75 (17 January 1983), which committed the USA to first the containment and then the reversal of soviet expansionism. The doctrine inspired the 'squeeze strategy' against the USSR, SDI, the contemplation of the first use of nuclear weapons against the USSR in the event of a conventional war, the funding of anti-soviet insurgents in Afghanistan, Angola and Nicaragua, and anti-soviet civil society groups in east-central Europe.

Charter of Paris (for a new Europe): was signed in November 1990 by the participating members of the Conference on Security and Co-operation in Europe. It built upon Gorbachev's idea of a 'Common European Home' and was in part a response to the collapse of soviet-style socialism in east-central Europe. The Charter marked the end of the cold war.

Useful websites:

The National Interest – the journal of both the neo-Cons and the neo-realists, published jointly by the National Interest and the Nixon Center think tanks. http://www.inthenationalinterest.com/index.html

National Security Council – National Security Directive 75 – http://www.fas.org/irp/offdocs/nsdd/nsdd-075.htm

The Paris Charter for a new Europe – http://www.osce.org/documents/mcs/1990/11/4045_en.pdf

the soviet forces and their allies in Afghanistan. The financial and human costs of this prolonged war ultimately forced the USSR to withdraw their troops in 1988–89. By 1981 Poland was in turmoil as Solidarnošc (Solidarity) an anti-communist trade union, challenged the Polish Communist Government. On Moscow's orders martial law was imposed in Poland and a military man, Marshall Jaruzelski, established a new government. The USA's public response to martial law was to embargo the sale of high technology and postpone talks on grain exports to the USSR. At the same time the USA also covertly channelled funds to Solidarity and, as the 1980s progressed, to other civil society groups in east-central Europe. American funding on its own is not sufficient explanation for the development of civil society groups in the region or for their role in the destabilisation and ultimate downfall of communist regimes in 1989, but it does indicate the willingness of the USA under Reagan to use a range of devices to roll back communism.

Reagan: from essentialist to interactionist?

Reagan and Gorbachev at the Washington Summit in 1987.

According to some Kremlin insiders such as Georgi Arbatov (1992), director of the USSR's Institute for the USA and Canada studies, Reagan's tough talking and 'squeeze strategy' actually made it more difficult for the would-be reformers within the USSR and delayed the prospect of reform until after Brezhnev's death in November 1982. On 11 August 1984, not realising that his words were being broadcast, Reagan joked, 'My fellow Americans, I am pleased to tell you that I've signed legislation that will outlaw Russia forever. We begin bombing in five minutes' (see Oberdorfer, 1991: 85–6). Such pronouncements did not go down well in Moscow and provided evidence to soviet hardliners of the need to maintain vigilance in the face of American intransigence. Reagan's second term as president coincided with Gorbachev's tenure as general secretary and the personal rapport developed by the two men helped to cement a change in Reagan's approach to the USSR. George Shultz (1993: 9) was impressed by Gorbachev and his foreign Minister Eduard Shevardnadze. Jack Matlock, the US Ambassador to Moscow, believed that the new 1986 CPSU Party Programme signalled real changes. The squeeze strategy was effectively abandoned and relations between the two superpowers were considerably eased. By the Moscow summit in 1988 Reagan even said that talk of an 'evil empire' now belonged to another time and another place. Reagan moved from an 'essentialist' to a more 'interactionist' approach (Farnham, 2001); he downplayed the importance of soviet ideology and instead took a more neo-realist approach, stressing the dynamics of superpower conflict, the dangers of mutual misperceptions and fears, and was more willing to talk and do deals with the USSR.

Gorbachev and *perestroika* as American victories?

American Republicans such as Reagan's Vice-President George H. W. Bush claim that Gorbachev's decision to pursue *perestroika* and to adopt his 'new thinking' on foreign policy were due to the American Government's 'squeeze strategy' and especially the development of SDI (Dumbrell, 1997: 116). During the 1992 US presidential election campaign George Kennan (1992) wrote in the *New York Times* that it was ridiculous for the Republicans to claim that they had won the cold war, an interpretation that Pipes (1992) swiftly rejected in a letter to the editor. In 1994 Peter Schweizer called his book on Reagan simply *Victory*, claiming the end of the cold war as victory for Reagan. The common thread to these triumphalist claims is that Reagan ran the soviet economy into the ground through the renewed arms race and pursued a squeeze strategy. The arms race and economic squeeze exacerbated existing economic problems within the USSR but it did not cause them. As John Dumbrell (1997: 70–4) points out the squeeze strategy was not consistently pursued. The grain embargo imposed on the USSR by President Carter after the declaration of martial law in Poland in December 1981 was lifted by Reagan in 1982 and by 1983 technology sales were gradually being encouraged again. Even while the Americans were applying the economic 'squeeze' the western Europeans and the Japanese continued to supply the USSR with technology and the Australians, Argentinians and Canadians supplied grain. It is also not clear that the USSR even tried to match US arms spending in the 1980s (Hessing Cahn, 1998: 53–4). Gorbachev knew that he could not fund domestic economic and social reforms and match western spending on the arms race; and so he signed the Intermediate Nuclear Forces (INF) Treaty (1987), unilaterally announced a reduction in conventional forces (1988) and pursued a Strategic Arms Reduction Treaty (1991). It is, however, highly debatable whether he was forced into this by the US arms race or by the simple recognition of the poor state of the soviet economy.

Box 2.5 Neo-realists versus constructivists on *perestroika* and the end of the cold war

Neo-realists: argue that soviet-style planned economies are innately inefficient and find it difficult to innovate and so, not surprisingly, the soviet economy was in crisis. The USSR could not compete with the economically stronger USA in defence spending. Gorbachev introduced *perestroika* and sought better relations with the USA because the power dynamic between the two superpowers was to the USA's advantage.

Neo-realist writers include: Daniel Deudney and G. John Ikenberry (1991 and 1991–2); Stephen G. Brooks (1997); William C. Wohlforth and Stephen G. Brooks (2000–1); William C. Wohlforth and Nina Tannenwald (eds) (2005); and William C. Wohlforth (1996, 2001, 2003).

Constructivists: recognise that the soviet economy was experiencing major difficulties and talk about the conjuncture of factors (see Chapter 1) that brought Gorbachev to office. They stress the way in which Gorbachev and his westernised advisers, brought new ideas and a new vision to the USSR's domestic and international policies exemplified by *perestroika* and the 'new thinking' on foreign policy. Constructivists place great importance on both Gorbachev's ideas and his agency (role) to the introduction and fate of *perestroika* and the ending of the cold war.

Constructivist writers include: Archie Brown (1997, 2004); Robert English (2000); Matthew Evangelista (2001, 2004a, 2004b); Rey Koslowski and Friedrich V. Kratochwil (1994); and Vladislav Zubok (2000).

The end of history?

Francis Fukuyama and the end of history

In 1989 Francis Fukuyama, who was then a deputy director of the US State Department's Policy Planning Staff, published an article entitled, 'The End of History?' in the summer issue of *The National Interest*. At this time the USSR was sliding into chaos and its grip on east-central Europe was loosening, soviet socialism was in retreat. He declared that, 'What we are witnessing is not just the end of the cold war, or the passing of a particular period of post war history, but the end of history as such: that is, the endpoint of mankind's ideological evolution and the universalization of Western liberal democracy as the final form of human government' (Fukuyama, 1989: 4). Fukuyama acknowledges that his approach to history is greatly influenced by the ideas of the German idealist philosopher Georg Hegel (1770–1831) and particularly the interpretation of Hegel's ideas by the Russo-French philosopher Alexandre Kojève (1902–68). So by 'the end of history' Fukuyama did not literally mean that there would be no more daily happenings or events, but rather the end of 'history' as an evolutionary process. For Fukuyama political and economic liberalism is the end of history because it is the best at fostering freedom and history has been evolving towards freedom. He was not claiming that all countries would immediately become liberal democracies, nor that nationalism or religious fundamentalisms would disappear overnight, rather that liberalism was already victorious in the realm of ideas or consciousness as in the twentieth century liberalism had seen off its great ideological rivals: Fascism and Bolshevism (Fukuyama, 1989: 3). It is one thing to claim the 'end of history' and quite another to prove it. To dismiss the continuing importance of nationalism and religious fundamentalisms also seems to exhibit a rather sweeping disregard for reality.

Fukuyama, modernisation, civil society and the end of the USSR

According to Fukuyama (1989 and 1992) liberal democracy and a market-oriented economy are the only viable options for modern societies. They lead to free and prosperous countries and a safer world. He argues that socio-economic modernisation, such as urbanisation and growing education levels, has a major impact on political and social attitudes and lead to demands for individual rights and political participation. The USSR was not exempt from these social changes but nonetheless maintained restrictions on independent social and political action (Fukuyama, 1993). In addition soviet socialism could not cope with the imperatives of industrial maturity; the lack of freedom meant that modern technological society could not flourish. The USSR therefore entered the 1980s with major economic problems and a political system that did not respond to social needs. Fukuyama, unlike Jerry Hough for example, does not believe that there were genuine opportunities for participation and that the USSR only had a proto civil society. *Perestroika* therefore was not a 'revolution from below', but a 'revolution from above' that received support or acquiescence from below. Fukuyama also believes that Reagan's policies played a significant role in bringing down the USSR.

The 'end of history' in the former USSR

Fukuyama tends to equate 'socialism' with soviet socialism, so the demise of the USSR is the demise of socialism. Socialism, however, takes many forms and still has adherents around the globe. The collapse of the USSR has not led to democracy throughout the former Soviet Union (FSU) and an assessment of Russia's democratic credentials is a major focus of this book. There are authoritarian regimes in the FSU whose leaders ignore any constitutional limits on their powers, and where there is a routinised denial of basic political freedoms and human rights, allied with abuses of electoral processes. The former soviet republics of Azerbaijan, Belarus, Kazakhstan, Turkmenistan and Uzbekistan are not liberal democracies. There have been pro-democracy revolutions, dubbed 'Colour Revolutions', in some former soviet republics. President Askar Akayev of Kyrgyzstan for example was ousted in a 'Tulip Revolution' following popular demonstrations during which he was accused of presiding over rigged parliamentary elections held in the spring of 2005. During the 'Pink Revolution' Eduard Shevardnadze was ousted as president of Georgia, which he had led since 1992. He was accused of electoral irregularities and presiding over a corrupt and ineffective leadership. Georgia's Pink Revolution led to the election of the pro-western Mikheil Saakashvili, a US-educated lawyer, in January 2004. Electoral irregularities in the October 2004 presidential elections in Ukraine led to mass demonstrations and protests called the 'Orange Revolution'. The elections were re-run resulting in the victory of the pro-western candidate Viktor Yushchenko and the defeat of the pro-Russia Viktor Yanukovych. Just as the USA helped to finance civil society groups in east-central Europe in the 1980s, they also provided funds and know-how to the civil society groups involved in these 'Colour Revolutions' (Traynor, 2004). The role of the financier George Soros and his Open Society Institute in providing funds for Georgia's Pink Revolution have resulted in it being dubbed the 'made-in-America coup'. The Colour Revolutions were part of President George W. Bush's policy of regime change to promote democracy and capitalism. In 1917 Lenin pushed for revolution even though, in Marxist terms, Imperial Russia (on its own) was an economically backward country and not ready for a workers' revolution. George W. Bush also gave the 'end of history' a push in the FSU.

The world economy and the demise of the USSR

The USSR's semi-isolation from the world economy

The relationship between the USSR and the rest of the world's economy played an important and often underestimated role in both the decision to introduce *perestroika* and its failure. The impact of the USSR's long-term semi-isolation from capitalism and globalisation, in addition to short-term factors such as the fall in commodity prices and the refusal of western economic institutions and governments to lend or give money to the USSR and its allies, must all be considered. Following Marx's analysis the CPSU believed that socialism was superior to capitalism and that capitalism would collapse under the weight of its contradictions and crises. In the early 1920s the Bolsheviks set out to create socialism in a backward and isolated country. Their revolution had been premature in that it had not happened in an advanced capitalist country as Marx had predicted. The USSR was also isolated as the revolutions in the advanced capitalist countries that Lenin had anticipated failed, leaving the USSR as the only socialist country in the world. Against Trotsky's arguments they set about creating 'socialism in one country' – a slightly deceptive term as, while it did entail using domestic resources to develop socialism, it also involved limited trading with the capitalist enemy in order to buy the goods that were needed to create socialism but could not be produced within the USSR. The soviet leadership believed that they were isolating their country from capitalism's pernicious contradictions but it also meant that the USSR was cut off from investment, ideas and new technologies.

In 1949 Comecon was set up to integrate the economies and coordinate five-year plans of the soviet bloc countries. Comecon's 'Basic Principles of the International Socialist Division of Labour' in 1962 envisaged a supranational planning agency, but this idea was shelved in the face of opposition from member countries, notably Romania. Comecon's 'Complex Programme of Socialist Economic Integration', which was adopted in 1971, achieved some production specialisation among member states. It also saw the creation of transnational vertically integrated production networks, whereby different stages in production processes – notably in the car, chemical, computer technology and metallurgy industries – were carried out in different Comecon countries. The 1970s saw this growing regionalisation but it was also a period of growing transnationalisation. Although the Comecon countries produced some new technologies of their own, their isolation from the world economy nonetheless made it difficult for them to adapt to the technological revolution. During the 1970s détente period, awareness of growing economic problems and also domestic social tensions encouraged the Comecon countries both to increase their trade with non-Comecon countries and to borrow heavily from the West, which further enmeshed them in the global capitalist economy.

Box 2.6 The international economy

Globalisation: is the closer integration of the global economy made possible by the rapid development of new technologies since World War II. It is characterised by the breakdown of the barriers to the flow of capital, knowledge, goods, services and, to a more limited extent, people. Globalisation results in the rapid expansion of world trade and the rise of transnational vertically integrated production networks, whereby different stages in the production of goods are conducted in different countries. Transnational corporations (TNCs) are important agents of globalisation.

Comecon (1949–91): was also known as the Council for Mutual Economic Assistance (CMEA). Comecon's founder members were Bulgaria, Czechoslovakia, Hungary, Poland, Romania and the USSR and it was later joined by Albania (1949–61), East Germany (1950), Mongolia (1962), Cuba (1972) and Vietnam (1978). It was set up in response to the American Marshall Plan and was part of the institutionalisation of Moscow's control over east-central Europe. Its purpose was to facilitate the adoption of centrally planned economies and to integrate the national economies through the development of 'fraternal economic cooperation'.

Globalisation: international capitalism and the end of the USSR

As early as the 1950s and 1960s the soviet economy was falling behind the West, lacking in economic innovation and failing to upgrade its technology. It could not maintain any kind of parity with the USA in weapons technology without access to world markets, but increased access to world markets undermined the very foundations of the soviet economy (Lockwood, 2000). Once the USSR was entrenched in the global capitalist economy, notably through its sales of oil, gas and other commodities, the USSR was subject to the same problems and developmental forces as capitalist countries. Domestic economic problems were compounded by adverse short-term international economic factors that prompted it to first introduce *perestroika* and then helped to precipitate its demise. Michael Cox has argued that it was not the American 'squeeze strategy' that pushed the USSR to reform rather: 'What hurt the Soviet Union after 1980 was not US economic pressure as much as the drop in the price of oil, the devaluation of the dollar, and the economic decision by western bankers not to lend any more money to Moscow's indebted East European allies' (Cox, 1990: 164). According to Alex Callinicos (1991: 45), 'The globalization of capital left the Stalinist states stranded. The forms of organization which had transformed the Soviet Union into a superpower and industrialized Eastern Europe no longer corresponded to world-wide patterns of development'. Another characteristic of globalisation is that it undermines a state's capacity to run its own economy, especially if the state's economic decision making is motivated by political rather than market-driven concerns (see Lockwood, 2000; Chase-Dunn, 1992). For Alex Callinicos (1991) the collapse of the USSR and the other Stalinist regimes in east-central Europe (1989–91) was part of the global transition from nationally organised to globally integrated capitalism.

Chapter summary

In order to explain the demise of soviet socialism, the collapse of the USSR and the accompanying end of the cold war, it is vital to understand the nature of the USSR. The essentialist-totalitarian, revisionist and Marxist analyses provide quite different assessments of the viability of soviet socialism and its ability to devise, implement and survive *perestroika*. The difficulties encountered in devising and implementing *perestroika*, and the impact of Gorbachev's leadership – the Gorbachev factor – have already been examined in Chapter 1. For American Republicans the 'Reagan factor' explains Gorbachev's decision to reform, and ultimately the end of the cold war and the demise of soviet socialism. For Francis Fukuyama, Reagan's policies provided an important advance in the inexorable progress to 'the end of history', marked by the triumph of democracy and capitalism and the concomitant defeat of rival ideologies. Finally, the USSR inhabited a world that was dominated by international capitalism, which since World War II had been increasingly affected by globalisation. The USSR could not resist the impact of globalisation, which also contributed to its demise.

Discussion points

- Was the Soviet Union unreformable?
- How did the Soviet Union manage to survive for 74 years?
- Did the USA win the cold war?
- Why was the USSR so vulnerable to globalisation?

Further reading

For an accessible introduction to models of the USSR go to Archie Brown (1974) *Soviet Politics and Political Science*, London: Macmillan. For two very different evaluations of the USSR see Hillel Ticktin (who edits the journal *Critique*) (1992) *Origins of the crisis in the USSR: Essays on political economy of the disintegrating system*, New York: M.E. Sharpe, and Walter Laqueur (1994) *The Dream that Failed. Reflections on the Soviet Union*, Oxford: Oxford University Press. The CIA's website includes a number of entries produced for or on behalf of its Center for the Study of Intelligence. These include assessments of the USSR and evaluations of these assessments. 'CIA's Analysis of the Soviet Union, 1947–1991', produced in 2001, provides a useful overview of CIA assessments; Gerald K. Haines (1999) 'At Cold War's End: US Intelligence on the Soviet Union and Eastern Europe, 1989–1991'; and Gerald K. Haines and Robert E. Leggett (eds) (2008) *Watching the Bear. Essays on CIA's Analysis of the Soviet Union*, which includes contributions from Zbigniew Brzezinski, Raymond Garthoff, Jack Matlock and Vladimir Treml. These four publications are also available online from the CIA website library: http://www.cia.gov/library/index.html.

For the argument between Richard Pipes who stresses the 'Reagan factor' and Raymond Garthoff who believes that *perestroika* was introduced because of a particular conjuncture of factors and stresses the 'Gorbachev factor', see Raymond Garthoff (1994) *The Great Transition: American-Soviet relations and the end of the Cold War*, Washington, DC: Brookings Institution, and Richard Pipes (1995) 'Misinterpreting the Cold War: The Hard Liners had it Right', *Foreign Affairs*, 74 (1) January–February, 153–60. Useful analyses of the failure of *perestroika* and the break up of the USSR are provided by Alexander Dallin (1992) 'Causes of the collapse of the USSR', *Post Soviet Affairs* (8) 4, 279–302; B. William Babour and Carol Wekesser (eds) (1994) *The Breakup of the Soviet Union: Opposing Viewpoints*, San Diego, CA: Greenhaven Press; Michael Cox (ed.) (1998) *Rethinking the Soviet Collapse: Sovietology, the death of communism and the new Russia*, London: Pinter; and Anne de Tinguy (1998) *The Fall of the Soviet Empire*, East European Monographs (481), distributed by Columbia University Press. The journal *Slavic Review* 63 (3), Fall 2004 carried a discussion on the theme 'Was the Soviet System Reformable?'.

For analyses of the end of the cold war see: Richard K. Hermann and Richard Ned Lebow (eds) (2004) *Ending the Cold War*, Basingstoke: Palgrave; M. Hogan (ed.) (1992) *The end of the Cold War: Its meaning and implications*, Cambridge: Cambridge University Press. Also see William C. Wohlforth (1996) *Witnesses to the End of the Cold War*, Baltimore, MD: The John Hopkins University Press, which is a collection of transcripts of discussions by key US and Soviet participants in the end of the cold war, with interpretive essays. John Lewis Gaddis (1992/3) 'International Relations Theory and the End of the Cold War', *International Security*, 17 (3), Winter, 5–58 explores why International Relations failed to predict the end of the cold war. In February and March 1989 the *New York Times* carried a series of opinion articles by leading experts under the rubric 'Is the Cold War Over?'. On developments within global capitalism see Benjamin R. Barber (1995) *Jihad vs. Macworld*, New York: Ballantine Books; David Held (1999) *Global Transformations: Politics, Economics and Culture*, Stanford, CA: Stanford University Press; Robert Gilpin (2000) *The Challenge of Global Capitalism*, Princeton, NJ: Princeton University Press; and Jeffrey Frankel (1997) *Regional Trading Blocs in the World Economic System*, Washington, DC: Institute for International Economics.

Useful websites

The Marxist Archive: http://www.marxists.org/

Includes the works of leading Marxists, including leaders of the USSR, Tony Cliff and Ernest Mandel.

Aleksandr Buzgalin's 'Alternatives' site: http://www.alternativy.ru/en

References

Aksiuchits, V. (1995) *Ideokratiia v Rossii*, Moscow: Vybor

Amalrik, A. (1970) *Will the Soviet Union Survive until 1984?*, Harmondsworth: Penguin Books

Andreyeva, G. (1988) 'I Cannot Forego My Principles', *Sovetskaia Rossiia*, 13 March

Arbatov, G. (1992) *The System: An Insider's Life in Soviet Politics*, New York: Time Books/ Random House

Bialer, S. (1986) *The Soviet Paradox: External Expansion, Internal Decline*, New York: Knopf

Brooks, S. G. (1997) 'Dueling Realisms (Realism in International Relations)', *International Organization*, 51 (3), Summer, 445–77

Brown, A. (1997) *The Gorbachev Factor*, Oxford: Oxford University Press

Brown, A. (2004) 'Gorbachev and the End of the Cold War', in R. K. Herrmann and R. N. Lebow (eds) (2004) *Ending the Cold War: Interpretations, Causations and the Study of International Relations*, Basingstoke: Palgrave

Brzezinski, Z. (1956) *The Permanent Purge: Politics in Soviet Totalitarianism*, Cambridge: Harvard University Press

Brzezinski, Z. (1962) *Ideology and Power in Soviet Politics*, New York: Praeger

Brzezinski, Z. (1989) *The Grand Failure: The Birth and Death of Communism in the Twentieth Century*, Basingstoke: Macmillan

Buzgalin, A. and Kolganov, A. (2003) *Stalin i raspad SSSR*, Moscow: URSS

Callinicos, A. (1991) *The Revenge of History. Marxism and the East European Revolutions*, Cambridge: Polity Press

Chase-Dunn, C. (1992) 'The Spiral of Capitalism and Socialism', *Research in Social Movements, Conflicts and Change*, (14), 165–87.

Cliff, T. (1974) *State Capitalism in Russia*, London: Pluto Press

Cohen, S. F. (1985) *Rethinking the Soviet Experience*, Oxford: Oxford University Press

Cox, M. (1990) 'Whatever Happened to the "Second" Cold War? Soviet-American relations: 1980–1988', *Review of International Studies*, (16), 15–172

Deudney, D. and Ikenberry, G. J. (1991) 'Soviet Reform and the End of the Cold War: Explaining Large-scale Historical Change,' *Review of International Studies*, 17, Summer, 225–50

Deudney, D. and Ikenberry, G. J. (1991–92) 'The International Sources of Soviet Change,' *International Security*, 16, Winter, 74–118

Dumbrell, J. (1997) *American Foreign Policy. Carter to Clinton*, Basingstoke: Macmillan

English, R. (2000) *Russia and the Idea of the West: Gorbachev, Intellectuals, and the End of the Cold War*, New York: Columbia University Press

Evangelista, M. (2001) 'Norms, Heresthetics, and the End of the Cold War', *Journal of Cold War Studies*, 3 (1), Winter, 5–35

Evangelista, M. (2004a) 'Explaining the End of the Cold War: Turning Points in Soviet Security Policy', in O. Njølstad (ed.) *The Last Decade of the Cold War: from Conflict Escalation to Conflict Transformation*, London: Frank Cass

Evangelista, M. (2004b) 'Turning Points in Arms Control' in R. K. Herrmann and R. N. Lebow (eds) (2004) *Ending the Cold War: Interpretations, Causations and the Study of International Relations*, Basingstoke: Palgrave

Farnham, B. (2001) 'Ronald Reagan and the Gorbachev Revolution: Perceiving the End of the Threat', *Political Science Quarterly*, 116 (2), July, 225–52

Fitzpatrick, S. (1982) *The Russian Revolution 1917–1932*, Oxford: Oxford University Press

Fitzpatrick, S. (1999) *Everyday Stalinism*, Oxford: Oxford University Press

Friedrich, C. J. and Brzezinski, Z. K. (1956) *Totalitarian Dictatorship and Autocracy*, Cambridge: Harvard University Press

Fukuyama, F. (1989) 'The End of History?', *The National Interest*, 16, Summer, 3–16

Fukuyama, F. (1992) *The End of History and the Last Man*, Harmondsworth: Penguin

Fukuyama, F. (1993) 'The modernizing imperative: the USSR as an ordinary country – Special Issue: The Strange Death of Soviet Communism', *The National Interest*, 31, Spring, 10–11

Gorbachev, M. (1991) *The August Coup: The Truth and the Lessons*, London: HarperCollins

Hessing Cahn, A. (1998) *Killing Détente: The Rights Attacks the CIA*, University Park: Pennsylvania State University Press

Hough, J. (1969) *The Soviet Prefects*, Cambridge: Harvard University Press

Hough, J. (1977) *The Soviet Union and Social Science Theory*, Cambridge: Harvard University Press

Hough, J. (1979) *How the Soviet Union is Governed*, Cambridge: Harvard University Press

Kagarlitsky, B. (1988) *The Thinking Reed. Intellectuals and the Soviet State from 1917 to the Present*, London: Verso

Kennan, G. (1946) 'Long Telegram'. Available on the George Washington University website http://www.gwu.edu/~nsarchiv/coldwar/documents/episode-1/kennan.htm

Kennan, G. F. (1992) 'The GOP Won the Cold War – Ridiculous', *New York Times*, 28 October

Kirkpatrick, J. (1992) *The Withering Away of the Totalitarian State – And other Surprises*, Washington, DC: AEI Press

Koslowski, R. and Kratochwil, F. V. (1994) 'Understanding Change in International Politics: The Soviet Empire's Demise and the International System', *International Organization*, 48 (2), Spring, 215–47

Lewin, M. (1988) *The Gorbachev Phenomenon: An Historical Interpretation*, London: Radius

Lockwood, D. (2000) *The Destruction of the Soviet Union: A Study in Globalization*, Basingstoke: Macmillan

Malia, M. (under the pseudonym Z) (1990) 'To the Stalin Mausoleum', *Daedalus*, 169 (1), Winter, 295–344

Malia, M. (1994) *The Soviet Tragedy: A History of Socialism in Russia, 1917–1991*, New York: The Free Press

Merridale, C. (1991) '*Perestroika* and political pluralism: past prospects', in C. Merridale and C. Ward (eds) (1991) *Perestroika. The Historical Perspective*, London: Edward Arnold

Oberdorfer, D. (1991) *The Turn: From Cold War to a new era, the United States and the Soviet Union, 1983–1990*, New York: Poseidon

Pipes, R. (1977) *Russia under the Old Regime*, Harmondsworth: Penguin

Pipes, R. (1984) 'Can the Soviet Union Reform?', *Foreign Affairs*, 63 (1), Fall, 47–61

Pipes, R. (1986) *Survival is Not Enough Soviet Realities and America's Future*, Touchstone Books: New York

Pipes, R. (1992) 'Letter to the Editor', *New York Times*, 6 November

Schapiro, L. (1972) *Totalitarianism*, London: Macmillan

Schwartz, J. J. and Keech, W. R. (1968) 'Group influence and the policy process and Soviet Union', *American Political Science Review*, LXII (3), September, 840–51

Schweizer, P. (1994) *Victory. The Reagan Administration's Secret Strategy that hastened the collapse of the Soviet Union*, New York: Atlantic Monthly Press

Shultz, G. P. (1993) *Turmoil and Triumph: My years as secretary of state*, New York: Macmillan

Skilling, H. G. (1966) 'Interest Groups and Communist Politics', *World Politics*, XVIII (3), April, 435–51

Suny, R. (1980) 'Georgia and the Soviet Nationality Policy', in S. F. Cohen et al. (eds) *The Soviet Union Since Stalin*, London: Macmillan, 200–26

Traynor, I. (2004) 'US campaign behind the turmoil in Kiev', *The Guardian*, 26 November, http://www.guardian.co.uk

Trotsky, L. (1937) *The Revolution Betrayed: What is the Soviet Union and Where is it Going?*, Published in 1972 by New York: Pathfinder Press (trans: Max Eastman)

Volkogonov, D. (1998) *The Rise and Fall of the Soviet Empire: Political leaders from Lenin to Gorbachev*, London: HarperCollins (trans and ed. Harold Shukman)

Waltz, K. N. (1979) *Theory of International Politics*, Reading, MA: Addison-Wesley

Waltz, K. N. (1990) 'Realist Thought and Realist Theory', *Journal of International Affairs*, 44 (1), 21–37

Wendt, A. (1992) 'Anarchy is what states make of it: the social construction of power politics', *International Organization*, 46 (2), 391–425

Wendt, A. (1999) *Social Theory of International Politics*, Cambridge: Cambridge University Press

White, S. (1979) *Political Culture and Soviet Politics*, London: Macmillan

Wohlforth, W. C. (ed.) (1996) *Witnesses to the End of the Cold War*, Baltimore, MD: Johns Hopkins University Press

Wohlforth, W. C. (2001) 'The Russian-Soviet Empire: A Test for Neorealism', *Review of International Studies*, December, 27 (5), 213–35

Wohlforth, W. C. (2003) *Cold War Endgame: Oral History, Analysis, Debates*, University Park: Pennsylvania State University Press

Wohlforth, W. C. and Brooks, S. G. (2000–1) 'Power, Globalization, and the End of the Cold War: Reevaluating a Landmark Case for Ideas', *International Security*, 53 (3), Winter, 5–53

Wohlforth, W. C. and Tannenwald, N. (co-eds) (2005) 'Ideas and the End of the Cold War', *Journal of Cold War Studies*, 7 (2), Spring, Special Issue

Zubok, V. (2000) 'Why did the Cold War End in 1989? Explanations of "The Turn" ', in O. A. Westad (ed.) *Reviewing the Cold War: Approaches, Interpretations, Theory*, London: Frank Cass

Chapter 3

Russia in transition

Learning objectives

- To introduce the problems of Russia's dual transition.
- To examine the concept and course of democratisation.
- To introduce the Washington consensus policies and explain their impact.
- To analyse the legacy of the soviet system on Russia's reforms.

Introduction

In 1992 under the leadership of President Boris Yeltsin, Prime Minister Yegor Gaidar and Foreign Minister Andrei Kozyrev, the Russian Federation (RF) began its transition from soviet socialism to capitalism and liberal democracy. This westernising or Atlanticist agenda as it became known, was influenced by western ideas and institutions. The leading seven capitalist countries (the G7), the International Monetary Fund (IMF), the World Bank and the American economist and IMF representative Jeffrey Sachs, were all actively engaged in devising the goals and substance of Russian reform. The views of the Russian people, however, were not canvassed at this crucial time. While the stated dual goals of Russia's transition were democratisation and the creation of capitalism, economic reforms were given precedence with the introduction of economic 'shock therapy' in January 1992. This dual transition raises important questions about the pace, interrelationship and sequencing of economic and political reforms. The concept of 'transition' is also contested, as it might seem to imply a simple, linear progression through a series of steps to a clear and achievable final goal. In reality transitions are very complicated phenomena, whose outcomes are determined by the interplay of a variety of factors including not only the suitability of the reform programme itself and whether there is an elite and/or popular consensus supporting it, but also the legacy of the former regime and the impact of international influences.

Democratisation

Democratisation – the end of soviet socialism

Russia is now described as post-communist. The Communist Party of the Russian Federation (KPRF) no longer enjoys the monopoly of political power once exercised by the Communist Party of the Soviet Union (CPSU). Marxism-Leninism is no longer the official state ideology and communism is no longer seen as the final, inevitable stage of history. Communism may have collapsed in 1991 but the soviet state, institutions, organisations and ways of thinking did not. In Russia there was no pro-democratic education, no purges, no Truth and Reconciliation Commission and no putting the old regime on trial. In 1992 President Yeltsin even ordered the soviet secret police (KGB) archives to be closed, so frustrating investigation of the crimes of the communist era. The new Russian state also inherited its personnel and institutions from the Russian Soviet Federative Socialist Republic (RSFSR). It did not have a new constitution, reformed representative institutions and founding elections until 1993. The 1978 RSFSR Constitution with a few amendments provided an inappropriate and contradictory legal foundation for the new democracy during the crucial first two years of democratisation. There was also continuity of political and economic elites at all levels and throughout the country. According to research conducted by the Russian Academy of Sciences (RAN), Institute of Sociology, in the mid-1990s 75 per cent of the Russian Federation's political elite and 61 per cent of the business elite came from the old soviet elite, the *nomenklatura*. Yeltsin had become the chair of the RSFSR Supreme Soviet in May 1990 and only left the CPSU in July 1990. In June 1991 he was elected to the new post of president of the RSFSR and it was not until 1993 that he was formally elected president of the new Russian Federation. The CPSU was never defeated at the polls and although it was briefly banned (from November 1991 until early 1992) the Communist Party of the Russian Federation (KPRF) remained a potent political force throughout the 1990s.

Box 3.1 The continuity between the Soviet and the Russian political and economic elites (in percentages)

	President's inner circle	Party leaders	Regional elite	Government	Business elite
Total from the soviet *nomenklatura*	75.0	57.1	82.3	74.3	61.0

Source: Olga Kryshtanovskaia (1996) 'The Financial Oligarchy in Russia', *Izvestia*, 9 January, 5. Olga Kryshtanovskaia is the head of the sector for the study of the elite, Institute of Sociology, RAN

Soviet socialism was finally destroyed when sections of the CPSU leadership, including Yeltsin, decided it was beyond reform. The Russian people were not mere bystanders in this, but until *perestroika* they had not been able to set up the political parties, interest groups, charitable organisations, free trade unions and religious groups that are the basis of a civil society. Western democracies are the products of long and gradual evolution, so it would be unrealistic to expect Russia to democratise overnight, especially as it lacked these basic institutional underpinnings. The functional or structural model of democratisation (see Box 3.3) also places importance on the cohesiveness of a country, the level of economic development and education attainment, as well as cultural support for democracy, to the process of democratisation.

Democratisation 1992–93

Throughout 1992–93 the Congress of People's Deputies (CPD, the lower house of the parliament) was dominated by communists and nationalists (the Red-Browns) who opposed Yeltsin's Atlanticist orientation and economic shock therapy. Congress and President Yeltsin were soon embroiled in an increasingly acrimonious deadlock. Congress believed that it could legitimately act as the voice of the people in the face of Russia's international decline and mounting domestic problems. This championing of the people mostly took the form of criticism and obstructionism of the president, rather than constructive suggestions or a willingness to take any responsibility. Yeltsin for his part would brook no criticism of his reforms, and presented himself as the champion and guarantor of democratic and economic reform. In 1993 President Yeltsin declared a state of emergency and opened fire on the recalcitrant parliament (see Chapter 6). The sight of the White House, the Russian parliament building, under fire graphically symbolised the fragility of Russian democracy. It was also a potentially dangerous precedent for the armed forces rather than democratic procedures to be used to settle disputes between president and parliament.

Despite this inauspicious beginning important changes were made at this time. First, Russia had a new constitution in 1993 which enshrined democratic values such as individual and human rights, and a separation of executive, legislative and judicial functions. While in reality the new constitution only established a rudimentary system of checks and balances between these institutions, it was nonetheless an important step. Secondly, multi-candidate, multi-party elections were held in December 1993. Thirdly, the Russian parliament was restructured. On the debit side the constitution endowed the president with extensive powers, which first Yeltsin and then Putin used to maximum effect, variously ignoring or controlling the parliament, with little challenge from Russia's weak civil society. Elections are held, however political parties are not grass-roots organisations representing the people, but rather vote harvesting machines set up by political and economic elites. To this day the judiciary has not established its independence and the institutions of law enforcement, like all government institutions, are neither popularly accountable nor are their activities transparent. After a period of freewheeling pluralism in the 1990s, the mass media under Putin came increasingly under Kremlin domination. All these developments reflect the problems that Russia is still experiencing in moving from the procedural democratisation initiated in the early 1990s towards substantive democracy.

Box 3.2 Democratic transition

Transition: the period between the end of soviet socialism or another authoritarian regime and the final emergence of a fully functioning democracy.

Political liberalisation: is the partial opening of an authoritarian regime but does not include the selection of political leaders through free and open elections. Under Gorbachev political liberalisation included: the reduction of censorship, growth of civil society, freer debate, reforms to the electoral system including multi-candidate elections and the release of some political prisoners.

Democracy: literally rule or government by the people, who are considered the primary source of political power. This rule may be exercised directly or more usually through elected representatives. Parliamentary and presidential regimes may both be democracies.

Democratisation: has two main stages. The first or transition stage is marked by the end of the old authoritarian regime and the beginning of a new democratic regime. The critical point in stage one is the replacement of the authoritarian government by one freely elected in open and fair, competitive elections (procedural democracy). The second or consolidation stage is characterised by the institutionalisation of democracy, when there is no alternative to democracy and no possibility of reverting to authoritarianism (substantive democracy).

Procedural democracy: concerns the procedures through which governments should take decisions and these include: the holding of competitive elections, the existence of basic formal institutions to guarantee competitiveness and the observance of electoral rules. All votes count equally and decisions are taken by a majority vote.

Substantive democracy: concerns the principles such as minority and civil rights, which must be incorporated into government. For example, minority rights could be abused while observing procedural democracy's majority decision-making requirement.

Box 3.3 The functional or structural model of democratisation

For further reading on this approach to democratisation see: Moore (1966); Lipset (1959, 1994); Lipset et al. (1993); Rustow (1970); and Huntington (1991–2, 1993).

Factors affecting democratic transition and consolidation	The Russian experience
Structural factor 1: Statehood	The Russian state was founded in Kiev in 988 and since then both its geographical centre and its boundaries have moved. After the Bolshevik Revolution, Russia (RSFSR) was just one of the USSR's 15 republics. Russia only became an independent state with the break up of the USSR. It inherited its state institutions, organisations and personnel from the RSFSR.
Structural factor 2: A sense of national unity and identity helps to underpin democracy whereas a growth in nationalist movements and strife make democratisation difficult or impossible	There are debates within Russia about what it means to be a Russian, especially as Russia is a multinational and multi-faith country. In 1991 the Muslim republics declared themselves independent of Russia, but through a series of private and unconstitutional bilateral treaties, Yeltsin maintained Russia's territorial integrity. Chechnia's rejection of a treaty was followed by two wars with Moscow: 1994–96 and 1999–2002. Moscow's tactics in this domestic war on terror, against combatants, the civilian population, journalists and NGOs have inhibited Russia's democratic consolidation.
Socio-economic factors or prerequisites: Democracy is best built in conditions of, if not affluence, then at least not mass poverty. High educational levels also better equip citizens for democracy by making them more tolerant and resistant to demagogues. Affluence and education strengthens the middle class who form the social base of democracies	Soviet modernisation created a literate and well-educated population. Economic reforms (1992–3) meant savings lost their value and led to plummeting living standards. The 1998 financial collapse again wiped out the savings of many aspiring middle-class Russians. The size of the Russian middle class is difficult to calculate, according to Tatyana Zaslavskaia (1997: 17) in the mid-1990s it consituted about 25 per cent of the population compared to 60–80 per cent in most western countries. A more recent study found that while 39.5 per cent of respondents identified themselves as middle class, only 19 per cent could really be considered middle class (Maleva, 2003). Although Vladimir Zhirinovsky, an undoubted demagogue, did well in the December 1993 elections his party's fortunes have since fallen. The electorate prefer candidates, such as Putin, who offer practical success rather than just words.
Cultural-normative conditions: Norms and values supportive of democracy such as an acceptance of pluralism tolerance, trust, civic duty	Russians took advantage of first *perestroika* and then democratisation to participate in politics through for example NGOs, lobbying and participation in elections. Electoral turnout remains high at 60–70 per cent, although this may in part be the legacy of compulsory voting in the soviet era. Public opinion surveys repeatedly show support for democratic values, however there is also fear that without strong authority there would be chaos (*khaos*) and that people would indulge in '*bespredel*', literally behaviour without limits.

Yeltsin, the Atlanticist agenda and the Washington consensus

The lack of a transition blueprint

The sheer geographical size of Russia, together with the experience of over 70 years of soviet socialism following on from centuries of Tsarist autocracy have left their mark. Russia's democratisation forms part of what Professor Samuel Huntington (1991) has identified as the world's third wave of democratisation, which began in the 1970s in southern Europe (Spain, Portugal and Greece), spread to Latin America in the 1980s, and then in the 1990s to the former soviet states in east-central Europe and some states in the former Soviet Union (FSU). In the early 1990s analogies were drawn between the post-authoritarian experience in Latin America and southern European countries and the Russian situation. While Russia shared certain similarities with these fellow 'third wave' countries, there were significant differences that render comparisons unhelpful. Certainly in the USSR, Latin American and southern Europe the authoritarian states tried to control all political activities and to prevent the development of civil societies which might challenge this state dominance. In Latin America and southern Europe, however, the Catholic Church provided an alternative ideology and an organisation that was not successfully controlled by the state. In contrast, in the USSR, the Russian Orthodox Church was deeply compromised by its symbiotic relationship with the soviet state and was unable to play an independent role. Nevertheless the USSR did have the beginnings of a civil society which was increasingly active during Gorbachev's *perestroika* period, 1985–91. Again while the economies of Latin America, southern Europe and the USSR shared a general need to modernise, there are more important and profound differences. The Latin American and southern European countries were already capitalist while under authoritarian rule. They began their post-authoritarian modernisation with, for example, private property laws in place and they already had private commercial banks and stock exchanges. The economies also had quite different structures: Latin American and southern European countries had small and medium size businesses whereas the soviet economy had a massive military-industrial complex which accounted for approximately one-third of its gross domestic product (GDP). In Russia, therefore, economic modernisation entailed a daunting array of tasks such as passing new laws, setting up a range of new institutions and grappling with these giant industrial dinosaurs. Thus post-authoritarian countries in southern Europe and Latin America could not provide Russia with a simple blueprint for its dual (political and economic) transition.

Even the former soviet states in east-central Europe did not share the same legacy as Russia. They had a much shorter experience of soviet-style socialism and had more highly developed civil societies, with independent political and social organisations and highly active churches. Their economies were also more diverse than the USSR's, in some cases including independent farming and private workshop production. These countries were smaller and geographically closer to western Europe; they were also viewed in the West as having been liberated from the soviet empire and, as such, deserving of the West's support. In contrast Russia with its nuclear arsenal had stood at the heart of the soviet superpower, so it was hard to see it as a victim of soviet socialism. In the 1990s the G7 countries saw Boris Yeltsin and his administration as the best guarantor of Russia's transition and provided him with substantial financial support and advice, using the same prescriptions they had given to Poland and the Czech Republic.

Russia's *kamikadze* reformers and the importance of rapid reform

The coalition of forces that had finally destroyed soviet socialism included reformist communists such as Vice President Aleksandr Rutskoi (1991–3) through to Yeltsin's Atlanticist allies. Once soviet socialism was defeated the differences, in some cases the chasms, in opinion among this loose coalition became increasingly evident. It is doubtful whether many Russians, even those who had worked for the end of soviet socialism in the name of democracy and the market, truly understood the path their country was about to take. The collapse of the Union of Soviet Socialist Republics (USSR), the loss of its superpower status, and the demise of soviet socialism and its certainties, left many Russians feeling vulnerable and disorientated. There was no popular consensus about what form Russia's post-communist economic and political systems should take. According to data collected by the All-Russian Centre of Public Opinion Studies (VTsIOM) in 1997, 60 per cent of Russians rejected the western capitalist model for their country and believed that in the 1990s Russia had set out on the wrong course (Shlapentokh, 1998: 209).

Government policy making, however, was dominated by the young Atlanticist reformers who called themselves *kamikadzes* (*kamikazes*) to capture the image of their 'do or die' approach to economic reform. Their rhetoric was curiously reminiscent of soviet maximalist, military rhetoric such as 'storming the steel front'. The *kamikadzes* shared their soviet predecessors' belief in the absolute correctness of what they were doing, believing that there was no alternative to the economic shock therapy advocated by their western advisers. Curiously, they also shared the soviet belief in the primacy of economic relations, namely that if they got the economy right then this would have beneficial political and social consequences. They believed that economic reform had to be accomplished as quickly as possible for three main reasons. First, in order to break the CPSU's power base in the state-owned and run economy. Secondly, the *kamikadzes* feared that the inevitable dislocation generated by economic reform, if prolonged, could lead to social revolt and the danger of a Communist Party restoration. Thirdly, the privatisation of state assets was also supposed to provide the new economic and political system with popular authority and legitimacy. Therefore, starting in 1992 all Russians were issued with vouchers (see Chapter 14) in order to give them the opportunity literally to buy a stake in the new Russian economy.

Box 3.4 The Washington consensus and Russia

- The Washington consensus is so named because it was devised by the International Monetary Fund (IMF) and the World Bank whose HQs are in Washington, USA.
- In the late 1980s and early 1990s the Washington consensus favoured 'shock therapy' or a 'big bang' approach of rapid economic reform to develop a market economy based on private property as quickly as possible.
- Yegor Gaidar and the IMF-appointed American economist Jeffrey Sachs devised macroeconomic stabilisation policies for Russia in order to stabilise the rouble, eradicate inflation, and eliminate the budget and balance of payments deficits.

	The Washington consensus approach	What happened in Russia
Attitude to reform	The inefficiencies of the soviet legacy will be removed by the adoption of a neo-liberal approach to the economy.	In January 1992 the Yeltsin Government introduced shock therapy, with the beginning of the privatisation of state enterprises and price liberalisation.
Political economy of reform	The collapse of soviet socialism provides a window of opportunity, which must be seized to push through reforms as quickly as possible so that they will be irreversible.	In the face of hyperinflation, falling production, rising unemployment and poverty the Yeltsin Administration abandoned shock therapy in 1993–4.
Attitude to gradual or partial reforms	Gradualism will enable old and vested interests to block and oppose further reforms.	While price liberalisation was very rapid, by the end of 1993 most of Russian industry was still in state hands and no agricultural land had been privatised; the budget and the balance of payments were not balanced.
		Conflict between Yeltsin's team and opposition forces in the Congress of People's Deputies led by Aleksandr Rutskoi and Ruslan Khasbulatov over the future of Russian reform, culminated in October 1993 when Yeltsin ordered the army to open fire on the parliament building.
	Recognises that initially standards of living will fall, so it is important that the transition is not prolonged or the people may develop 'transition fatigue' and oppose reform – hence the need for rapid reform.	The poverty provoked by the shock therapy led to victory for anti-shock therapy communists and nationalists (Red-Browns) in the December 1993 Duma elections.

Box 3.4 (*Continued*)

	The Washington consensus approach	What happened in Russia
View of the relationship between the different components of reform	The economic reforms are complementary and must be introduced simultaneously.	Price liberalisation was introduced in January 1992. Privatisation was conducted in stages and was not completed under Yeltsin. Stabilisation policies were inconsistently pursued.
Reform supporters	The owners of the newly privatised enterprises will provide the main social base for reform.	The main beneficiaries of the first round of privatisation were those indulging in various forms of 'insider privatisation' including the '*nomenklatura* capitalists' and the oligarchs. They certainly did not want the return of soviet socialism but are also powerful vested interests in their own right.
	At this point it is important to continue reform, which will ultimately create more beneficiaries and supporters.	Voucher privatisation between October 1992 and June 1994 was supposed to give all citizens a vested interest in reform, but it did not create a share-owning citizenry.
		The failure to develop popular support for the reforms led Yeltsin to court the support of the oligarchs in the 1996 presidential elections.
		The oligarchs came to dominate economic policy and benefited from fresh rounds of privatisation. Most Russians resent the concentration of wealth in a few hands and view it as illegitimate and corrupt. This could undermine political stability and the legitimacy of the regime.
Attitude toward legal and institutional change	It is important to introduce laws and institutions that underpin capitalism, such as those supporting the rights of private property owners, creditors and shareholders. Anti-monopoly regulations and a revised tax system are also important.	In 1992 all Russia's laws and institutions needed to be reformed. This was a gigantic undertaking which progressed very slowly in the 1990s but gained pace under Putin.
		Complementary reforms in the organisation and functioning of government, judiciary and law enforcement at the national level and below, as well as social norms fostering respect for legality and entrepreneurship, have been slow to develop.
Attitude toward initial conditions	It is imperative to create a clean slate by breaking existing communist state structures and institutions. This will stop reforms being sabotaged by the former *nomenklatura* and conservative communists.	Russia inherited the state structures, institutions and personnel from the USSR and used these to implement reform.

Box 3.4 (*Continued*)

	The Washington consensus approach	What happened in Russia
Main view of markets and liberalisation	Markets will develop spontaneously provided government does not intervene.	Uncertainty over property rights and their enforcement, together with the importance of business and market networks have hindered the development of markets.
Main attitude toward inefficient enterprises	They should be allowed to go bankrupt and close down.	In the 1990s enterprises remained open even if they had little or no work, especially in one-industry towns where their closure would have had catastrophic social consequences.
The role of government	The role of government should be reduced overall and it should not meddle with the economy.	The government was the instigator of major reforms. While privatisation, for example, reduced its role in the direct planning and management of the economy, the government maintained an interventionist approach to the economy. Under Putin, major industries were de facto brought back under state control.
Main emphasis of government reform	To slim the government's size and scope, and to balance the budget.	In 1993 'founding elections' for the Duma were held and a new Constitution, enshrining the principles of the separation of powers, checks and balances between branches of government, as well as between the centre and the regions were introduced. These were supposed to create legitimate and accountable institutions, and to build solid constituencies for reform.
		Government agencies were taken over by interest groups, such as monopolies and organised crime groups.
		As the economy went into crisis in the 1990s, government welfare and social spending increased rather than decreased.
		Attempts to reform the civil service were delayed and it has grown in size.
Overall assessments of the impact of 'shock therapy'	Shock therapy did not fail, nor was it inappropriate for Russian conditions. Shock therapy was not applied consistently and was abandoned prematurely. Shock therapy was a success in Poland and the Czech Republic and could have been in Russia.	For Russian Red-Browns, shock therapy was an inappropriate programme born of western, neo-liberal triumphalism, which had ruinous consequences for Russia and its people.
		Russian liberals such as the more social-democratic leaning Grigory Yavlinsky believed that there was 'Too much shock and not enough therapy'.

The Washington consensus: marketisation and/or democracy?

The western bodies involved in Russia's reforms: the IMF, World Bank, Organisation for Economic Co-operation and Development (OECD) and the G7 countries all spoke in favour of the dual goals of liberal democracy and capitalism, but did not make Russian receipt of economic aid conditional upon democratisation. In contrast the European Bank for Reconstruction and Development (BERD), which was set up in the wake of the 1989 revolutions in east-central Europe, made a clear commitment to such conditionality. BERD's 1990 Articles of Agreement state, 'In contributing to economic progress and reconstruction, the purpose of the Bank shall be to foster the transition towards open, market-oriented economies and to promote private and entrepreneurial initiative in central and eastern European countries committed to and applying the principles of multiparty democracy, pluralism and market economics' (Ascherson, 1992: 25). Unfortunately under its first chair, Jacques Attali, BERD was slow to disburse funds to former communist countries but quick to spend lavishly on its own London headquarters. It has been suggested that Attali also fell out of favour because he advocated 'a more state capitalist, planned form of reconstruction in the east' in contrast to the neoliberal approach of the Washington consensus (Gill, 1997: 155). In 1993 Attali was replaced by a former managing director of the IMF, Jacques de la Rosière who served as BERD chair until 1998. For his part Michel Camdessus the managing director of the IMF (1987–2000) tended to sidestep the question of how the IMF would respond if Russia seemed to be abandoning democratisation.

The Washington Institutions and the G7 leaders saw Yeltsin as the best guarantor of reform, believed that it was vital to break the power of the Communist Party and to forge ahead with economic reform; democratisation while desirable could come later. In 1996 the IMF provided the Russian government with funds in the run up to the presidential election, which Yeltsin was able to use to promote projects in the regions that helped to swing votes his way. The democratic procedure of an election did take place, and the West and Russia's new business elite had their preferred candidate back in office, but this was hardly an open and fair election.

The development of the new political and economic elite

Nomenklatura capitalists

Private economic activity was illegal in the USSR until Gorbachev legalised co-operatives and the leasing of land (see Chapter 1). This, combined with the value of savings being wiped out by currency reforms, meant that there were not large numbers of Russian citizens with money to set up new businesses. Despite the issuing of privatisation vouchers, the main beneficiaries of the privatisation of state assets were the former soviet elite, the *nomenklatura*. Membership of the *nomenklatura* was by invitation only and was a prerequisite for the USSR's top jobs. Given the continuity of elites between the RSFSR and the Russian Federation, the *nomenklatura* were well-placed to take advantage of Russia's privatisation process. They had money, know-how and contacts – not to mention control over the privatisation process itself.

In the aftermath of the failed August 1991 coup, a senior CPSU official Nikolai Kruchina died in a mysterious fall from his balcony. The KGB were quick to say it was suicide, but the real reason for Kruchina's death undoubtedly lay in his responsibility for CPSU finances. Through its control of the soviet state's assets the CPSU had become extremely rich 'owning' property, foreign investments and bank deposits. The true extent of what has been called the 'party gold' will probably never be known. Kruchina was killed because he knew too much. The existence of this party gold meant that elements within the former *nomenklatura* were in a financial position to take advantage of the privatisation of state assets. Privatisation provided the *nomenklatura* with a fabulous opportunity to get rich quickly, whether they had access to party gold or not. Through privatisation, about one-third of Russia's GDP passed into the hands of members of the *nomenklatura*. So well did they do that Yegor Gaidar, the architect of Russia's radical economic reform, refers to '*nomenklatura* privatisation', '*nomenklatura* capitalism' and even somewhat strangely to '*nomenklatura* democracy' (Gaidar, 1995: 104). The December 1992 appointment of Viktor Chernomyrdin replacing Yegor Gaidar as prime minister marked the arrival of the *nomenklatura* in the Kremlin. Chernomyrdin had made his fortune from his post as Minister of the Gas Industry (Gazprom) which provided him with control of a (perfectly legal) giant monopoly.

In the period before price liberalisation *nomenklatura* capitalists were able to buy raw materials such as oil, gas and metals from the state at prices typically less than one per cent of the world price; they then sold these on the world market becoming instant billionaires. The directors of state economic enterprises also used Gorbachev's reforms to set up their own businesses. Typically they would set up a co-operative within and parasitical upon their state enterprise, as a means to channel raw materials, goods and, therefore, profits to themselves. The directors then had the finance to buy their workers' vouchers during privatisation and so became the private owners of an enterprise they had formerly managed for the state. Some directors simply took advantage of the chaos of the time to seize state assets. The result is that many privatised enterprises are owned by individual members or partnerships of former *nomenklatura* members, using the money amassed during the soviet era.

The Komsomolers

The Komsomol was the CPSU's youth organisation whose members ranged from teenagers to people in their early thirties. Membership of the Komsomol was a stepping stone to party membership and, as such, was an important testing ground for the future soviet elite. During *perestroika* some Komsomol members were encouraged to engage in the newly legalised forms of economic activity. The CPSU leadership wanted to develop a cohort of young people with entrepreneurial skills, particularly in the area of new technologies, and to establish small and medium-sized businesses. In 1987–88 Youth Centres for Scientific and Technical Creation

(NTTM) were created under the aegis of Moscow district party committees. The NTTMs were provided with start-up funds of 50,000 roubles, granted a five year tax holiday and were told to make a profit. The NTTMs provided the vehicle for some Komsomol members to become members of the new post-communist financial and political elite. One such NTTM was the Centre for Inter-branch Scientific and Technical Programmes known by its Russian acronym Menatap, which traded in computers and software. Under Mikhail Khodorkovsky, Menatap became one of Russia's major financial-industrial groups and Khodorkovsky became a leading oligarch. Crucially NTTMs were the only organisations, apart from the state itself, which could legally engage in foreign trade. Oneximbank (the United Export-Import Bank) was founded after 1991 but by Komsomolers who had got an early start in the highly lucrative import trade. Konstantin Borovoi used NTTM profits to set up his own co-operative in 1987, he then went on to set up the Russian Commodities and Raw Materials Exchange (RTSB) one of Russia's first and largest commodities exchanges. Sergei Kiriyenko, who was briefly prime minister in March–August 1998, also began his political and economic career in the Komsomol and the NTTMs (Coulloudon, 1998: 539–40).

The New Russians

The rich in post-communist Russia are known as the New Russians. They include Komsomolers, *nomenklatura* capitalists and others who took advantage of the new opportunities in the late 1980s and early 1990s to get rich. Olga Kryshtanovskaya found that the New Russians are differentiated by their past experience, educational and cultural levels, lifestyles and political aspirations. There are also the not-so-well-educated low-level entrepreneurs, who are inclined to be involved in rather shady or risky business ventures. These include the shuttlers (*chelniki*) who travel to and from neighbouring countries, bringing back goods for sale in markets, pavement kiosks or small shops. According to Kryshtanovskaya, these New Russians like to flaunt their wealth and indulge in lavish displays of conspicuous consumption, but they are not interested in politics. There is also a business elite of respectable, highly educated businessmen who hold high-level positions in legal commercial structures; they do not flaunt their wealth but like to live well (Kryshtanovskaya, 1994, 1995). The business elite, which includes the *nomenklatura* capitalists and the former Komsomolers are also marked according to Kryshtanovskaya by their efforts to influence the political process.

The clan system

The *nomenklatura* system encapsulated the patron–client relationships, institutional or corporate pluralism (see Chapter 2), nepotism, clan politics and informal networks that were vital to the functioning of the soviet system. As president and parliament battled for formal domination of the Russian Federation's government and politics in the 1990s, these networks and clans adapted to the new political and economic realities. The clans are based upon a common economic interest and

Table 3.1 The development of the Russian business elite

Period	Name of the stage	Characteristics of the business elite	Characteristics of the economic process
1986–1989	Creation of 'Komsomol economics'.	Creation of experimental groups of businessmen from the nomenklatura.	Monopolisation of the superprofitable quick turnover sectors of the economy.
1989–1992	Latent privatisation: 'Privatisation of the state by the state'.	Formation of a class of authorised agents.	Privatisation of financial and administrative structures. Concentration of financial capital.
1992–1994	Open privatisation of industry.	Formation of a business elite.	Struggle of Moscow banks to divide up industry.
1994–1998	Shares for loans auctions.	Formation of the Yeltsin oligarchy.	The acquisition by the Moscow banks of the major industrial enterprises. The foundation of financial–industrial groups and vertically integrated companies.
1998–2001	1998 economic crisis and post-crisis development.	Formation of regional oligarchies.	The appearance of leading holdings, business specialisation.
2002	Policy of separating business from power.	Big business becomes part of the new nomenklatura.	Business is forbidden to finance its own political schemes.
2004	Formation of a new oligarchy.	Formation of the Putin oligarchy.	Strengthening of state supervision of business.

Source: Olga Kryshtanovskaya (2005) *Anatomiia Rossiiskoi elity*, Moscow: Zakharov, 295–6

through their representatives within the government and/or the presidential administration, compete for influence, power, resources and money. There are industry-based clans, for example, Viktor Chernomyrdin headed the energy clan and Oleg Soskovets the military-industrial complex clan. Until 1996 when he was sacked as deputy prime minister, Soskovets was the third ranking figure in the government hierarchy after the then prime minister Viktor Chernomyrdin and President Boris Yeltsin. The government also had a security clan which was also known as the War Party due to its support for the Chechen war (1994–6). The security clan included Aleksandr Korzhakov the head of Yeltsin's presidential guard of 17,000 men until he was sacked in 1996. The Security clan also included Mikhail Barsukov the head of the Federal Security Service (FSB), Defence Minister Pavel Grachev and Oleg Soskovets, whose military-industrial interests chimed with the security-minded Korzhakov, Barsukov and Grachev. A Moscow clan based on shared banking and property interests, and headed by Moscow's mayor, Yuri Luzhkov also emerged in the 1990s; as did sub-clans representing individual regions or less powerful economic interests such as agriculture.

The clan system, although not necessarily the same clans, still operates at all levels of the Russian state and in all regions of Russia. In Russia's super-presidential

Table 3.2 The Yeltsin oligarchy

Group	Oligarch	Financial interests	Industrial interests	Media interests
Lukoil	Vagit Alekperov	Bank Imperial (with Gazprom)	Lukoil (oil)	*Izvestia* newspaper with Oneximbank
Berezovsky	Boris Berezovsky	Obyedinenny Bank Logovaz (car dealership)	Sibneft (oil) merged with Yukos (oil) in 1998 to form Yuksi	ORT television company (with others), *Nezavisimaia gazeta* newspaper and *Ogonyok* magazine
Alfa	Mikhail Fridman	Alpha Bank	Tyumen oil and various trading forms	
Most	Vladimir Gusinsky	Most-bank		*Sevodnia* newspaper, *Itogi* magazine, NTV television company (with Gazprom)
Menatap	Mikhail Khodorkovsky	Bank Menatap	Yukos merged in 1998 with Sibneft to form Yuksi	Independent Media news groups
Oneximbank	Vladimir Potanin	Oneximbank	Sidanco (oil), Norilsk (metals), Sviazinvest (telecom)	*Komsomolskaia Pravda, Russkii Telegraf* newspapers, *Izvestia* newspaper (with Lukoil)
SBS-Agro	Alexander Smolensky	SBS-Agro Bank		*Kommersant* newspaper
Gazprom	Rem Vyakhirev	Bank Imperial, Gazprom Bank, National Reserve Bank	Gazprom (oil and gas)	*Trud* and *Rabochaia Tribuna* newspapers, NTV television company (with Most)

Note: For up-to-date information about the oligarchs, see Chapter 14

system these groups focus their energies on gaining access to the president's court and in the units of the Federation to the mayor, governor or chief executive. They are quite ruthless and will use compromising material, blackmail, bribes, threats and in extreme instances even assassination to get their way. They are not generally committed democrats but see democratic procedures such as elections as useful weapons in their power struggles. The Russian government is very sensitive to this analysis of Russian politics. On 23 November 1995 the newspaper *Nezavisimaia Gazeta* carried an article by Thomas Graham, a first secretary at the American Embassy in Moscow, about the 'warring clans' at the top level of government. The USA received an official protest from the Russian government accusing Graham of violating diplomatic protocol. Graham stated that 'these clans contain few staunch supporters of democracy, and none of these clans are devoted to democratic ideals, despite public assurances to the contrary' (cited in *Izvestia*, 29 November 1995: 3).

By 1997 Olga Kryshtanovskaya, Russia's leading researcher on the new elites, was arguing that Russia was ruled exclusively by clans which enjoyed varying degrees of influence (Kryshtanovskaia, 1997). Further evidence of the clan wars came in 1997 when Chernomyrdin's Energy clan came into conflict with the Western clan headed by Anatoly Chubais and Yeltsin's daughter Tatyana Dyachenko. The conflict was provoked by a new round of privatisations of state oil assets. The competing clans wanted the power to direct these privatisations to their advantage, the economic stakes in the power struggle were enormous, with some of Russia's richest assets literally up for grabs. Korzhakov, who hated both the Western and the Energy clans, claimed to have compromising material allegedly showing that Chernomyrdin had millions of dollars in Swiss bank accounts. In January 1997 Chubais was accused of tax evasion. During the final years of Yeltsin's presidency the use of such compromising materials (*kompromat*) increasingly became a weapon in these inter-clan battles at the highest levels. The end of the Yeltsin era did not see the end of the clans and their tactics (see Chapter 5). Putin was the choice of the St Petersburg and the *siloviki* (literally the power-wielders) clans for the presidency, and these clans disseminated compromising materials against his electoral opponents. Putin was elected president in a multi-candidate election, but it was hardly a shining example of even procedural democracy.

The Russian oligarchs

In the early 1990s a small group of men known as the oligarchs developed vast financial and industrial empires (FiGs). By the time Yeltsin retired the oligarchs controlled over 50 per cent of the Russian economy in GDP terms. The oligarchs also sought political power and influence to augment their economic power by allying themselves with the centres of political power in Moscow and the regions (for up-to-date information about them, see Chapter 14). As the 1996 presidential election drew nearer, it seemed almost certain that Yeltsin would lose to Gennady Zyuganov, the head of the KPRF. Yeltsin and the oligarchs feared that a Gennady Zyuganov victory would mean a return of communism and an end to their riches. The oligarchs and Anatoly Chubais, Yeltsin's trusted first deputy prime minister and the head of the State Property Committee responsible for privatisation, formed a stop-Zyuganov alliance. The oligarchs financed and – with Anatoly Chubais – largely ran Yeltsin's 1996 re-election campaign. During the campaign Chubais's Centre for the Defence of Private Property, received an unsecured, no-interest loan of US$14 billion from the Alexander Smolensky's Stolichny Bank (later SBS-Agro) to help promote a civil society, which in reality meant to get Yeltsin re-elected. Following Yeltsin's re-election the oligarchs were repaid for their support with broadcasting and commercial licences and by a further round of privatisation of some of Russia's most valuable energy, transportation and communications assets. Chubais and four associates also received an extremely generous US$450,000 advance for a book on privatisation from a publishing house controlled by Vladimir Potanin's

Oneksimbank. At the time Oneximbank was a bidder for Sviazinvest, a telecommunications company. All these new privatisations were conducted at absurdly low fixed prices, depriving the government of both assets and funds that would have helped them to weather the summer 1998 economic crash. Anatoly Chubais became Yeltsin's chief-of-staff in the new administration, which was an important position particularly given Yeltsin's declining health and withdrawal from day-to-day affairs. Chubais championed the appointment of the leading oligarch Boris Berezovsky as a deputy minister of security. Berezovsky started his economic empire with the Logovaz car business and did not have any particular skills for his new post. However, Berezovsky's oil interests meant that he was keenly concerned with the impact of the first Chechen war on Russia's oil industry and his new government post gave him access to policy making on Chechnia. As Yeltsin had failed to nurture popular support for his reforms, he was forced to fall back on the support of the oligarchs.

State corporatism

> **Box 3.5** Definition of a corporate state
>
> A state in which government represents and is answerable, not to individual citizens, but to the various corporations of which the individual is a functional part.
>
> *Source*: Iain Mclean (ed.) (1996) *Concise Oxford Dictionary of Politics*, Oxford: OUP (abbreviated and adapted)

In the 1990s Russia developed a system of state corporatism in which various groupings, but primarily the *nomenklatura* capitalists, clans and the oligarchs, compete for both economic and political power. The manner in which privatisation was conducted effectively legalised insider trading and led to the creation of private monopolies. It also helped to perpetuate and promote the importance of contacts and networks, particularly those providing linkages between business and the state. Russia developed a business structure of large financial-industrial groups (FiGs) similar to those in nineteenth century Tsarist Russia, and to the contemporary Japanese *keiretsus* and South Korean *chaebols*. The FiGs prosper economically by their proximity to Russia's centres of political power. For example in the 1990s Russia's new banks were often set up with the support of the state and its funds. Banks, particularly those that had supported Yeltsin in his 1993 conflict with the parliament, were given the right to handle government funds and to represent the state in export dealings; they also had the help of state bodies in obtaining export licences. In 1993, for example, Vladimir Potanin's Oneximbank was commissioned by the government to administer federal budgets. In 1995 Oneximbank became the bank of the State Committees for Bankruptcy and Privatisation and then took on the management of funds allocated for the rebuilding of Chechnia (Coulloudon, 1998: 539). Under Yeltsin banks also made even greater profits from their handling of state funds by delaying the transfer or payment of state obligations, such as salaries or pensions, and then using these funds to provide highly lucrative short-term credits. The FiGs thus benefit from patronage and this would be endangered by further democratisation. They finance politicians and political parties, and use their media empires to promote their own and their patrons' shared interests; the 1996 election of Yeltsin was just the tip of the iceberg. They make use of the procedural democratic practices and in doing so undermine the development of substantive democracy. It is not in their interest for Russia to develop a truly pluralistic, transparent, open and accountable democracy. Therefore, they share Putin's concept of the 'vertical state' in which the president, standing at the apex of the state, sends orders down the state structures rather than power and authority lying with the people.

The legacy of the Imperial Russian and Soviet states

Soviet socialist states have been described by George Schöpflin (1994: 133) as 'over regulated' and 'soft'. These terms provide a timely antidote to the image of the all-powerful soviet state. First, soviet states were over regulated because the centre issued 'streams of directives, decrees, and other forms of instruction . . .' (ibid.). As it was impossible to comply with all the directives and regulations, legality became devalued. Party/state officials became selective about what instructions they implemented and adept at filing reports that made it appear as if they were doing what was required. The capricious nature of Yeltsin's decision making and his penchant for rule by decree in the face of opposition from the parliament, the form of super-presidentialism that emerged after 1993 and the increasing assertiveness of local elites, compounded the soviet tradition of ignoring central directives. The soviet state was also 'soft' as 'the state administration under communism lacked the will and the means to enforce the rules it issued, both politically and in practice, thereby encouraging corruption, a lackadaisical approach to regulation, and disregard for the legal sphere' (ibid.).

Again there are continuities in the Russia Federation, most obviously in the sphere of tax collection. These problems began with a long delay in creating new tax codes that reflected the changing nature of the Russian economy. In the 1990s tax codes were so complicated that it was impossible to abide by them and make a profit. Not surprisingly a 1997 survey found that 61 per cent of Russians believed that tax evasion was not a crime (Anichkina, 1997: 3). Tax evasion was the norm at all levels of business. It was only after Yeltsin sacked Viktor Chernomyrdin as prime minister in 1998 for example, that the authorities pursued his Gazprom company for payment of 4.2 billion roubles (US$675 million) in back taxes. In 1997 a new paramilitary Tax Police was formed to combat tax evasion. It consisted of a special 500-man SWAT (special weapons and tactics) team armed with AK-47 assault weapons, sniper rifles, tear gas, grenades, shotguns, bullet proof body armour, heavy duty saws and mountaineering equipment (ibid.). While it may seem counter-intuitive to argue that such paramilitary policing is evidence of a soft state, the SWAT team's existence demonstrates the inability of the state to frame appropriate legislation and to establish a routinised compliance with laws, decrees and instructions.

Imperial Russia and the USSR: the people and the state

Before the 1917 Bolshevik Revolution Russians lived in an autocracy; after they lived in a one-party authoritarian state. Historically the Russians have had a rather ambivalent attitude towards the state, simultaneously seeing a strong state as the best guarantor of their security but also as something beyond themselves to which they held no duty of obedience. The state was protector but also oppressor. Both the Imperial and the Soviet states could be completely arbitrary in their dealings with the people; there was no rule of law and no regard for individual rights. Under Stalin whole categories of peoples, whether they were the so-called rich peasants (the kulaks) or nationalities accused of collaboration with the Nazis, could be crushed, physically annihilated or exiled. Certainly, by the 1950s the application of law was largely routinised but the judiciary was not autonomous and when the state or the CPSU decided to intervene in legal procedures – even when this intervention contravened soviet law – the individual had no recourse. The result was that the state commanded fear rather more than respect and most people gave at least the appearance of conformity. To this day, this phenomenon encourages people to see the state and its laws as something alien, to be got around and subverted. The people are used to falling back on their families, friends, networks and communities, or in the case of criminals their gangs, for support and protection against the state. Russians talk of having a 'roof' (*krysha*): a powerful person, a criminal or an official, who provides protection in return for payment, services, support or favours. The instability and economic insecurity experienced by most Russians during the 1990s also encouraged them to fall back on their networks and patron–client relationships.

Patrimonialism, '*kormlenie*' and corruption

In both Tsarist Russia and in the USSR political power was closely linked to property ownership or the control of economic resources. Imperial Russia was a patrimonial regime 'where the rights of sovereignty and those of ownership blend to the point of becoming indistinguishable, and political power is exercised in the same manner as economic power' (Pipes, 1977: 22–3). The Tsar rewarded nobles with economic privileges in return for their service and support. In 1722 Peter the Great established a 'table of ranks' which divided state service into armed services, civil service and court. The CPSU leaders of the soviet state also disposed of political and economic power and authority; the CPSU also had its own rough equivalent of a table of ranks in the *nomenklatura* system. The Imperial Russian nobility were in effect the elite of the civil service and, like all the other civil servants, they indulged in *kormlenie* or 'feeding'. They performed their service to the Tsar, such as tax collection, but kept a portion back for themselves. This approach to public service did not disappear with the Bolshevik Revolution. Under Gorbachev for example anyone wishing to set up a co-operative or to lease land had to pay bribes in order to get the necessary permissions and licences.

Kormlenie or, less euphemistically, corruption – the use of public resources for personal gain – also characterises post-communist Russia. The privatisation process provided highly lucrative opportunities for corruption. These include activities that in the West would be classified as a conflict of interest or insider trading, but which were not then covered by Russian law. They also include the illegal use of state funds or the preferential granting of licences in return for a personal reward. The Norilsk loans-for-shares scandal uncovered by the Russian Audit Chamber in 1997 is just one example of such activities. Norilsk is one of Russia's major hard-currency earners, producing 90 per cent of Russia's nickel, 80 per cent of its cobalt and all of its platinum. In 1995 the oligarch Vladimir Potanin's Oneximbank acquired a 38 per cent share in Norilsk nickel for a US$170 million loan to the government, in 1997 Oneximbank paid a further $250 million. Once the government paid back the loan it had, in effect, sold a major state asset for only US$80 million. The scandal was heightened by the fact that Norilsk workers were not being paid. Potanin was an ally of Anatoly Chubais, the chair of the State Property Committee. There is an expectation, born of long experience, that individuals will use state service or links with the state for personal gain.

Corruption to this day pervades all levels of the Russian state, although it is difficult to gauge the scale of such activities as they are obviously neither recorded nor publicised. The role of the state and, therefore, civil servants in privatisation or tax collection provides ample opportunities for corrupt behaviour. Customs officials do deals with criminal gangs, receiving a cut of the profits in return for not collecting import taxes. The FSB (successor organisation to the KGB), the police and members of the armed forces are all known to sell security services. These services range from performing their normal state function for private reward, to using their capacities (know-how, contacts, weapons) as state functionaries for illegal purposes. The lack of an adequate legal framework, low wages, a loss of mission on the part of the security forces, the state's inability to provide security and the tradition of using positions for personal power, have all contributed to this phenomenon.

Box 3.6 President Putin on corruption

I note what has become a characteristic feature of our country's political life, namely, low levels of public trust in some of the institutions of state power and in big business. The reasons for this situation are understandable.

The changes of the early 1990s were a time of great hopes for millions of people, but neither the authorities nor business fulfilled these hopes. Moreover, some members of these groups pursued their own personal enrichment in a way such had never been seen before in our country's history, at the expense of the majority of our citizens and in disregard for the norms of law and morality. . . .

[D]espite all the efforts we have made we have still not yet managed to remove one of the greatest obstacles facing our development, that of corruption. It is my view that social responsibility must lie at the foundation of the work of civil servants and business, and they must understand that the source of Russia's wellbeing and prosperity is the people of this country.

Source: Vladimir Putin (2006) 'Annual Address to the Federal Assembly of the Russian Federation', 10 May, President of Russia Official Web Portal, http://www.kremlin.ru/eng/

The great criminal revolution

In the 1990s the greatest threat to Russia's reforms came not from the Russian people, suffering from 'transition fatigue' and voting for the Red-Browns, but from crime and corruption. Capitalist markets and democracy both need the rule of law, and law and order. The soviet legacy and the post-communist reforms created the conditions in which crime and corruption flourished. The USSR had its own criminal underworld and organised crime gangs. After the death of Stalin (1953), but more decisively under Leonid Brezhnev's leadership (1964–82), there was a growth in both criminal organisations and their interconnection with the *nomenklatura*. Criminals and members of the *nomenklatura* used the shortages that were endemic in the soviet economy to make money. The structure and the activities of the *nomenklatura* led the soviet investigative journalist Arkady Vaksberg (1991) to describe the soviet regime itself as a mafia. According to Stanislav Govorukhin, an anti-Yeltsin film maker and nationalist Duma member (1993–2003), Russia experienced a criminal revolution in the early 1990s. In first a documentary and then a book entitled *The Great Criminal Revolution*, Govorukhin charged the Kremlin presidency with turning the country into a 'camp of criminals' (Govorukhin, 1993: 35), characterised by general lawlessness, organised crime, corruption and the criminalisation of the Russian state itself.

It was extremely difficult for the new Russian state to maintain the rule of law and law and order, partly as the country lacked appropriate laws to enforce. Privatisation in the 1990s took place in an environment in which there was no clear distinction between legal and illegal activities and a generally lawless atmosphere. Little wonder then that most Russians use the western word 'businessman' (*biznesman*) ironically, to mean a criminal. The lack of a legal framework facilitated the criminalisation of economic activities and has also frustrated the development of a market economy. The lack of anti-monopoly legislation for example meant that privatisation resulted in the transformation of gigantic state monopolies into private monopolies and the creation of a small group of super rich: the oligarchs. As Russia developed in the 1990s, crime and criminality stretched into the heart of the Russian state, frustrating further democratisation.

Democracy, crime and corruption

While long-standing democracies are not immune to corruption, 'fledgling democracies where a procedural transition has not been accompanied and underpinned by a spread of "real" or substantive democracy' (Harriss-White and White, 1996: 3) are particularly vulnerable. In the long term, democratisation by promoting competition, transparency and accountability should work against corruption and crime. Democratisation does, however, also provide greater opportunities for corruption. Russian political parties are still poorly developed institutions, often lacking in organisation and funds, and election campaigns are expensive. Little wonder then that Russia's new economic elite set up their own well-funded political parties, with preferential access to the media, and supported Yeltsin in 1996. In the 1990s Russia's central and local governments were privatising state assets including industrial enterprises, raw materials and housing. The combination of these two factors generated tremendous criminal interest in Russia's democratic institutions.

In 1997 Mikhail Manevich, the head of St Petersburg's City Property Committee was assassinated after attacking insider deals in the privatisation of the city's property. During the December 1998 elections to the St Petersburg City Legislative Assembly, political parties backed by criminals openly bought votes, particularly from older voters who had been especially hard hit by the economic reforms. Galina Starovoitova a co-Chair of the reformist Democratic Russia party, was murdered on 20 November 1998 after she threatened to expose the criminal gangs who were trying to take over the running of St Petersburg. Her aide Ruslan Linkov, who was also gravely wounded in the attack, stated, 'I believe the people who ordered the killing were extremely powerful, well-connected among the police and the FSB – they know how to put pressure on people to ensure the case is not resolved' (Gentleman, 1999: 22). Only in June 2005 were two men – Yury Kolchin, a former intelligence officer, and Vitaly Akishin – found guilty of Starovoitova's murder, described by the St Petersburg City Court as politically motivated and a terrorist act. Those who ordered the assassination have not been formally identified. Criminalisation has subverted the very state institutions that are charged with providing the law and order that democracy needs in order to thrive. Investigative journalists who have attempted to expose malfeasance or anti-democratic practices have also been subjected to harassment and even assassination (see Box 11.5, Chapter 11).

Does Russia need a transitional authoritarianism?

The Asian Tiger economies as modernising dictatorships

Politicians such as Aleksandr Rutskoi looked east to the state capitalist model of economic development employed by the Asian Tiger economies (South Korea, Taiwan and Singapore) and also to Japan for inspiration. He argued that state capitalism was better suited historically and culturally to Russia than the Washington consensus neo-liberalism and shock therapy. Rutskoi shares with many Russian nationalists and communists the belief that Russia is a Eurasian rather than a European country and should, therefore, follow an Asian model of development. In the early 1990s Rutskoi was particularly interested in the lessons that Russia could learn from South Korea. Rutskoi favoured gradual reform and also argued that state capitalism is in keeping with Russia's pre-communist tsarist economic development, which was characterised by high levels of state intervention in the economy, with the state encouraging investment and even acting as an entrepreneur (Steele, 1994: 333–4). Rutskoi admired Pyotr Stolypin, Tsar Nicholas II's prime minister (1906–11), who advocated economic reform combined with a strong state. The Asian Tigers' policy of protecting domestic markets seems to offer a weakened and vulnerable Russia a better chance of achieving the rapid economic modernisation and restructuring that it so desperately needs, than does opening up to the forces of global capitalism. Among the G7 countries it is not surprising that Japan tended to favour a state capitalist model of development rather than shock therapy for Russia (Gill, 1997: 160). Another feature of the Asian Tiger and Japanese model of development is that economic reform took precedence over democratisation; South Korea achieved economic modernisation and growth without being a democracy. In the 1990s Aleksandr Rutskoi did not advocate the abandonment of Russia's nascent democratisation in order to be more like South Korea's modernising dictatorship, but argues that Russia needs a strong state: a state that stands up for Russian interests in the world, maintains its integrity against internal threats such as crime and ethnic dissent, while forging ahead with economic modernisation. In the early 1990s, when Russia began its transition process the Washington consensus held that 'the greatest threat to freedom and capitalism . . . came from totalitarian states' (Gray, 1999: 200). The thrust of reform was therefore to weaken the state.

General Pinochet's Chile as a model for Russia

Russia began democratisation and marketisation under Gorbachev but even then the interrelationship between the two was hotly contested. The problem is that capitalism does not need democracy; it needs markets and stability. Democracy, particularly at a time of heightened expectations but lowering standards of living, is not necessarily conducive to capitalism. Russian democrats and capitalists (who are not necessarily the same people) feared that even the legendary patience of the Russian people would run out and that they would vote the Red-Browns into government. In 1990 the political analyst Andranik Migranyan (1990) argued that Russia needed a form of transitional authoritarianism in order to give the new leadership the time and the powers to push through reforms without the disruption of popular opposition. Only once the reforms had been accomplished, and the Russian people were reaping their benefits, could authoritarianism be safely abandoned in favour of democratisation. Russian public opinion survey data in the early 1990s did not support the idea that Russians were looking for a strong leader like Chile's General Pinochet to push through market reforms with what is euphemistically called a 'firm hand', that is with the suppression of democracy. The public opinion analyst Igor Kliamkin, while equally sceptical about the prospects for both Russian parliamentarism and authoritarianism, specifically took issue with Andranik Migranyan's advocacy of a transitional authoritarianism. Kliamkin acknowledged that the prerequisites for successful democratisation, such as the existence of private property and a civil society, were not firmly entrenched in Russia. At the same time, however, his findings raised doubts about the readiness of the people and influential elite groups such as economic managers, administrators and even the armed forces to push through reform with a 'firm hand'. In a nationwide survey conducted in August–September 1993, respondents were asked to choose the political figures closest to their ideal. Pinochet came second to last with only one per cent of the votes, pipped for last place by Saddam Hussein of Iraq. In the two top spots, separated from the others by a wide margin, were Yuri Andropov and Margaret Thatcher. Kliamkin interpreted these results as evidence that Russia was ready for a strong leader but that: 'It is wavering between the democratic authoritarianism of the "Iron Lady", who improved British capitalism, and the authoritarianism – not at all democratic, but not dictatorial in the Stalin style either – of one of the last Communist general secretaries, who tried to use administrative measures to improve Brezhnev's "developed socialism"' (Kliamkin, 1993: 4).

Box 3.7 Igor Kliamkin on authoritarianism

In the modern understanding of the term, an authoritarian regime is an agreement among influential groups that control the economy and the 'structures of power' to curtail or to restrict political freedoms in order to close the legal channels through which social discontent can be manifested and to break, if necessary with force, the resistance of that segment of the population that prefers the ideal of just distribution to the ideal of economic freedom and efficiency.

Source: Igor M. Kliamkin (1994) 'What Kind of Authoritarian Regime Is Possible in Russia Today?' *Russian Politics and Law*, 32 (6), November–December, 37. Igor Kliamkin is a political scientist and the general director of the Independent Institute of Sociological Analysis in Moscow

---

Kliamkin also rejected the interpretation of the findings that the majority of Russians supported the imposition of the state of emergency in 1993 as evidence that they would support a 'firm hand'. Kliamkin argues, 'Most of the supporters of a "firm hand" in today's Russia envisage it not as a political dictatorship to ensure economic freedom but as something quite different – as authoritarian regulation of the economy and protection of the individual from arbitrariness and lawlessness while preserving political freedoms' (Kliamkin, 1994: 39). The Russians do not yearn for a strong state for its own sake; what they want is an effective state that is able to provide stability and law and order. For the majority of Russian people the 1993 impasse between president and parliament was associated with plummeting standards of living and lawlessness, they supported the state of emergency not because they wanted a dictatorship but because they wanted something done.

Democratisation to build consensus, authority and legitimacy

In 1990 the Hungarian economist Janos Kornai, who would later be a colleague of Jeffrey Sachs, stressed the importance of simultaneous democratisation and marketisation in order to break the communist bureaucratic monopolies and to develop the public support and consensus necessary to see a country through the disruption of economic reform (Kornai, 1990). Kornai rejects the idea that democratisation presents a threat to economic reform through political elites being thrown off course by a discontented electorate. For Kornai democratisation is a vital adjunct to economic reform as it promotes the further development of a civil society, which in turn strengthens a sense of personal responsibility among citizens, respect for the authority and legitimacy of the government and its laws, and promotes social and political stability. All these factors are vital to the operation of a capitalist economy.

The argument that democratisation should be delayed until after economic reform is also based on the dubious assumption that an elite is able to identify the national interest and to push it forward. The Russians have rid themselves of the CPSU, a self-appointed elite whose ideology of Marxism-Leninism was claimed to enable the party to identify what was best for the country, but which had such disastrous consequences. Without being subjected to democratic controls, no matter how flawed and frustrating they may be, there is no guarantee that a new elite would be any more successful in defining the national interest or interests. Equally, without democratic accountability, there is nothing to stop the new elite from merely pursuing their own sectional interests in the name of the national interest. The suppression of democracy would not necessarily promote national economic development but it would enable the suppression of any popular objections to the excesses of what Russians call their 'wild capitalism'. It is not surprising then that immediately after the March 2000 presidential election Pyotr Aven, a former foreign trade minister and a leading oligarch who heads the Alfa group, said that Putin should 'resort to totalitarian methods to push through radical economic reform . . .' (Traynor, 2000b). He also argued that '. . . Mr Putin should model his regime on that of Augusto Pinochet of Chile, combining Reaganomics with dictatorial controls' (ibid.).

President Putin and managed democracy

Putin made it clear that there could be no return to the soviet past, described socialism as a 'spent force' and argued that Russia's future was as a democracy with a market economy. In his first speech as acting president, he also declared that, 'Freedom of speech, freedom of conscience, freedom of the press, the right to private property – these basic principles of a civilised society will be protected' (Traynor, 2000a); but in the same year he also supported the concept of a strong Russian state (*gosudarstvennost'*) characterised by order, security and stability. While disorder, insecurity and instability are not conditions in which democracy thrives, Putin strengthened the state – especially the presidency and the security forces – at the expense of democratic institutions and practices. He asserted that Russia needed a 'managed democracy', which entailed using democratic means to solve problems that can be solved democratically, but an authoritarian approach when a democratic one was inappropriate. Putin and his administration were the arbiters of which approach was applicable in any given situation. This meant, for example, that elections were held but they were 'managed' to achieve the necessary results (see Chapter 12). NGOs were tolerated but controlled and co-opted as far as possible (see Chapter 10). Under Putin the regions were brought back under presidential control (see Chapter 7), together with the Federation Council, the upper house of parliament (see Chapter 6). Putin also moved against those, such as Chechen rebels, selected oligarchs, journalists (see Chapter 11) and environmentalists, who he believed endangered or weakened Russia.

Chapter summary

The transition from President Yeltsin to Putin was an important indicator of the state of Russian democracy. On the plus side, Yeltsin stepped down and there was the formality of an election, which saw the peaceful transition from one president to the next. However, the secret selection of the largely unknown Putin as the 'chosen successor' by the clans that dominate elite level politics and the manipulation of the electoral process, speaks to the limits of democratisation. Yeltsin's legacy was a country in which procedural democracy had been initiated, but one in which substantive democracy had not developed – nor, importantly, had it been encouraged to develop by the political and economic elites. Russian democratisation rotted from the top, not least through the cultivation of the oligarchs as a wealthy band of supporters to finance Yeltsin's 1996 presidential election. This had disastrous economic and political consequences. First, it further fuelled the crony capitalism and corruption that was already undermining marketisation. Secondly, the concentration of economic power in a few hands took resources away from the state and also slowed the development of a propertied middle class who might have a financial stake in a new, democratic regime. Thirdly, although the support of the oligarchs came at a high price, Yeltsin put little effort into building a domestic consensus to support his reforms. The result was that both marketisation and democratisation were distorted and, by the time that Putin became President, had already failed to deliver on the high hopes of 1992. For his part Putin was committed to the twin goals of marketisation and democratisation, but was willing to sacrifice both to the greater goal of strengthening of the Russian state.

Discussion points

- Did Yeltsin have any choice other than to court the support of the oligarchs in 1996?
- What aspects of the soviet legacy either helped or hindered the Russian Federation's democratic transition?
- What were the achievements of Russian democratisation under Yeltsin?
- Does the Russian state need to be strengthened or weakened?

Further reading

Peter Truscott's (1997) *Russia First. Breaking With the West*, London: I. B. Tauris analyses the ups and downs of Russia's reforms and Lilia Shevtsova's (1999) *Yeltsin's Russia. Myths and Reality*, Washington, DC: Carnegie Endowment for International Peace provides a compelling analysis of the origins, course and consequences of the Yeltsin presidency. Leon Aron (2000) *Yeltsin: A Revolutionary Life*, New York: St Martin's provides a generally positive view of Yeltsin while Peter Reddaway and Dmitri Glinski (2001) in *The Tragedy of Russia's Reforms: Market Bolshevism against Democracy*, Washington: U.S. Institute of Peace argue that Yeltsin and Washington set out to destroy the CPSU and sacrificed everything, including legality, to do it. On the economy, Paul Marer and Salvatore Zecchini (1991) *The Transition to a Market Economy*, Paris: OECD, look at the issues raised by the appropriate sequencing of reform. While Marshall Goldman in his (1994) *Lost Opportunity: Why Economic Reforms in Russian Have Not Worked*, New York: W. W. Norton, his (2003) *The Piratization of Russia: Russian Reform Goes Awry*, London: Routledge; and Chrystia Freeland (2000) *Sale of the Century. Russia's Wild Ride from Communism to Capitalism*, London: Little, Brown & Co. provide gloomy assessments of Russia's economic reforms.

For comparisons of Russia's and other post-authoritarian transitions, see Tina Rosenberg (1995) 'Overcoming the Legacies of Dictatorship', *Foreign Affairs*, 74 (3), May–June, 134–52 and Melvin Croan et al. (1992) 'Is Latin America the Future of Eastern Europe?', *Problems of Communism*, 41 (3) May–June, 44–57. On the interrelationship of economic and political reform see Michael McFaul (1995) 'Why Russia's Politics Matter', *Foreign Affairs*, 74 (1), January–February, 87–99 and Neil Robinson (1994) 'From coup to coup to . . .?

The post-communist experience in Russia, 1991–1993', *Coexistence*, 31 (4), 295–308. Analyses of the conditions necessary for democratisation and democratic consolidation are provided by Nancy Bermeo (ed.) (1992) *Liberalization and Democratization. Change in the Soviet Union and Eastern Europe*, Baltimore, MD: Johns Hopkins University Press; Larry Diamond and Marc F. Plattner (eds) (1993) *The Global Resurgence of Democracy*, Baltimore, MD: Johns Hopkins University Press; Geoffrey Pridham (2000) *The Dynamics of Democratization: A Comparative Approach*, London: Continuum; Larry Diamond (1999) *Developing Democracy. Toward Consolidation*, Baltimore, MD: Johns Hopkins University Press; Vladimir Gel'man (2003) 'Post-Soviet Transitions and Democratization: Towards Theory-Building', *Democratization*, 10 (2), 87–104; and V. Gel'man, S. Ryzhenkov and M. Brie (2003) *Making and Breaking Democratic Transitions. The Comparative Politics of Russia's Regions*, Lanham, MD: Rowman and Littlefield. On crime and corruption, see Stephen Handelman (1995) *Comrade Criminal: Russia's New Mafiya*, New Haven, CT: Yale University Press; David Satter (2004) *Darkness at Dawn: The Rise of the Russian Criminal State*, New Haven, CT: Yale University Press; and Frederico Varese (2005) *The Russian Mafia: Private Protection in a New Market Economy*, Oxford: Oxford University Press.

For information about Russia's oligarchs go to the *Forbes* magazine for articles by Paul Klebnikov (ed.) (2004) 'The 100 Richest Russians', available on the *Forbes* magazine website: http://www.forbes.com/home/lists/2004/07/14/04russialand.html. Also see his (2000) *Godfather of the Kremlin: Life and Times of Boris Berezovsky*, New York: Harcourt, Inc; Dominic Midgley and Chris Hutchins (2004) *Abramovich: The Billionaire from Nowhere*, London: HarperCollins; David E. Hoffman (2002) *The Oligarchs. Wealth and Power in the New Russia*, New York: Public Affairs; Stephen Fortescue (2006) *Russia's Oil Barons and Metal Magnates: Oligarchs and the State in Transition*, Basingstoke: Palgrave. On Russia's political elite see David Lane's (1996) 'The Transformation of Russia: The role of the political elite', *Europe-Asia Studies*, 48 (4), 535–49; Lane (1998) with Cameron Ross, 'The Russian Political Elites, 1991–1995: Recruitment and Renewal' in John Higley, Jan Pakulski and Wlodzimierz Weselowski (eds) *Postcommunist elites and democracy in Eastern Europe*, St Martin's Press: London, 4–28; and David Lane and Cameron Ross (1999) *The transition from communism to capitalism: ruling elites from Gorbachev to Yeltsin*, Basingstoke: Palgrave.

Useful website

Freedom House: http://www.freedomhouse.org/

An American site which produces yearly 'Nations in Transit' reports, which allocate numerical scores for different aspects of democratisation. For criticism of Freedom House's and other measurements of democracy see Gerardo L. Munck and Jay Verkuilen (2002) 'Conceptualising and Measuring Democracy: Evaluating Alternative Indices', *Comparative Political Studies*, 35 (1), February, 5–34.

References

Anichkina, M. (1997) 'Russian tax police go to work with AK-47 rifles', *The European*, 3–4 February, 3

Ascherson, N. (1992) 'The bank that likes to say "only on condition . . ."' *The Independent on Sunday*, 12 July, 25

Coulloudon, V. (1998) 'Elite Groups in Russia', *Demokratizatsiya*, 6 (3), Summer, 535–49

Gaidar, Y. (1995) *Gosudarstvo i evoliutsiia*, Moscow: Evraziia

Gentleman, A. (1999) 'St Petersburg in grip of assassin's terror', *The Guardian*, 20 November, 22

Gill, S. (ed.) (1997) *Globalization, Democratization and Multilateralism*, Basingstoke: United Nations Press, Macmillan

Govorukhin, S. (1993) *Velikaia kriminal'naia revoliutsiia*, Moscow: Andreevskii flag, 35

Gray, J. (1999) *False Dawn. The Delusions of Global Capitalism*, London: Granta

Graham, T. (1995) *Nezavisimaia gazeta*, 23 November; cited in *Izvestia*, 29 November, 3

Harriss-White, B. and White, G. (1996) 'Corruption, Liberalization and Democracy', *IDS Bulletin*, 27 (2), April, 1–6

Huntington, S. P. (1991) *The Third Wave: Democratization in the late Twentieth Century*, Norman, OK: University of Oklahoma Press

Huntington, S. P. (1991–92) 'How Countries Democratize', *Political Science Quarterly*, 106 (4), Winter, 579–616

Huntington, S. P. (1993) 'Democracy's Third Wave', in L. Diamond and M. F. Plattner (eds) *The Global Resurgence of Democracy*, Baltimore, MD: Johns Hopkins University Press, 3–25

Kliamkin, I. (1993) 'Russia Faces a Choice: THATCHER, PINOCHET OR ANDROPOV?, *Izvestia*, 4 November, 4. Available in English in the *Current Digest of the Post Soviet Press*, XLV (45), 19–20

Kliamkin, I. M. (1994) 'What Kind of Authoritarian Regime Is Possible in Russia Today?', *Russian Politics and Law*, 32 (6), November–December, 37

Kornai, J. (1990) *The Road to a Free Economy*, New York: W. W. Norton

Kryshtanovskaia, O. V. (1994) '*Politicheskaia elita i krupnyi kapital uzhe ne mogyt sushestvovat' drug bez druga*', *Rossiiskoe Obozrenie*, (41), 12 October, 3–4

Kryshtanovskaia, O. (1995) '*Kto nami pravit?*', *Otkrytaia Politika*, (1), January 13–19

Kryshtanovskaia, O. (1996) 'The Financial Oligarchy in Russia', *Izvestia*, 9 January, 5

Kryshtanovskaia, O. (1997) '*Kto segodnia pravit bal v Rosii*', *Argumenty i Fakty*, 21 May

Kryshtanovskaia, O. (2005) *Anatomiia Rossiiskoi elity*, Moscow: Zakharov, 295–6

Lipset, S. M. (1959) 'Some Social Requisites of Democracy: Economic Development and Political Legitimacy', *American Political Science Review*, (53) 1, March, 69–105

Lipset, S. M. (1994) 'The Social Prerequisites of Democracy Revisited: 1993 Presidential Address', *American Sociological Review*, (59), 1–22

Lipset, S. M., Seong, K.-R. and Torres, J. C. (1993) 'A Comparative Analysis of the Social Requisites of Democracy', *International Social Science Journal*, 136, 155–75

Maleva, T. (ed.) (2003) *Srednie klassy v Rossii. Moskovskii Tsentr Karnegi* Moscow: Gendol'f

Migranyan, A. (1990) 'Gorbachev's Leadership: A Soviet View', *Soviet Economy*, 6 (2), April–June, 155–9

Moore, Jr., B., (1996) *Social Origins of Dictatorship and democracy: Lord and Peasant in the Making of the Modern World*, Boston, MA: Beacon Press, Chapter 7, 'The Democratic Route to Modern Society'

Pipes, R. (1977) *Russia under the Old Regime*, Harmondsworth: Penguin

Putin, V. (2006) 'Annual Address to the Federal Assembly of the Russian Federation', 10 May, available on President of Russia Official Website, http://www.kremlin.ru/eng/

Rustow, D. (1970) 'Transitions to democracy', *Comparative Politics*, 2 (3), April, 337–63

Schöpflin, G. (1994) 'Post communism: Problems of Democratic Construction', *Daedalus*, 123 (3), Summer, 127–41

Shlapentokh, V. (1998) '"Old", "New" and "Post" Liberal Attitudes Toward the West: from Love to Hate', *Communist and Post Communist Studies*, 31 (3), September, 199–216

Steele, J. (1994) *Eternal Russia*, London: Faber and Faber

Traynor, I. (2000a) 'Profile: Vladimir Putin', *The Guardian*, 14 January

Traynor, I. (2000b) 'Putin urged to apply the Pinochet stick', *The Guardian*, 31 March

Vaksberg, A. (1991) *The Soviet Mafia*, London: Weidenfeld and Nicolson (trans: J. and E. Roberts)

Zaslavskaia, T. I. (1997) 'Social Disequilibrium and the Transitional Society', *Sociological Research*, 36 (3), May–June, 6–21

Chapter 4

Russia and the Russian peoples

Learning objectives

- To identify and locate Russia geographically and historically.
- To explain the 'multinational' nature of Russia, the concepts of 'Russian' and 'Russian citizen'.
- To examine the importance of the Russian Orthodox Church.
- To examine the 1993 Constitution and its statements about the nature of Russia.

Introduction

The Preamble to the 1993 Constitution of the Russian Federation begins: 'We, the multinational people of the Russian Federation', so while bearing the name of its numerically dominant nationality, the Russians, the Constitution recognises that Russia is a multinational state. The preamble also talks of the peoples of Russia as 'united by a common destiny on our land', implying a shared Russian identity that transcends the individual identities of Russia's over 160 different nationalities. Russian is the official language but over one hundred languages are spoken. Articles 1 and 3 of the Constitution describe Russia as a democratic, federative republic with its peoples as sovereign. This immediately raises questions about the relationship between the Russian state and nationality and, therefore, citizenship and nationality. In 1991–2 the Yeltsin leadership took the strategic decision to turn the former RSFSR into a western-style, democratic country with a capitalist economy. Although Russia's liberal reformers stressed Russia's western or European identity, Russia geographically and culturally straddles the Eurasian land mass. Yeltsin promoted a civic concept of a Russian (*rossiiskaia*) nation, encompassing all RF citizens irrespective of their nationality, culture or religion. National unity and the legitimacy and authority of the law-governed state, would be achieved through a shared loyalty to the democratic values of an open, civil society. Article 13 of the 1993 Constitution expressly forbade the creation of a new state ideology, such as existed in Imperial Russia and the USSR. Such top-down expressions of state power were to have no place in a country whose citizens were supposed to be united by their support for the new Constitution and emerging democratic, political institutions.

The Russian Federation inherited its international borders from the internal administrative boundaries of the Russian Soviet Federative Socialist Republic (RSFSR) of the USSR. This meant that in 1992 25 million ethnic Russians were living outside of Russia, while the Islamic Tatars, Bashkirs, Chuvashs and Chechens living within Russia had already declared their independence. So in the 1990s Russia was facing highly complex questions about the relationship between nationality, citizenship and land, while simultaneously struggling to build a democratic state.

The Russian flag, state emblem, anthem and national holiday

The flag and state symbols

In 1992 Yeltsin needed to create a new Russian identity and to remove the symbols of the USSR. He drew upon Russia's pre-revolutionary imperial past and adopted, by Presidential decree and without the approval of the Duma, the white, blue and red tricolour flag and the double-headed eagle as the state emblem. In 1997 communists in the Duma failed in their bid to resurrect the soviet red flag and the hammer and sickle as the state emblems. The two-headed eagle appears on the front of Russian Federation passports. The three crowns above the eagle symbolise the three Khanates of Kazan, Astrakhan and Siberia, which Ivan the Terrible captured from the Tatars in the sixteenth century. The crowns are adorned with Orthodox Christian crosses. For Russia's Islamic Tatar people this literally symbolises their ethnic and religious subjugation. The passport is also only in the Russian language. The problem for Russia today is to create a unified state that not only recognises Russia's diversity but also incorporates this diversity within its state structures and institutions. Yeltsin by choosing Imperial Russian symbols stressed the historical continuity between Imperial Russia and the Russian Federation. The problem here is that in the nineteenth century Imperial Russia adopted aggressive Russification programmes among its non-Russian subjects. The resulting alienation of Imperial Russia's subject peoples contributed to the instability and discontent that helped to fuel the 1917 Bolshevik Revolution and the destruction of Imperial Russia.

Holidays

National holidays usually reflect significant dates in a country's history or encapsulate an important aspect of their identity. Since 1991 Russia has created new holidays and amended old holidays to move away from its soviet past and to celebrate its new, evolving identity as a democratic state and under Putin as a strong Russian state. Victory Day commemorating the USSR's victory over Nazi Germany in 1945 remains a constant and is still celebrated on 9 May as it was in soviet times. The

USSR's two other leading holidays, International Workers' Day (May Day) on 1 May and the 7 November holiday in honour of the 1917 Bolshevik Revolution had tremendous ideological significance and in soviet times were both celebrated with huge parades throughout the country. May Day is now called Spring and Labour Day and is no longer celebrated with official parades, but remains popular with older Russians. In commemoration of the RSFSR's declaration of sovereignty on 12 June 1990, Yeltsin established 12 June as Independence Day in 1991. In 1994 it was rather clumsily renamed, Day of the Adoption of the Declaration of Sovereignty of the Russian Federation and although it was welcomed by some Russians for others it was too associated with the break up of the USSR and Yeltsin's reforms to be a day of celebration. In 2002 in a bid to overcome the divisive nature of the 12 June holiday and in accordance with his nationalist agenda, Putin renamed 12 June, Russia Day. Yeltsin had established 12 December as Constitution Day to celebrate the adoption of the new RF Constitution on that day in 1993, but it too divided Russian opinion and was abandoned in 2004 on the grounds that it duplicated Russia Day.

In the 1990s Zyuganov's Russian Communist Party was still a potent force and Yeltsin knew better than to try to end the 7 November soviet-era holiday in honour of the Bolshevik (Great October) Revolution. However, the holiday championed soviet socialism and did not correspond to Yeltsin's dual transition to democracy and the market. Yeltsin abandoned the soviet-era parades and renamed 7 November National Reconciliation Day, but this revamped holiday never really caught the public imagination. In honour of Russia's multinational population Putin replaced National Reconciliation Day with a new patriotic holiday, People's Unity Day on 4 November, thus cutting ties with the soviet past. On 4 November 1612 Moscow was liberated from Polish-Lithuanian occupation and in 1613 the Romanov dynasty which survived until 1917, was founded. This was the end of the chaos and weak rule of the 'Times of Trouble' and marked the revival and geographical expansion of the Russian state (Yasmann, 2005). The Russian Orthodox Church (ROC) attributes victory in 1612 to the Our Lady of Kazan icon, Russia's second most popular icon of the Virgin Mary which until 1917 was venerated on 4 November. The new holiday was welcomed by Patriarch Alexii II and the Inter-Confessional Council, which includes pro-Kremlin Christian, Muslim and Jewish leaders. Putin was also careful to stress that this was a holiday celebrating the unity of all Russia's peoples, and that Tatars had helped to repel the invaders in 1612. In the Duma, People's Unity Day was supported by the pro-Putin Unified Russia party, nationalist parties such as *Rodina* (Motherland) and the Liberal-Democratic Party of Russia, although communists opposed the loss of the 7 November holiday. Russian schools and national TV channels held special classes and broadcast documentaries to explain the historical significance of the new holiday.

The first celebrations of People's Unity Day in 2005 were hijacked by Russian nationalists and ultra-nationalists, who tried to turn it from a day of unity of all Russia's peoples into a 'Russian march' for ethnic Russians only. In Moscow marchers included the 'Movement Against Illegal Immigration' (DPNI), *Pamyat*, the Slavonic Union, the National Socialist Organisation, the Eurasian Youth Movement (part of Aleksander Dugin's Eurasian Movement); there were Nazi-style salutes, flags and swastikas and slogans included the Nazi *Sieg Heil*, as well as 'Glory to Russia',

'Russia for the Russians' and 'Long live the Empire'. The cities of Moscow and St Petersburg responded by banning right-wing demonstrations planned for 4 November 2006. A survey conducted in October 2006 by the Yury Levada analytical centre found that the new holiday had not yet captured the people's imagination. Only 20 per cent of respondents could correctly name the new holiday, which was at least an improvement on the 8 per cent figure in 2005. While 51 per cent either could not name the holiday or found it difficult to reply in 2005, the corresponding figure was still 43 per cent in 2006 (Levada Tsentr, 2006). Asked which holiday they intended to celebrate in 2006, 12 per cent said National Unity Day on 4 November; 23 per cent said October Revolution Day on 7 November; 58 per cent said 'neither one nor the other'; and 12 per cent said they 'did not know' or 'found it difficult to answer' (respondents could give more than one answer). People's Unity Day is still a comparatively new holiday and has yet to capture the hearts of Russia's peoples; it is in danger of being taken over by extremist elements.

National anthem

From 1990–2000, Russia had a patriotic tune by Glinka, but Yeltsin and the parliament could not agree on the words for a national anthem (or hymn). In 1997

Box 4.1 The anthem (hymn) of the Russian Federation, 2000

Russia, our holy state (*derzhava*)!
Russia, our beloved country!
A mighty will, a great glory,
Are your inheritance for all time!

Chorus
Be glorious, our free Fatherland (*otchestvo*),
Eternal union of fraternal peoples,
Common wisdom given by our forebears,
Be glorious, our country! We are proud of you!

From the southern seas to the polar region
spread our forests and fields.
You are unique in the world, you are without compare
Our Native land protected by God!

Chorus
Wide spaces for dreams and for living
Are opened for us by the coming years.
Faith in our native land (*otchizna*) gives us strength.
Thus it was, so it is and always will be!

Chorus

Useful website: Russian Anthems museum, contains recordings of the Imperial Russian, Soviet and Russian Federation anthems. http://www.hymn.ru/index-en.html

communists in the Duma urged a return to Stalin's 1944 anthem, composed by Aleksandr Aleksandrov with words by Sergei Mikhalkov, but with the Marxist rallying cry of 'Proletarians of the world unite' replaced by the more nationalistic: 'Be glorious, Russia'. The communist proposal was defeated and, despite a competition to find new lyrics, the deadlock continued. The absence of lyrics was particularly obvious at international sporting events, such as the summer 2000 Olympic Games. The impasse was finally broken when in December 2000 the Duma voted in favour of Putin's suggestion to revert to Aleksandrov's stirring music and to use new lyrics by the now 87-year-old Mikhalkov. References to Lenin and communism were dropped and those to God and Russia introduced.

The new anthem was officially played for the first time in the Kremlin on 30 December 2000 and Putin described it as 'a symbol that Russia had overcome many of its problems' and stated, 'approval of the anthem is an important indication that we have finally managed to bridge the disparity between past and present' (BBC Monitoring, 2000). Putin's comments were also indicative of his approach to Russia's past and present. He retained the Imperial state flag and symbols while adopting a modified version of a soviet national anthem, so synthesising elements from very different periods of Russian history to create symbols for the present and future.

Locating Russia and the Russians

Russia's moving geographical location

Geographically Russia is predominantly in Asia but the majority of the population live in European Russia, west of the Urals. The 2002 All-Russia Population Census found that 103 million Russian citizens live in Europe and 42 million in Asia. A country without natural frontiers, through the centuries Russia has been invaded by the Mongols, Ottoman Turks, Poles, Swedes, French and Germans. Conversely throughout its history, while sometimes losing territory, Russia has also been able to expand into neighbouring areas. Russia has, therefore, experienced a mixture of vulnerability and expansionism in the course of its state building. Western European countries only conquered their overseas empires after having developed their nation states. Russia, by contrast, conducted a simultaneous process of state-building and imperial expansion (Dawisha and Parrott, 1994: 26). The geographical centre of gravity of the Russia state has shifted, for example from Kiev (Kyiv, the capital of modern-day Ukraine) to Muscovy following the Mongol conquest in 1240, and Russia's borders have been subject to constant change.

The response to Russia's vulnerability from Ivan III (the Great, 1462–1505), Vasily III (1505–33) and then Russia's first Tsar, Ivan IV (the Terrible, 1533–84) was to conquer surrounding territories and to create a centralised, militarily powerful, autocratic state. A weak state and military inability laid Russia open to foreign intervention and internal dissension, as exemplified by the Time of Troubles (1598–1613) with occupation by the Poles. Further periods of external expansion brought parts of Poland, the Baltic territories, Central Asia and the Caucasus under Imperial Russian control. The history of the development of the Russian state, therefore, has two key features: the vital importance of an authoritarian and militarily powerful state and the ethnic Russians as an imperial people.

Russia: a multinational federation

Ethnic Russians constitute almost 80 per cent of Russia's people, which means that just over 20 per cent are from the estimated 160 other nationalities to be found in Russia today. The traditionally Islamic Tatar, Bashkir, Chuvash and Chechen peoples, all number over one million and together constitute just over 7 per cent of the population. In 1989 Russia's Tatars celebrated the 1,100 anniversary of their conversion to Islam. They had had their own state from the eighth century until their conquest by Ivan the Terrible in 1552. While for Russians 1552 is the turning point in the eventual establishment of a powerful Russian state, for the Tatars it was the beginning of their Russian yoke (*igo Rossii*). In 2002 Buddhist Kalmyks numbered just 155,938 people, while 80 other nationalities numbered just over 10,000 each. Many Russian citizens have mixed or multiple ethno-cultural identities, so for example a Cossack might also be a Russian or a Ukrainian.

Changing definitions of Russian citizenship

As a multinational, democratic state Russia needs to develop a civic identity which includes all its citizens rather than a Russian national identity. The Russians have two words which are both translated into English as Russian: *Russkii* refers to the Russian language and ethnicity, while *Rossiiskii* refers to the Russian state and therefore citizenship. A Russian citizen is a *Rossiianin* from *Rossiiskii*. A Russian citizen (*Rossiianin*) is not necessarily an ethnic Russian (*Russkii*) and an ethnic Russian is not necessarily a Russian citizen. When talking of the Russian people Yeltsin was very careful to use the term *Rossiianye* meaning Russian citizens rather

Table 4.1 Nationalities numbering over one million in Russia

Nationality	Total number	In %
Russians	115,889,107	79.83
Tatars	5,554,601	3.83
Ukrainians	2,942,961	2.03
Bashkirs	1,673,389	1.15
Chuvashs	1,637,094	1.13
Chechens	1,360,253	0.94
Armenians	1,130,491	0.78

Total RF population approximately 145 million

Source: All-Russia Population Census, October 2002. http://www.perepis2002.ru/

than *Russkie* the ethnic Russians. In the 1991 Russian citizenship law, there was no requirement to be an ethnic Russian or even to speak the Russian language for citizenship. The Law on RF Citizenship, introduced in February 1992, granted Russian citizenship to all permanent residents in Russia and to all former soviet citizens, regardless of nationality, who moved to Russia. In effect anyone who held a Soviet passport could virtually automatically become a Russian citizen. The 2002 amendment to the Law on RF Citizenship, however, established more stringent criteria. Although former soviet citizens are still eligible to apply for citizenship without a waiting period, a person with relatives in Russia must live in Russia for 5 or more years, and a person without relatives for 10 years, before they are eligible to apply for citizenship. Would-be Russian citizens now have to be familiar with the Constitution and speak Russian, and preference is given to those with a secondary education or who are prepared to join the armed forces. One effect of this amendment, together with the 2002 Law on the Legal Status of Foreign Citizens in the Russian Federation, is that former Soviet citizens who had legally resided in Russia but who had not taken out Russian citizenship are now classified as illegal migrants.

Citizenship and nationality: to record or not to record?

In soviet times every adult had an internal passport which recorded their citizenship (*grazhdanstvo*) and in the 'fifth point' their nationality (*natsional'nost'*). This 'fifth point' proved a contentious issue. Even before the collapse of the USSR Russian democrats were calling for the removal of the fifth point, as an important step in ending nationality-based discrimination and towards the development of a democratic, civic concept of citizenship including all the peoples of Russia. The question of whether or not to record nationality on an individual's passport was not so simple, however. While information about nationality may be used to discriminate against an individual, it can also be used to justify spending on teaching in a language other than Russian for example and to support other minority rights. When the Yeltsin Government finally began issuing new passports without the fifth point in October 1997, there was uproar. Although Russia's democrats and non-Russian nationalities still acknowledge the importance of a civic identity, they also recognised the importance of officially recording a person's nationality. The new fear was that if a person's nationality is not recorded, that if the differences among Russian citizens are not recognised, this would lead to creeping Russification, assimilation and the undermining of the autonomy of the Russian Federation's nationality-based republics. In the 1990s for example, the Red-Browns were calling for the abolition of these republics and for a return to the pre-1917 practice of dividing the country into territorially-based provinces (*guberniia*). Yeltsin rejected these calls and concluded a series of bilateral treaties with Russia's republics. Under the treaty agreed with Tatarstan in February 1994 and according to the Tatarstan Constitution, the people of the Tatarstan republic had dual Russian Federation and Tatarstan republic citizenship. The new Russian Federation passport gave no sense of this dual nationality, which led to calls for Tatarstan to issue its own passport. The parliament of Tatarstan with the support of their president,

Mintimer Shamiyev, stopped issuing the new Russian Federation passports in 1997 (Khasanova, 1997).

Putin came to office determined to strengthen what he calls 'the power vertical', the line of command running from the Kremlin in Moscow down through the republics and regions. Believing that too much local autonomy had undermined the state, he ended bilateral treaties, insisted that the republics' constitutions conform to the RF Constitution, and amalgamated republics and regions into new federal districts, which are not nationality based. In 2005 the Duma discussed a bill to define all the RF population as simply *Rossiiskii*, as citizens of the Russian state. This debate plus the undermining of the power of the ethnically-based republics and regions, once again raised fears that Putin was not motivated by democratic imperatives but rather by the desire to strengthen the Russian state. In March 2005 Shamiyev was nominated by Putin for another term as president of Tatarstan and the two men also concluded an agreement allowing residents of Tatarstan the right to a passport with an insert bearing Tatarstan's state symbol.

The lost Russians: the diaspora

The Russian diaspora are the 25 million ethnic Russians left outside the Russian Federation in the 14 other former union republics of the USSR. The USSR was a highly geographically mobile society and Russians spread out throughout the Union to hold key positions in local power structures or simply to augment the local labour force. As the Russian nationality was so closely associated with the soviet state, the Russians were and often still are, viewed as imperial colonisers and the unwanted remnants of the soviet empire. In the newly independent states of the former USSR, in what the Russians call the 'Near Abroad', ethnic Russians are often viewed as Moscow's fifth column providing Moscow with an excuse to meddle in their now sovereign neighbours' domestic affairs. The diaspora is vulnerable; they have been subjected to physical harassment, discriminatory laws and treated as second class citizens and so symbolise Russia's diminished status and its inability to protect ethnic Russians.

In the 1990s the diaspora became a political issue within Russia with politicians vying to express their concern. As Russia is a multinational state, the selection of ethnic Russians for protection and not Russia's other peoples in the Near Abroad, contradicted the Constitution. Russian liberals tended to stress the importance of all states adhering to international human rights conventions in the treatment of ethnic minorities. Yeltsin spoke of Russia's concerns for its compatriots (*sootech-estvenniki*) in the Near Abroad and promised that the Russian government would champion their rights and protect them against persecution; at the same time the Red-Browns argued that Russia's borders should be moved to bring all Russians into Russia. In his April 2005 Annual Address to the Federal Assembly, Putin said that 'the collapse of the Soviet Union was a major geopolitical disaster of the century. As for the Russian nation, it became a genuine drama. Tens of millions of our co-citizens and compatriots found themselves outside Russian territory' (Putin, 2005). However, in 2006 Putin noted that most Russians living outside Russia do so voluntarily, he described supporting and defending their rights as a national

Table 4.2 The size and distribution of the Russian diaspora

New state	Total population (in millions)	The Russian minority (as a percentage of the population)
Ukraine	52	22
Kazakhstan	17	36
Belarus	10	13
Moldova	4	13
Latvia	3	35
Estonia	7	6
Georgia	5	6
Uzbekistan	20	8
Tajikistan	5	7
Kyrgyzstan	4	22
Turkmenistan	4	9

Source: Anthony Hyman (1993) 'Russians Outside Russia', *The World Today* 19 (11), 206

priority, and announced programmes to provide the disapora with cultural, educational and social support, and to provide help with resettlement for Russians wishing to settle in Russia (Putin, 2006).

The lost Russians?: The eastern Slavs

It was the leaders of Russia, Ukraine and Belarus who signed the December 1991 Belovezha (Minsk) Agreement which brought an end to the USSR. Russia's westernising reformers typically believed that Russia's best hope for reform was if it were no longer at the centre of an empire. In contrast the Communist Party of the Russian Federation (KPRF) is particularly keen to project itself as leading the drive to reintegrate the countries of the former USSR. Russian nationalists such as Aleksandr Solzhenitsyn typically believe that the Russian state should encompass all the eastern Slavs, the Russians, Ukrainians and Belarussians, as well as the Russian population of Kazakhstan. These ideas have a long heritage. In the nineteenth century Russian historians such as Nikolai Karamzin (1766–1826), Sergei Solovoyev (1820–79) and Vasily Klyuchevsky (1841–1911) stressed the unity of the eastern Slavs, the Russians, Ukrainians and Belarussians; although the eastern Slavs had certain regional differences they were portrayed as one Russian nation. There is a sense that Russia has been territorially, economically and also culturally diminished by the loss of the eastern Slavs. Twenty-two per cent of Ukraine's population are ethnic Russians; its independence was a strategic and economic loss to Russia. More importantly for Russian nationalists, Ukraine's capital Kiev was the cradle of the Russian state, the medieval principality of Kievan Rus.

On 15 March 1996 the Red-Brown dominated Duma voted to revoke the Belovezha Agreement, so ringing alarm bells in all the former soviet republics. Gennady Zyuganov's programme for the 1996 presidential election demanded the abrogation of what he called the 'Belovezha Putsch'. He tried to assure Russia's neighbours that no new state would be forcibly annexed nor was their sovereignty under attack. Zyuganov did however commit Russia – if he became president – to take all necessary measures to restore 'fraternal ties' particularly between Russia, Ukraine, Belarus and Kazakhstan as the foundation for a planned and voluntary restoration of a union state. Yeltsin condemned the Duma vote and instead sought to strengthen the Commonwealth of Independent States (CIS). Ukraine continues jealously to guard its independence but President Lukashenko of Belarus has supported Belarus–Russian integration. In April 1997 Yeltsin and Lukashenko signed an outline union treaty committing the two countries to closer military, economic and social cooperation, while maintaining each country's sovereignty. Further treaties followed in December 1998, culminating in December 1999 with a new Union Treaty committing Belarus and Russia to form a confederation.

The Cossacks

Cossacks are Russian Orthodox Christians and Russian nationalists with a powerful martial tradition. They are the descendants of Russian and Ukrainian peasants who fled serfdom to live in the borders areas of the imperial Russian empire in the Rostov and Volgograd regions, Krasnodar and Stavropol territories, Kazakhstan, Siberia and the Far East. The Cossacks lived as free people and had their own organisations, including military forces (*voyska*) which loyally served the tsars. Their support for the tsars led to their persecution by the Bolsheviks. In 1992 Yeltsin set up a Council on Cossack Affairs and the Cossacks were classified as among the oppressed peoples of the soviet period but were denied the status of a distinct ethnic group. According to the 2002 Russian census there are 140,000 Cossacks, although retired General Gennady Troshev (2002: 210), the presidential adviser on Cossack Affairs, claims there are 660,000 living in 56 of Russia's federal subjects. Putin's 'Law on Cossack Service' (2005) even gives Cossacks a role in children's patriotic education. In 2005 Cossacks began a campaign for the merger of Rostov and Volgograd *oblasts* to form a Don Cossack *oblast*. Such a merger would, in effect, revive the republic of Don Cossacks founded in the sixteenth century but it is unlikely to happen.

Religion and the Russian state

The Russian Orthodox Church and the Russian state

The adoption of Christianity by Prince Vladimir in Kiev in 988 is the defining moment in the development of Russian culture and statehood. The identification of the conversion to Christianity as the beginning of the Russian state highlights the interrelationship of state and church in Russia. From 988 until 1917 Russian Orthodoxy was the state religion. Peter I, the Great (1689–1725), the great westerniser seen by some as the enemy of Holy Mother Russia, brought the Russian Orthodox Church (ROC) within the state apparatus. The Holy Ruling Synod under the leadership of the tsar's representative the ober-procurator managed church affairs.

The ROC held a privileged position as the national church, was in a symbiotic relationship with the Russian state and played a major role in the development of a Russian identity. The ROC is not just a religion it is the cradle of Russian history and culture, a repository of art and music. In 2006 a feature-length Disneyesque animated cartoon called *Prince Vladimir* was released on the eve of the Defenders of the Fatherland Day, which is celebrated on 23 February. The cartoon had the blessing of Patriarch Alexii II, the head of the Russian Orthodox Church, and is just one of the films that have been released in recent years with a patriotic theme. *Prince Vladimir* took US$2 million in its first weekend, outperforming *Shrek 2* (Abelsky, 2006: 45).

The Russian Orthodox Church and the soviet state

The soviet state was officially both secular and atheistic. As early as the 1920s, however, the ROC began to collaborate with the state in return for a limited and controlled existence while other religions and religious groups were persecuted. Stalin and the ROC made common cause during the Great Patriotic War (1941–45) to defend Mother Russia against the Nazi invaders. In 1987 Gorbachev abandoned anti-religious propaganda and instead reinvented himself as a champion of the Russian Orthodox revival. At a time when the USSR seemed to be in imminent danger of collapse and Russians were bemoaning their exploitation within the Soviet Union, the soviet media were full of articles and programmes about the forthcoming millennium of Orthodoxy in Russia and links were made between the importance of Orthodoxy to Russian culture and the strength of the Russian state. In 1988 Gorbachev took the opportunity of the 1,000 anniversary of the baptism of Prince Vladimir to court Russian nationalists and invited the head of the ROC, Patriarch Pimen, and members of the Holy Synod to the Kremlin. In 1990 a new Law on the Freedom of Religion promised to protect the rights of people of all faiths, not to regulate religious life and affirmed the equality of treatment of all religions.

The Russian Orthodox Church in the Russian Federation

The 1993 Constitution provides for freedom of religion and recognises the equality of all religions before the law; it also describes Russia as a secular state and prohibits the establishment of a state religion. Reality is somewhat different, as the ROC and the Russian state have developed a new mutually beneficial relationship. For Yeltsin, a former communist who had been accused of selling-out to the West, association with the national church helped to strengthen his Russian national credentials. In return he consulted the ROC on certain policy issues particularly concerning morality, the family and the role of women. Yeltsin also glossed over any discussion of the ROC's collaboration with the soviet state.

While Yeltsin was an atheist, Putin is a baptised member of the ROC who regularly attends communion and confession. Putin's spiritual adviser is the Archimandrite Tikhon, the Father Superior of the Sretensky Monastery in Moscow. In August 2001 Putin made a pilgrimage to the holy places of Russian Orthodoxy and enjoys a close relationship with the Patriarch of All Russia, Alexii II. ROC infiltration of state structures begun under Yeltsin has continued under Putin. In the 1990s the ROC signed various agreements with the Ministry of Internal Affairs, the Federal Border Service and the Ministry of Defence. In images reminiscent of Imperial Russia, Orthodox priests now bless Russian service personnel and equipment. This association of the armed forces with the ROC is opposed by groups such as the International Union of Soviet Officers. In 2006 they denounced the unconstitutional 'clericalisation' of the armed forces by the ROC. They claim that the ROC encourages xenophobia, national and religious hatred, Islamophobia, and falsely depicts the conflict in Chechnia as a clash between Christianity and Islam – all in the name of patriotism (Goble, 2006). Under Putin the ROC also made inroads into state education; starting in September 2006 schools in Bryansk, Kaluga, Smolensk and Belgorod *oblasts* introduced compulsory classes dealing with moral and social issues with an Orthodox Christian element, despite protests from Muslim and Jewish leaders. Similar courses are also electives in 11 other regions.

Box 4.2 Russia's 'official' or 'traditional' religions

Russian Orthodoxy (see above) – According to the 2002 census 58 per cent of Russians are Orthodox Christians.

Russian Orthodox website: http://www.pravoslavie.ru/english/

Islam – The Muslim nationalities according to the 2002 census constitute 14.5 million people and Muslims are Russia's largest religious minority. Geographically most Muslims live in the Northern Caucasus and the Middle Volga: in the republics of Bashkortostan, Tatarstan and Chuvashia; Perm Krai; Ulyanovsk, Samara, Nizhnii Novgorod, Moscow, Tyumen and Leningrad *oblasts*. Most Muslims are Sunnis although there are some Shi'ites in the Northern Caucasus and in Chechnia there is a

Putin meets Supreme Mufti Talgat Tajuddin, in Ufa, 2003.

tradition of Sufism. The Kremlin is careful to distinguish between moderate Muslims whose leaders and organisations are represented in the pro-Kremlin Russian Council of Muftis led by Mufti Ravil Gainudtin and radical Muslims whose mosques, schools and organisations are forced to close. In 2006 the Russian Council of Muftis set up a Moscow Centre for the Dissemination of Moderate Islam aimed at young Muslims. Ravil Gainudtin and Talgat Tajuddin, the head of the Central Muslim Spiritual directorate, supported Putin's description of the war in Chechnia as one against the separatist, radical Wahhabi sect of Islam. In 2003 however, Gainutin announced the removal of Tajuddin from his posts for damaging the authority of

Box 4.2 (Continued)

Russia's Muslim organisations at home and abroad, after Tajuddin called for a jihad against the US for their actions in Afghanistan and Iraq. The 1997 ruling by the Ministry of the Interior forbidding Muslim women from wearing head scarves in passport photographs was overturned by the Russian Supreme Court in 2002.

Council of Russian Muftis website (Russian only): http://www.muslim.ru/

Buddhism – Predominantly the Karma Kagyu school of Tibetan Buddhism, practised primarily by the indigenous peoples of the republics of Kalmykia, Buryatia and Tyva; Khabarovsk Krai; Chita and Amur *oblasts*. Estimates of the number of Buddhists in Russia vary between 300,000 and 700,000. The Central body of Russian Buddhism is the Karma Kagyu Buddhist Association of the Russian Federation. Some Buddhists also practice Shamanism, in which holy people called Shamans mediate between the spirit worlds and the visible world.

Russian Buddhism on the Internet website: http://buddhist.ru/welcome/modules/wfchannel/

Karma Kagyu Buddhist Association of Russia website: http://www.buddhism.ru/eng/

Judaism – In Russia the word '*Yevrei*' (Hebrew) denotes Jewish ethnicity and the more rarely used '*Iudei*' – Judean – a Jewish believer. Since the late 1980s over half of Russia's Jewish population have emigrated, leaving 30,000 Jews in Russia according to the 2002 census. The Federation of Jewish Communities of the CIS was founded in 1998 to restore Jewish life and culture. Since 1991 there has been a growth in anti-Semitism at all levels, ranging from verbal, written and physical attacks on Jews mainly by Russian nationalists and neo-Nazis. In 2005 15 Duma deputies demanded Judaism and Jewish organisations be banned from Russia; the Nationalist *Rodina* party condemned Jewish texts as anti-Russian and in January 2006 eight Jews in a Moscow synagogue were stabbed by a man with neo-Nazi links. The Russian government officially opposes anti-Semitism.

Federation of Jewish Communities of the CIS website: http://www.fjc.ru/default.asp

The Interreligious Council of Russia – Established in 1997 to bring together representatives of the traditional religions, the founder members were: Metropolitan Kirill of Smolensk and Kaliningrad; Talgat Tajuddin, Chair of the Central Board of Muslims in Russia and the CIS; Ravil Gainutdin, Chair of the Council of Muftis in Russia; Rabbi Arthur Shaevich, Supreme Rabbi of the CIS; and Pandito Khambo-lama Damba Ayushev, head of the Tradition of Buddhist Sangha in Russia. The Council's aim is to find shared ways to solve Russia's urgent problems, including social problems, anti-Semitism, Islamophobia, Russophobia and to oppose domestic religious sects such as neo-Pentecostalists, the Vissarion Community in Siberia, and the Radasteya in the Urals. They also oppose the activities of 'foreign' religions and sects in Russia, including Jehovah's Witnesses, Scientologists, Mormons, Seventh-Day Adventists, and the Salvation Army. In 2004 they opposed the building of a Hindu temple and Vedic centre in Moscow. In 2006 the ROC, Tajuddin, Gainutdin and Shaevich also opposed a proposed Gay Pride march in Moscow.

Russia's 'traditional' and 'official' religions

Russia does not have a state religion but it does have official or traditional religions. The 1997 Law on Freedom of Conscience and on Religious Associations required religious groups to register and made the process particularly difficult for those which could not prove they were 'traditional' religions that had existed in Russia for at least fifteen years. This had the effect of requiring religious organisations to have existed during the atheistic soviet period, when only the ROC, Islam, Buddhism and Judaism had any kind of official existence. Without registration under the 1997 law religious organisations experience difficulties in building, owning or renting property; they cannot invite speakers from abroad or conduct educational, publishing or charitable activities. The 1997 law has been used against Russia's minority faiths, denied official recognition during the soviet period, such as the Pentecostal Church and the Jehovah's Witnesses. Baptists and Seventh-Day Adventists, which had existed in Russia since before the 1917 revolution have also been particularly hard hit. Patriarch Alexii II, the head of the ROC, also claimed that the only Catholics in Russian before the revolution were Poles or foreign diplomats and so Catholicism should also be restricted. From 1991 Russia had experienced an influx of western missionaries, whose ideas and activities were viewed by many Russians as part of a general assault by the West that had already led to the collapse of the USSR and the imposition of economic shock therapy. The 1997 law provided a form of religious protectionism against various Protestant sects and Roman Catholicism, and has also been used against eastern faiths such as Hinduism. The Roman Catholic Church has since been given the status of a long-established religion but the activities of Jesuits are still restricted, and relations between the ROC and Rome remain tense. In October 2004 Putin created a new federal registration service within the Ministry of Justice for religious groups, political parties and social organisations. The service's stated role is to ensure that such bodies abide by the terms of their statutes, but it also provides the state with opportunities to, in effect, ban or interfere in their activities. The Interreligious Council of Russia, which unites the leaders of Russia's traditional religions in a pro-Kremlin lobby, approves these registration requirements. The Council argues that registration should be denied to non-traditional groups and foreign sects, which they deem to be a threat to Russia's national security.

Russia, between East and West

The nineteenth-century debate about Russia's identity and modernisation

The contemporary debates about Russia's identity and optimum course of development have a long historical precedent. From the time that Peter the Great (1689–1725) adopted western ideas in order to force Russia into breakneck modernisation, the question of the relevance of western ideas to Russia has polarised Russian thinkers. In the nineteenth century the debate about Russia's identity and destiny took the form of a clash between the Westernisers (*zapadniki*) and the Slavophiles (*slavianofily*). The Slavophiles stressed Russia's uniqueness (*samobytnost'*) and its organic history, condemning both Peter the Great's forced modernisation and his importation of alien western ideas as destructive of Russia. Slavophilism was centred on a belief in the superior nature and supreme historical mission of Orthodoxy and Russia. The Slavophiles depicted western society and culture as divided and western rationalism as a source of evil. They also stressed the collectivist nature of Russia, embodied in the patriarchal family, peasant commune (*mir*) and in the religious sphere by the concept of *sobornost'*. *Sobornost'* is usually translated as community, but this does not fully convey its true meaning as an organic, harmonious, community of Orthodox Christian believers. Slavophiles believed that only within, and by submission to, this community can people find love, truth and ultimately freedom. They were profoundly opposed to western notions of individualism and, therefore, parliamentarism and constitutionalism. Slavophiles such as Ivan Kireevsky (1806–56), Alexei Khomiakov (1804–60), Konstantin Aksakov (1817–60), and his brother Ivan Aksakov (1823–86), rejected westernisation and argued that Russia must proceed along its own path, not simply replicating the western course of development.

In contrast to the Slavophiles the Westernisers stressed the imperative of following a western path of development. The Westerniser Peter Chaadaev (1794–1856) in his 'Philosophical Letter' (1836) argued that 'Russia had no past, no present, and no future' (cited in Riasanovsky, 1984: 361); that Russia belonged to neither East nor West and had contributed nothing to culture; and that, in order to fulfil its historical mission, Russia must westernise. Chaadaev was declared mad by the authorities. Rather than demonising Peter the Great, Westernisers praised his efforts to modernise Russia along European lines. Orthodoxy was also of no great importance to the Westernisers; some were Orthodox in their personal faith but others were agnostic or even militant atheists. The Westernisers favoured political reform including the end of autocracy, the adoption of a constitution and the establishment of a parliament.

Russia as a European country

The importance for reformers in establishing Russia as a European country lies in the putative link between European culture and democracy and capitalism. If it can be established that Russia is indeed a European country then whatever problems Russia is currently experiencing can be explained as due to the soviet legacy or transitional problems. The counter argument is that Russia is historically and culturally ill-disposed towards western liberal democracy and capitalism. Russian nationalists argue Russia is unique; if this is so the political institutions and economic arrangements that work in western countries are likely to be inappropriate for Russia. If this is the case, Russia has been on the wrong course since the end of communism; western-style liberal democracy and capitalism are not just experiencing teething troubles that will eventually pass but are doomed to catastrophic failure. The logic of this argument is that rather than following western models of development Russia must seek out its own path.

Russia's European credentials seem rather limited. Russia was never part of the Roman empire, did not directly experience the defining events of European history such as the Renaissance and the Reformation, and took no part in the maritime discoveries and the scientific and technological advances of the early modern period. In the eighteenth century Catherine the Great (1762–96) did encourage the assimilation of Enlightenment ideas, but these only influenced some of the aristocracy and the intelligentsia. Nevertheless in the nineteenth century Russians made significant contributions to European art forms such as the novel, opera and ballet. Gorbachev advocated the concept of a Common European Home and defined the USSR as a European country. He allied himself with the historian Dmitrii Likhachev (1906–99), who combined a liberal Russian nationalism with a firm belief in Russia's European heritage. Likhachev argued for example that medieval Russia constituted a distinctive civilisation within the European whole, that Prince Vladimir's adoption of Orthodox Christianity (988) brought Russia into the Byzantine civilisation which contributed to Europe's pre-Renaissance culture. Therefore, according to Likhachev, Russia experienced the Renaissance but through Byzantium rather than Rome. Following this line of argument Russia combines both Russianness and a European identity. Likhachev was dismissive of notions of a mysterious Russian soul defining and restricting its likely course of development, instead he believed that Russia could create its own destiny.

Russian and Asia

Geographically Russia is predominantly an Asian country but Russians have a rather ambivalent attitude towards Asia, recognising Russia's Asian heritage but also disparaging it and depicting it as responsible for the negative aspects of Russian culture. It is easy to overstate the impact of the 1240 Mongol invasion on the Russians. The Mongols respected and tolerated the ROC which was able to serve as a rallying point and focus for Russian loyalty. The Mongol invasion did, however, feed the Russian sense of vulnerability and was invoked by Russian tsars and emperors to justify territorial expansion and the need for a strong autocratic state to preserve Russia. Imperial Russia's expansion eastward into Siberia was depicted as part of Russia's manifest destiny to bring civilisation and economic development to Asian peoples. The term 'Asian' tends to be used pejoratively among Russians, for example in 1917 Lenin accused some Bolshevik officials as having a semi-Asiatic mentality. Similarly, Lenin ascribed Stalin's crude behaviour and authoritarian manner to his being an Asian. Stalin was a Georgian and educated at an Orthodox Christian seminary, but evidently Caucasian people were also classified as Asian. Russia's 'Asian characteristics' are blamed for making Russia resistant to modernisation, prone to authoritarianism, with a weak civil society and a dominant state.

Eurasianism

The 1980s saw renewed interest by Russia's Red-Browns in the idea of Russia as a Eurasian country and culture. Eurasianism was first developed in the 1920s as an alternative to Bolshevism by Prince Nikolai Trubetskoi, George Florovsky and Pyotr Savitsky in their *Exodus to the East (Iskhod k vostoku)* published in Sofia in 1921. In 1989 Sergei Zalygin the editor of the influential journal *Novy Mir* reprinted an article by the Eurasianist thinker Nikolai Berdyaev (1874–1948). Berdyaev believed that material development with its need for a market, private property and scientific-technical progress was a universal value and necessary for Russia. Nonetheless he contrasted the struggle between Russia and the West as one of the 'spirit' versus 'machine'. According to Berdyaev Russians do not worship the golden calf (money and material possessions) and Russian civilisation has not become a world of things unlike the West (Berdyaev, 1947).

Box 4.3 Russians as Eurasians

Berdyaev argued:

The inconsistency and complexity of the Russian soul may be due to the fact that in Russia two streams of world history – East and West – jostle and influence one another. The Russian people is not purely European and it is not purely Asiatic. Russia is a complete section of the world – a colossal East-West. It unites two worlds, and within the Russian soul two principles are always engaged in strife – the Eastern and the Western.

Source: Nicolas Berdyaev (1947) *The Russian Idea*, London: The Centenary Press, 2 (trans: R. M. French)

In the 1980s Zyuganov worked with Russians within the CPSU to elaborate a Russian-oriented form of communism. From 1988 the CPSU began to publish a wide range of non-communist Russian thinkers including the works of the Eurasianist Lev Gumilev. This seems a very strange partnership as Gumilev was vehemently anti-Marxist and believed that Bolshevism was totally alien to Russians. For Gumilev, Marxism and Bolshevism embodied alien western and Jewish values, and so could bring nothing but harm to Russia. In Eurasianism they found ideas that stress the differences between Russian and European civilisations, are sceptical of capitalism, and depict Russia as a unique historical and cultural fusion of Slav and Turkic, Orthodox and Moslem elements. Zyuganov worked quite closely with Aleksandr Prokhanov, the editor of the Russian nationalist weekly *Den* (Day), renamed *Zavtra* (Tomorrow) in 1993 which had a page devoted to Eurasianism, providing a forum for Russian Nationalists and Muslims.

In contrast to the Marxist focus on class Gumilev argued that history is the history of nations, which he termed 'ethnoses'. Gumilev argued that it was possible for two or more nations to unite to form a super-ethnos and that five hundred years ago the eastern Slavs, Mongols and Tatars had fused to form such a super-ethnos (Gumilev, 1992: 10–11). A thousand years before a Teuton and Latin super-ethnos had formed in western Europe, presenting a constant threat to the Slav-Tatar-Mongol super-ethnos. In contrast to the idea that Russia had saved Europe and Christendom from the Mongol hordes, Gumilev argued that it was the military prowess of the Mongols that had saved the eastern Slavs from the predation of the West. Gumilev's concept of an ethnos is not defined in racial terms but rather in terms of the link between an ethnos and its ancestral lands. This gives rise to the concept of a parasite ethnos, an ethnos which has lost its ancestral land and survives as a parasite on another ethnos; in Russia this means the Jews. According to Gumilev there are also parasite states which lack their own dynamism and survive by living off the resources and culture of another ethnos, the USA is a parasite state.

The KPRF under Zyuganov has found Eurasianism more attractive than Marxism: its anti-westernism is appealing, it provides a concept of a multinational Russia which condones anti-Semitism, and the idea of a super-ethnos can also be used to justify Russia as a great power. In the early 1990s other Red-Browns such as the Russian Party and the National Republican Party also adhered to Eurasianist ideas. Since the mid-1990s Eurasianism has been challenged by more narrowly focused Russian Nationalist ideas, which are anti-western, anti-Asian and anti-Semitic. The humiliation of the Russian armed forces in the first Chechen war (1994–96), continuing instability in the Caucasus and fear of Chinese expansionism have provoked a reappraisal of attitudes particularly towards the Islamic world and China. By 1996 even Aleksandr Prokhanov was no longer such a devoted Eurasianist and now argued that it would be the Islamic and Chinese worlds which would really enjoy the dissolution of Russia (Shlapentokh, 1997: 12).

The Russian idea – a new state ideology?

The state ideology

In 1992 certain strategic decisions were taken about Russia's future. The Yeltsin leadership committed Russian to becoming an open society, which included a competitive market economy, a civil society (*grazhdanskoe obshchestvo*) and a law-governed state (Kortunov, 1995: 5). A continuing problem is that Russian politics are polarised between liberal democrats on one side and Red-Browns on the other, so that the very legitimacy and authority of the state are contested. Alexander Tsipko of the Gorbachev Foundation neatly encapsulates the problem as: 'Old Russia was united by ideology combining Christian Orthodoxy and Russian identity. Soviet Russia was united, at least outwardly, by communist ideology. But what ideology can unite the patriots and the democrats, the Russians with traditional Russian identity and the Russians with Soviet identity?' (Tsipko, in Ieda, 1993: 191). Tsipko believes that Russia's democrats need to offer the Russian people a new national idea to challenge the national ideas and ideologies provided by the communists and the nationalists.

In the new states of the former USSR nationalism was mobilised to promote the legitimacy and integration of the new states. Yeltsin used Russian nationalism and the slogan 'Russia First' (see Chapter 2) in his bid to break free from the USSR, but resisted adopting Russian nationalism as a new state ideology. In a multi-national state Russian nationalism would be a divisive rather than integrative force and also would not sit easily with Yeltsin's westernising agenda. Once Yeltsin was in power his most virulent critics were Russian nationalists. Article 13 of the Russian Federation Constitution (1993) specifically forbids the adoption of a state ideology. For Russia's democrats the concept of an official state ideology is too reminiscent of Imperial Russia and the USSR to be appropriate for a new democracy. In the new Russia democratic principles and institutions were supposed to promote a cohesive civic Russian identity which was to provide a firm foundation for the new state. However, after Yeltsin's re-election in 1996 he called for the formulation of a national ideology to unite all the citizens of Russia and set up a commission to investigate Russia's identity.

A new state ideology: back to the future?

In the last two hundred years Russia has had two state ideologies. Marxism-Leninism and the Official Nationality Doctrine. The Official Nationality Doctrine was the Imperial Russian state ideology from 1833 to 1917, although briefly dropped by the reformist Tsar Alexander II (1855–81). The Official Nationality Doctrine was elaborated by Minister of Education Count Uvarov and had three elements: Orthodoxy (*pravoslaviye*), Autocracy (*samoderzhaviye*) and nationality (*narodnost'*). Orthodoxy referred to the pre-eminence of the ROC, Autocracy to the absolute powers of the tsar as the foundation of the Russian state, and Nationality placed Russians as the principal people in the empire (Hoskings, 1997: 147). Could the Official Nationality Doctrine provide the basis for a new Russian state ideology updated for the new millennium? Russian Orthodoxy is being revived as the state religion, and the numerically and culturally dominant ethnic Russians do seem to be the 'principal people' of the Russian Federation. As for Autocracy, however, there seems no ground swell of support to return to tsarism. In 1991 Yeltsin invited Vladimir Kirillovich Romanov, the father of the pretender to the Russian throne to St Petersburg. At that time about 20 per cent of the Russian population supported the restoration of the monarchy; by 1995 only 7 per cent were in favour (Figes, 1998: 102). The last Tsar Nicholas II and his family were exhumed from a bog near Yekaterinburg in 1991 and finally interred in St Petersburg's Peter and Paul Fortress on 17 July 1998. In his funeral oration President Yeltsin described the burial as a 'symbolic moment of national repentance and unity' (ibid.: 98). This is rather ironic as when Yeltsin was the Communist Party Secretary in Sverdlovsk (Yekaterinburg) he had followed Kremlin orders and demolished the Ipatiev house where the Romanovs were executed on 17 July 1918. Russia's communists objected to this state burial as it could constitute not just an apology for the deaths of the Romanovs but also a rejection of the Bolshevik Revolution and the entire soviet era. The ROC, for whom Nicholas is a saint, boycotted the burial as despite exhaustive scientific testing they do not believe the remains are authentic. Autocracy in the form of tsarism would not be part of a new state ideology.

It seems likely that if Russia were to develop a new state ideology it would include the concepts embodied in the Russian Idea. Drawing on the ideas of the Slavophiles and the Eurasianists, the Russian Idea holds that Russia is a unique civilisation with its own cultural and historical traditions which set it apart from the West. For advocates of the Russian Idea it is these ideas that will promote stability, harmony and development in Russia. The three main features traditionally associated with the Russian Idea are: the Orthodox Church, the tsarist state and the peasant commune (McDaniel, 1996: 31). In Russia today there would be a belief in a strong Russian state in alliance with the Orthodox Church. It would not necessarily mean an end to elections or attempts to quash Russia's developing political pluralism; it would, however, be a state with a strong emphasis on military might and patriotism and anyone challenging these values would be given short shrift. The Russian political scientist Aleksei Kiva (1996: 2) suggested that,

---

Box 4.4 Prime Minister Vladimir Putin, 'Russia at the turn of the millennium', 30 December 1999

In this speech Putin set out his understanding of Russia and his vision for the future. According to Putin the Russian people believe in new things such as:

> freedom of expression, freedom to travel abroad and other fundamental political rights and human liberties – value that they can have property, engage in free enterprise and build up their own wealth . . .

But they also believe in traditional Russian values (paraphrased below).

Patriotism – in the positive sense of pride in one's country, its history and accomplishments, the striving to make one's country better, richer, stronger and happier; not in the negative sense of nationalist conceit and imperialist ambition.

The greatness of Russia – Russia has and will always be a great power (*derzhava*) due to the inseparable characteristics of geopolitical, economic and cultural existence, which have determined the mentality of the people and government policy throughout its history and in the future. Great powers are now marked by their ability to be leaders in technology, to promote the wellbeing of their people, to uphold their security and national interests, rather than just by their military strength.

Statism – Russia is not like the USA or Britain in which liberal values have deep historic traditions. In Russia the state and its institutions have always played an exceptionally important role in the life of the country and its people. Russians see a strong state as the source and guarantor of order and the initiator and main driving force of any change. Russians today do not equate a strong and effective state with a totalitarian state. Russians now value democracy, a law-based state, and personal and political freedom; but they are also alarmed by the weakening of state power and so look forward to a restoration of the guiding and regulating role of the state on the basis of traditions and the present state of the country.

Social solidarity – collectivist rather than individualist forms of activity have always prevailed in Russia; paternalism is deeply rooted. Most Russians are used to looking to the aid and support of the state and society for improvements in their conditions, rather than relying on their own initiative and flair for business.

Source: http://www.geocities.com/capitolhill/parliament/3005/poutine.html

'It would seem that the following could be components of a national idea: the idea of a strong and flourishing Russia; the idea of statehood, patriotism and solidarity; the idea of freedom; the idea of prosperity; the idea of spirituality; the idea of constitutional order and safety; the idea of justice; the idea of civil peace and accord; and the idea of openness to the world'.

In a speech entitled 'Russia at the turn of the millennium', Putin (1999) noted that Russia was experiencing social and political divisions and drew analogies between Russia after October 1917 and the 1990s. According to Putin accord and unity had been achieved after the Bolshevik Revolution more through persecution and repression than ideology and education. Putin, therefore, rejected the term state ideology because of its association with Russia's recent soviet past, with its state-sponsored ideology and 'practically no intellectual, spiritual freedom, ideological pluralism freedom of press, political freedom' (ibid.). Putin also specifically rejected the adoption of a new official state ideology and instead believes that a voluntary, civil-social accord will slowly develop. He stated, 'I suppose that the new Russian idea will come about as an alloy or an organic unification of universal general humanitarian values with traditional Russian values which have stood the test of the times, including the test of the turbulent 20th century. This vitally important process must not be accelerated, discontinued and destroyed' (ibid.).

Chapter summary

The debate about Russia's identity is a debate about Russia's future. Those who stress Russia's uniqueness (*samobytnost'*) tend to argue that western models of development are not appropriate for Russia. Conversely those who stress Russia's European identity do so to support a modernising project based on capitalism and democracy. As a multinational state the question of the Russianness of the state is also highly contentious. So far democratic principles and a civic concept of identity have had little success in integrating state and society. Russia is, therefore, looking for a new state ideology which is likely to draw upon Russian nationalism. Eurasianists and some Russian nationalists stress that their nationalism is based upon an inclusive concept of Russianness, not upon a 'blood'-based definition and that it can, therefore, incorporate all Russia's peoples.

Discussion points

- Explain why Russia has drawn upon Imperial Russian (pre-1917) and soviet state emblems.
- How Russian is Russia?
- Is Russia really a secular state?
- Does Russia need a new state ideology?

Further reading

For a fascinating and wide-ranging analysis of Russian history and culture by Russia's leading liberal nationalist historian, try Dmitrii S. Likhachev's (1991) *Reflections on Russia*, Boulder, CO: Westview Press. Vera Tolz (2001) *Russia. Inventing the Nation*, London: Arnold provides a comprehensive and accessible analysis of the nature of Russia. For an extensive high level American–Russian discussion on Russian identity, try James H. Billington and Kathleen Parthé (2003) *The Search for a New Russian National Identity: Russian Perspectives*, issued by the Library of Congress and available online at http://www.loc.gov/about/welcome/speeches/russianperspectives/index.html

On the Russians and the development of Russian nationalism there are two very useful books: Geoffrey Hoskings (2006) *Rulers and Victims: The Russians in the Soviet Union*, Harvard University Press and Hoskings and Robert Service (eds) (1998) *Russian Nationalism. Past and Present*, Macmillan: London.

For accounts of the nature and treatment of the Russia diaspora go to Jeff Chinn and Robert Kaiser (1996) *Russians as the new minority*, Boulder, CO: Westview Press; Paul Kolstoe (1995) *Russians in the former Soviet republics*, London: Hurst and Co.; and Neil Melvin (1995) *Russians Beyond Russia. The Politics of National Identity*, London: RIIA, Pinter.

Useful articles on religion in Russia include Mark A. Smith (2002) 'The Russian Orthodox Church', C109; and his (2006) 'Islam in Russia', *Russian Series* November, 06/53, November, both available on the website of the Conflict Studies Research Centre of the UK Defence Academy (http://www.defac.ac.uk). See also G. G. Yemelianova (1995) 'Russia and Islam: The History and Prospects of a Relationship', *Asian Affairs*, 82 (3), 278–90 and Geraldine Fagan (2001) 'Buddhism in Postsoviet Russia: Revival or Degeneration?', *Religion, State & Society*, 29 (1), March, 9–21.

A comprehensive analysis of the Russian Idea is provided by Tim McDaniel (1996) *The Agony of the Russian Idea*, Princeton, NJ: Princeton University Press.

On Russia's European identity and its relationship with Europe see Paul Dukes (1998) 'Globalization and Europe: The Russian Question', in Roland Axtman (ed.) *Globalization and Europe*, London and Washington: Pinter; and Iver B. Neumann (1996) *Russia and the Idea of Europe*, London: Routledge.

Useful websites

On religion in Russia

Interfax Information Services – Religion portal for Russia: http://www.interfax.ru/?lang=e

Keston Institute: http://www.keston.org/

Russia Religion News, Stetson University, USA: http://www.stetson.edu/~psteeves/relnews/

On Eurasianism

Alexander Dugin's Arctogaia Eurasian Movement: http://www.arctogaia.com/public/eng

The Scientific Heritage of Lev Gumilev: http://gumilevica.kulichki.net/English/index.html (includes some of Gumilev's books in English)

The Eurasian Politician: http://www.cc.jyu.fi/~aphamala/pe/index.htm

References

Abelsky, P. (2006) 'Redrawing Russian History', *Russia Profile*, III (4), May, 45–6

BBC Monitoring (2000) 'Russian president makes New Year speech at Kremlin reception', available from *Johnson's Russia List*, 4716, 31 December, http://www.cdi.org/russia/johnson/4716.html

Berdyaev, Nicolas (1947) *The Russian Idea*, London: The Centenary Press (trans: R. M. French)

Chaadaev, P. (1836) 'The Philosophical Letter', *The Telescope*

Dawisha, K. and Parrott, B. (1994) *Russia and the New States of Eurasia. The Politics of Upheaval*, Cambridge: Cambridge University Press

Figes, O. (1998) 'Burying the Bones', in 'Russia: the Wild East', *Granta*, 64, 95–111

Goble, P. (2006) 'Russian officers denounce "Clericalization of the Military"', *Window on Eurasia*, http://www.freemediaonline.org/goble_window_russian_officers_denounce_29june2006.htm

Gumilev, L. N. (1992) *Ot Russiia k Rossii: ocherki etnicheskoi istoriia*, Moscow: Ekopros

Hoskings, G. (1997) *Russia People and Empire 1552–1917*, London: HarperCollins

Hyman, A. (1993) 'Russians Outside Russia', *The World Today*, 19 (11), 206

Khasanova, G. (1997) 'Russia's new identity document creates uproar in Tatarstan', *Prism*, 3 (21), 19 December, http://www.jamestown.org/

Kiva, A. (1996) 'Ideas are not cast on paper but in the public mind', *Rossiiskaia gazeta*, 1 August, 2

Kortunov, S. (1995) '*Natsional'naia sverkhzadacha. Opyt rossiiskoi ideologii*', *Nezavisimaia gazeta*, 1 October, 5

Levada, T. (2006) '*Kakoi prazdnik budut otmetat' rossiiane 4 noiabria . . . ?*', 1 November, Levada Centre website, http://www.levada.ru/press/2006110101.html

McDaniel, Tim (1996) *The Agony of the Russian Idea*, Princeton, NJ: Princeton University Press

Putin, V. (1999) 'Russia at the turn of the millennium', downloaded from geocities website 19 July 2007, http://www.geocities.com/capitolhill/parliament/3005/poutine.html

Putin, V. (2005) 'Annual Address to the Federal Assembly', 25 April, Kremlin website, http://www.kremlin.ru/eng

Putin, V. (2006) 'Opening Address at the World Congress of Russians Abroad', Kremlin website, http://www.kremlin.ru/eng

Riasanovsky, N. V. (1984) *A History of Russia*, Oxford: OUP

Shlapentokh, V. (1997) 'How Russians Will See the Status of Their Country by the End of the Century', *Journal of Communist Studies and Transition Politics*, 13 (3), September, 1–23

Troshev, D. (2002) 'Cossacks' participation in the 2002 All-Russia population census', *International symposium 'The Russians in the Mirror of Statistics: All Russian population Census 2002'*, 210–12, http://www.perepis2002.ru/ct/doc/symposium_eng.doc

Tsipko, A. (1993) 'Dialectics of the Ascent of a New Russian Statehood', in O. Ieda (ed.) *New Order in Post-Communist Eurasia*, Sapporo, Japan: Slavic Research Centre, Hokkaido University

Trubetskoi, N., Florovsky, G. and Savitsky, P. (1921) *Exodus to the East*, Sofia: Rossiisko-Bolgarsko knigo

Yasmann, V. (2005) 'Russia: New Russian Holiday Has More behind It than National Unity', *RFE/RL Feature Article*, 4 November, *RFE/RL* website, http://www.rferl.org/

Part 2

THE EXECUTIVE AND THE LEGISLATURE

Chapter 5

The federal executive: the president and the government

Learning objectives

- To examine and analyse the Russian presidency.
- To examine and analyse the government.
- To explain the importance of networks and clans.
- To introduce the reform of the state service.

Introduction

The president and the government are the federal executive of the Russian Federation. The 1993 RF Constitution endorsed liberal democratic principles; a separation of executive, legislative and judicial powers; and established a mixed presidential-parliamentary republic with a dual executive consisting of a president and a prime minister. The constitution also created a super-presidency with the president and the presidential administration at the apex of political and economic life. The components of this super-presidency are a strong executive presidency, a weak legislature and a poorly developed judiciary. The president has extensive powers of appointment, dominates the work of government and can bypass parliament by issuing decrees. Russia is ruled from the president's headquarters in the Kremlin; the government based in the Old Square and the parliament in the White House play subsidiary roles. The symbolism here is immense as the Kremlin was previously the home of the Politburo (the highest body of the CPSU) and of the party General Secretary (the leader of the USSR). In the USSR the parliament and the government were subordinate to the CPSU Politburo. The presidential administration and the government even replicate the former division between the Party Politburo and the soviet government, the Council of Ministers (Minasov, 1992: 2). The presidential administration today bears remarkable functional similarities to the CPSU Central Committee apparatus – and has even more staff (see Chapter 16).

The Constitution is just the starting point for understanding the nature and powers of the executive. The personalities and skills of the ailing Yeltsin and the younger and healthier Putin, together with the other resources at their disposal and the general

Table 5.1 Russia's presidents

Name	Election dates
Boris Yeltsin	12 June 1991* and 3 July 1996
Vladimir Putin	26 March 2000** and 14 March 2004
Dmitry Medvedev	2 March 2008

Notes:
* In 1991 Yeltsin was elected president of the RSFSR of the USSR
** Acting president since 31 December 1999

context, have all affected the operation of the executive. Yeltsin initiated major institutional and policy reforms to move the country away from communism, without a popular and elite consensus about the desirability of these reforms and goals. In order to stay in office, push through his reforms and to maintain Russia's territorial integrity, Yeltsin compromised with powerful vested interests – notably the republican and regional bosses and the oligarchs. In contrast, by the time Putin became president in 2000, there was no longer a realistic possibility of a communist restoration. He wanted to rein in the republican and regional bosses and the oligarchs, and to maintain the country's integrity in the face of secessionist movements, notably in Chechnia. Putin also had an extensive reform agenda encompassing all areas of Russian life. To achieve this and to ensure effective policy implementation, Putin stressed the need to reform the state (civil) service and to 'strengthen the power vertical', that is the line of command running from the president down through and to the political institutions at all levels.

Box 5.1 The presidential oath

At the inauguration ceremony the president swears this oath:

> In performing my duties as the President of the Russian Federation, I pledge to respect the rights and liberties of every citizen, to observe and protect the Constitution of the Russian Federation; to protect the sovereignty and independence, security and integrity of the state and to serve the people faithfully.

Source: Article 82 of the RF Constitution, 1993

The president

The constitutional position of the Russian president, including the restrictions that apply, is discussed in Boxes 5.2 and 5.3. Discussion of how this works in practice is also provided, along with the voting patterns in the failed impeachment of Yeltsin (see Table 5.2).

Box 5.2 The Russian President*

According to the Constitution	Notes
The basic requirements A candidate: ■ Must be at least 35 years old. ■ Must be a Russian citizen. ■ Must be resident in Russia for at least ten years. ■ Is directly elected for a four-year term. ■ May serve no more than two consecutive terms in office.	■ In most democracies, there are restrictions on the type of person who can stand for election. US presidents may also only serve two terms in office. ■ Yeltsin floated the idea that he should be allowed to stand again in 2000, as when he was first elected in 1991 it was as RSFSR not RF president. The Constitutional Court ruled against this interpretation in 1998 and Yeltsin had to stand down.
The president is the guardian of the state ■ Is the head of state. ■ Is required to take measures to protect Russia's sovereignty, independence and state integrity and to ensure the concerted functioning and interaction of all bodies of state power. ■ In the event of a dispute between Moscow and a region or between regions, the president may use conciliation processes. If these fail, the president is empowered to suspend the enactments of a federal unit's executive that conflict with the RF Constitution or violate civil rights and freedoms, pending a decision by the courts. ■ Is empowered to introduce martial law and to declare a state of emergency, subject to confirmation by the Federation Council. ■ Heads the armed forces and approves the Military Doctrine. ■ Chairs the Security Council and the Defence Council. ■ Appoints and dismisses the Armed Forces Command. ■ Determines the guidelines of domestic and foreign policies.	■ The president is charged with protecting Russia against both internal and external threats. ■ As Russia was born out of the disintegration of the USSR, combating centrifugal forces, such as bids for autonomy or independence by Russia's federal subjects and the delineation of authority between Moscow and the federal units, have been an important focus of presidential action. Yeltsin and Putin used negotiations, threats, judicial and (e.g. in the case of Chechnia) armed force to prevent the RF from disintegrating. ■ All the 'power ministries' (Defence, Interior, Foreign Affairs, Civil Defence, Emergencies and Disaster Relief) and the heads of the Federal Security Service (FSB) and Foreign Intelligence Service (SVR) answer directly to the president rather than to the prime minister.
The president is guardian of the Constitution, civil rights and freedoms	■ The Minister of Justice answers directly to the president not the prime minister. ■ Putin's advocacy of a 'managed democracy' has made civil society activities more difficult.
The president has an international role ■ Represents Russia abroad. ■ Attends and hosts summits and meetings of world leaders. ■ Determines the guidelines of foreign policy. ■ Appoints Russia's diplomatic representatives to foreign states and	■ In the 1990s, Russia was grappling with its diminished international status as a former superpower. Yeltsin, however, did not always behave with the dignity expected of an international statesman, appearing drunk at a number of international gatherings.

Box 5.2 (*Continued*)

According to the Constitution	Notes
international organisations, after consultation with the representative committees or commissions of the Federal Assembly; also accredits foreign ambassadors to Russia.	▪ In contrast, Putin always behaved with great dignity; he has travelled widely and hosted world leaders in Moscow and St Petersburg. He ensured that Russia regained its status as a major global actor.

The president has extensive powers of appointment and dismissal (patronage)

According to the Constitution	Notes
▪ Appoints judges to the Constitutional Court, Supreme Court and Higher Arbitration Court and the prosecutor-general, subject to confirmation by the Federation Council. Appoints judges to other federal courts.	▪ These powers contradict the principle of the separation of the executive, legislative and judicial powers, as they place the president in the dominant position.
▪ Appoints and dismisses the prime minister; deputy prime ministers, federal ministers proposed by the prime minister; the chair of the Russian Central Bank, subject to approval by the Duma.	▪ These powers enable the president to dominate the prime minister and the government.
▪ If the Duma rejects the president's nominations for prime minister three times, the president may dissolve the Duma and call new elections.	▪ While the Duma has the right to reject a presidential nomination for prime minister, the threat of a new election can be used to bring them into line.
▪ Appoints the members of the Security Council, the Defence Council and the Presidential Administration.	▪ Putin used presidential decrees to extend his powers of appointment beyond those listed in the Constitution.
▪ Appoints the presidential plenipotentiary envoys to the seven federal districts created in 2000.	▪ Yeltsin and Putin used patronage to move their supporters into key positions. This is an important way of strengthening presidential power bases and the informal political networks that are vital to the functioning of Russian politics.
▪ Since 2004 appoints regional governors, subject to confirmation by the local legislature.	
▪ Since December 2004 appoints Audit Chamber heads.	

The president has a legislative role

According to the Constitution	Notes
▪ Issues decrees (*ukazy*) and executive orders and regulations (*rasporiazhenie*), which are binding throughout the RF and do not have to be submitted to parliament or the people.	▪ Yeltsin and Putin both made extensive use of decrees to push through their agendas, while avoiding parliamentary scrutiny.
▪ Presents draft laws to the Duma for consideration.	▪ The Presidential Administration draws up the president's decrees, so taking on a role usually performed by governments.
▪ May veto Federal Assembly laws.	
▪ Signs federal laws.	

Other powers

According to the Constitution	Notes
▪ The president may call a referendum.	▪ These powers have not so far been used.
▪ The president may dissolve the Duma.	

* See Chapter Four of the RF Constitution

Box 5.3 The restrictions on the president

According to the Constitution	Notes
The president cannot dissolve parliament:	
▪ Within one year of a parliamentary election.	▪ Yeltsin and Putin more successfully, bypassed 'the need' to dissolve parliament, by making sure that it has became an increasingly pliant body, dominated by pro-Kremlin parties.
▪ If the parliament has filed impeachment charges against president.	
▪ If the president has declared a state of emergency.	
▪ Within six months of the expiration of president's term of office.	
The president	
▪ Is subject to the Constitution and Russia's other laws.	▪ Immunity for the president (and deputies) was introduced to stop their work from being frustrated by malicious lawsuits.
▪ Enjoys immunity.	▪ Putin's first decree was to grant Yeltsin and his family immunity from prosecution, despite mounting evidence of corruption.
The judiciary	
▪ The Constitutional Court is empowered to consider the constitutionality of the president's actions.	▪ Top level judges and the procuracy are appointed by the president and so benefit from presidential patronage.
▪ The Constitutional Court together with the Supreme Court may confirm that there is evidence the president is guilty of 'high treason' or a similar 'grave crime' and verify that the correct procedures have been followed.	▪ The judiciary were gradually becoming independent of the executive under Yeltsin, but Putin reversed this trend.
▪ In 2002, the Supreme Court ruled that private citizens have no right to challenge presidential decrees. This was overturned in February 2003.	
The Federal Assembly (parliament)	
▪ The lower house, the Duma, may pass laws and its approval is required for some of the president's appointments.	▪ The 1993 and 1995 elections produced Dumas that were too fragmented to mount an effective challenge to the president.
▪ The approval of the upper house, the Federation Council, is required for some of the president's appointments.	▪ The 1999, 2004 and 2007 elections produced Dumas that were increasingly dominated by pro-Kremlin political parties.
	▪ The Federation Council was initially composed of Yeltsin appointees. In the mid-1990s its members began to be elected and to be more assertive. Putin introduced the presidential appointment of Federation Council members again.

Box 5.3 (*Continued*)

According to the Constitution	Notes
If the president is incapacitated ■ Presidential power is ceded temporarily to the prime minister. ■ If the president demonstrates a persistent inability to exercise his powers for health reasons, the prime minister becomes acting president, and new presidential elections must be held within three months.	■ The president decides on their own capacity to carry out their duties. ■ In the 1990s the Duma pushed unsuccessfully for a commission to rule on health-related issues of competency for all leading politicians, but this was resisted by Yeltsin. ■ When ill in September 1996, Yeltsin made a token delegation of power when the foreign, interior, intelligence and defence ministers were told to report to the prime minister, Chernomyrdin. ■ In November 1996, before undergoing a seven-hour quintuple heart bypass operation, Yeltsin ceded full powers and the nuclear trigger to Chernomyrdin – but only until the operation was over. ■ Throughout Yeltsin's illnesses, the presidential administration wielded more effective power than the prime minister. According to Aleksandr Korzhakov, Anatoly Chubais the head of the Presidential Administration acted like a regent.
Impeachment ■ The president may be impeached on the initiative of a two-thirds majority in both chambers of the Federal Assembly.	■ The impeachment procedures are extremely cumbersome. A proposal to impeach Yeltsin did not receive the necessary two-thirds Duma vote (see Table 5.2). ■ Presidential domination of the Duma makes an impeachment initiative unlikely to succeed.

Table 5.2 The failed attempt to impeach President Yeltsin, 13 May 1999

The charges	Votes for	Votes against
Destroying the USSR	239	39
Illegally destroying the Parliament in 1993	263	60
Sending troops into Chechnia	283	43
Undermining the armed forces	241	77
Committing genocide against the Russian people	238	88

Source: Keesing's Record of World Events, 45 (5), 1999, 42,950

The president: beyond the constitution

The president is above politics and the personalisation of leadership

Post-communist Russian presidents depict themselves as above 'mere' politics. The president, so the argument goes, represents the whole country and not just those who voted for him. However, the president is no mere ceremonial figurehead; Yeltsin's westernising agenda, for example, heralded in the greatest changes in Russia since 1917. These were highly controversial and actively opposed by many citizens, despite Yeltsin's claims that the reforms were in the interests of all. More recently, Putin has claimed that strengthening the state is in the interest of all Russian citizens, but this led to restrictions on civil society organisations and a military campaign against Chechnia. Russian presidents are not nominal heads of state standing above politics; they are deeply embroiled in politics and take the lead in both policy making and defining Russia's general course.

The self-image of being above politics, contributes to the personalisation of the style and substance of political leadership. In contrast to soviet leaders who traditionally held themselves aloof from the people, Yeltsin like Gorbachev before him, had a more easy-going style. During the 1996 presidential election campaign Yeltsin travelled a great deal throughout Russia, indulging in some extremely boisterous folk and disco dancing with the electorate and seemed to genuinely relish being out among his people. This was typical of his general approach to politics and government, preferring direct contact with the people without having to bother with intervening institutions such as political parties or indeed parliament. Putin shared Yeltsin's belief that the president is above the political fray and when he spoke as president, in the best tradition of his KGB service background, he expected support and for his orders to be carried out. It would be difficult, however, to imagine Putin climbing on a tank and rallying the crowd as Yeltsin did in August 1991. Putin is not an inspirational speaker and does not have Yeltsin's easy way with people. Medvedev is also a fairly reserved character, who is a technocrat rather than a politician.

Another aspect of this personalisation of politics is that Yeltsin, Putin and Medvedev are not members of a political party (see Chapter 12). Yeltsin resigned as chair of Democratic Russia when he became chair of the RSFSR Parliament in 1990 and while RF president he never established a presidential party. He did benefit from the support of Chernomyrdin's pro-Kremlin party, 'Our Home is Russia', but never joined it. Putin benefited from the support of the *Edinstvo* (Unity) party, the largest faction in the 1999–2004 Duma and then of United Russia in the 2004–2007 Duma. Putin did not even join United Russia when he headed their party list of candidates for the 2007 Duma elections. United Russia also supported Medvedev's candidature for the 2008 presidential election, but he is not a party member. An advantage of not being a party member is that the president is not then subject to party discipline, which gives them room for manoeuvre. Putin did not produce a manifesto for the presidential elections in 2000 and 2004, which meant that voters were asked to vote for Putin the man. This personalisation of politics enabled Putin to appeal to voters across a wide range of party allegiances and ideological orientations, from pro-market liberals through to communists and nationalists. It served him well as he won two elections on the first round and has consistently high approval ratings (FOM database, 1999–onwards). The first time that Medvedev ever stood for election for any post was the presidential elections in 2008. He did not produce an election manifesto and his election was a personal vote of approval not for Medvedev but for his mentor, Vladimir Putin.

This personalisation, however, has a negative impact on democratic consolidation and potentially on political stability. For the 2000 presidential election Putin supporters set up reception points, whose staff received electors' requests for housing and financial support, and complaints about the non-payment of wages and pensions. This is reminiscent of courtiers collecting petitions from the people to pass on to a tsar. In tsarist Russia it was all too common for people to believe that it was those standing between the 'Little Father Tsar' and the people – the courtiers, bureaucrats and aristocracy – who were responsible for their problems. In democracies, while voters do approach their representatives with individual requests, most popular demands are processed by political parties, autonomous social and political organisations or parliament and not by ad hoc groups of election workers on behalf of the president. The personalisation of politics encourages issues to be appealed up the political system, rather than the establishment of a clear delineation of authority and responsibility between different government institutions and regularised procedures for dealing with citizens' inputs. By diminishing the role and status of institutions such as parliament, these practices frustrate the further institutional development that is vital to democratic consolidation.

Parallelism and institutional improvisation

Although the 1993 Constitution gave Yeltsin the powers of a super president, he was nonetheless at times politically vulnerable and increasingly physically frail. Yeltsin tried to counteract these problems by what is best characterised as institutional improvisation. He created rival institutions with competing or overlapping and shifting competencies, played the role of arbiter between them, and used his appointment prerogatives (patronage) to advance allies and reward support. Putin continued the practice of balancing groups within the political and economic elite by playing them off against each other. Within the executive Yeltsin encouraged rivalries between the prime minister and the government on one side and the presidential administration on the other, and created a range of competing 'power wielding' institutions (see Chapter 9). These individual groups enjoyed a degree of autonomy, duplicated each others' responsibilities, while being encouraged to compete for presidential favour. The political and economic groups closest to the president at any one time had greater influence on policy making than the relevant government institutions. This approach made it difficult to formulate and implement consistent policies.

The political rise and fall of the oligarchs?

The political rise of the oligarchs was an important consequence of the absence of a presidential political party under Yeltsin. The oligarchs had already benefited economically from the reforms of the early 1990s and they did not want KPRF leader Gennady Zyuganov to win the 1996 presidential election. As the remnants of the soviet-era CPSU, the KPRF had branches throughout the country and experienced personnel able to get Zyuganov's message out to the electorate. The absence of a political party meant that Yeltsin did not have an organisation capable of rallying the electorate on his behalf. Anatoly Chubais, the head of the Presidential Administration and a close ally of Yeltsin's daughter Tatyana Dyachenko, met with the leading oligarchs led by Boris Berezovsky who agreed to back Yeltsin. The oligarchs were rewarded by preferential treatment in the next round of economic privatisation and were, de facto brought into policy making. Putin came to office claiming that he would destroy the oligarchs as a class. The oligarchs, together with the republican and regional bosses, were the two main centres of independent power that could challenge the president; their powers had to be curbed in order to strengthen the presidency.

Putin was not entirely against the oligarchs' involvement in politics, he had after all personally benefited from their financial and media backing during his election in 2000. Putin's aim was to ensure that any political activity by an oligarch was pro-Kremlin. In 2001 Putin took on the two oligarchs, first Boris Berezovsky and then Vladimir Gusinsky, who were not prepared to toe the new line. For the 2000 presidential election Gusinsky had backed the Primakov–Luzhkov challenge to Putin. Gusinsky's Media-MOST conglomerate was already in debt, surviving on loans from Gazprom and the Bank of Moscow. Within a year Media-MOST was bankrupt, denied credit by businesses that were either owned by or allied to the state, and facing action in the criminal and civil courts. From would-be king maker, Gusinsky became a self-imposed exile. Berezovsky had backed Putin in 2000 even helping to set up the *Edinstvo* (Unity) party, but then criticised him over the war in Chechnia, the Kursk submarine disaster and changes to the government structure. Berezovsky was charged with corruption and fled the country. In 2003, Putin moved against Russia's richest man Mikhail Khodorkovsky who was funding anti-Kremlin liberals and communists; Khodorkovsky is now in prison (see Chapter 8). Most oligarchs, including Vladimir Potanin and Roman Abramovich, quickly realised the dangers of confronting Putin and adapted to the new realities in order to keep their fortunes. Although Abramovich was a protégé of Boris Berezovsky, he became staunchly pro-Kremlin and in 2005 Putin reappointed him governor of the Chukotka AO. Putin pursued a policy of 'equal proximity' of the elite business groups to the presidency, which reduced their individual roles in policy making.

Putin and 'strengthening the power vertical'

Putin (2000b) argued in his first Annual Address to the Federal Assembly on 8 July 2000 that, in order to respond to the many challenges facing Russia, it was imperative to strengthen the state. Acknowledging that this would lead to speculation about dictatorship and authoritarianism, he continued that the word 'effective' could be substituted for 'strong' and that, 'an effective state and a democratic state is capable of protecting civil, political and economic freedoms, capable of creating conditions for people to lead happy lives and for our country to flourish' (ibid.). Certainly, if a state is unable to maintain security and the rule of law, the result is not freedom but instability and anarchy, which disproportionately affects the weak and vulnerable. For example in the 1990s, some Russians became super-rich, but the state's tax gathering problems contributed to its failure to address mounting social problems. Putin argued that Russia needs to strengthen the state and the power vertical (see Box 5.4) which entailed centralising power in the Kremlin and creating an even stronger presidency.

Box 5.4 The main features of strengthening the power vertical

Overall: a super-presidency and a powerful presidential administration dominating all other political, judicial, social and economic bodies. This has been achieved by:

- The creation of seven new federal districts headed by presidential plenipotentiaries or envoys.
- Presidential appointment of republican and regional governors, subject to only formal confirmation by the local legislatures.
- The domination of the Federal Assembly by the 'party of power', so the Duma waits for directives from the president rather than taking independent initiatives.
- Selective 'justice', such as the targeting of certain oligarchs and campaigners for investigation and prosecution.
- State-controlled TV and the ownership of newspapers by state-controlled companies.
- Moves to control civil society organisations, including since 2002 the right to suspend political parties and NGOs accused of extremism; legal pressures on journalists and media outlets; and state monitoring of emails and the Internet.

In 2000, as part of reducing the power of the republican and regional bosses, Putin reorganised the Federation Council, the upper house of the Federal Assembly. The Federation Council had been composed of the regional governors, presidents of the republics, and heads of the republican and regional legislatures. The Federation Council is still composed of two representatives for each federal subject, but these representatives are now presidential appointees. In May 2000, Putin issued a decree establishing seven new federal districts (*okrugs*) each composed of around twelve republics and regions. The federal districts are headed by a presidential representative, most of whom have some kind of a security background. As part of the strategy of bringing the republics and regions into line, one of the most important tasks for the new presidential representatives was to ensure that the charters, constitutions and legislation in their district did not contradict the RF Constitution and federal laws. Putin also persuaded the Duma to pass a law giving him the right to remove governors and republican and regional legislatures if their legislation contradicted the RF Constitution and federal laws. The presidential representatives also coordinate the work of the federal bureaucracy. Putin believed that stronger measures were needed to bring Chechnia back under Moscow's control and in June 2000 launched a military campaign and issued a decree establishing direct presidential rule in the republic (see Chapter 7).

The overall result of 'strengthening the power vertical', has not been the creation of a strong and effective vertical chain joining the republics and the regions to Moscow, but rather the strengthening of presidential power. This added to the continuing personalisation of power in Putin and the over-concentration of power in the post of the president. The overemphasis on strengthening the power vertical has been at the expense of adequate attention to the development and coordination of the institutions at the different (horizontal) levels of representation and government – that is, at the republican, regional and local levels. Attention needs to be paid to regularising the delegation of power and authority down the vertical, while maintaining central oversight. The republican and regional bosses who emerged in the 1990s were a varied bunch, including committed democrats and go-ahead reformers but also mini dictators who were often corrupt and inefficient. In reining in the republican and regional bosses, Putin moved against the corrupt and power hungry, but he also inhibited positive initiatives at the regional level, which has frustrated the consolidation of democracy.

Presidential networks

Presidential networks: the Yeltsin presidency

Most political leaders in democracies rise to and remain in power with the backing of a political power. In Russia these functions are performed by informal but very powerful presidential support networks, which a president is able to promote and nurture through presidential patronage. Yeltsin's immediate circle operated like a court, with individuals vying for access (for more on Yeltsin's presidency, see Chapter 3). An important figure was Aleksandr Korzhakov, who had been appointed the head of Yeltsin's bodyguard on his arrival in Moscow in 1986 and became a close friend and confidant. Yeltsin had two main clans or networks that supported him in power: the Security clan and the Western clan, headed by Anatoly Chubais and supported by Yeltsin's daughter Tatyana Dyachenko and Boris Berezovsky. In 1996 conflict between the Security and the Western clans took place at the very heart of the court of 'Tsar Boris'. In January 1996, Korzhakov manoeuvred the sacking of Sergei Filatov as head of the presidential administration and had him replaced by Nikolai Yegorov. Korzhakov believed that Yeltsin could not win the forthcoming presidential election and that it should be postponed, but found himself increasingly sidelined by Chubais and Dyachenko. At the instigation of the Western clan, the Security clan plus seven leading generals were sacked in between the two rounds of the 1996 presidential elections.

The clan system, with its associated lack of popular accountability and transparency in decision making, encouraged corruption. By the late 1990s, the media increasingly carried corruption allegations against what they dubbed 'the Family'. The Family included Yeltsin's biological family, his political associates such as Anatoly Chubais and Aleksandr Voloshin, the head of the presidential administration; the Western clan; and representatives of big business and the oligarchs such as Boris Berezovsky. In February 1999, Prime Minister Primakov and the Prosecutor General Yury Skuratov launched an anti-corruption campaign specifically targeting the Family. In April the Prosecutor General's office issued a warrant for the arrest of Berezovsky and Nikolai Glushkov, a former director of the state airline Aeroflot, on charges of diverting hard currency profits from the airline to Swiss-based companies owned by Berezovsky. The Director General of Aeroflot was, and continues to be, Yeltsin's son-in-law Valery Okulov. The anti-corruption campaign was closing in on the Family who used the powers of the presidency and the financial and media might of the oligarchs to try to crush the individuals involved. Skuratov was threatened with the release of a fabricated, compromising video and so resigned on 'health grounds'; once the video was released Yeltsin suspended him from office, supposedly due to this sex scandal.

Crucially, the Federation Council and the Constitutional Court acted independently of the president at this time. The Federation Council refused to accept Skuratov's resignation and Yeltsin's attempt to dismiss him; then the Constitutional Court ruled that Yeltsin could suspend Skuratov but that he could not overrule the Federation Council's rejection of his dismissal of Skuratov. On 12 May, Yeltsin used his presidential powers to dismiss Primakov and his government and to replace Primakov with Sergei Stepashin. The Family were concerned by Primakov's anti-corruption campaign and wanted some leverage over the Duma which was due to start impeachment proceedings against Yeltsin on the following day. In the event the Duma failed to muster the 300 votes necessary for the impeachment procedures to continue and Yeltsin was saved. However, by the time Yeltsin resigned as president the Russian public were exasperated by his antics, his failure to address Russia's mounting problems, and the corruption that went to the heart of the presidential family and administration.

Yeltsin and operation successor

Yeltsin had always assiduously avoided creating an heir apparent, but now he needed to pass his reforms into a safe pair of hands and seek protection for 'the Family'. In 1998 most people in Russia had not heard of Vladimir Putin, but within a year he was appointed prime minister and six months later elected president. In 1997 when Yeltsin was frequently absent due to ill health, the Russian and western media were full of speculation about who would succeed him but no-one seems to have identified Putin as a possible successor. The manoeuvring began with the simultaneous announcement that Duma elections would be held on 19 December 1999 and the naming of Putin as acting prime minister. The Duma approved Putin's appointment on the first vote, by 232 votes to 84 with 17 abstentions, as they knew that if they endorsed Putin the Duma elections would go ahead as scheduled.

Box 5.5 Boris Yeltsin

Born in 1931 into a peasant family in Butka, a village in Sverdlovsk province in the Urals. In 1955 he graduated as a construction engineer from the Urals Technical Institute and began work as an engineer in the construction industry. In 1961 Yeltsin joined the CPSU and from 1976–85 he was the CPSU first secretary in Sverdlovsk. In 1976, he was elected as a deputy to the USSR Supreme Soviet.

In 1986 Gorbachev appointed Yeltsin to the CPSU Politburo and, as Moscow party boss, Yeltsin used his position to attack *nomenklatura* privileges and corruption. By 1987 Yeltsin had fallen out with Gorbachev who sacked him. Yeltsin suffered a major heart attack. Despite this, in March 1989 Yeltsin won a seat in the USSR Congress of People's Deputies with 89.6 per cent of the vote and rapidly became the figurehead for anti-Gorbachev, liberal Russian nationalism and a leading member of the Inter-Regional Group.

Boris Yeltsin.

In March 1990 he was elected to the RSFSR Congress of People's Deputies for Sverdlovsk and in May 1990 was elected chair (president) of the RSFSR. Yeltsin finally left the CPSU in July 1990. In June 1991 he was directly elected president of the RSFSR winning 58 per cent of the vote. Later that year Yeltsin led opposition to the August 1991 coup and organised Gorbachev's release form Foros. Yeltsin was elected RF President on 3 July 1996. Already suffering ill-health, however, he was frequently absent from the Kremlin. Yeltsin died in 2007.

Primakov and Moscow Mayor Yury Luzhkov formed the main opposition to Yeltsin and Putin, but were unable to prevent Putin's inexorable rise. In his speech to the Duma before the vote, Putin said the sort of things that most Russians wanted to hear. He promised to make sure that wages and pension arrears would be paid and that he would also help the farming sector and strengthen the defence sector. He promised that the elections would be honest, to restore discipline to the country and to fight economic crime. He also vowed to defend the interests of Russians in the Near Abroad and to restore order in the Northern Caucasus, an area that includes Chechnia.

The December 1999 Duma elections augured well for Putin. The recently formed pro-Putin Unity party gained 72 deputies, coming second to the 113 KPRF deputies. Yeltsin surprised Russia and the world by announcing his resignation on 31 December 1999, so making Putin acting president. In his televised resignation address, Yeltsin specifically endorsed Putin for the presidential elections, describing him as a leader who would be able to draw society together and to gain broad political support so ensuring the continuation of reform. A few days after Yeltsin resigned,

Box 5.6 Vladimir Putin

Born in 1952 in Leningrad. Putin describes himself as being a bit of a tearaway as a teenager, who grew to harbour a burning desire to join the KGB. In 1975, he graduated from the International Department of the Law Faculty of Leningrad State University (LGU) and the same year joined the KGB. Putin was a loyal KGB functionary serving 15 years, mainly in Leipzig and Dresden in East Germany. In his biography *Ot Pervogo Litsa* (*First Person*) (Putin, 2000a) he records that his early duties included suppressing dissidents.

At the end of 1989, the Berlin Wall fell and Putin returned to the USSR. In the following March he began to work for his former law professor Anatoly Sobchak, who was Leningrad's first democratically elected mayor. In June 1990, Putin began work in LGU's International Affairs Department, in a role traditionally fulfilled by a KGB agent. At

Vladimir Putin.

this time, Leningrad was one of Russia's main centres of anti-communist, radical dissent and Sobchak was one of the leading figures in the democratic movement. Quite how Putin, the KGB functionary, fitted into this environment remains unclear. It is quite possible that the KGB wanted to have one of their men working on the inside, keeping an eye on what the democrats were doing. In June 1991, Putin was appointed head of the International Committee of the mayor's office, with responsibility for promoting international relations and foreign investments. Sobchak and his team sided with Yeltsin during the August 1991 attempted coup and ordered the military to stay in their barracks, which they willingly did. Putin formally resigned from the KGB during the coup. In September 1991, Leningrad reverted to its pre-revolutionary name of St Petersburg. Throughout the momentous events of the final collapse of the USSR and the early 1990s Putin kept a low profile; not turning himself into a politician or an orator, he seems to have worked diligently at his job. In 1994, he was promoted to first deputy chair (mayor) of the city government, a post that involved dealing with western business people and investors. In 1996 Sobchak, who was accused of corruption, lost the mayoral elections to one of the deputy mayors, Vladimir Yakovlev, whom Putin labelled Judas during the campaign. In the murky world of St Petersburg politics, the charges were probably the malicious concoction of Sobchak's political enemies. In 1999, Putin had the charges against Sobchak dropped; the two men remained loyal to each other. In February 2000, Sobchak returned from self-imposed exile and died of a heart attack while campaigning for Putin's election as president.

In August 1996, Anatoly Chubais a fellow St Petersburger brought Putin into the Yeltsin administration in Moscow. From July 1998 to August 1999 Putin served as the first civilian head of the secret police (FSB) and from March to August 1999 was the secretary of the Security Council. His rise from obscurity was then very rapid: in August 1999 he was appointed acting prime minister and on Yeltsin's resignation he became acting president on 31 December 1999. He was elected president in March 2000 and re-elected in March 2004.

Putin issued a decree guaranteeing Yeltsin and his biological family immunity from criminal or administrative charges and from being arrested, searched, interrogated, or subjected to a body search. In a signal that 'the Family' were being distanced from power, Putin's first dismissal was Tatyana Dyachenko.

Presidential networks: the Putin presidency

In Russia, elections and political parties have little impact on the formation of government, rather presidential appointments reflect the personal preferences of the individual president. When making an appointment a president is looking for personal loyalty and will, therefore, tend to draw on the networks they have developed over the course of their career. Putin inherited the support of members of the business community, most of the oligarchs and 'the Family' from Yeltsin. Yeltsin's inner-circle had carefully selected and groomed Putin for the presidency because they wanted someone who would maintain their economic reforms and protect them personally. Although Putin immediately sacked Yeltsin's daughter Tatyana Dyachenko as a presidential adviser, he inherited Yeltsin's Presidential Administration. Aleksandr Voloshin, the head of Yeltsin's Presidential Administration and a prominent Family member, resigned but was immediately reinstated by Putin, even though he doubted the loyalty of anyone closely associated with Yeltsin's clans and networks. At first Voloshin and his ally Prime Minister Mikhail Kasyanov were able to maintain considerable control over the general direction and policies of the new government. However, first Voloshin was eased out; he resigned in October 2003 and was replaced by Putin's St Petersburg ally Dmitry Medvedev, who rapidly emerged as the Kremlin power broker. The replacement of Kasyanov by Mikhail Fradkov in 2005 marked the removal of the last vestige of the Yeltsin-era Kremlin and the final stage in Putin's takeover. Like Yeltsin before him, Putin had assiduously used his powers of appointment to place his supporters in key positions, in order to facilitate his domination over the political and economic life of the country.

The categorisation of Putin's networks is very complex as they overlap and there is a variety of sub-networks. There are two main networks: first, the *siloviki*, literally the power people from the armed forces and security forces, and secondly the Petersburgers from his time in St Petersburg. Some of the *siloviki* (the singular is a *silovik*) also come from St Petersburg, this group are known as the Petersburg Chekists (*chekisty*); the Chekists were the post-1917 secret police. Viktor Cherkessov, Putin's envoy to the North West Federal District (2000–2003); Sergei Ivanov the defence minister; Igor Sechin, the deputy chief of staff of the presidential administration who also worked for Sobchak (1991–96); and Viktor Ivanov, the deputy head of the presidential administration are all former KGB officers from St Petersburg. Putin looked for loyalty and honesty in his appointments, which he believes are qualities demonstrated by service personnel. In an interview with American ABC television on 24 March 2000, Putin declared, 'I am bringing into my inner circle people from the law enforcement bodies who are in no way connected with the people and structures which may be associated with any form of corruption' and that, 'I have known them for many years and I trust them. It has nothing to do with ideology. It's simply a matter of their professional qualities and personal relationships' (Traynor, 2000: 15).

Putin's championing of the strong state, including the renewed war in Chechnia, commitments to higher defence spending and new weapons systems, combined with a more assertive foreign policy concept and defence doctrine, all reflected Putin's personal preferences and the imprint of the *siloviki* on policy making. The *siloviki* provided Putin with the institutional support and personnel needed to carry out his reforms. The *siloviki* are not particularly interested in the preservation and continuation of the radical economic reforms of the 1990s, they are more concerned with the preservation of Russia as a great state (*gosudarstvennost'*). In this they hold true to many of the traditions of the soviet state combined with a conservative Russian nationalism. They therefore contributed a centralising and anti-democratic impulse to Putin's Administration, wanting, for example, restrictions placed on civil society.

For Putin the advantage of bringing St Petersburg outsiders to Moscow was that they were not part of the entrenched clans and networks that had developed under Yeltsin and which now frustrated reform. Alexei Kudrin the Finance Minister and German Gref the Economic Development and Trade Minister had both worked with Putin in St Petersburg. Kudrin had been a deputy mayor and Gref had been in charge of the city's privatisation. These Petersburgers are economic liberals who want to continue the radical economic reforms that had stalled by the end of the 1990s. Like Putin they had also left St Petersburg in 1996, when Sobchak was defeated. Anatoly Chubais, an economic liberal who had overseen the federal privatisation programme in the 1990s, brought Kudrin and Putin to Moscow. Chubais had emerged from this time with a private fortune and as head of the Russian energy conglomerate RAO-Unified Energy Systems. Russia's economic liberals often have a personal and pragmatic stake in making sure that the economic reforms of the 1990s are not reversed. In this, they tended to come into conflict with the *siloviki*, who favour the renationalisation of Russia's strategic industries and greater economic protectionism. Curiously, Putin pursued the policy preferences of both these two networks. The economic liberals inspired policies such as the reform of health and welfare spending, the bid to join the WTO and the general opening up of Russia to the global economy. In contrast the *silovki* pushed for the effective renationalisation of Russia's major energy, metals and media companies through the creation of Kremlin front-companies (see Chapters 11 and 14). Putin's close St Petersburg ally Igor Sechin, for example, who was the deputy of the presidential administration from 1999 to 2008 heads the state-owned *Rosneft* oil company and this is typical of the intertwining of the Kremlin and business. In 2005 the newspaper *Nezavisimaia gazeta* (26 July 2005) even carried an article entitled 'Kremlin Inc. has performed well', about this phenomenon, which marked a victory for the *siloviki* over the liberals within Putin's administration.

Presidential institutions

Presidential Administration

The Presidential Administration, also known as the Presidential Executive Office and as the Presidential or Kremlin staff, is a government body formed in accordance with Article 83 of the Constitution to provide the president with the administrative support and coordination necessary to carry out his role as head of state. In 2004, 2,000 people worked for the Presidential Administration (Kremlin website, 2007a). The Presidential Administration includes research and analytical departments, which analyse domestic and international political, economic, social and legal trends; advisory bodies, together with policy-making and policy-implementation agencies. They draft the president's Annual Address to the Federal Assembly as well as his speeches, decrees, instructions and orders, and draw up presidential bills to be submitted to the Duma. They also monitor the enforcement of federal laws and presidential decrees, which means they play a major role in strengthening the power vertical, by both ensuring the compliance of republican and regional legislation with the Constitution and federal laws and ensuring effective policy implementation throughout Russia.

Box 5.7 Heads of the Presidential Administration

Yury Petrov	19 July 1991 to 19 January 1993
Sergei Filatov	19 January 1993 to 22 February 1996
Nikolai Yegorov	22 February 1996 to 16 July 1996
Anatoly Chubais	16 July 1996 to 9 March 1997
Valentin Yumashev	9 March 1997 to 7 December 1998
Nikolai Bordyuzha	7 December 1998 to 19 March 1999
Aleksandr Voloshin	19 March 1999 to 30 October 2003
Dmitry Medvedev	30 October 2003 to 14 November 2005
Sergei Sobyanin	14 November 2005 to 12 May 2008
Sergei Naryshkin	12 May 2008–

The president appoints his Kremlin staff, making them politically appointed state employees drawn from the president's networks, who serve as presidential aides. Before coming to Moscow in 1986, Yeltsin's career had been in Sverdlovsk and he drew on his Sverdlovsk network when he began creating his RSFSR Presidential Administration. Gennady Burbulis, a former Professor of Marxist philosophy in Sverdlovsk, laid the foundations of the Administration, ran Yeltsin's 1991 presidential election campaign and remained a close adviser until November 1992 when parliamentary pressure led to his sacking. Yury Petrov, the first Presidential Administration head, was a former Communist Party boss who was also from Sverdlovsk. Yeltsin's daughter Tatyana Dyachenko was a presidential adviser and in 1996 Anatoly Chubais (a prominent member of the Family) was appointed head of the Presidential Administration. As a Yeltsin-era creation the presidential administration still suffers from the parallelism and institutional improvisation that

bedevilled his other institutions. Yeltsin's appointments to the Presidential Administration were used to promote allies and to ensure their continued support. This
involved playing different groups off against each other, with the result that the
presidential administration developed into a series of competing and overlapping
hierarchies. Although Yeltsin told Chubais to reduce its size, this proved and remains
an intractable problem as fewer posts means fewer opportunities for patronage.
The head of the Presidential Administration is a major focus for lobbying and plays
an important role in developing and maintaining a working relationship with the
government. The head of the Presidential staff is very much a Kremlin insider and
close to the president. Putin inherited Aleksandr Voloshin from Yeltsin, but in 2003
replaced him with his close St Petersburg ally Dmitry Medvedev, who was then
promoted to first deputy prime minister in 2005. Sergei Sobyanin, the next head
of the Presidential Administration played an important role in organising Putin's
'operation successor'. Sobyanin ran Medvedev's presidential election campaign in
2008, ensuring that Putin's chosen successor was duly elected.

The Security Council

In 1992 Yeltsin established the first Security Council. According to Article 83 of
the 1993 RF Constitution the president appoints its members, and chairs and sets
the agendas for its meetings. As its name suggests the Security Council is concerned
with national security in its broadest sense, including all internal and external threats
to the individual, society and the state. It is a deliberative, special advisory body
accountable to the president; its role is to provide analysis and strategic planning,
to draft presidential decisions and policy proposals, and to provide coherence to
state policy across the range of security issues. This entails bringing together and
harmonising the views, interests and resources of the power ministries (Defence,
Interior, Foreign Affairs, and Emergencies and Disasters Relief) and the security
agencies, whose heads form the core of its membership. In 2004, Putin signed a
decree setting out the Security Council's membership during his second presidency.
The decree established that the Security Council includes the prime minister, the
power ministers, the heads of the Foreign Intelligence Service and Federal Security
Service, the Duma and Federation Council speakers, the head of the Presidential
Administration, the head of the Russian Academy of Sciences and the president's
Plenipotentiary Envoys to the seven federal districts.

The Security Council's work is overseen by a secretary, who answers directly
to the president. Security Council secretaries are people of considerable standing,
drawn from the armed forces, power ministries or security agencies. Putin briefly
held the post in 1999; he was succeeded by Sergei Ivanov who went on to be Defence
Minister, Vladimir Rushailo who had been interior minister before becoming the
secretary, Igor Ivanov a former foreign minister and the current incumbent,
Valentin Sobolev, is a former KGB operative. Under Yury Skokov, its first secretary, the Security Council began to parallel and supplant the formal government
policy-making bodies, particularly in the areas of foreign policy and security. For
example, it was the Security Council which took the decision to send the Russian

---

Box 5.8 The Presidential Administration (Kremlin staff)

The Kremlin staff consists of the following posts:

- Chief of staff of the Presidential Executive Office
- Deputy chiefs of staff of the Presidential Executive Office and presidential aides
- Presidential aides
- Press attaché
- Chief of presidential protocol
- Presidential advisers
- Plenipotentiaries to the power bodies

The Kremlin staff's subdivisions:

- Security Council Office
- Offices of the Presidential Plenipotentiary Envoys in the Federal Districts
- Presidential Advisers' Office
- Presidential State-Legal Directorate
- Presidential Chancellery
- Presidential Control Directorate
- Presidential Speechwriters Directorate
- Secretariat of the Chief of Staff of the Presidential Executive Office
- Presidential Domestic Policy Directorate
- Presidential Foreign Policy Directorate
- Presidential Personnel and State Decorations Directorate
- Presidential Civil Service Directorate
- Presidential Directorate for Protecting Citizens' Constitutional Rights
- Presidential Document Processing Directorate
- Presidential Directorate for Communication and Public Feedback
- Presidential Press and Information Office
- Presidential Protocol and Organisation Directorate
- Presidential Experts' Directorate
- Presidential Directorate for Interregional Relations and Cultural Contacts with Foreign Countries

Source: Kremlin website, http://www.kremlin.ru/eng/administration.shtml

---

Army into Chechnia in 1994. The Security Council draws up Russia's National Security and Foreign Policy Concepts and its Military, Information Security and Navy Doctrines. The Security Council is the major forum where foreign and security related policies are made; the relevant government institutions then execute these policies.

Box 5.9 Secretaries of the Security Council

Yury Skokov	3 April 1992 to 11 June 1993
Yevgeny Shaposhnikov	11 June 1993 to 18 September 1993
Oleg Lobov	18 September 1993 to 18 June 1996
Aleksandr Lebed	18 June 1996 to 19 October 1996
Ivan Rybkin	19 October 1996 to 2 March 1998
Andrei Kokoshin	3 March 1998 to 14 September 1998
Nikolai Bordyuzha	14 September 1998 to 29 March 1999
Vladimir Putin	29 March 1999 to 9 August 1999
Vladislav Sherstyuk	9 August 1999 to 15 November 1999
Sergei Ivanov	15 November 1999 to 28 March 2001
Vladimir Rushailo	28 March 2001 to 9 March 2004
Igor Ivanov	9 March 2004 to 18 July 2007
Valentin Sobolev	18 July 2007–

The State Council

In September 2000 Putin issued a decree establishing a new advisory body to the president called the State Council. According to the Kremlin website (2007b), Putin formed the State Council in order to harness the potential of regional leaders. Regional governors and presidents form the core of its membership and the RF president, who chairs the State Council, may also co-opt other members. Putin appointed one of his presidential aides Aleksandr Abramov as the secretary of the State Council; Abramov was reappointed to the Kremlin staff by Medvedev and remains as the secretary. There is also a State Council Presidium, whose membership includes the leaders of one of the republics, territories or provinces from each of the seven federal districts established in 2000. The membership is rotated every six months. The Presidium sometimes has joint sessions with the Security Council and the presidential advisory bodies. The Presidium prepares the State Council sessions, which are devoted to single topics and are held four times a year. The formation of the State Council was part of Putin's bid to strengthen the power vertical, as its role according to the Kremlin website is to 'ensure the concerted functioning and interaction of various governmental bodies' (ibid.).

The Council of Legislators

The Council of Legislators is a consultative group set up in May 2002. It is the second new body, the first being the State Council, that Putin created in order to reform the relationship between the presidency and the republics and regions. The

Council of Legislators includes the heads of the 80 regional parliaments and members of the Federation Council. It meets every three months at the Federation Council and once every six months at the Kremlin, when it is chaired by the president. The main aim of the Council is to improve the overall quality of legislation and to coordinate legislative activity; it provides a useful forum where the impact of proposed legislation in a particular region or regions can be aired. This is an especially important matter as in 2005 Putin initiated four national projects on healthcare, education, housing and agriculture, under the overall direction of Dmitry Medvedev. The Council of Legislators contributes to the process of turning these projects into legislation, with the aim of ensuring the projects' implementation throughout Russia.

Presidential Commissions and Councils

The president may set up Presidential Commissions and Councils to perform specific functions or to investigate a particular question or issue. For example, there was

---

Box 5.10 Federal Boards, Commissions and Councils answerable to the president

- Directorial Board for Special Programmes of the RF President (a federal agency)
- Administrative Board for the RF President (a federal agency)
- Presidential Commission for Military-Technical Co-operation of the RF with Foreign States
- Presidential Commission on Federative and Local Self-Government Issues
- Presidential Commission for Citizenship
- Presidential Commission for Screening Candidates for Federal Judges
- Presidential Commission for State Decorations
- Presidential Commission for the Rehabilitation of the Victims of Political Repression
- Council for Implementing Priority National Projects
- Council for Combating Corruption
- Culture and Art
- Heraldic Council
- Council for the Enhancement of the Judicial System
- Council for the Codification and Enhancement of Civil Legislation
- Council on Science, Technologies and Education
- Council for Interaction with Religious Organisations
- Council on Physical Culture and Sport
- Council for Facilitating the Development of Civil Soviety Institutions and Human Rights

a temporary Presidential Commission on Prisoners of War, Missing and Interned Persons set up specifically to investigate what had been happening in Chechnia since 1994.

The prime minister and the government

The role of the government

The major role of government is the execution (implementation) of policy. The government has a limited policy-making role in the areas of health, social security, environment, culture, science, education. Foreign, defence and security policy making are the preserve of the presidency. The government has various formal functions, such as the protection of the rule of law, human and civil rights, and property rights and taking action against crime, which are roles it shares with the president. It also has an important financial role, which includes executing credit and monetary policies, formulating the state budget and submitting it to the Duma, and issuing a report on the budget's implementation. If the Duma rejects the budget it is referred to a conciliation commission comprised of members from the Duma and government. It also has the prerogative of scrutinising any bill presented to the Duma that has financial implications. The government also has a legislative role as it can present bills to the Duma and issue decrees and directives in order to implement policy; but these may be rescinded by the president if they contradict existing legislation or presidential decrees.

Prime minister or chair of the government

Russia has not had a vice president since 1993 and in formal terms the prime minister holds the second most important post in the country. The Constitution describes the president as the policy maker and the prime minister as the executor. Part of the weakness of the prime minister is that while the president is directly elected, the prime minister is selected by the president and subject to confirmation by the Duma. This means that a prime minister does not necessarily have their own power base and there is also no requirement that they should be selected from the largest single party or a majority coalition in the Duma. For example, Chernomyrdin remained prime minister after the December 1995 Duma elections, even though his party Our Home is Russia only secured 10 per cent of the vote. In formal terms the prime minister is responsible for Russia's day-to-day administration and, with the other government ministers, helps the president and his advisers to formulate policy. The prime minister also acts as a bridge between the president and parliament and is the chief advocate of government policy in parliament. Yeltsin's longest serving prime minister was Viktor Chernomyrdin who proved particularly 'adept at forging agreements and building consensus among executive bodies, with legislators and lobbying groups. As founder of Our Home is Russia Chernomyrdin spearheaded an effort to bridge the institutional and policy interests of regional elites, enterprise directors and other executives who [were] so critical to the fortunes of the Yeltsin-Chernomyrdin regime' (Willerton, 1997: 50).

Yeltsin and his prime ministers

In his battles with first Gorbachev and then with the Congress of People's Deputies, Yeltsin concentrated on getting power for himself as RSFSR president and then as RF president. Even when firmly entrenched in the super-presidency after 1993 he was still not prepared to tolerate the emergence of any political figure who might challenge him or who might appear to be an heir apparent. Prime ministers also provided useful scapegoats for the failures of presidential policies; Yegor Gaidar was the first casualty, being blamed for the excesses of economic shock therapy. Chernomyrdin was similarly unceremoniously dumped, despite absolute public loyalty to Yeltsin, but was being widely spoken of as a future president. Yeltsin sacked Chernomyrdin in March 1998 on the grounds that the government lacked dynamism and needed new ideas and approaches, but then tried to bring him back in August–September 1998 arguing that the country needed continuity and stability. Prime Minister Sergei Kiriyenko, who was hated by the oligarchs and the business community for his attempts to enforce tax collection and by the Red-Browns for his economic liberalism, was blamed for the summer 1998 economic crisis and fired by President Yeltsin on 23 August. The oligarchs wanted Chernomyrdin back as prime minister because it would give him a power base for the presidential elections and he was their preferred post-Yeltsin president. When Primakov was sacked in May 1999, Yeltsin thanked him for bringing stability but criticised him for failing to restructure the economy. The real reason for getting rid of Primakov was that he was being spoken of as a natural candidate for the year 2000 presidential election, far outshone Yeltsin in popular approval ratings, had not been firm enough in his rebuttal of the Duma's attempts to impeach Yeltsin and was attacking the oligarchs. Primakov was replaced by another Yeltsin loyalist, the Interior Minister Sergei Stepashin, who was soon replaced by Vladimir Putin. The increasingly mercurial Yeltsin had four prime ministers in his last 18 months in office.

Putin and his prime ministers

In contrast to Yeltsin, Putin had only three prime ministers. His first prime minister, Mikhail Kasyanov, was closely associated with the Yeltsin Family and openly disagreed with Putin on administrative reform, tax policy in the oil industry and opposed the prosecution of the oligarch Mikhail Khodorkovsky. His sacking in February 2004, just three weeks before the presidential elections, was the last major step in Putin's emergence from Yeltsin's shadow. As the pro-Putin United Russia party had dominated the Duma since December 2003 the confirmation of Mikhail Fradkov, a little known bureaucrat, as prime minister was a formality. Fradkov was not closely associated with any of the rival clans and networks and, as such, had no powerbase of his own. He was essentially a technocrat rather than

Box 5.11 Russia's prime ministers from 1991 onwards

The prime ministers' names are followed by the dates of their period in office, in brackets, and biographical information.

Boris Yeltsin (6 November 1991 to 15 June 1992)
For biographical details see Box 5.5.

Yegor Gaidar* (15 June 1992 to 14 December 1992)
Born in 1956. In 1978 he graduated in economics from Moscow State University. In 1990, established a think-tank called the Institute of Market Reform. In 1991 he left the CPSU and joined Yeltsin's government as finance minister; he went on to be the architect of economic shock therapy. From 1991–2 and September 1993 to January 1994, he was also the first deputy prime minister. He was appointed first economics minister and then from June to December 1992 was acting prime minister, being dropped to appease parliament. In 1993 he was briefly economics minister, but left the government in 1994. In 1993, he co-founded the Democratic Choice political movement which won 94 seats in the Duma elections that year. In 1995 he lost his Duma seat. In 1999 he was a founder member and co-chair with his long-term political ally, Anatoly Chubais, of the Union of Rightist Forces (SPS); the following year Democratic Choice and SPS merged. From 1999 to 2003 he served as a deputy to the Duma, but SPS fared badly in the 2003 elections and Gaidar now concentrates on his economic research and writing. He is director of the Institute for the Economy in Transition; its website address is http://www.iet.ru/index.php?&lang=en

Viktor Chernomyrdin** (14 December 1992 to 23 March 1998)
Born in 1938. Attended a technical college and began work as an oil refinery mechanic; between 1967–73 and 1978–82 he worked for the CPSU. Chernomyrdin worked his way up through the state oil and gas industries; in 1982 he was appointed deputy Minister and in 1985 the Minister of oil and gas. In 1989, the gas and oil industries were split and the gas section became Gazprom, a government company headed by Chernomyrdin, which was Russia's biggest enterprise and the world's largest gas company. Chernomyrdin became an oligarch in his own right. In May 1992 he was appointed deputy prime minister in charge of fuel and energy. In April 1995, he founded the centrist political block Our Home is Russia (NDR). In August 1998 the Duma rejected Chernomyrdin's re-appointment as prime minister. Putin appointed Chernomyrdin Russia's ambassador to Ukraine in 2001, reportedly to keep him out of politics in Russia.

Sergei Kiriyenko (23 March 1998 to 23 August 1998)
Born in 1962. An engineer. From 1987 he worked for the Komsomol in Gorky. From 1991–94 he was president of the Kontsern AMK. In January 1994 he founded and became president of the *Guarantiia* Bank in Nizhnii Novgorod (formerly Gorky) and in 1996–97 headed the Nizhnii Novgorod oil refinery company Norsi-oil. In 1997 he was appointed first deputy minister of fuel and energy, later that year succeeding his mentor Boris Nemtsov as minister. On 23 March 1998 he became acting prime minister, but he only gained Duma confirmation of his appointment on the third vote on 24 April 1998. He was blamed for Russia's inability to weather the 1998

Box 5.11 *(Continued)*

economic crisis and for the devaluation of the rouble and was sacked as prime minister. Politically he is allied to the Union of Rightist Forces. In November 2005 he was appointed to head *Rosatom*, the Federal Atomic Energy Agency.

Viktor Chernomyrdin* (23 August 1998 to 11 September 1998)
See above.

Yevgeny Primakov (11 September 1998 to 12 May 1999)
Born in 1929. Graduated in 1953 from the Moscow State Institute of Oriental Studies, he is a Middle Eastern specialist and an Arabic speaker with considerable academic, diplomatic and intelligence experience. From 1956–70 he worked as a journalist in the Middle East and is assumed to have been a KGB operative during this time. In the 1970s and 1980s he held prestigious academic posts. From 1990–91 he was a member of Gorbachev's Presidential Council and served as Gorbachev's special envoy to Iraq before the Gulf War. After the failed August 1991 coup Primakov was appointed the first deputy chair of the KGB and then from 1991–96 he was the Director of the RF's Foreign Intelligence Service (SVR). In 1995 he was appointed to the president's Foreign Policy Council. From January 1996 to September 1998 he served as foreign minister and championed a state-realist-centrist approach to foreign policy. He was appointed prime minister in September 1998 when the Duma rejected Chernomyrdin's candidature. As prime minister Primakov earned respect across the political spectrum and even managed to push through tax reforms. His moves to stamp down on corruption alienated the oligarchs and Yeltsin was alarmed by Primakov's presidential ambitions. In 1999, he supported the Fatherland-All Russia election faction, the main opposition to Putin's pro-Putin Unity party. In November 2004 he testified in defence of the former Yugoslav President Slobodan Milošević, who was on trial for war crimes.

Sergei Stepashin (12 May 1999 to 9 August 1999)
Born in 1952. From 1973–90 he served in the Interior Ministry troops gaining a doctorate in 1986. In 1990, he was elected to the Russian Supreme Soviet and served as the chair of its Security Committee. From 1991 he served as deputy minister then first deputy minister of security, in 1993 joining the Security Council. In December 1993 he became the first deputy director of the Federal Agency for Counter-Intelligence and then from March 1994 to July 1995 was the Director of the FSB, but he either resigned or was dismissed due to the failed attempt to rescue the Buyonnovsk hostages. He became the head of the government's administrative department and then from 1997–98 was the minister of justice. In March 1998 he was appointed minister of the interior. In May 1998 he was sent by Yeltsin to Chechnia to negotiate with the Chechens and seems to have been taken hostage. A Yeltsin loyalist, in April 1999 he was appointed to the additional post of first deputy prime minister. During May–August 1999 he was prime minister, but it was always clear that he would only hold the post temporarily. In June 1999 he took Primakov's post as a permanent member of the Security Council. Since 1999 he has supported the liberal Yabloko political party and in 2001 was elected to the Duma. He resigned his seat to become head of the RF Accounts Chamber.

Box 5.11 (*Continued*)

Vladimir Putin (9 August 1999 to 7 May 2000)
For biographical details see Box 5.6.

Mikhail Kasyanov (7 May 2000 to 24 February 2004)
Born in 1957. Graduated from the Moscow Automobile Institute and Gosplan's Higher Economic Programme. Between 1981 and 1990 he worked for Gosplan as an economist and financial expert, and is a fluent English speaker. In 1991 he was appointed head of foreign economic relations in the Ministry of Finance and then from 1993–95 headed the department of foreign credit and debt in the Ministry of Finance and negotiated Russia's debt repayments with the IMF and western officials. In 1995 he was appointed deputy finance minister, in 1999 first deputy minister, and then minister of finance. In January 2000 he was also appointed first deputy prime minister and the following month renegotiated the terms of Russia's commercial debt to western banks, getting more than one-third written off. In 2006 he announced his intention to stand for the presidency in 2008, but his candidacy was barred.

Viktor Khristenko* (24 February 2004 to 5 March 2004)

Mikhail Fradkov (5 March 2004 to 14 September 2007)
Born in 1950. An economist with a specialism in foreign economic relations, graduated from the Foreign Trade Academy in 1981. From 1991 to 1992 he was Russia's deputy permanent representative to GATT. In 1992 he was deputy minister, then in 1993 first deputy minister and in 1997 minister of Foreign Economic Relations. In 1998–99 he was the chair and general director of the *Inosstrakh* insurance society. In May 1999 he was appointed Minister of Trade. From May 2000 he was the first deputy secretary of the Security Council and from March 2001, director of the Federal Tax Police Service. In May 2003, Fradkov became Russia's permanent representative to the European Union in Brussels, with the rank of minister.

Viktor Zubkov (14 September 2007 to 8 May 2008)
Born in 1941. In 1965 Zubkov graduated in Economics from the Leningrad Agricultural Institute and ran collective farms in Leningrad *oblast* until 1985 when he began work for the *oblast* administration. From 1991 to 1993 he was the deputy chair of the St Petersburg Administration's External Relations Committee, which was chaired by Putin. Between 1993 and 2000 he worked for the Federal Tax Service and the Tax Ministry. In 1999 he unsuccessfully stood for election as the governor of Leningrad *oblast*. In 2001 he became the director of the newly created Federal Financial Monitoring Service, which battled money laundering and was part of Putin's campaign against the oligarchs. In 2004 he announced that the licences of some banks would be withdrawn, prompting a banking crisis. He was a surprise appointment as prime minister as he had a low personal profile and was aged 66. A member of the St Petersburg clan, his daughter is married to the Defence Minister Anatoly Serdyukov.

Vladimir Putin (8 May 2008–)
For biographical information go to Box 5.6.

* Acting prime ministers only
** When first appointed, Chernomyrdin was the Chair of the Council of Ministers

a politician, an economic reformer who had come into contact with the *siloviki* while head of the Federal Tax Police. Fradkov and the deputy prime minister Aleksandr Zhukov were selected to carry through the key reforms of Putin's second presidency, which included further economic, tax and administrative reform. Above all Putin wanted a prime minister who would faithfully execute the policies devised by the president; he did not want a prime minister who wanted to play a more political role. Fradkov's appointment made the Putin presidency even stronger than before, as he now had a pliant parliament and prime minister, which reinforced the already gathering trend for policy initiative to originate in the Kremlin rather than in the government.

Putin and the changing structure of government

The Russian government structure in the 1990s reflected Yeltsin's institutional improvisation; it consisted of too many bodies with overlapping and poorly defined roles and was grossly overstaffed. Putin established a working party under a deputy prime minister, Boris Aleshin, to identify ways of streamlining the government structure. Following his own re-election and Fradkov's appointment as prime minister, Putin signed a presidential decree 'On the system and Structure of Federal Executive Bodies' on 9 March 2004, which reformed the government structure. The number of ministries was reduced from 24 to 15 by merging responsibilities and reducing the status of some ministries to federal agencies, most of which were still headed by their former minister. The reorganisation also provided an opportunity to sideline ministers and officials who had ties with the Yeltsin era. Putin's allies – Sergei Ivanov at Defence, Alexei Kudrin at Finance, German Gref at Economic Development and Trade, Alexei Gordeyev at Agriculture, Sergei Shoigu at Emergency Situations and Yury Chaika at Justice – all remained in post. The reform also established three tiers of government with different functions. The ministries form the first tier; their role is to generate policy within their sphere of competence and to issue normative orders. Although under Putin the presidency dominated policy initiative, as he rather than the prime minister had selected the ministers, the ministries could be relied upon not to challenge Putin's policy agenda. The 18 federal services form the second tier and they have the purely executive role of ensuring implementation and compliance. The 25 federal agencies which deliver state services to the people form the third tier. Wholly or partially owned state companies are not formally a part of the government, however, they also de facto execute the Kremlin's policies. For example, Gazprom's prices are set to serve the Kremlin's domestic and foreign agendas.

Deputy prime ministers

Under Yeltsin the practice developed of having a varying number of first deputy and deputy prime ministers. A few deputy prime ministers were also ministers, but their main role was to oversee the work of a group of ministries. The prime minister and his deputies formed a small inner cabinet that would meet regularly to discuss the work of government. By the end of Putin's first term there were six deputy prime ministers. In 2004 the new Prime Minister Mikhail Fradkov announced that in future there would only be one first deputy prime minister and two deputy prime ministers. The first deputy prime minister is, as the name suggests, the person who stands in when the prime minister is unavailable for any reason. Putin ensured that two of his closest allies, Dmitry Medvedev and Sergei Ivanov were deputy prime ministers, and the third Aleksandr Zhukov was an extremely able technocrat. Zhukov was put in charge of a special commission to bring government spending under control. While Putin was president, the role of the deputy prime ministers was reduced and the practice of holding the inner cabinet meetings ceased.

Box 5.12 Heads of the Government Administration (chiefs of staff)

Vladimir Kvasov	6 January 1994 to 11 November 1994
Vladimir Babichev	15 November 1994 to 23 March 1998
Nikolai Khvatkov	8 May 1998 to 28 August 1998
Igor Shabdurasulov	28 August 1998 to 14 September 1998
Yury Zubakov	14 September 1998 to 25 May 1999
Andrei Chernenko	25 May 1999 to 19 August 1999
Dmitry Kozak	19 August 1999 to 18 May 2000
Igor Shuvalov	18 May 2000 to 28 May 2003
Konstantin Merzlikan	28 May 2003 to 9 March 2004
Dmitry Kozak	9 March 2004 to 13 September 2004
Sergei Naryshkin	13 September 2004–

The Cabinet staff or government administration

In March 2004 Putin described the government administration as 'for all practical purposes almost a shadow ministerial cabinet' and that it needed to 'transform itself into an effective and modern administrative instrument' (Putin, 2004). There is tremendous rivalry between the deputy prime ministers and the chief of the Cabinet staff. Putin's appointment of his fellow Petersburgers, first Dmitry Kozak and then Sergei Naryshin, as Cabinet chiefs of staff shifted influence away from the government and towards government administration. Putin also ensured that their allegiance was to him rather than to their immediate superior, Prime Minister Fradkov. On his appointment Kozak immediately announced that the ministries had to dramatically reduce their staff numbers. At the end of March 2004 Kozak announced that ministries were to be allowed only two deputy ministers each. At that time Gref's Ministry of Economic Development and Trade had 12 deputy ministers and three first deputy ministers. Then in April 2004 Kozak announced that the overall number of deputy ministers would be reduced from 250 to 18.

Ministerial departments were also allowed only two deputies each. What tended to happen, however, was that rather than there being an overall reduction in staff numbers, staff were simply reallocated to other posts. For example, many ministries created new quasi-governmental services and agencies which performed similar functions to the old agencies and services.

Medvedev and the Russian government

In September 2007 Mikhail Fradkov stood down as prime minister and was replaced by a close ally of Putin, Viktor Zubkov. Zubkov was only ever intended to be an interim prime minister and it was understood that he would step down once Medvedev was elected president in order for Putin to be appointed prime minister.

Box 5.13 Medvedev's prime ministers

The Prime Minister

Vladimir Putin

Two First Deputy Prime Ministers

- **Viktor Zubkov:** the former prime minister, who now heads the government commissions on the national project in agriculture, fisheries, forestry and the agrarian-industrial sector.

- **Igor Shuvalov:** a former presidential aide and one of Putin's top economic advisers, he now oversees economic and social issues and foreign economic ties, including negotiations with the WTO.

Five Deputy Prime Ministers

- **Sergei Ivanov:** a former first deputy prime minister and defence minister. This is a demotion for Ivanov who has not been given a specific role.

- **Sergei Sobyanin:** the former head of Putin's Presidential Administration (Kremlin staff), he oversees the division of power between federal bodies. He also takes on the role of government chief of staff.

- **Aleksandr Zhukov:** a former deputy prime minister in the previous Cabinet. He is now in charge of priority national projects as well as overseeing state policy on culture, arts, sport, education, healthcare and the social sector.

- **Igor Sechin:** the former deputy head of Putin's Presidential Administration (Kremlin staff). He now oversees the state industrial policy (but not the defence sector), energy policy, mineral extraction and environmental protection. He is also the chair of the state-run *Rosneft* oil company.

- **Alexei Kudrin:** a former deputy prime minister in the previous Cabinet, he is in charge of social and economic development. He is also Finance Minister and is in charge of the implementation of a single fiscal and monetary policy, financial planning, the state budget, investment policy and state debt management.

The executive bodies of the Russian Federation

President of the Russian Federation

Prime Minister (Chair of the RF Government)

Deputy Prime Ministers (Deputy Chairs of the RF Government)

Ministry of the Interior
- Federal Migration Service

Ministry of Civil Defence Matters, Emergencies and the Liquidation of the Consequences of Natural Disasters (MChS)

Ministry of Foreign Affairs
- Federal CIS Affairs Agency

Ministry of Defence
- Federal military-technical cooperation service
- Federal technical and export supervision service
- Federal defence contracts service
- Federal special construction agency

Ministry of Justice
- Federal punishment service
- Federal bailiff service

Ministry of Healthcare and Social Development
- Federal service for the supervision of the defence of consumer rights and well-being
- Federal healthcare and social development supervision service
- Federal labour and employment service
- Federal bio-medical agency

Ministry of Culture
- Federal service for the supervision of the observance of legislation on the protection of the cultural legacy
- Federal archive agency

Ministry of Education and Science
- Federal education and science supervision service
- Federal intellectual property, patents and trade marks service
- Federal education agency
- Federal science and innovation agency

Ministry of Natural Resources and Ecology
- Federal hydrometeorology and environmental monitoring service
- Federal natural resources management service
- Federal ecological, technological and atomic management service
- Federal water resources agency
- Federal subsoil resources management agency

Ministry of Industry and Trade
- Federal technical regulation and metrology agency

Ministry of Regional Development

Ministry of Communications and Mass Media
- Federal communications and mass media supervision service
- Federal information technology agency
- Federal press and mass media agency
- Federal communications agency

Ministry of Agriculture
- Federal veterinary and plant health inspection service
- Federal forestry agency
- Federal fisheries agency

Ministry of Sport, Tourism and Youth Policy
- Federal youth affairs agency
- Federal tourism agency
- Federal physical culture and sport agency

Ministry of Transport
- Federal air navigation service
- Federal transport supervision service
- Federal air transport agency
- Federal roads agency
- Federal railway agency
- Federal sea and rivers transport agency

Ministry of Finance
- Federal tax service
- Federal insurance supervision service
- Federal financial and budgetary supervision service
- Federal treasury service

Ministry of Economic Development
- Federal state statistics service
- Federal registration service
- Federal geodesy and cartography agency
- Federal state reserves agency
- Federal real estate registry agency
- Federal agency for state property management
- Federal agency for the administration of special economic zones

Ministry of Energy

Federal Government Services and Agencies (reporting to the government)

Antimonopoly Service, Customs Service, Tariff Service, Financial Monitoring Service, Financial Market Service, Space Agency, Agency for the Delivery of Military, Technical and Material Means

Federal Government Services and Agencies (reporting to the president)

External Intelligence, Federal Security Service, Federal Narcotics Control Service, Federal Protection Service, State Messenger Service, the Main Administration for the President's Special Projects, the Presidential Administration

Source: 'Federal'nye organy ispolnitel'noi vlasti', Russian government website, http://www.government.ru/content/executivepowerservices/#

On 12 May 2008 Putin's close ally Sergei Naryshkin was appointed the new head of the Presidential Administration but retained his post as head of the government administration. Naryshkin therefore has the task of ensuring that the presidential and government staffs work together. Also on 12 May 2008 President Medvedev issued a decree on the 'System and Structure of the Federal Executive Bodies of Power' (Kremlin, 2008) which established a new Ministry of Sport, Tourism and Youth Policy. It also reorganised existing ministries and redistributed some functions between ministries and other executive bodies. For example, the former Ministry of Information Technology and Communications is now the Ministry of Communications and Mass Media, headed by Putin's former head of protocol Igor Shchyogolev. The functions of the former Ministry of Industry and Energy have been split; there is now a Ministry of Industry and Trade and a separate Ministry of Energy (ibid.). The number of ministries is now 18. The decree also increased the number of deputy prime ministers to seven, including two first deputies as before (see Box 5.13).

Medvedev has also made changes to the federal agencies, six of which have been abolished and their functions transferred to the relevant ministry. The Federal Agency for Federal Property Management is now the Federal Agency for State Property Management and it will oversee the sale of privatised federal property through the Federal Property Fund. The decree also stipulated that federal ministers have the right to issue binding instructions to the heads of the federal services and agencies under their responsibility and, if necessary, to suspend decisions taken by these federal services and agencies (by their heads) or cancel these decisions in the absence of other procedures for their cancellation set by federal law (ibid.).

Reforming the state service and creating a civil service?

The reform imperative

The transformation of the soviet state service into a Russian civil service is a vital part of the democratisation process. Russia needs a rational, rules-based, effective, impartial, accountable and democratic civil service in order to carry out reform. The soviet state service (or administration) was highly centralised and accountability ran upwards to superiors not to the people. Neil Parison (2000: 5) also argues that there was 'a lack of other forms of accountability (legal, financial, or public). Informal and personalistic systems for resolving disputes, allocating resources, and making appointments were the norm. Administration was not seen as a "public service" serving the soviet people, but rather as "state service" and the CPSU was effectively the state'. State service reform also includes reducing the number of employees (known as *kadry* or cadres) both to cut costs and to reflect the state's reduced role in the life of the country, notably in the economy. Given the continuity of personnel, retraining was also essential as the vast majority of cadres did not have the skills that are required in post-communist Russia. Salary scales and career structures also needed to be revised in order to retain and attract younger, better-qualified people in the face of stiff competition for personnel from the growing private sector.

State service reform under Yeltsin

In November 1991 the Communist Party Schools, which for decades had trained communist party functionaries, were charged with creating and training a new Russian civil service. A new body called the Chief Department for Personnel Training or more informally *Roskadry* (Russian cadres), was established within the Russian government in 1992. Under Prime Minister Yegor Gaidar the government initiated reforms similar to those adopted by the other former communist countries of east-central Europe to turn communist bureaucrats into western-style civil servants. Know-how, funding and training were provided by western governments and organisations, which saw transformation of the bureaucracies as vital to the reform of communist states. In response, *Roskadry* initiated the retraining of existing staff and tried to set new professional entry requirements. Retraining focused on the eradication of soviet practices and the development of new skills, particularly in the areas of law, finance and personnel management. In a vain attempt to stamp out corruption, civil servants were forbidden to take part in private economic activities and were required to declare their outside interests. There were also moves to reduce the number of ministries and agencies and the overall number of civil servants, in response to the state's changing functions. Gosplan, the soviet central economic planning body, was no longer required as Russia pursued marketisation and so was disbanded. However, new ministries, agencies and services were created to carry out the state's new functions. During the early to mid-1990s Russia acquired, among other institutions, a Bankruptcy Agency, an Antimonopoly Ministry and a Securities and Exchanges Commission. Ministries with an enhanced role in the new conditions, such as the Ministry of Tax and Revenues, saw their staff numbers grow dramatically. The growth of the Presidential Administration, and the creation of new bodies both at the federal level and within the republics and regions, led to an increase rather than the desired decrease in the number of civil servants. It is estimated that in 1985 the whole USSR had 800,000 civil servants but that by 1994 Russia alone had one million civil servants; by 2001 this figure had risen to 1.2 million (Weir, 2002).

At the end of 1993 *Roskadry* complained about the lack of progress in civil service reform and made a radical call for the creation of a unified civil service, with central control of merit-based appointments. This was a step too far and proved to be *Roskadry*'s final act before it was dissolved in January 1994. Government ministries opposed this proposal, which endangered the complex network of favours and patronage that they enjoyed. As privatisation of state assets progressed in the 1990s, ministries developed into unofficial, semi-independent, ministerial-businesses (Afanasyev, 1997). A unified civil service would have threatened the money-making opportunities that the 'civil' servants enjoyed. The 1995 Civil Service Law went some way to defining the status, duties, career structure and code of ethics for the civil service. Civil servants were not allowed to engage in outside work apart from teaching, scientific or creative work; they could not be a member of a legislative body, engage in economic or commercial activities, or use their office to promote the interests of a political party, public organisation or a religious organisation. The law failed to provide any effective mechanisms to ensure that its provisions were enforced. This, together with the weakness of Russia's law enforcement agencies and bureaucratic resistance, meant that little progress was made in implementing reform; corruption flourished and little progress was made in developing accountable and transparent governance. Another problem was that there was no clear distinction made between career state employees and political appointees, with the result that patronage rather than open appointments based on merit dominated. The dominant patrimonial culture (see Chapter 4) meant that careers depended upon pleasing a patron rather than necessarily doing a good job and it also encouraged corruption.

State service reform under Putin

Putin inherited a state service that was largely ineffective, often corrupt and not fit for purpose. In his Annual Message in 2002, Putin described Russia's state service as behaving in an 'arbitrary manner' (*proizvol*) (Putin, 2002). The Russian political scientist Vladimir Gelman also argued: 'Our bureaucrats are unprofessional, badly paid and, most important, they exercise power not in the public interest but in their own. Until the state machinery in this country is completely redesigned from top to bottom, no other reforms can be reliably implemented' (Weir, 2002). For Putin, state service reform was a vital component of his broader agenda of state modernisation.

In 2001 a Presidential Commission 'For the Reform of Government' headed by Prime Minister Mikhail Kasyanov and an inter-ministerial working group headed by Dmitry Medvedev, who was then a presidential aide, were set up. The work on state service reform was highly contentious, there was a good deal of infighting as groups tried to protect their vested interests and the reforms were not as radical as anticipated. In 2002 government service and its key principles were defined, the relationship between the different branches of government were clarified and more detailed arrangements for personnel management were set out. There was also a new Code of Conduct, which was supposed to make state servants more responsible, less corrupt, more transparent in their work and more controllable by, and accountable to, the public. Unfortunately, the code did not contain procedures for verifying compliance with its provisions. In 2003, the state service was divided into civil, military and law enforcement servants. The military and law enforcement services are part of the federal level, but the civil service is divided between the federal and the republican-regional levels. Anyone receiving a salary from a republican-regional or federal budget is defined as a civil servant.

Continuing problems

Putin's reforms went some way towards modernising and reforming the state service, but they did not create a civil service and problems persist. Russia's political elites still view the civil service as an extension of their power and authority, and patronage remains an important career prerequisite. While most democracies have some political appointees who are paid by the state, in Russia this practice is on a much larger scale. At the highest level the members of the Presidential Administration are both government employees and political appointees. Similar patterns exist at the republican and regional levels. The concept of a conflict of interests between one's public employment on the one hand and one's private activities, beliefs and allegiances on the other is also not widely understood. Furthermore, through his endeavours to control civil society and the media, Putin all but eliminated social oversight of the bureaucracy. Similarly, the strengthening of presidential control over the legislature and the judiciary also weakened other potential sources of oversight. Far from strengthening the state, as he wished, this will ultimately weaken it. An important lesson from the Brezhnev to Chernenko (1964–85) period was that the bureaucracy cannot be effectively controlled from above, even with extensive use of the police and secret police. Russia still needs an honest and professional civil service to implement reform, but this can only be created within the context of further democratisation.

Chapter summary

Putin continued the creation of a super-presidential system begun under Yeltsin. There are major weaknesses in the super-presidential system, not least the very personalistic style of leadership assumed by both Yeltsin and Putin, their promotion and reliance on networks, and the lack of a clear separation of political and administrative roles within the executive. Putin's personal popularity ratings remain high and few mourn the loss of power and influence by certain oligarchs and regional bosses. However, the concentration of power in the presidency and the weakening of other institutions such as the Federal Assembly and republican and regional legislatures ultimately weakens Russia's policy capacity. The separation of powers in democracies is not just about preventing authoritarianism and corruption; it also encourages engagement in public life by a range of social actors and helps to promote efficiency, new ideas and initiatives. Putin gave the impression of effective and decisive leadership, he could be assured that the parliament would pass his legislation and the president can also rule by decree. However, the weakening of other institutions and attempts to co-opt civil society bodies (see Chapter 10) encourage personalism, corruption and clientalism and ultimately weakens the immediate prospects for democratic consolidation.

Discussion points

- How useful is the RF Constitution (1993) to our understanding of the nature and role of the president?
- Why are clans and networks so important to Russian presidents?
- Do you think Putin needed to strengthen the power vertical and, if so, why?
- Does Russia have a democratic government?

Further reading

Analyses of the Putin presidency are provided by: Peter Truscott (2004) *Putin's Progress*, London: Simon & Schuster; Andrew Jack (2004) *Inside Putin's Russia*, London: Granta Books; the late Anna Politkovskaya (2004) *Putin's Russia*, London: The Harvill Press (trans: Arch Tait); Lilia Shevtsova (2003) *Putin's Russia*, Washington, DC: Carnegie Endowment for Peace (trans: Antonina W. Bois); Richard Sakwa (2004) *Putin: Russia's Choice*, London: Routledge; Peter Baker and Susan Glasser (2005) *Kremlin Rising: Vladimir Putin's Russia and the End of the Revolution*, New York: Simon & Schuster; Yuri Felshtinsky and Alexander Litvinenko (2007) *Blowing up Russia: The Return of the KGB*, London: Gibson Square Books; and Yuri Felshtinsky and Vladimir Pribylovsky (2008) *The Age of the Assassins. The Rise and Rise of Vladimir Putin*, London: Gibson Square Books.

For analyses of presidentialism and presidentialism versus parliamentary systems see Juan J. Linz and Aturo Valenzuela (eds) (1994) *The Failure of Presidential Democracy*, Baltimore, MD: Johns Hopkins University Press; Arend Lijphart (ed.) (1992) *Parliamentary Versus Presidential Government*, Oxford: Oxford University Press; Steve Fish (1997) 'The Pitfalls of Russia Superpresidentialism', *Current History*, 96 (612), October, 326–30; and Timothy J. Colton and Cindy Skach (2005) 'The Russian Predicament. A Fresh look at Semipresidentialism', *Journal of Democracy*, 16 (3), July, 113–26.

Useful websites

Constitution of the Russian Federation, 1993: http://www.departments.bucknell.edu/russian/const/constit.html

President of Russia (Kremlin): http://president.kremlin.ru/eng/ and http://www.kremlin.ru/eng/

Security Council (Russian only): http://www.scrf.gov.ru/

Satirical short stories about Vladimir Vladimirovich (aka Putin) by the journalist Maxim Kononenko (aka Mr Parker): http://vladimir.vladimirovich.ru/english

The Public Opinion Foundation (FOM) website carries the results of numerous surveys on a wide variety of topics.

For surveys about the president: http://bd.english.fom.ru/cat/policy/president2

For a survey of public opinion on the civil service: http://bd.english.fom.ru/report/cat/soc_real/number_05_04/egur050406

References

Afanasyev, M. (1997) *Klientelism i rossiiskaya gosudarstvennost'*, Moscow: *Tsentr konstitutsionykh issledovanyi moskovkogo obshchestvennogo nauchnogo fonda*

FOM Database (1999– onwards) 'Putin's ratings', Public Opinion Foundation website, http://bd.english.fom.ru/cat/policy/president2/putin

Kremlin website (2007a) 'The Presidential Executive Office', downloaded 19 July 2007, http://www.kremlin.ru/eng/administration.shtml

Kremlin website (2007b) 'The State Council', downloaded 19 July 2007 http://www.kremlin.ru/eng/articles/council.shtml

Kremlin (2008) 'President Dmitry Medvedev signed decree on the System and Structure of the Federal Executive Bodies of Power', 12 May, Kremlin website, http://www.kremlin.ru.eng/

Minasov, R. (1992) 'Nomenklatura prepares to take revenge', *Rossiiskaia Gazeta*, 4 March: 2 (reprinted in English in *Current Digest of the Post Soviet Press*, XLIV (9), 1992, 22–3)

Parison, N. (2000) 'Russia: Public Administration reform: Issues and Options', ECSPE, The World Bank Conference on Post Election Strategy, Moscow, April 5–7, 1–12. Available online at http://www.imf.org/external/pubs/ft/seminar/2000/invest/pdf/parison.pdf

Putin, V. (2000a) *Ot pervogo litsa*, Moscow: Vagrius

Putin, V. (2000b) 'Annual Address to the Federal Assembly', 8 July, Kremlin website, http://www.kremlin.ru/eng

Putin, V. (2002) 'Annual Address to the Federal Assembly', 18 April, Kremlin website, http://www.kremlin.ru/eng

Putin, V. (2004) quoted in 'Vladimir Putin: Government must be effective administrative instrument', *Pravda*, 9 March, http://www.pravda.ru/

Traynor, I. (2000) 'Putin puts his trust in KGB honesty', *The Guardian*, 25 March, 15

Weir, F. (2002) 'Putin's duel with the bureaucrats', *Christian Science Monitor*, 22 February, http://www.csmonitor.com

Willerton Jr, J. P. (1997) 'Presidential Power', Chapter 3, in S. White, A. Pravda and Z. Gitelman (eds) *Developments in Russian Politics 4*, Basingstoke: Macmillan

Chapter 6

The Federal Assembly

Learning objectives

- To introduce the development of the Federal Assembly under Yeltsin.
- To describe the composition and functions of the State Duma.
- To describe the composition and functions of the Federation Council.
- To examine the impact of Putin's reforms on the Federal Assembly.

Introduction

Russia began its post-communist transition with some slightly reformed soviet era institutions, which had been created for an entirely different political system. One of the major results of Gorbachev's reforms was that political power within

Emblem commemorating 100 years of the State Duma in Russia.

Russia had become very diffuse. The writing of a new Constitution and creation of new institutions, therefore, took place amid struggles between different power centres: the presidency, the Congress of People's Deputies and its standing body the Supreme Soviet, the government and the increasingly assertive regional authorities. The power struggle culminated in October 1993 with armed confrontation between the parliament housed in the White House and the Yeltsin presidency. Ultimately Yeltsin won and the new RF Constitution adopted in December 1993 reflected his preference for a strong, super-presidency and a correspondingly weak parliament. According to the 1993 Constitution, the new Federal Assembly (parliament) is 'the permanently functioning, representative and legislative organ of the Russian Federation'. The upper chamber is the Federation Council and the lower chamber is the State Duma (hereafter Duma). The Federal Assembly's structure, formation and jurisdiction are set out in Chapter 5 of the 1993 Constitution. The two chambers of the Federal Assembly are not housed in the same building or even on the same site in Moscow. The Duma is housed in the White House while the Federation Council is housed in the Main Building on Bolshaia Dmitrovka Street with additional offices and committee rooms on Novy Arbat Street. The Duma and the Federation Council sit separately and only meet together to hear messages from the president, the Constitutional Court and addresses from foreign heads of state (Art. 100). This chapter examines the context and issues surrounding the creation of the Federal Assembly; the relationship between the two houses; their compositions and legislative and representative functions.

From soviet institutions to a new Constitution, 1990–1993

From Russian Socialist Federal Soviet Republic (RSFSR) to Russian Federation parliament

Gorbachev's democratisation included a reduction in the powers of the Communist Party of the Soviet Union (CPSU) and an increase in the powers of the soviets and their chairs at all levels. This apparent deconcentration and decentralisation of power and authority had been countered by the creation of a strong executive presidency for the USSR. In May 1990 Yeltsin was elected the chair of the RSFSR Supreme Soviet, which was the standing body of the Congress of People's Deputies. He now held the most powerful non-Communist Party post in Russia. In a gesture designed to appeal to Russia's regions, Yeltsin chose Ruslan Khasbulatov, a Chechen, as his first deputy. In July 1990 in another move designed to appeal to Russia's regions, Yeltsin created a Federation Council within the office of the chair of the RSFSR Supreme Soviet. The Federation Council included the 31 chairs of the soviets of the autonomous republics, *oblasts* and *okrugs*, as well as a further 31 chairs of selected *oblast*, *krai* and city soviets. From 1991 the Federation Council also included the chairs of the 88 (later 89 after the republic of Chechnia-Ingushetia split into two) subjects of the Russian Federation. Then in a move that paralleled the creation of the USSR executive presidency, the RSFSR agreed in a March 1991 referendum to create a new post of RSFSR president. Yeltsin argued that the RSFSR needed a strong presidency for two main reasons. First to counter and challenge President Gorbachev's central power and his opposition to the RSFSR's reforms and, secondly, to maintain Russia's own integrity by preventing its regions from seeking independence from Russia. Yeltsin was duly elected RSFSR president on 12 June 1991 and Khasbulatov became the chair of the Supreme Soviet. At this time Khasbulatov and the Russian Parliament accepted the need for a strong Russian presidency. The Congress of People's Deputies even granted Yeltsin emergency powers to rule by decree for one year until the end of 1992.

Box 6.1 Supreme Soviet (Council) chairs*

Boris Yeltsin 29 May 1990 to 10 July 1991

Ruslan Khasbulatov** 10 July 1991 to 4 October 1993
Born in 1942, a Chechen. An economics professor and corresponding member of the Russian Academy of Sciences, he had also worked in the Komsomol apparatus (full-time staff). In 1990 he was elected to the RSFSR parliament and in 1991 he became the chair of the RSFSR Supreme Soviet. He became increasingly critical of Yeltsin's economic programme and was one of the leaders of the parliament's armed opposition in October 1993. He was arrested and imprisoned but was granted a parliamentary amnesty in 1994. He then became briefly active in Chechen politics, advocating limited sovereignty for Chechnia, and in 1995 considered (but did not run for) the Chechen presidency. He is currently a professor at the G. V. Plekhanov Economics Academy. He is the founder and head of the International Economy department at the Russian Economic Academy.

* Dissolved by presidential decree 21 September 1993, but the decree was not recognised by the Supreme Council. The decree was finally enforced on 4 October 1993

** acting to 29 October 1991

The parliamentary and presidential consensus ends

When the USSR was disbanded in December 1991, the consensus between the Russian president and parliament began to pull apart. Following the defeat of the August 1991 coup Yeltsin's prestige was at its highest, not least because he had delivered Russian independence. He should have seized the initiative: dissolved parliament, called fresh elections, started work on a new constitution, and initiated reform of institutions and structures. Instead, in a pattern of behaviour that was to mark his leadership, he followed the period of furious activity that had defeated the coup by withdrawing to his dacha for several months. All the while Russia was drifting into chaos. When Yeltsin did re-emerge he declared that the important thing was to get down to economic reform and that there was no time to talk. He used the powers granted to him by the Congress of People's Deputies to launch economic shock therapy and appoint key government ministers and regional officials. Through 1992 president and parliament worked together somewhat uneasily. While Khasbulatov was highly critical of shock therapy he shared Yeltsin's belief in the importance of Russian unity and resisted attempts by the republics to achieve greater autonomy let alone independence. Khasbulatov also ensured that most presidential legislation successfully passed through the parliament, even though it was dominated by communists and nationalists (the Red-Browns). However, parliament increasingly used its control over the administration of legislation to block the implementation of presidential policies.

During 1992, as Russia was plunging deeper and deeper into economic and political chaos, the conflict between the parliament and the president grew. At the root of the conflict was a competition for power. Between 1990 and mid-1993 the RSFSR Constitution was amended over 300 times, leading to a confused situation in which supreme state power was granted to both the legislative and the executive branches. Khasbulatov argued for a return to the pre-June 1991 situation in which the chair of the parliament rather than the president was Russia's leader. In contrast Yeltsin held firm to his belief that Russia needed a strong executive presidency. Khasbulatov could legitimately find constitutional provisions that supported his advocacy of a parliamentary system with the president reduced to a ceremonial role, but it is also clear that he was personally ambitious and had turned parliament into his personal power base. He distributed perks and privileges such as apartments and trips abroad to gain supporters. For his part Yeltsin ignored, insulted or attacked the Congress of People's Deputies and made little attempt to establish a working relationship with it. Yeltsin also lost the support of Aleksandr Rutskoi, his vice-president since the 1991 RSFSR presidential elections. Rutskoi was the leader of the party Communists for Democracy, which opposed shock therapy and sided with Khasbulatov. By the late summer of 1992 it was clear that the political institutions had failed to resolve the conflict and, in an increasingly volatile atmosphere, there were allegations and counter allegations of coup plots. Yeltsin's supporters urged him to suspend parliament and introduce direct presidential rule; parliament accused Yeltsin of seeking dictatorial powers and of failing to implement an effective reform programme. Although failing in a bid to impeach Yeltsin, parliament refused to extend his emergency powers which expired in December 1992 and Yeltsin countered by accusing parliament of blocking desperately needed reforms and of being dominated by undemocratic deputies.

It would have taken a president of consummate political skills to have worked with the Russian parliament at this time. Yeltsin lacked such skills. In December 1992 Valery Zorkin the chair of the Constitutional Court brokered a temporary compromise solution between Yeltsin and Khasbulatov, which included the sacking of some of Yeltsin's closest allies including the replacement of acting Prime Minister Yegor Gaidar by the more centrist Viktor Chernomyrdin. The Congress of People's Deputies also won the right to approve presidential appointments and dismissals in the key areas of finance and foreign affairs. In return the Congress of People's Deputies agreed to drop their demand for constitutional amendments to weaken the presidency and to accept a referendum on a new constitution to be held on 11 April 1993. The referendum would decide whether Russia would have a presidential or a parliamentary system.

Table 6.1 The April 1993 Referendum: a mandate for Yeltsin?

Question	Percentage of the vote	
	Yes	No
1. Do you have confidence in the president of the RF, B. N. Yeltsin?	58.7	39.2
2. Do you approve of the socio-economic policies carried out by the president of the RF and the government of the RF since 1992?	53.0	44.6
3. Do you consider it necessary to hold early elections for the president of the RF?	49.5	47.1
4. Do you consider it necessary to hold early elections for the People's Deputies of the RF?	67.2	30.1

Source: Adapted from *Keesings Record of World Events. News Digest*, April 1993: 39421

The April 1993 referendum

Yeltsin sought a personal mandate to end the deadlock by appealing, over parliament, directly to the Russian people via a referendum. Yeltsin emerged a narrow victor from the April referendum and could take some comfort from the fact that over 67 per cent of the voters favoured early elections to the Congress of People's Deputies. The percentage of voters expressing no confidence in Yeltsin, his reforms and wanting early presidential elections was still substantial, however. Voters were also consistent in their voting across the four referendum questions. In the regions where the majority expressed no confidence in President Yeltsin, they also did not approve of his socio-economic policies and favoured early presidential elections. Yeltsin's victory was largely confined to the big cities and he fared badly in small towns and in Russia's heartlands which had been particularly hard hit by shock therapy. Similarly he lacked support in those areas of Siberia that were not cushioned by oil, coal and diamonds earnings. While parliament and president were fighting over power in Moscow, Russia's non-Russian republics were demanding greater autonomy or outright independence. Ten of Russia's republics, including the Volga republics of Bashkortostan, Marii-El, Mordovia and Udmurtia, passed votes of no confidence in Yeltsin. In the republic of Tatarstan voter turnout in the referendum was so low that its vote was declared invalid. Yeltsin also fared badly in the Caucasus; in the republic of Dagestan only 15 per cent and in Chechnia-Ingushetia only 2 per cent of voters expressed confidence in Yeltsin. The referendum results did not give Yeltsin a decisive mandate and they did not resolve the stand-off between president and parliament.

The final showdown: parliament versus the president

The impasse between president and parliament continued through the spring and into the autumn of 1993. Since 1990 work had been under way on a new constitution; in May 1993 Yeltsin hastened matters along by setting up a special Constitutional Assembly which produced a new draft constitution on 12 July. The draft was a contradictory hybrid of a presidential and a parliamentary system. The

A soldier stands on top of a tank at the Russian White House on 4 October 1993.

constitutional crisis escalated and in mid-September Khasbulatov and Rutskoi, warned that Yeltsin was planning direct presidential rule and a dictatorship. On 21 September Yeltsin issued Decree no.1400 'On Gradual Constitutional Reform in the Russian Federation' dissolving parliament. Parliamentary powers were to be vested in a new Federal Assembly, with the existing Federation Council as the upper chamber. He ordered the Constitutional Assembly to agree a final version of the Constitution with the parliament's Constitutional Commission, announcing that a referendum on the new constitution and parliamentary elections would be held on 12 December 1993.

An emergency meeting of the Constitutional Court ruled by nine to four that Yeltsin's statements were in violation of the Constitution. The Supreme Soviet responded by declaring Rutskoi acting president, setting up an alternative government and refusing to comply with the order to dissolve parliament. They also summoned an emergency parliamentary session which was attended by 658 of the possible 1,033 deputies. Yeltsin replied by sealing off the Russian parliament building, the White House, and cutting off the electricity and water supply with around 100 – mostly Red-Brown – deputies left inside. Armed insurrection followed on 3 October when around 15,000 supporters of the parliamentary rebels managed to breach the cordon of Interior Ministry troops and enter the White House. The stand-off between president and parliament had rapidly moved to a stage when it could only be resolved by force. Khasbulatov and Rutskoi emboldened by the rebels' success believed that the Russian security forces were deserting Yeltsin and so ordered their supporters to attack the office of Moscow's mayor and the Ostankino television centre. Yeltsin declared a state of emergency that continued until 18 October.

Box 6.2 Were Yeltsin's actions against the parliament in October 1993 justified?

Arguments in favour of Yeltsin:

- The Congress of People's Deputies was dominated by communists and nationalists who opposed reform.

- Congress was elected in March 1990 when the CPSU was the only legal political party and, while a truer reflection of public opinion than the previous Congress, it was not freely elected.

- Yeltsin was elected with a personal popular mandate. Public opinion polls regularly demonstrated that he had more support than Congress.

- Yeltsin was the best guarantor of democracy and economic reform. Khasbulatov and his allies were only interested in power.

- Yeltsin had no choice but to use the armed forces because the Congress rebels used force and would not compromise.

- Yeltsin was the only person in 1991 with the stature and support to prevent a hardline restoration. Democratisation could only be achieved by hard measures against those who opposed it.

Arguments against Yeltsin:

- Congress passed the declaration of sovereignty and took the first steps towards a separation of powers and a Constitutional Court.

- By 1990 the CPSU was so pluralistic that the party label tells little about deputies' allegiances. The CPSU included Stalinists, Social Democrats, Communists and free marketeers. Yeltsin himself only left the CPSU in July 1990.

- Yeltsin's campaign for the 1991 presidential elections did not include any of the economic reforms that he introduced after the elections. There was no electoral mandate for shock therapy.

- Yeltsin should have tried to negotiate with parliament and broaden his support there.

- A true democrat does not use force to resolve deadlock. Yeltsin was only interested in power.

Russian armed forces were reluctant to get involved in this conflict between civilian politicians and institutions, but Defence Minister Gen. Pavel Grachev finally relented and on 4 October the White House was bombarded for 10 hours. The rebels surrendered and were arrested; 189 people were killed during the fighting in Moscow.

Yeltsin victorious

> **Box 6.3** Referendum on the RF Constitution, 12 December 1993
>
> In response to the referendum question: 'Do you approve of the Constitution of the Russian Federation?' the electorate (on a turnout of 54.8 per cent) voted as follows:
>
> | Votes | Percentage of the electorate | Percentage of the valid votes |
> |---|---|---|
> | In favour | 31.0 | 58.4 |
> | Against | 22.1 | 41.6 |
> | Invalid votes | 1.7 | |
> | Total votes | 54.8 | |
>
> Source: Rossiiskie vesti, 25 December 1993, 1

Following his victory in October 1993 and with his chief opponents in prison, Yeltsin was able to dominate the framing of the new constitution. The Constitutional Assembly was reorganised and headed by Sergei Filatov, the head of the Presidential Staff. The final version of the constitution produced on 10 November enshrined Yeltsin's preference for a strong presidency and a weak parliament. Yeltsin was not due to submit himself for re-election until 1996 but the Duma, the lower house of the Federal Assembly (parliament) was elected on the same day as a referendum on the Constitution was held. The elections were held as if the Constitution, establishing the new principles and institutions, had already been approved. The new Constitution's section on 'Concluding and Transitional Provisions' even states that 'The day of the nationwide vote – 12 December 1993 – is deemed the day of the adoption of the Constitution of the Russian Federation'. It was assumed that the Constitution would be approved; in the event 58.4 per cent of votes cast were in favour, but this represented approval by only 31 per cent of the possible electorate. This was hardly a resounding endorsement for Yeltsin's Constitution. Similarly, the results of the Federal Assembly elections produced a decidedly anti-Yeltsin majority. A sign that relations between the president and parliament were not gong to be easy came in early 1994 when the Duma granted an amnesty to all the rebels who had taken part in 'the events' of October 1993.

Box 6.4 The Federal Assembly established in 1993*

Federation Council
178 members (*chleny*)
Two seats for each of the republics and regions
Members serve a four-year term

State Duma
450 deputies (*deputaty*)
Deputies serve a four-year term
Each voter casts one vote for a constituency candidate and a second vote for a party on the list

Constituency seats	Party list seats
225 deputies elected by single-member constituencies	225 deputies elected by Russia-wide party lists
First-past-the-post system	Proportional representation
A valid vote requires a 25 per cent turnout	A party list must receive a minimum of 5 per cent of the national vote to gain representation
	If a party list candidate wins a constituency seat (s)he is replaced by the next candidate on the list

* The way the membership of the two chambers is selected was changed by President Putin in 2007

The Duma

The Duma is the standing body of the Federal Assembly and its deputies work full-time in the legislature. It has the primary role in the consideration of all legislation. Deputies do not have a significant role in government, however, and it is the government – in its turn dominated by the president – which has the greater role in the legislative process (see Chapter 5). The weakness of the Duma in relation to the executive also has the effect of severely limiting the input of the Russian electorate, represented by the deputies, into the legislative process.

The Duma deputies

According to the Constitution the Duma's terms last four years. The first Duma elected in December 1993 was considered transitional and so was elected for only a two-year term. Those who wanted to stress continuity with Imperial Russia's four State Dumas (1906–1917) called the 1993–1995 Duma the 5th Duma. Until 2007 the Duma's 450 deputies were elected for a four-year term by two different

Box 6.5 The Duma's jurisdiction

- **Legislative initiative and review:** The Duma shares with the president and the Federation Council the right of legislative initiative and may also review government legislation. The Duma adopts federal laws (*postanovleniia*) by a simple majority (266) vote of the deputies. Within five days of adoption these are passed to the Federation Council for approval. Once approved by the Federation Council the laws are signed by the president. The Federation Council may reject a bill by a two-thirds majority. In this case a joint commission is set up to try to settle the differences. This has generally proved possible. The Duma then votes on the compromise bill; if the Duma rejects the Federation Council's proposals during the conciliation process, it may vote by a two-thirds majority to override the Federation Council's veto and send its version to the president for signature. The president may veto a law. For the Duma to override a presidential veto requires a two-thirds majority (300 votes) of the Duma, supported by a two-thirds majority vote in the Federation Council. A two-thirds majority vote by the Duma with presidential support overrules a Federation Council rejection. To pass a federal constitutional law requires a two-thirds vote of the Duma and a three-quarters vote of the Federation Council.

- **To amend the Constitution:** By a two-thirds majority, which must then be approved by the Federation Council and signed by the president.

- **Approves or rejects the president's nominee for prime minister:** This power is severely limited because the Duma must decide within one week to confirm or reject a candidate once the president has placed that person's name in nomination. If it rejects the president's choice three times, the president is empowered to appoint a prime minister, dissolve the parliament, and schedule new Duma elections. The Duma does not have the right to approve government ministers.

- **Appoints:** The chair of the RF Central Bank, the chair and deputy chair of the Accounting Chamber and half of its staff of auditors, the High Commissioner (Plenipotentiary) for Human Rights, 5 of the 15 members of the RF Central Electoral Commission and the Duma representatives to the Council for Public Services.

- **May initiate impeachment procedures against the RF president:** This requires a two-thirds majority (300 votes). Impeachment also requires a two-thirds majority (119 votes) by the Federation Council, plus a Supreme Court ruling of evidence of a crime and a Constitutional Court ruling that the correct procedures have been followed.

- **May pass motions of confidence or no confidence in the government and force the resignation of the government:** This requires a simple majority (266 votes). However, the president may disregard the motion and instead dismiss the Duma. The government's position is further strengthened by another constitutional provision that allows the government to demand a Duma vote of confidence at any time; refusal to do so is grounds for the president to dissolve the Duma. After resignation a government continues to work until the Duma appoints a new prime minister.

- **Grant amnesties:** By a simple majority (266 votes). Amnesties have been granted to some of the participants in the August 1991 coup attempt, and the May and September–October 1993 conflicts between Yeltsin and the parliament.

methods. Half of the deputies (*deputaty*) were elected in single-member constituencies under a first-past-the-post system. The remaining deputies were elected from federal party lists under a proportional representation system. In order to reduce the political fragmentation in the Duma and to prevent extremist parties from benefiting from proportional representation, a party had to surmount a 5 per cent threshold to achieve representation. Parties that won seats through the party list system automatically acquired the status of a party faction (*ob"edinenie*), which the deputies elected for the single-member constituencies could also join. Independent and other deputies could join an existing party faction, or form a new faction if they could gather a membership of at least 35 deputies. Party factions tended to be quite fluid with deputies changing factions and/or voting with another faction. There were also party groups composed of deputies elected in single-member constituencies.

Box 6.6 Requirements of a Duma deputy

A Duma deputy must:

- be a Russian citizen.
- be at least 21 years old.
- not be simultaneously a member of the Federation Council, or a deputy to another representative body at federal or sub-federal level, or a civil servant.
- work in the Duma on a permanent and professional basis.

The Duma holds hearings (*sluzhaniia*) on questions within its jurisdiction on the initiative of the Council, Committees and Commissions and deputy factions of the Duma. Deputies and invited others may discuss draft laws requiring public discussion; international agreements, presented for ratification; the draft federal budget and the account of its fulfilment; legislation and other legal acts recommended by the CIS interparliamentary organisation and other interparliamentary organisations' assembly; and other major domestic and foreign policies. In addition to attending sessions of the Duma and participating in the work of committees and commissions, deputies are expected to work with voters. This involves responding to correspondence and conducting surgeries in the district that has been allocated to them by the electoral society, forwarding suggestions to the relevant government body or social organisation, and keeping voters informed about their activities.

The chair or speaker of the Duma

Leadership of the Duma is provided by its chair (*predsedatel'*) or speaker and the incumbent of this post is able to facilitate or frustrate the ambitions of the president. Yeltsin and Khasbulatov literally fought for power in 1993 and Putin was not able to oust Gennady Selesnyov of the KPRF until 2003. The chair and the deputy chairs are elected by a secret ballot of the deputies. Following the 2007 Duma elections the pro-Kremlin United Russia has 315 of the 450 deputies which meant that Boris Gryzlov, who was the chair during the Duma's fourth convocation and is the leader of the United Russia party faction in the Duma, was assured of re-election; the first deputy chair is also from the United Russian party. There are also nine deputy chairs. The result is that the Duma's work is organised by the pro-Kremlin United Russia party, as are the Duma's interactions with the executive, the government and the judiciary.

The chair presides over the Duma sessions, supervises its operation and is in charge of its work. The chair publishes directions, gives instructions, signs the Duma's resolutions, and nominates and dismisses the head and first deputy of the Duma apparatus (civil service). The chair sends legislative proposals and materials for consideration to the deputy groups and factions, allocating them to the relevant

---

Box 6.7 Duma chairs

Ivan Rybkin: Chair from 14 January 1994 to 17 January 1996
Born in 1946. He is a graduate of the Volgograd Agricultural Institute and the Academy of Social Sciences attached to the CC CPSU, a candidate of technical sciences and a doctor of political science. He was elected a deputy of the RSFSR, a member of the Supreme Soviet of the RF, and a deputy of the Duma during the first and second sessions. He was the Duma chair during its first session. In 1996 he became the Security Council secretary and in March 1998 the deputy chair of the RF government. From 1998 to 2000 he was the plenipotentiary representative of the RF President to the CIS governments.

Gennady Selesnyov: Chair from 17 January 1996 to 29 December 2003
Born in 1947. Graduated in journalism from Leningrad State University, then worked in journalism becoming the head editor of *Pravda* between 1991 and 2003. He was elected a Duma deputy in 1993 and in 1995 became its deputy chair. He served as chair during the Duma's second and third sessions. From 1997 he was the chair of the parliamentary meeting of the Union of Belarus and Russia.

Boris Gryzlov: Chair from 29 December 2003
Born in 1950. A graduate of the Leningrad Electrical Technical Institute, a radio engineer with a specialism in cosmic communications and also a candidate of political science. From 1997–1999 he headed the teaching-methodological centre for new technology of the Baltic State Technical University. In 1999 Gryzlov started work for 'The Development of the Regions' business in St Petersburg. In October 1999 he became head of the St Petersburg branch of the *Edinstvo* (Unity) movement. From December 1999 to March 2001 he was a Duma deputy and leader of the *Edinstvo* faction. In May 2000 he became the chair of the Policy Council (*Politsoviet*) of the *Edinstvo* party. From March 2001 to December 2003 he was the RF Minister of the Interior. In November 2002 he also became chair of *Edinaia Rossiia*'s (United Russia's) Supreme Council. In December 2003 he was re-elected to the Duma, became its chair and the leader of United Russia's deputy faction. In 2007 he was re-elected to the Duma and became the chair again.

Duma committee. The chair is the lynchpin of the Duma's interactions with international, federal and sub-federal bodies and organisations. The chair also represents the Duma in its dealings with the Federation Council, Government, Constitutional Court, Supreme Court, Central Electoral Commission, the RF Central Bank, Human Rights Ombudsman, Accounting Chamber, international, public and other organisations, and the parliaments and officials of foreign states. The chair represents the Duma in its dealings with the president, forwards laws passed by the Duma to the president and participates in the president's procedures to resolve differences of opinion between federal and sub-federal state bodies and between sub-federal-level bodies.

The State Duma Council

The Duma Council is a small body with only a few duties. It prepares the draft agendas and timetables for the Duma sessions (*zasedanie*), decides which draft laws (*zakonoproekt*) are to be considered; it also allocates draft laws to the relevant Duma committees; refers draft laws for examination to deputy factions and when necessary to other bodies with the right of legal initiative; calls parliamentary hearings; and distributes duties between the Duma's deputy chairs. In carrying out these tasks it will, in reality, follow the instructions it receives on behalf of the government and the president. At the suggestion of the president, the Duma chair or not less than one fifth of the deputies, the Duma Council may convene extraordinary Duma sessions. These tasks appear pretty routine but they contain the potential to direct the Duma's deliberations along a particular path. The Duma Council's membership reflects the composition of the Duma and includes the Duma chair and the chairs or representatives of the Duma's registered factions and groups. These groups have the deciding vote and the deputy chair of the Duma and the Committee chairs have a consultative role. The following may also participate in the Council sittings: the government's plenipotentiary (envoy) in the Duma; the president's plenipotentiary (envoy) in the Duma; representatives of a federal subject if the Council is examining a draft law in an area for which the subject has a right of legal initiative; and finally any Duma deputy. The Duma has the right to repeal a decision of the Council of the State Duma.

Committees and commissions of the State Duma

The Duma has a system of committees on the major policy areas and temporary commissions may also be set up as necessary. The number of committees is not static; during the fourth Duma convocation 2003–2007 there were 29 committees and for the current fifth convocation 2007–2011 there are 33. The committees review legislation and make recommendations to the government. Each deputy (except the chair, deputy chairs and faction leaders) is expected to serve on one of the committees. The Duma decides on the composition of a committee or a commission, but it is usually based on the proportional representation of each of the deputy factions/groups within the Duma. Each committee or commission usually has between

Box 6.8 State Duma committees and commissions: fifth convocation, 2007–2011

Committee on Constitutional Legislation and State Construction

Committee on Civil, Criminal, Arbitration and Procedural Legislation

Committee on Labour and Social Policy

Committee on the Budget and Taxes

Committee on the Financial Market

Committee on Economic Policy and Business

Committee on Property

Committee on Construction and Land Issues

Committee on Science and Scientific Technology

Committee on Energy

Committee on Transport

Committee on Defence

Committee on Security

Committee on International Affairs

Committee on CIS Affairs and Links with Compatriots

Committee on Federal Affairs and Regional Policy

Committee on Questions of Local Self-government

Committee on the Regulation and Organisation of the Work of the State Duma

Committee on Information Policy, Information Technology and Communications

Committee on Healthcare

Committee on Education

Committee on the Family, Women and Child Affairs

Committee on Agricultural Questions

Committee on Natural Resources, their Exploitation and Ecology

Committee on Culture

Committee on the Affairs of Public and Religious Organisations

Committee on Nationality Affairs

Committee on Physical Culture and Sport

Committee on Youth Affairs

Committee on Problems of the North and the Far East

Committee on Veteran Affairs

Commission on Mandate Questions and Questions of Deputy Ethics

The State Duma website also lists the following two commissions separately:

The State Duma Audit Commission

The State Duma Commission on the Examination of Expenditure on the Federal Budget on the RF's Defence and Security

Source: 'Sostav i struktura gosudartsvennoi dumy. Komiteti i komissii', State Duma website, http://www.duma.gov.ru/

12 and 35 members. The committees and commissions conduct a preliminary examination of questions under their jurisdiction and present draft laws to the Duma for examination. They then write up the findings and conclusions on draft laws, draft decisions and resolutions (*postanovleniia*). On the instruction of the Duma they prepare inquiries for the Constitutional Court, organise Duma hearings (*sluzhaniia*) and comment on the relevant sections of the draft federal budget.

The State Duma and Federal Assembly apparatus

The Duma chair heads the Duma apparatus (civil servants), appoints and dismisses the head of the apparatus with the agreement of the Duma Council and the Committee on Regulations and Organisational Work of the Duma, which supervises the work of the civil service. The apparatus's role is to support the work of the Duma. Since the mid-1990s the Duma apparatus has undergone considerable change; new technologies have been introduced and particular attention has been paid to upgrading skills (Gryzlov, 2004: 306).

Presidents and the Duma

Putin and the Duma

Putin was not content for the Duma to be disorganised and obstructionist as it had been under Yeltsin, so he moved to further strengthen the executive at the cost of the Duma. Under Yeltsin Duma deputies had used close ties with government ministries and agencies to lobby on behalf of their departments. The deputies had also been adept at using intra-governmental rivalries and conflicts to promote their interests. In April 2000 Putin banned this practice and government departments were ordered to deal with the Duma only through the government's official envoy in the Duma. Putin was also quick to criticise the slow pace at which the Duma had passed legislation in 2001. Pressure was applied and during the Duma's spring session in 2002 it passed 62 bills on their third and final reading. A report in the liberal Moscow newspaper *Vremya MN* on 28 June 2002 described the session's last days as working at a frantic pace and quoted a comment from Grigory Yavlinsky, the liberal Yabloko party leader, that 'even members of specific committees lack time to understand the contents of laws, much less the deputies who vote on them.' The article complained that laws sponsored by the executive were being pushed through 'no matter what' and that the deputies were only given the text on the day that is was to be discussed and not three days before as the rules required.

Although Putin had managed to galvanise the Duma into action he wanted to strengthen his control over its work even further. He encouraged the creation of a new party of power (see Chapter 12) called *Edinstvo* by the merger in 2001 of the pro-Kremlin Unity party and Fatherland-All Russia party, which effectively consolidated the centre of Russian politics into one pro-presidential political party,

Box 6.9 Explaining the weakness of the Duma under Yeltsin

- The constitutional provisions establishing a super-presidency.

- The deputies do not have a significant role in government. The prime minister does not have to be a member of the Duma and the Duma's role in the selection of the prime minister is either to accept or to reject the president's choice, reducing even further the Duma's role in the legislative process.

- No single party or block had a majority in the Duma and party discipline was also very weak. This meant that Yeltsin was able to make frequent use of his power to veto Duma bills and the Duma was unable to act together to overturn the veto.

- This fragmentation meant that debates in the Duma were often polarised so making it difficult to achieve a consensus and act in a concerted manner.

- This fragmentation also meant Duma legislation tended to be the product of back-room trading, which both slowed down the legislative process and produced laws that tended to be fairly general and/or to contain contradictory elements, so making implemention difficult.

- Deputies did not always conduct themselves in a professional manner, so reducing their public standing. Deputy immunity from prosecution encouraged corruption and led to criminals standing for election to benefit from both the immunity and the – albeit limited – opportunities to influence legislation that a deputy enjoys. Some deputies, notably from the RF Liberal Democratic party, were prone to even fighting in the chamber.

- Yeltsin was adept at using his powers of patronage to buy support.

- The Duma's weakness and the disdain with which Yeltsin treated it reinforced and encouraged negative patterns of behaviour. The Duma tended to behave in an obstructionist manner rather than building a constructive relationship with the executive.

isolating reformist liberals and further marginalising the left. Putin's interior minister, Boris Gryzlov, became the head of the new United Russia's ruling Higher Council in November 2002. There was a potential 'minor' obstacle as the RF Law on Political Parties forbad top state officials, including ministers, from simultaneously working in the executive bodies of political organisations such as political parties. Gryzlov rather disengenuously argued that he was primarily a minister who just happened to support a particular political party in his spare time, but that he was not actually a party member. His situation was regularised in October 2004 when the Duma legislated to allow government ministers to not only join political parties, but also to hold leadership positions within them.

In 2002 Putin's supporters and other anti-communist parties in the Duma united to begin the process of removing communists from the chairs of Duma Committees. The communists were accused of using their committee leaderships to frustrate much-needed legislation. The loss of the committee leaderships also deprived them of financial and administrative resources in the run-up to the 2003

Duma elections. Although the communists emerged from the 2003 elections as the second largest party in the Duma, the leaderships of all the Duma Committes were given to United Russia party members. United Russia's domination of the Duma was further consolidated in January 2003 when Boris Gryzlov, a close ally of Putin's, replaced KPRF party member Gennady Selesnyov as Duma chair.

United Russia's domination of the Duma has had major repercussions both for the functioning of the Duma and Russian democratisation. First, bills undoubtedly move through the Duma stage of the legislative process much faster than before. While this removed the Duma's obstructionism and foot dragging, fast legislation does not necessarily mean good legislation that has been thoroughly scrutinised. Secondly, lobbying the Duma steeply declined as United Russia now, in effect, handles all legislative decision making on behalf of first Putin and now Medvedev – meaning that the Duma's role in the legislative process has become increasingly formalistic. This raises broader questions about Russia's democratisation as the legislature is not truly independent because it is so dominated by the executive. This also means that the electorate's inputs into the legislative process are crowded out by the dominance of United Russia. United Russia is a top-down political party, concerned with discipline and 'getting the vote out' on behalf of first Putin and now Medvedev, rather than listening to the electorate. United Russia's party elite share a general conservatism and benefit from presidential patronage, but they have no incentive to reach out and listen to voters. This lack of engagement with the electorate leaves the Duma increasingly isolated from the people and, not surprisingly, there is widespread disillusionment with the Duma. A survey conducted in 2007 asked Russians, 'Would you rate the way most State Duma deputies handle their jobs as excellent, good, fair, poor or very poor?'. It found that only 6 per cent of respondents rated deputies' work as excellent or good, 31 per cent rated it as fair, 45 per cent rated it as poor and very poor, with 13 per cent saying they found it hard to say (FOM, 2007).

The Duma and votes of no confidence

According to the Constitution the executive is accountable to parliament (see Chapter 5). For example, the Duma may pass a vote of no confidence in the government and the parliament may reject the president's candidate for the premiership. In both these cases if the Duma persists in opposing the president the Duma may be dissolved, so they are risky strategies. To succeed, a no confidence vote requires a simple majority of the Duma. There have been three attempts to bring down the government under Putin, all of which failed to gather the necessary votes. The first attempt was led by the KPRF in March 2000. Then in late April 2003 the KPRF and the liberal Yabloko party joined forces and tried to dislodge Prime Minister Kasyanov. Most recently in February 2005 the KPRF and the nationalist *Rodina* party tried to bring down Prime Minister Fradkov. Even though Russia was experiencing mass public protests against the replacement of the soviet-era welfare benefits system, the move failed. The pro-Putin majority of deputies always voted for the government.

The Public Chamber

The Public Chamber (*obshchestvennaia palata*) is yet another one of Putin's post-Beslan initiatives. It is an oversight committee with consultative powers, whose role is to analyse draft legislation and to monitor the activities of the Federal Assembly, the Federal government, government bodies in the federal subjects, and federal and regional administrative bodies. It is empowered to hold public hearings and call officials to account; its members may attend government meetings and request information from officials, but its resolutions are only recommendations. The Duma approved the creation of the Public Chamber in March 2005 by 345 votes to 50. The Chamber has 126 members: one-third are chosen by the president from the great and the good of Russia and a second third are nominated by civil society organisations. Once the first two-thirds are installed they select the remaining 42 members. Each Public Chamber convocation serves for two years and the first one started work in 2006. Putin's choice of members ranged from Irina Rodnina an ice skater, TV personality Eduard Sagalayev, Leonid Roshal a children's doctor to Russia's Chief Rabbi Berl Lazar. One of Putin's choices, the nuclear physicist and Russian Academy of Sciences member Yevgeny Velikhov, became the secretary of the Public Chamber. The Duma is undoubtedly unpopular but, rather than reforming the Duma, Putin's approach was to dominate it and create another body to usurp its functions. It is hard to see how the Public Chamber will encourage popular participation in politics or encourage the Duma to represent the people and fulfil its function of overseeing the executive.

The Federation Council

The Council of the Federation, Federation Council or *Sovet Federatsii* was originally created in July 1993 – before the 'October events' – with representatives of all the republics and regions except Chechnia, which had already declared independence. At this stage Yeltsin wanted the Federation Council to approve his latest draft constitution. This was rather overtaken by the escalating conflict between Yeltsin and the parliament, but the Federation Council survived to form the upper house of the new Federal Assembly. The Federation Council is composed of members from the republics and regions. Although it shares with the Duma the right to initiate legislation it is the weaker of the two Federal Assembly chambers and is more a consultative and scrutinising body. The weakness is compounded by the fact that its members only work part-time for the Federation Council, combining their monthly visits to Moscow with a highly demanding, full-time post back in their republic or region. Overall the structures supporting the Federation Council's work are smaller and much less developed than those found in the Duma. Although the Federation Council has a long list of committees and commissions, it traditionally has fewer than the Duma and its members do not have the same time to devote to this work as do Duma deputies.

Box 6.10 The areas of competence of the Federation Council*

- Approves changes to borders between RF subjects
- Approves presidential decrees on the introduction of martial law and the introduction of a state of emergency
- Decides on the use of RF armed forces outside of Russian territory
- Declares presidential elections
- The impeachment of the president: The Federation Council may confirm the impeachment of a president initiated by the Duma. It may also impeach the president but only after a lengthy series of referrals to the Supreme Court and confirmation by a two-thirds majority of both chambers of the Federal Assembly.
- Appoints and dimisses judges: to the RF Constitutional Court, the Supreme Court and the Supreme Court of Arbitration on the recommendation of the president. The judges are sworn in by the Federation Council chair.
- Appoints and dismisses: the RF prosecutor-general, the deputy chair of the Accounting Chamber and half of its staff.
- Participates in the legislative process: All bills, even those proposed by the Federation Council (FC), must first be considered by the Duma. Federal laws on questions of war and peace, the status and defence of Russia's state borders, the ratification and rejection of international treaties, the federal budget, federal taxes and duties, financial and monetary matters, credit, customs regulation, monetary emission, passed by the Duma are subject to obligatory review by the Federation Council. The Duma passes draft laws to the Federation Council for consideration. The Federation Council passes a bill by a simple majority vote. A bill is considered passed if the Federation Council does not consider it within 14 days. If the Federation Council does not pass a bill, a joint conciliation commission is set up with the Duma to work out a compromise version of the legislation. Although the FC has the power to review and force compromise on legislation, in practice its role has been primarily as a consultative and reviewing body.
- The right of legislative initiative and scrutiny and to pass resolutions: Legislation is passed by a majority vote.
- Approves the appointment of: members of the Presidium of the Supreme Court, five of the fifteen members of the Central Electoral Commission, two Federation Council representatives to the National Banking Council (NBC), Duma representatives to the Council for Public Service presided over by the president, deputy prosecutor-generals (proposed by the prosecutor general).

*See: Article 102 of the RF Constitution

Federation Council committees and commissions

The Federation Council committee and commission system is much less developed than the Duma's. There are currently 16 committees and 10 commissions, but in the 1990s it had only 7 committees at a time when the number of Duma

Committees was steadily growing. All members of the Federation Council are expected to serve on a committee or commission, with the exceptions of the chair, the first deputy chair and the deputy chair. The chair allocates the leadership of the committees and commissions and monitors their work. Committees and commissions have equal rights and responsibilities in carrying out the Federation Council's responsibilities, these include, examining federal laws passed on by the Duma, drafting laws and other normative acts and conducting parliamentary hearings.

Box 6.11 Federation Council committees and commissions, May 2008

Committee on Constitutional Legislation

Committee on Judicial and Legal Affairs

Committee on Federal Affairs and Regional Policies

Committee on Local Self-Governance

Committee on Defence and Security

Committee on Budget Issues

Committee on Financial Markets and Monetary Circulation

Commission for Interaction with the Accounts Chamber of the Russian Federation

Committee for Foreign Affairs

Committee on the Commonwealth of Independent States Issues

Commission on Standing Orders and Parliamentary Performance Organisation

Commission on Ways and Means of the Council of the Federation's Constitutional Powers Implementation

Committee on Social Policy Issues

Committee for Science, Education, Public Health and Ecology

Commission on Youth and Sports Issues

Committee on Economic Policy, Business and Ownership

Committee for Industrial Policy

Commission on Natural Monopolies

Committee on Natural Resources and Environmental Protection

Committee for Agriculture, Food Policy and Fishery

Committee on Northern Territories and Indigenous Minorities Issues

Commission for Information Policy

Commission for the Council of the Federation Performance Maintenance Monitoring

Commission for National Maritime Policy

Commission on Culture

Commission for Housing Policy and Utilities Services

Source: 'Committees and standing commissions of the Federation Council', Federation Council website, http://www.council.gov.ru/eng/committee/index.html, downloaded 18 May 2008

The Federation Council chair (speaker)

The Federation Council elects a chair, first deputy chair and deputy chair from among its members. The chair draws up a draft agenda for the Federation Council's approval, convenes and presides over its sessions, allocates the leadership of the committees and commissions, coordinates and monitors their work, and allocates duties to the other chairs and deals with general organisational issues. The chair also supervises the work of the Federation Council's apparatus (civil service), which entails approving its structure and staffing numbers, and appointing and dismissing the head of the apparatus. The chair represents the Federation Council in the Federal Assembly and signs the resolutions that are passed to the Duma or to the president. The chair also represents the Federation Council in its dealings with the RF president, other federal and regional state bodies, public organisations, foreign parliaments and international organisations, and with the state and public leaders of foreign countries. The chair participates in the president's conciliation procedures to resolve disputes between federal state bodies and regional state bodies, publicises new laws and constitutional amendments and passes approved RF laws to the republican and regional legislatures. Finally, the chair appoints Federation Council members to serve as its plenipotentiaries (envoys) to the Duma, government, Constitutional Court, Supreme Court, Higher Arbitration Court, Accounting Chamber, General Prosecutors Office, Central Electoral Commission and the Ministry of Justice.

Federation Council chairs: from Yeltsin to Putin

Yeltsin had two Federation Council chairs while he was president. The first, Vladimir Shumeiko, was typical of the industrial directors that Yeltsin liked to promote and was once even tipped as a possible successor to Yeltsin. Shumeiko lost his Federation Council seat in 1996 and was replaced by Yegor Stroyev, a member of the KPRF. Stroyev carefully nurtured his place within Yeltsin's coterie but after the 1998 economic crisis he started to pull away from Yeltsin. Stroyev was a dual-post holder: chair of the Federation Council and governor of Oryol. Following Putin's changes to the composition of the Federation Council, Stroyev could not keep both posts. In the end the decision was made for him: he lost the chairmanship and had to go back to Oryol. Stroyev was the last Yeltsin-era figure in the Federation Council. Stroyev was manoeuvred out of office by the pro-Kremlin 'Federation Group' of over 100 Federation Council members set up in March 2001. Although it is expressly forbidden for political parties or factions to organise in the Federation Council, Valery Goreglyad set up the Federation Group with two clear aims: to support Putin's reforms and to get rid of Stroyev (Malyakin, 2001; Litvinovich, 2001). The Federation Group were dubbed 'Putin's fan club' by the Russian media. It seems that the Federation Group assumed that once they had got rid of Stroyev, Goreglyad would become chair. However, Putin preferred Sergei Mironov who had only been elected to the Federation Council in June 2001 but was a member of Putin's network of Petersburgers. The Federation Council members who were Putin's appointees duly voted for the little known Mironov. In 2002 Mironov ordered the Federation Group to disband.

Box 6.12 Federation Council chairs

Vladimir Shumeiko: Chair from 13 January 1994 to 23 January 1996
Born in 1945. In 1991 he was appointed chair of the RSFSR Supreme Soviet. In June 1992 he became the first deputy prime minister. He lost his Federation Council seat in 1996. Although a long-time Yeltsin ally, during the 1996 gubernatorial elections his Reforms–New Course movement did not always support Yeltsin's preferred candidates. In 1997 he was involved in the founding of a broad-based political coalition called the Union of Progressive Forces.

Yegor Stroyev: Chair from 23 January 1996 to 5 December 2001
Born in 1937 in Orlov *oblast*. He trained as an agronomist and worked on collective farms during 1955–63 and then began work for the CPSU, rising to first secretary of Oryol. In 1984 he became a member of the CPSU Central Committee and from 1989 the CC CPSU Secretary for agriculture, joining the Politburo in 1990. In 1993 he was elected head of the Oryol *oblast* administration. In 1995 he joined the 'Our Home is Russia' party. He became a member of the Federation Council in 1996.

Sergei Mironov: Chair from 5 December 2001
Born in 1953 in Leningrad and worked as a geophysicist. In 1993 he received a RF Ministry of Finance certificate to work on the securities market and started a business career. In 1994 he was elected to the St Petersburg Legislative Assembly and went on to serve as its deputy chair and chair. In June 2001 he became a member of the Federation Council and joined its Committee on Constitutional Legislation and Judicial and Legal Affairs, in October 2001 becoming the committee's deputy chair. In December 2001 he was elected Federation Council chair, although he lacked experience of the Federation Council. In January 2003 Mironov was re-elected to the St Petersburg Legislative Assembly and re-elected chair of the Federation Council. He is the chair of the pro-Kremlin Russian Justice, Fatherland/Pensioners political party. For further information see Sergei Mironov's website: http://mironov.info/sitemap

Yeltsin and the Federation Council

The 1993 RF Constitution describes Russia as a federative republic. In the 1990s there was a real fear among Russia's ruling elite that Russia would break up into independent countries. The Federation Council was a means to ensure that all Russia's republics and regions had a voice in Moscow. The 1993 Constitution established a Federation Council that was composed of 178 members (*chleny*), aged 30 or over, two from each of the federal subjects, the republics, regions, districts, and the two cities with federal status, Moscow and St Petersburg. This provision ensured that the smaller ethnic-national territories were over-represented for their numerical size. One of a federal subject's Federation Council members came from its legislative body and the other from its executive (Art. 95.2). As part of the transitional arrangements the 1993 Constitution also required that the Federation Council's first convocation (1993–96) should be directly elected by the people on

12 December 1993. Yeltsin issued a presidential decree stating that candidates would be elected for only two years and that they needed at least 2 per cent, or 25,000 signatures, whichever was the highest from their republic or region. This had the effect of helping the elected republican and regional elites to either gain or maintain a presence at federal level in Moscow.

In 1995 a new Federation Council Law replaced the direct election of Federation Council members with the *ex officio* appointment of the heads of executives (governors, presidents and mayors) and the heads of the legislatures (chairs or speakers) from each federal subject. The system of *ex officio* appointment meant that the composition of the Federation Council gradually changed as the heads of the executives and legislatures changed throughout the federation. Due to these changes it was anticipated that the second Federation Council convocation formed in January 1996 would serve for an unlimited term. The new selection procedure meant that President Yeltsin was dealing with a fairly pliant body. The presidents of Russia's republics and the regional governors had been appointed by Yeltsin and their posts only started to be elected in 1993. By 1995 only 66 of the 89 regional governors and presidents of the republics had been elected. The Federation Council's substantial corps of presidential appointees contradicted the constitutional principle of a separation of powers. It also meant that the Federation Council contained members who owed their political careers to Yeltsin rather than to the electorate of the area they were supposed to represent. Another problem was that Russia did not have the same government structure in each of the republics and regions, making the identification of the head of the legislature and the head of the executive more complex than it might at first appear. For example, some had presidents, others prime ministers and a third group had collective heads of government.

Between the presidential elections in June–July 1996 and January 1997 there were elections in 40 federal subjects which saw 56 per cent of Yeltsin's former appointees failing to be elected as governors. Of their replacements 15 belonged to the opposition, 8 were independents and only 12 were Yeltsin supporters. At this time the KPRF and Chernomyrdin's pro-Yeltsin Our Home is Russia party were the two largest parties. Unlike Duma deputies, Federation Council members were not allowed to establish party factions and many did not have a specific party allegiance. Even for those Yeltsin appointees who had survived the election process, political survival now required them more assiduously to promote their home republic's or region's interests. The Federation Council had always been a major lobby for regional interests, now this tendency grew. The governors had substantial executive power in their republics and regions, controlling budgets and in effect deciding how much money their region should transfer to the federal coffers. They were, therefore, politicians of some power and stature who had their own power bases and were not dependent on presidential patronage. The first signal that the Federation Council was becoming more assertive came in December 1996 when it voted for the return of Sevastopol in the Crimea from Ukraine to Russia, against Yeltsin's wishes. In 1999, Yeltsin's final year as president, the Federation Council twice refused to accept Yeltsin's dismissal of Prosecutor General Yuri Skuratov, who had initiated investigations into corruption in the executive branch and the presidential administration, even issuing a warrant for the arrest of Yeltsin's ally Boris Berezovsky.

Putin and the Federation Council

Putin came to office with two main aims for the Federation Council. First, to turn it back into a pliant second chamber so that his legislative programme would enjoy a speedy passage through the Federal Assembly. Secondly, as part of his broader aim of strengthening the power vertical, to bring the republican and regional elites who make up the Federation Council into line. The Federation Council in 2000 was hardly a model democratic body representing the interests of ordinary Russian citizens. The republican and regional elites were adept at using their dual-posts in their home areas and membership of the Federation Council, to further their own political and economic interests. However, Putin's reforms far from democratising the Federation Council turned it into a rubber stamp for the federal executive.

In 2000 Putin unveiled, though for the Federation Council it must have felt more like unleashed, a new federal law on the Federation Council. The law set out that the Federation Council would, as before, consist of two represent-atives from each of the republics and regions. The difference was that now one would be appointed by the head of the executive (governor), subject to confirma-tion by the legislature, and the legislature would elect the other. The incumbents did not go quietly; they faced losing a valuable forum where they could lobby for their area, as well as losing their right to immunity from arrest, search and detention, and material privileges. Putin responded with threats to initiate criminal investigations into the governors' activities and the Duma threat-ened to overrule the Federation Council's veto and side with the president. In July 2000 the Federation Council capitulated and accepted the new law. This meant an end to the previous practice of combining the post of head of a regional executive with membership of the Federation Council; by 2002 the last of the old-style dual-office holders had left the Federation Council. There is no set national date when all the Federation Council members come up for election. Federation Council members hold office while the regional bodies that originally selected them hold office. From 2001 these regional bodies also made extensive use of their new right to recall their senator, as Federation Council members are now often called. A new law in December 2004 required that recall proce-dures be initiated only by the chair of the Federation Council and so recalls have disappeared.

In 2004 Putin tightened his grip on the Federation Council still further when he replaced the direct election of regional governors by presidential appointments, subject to confirmation by the relevant regional legislature. This meant that the RF president now selects the governors, who then choose one of a republic's or region's Federation Council members. As the Federation Council usually only has day-long sessions twice a month, it simply does not have the time to adequately examine legislation. It now passes bills by large majorities with almost unseemly haste, and it is hard to see how it can possibly be acting as a check and balance on the executive and the Duma. The Federation Council's original role as a forum in Moscow for the views and interests of the republics and regions has also been lost. As mergers have led to fewer federal subjects, the Federation Council now has 168 senators representing the 84 federal subjects.

Chapter summary

In the aftermath of the 1993 confrontation between President Yeltsin and the Congress of People's Deputies, Yeltsin was able to establish a super-presidential system in the new RF Constitution in 1993. In the 1990s the Duma was highly fragmented and, while the Federation Council became increasingly assertive, the Federal Assembly was unable to mount an effective challenge to the president. As part of his bid to create a managed democracy Putin turned the Federal Assembly into an increasingly pliant body, with the Federation Council filled by presidential appointees and their allies, and the Duma dominated by the pro-Kremlin party of power, United Russia. This means that legislation moves much more swiftly through the required stages than under Yeltsin, but has not enhanced the Federal Assembly's supposed role as a representative body for the Russian people.

Discussion points

■ Did Yeltsin have to launch a military assault on the parliament to save Russian democracy?

■ In 2005 Boris Gryzlov said, 'the Parliament is not a place for discussion' (Zarakhovich, 2007). What do you think he meant and what are the implications of his comment?

■ What was the impact of strengthening the power vertical on the Federation Council?

■ Have developments in the composition and activities of the Federal Assembly promoted or frustrated Russia's democratic consolidation?

Further reading

An analysis of the Russian parliament during the early transition period before the adoption of the new RF Constitution in 1993 is provided by Josephine Andrews (2002) *When Majorities Fail: The Russian Parliament, 1990–1993*, Cambridge: Cambridge University Press. For the period after 1993, go to Tiffany A. Troxel (2003) *Parliamentary Power in Russia, 1994–2001*, Basingstoke: Palgrave. Examinations of the development and operation of the Federal Assembly are provided by Thomas F. Remington in his (2001) *The Russian Parliament: Institutional Evolution in a Transitional Regime*, New Haven, CT: Yale University Press; 'Putin, the Duma and Political Parties', in Dale Hersping (ed.), *Putin's Russia: Past Imperfect, Future Uncertain*, London: M.E. Sharpe; and (2003) 'Majorities Without Mandates: The Russian Federation Council since 2000', *Europe-Asia Studies*, 55 (5), 667–91; and finally his (2006) 'Presidential Support in the Russian State Duma', *Legislative Studies Quarterly*, XXXI, 5–32. Paul Chaisty provides a fascinating analysis of the interrelationship of economic and political power in his (2006) *Legislative Politics and Economic Power in Russia*, Basingstoke: Palgrave, and also an examination of the work of the Duma with Petra Schleiter in their (2002) 'Productive but not Valued: The Russian State Duma, 1992–2001', *Europe-Asia Studies*, 54 (5), 701–23.

Useful websites

Federation Council: http://www.council.gov.ru/eng/

State Duma: http://www.duma gov.ru/

Federal Assembly (Russian only): http://www.gov.ru/main/page7.html

Biographical information about Russia's deputies is available on the **US State Department's website**: https://www.usrbc.org/government/russian_government/russian_government_state_duma/deputies_alphabetical/4

References

FOM (2007) 'The Performance of State Duma Deputies', 19 July, FOM website: http://bd. english.fom.ru/report/map/ed072910

Gryzlov, B. V. (obsh. red.) (2004) *Gosudartvennaia Duma. Federal'naia Sobranie Rossiiskoi Federatsii v 1993–2004 godakh.* Moscow: Gos Duma

Keesings Record of World Events (1993) *News Digest*, April: 39421, *Rossiiskie vesti* (1993) 25 December: 1

Litvinovich, D. (2001) 'The intrigues in the Federation Council', *Pravda*, 7 December, http://english.pravda.ru/russia/

Malyakin, I. (2001) 'The Putin Appreciation Club in Russia's Upper House: Everyone's a member', *Prism*, 7 (6), 30 June. Available from: http://www.jamestown.org/publications

Zarakhovich, Y. (2007) 'Russian Protest Putin's Rule', 4 March, *Time*, http://www.time.com/time/world/article/0,8599,1595828,00.html

Chapter 7

Russian federalism

Learning objectives

- To describe the structure, institutions and development of Russian federalism.
- To examine the relationship between nationality and federalism.
- To analyse Putin's 'strengthening of the power vertical'.
- To introduce local government.

Introduction

The Russian Federation (RF) is the largest country in the world, slightly over 1.8 times the size of the USA, covering 17,075,200 sq km or one-seventh of the world's land surface and 11 time zones. The problems of maintaining the geographical integrity of such an enormous and diverse country are immense. In Imperial Russia and the USSR the tsars and the communist leadership tried to run the country from the capital and, although the country was divided into administrative areas, power resided at the centre. Russia today needs to maintain its territorial integrity, for Moscow to serve as a unifying centre and for the government to operate democratically, effectively and evenly throughout the country. The Preamble to the RF Constitution describes Russia as a democratic federation based on the equality and self-determination of its multinational people. Russia's non-Russians do not want to live in an updated Russian empire and even before the Russian Federation came into existence it was faced by strong secessionist demands, notably from some of its predominantly Muslim areas. Conflict between President Yeltsin and the parliament in the early 1990s created a situation in which Russia's non-ethnic Russian nationality-based republics and its predominantly ethnic Russian regions simply grabbed as much power as they could from Moscow. In this free for all, democracy was often the loser as republican and regional bosses set up their own mini fiefdoms. A federal system requires a clear delineation of jurisdiction and competences between the different levels of government: federal, republican and regional down to local self-government. However, in order to counteract the centrifugal forces that threatened to tear the country apart Yeltsin employed a variety of devices – bilateral treaties, presidential representatives, first appointed and then elected governors, and in the case of Chechnia a war – both to assert central control and to procure the support of the regions. The result was that Russia developed a form of asymmetrical federalism, in which its federal subjects were far from equal, but the federation remained largely intact.

President Putin came to office determined to reassert not just Moscow's but the RF president's supremacy and to impose his rule throughout the country. To achieve this he stressed the need to 'strengthen the power vertical' (see Chapter 5), that is the vertical chain of executive authority running from the president down to the lowest level of government. In 2001 even before Putin began talking of strengthening the power vertical, he had already set up a presidential commission to investigate the demarcation of jurisdiction and competence between the federal and other levels of government. It was chaired by Dmitry Kozak, Putin's trusted Petersburger ally who was then deputy head of the Presidential Administration. Putin also stressed the dictatorship of law (see Chapter 8) and the need for Russia to be a unified legal space. Putin, therefore, ended Yeltsin's bilateral treaties and began to merge federal subjects, created seven federal districts led by presidential plenipotentiaries many of whom were from his *siloviki* network, replaced elected governors with presidential appointees, created a new State Council (see Chapter 5) and went to war against Chechnia to keep the federation together.

From RSFSR to the Russian Federation

The myth of soviet federalism

According to each soviet constitution the USSR was 'a voluntary union of sovereign republics, that their borders could not be changed without their consent, that each republic retain[ed] the right of secession, that the powers not specifically assigned to the union government [were] reserved for the governments of the republics . . .' (Unger, 1981: 274). Although the USSR had a federal structure it did not operate as a true federal system. Nationalist sentiments were suppressed before they could become demands for secession and borders were routinely changed without consultation. The Communist Party of the Soviet Union (CPSU) rather than the government was the real power in the country. The practice was for the Communist Party boss in each of the union republics to be a local person, but the Politburo in Moscow usually appointed the second in command from outside the republic. The CPSU together with the economic institutions that ran the centralised economy, the armed forces and security services pulled the country together in a bid to ensure that the Kremlin's writ ran throughout the country. In the USSR's 'soft state' (see Chapter 3) reality increasingly fell far short of these aspirations and contributed to the weakening of the soviet system. Added to this, as Gorbachev reformed the USSR nationalist aspirations grew and the union republics began to turn the USSR's mythical federalism into reality. One by one in a 'parade of sovereignty' the union republics claimed their right to secede from the Union.

The Russian Soviet Federative Socialist Republic (RSFSR)

The Russian Soviet Federative Socialist Republic (RSFSR) which was one of the USSR's 15 union republics declared its state sovereignty on 12 June 1990. At this time the RSFSR comprised 31 ethno-federal subjects which included 16 autonomous republics, 5 autonomous *oblasts* and 10 autonomous *okrugs*. In August 1990 during a visit to Tatarstan, an autonomous republic of the RSFSR, the newly elected RSFSR chair Boris Yeltsin famously urged Tatarstan to 'Take as much independence as you can'. Yeltsin's support for national self-determination was partly designed to undermine Gorbachev's attempts to negotiate a new union treaty that might have preserved the USSR (see Chapter 1). However, Russia's autonomous republics led by Chechnia-Ingushetia, Tatarstan and Bashkortostan, and Russia's regions began pushing for greater autonomy from both the USSR and the RSFSR.

In December 1990 the RSFSR Constitution was amended and the RSFSR's autonomous republics became simply republics. Then in July 1991 the Supreme Soviet elevated four of the five autonomous *oblasts* (Adygeya, Gorno-Altai, Karachaevo-Cherkessia and Khakassia) to republics, leaving only the Jewish autonomous *oblast*. The republics also unilaterally raised their status by electing their own presidents. Tatarstan elected its president on 12 June 1991 the same day as Yeltsin was elected president of the RSFSR, and by the end of 1991 Kabardino-Balkaria, Marii El, Mordovia, Chechnia and Tyva all had their own presidents. The privatisation of state assets such as economic enterprises, land and buildings added to these centrifugal forces. Moscow both as the capital of the USSR and of the RSFSR came into conflict with the union republics, and Russia's republics and the regions, over ownership of these state assets. Tatarstan's declaration of sovereignty on 30 August 1990 was not only about national self-determination but also about securing Tatarstan's ownership of the republic's assets which included its mighty oil industry. At this time ethnographer Galina Starovoitova, who was also Yeltsin's main adviser on nationality issues, talked of the USSR as being like a Russian Matrioshka, a nest of dolls with each one opening up to reveal an even smaller doll. In the early 1990s there were very real fears that the same forces that had led to the disintegration of the USSR would continue and lead to the disintegration of Russia (see Szajkowski, 1993).

Why federalism?

Unitary and federal states may be equally democratic, but for Russia a federal system seems to better answer its needs. Given Russia's history, the centralism of a unitary state runs the risk of being or tending towards authoritarianism and imperialism. Federalism is better suited to the sheer geographical scale of Russia. Federalism also has the potential to provide a regularised and democratic coherence to the relations between the federal and other levels of government. Article 4 of the RF Constitution states that, 'The Constitution of the Russian Federation and federal laws shall have supremacy throughout the entire territory of the Russian Federation'. This is a fairly standard requirement in federal systems, to ensure the benefits and costs of federation membership fall equally on all its members.

However, to achieve this in a way that values and nurtures the social, cultural and economic diversity of the regions, while respecting local autonomy is an immensely complicated and delicate task.

Glossary

Federal system of government

- In a federal system power is divided between a central authority and constituent political units.

- In Russia the central authority is the government in Moscow and the constituent political units (federal subjects – *subyekty federatsii*) are the republics, autonomous *okrugs*, autonomous *oblast*, *krais*, *oblasts* and cities of federal status. These are usually referred to collectively as the regions.

Unitary system of government

- In a unitary system power resides with the central government.

- The central government exercises the exclusive right to decide the powers and jurisdiction of the levels of government below the centre.

The structure of the Russian Federation

In the late 1980s and early 1990s debates about the future structure of an independent Russia produced three broad solutions. Proponents of an imperial vision of Russia with the Russians at the centre of a new great power, such as the Russian nationalists and Zhirinovsky's fascists, favoured a unitary state. Under this scheme the national-territorial subjects, the republics, autonomous *okrugs* and the one autonomous *oblast*, would be abolished and the country divided into territorially-based administrative regions like the tsarist provinces (*gubernii*). Not surprisingly this approach was vehemently opposed by the republics and by Russia's democrats who feared the potential dangers of a powerful, centralised unitary state. A second solution, that briefly found some support and a place in the 1991 draft constitution, envisaged a federal structure with a weak centre. Under this scheme Russia would have been divided into nationality-based republics and territorially-based lands or *zemli* (similar to the German länder), with the same status and rights. The republics rejected this scheme which they viewed as a diminution in their status and an attack on their sovereignty. The Federal Treaty adopted in 1992 and then incorporated into the 1993 RF Constitution in a slightly modified form enshrined a third approach. Russia is described as a federation, the republics' special status is recognised but there was also an attempt to enhance the rights of the regions. The Federal Treaty maintained the division of Russia into the 88 (soon to be 89) federal subjects inherited from the RSFSR (see Box 7.2). The republics are described as the homelands of the non-Russian nationalities. Each republic takes its name from its main non-Russian nationality or titular nationality. So, Bashkortostan after the Bashkirs and Chechnia after the Chechens. The autonomous *okrugs* are ethnically-based subdivisions of the territorially-based *oblasts* and *krais*, so for example Yamal Nenets is an autonomous *okrug* in Tyumen *oblast*.

Box 7.2 The RF national and territorial structure under Yeltsin

32 *nationality-defined federal subjects*

21 national republics:
Adygeya, Altai, Bashkortostan, Buryatia, Chechnia,* Chuvashia, Dagestan, Ingushetia,* Kabardino-Balkaria, Kalmykia, Karachaevo-Cherkessia, Karelia, Khakassia, Komi, Marii El, Mordovia, North Ossetia, Sakha (formerly Yakutia), Tatarstan, Tyva, Udmurtia.

10 autonomous *okrugs*:
Aginsk Buryat, Komi-Permyak, Koryak, Nenets, Taimyr (Dolgano-Nenets), Ust-Ordyn Buryat, Khanty-Mansi, Chukotka, Evenk, Yamal-Nenets

1 autonomous *oblast*:
The Jewish autonomous oblast

57 *territorially defined federal subjects*

6 *krais*:
Altai, Krasnodar, Krasnoyarsk, Primorie (Maritime), Stavropol, Khabarovsk

49 *oblasts*:
Amur, Arkhangelsk, Astrakhan, Belgorod, Bryansk, Vladimir, Volgograd, Vologda, Voronezh, Ivanovo, Irkutsk, Kaliningrad, Kaluga, Kamchatka, Kemerovo, Kirov, Kostroma, Kurgan, Kursk, Leningrad, Lipetsk, Magadan, Moscow, Murmansk, Nizhnii Novgorod, Novgorod, Novosibirsk, Omsk, Orenburg, Oryol, Penza, Perm, Pskov, Rostov, Ryazan, Samara, Saratov, Sakhalin, Sverdlovsk, Smolensk, Tambov, Tver, Tomsk, Tula, Tyumen, Ulyanov, Cheliabinsk, Chita, Yaroslavl

2 'cities of federal status':
Moscow, St Petersburg

* Chechnia-Ingushetia was originally one republic, but split into two republics in 1992.

Russia's other peoples and their lands

As Yeltsin had endorsed the principle of national self-determination within the USSR it was difficult to resist declarations of sovereignty by Russia's non-Russian republics. Put simply, if the 1.7 million Estonians could have their own sovereign country then why not the 5.5 million Tatars in Russia? In the early 1990s nationalism seemed to pose the main threat to Russia's integrity and yet, with the horrific exception of Chechnia, Moscow reached peaceful accommodations with its 20 nationally-based republics. It should be remembered that ethnic Russians

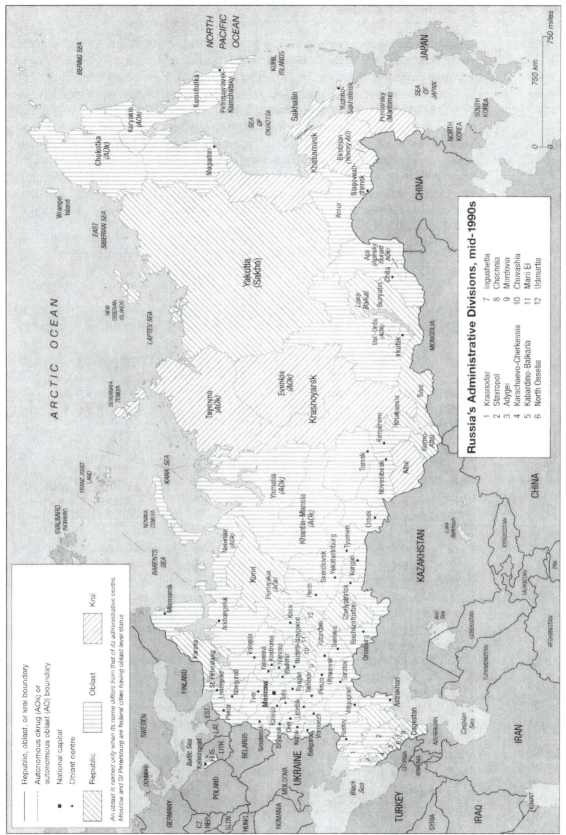

Russia's Administrative Divisions, mid-1990s

1 Krasnodar	7 Ingushetia
2 Stavropol	8 Chechnia
3 Adygei	9 Mordovia
4 Karachaevo-Cherkessia	10 Chuvashia
5 Kabardino-Balkaria	11 Marii El
6 North Ossetia	12 Udmurtia

Republic, oblast, or krai boundary

Autonomous okrug (AOk) or autonomous oblast (AO) boundary

■ National capital

• Oblast centre

Republic

Oblast

Krai

An oblast is named only when its name differs from that of its administrative centre. Moscow and St Petersburg are federal cities having oblast level status

ARCTIC OCEAN

BERING SEA

NORTH PACIFIC OCEAN

EAST SIBERIAN SEA

LAPTEV SEA

KARA SEA

BARENTS SEA

FRANZ JOSEF LAND

SVALBARD (NORWAY)

NOVAYA ZEMLYA

SEVERNAYA ZEMLYA

NEW SIBERIAN ISLANDS

Wrangel Island

SEA OF OKHOTSK

KURIL ISLANDS

SEA OF JAPAN

JAPAN

SOUTH KOREA

NORTH KOREA

CHINA

MONGOLIA

KAZAKHSTAN

Lake Balkhash

Aral Sea

KYRGYZSTAN

TAJIKISTAN

UZBEKISTAN

TURKMENISTAN

AFGHANISTAN

IRAN

IRAQ

KUWAIT

SYRIA

TURKEY

GEORGIA

ARMENIA

AZERBAIJAN

Caspian Sea

Black Sea

UKRAINE

MOLDOVA

ROMANIA

HUNG.

SLOV.

CZ. REP.

POLAND

GERMANY

DENMARK

SWEDEN

FINLAND

BELARUS

EST.

LAT.

LITH.

RUS. Kaliningrad

Baltic Sea

St Petersburg

Moscow

Karelia

Murmansk

Arkhangelsk

Vologda

Novgorod

Pskov

Tver

Smolensk

Bryansk

Kaluga

Orel

Kursk

Belgorod

Voronezh

Lipetsk

Tambov

Ryazan

Tula

Yaroslavl

Kostroma

Ivanovo

Vladimir

Nizhniy Novgorod

Kirov

Komi

Nenetsia (AOk)

Penza

Saransk

Ulyanovsk

Samara

Saratov

Volgograd

Rostov

Astrakhan

Dagestan

Kalmykia

Tatarstan

Bashkortostan

Perm

Permyakia (AOk)

Sverdlovsk

Yekaterinburg 9

Chelyabinsk

Kurgan

Tyumen

Khanti-Mansia (AOk)

Yamalia (AOk)

Omsk

Tomsk

Novosibirsk

Kemerovo

Altai

Gorno-Altai

Khakasia

Krasnoyarsk

Evenkia (AOk)

Taymyria (AOk)

Yakutia (Sakha)

Tuva

Irkutsk

Ust-Orda (AOk)

Lake Baikal

Buryatia

Chita

Aga Buryat (AOk)

Aginsky

Amur

Blagoveshchensk

Birobidzhan (Yevrey AO)

Khabarovsk

Yuzhno-Sakhalinsk

Sakhalin

Primorsky (Maritime)

Magadan

Petropavlovsk-Kamchatsky

Kamchatka

Koryakia (AOk)

Chukotka (AOk)

Orenburg

comprised barely half the population of the USSR but are 83 per cent of Russia's population. Despite Russia's estimated 126 nationalities it is still a fairly homogeneous country. Russia's largest ethnic minority the Tatars constitute only 3.8 per cent of the population (see Table 4.1). The existence of the nationality-based republics assumes a link between a nationality and a particular geographical area, but just as over centuries ethnic Russians moved across the Eurasian landmass so did Russia's other peoples. This makes it very difficult to establish clear, indisputable links between a nationality and a particular territory or homeland. The result is that Russia's internal administrative boundaries have been disputed, which has been a destabilising factor particularly in the Northern Caucasus. The dispute between the republics of Ingushetia and North Ossetia over Prigorny *raion* has still not been resolved.

Box 7.3 The Ingush–North Ossetian dispute over Prigorny *raion*

In 1944 Stalin dismembered the Chechen-Ingush Autonomous Republic (ASSR) and deported its population to Siberia and Central Asia for alleged collaboration with the German invaders. In 1957 Khrushchev rehabilitated the Chechen and Ingush peoples and the Chechen-Ingush ASSR was re-established. However, the Prigorny *raion* was not transferred back to the republic from North Ossetia. In 1991 the USSR adopted a 'Law on the Rehabilitation of Repressed Peoples', to address the problems of the 12 peoples deported from their lands during the Great Patriotic War. The law stated that Prigorny *raion* should be returned to the Chechen-Ingush autonomous republic, but did not establish when and how many Ingush unofficially resettled in Prigorny *raion*. According to Valery Tishkov, an ethnographer from the Russian Academy of Sciences and Chair of the RF State Committee on Nationalities Policy, although at the time of their deportation many Ingush had been living in Prigorny *raion*, only 20 years before it had been Cossack not Ingush land (Project on Ethnic Relations, 1992). Nonetheless, the Ingush see this as their land. In November 1992 Ingush and Ossetian militias fought, the latter with the active support of Russian Interior Ministry troops. The fighting in Prigorny *raion* left 500 dead; 9,000 Ossetians and 65,000 Ingush became refugees. The NGO Human Rights Watch/Helsinki Organization (1996) accused the Ossetians of war crimes and ethnic cleansing. The dispute continues unresolved with Ingush attempts to resettle Prigorny *raion* in any number blocked by Ossetian officials, who have settled Ossetian refugees from Georgia there.

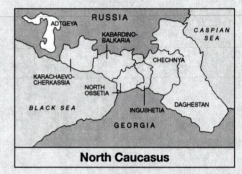

North Caucasus

The titular nationalities are actually the majority population group in only 10 of the 32 nationality-based federal subjects. These are Aga-Buryatia, Chechnia, Chuvashia, Dagestan, Ingushetia, Kabardino-Balkaria, Kalmykia, Komi-Permyak, North Ossetia and Tyva. In 18 of the nationality-designated federal subjects ethnic Russians are in the absolute majority, they are a plurality in three and form substantial majorities in the others. According to 1989 census data 51.3 per cent of people living in the various republics were actually ethnic Russians and only 48.7 per cent were from the titular nationalities. Within the RF nationality is clearly an important source of individual and group identities, a focus of political mobilisation and a rationale of inter-ethnic tensions, but the drive to wrest power from Moscow is not just about national self-determination. Ethnic Russians living in the republics also participated in the drive to gain more powers for the republics from Moscow and thus to benefit from the republics' higher status. In turn the republican constitutions generally recognised the multinational composition of their populations and stated that their peoples enjoy equal rights.

Russia's asymmetrical federalism

The Federal Treaty established the equal rights and obligations of all the federal subjects, but gave the nationality-based republics special privileges. In 1992 only the republics of Chechnia and Tatarstan refused to sign the Federal Treaty, on the grounds that only independence was acceptable. The Federal Treaty recognised the republics as sovereign states within the federation, that they could have their own constitutions, laws and supreme courts, and elect their own parliaments and presidents. The other federal subjects have no such privileges; they are allowed only charters rather than constitutions and until 1996 their governors (the heads of the administration) were appointed by the RF president rather than elected locally. In the mid-1990s Ilya Glezer described Russia as an asymmetrical federation in which the 23 million Russian citizens living in the republics lived in a federation while the remaining 124 million lived in a unitary state (Solnick, 1995: 52).

Reducing the number of federal subjects

The little-known but highly influential Council for the Study of Productive Resources (SOPS) of the Russian Academy of Sciences acts as a think-tank for the prime minister and the government. Under Putin it produced a plan to reduce the number of federal units from 89 to 28 (Yasmann, 2006). Russia's original 88/89 federal subjects were part of the legacy of the USSR's administrative divisions rather than any purposeful post-soviet design. The USA also has a federal system and although it is geographically smaller than Russia it has over double Russia's population, but is divided into just 50 states. There are, therefore, good and practical reasons to revisit the number of Russia's federal subjects. The Kremlin argues that a smaller number of larger-sized subjects will be easier to manage. However, the SOPS plan included two proposals that were particularly alarming to the non-ethnic Russian subjects. First, the formation of new regions by the merger of the

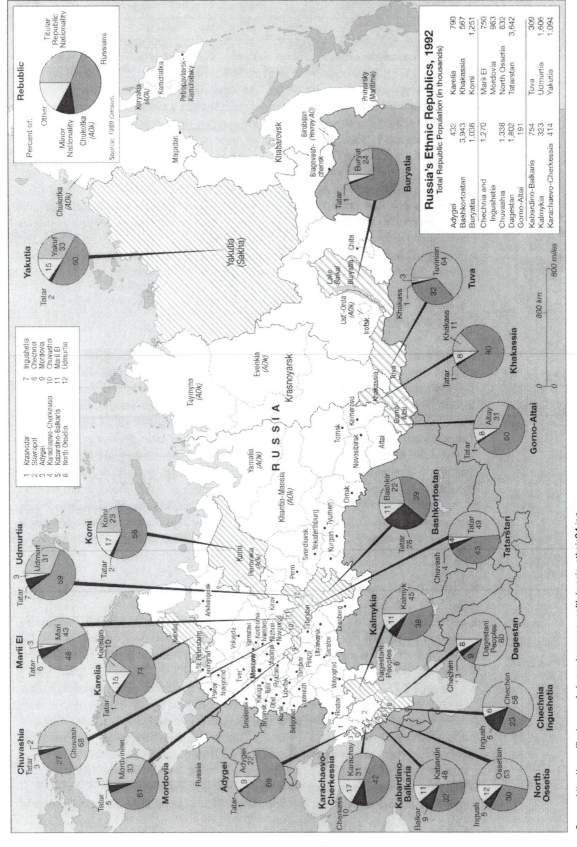

Russia's Ethnic Republics, 1992
Total Republic Population (in thousands)

Adygei	432	Karelia	790
Bashkortostan	3,943	Khakassia	567
Buryatia	1,036	Komi	1,251
Chechnia and		Marii El	750
Ingushetia	1,270	Mordovia	963
Chuvashia	1,338	North Ossetia	632
Dagestan	1,802	Tatarstan	3,642
Gorno-Altai	191		
Kabardino-Balkaria	754	Tuva	309
Kalmykia	323	Udmurtia	1,606
Karachaevo-Cherkessia	414	Yakutia	1,094

Rebublic

- Titular Republic Nationality
- Russians
- Other
- Minor Nationality

Percent of:

Source: 1989 Census.

Source: http://www.lib.utexas.edu/maps/commonwealth/russia_ethnic94.jpg

Box 7.4 The merger of federal subjects

1 December 2005	Perm *oblast* and Komi Permyak autonomous *okrug* became part of Perm *krai*.
1 January 2007	Evenk and Taimyr autonomous okrugs merged with Krasnoyarsk *krai*. The new unit is called Krasnoyarsk *krai*.
1 July 2007	Kamchatka *oblast* and Koryak Autonomous *okrug* merged to form Kamchatka *krai*.
1 January 2008	Ust-Ordyn Buryat Autonomous *okrug* merged with Irkutsk *oblast*. The new unit is called Irkutsk *oblast*.
1 March 2008	Chita *oblast* and Agin-Buryat autonomous *okrug* merged to form Zabalkaysky *krai*.

The RF national and territorial structure, May 2008

26 nationality-defined federal subjects

21 national republics:
Adygeya, Altai, Bashkortostan, Buryatia, Chechnia, Chuvashia, Dagestan, Ingushetia, Kabardino-Balkaria, Kalmykia, Karachaevo-Cherkessia, Karelia, Khakassia, Komi, Marii El, Mordovia, North Ossetia, Sakha (formerly Yakutia), Tatarstan, Tyva, Udmurtia.

4 autonomous *okrugs*:
Nenets, Khanty-Mansi, Chukotka, Yamal-Nenets

1 autonomous *oblast*:
The Jewish autonomous oblast

58 territorially defined federal subjects

9 *krais*:
Altai, Kamchatka, Krasnodar, Krasnoyarsk, Perm, Primorie (Maritime), Stavropol, Khabarovsk, Zabalkaysky

47 *oblasts*:
Amur, Arkhangelsk, Astrakhan, Belgorod, Bryansk, Vladimir, Volgograd, Vologda, Voronezh, Ivanovo, Irkutsk, Kaliningrad, Kaluga, Kemerovo, Kirov, Kostroma, Kurgan, Kursk, Leningrad, Lipetsk, Magadan, Moscow, Murmansk, Nizhnii Novgorod, Novgorod, Novosibirsk, Omsk, Orenburg, Oryol, Penza, Pskov, Rostov, Ryazan, Samara, Saratov, Sakhalin, Sverdlovsk, Smolensk, Tambov, Tver, Tomsk, Tula, Tyumen, Ulyanov, Cheliabinsk, Chita, Yaroslavl

2 'cities of federal status':
Moscow, St Petersburg

ethnic autonomous republics with neighbouring ethnic-Russian administrative areas. Secondly, the removal of any reference to ethnicity in the names of new provinces (ibid.). The plan also included proposed mergers, such as the creation of a North Caucasus Province from the ethnically-based Chechnia, Ingushetia, Dagestan, Kabardino-Balkaria and North Ossetia with the predominantly Russian Stavropol *krai*. A new federal law, drafted by the Council for the Study of Productive Resources, was passed in December 2001 and made it possible to merge two federal subjects with contiguous borders. A merger proposal has to be approved by the voters in both the subjects through a referendum and is then followed by the amendment of Article 6 of the RF Constitution.

Not surprisingly the fear, especially in the ethnically-based republics, is that the mergers are part of a broader agenda to turn Russia into a centralised, unitary state, divided into territorially based administrative units, like the tsarist provinces (*guberniia*). The Kremlin has met local opposition to its merger plans. Chechnia and Ingushetia have resisted all attempts to reunite them and so far the plan to unite all the ethnic groups of the Northern Caucasus with the predominantly Russian Stavropol *krai* has not happened. The Kremlin's merger of Irkutsk *oblast* and the Ust-Ordinsky Buryatsk autonomous *okrug* began in 2003, but initially floundered when the two governors argued over the control of financial assets. The dispute was only resolved and a referendum held when the Kremlin replaced Irkutsk *oblast*'s governor. The Kremlin also postponed its plans to merge the republic of Adygeya into the surrounding Krasnodar *krai* following fierce opposition from the Adygeya President Khazret Sovmen.

The development of Moscow's relations with the regions

Yeltsin's unconstitutional bilateral treaties with the republics

In the mid-1990s even those republics that had signed the Federal Treaty also concluded bilateral treaties with Moscow. The bilateral treaties were all different, but concerned the delineation of jurisdiction between Moscow and the republic. The treaties typically dealt with exports, the levels of taxes and revenues to be forwarded to the federal government coffers and the levels of subsidies from Moscow to the republic. The treaties contravened Article 5.4 of the RF Constitution, which states that, 'All subjects of the Russian Federation are equal with each other in inter-relations with federal bodies of state power.' Also, the jurisdictions of the federal government in Moscow and the federal subjects are set out in Articles 71 and 72 (see Box 7.5). The contents of these treaties were also kept secret and so evaded constitutional review.

From Moscow's perspective the treaties provided a device to stop the RF from disintegrating. In February 1994 Tatarstan finally concluded a bilateral treaty with Moscow which described Tatarstan as a state united with Russia on the basis of the constitutions of the two sovereign states (Hafeez, 1994). The treaty also stated that Tatars conscripted into the armed forces would serve in Tatarstan. Unlike Chechnia, Tatarstan is surrounded by the RF so even if it had achieved

> **Box 7.5** The jurisdiction of the federal government and the federal subjects
>
> The following articles are extracted from Chapter 3 of the RF Constitution. According to Article 71 the jurisdiction of the federal government includes:
>
> - The adoption and amendment of the RF Constitution and federal laws, and supervision over compliance with them;
> - The federal structure and territory of the Russian Federation;
> - Determining the basic principles of federal policy and programmes concerning the state structure, the economy, the environment, and the RF's social, cultural and national development;
> - The establishment of the legal framework for a single market; including financial, monetary, credit and customs regulation and the emission of money;
> - The foreign policy and international relations, international treaties, questions of war and peace;
> - The foreign trade relations;
> - Defence and security;
> - The law courts; Prosecutor's Office; criminal, criminal-procedural and criminal-executive legislation.
>
> According to Article 72 the joint jurisdiction of the RF and federal subjects apply equally to all federal subjects and includes:
>
> - Ensuring compliance of the constitutions and laws of the republics, charters, laws, and other regulatory legal acts of the other federal subjects with the RF's Constitution and federal laws;
> - The coordination of health issues, protection of family, motherhood, fatherhood and childhood; social protection including social security;
> - The establishment of general guidelines for the organisation of the system of bodies of state power and local self-government;
> - The coordination of the international and external economic relations of the federal subjects and compliance with the RF's international treaties.
>
> Article 76
>
> - On issues within the RF's jurisdiction any constitutional or federal laws it adopts apply throughout the RF.
> - The laws of the federal subjects may not contravene federal laws.
>
> *Source*: adapted from Chapter 3 of RF Constitution, available online: http://www.departments.bucknell.edu/russian/const/ch3.html

independence it would have had to come to terms with Moscow. Oil-rich Tatarstan and Bashkortostan and diamond-rich Sakha were typical of the resource-rich republics that had treaties enabling them to retain higher percentages of their tax revenues than other regions. In this way the treaties contributed to the development of 'fiscal federalism' which is characterised by 'a significant degree of decentralisation in fiscal authority' (OECD, 2000: 113). The treaties and fiscal federalism exacerbated the vast differences that already existed among and between the republics-regions; Tatarstan, for example, is able to fund extensive education, healthcare and welfare services that are the envy of the mostly Russian *oblasts*.

Fiscal federalism: follow the money

The flow of money between federal and regional levels is an important element of federal–regional relations. Yeltsin made significant financial concessions to regional leaders who either made credible threats of secession or who were loyal to him. These concessions were typically part of a bilateral treaty. The result was considerable disparity in the financial resources flowing between the federal and individual regional governments, which impacted upon individual regional governments' ability to implement federal policy and to carry out their constitutionally defined roles (see Box 7.5). Under Putin a new version of the Budget Code was introduced which defined and clarified the powers and jurisdictions of the federal and regional governments. The new Budget Code stipulates that most financial assistance to the regions is managed by five state funds (see Box 7.6).

Box 7.6 The five state funds managing assistance to the regions

- Financial Support Fund (established in 1994) grants subsidies based on a formal evaluation of a region's tax potential and normal expenditures.
- Compensation Fund provides money depending on the number of people in a region who qualify for federal compensation.
- Co-financing Social Expenditures Fund finances socially significant services.
- Regional Development Fund provides finance on a competitive basis to stimulate capital investment.
- Fund for Municipal and Regional Finance encourages budgetary reform in the regions.

Source: Alexei Makrushin and Ksenia Yudayeva (2005) 'Funding Federalism in the Power Vertical Age', *The Moscow Times*, 14 June. Available on the *Russia Profile* website, http://www.russiaprofile.org/

The regions may also apply for budget credits which are supposed to be used only to cover budget shortfalls caused by unexpected expenditures; however, in practice they are used to pay for predictable expenditures (ibid.). According to the Ministry of Regional Development only 20 per cent of Russia's regions are *not* dependent on federal subsidies. Federal budget subsidies to the regions during the period January–October 1996 amounted to 440 billion roubles (US$16.6 bn) or 14.61 per cent of the regions' budget revenues (Russia Profile, 2006).

The *oblasts* bid for republic status

Even before Moscow and the republics began to conclude bilateral treaties Russia's regions aspired to the status of republics. Led by their governor Eduard Rossel, the Sverdlovsk *oblast* soviet voted in July 1992 to become the Urals Republic and in October 1992 voted to adopt a republican Constitution (Levin, 1993). Rossel argued that the nationality-based republics were spurious creations as the titular nationalities were not typically in the majority within their republics, and that their existence encouraged rather than defused nationalist discontent. Rossel advocated the division of the RF solely on a territorial basis into provinces (*gubernii*), so that no nationality would be perceived as having a privileged status. In 1993 while Yeltsin and the parliament were locked in conflict in Moscow, a growing number of regions followed Sverdlovsk's lead and unilaterally declared themselves republics. Primorie (Maritime) *krai* called itself the Maritime Republic, Krasnoyarsk and Irkutsk *oblasts* formed the East Siberian Republic, Cheliabinsk became the South Urals Republic, Oryol *oblast* joined with other *oblasts* to form the Central Russian Republic, and in September several Siberian *oblasts* and republics formed the Siberian Republic (Teague, 1994: 45).

Fresh from defeating the parliamentary insurgents Yeltsin sacked Rossel in November 1993, but Rossel was soon elected to head the Sverdlovsk legislature; in August 1995 he was elected governor of Sverdlovsk *oblast* and threatened to take his case to the Constitutional Court. With the 1996 presidential elections fast approaching and his popularity waning, Yeltsin started to sign bilateral treaties with the regions, the first with Rossel on behalf of Sverdlovsk *oblast*. Rossel had got the deal he wanted for his *oblast* and so he stopped pressing for the creation of a Urals republic and supported Yeltsin in the 1996 presidential elections. The strategically important but economically impoverished Kaliningrad *oblast* was also one of the first *oblasts* to acquire a bilateral treaty. Other regions benefited from having patrons within Yeltsin's circle. Orenburg, the home area of Prime Minister Chernomyrdin, was an early recipient of a bilateral treaty as was Krasnodar *krai* which had close ties with Nikolai Yegorov, who was then the president's chief-of-staff.

The bilateral treaties stopped the *oblasts'* republicanisation demands and were a useful form of presidential patronage prior to the 1996 presidential elections to gather regional support for Yeltsin (Zlotnik, 1996). The treaties also encouraged the regions to compete for a good deal with Moscow, rather than to cooperate with each other against Moscow. The conclusion of bilateral treaties with the Russian-dominated regions also went some way to overcoming the discontent with the privileges enjoyed by the republics. In the 1990s there were practical reasons for these unconstitutional bilateral treaties in a country that seemed on the verge of disintegration and where civil war was raging in Chechnia (1994–96).

Putin's 'dictatorship of law'

When Putin became president he was faced with unconstitutional bilateral treaties, republican constitutions and regional charters, and an estimated 20,000 republican and regional laws which did not comply with the RF Constitution and/or federal laws (Traynor, 2000: 13). Putin wanted Russia to have a unified legal system which was to be achieved by what he termed 'a dictatorship of law'. Therefore, he put an end to the bilateral treaties and demanded that republican constitutions and laws, and regional charters and laws, be rewritten to comply with the RF Constitution and federal laws by mid-2005. He used both the courts and his plenipotentiaries to the seven federal districts to speed this process along. In the period 2000–2004 Putin gained the right for the president to dismiss governors who violate federal laws more than once or commit a serious crime; fail to either enforce federal laws or to bring their laws into compliance with federal laws; and, finally, if their area's debt exceeds 30 per cent of its budget revenues or if budget revenues are misused. The president also now has the right to disband republican-regional legislatures if they do not fulfil their role in bringing legislation into line with federal law. In order to control the regions Putin ensured that federal government now controls most of Russia's important tax revenues and federal subsidies are no longer determined by bilateral treaties. As world oil prices rose under Putin, the federal government was able to keep an increasing proportion of Russia's earnings without reducing funding for the regions.

The establishment of a 'dictatorship of law' goes to the heart of the question of which way power flows in the RF. The regions tend to believe that the federal centre should only have the powers that they allow and that they are better able to respond to the interests of their inhabitants. In contrast the Kremlin believes it should determine what powers are apportioned to the federal subjects. Putin had to compromise. In November 2006, for example, he signed – with very little publicity – a 10-year, power-sharing treaty with Tatarstan (Smirnov, 2006). The treaty gives the republic less autonomy than it had under Yeltsin, but does call for joint management of the republic's oil by federal and republican authorities and also grants Tatarstan tax exemptions on mineral resources. It established Tatar as the republic's official language; allowed that federal passports have inserts in Tatar and that candidates for the presidency of Tatarstan must speak Tatar. Putin, like Yeltsin in 1996, needed Tatarstan's President Shaimiev – who is also a senior official in the pro-Putin United Russia party – to deliver votes in the December 2007 Duma elections. In addition for Putin it was better to deal with Shaimiev than to have to confront a Tatar backlash led by the republic's increasingly popular separatist and radical Islamic groups (ibid.). The treaty was highly controversial and was opposed by Aleksandr Konovalev, the presidential plenipotentiary to the Volga district, and Sergei Mironov who was chair of the Federation Council; they feared that the Tatarstan treaty would lead to demands for treaties from other republics. Predictably in November 2006 civic organisations in Bashkortostan, with the support of their president Rakhimov, formed a movement called 'For Federative Russia' to campaign for a power-sharing treaty for their republic (Smirnov, 2007). Presidents Putin and Shaimiev signed the Tatarstan treaty (Tatarstan, 2007) on 26 June 2007 and to date there has not been a flood of new treaties.

Yeltsin's presidential representatives

In the aftermath of the August 1991 coup attempt Yeltsin wanted to prevent the disintegration of Russia and to introduce reform throughout the country; both aims required the assertion of Moscow's control over the regions. To this end Yeltsin created and made the appointments to two new posts, which initially had roughly equal status: the posts of regional governor (*gubernator*) and presidential representative (*predstavitel' prezidenta*) or envoy. Starting in 1991 presidential representatives were appointed to all the *oblasts* and *krais* and by 1998 they had been appointed to all the federal subjects with the exception of the republics of Karelia, Bashkortostan, Tatarstan and Sakha (Petrov, 1998).

In the early 1990s most regions and republics were still run by CPSU appointees and so the presidential representatives were supposed to be champions of Yeltsin's reforms, monitor local developments and report back directly to the president. As the power struggle between the president and the parliament escalated in 1992 and into 1993, the Supreme Soviet wanted to counter the influence of the presidential representatives by creating their own representatives. However, it failed to establish a new post of Supreme Soviet representative and then failed to get the presidential representatives abolished. The presidential representatives' role was to ensure the compliance of local laws with federal laws; they had the authority directly to impose presidential decrees without consulting the local leadership and could even recommend the dismissal of any local official they identified as undermining federal policies. Their duties were also extended to include overseeing the execution of the federal budget, the activities of federal agencies and the use of federal property within their area; as well as coordinating local government agencies. The presidential representatives sound very powerful but in reality their role was not clearly defined and they lacked the political authority or economic resources that might have encouraged the republican and regional leaderships to take notice of them. They also tended either to be co-opted by the republican-regional leaderships or to be actual or former members of the regional executives. Boris Nemtsov, for example, even served simultaneously as presidential representative and governor of Nizhnii Novgorod *oblast*. Presidential representatives soon became regional advocates to the president rather than presidential representatives in the regions. Little wonder that they were abolished by President Putin in 2000, when he created the new post of presidential plenipotentiary to the seven federal districts.

Putin's federal districts and presidential plenipotentiaries

In 1998 the Council for the Study of Productive Resources (SOPS) had proposed the creation of seven federal districts (Yasmann, 2006). This idea was adopted by Putin in a presidential decree of May 2000 that organised Russia's 89 federal subjects into seven federal districts. The same decree also dismissed the existing 89 presidential representatives to each region as a prelude to naming new presidential envoys or plenipotentiaries (*polpredy*) to the federal districts later the same month. The plenipotentiaries are directly accountable to the president and were soon dubbed 'governor generals', after their tsarist predecessors, by the Russian

Box 7.7 The federal districts and their presidential plenipotentiaries

Central (*Tsentralny*)

Composition: Belgorod, Bryansk, Vladimir, Voronezh, Ivanovo, Kaluga, Kostroma, Kursk, Lipetsk, Moscow, Oryol, Ryazan, Smolensk, Tambov, Tver, Tula and Yaroslavl *oblasts* and the city of Moscow.

Federal district centre: Moscow

Georgy Poltavchenko 18 May 2000–	Born 1953. Joined the KGB in 1979 serving in Leningrad *oblast*. In 1992 founded, and until 1999 headed, the St Petersburg Tax police; 1999 to 2000 served as the presidential representative to Leningrad *oblast*. A Putin loyalist he is a counterweight to the powerful Moscow mayor Yury Luzhkov.

Far Eastern (*Dalnevostochny*)

Composition: Republic of Sakha; Primorskii (Maritime) and Khabarovsk *krais*; Amur, Kamchatka, Magadan and Sakhalin *oblasts*; Jewish autonomous *oblast*; Koryak and Chukchi autonomous *okrugs*.

Federal district centre: Khabarovsk

Konstantin Pulikovsky 18 May 2000 to 14 November 2005	Born 1948. Rose to colonel general (now retd.) during a 33-year military career. In 1996 he was appointed commander of Russian forces in Chechnia and from 1996 to 1998 was the deputy commander of the North Caucasus Military District. Between 1998 and 2000 he held government positions in Krasnodar *krai*. A former member of the Presidential Administration.
Kamil Iskhamov 14 November 2005 to 30 October 2007	Between 1989 and 1991 he was a member of the Kazan (Tatarstan) city executive committee, then from 1991 to 2005 he was a member and chair of the Kazan City Council of People's Deputies and also head of the Kazan City Administration.
Oleg Safonov 30 October 2007–	Born 1960. Served in the KGB from 1982 to 1991. He then worked with Putin in the Committee for the External Relations of the St Petersburg Mayor's Office. Between 1996 and 2007 he was a deputy Interior Minister.

North Western (*Severo-Zapadny*)

Composition: republics of Karelia and Komi; Arkhangelsk, Vologda, Kaliningrad, Leningrad, Murmansk, Novgorod, Pskov *oblasts*; Nenets autonomous *okrug*; city of St Petersburg.

Federal district centre: St Petersburg

Viktor Cherkesov 18 May 2000 to 11 March 2003	Born 1950. Graduated in law from Leningrad State University. 1975 joined the KGB and developed a reputation as a dissident hunter; is loathed by Russia's liberals. Rose to head the FSB in St Petersburg and Leningrad *oblast*,

Box 7.7 (*Continued*)

	1992–8. In 1998 appointed First Deputy Director of the FSB under Putin. A St Petersburger-Chekist.
Valentina Matvienko 11 March 2003 to 15 October 2003	Born 1949. Graduated from the Leningrad Chemical Pharmaceutical Institute in 1972 and then had a career in the Leningrad Komsomol and CPSU committees in Leningrad. 1986–89 Deputy Chair of the Leningrad Soviet Executive Committee, 1989–90 Chair of the Supreme Soviet Committee on Women's Affairs, Protection of Families, Children and Motherhood. 1991–98 diplomatic postings and worked in the Foreign Affairs Ministry. From September 1998 a deputy prime minister.
Ilya Klebanov 1 November 2003–	Born 1951. 1997–8 worked in the St Petersburg City Administration. 1999 appointed deputy prime minister with responsibility for the defence industries. 2002 appointed Minister of Industry, Science and Technology.

Volga (*Privolzhsky*)

Composition: republics of Bashkortostan, Marii El, Mordovia, Tatarstan, Udmurtia, and Chuvashia; Kirov, Nizhnii Novgorod, Orenburg, Penza, Perm, Samara, Saratov and Ulyanovsk *oblasts*; Komi-Permyak *okrug*.

Federal district centre: Nizhnii Novgorod

Sergei Kiriyenko 18 May 2000 to 14 November 2005	Born 1962. During the 1980s was a Komsomol Secretary in Nizhnii Novgorod. 1991–94 President of AO Kontsern, 1994 founded and headed (until 1997) *Guarantiya* Bank. 1996–97 head of the Nizhniy Novgorod oil refinery company Norsi-oil. 1997 first deputy minister then Minister of fuel and energy. 1998 prime minister.
Aleksandr Konovalov 14 November 2005–	Born 1968. 1992–2005 worked in the St Petersburg Prosecutor's Office. February–November 2005 Chief Prosecutor in Bashkortostan.

Siberian (*Sibirsky*)

Composition: republics of Altai, Buryatia, Tyva and Khakassia; Altai and Krasnoyarsk *krais*; Irkutsk, Kemerovo, Novosibirsk, Omsk, Tomsk and Chita *oblasts*, Aga-Buryatia, Taimyr (Dolano-Nenets), Ust-Ordyn Buryati and Evensk autonomous *okrugs*.

Federal district centre: Novosibirsk

Leonid Drachevsky 18 May 2000 to 9 September 2004	Born 1942. Minister for Relations with the CIS 1999–2000.
Anatoly Kvashnin 9 September 2004–	Born 1946. A military career rising in 1992 to the General Staff of the Russian Armed Forces. In 1995 appointed Commander of the North Caucasus Military District, then May 1997 to July 2004 served as Chief of the Armed Forces General Staff and in 1997 became first deputy defence minister.

Box 7.7 (*Continued*)

Southern (*Yuzhny*)*

Composition: republics of Adygeya, Dagestan, Ingushetia, Kabardino-Balkaria, Kalmykia, Karachaevo-Cherkessia, North Ossetia and Chechnia; Krasnodar and Stavropol *krais*; Volgograd and Rostov *oblasts*.

Federal district centre: Rostov-on-Don

* Until June 2000 called the Northern Caucasus

Viktor Kazantsev 18 May 2000 to 9 March 2004	Born 1946. A military career serving in Transcaucasus, Turkmenistan and Central Asia. A general, he headed Russia's military campaign against Chechnia in 1999 to May 2000. A Hero of the Russian Federation.
Vladimir Yakovlev 9 March 2004 to 13 September 2004	Born 1944. 1996–2000 Governor (mayor) of St Petersburg.
Dmitry Kozak 13 September 2004 to 24 September 2007	Born 1958. Graduated in law from Leningrad State University in 1985 then in 1990 began work in the law department of the Leningrad/St Petersburg city administration, serving between 1994 and 1999 as head of the mayor's Legal Department and from 1996 to 1999 as deputy mayor of St Petersburg. In 1999 he was appointed deputy chief of the Presidential Administration. A Putin loyalist and close ally of Dmitry Medvedev he was appointed regional development minister on 24 September 2007.
Grigory Rapota 9 October 2007–	Born 1944. He had a long career in the KGB, serving as the deputy head of the SVR between 1994 and 1998, then was briefly a deputy secretary of the Security Council. From late 1998 to September 1999 he was a deputy director of the state's arms export agency *Rosvooruzheniye*, before becoming first deputy trade minister then deputy industry and energy minister. From October 2001 he was the general secretary of the Eurasian Economic Community.

Urals (*Uralsky*)

Composition: Kurgan, Sverdlovsk, Tyumen and Chelianbinsk *oblasts*; Khantsy-Mansi and Yamal-Nenets autonomous *okrugs*.

Federal district centre: Yekaterinburg

Col.-Gen. Pyotr Latyshev 18 May 2000–	Born 1948. A police career for the Ministry of the Interior in the Urals and in 1991 became head of the Ministry of the Interior in Krasnodar. 1990–93 a member of the Russian Supreme Soviet and first deputy minister of the interior. 1994–2000 deputy minister of the interior and vice chair of the Federal Anti-terrorism Commission.

media. Putin drew on his *siloviki* network for these appointments; of the original appointees only Sergei Kiriyenko and Leonid Drachevsky were civilians. As the new federal districts are designed to maintain the RF's integrity and security, their geographical composition closely mirrors the Interior Ministry and the Defence Ministry's military regions. This facilitates the plenipotentiaries' role in managing the activities of the 'power ministries' – Defence, Interior and Security – in their districts. The plenipotentiaries were also appointed to the Security Council, one of the key bodies of presidential power (see Chapter 5).

Overall, the plenipotentiaries' role is to ensure that the Kremlin's writ runs throughout the federation and to put an end to fragmentation. They also manage the activities of the Justice Ministry in their regions and one of their first tasks was to oversee the process of bringing republican and regional constitutions, charters and laws into conformity with the RF Constitution and federal laws. As well as being an assertion of central control, this process also led to the removal of authoritarian legislation that contravened citizens' constitutional rights. Another aspect of the plenipotentiaries' role is to ensure that federal agencies such as the tax and security services operate uniformly throughout the federation, rather than in the interest of local elites. They are also responsible for the rotation of federal employees throughout the RF, a policy which is supposed to prevent the development of cozy and possibly corrupt alliances with local politicians.

The regional governors under Yeltsin: from appointment to election

Yeltsin modelled the new post of governor on the tsarist governor generals and appointed them to head the administration in each of the federal subjects. Most of the governors were not the existing chairs of *oblast* or *krai* executive committees and this led to conflicts with local soviets who wanted to have their own chairs appointed governor. The governors, like the presidential representatives, were supposed to ensure that the president's reform programme was implemented in the regions and they were, therefore, given substantial executive powers such as control over the regional budget. They were also appointed *ex officio* to the Federation Council and so dominated the upper chamber of the Federal Assembly (parliament) in Moscow. A profound change to the status and function of the governors came with the May 1996 Constitutional Court order that the election of governors (gubernatorial elections) should begin later that year. While the gubernatorial elections did not mark a formal change in the governors' status, they gave the governors greater local legitimacy and authority and removed them from the presidential patronage system. The result was that the governors increasingly came to represent the regions in Moscow, rather than to be the president's placemen in the regions. The gubernatorial elections completed by 1 September 1996, saw only 14 of the 30 incumbents elected (Orttung, 1996). Gubernatorial elections also provided leading politicians with substantial regional power bases and platforms from which to challenge the federal government. For example, in October 1996 Aleksandr Rutskoi, Yeltsin's former vice-president and now vehement opponent, was elected governor of Kursk.

The regional governors under Putin: from election to appointment

Putin used the September 2004 terrorist attack on a school in Beslan to justify his next step in strengthening of the power vertical: the replacement of elected governors by presidential appointees. Putin claimed that this new system would help to protect Russia from terrorism; quite how appointment rather than election would do this is unclear, other than Putin's belief that anything that strengthened the centre would make Russia stronger. Putin was able to push through the loss of a

---

Box 7.8 Federal feudalism

Background: During the 1990s Moscow was unable to control developments in the regions. However, this was not necessarily a victory for local democracy over a central domination. The Russian media accused many local leaders including presidents Kirsan Ilyumzhimov of Kalmykia and Murtaza Rakhimov of Bashkortostan of acting like tsars or feudal lords rather than democratic leaders.

The republic of Kalmykia

In 1993 Ilyumzhimov, who calls himself the 'Kalmyk Khan', was elected president. He persuaded the republic's Supreme Soviet to abolish local soviets (councils), to dissolve the Supreme Soviet and replace it with a 25-member professional parliament. Ilyumzhimov then imposed direct rule through a network of personal representatives. The republic's democratic opposition was harassed by the police and the only opposition newspaper *Sovetskaia Kalmykia* closed; its editor Larissa Yudina was murdered in 1998. For the 1996 and the 2000 RF presidential elections, Ilyumzhimov got the vote out for Yeltsin and Putin. In 1995 he was the

only candidate in the republic's presidential elections and won another seven-year term amid allegations of electoral fraud; he was re-elected in 2002. Ilyumzhimov, who is also president of the World Chess Federation, has been accused of corruption and it was widely assumed that he would be sacked by Putin. However, although Kalmykia is desperately poor and economically underdeveloped it is stable, largely due to the continuing use of force to silence opposition and protestors. Ilyumzhimov is still president.

See Republic of Kalmykia website: http://kalm.ru/en/

Box 7.8 (*Continued*)

The republic of Bashkortostan

Elected president in 1993 Rakhimov is known as Babai (Grandad) and runs the oil-rich republic with other members of his family. His son runs the holding company that controls the oil industry. The local media are controlled and any signs of opposition immediately suppressed. For the 1996 and the 2000 RF presidential elections, Rakhimov got the vote out for Yeltsin and Putin. In the 1990s in defiance of federal law, Rakhimov appointed all the republic's judges and prosecutors, and controlled the local secret police and police force. According to the Bashkortostan constitution the republic's laws were on an equal footing with federal laws. In May 2000

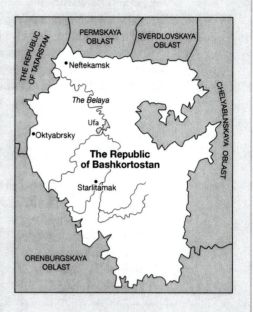

Putin ordered Bashkortostan to bring its constitution into line with the RF Constitution. He was re-elected president in 2003 amid allegations of election fraud and in 2006 he was appointed president by Putin.

democratic right because the RF Constitution does not specify that governors should be elected. Although most governors are believed to have opposed the move, they nonetheless publicly supported the change and quickly began to curry favour with the president. United Russia's dominance of the Duma ensured approval of the necessary legislation. Under the new system the RF president selects a candidate for governor on the advice of the presidential staff and plenipotentiaries. The president's choice is then subject to confirmation by the regional legislature. In the event that a legislature rejects the president's candidate three times, the president is empowered to disband the legislature and call new elections. The president would then appoint a new interim governor, who is subject to approval by the new legislature. There is no doubt that there was a major problem with the elected governors, who were often corrupt and sometimes little better than local tyrants; they controlled the media and used all the resources at their disposal to put pressure on the electorate in order to stay in power. This helps to explain why there was no great public outcry against the change. Although the popular accountability provided by the election of governors was far from perfect, in 2004 electors in Pskov, Ryazan and Arkhangelsk *oblasts* and Altai *krai* did remove unsatisfactory governors via the ballot box. Instead of centralising Putin could have devolved greater power to the mayors, in an attempt to build up local levels of self-government as a counterbalance to the governors within the regions. Instead he created a situation in which the appointment of governors has been removed from public oversight and made the governors accountable to federal rather than regional and local interests. The process of replacing or reconfirming governors in office will last until 2009. With only a handful of exceptions, Putin nominated incumbent governors to carry on serving as governors rather than sweeping away the existing corps of governors. Local legislatures have just rubber stamped the presidential appointments and the governors know that their survival in office depends on the support of the RF president.

Strengthening the power vertical: networks and parties of power

During the soviet period the Kremlin stood at the apex of a range of institutions: the CPSU, economic institutions, the armed forces and the security services that pulled the country together. Putin created similar structures using his *siloviki* network, both to provide key personnel and institutional support for his reforms and he increasingly also used his United Russia presidential 'party of power'. In March 2007 legislative elections were held in 14 regions under the new electoral system in which half the seats are elected by party list. The biggest share of the vote was taken by United Russia, on a low turnout of only 39.1 per cent (Reuters, 2007: 21). The election in Stavropol *krai* was narrowly won by the communists. Second place went to the pro-Kremlin Justice party, headed by Sergei Mironov, the speaker of the Russian Federation, which was created to take votes from the communists and so aid United Russia (EIU, 2007). What was happening was the ousting of republican and regional parties of power created by the regional leaders by Putin's party of power.

In 1998 the regional bosses had believed that they could take control of the Duma in the December 1999 elections. At this time the RF Communist Party and to a lesser extent Chernomyrdin's Our Home is Russia, were the only political parties organised throughout the country. Political elites in the regions formed their own parties and, once elected, these became the region's 'party of power'. The Fatherland-All Russia (OVR) movement was formed by former prime minister, Yevgeny Primakov, Yury Luzhkov the mayor of Moscow and President Shaimiev of Tatarstan. Konstantin Titov the governor of Samara *oblast* created Russia's Voice which was a coalition of the 'parties of power' from some of the regions. In the event OVR came a creditable third in the Duma elections. Putin wanted his United Russia party to act as a unifying force both by winning the December 2007 Duma elections and by tying republican and regional legislatures to the RF president. In 1996 the economist Philip Hanson noted that conflict between regional and national economic policy in Russia was not moderated by 'any effective chain of party loyalties tying the careers of regional politicos to their acquiescence in a particular party's national policies' (Hanson, 1996). The penetration of United Russia into the regions is designed to provide a conduit for views to pass to the Kremlin from the regions, but it is also to ensure the implementation of federal policies at all levels of government.

Chechnia

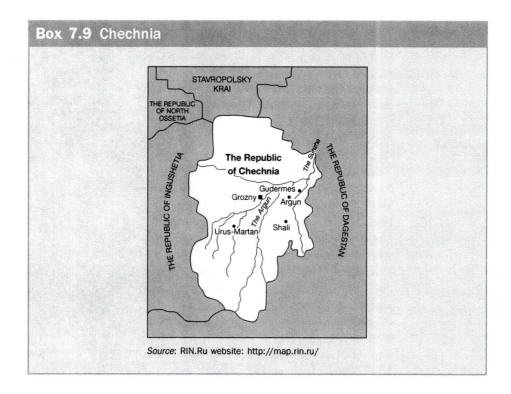

Box 7.9 Chechnia

Source: RIN.Ru website: http://map.rin.ru/

Chechnia, a reluctant part of Russia

Chechnia became part of the Imperial Russian Empire in 1858 after decades of fighting. As the USSR was disintegrating in 1991 Chechnia, which was an autonomous republic within the RSFSR, moved quickly to assert its independence from the USSR and Russia. Doku Zavgayev, Chechnia's communist leader was overthrown and Dzhokar Dudayev, a former soviet air force general was elected president and declared Chechen independence. In 1992 Chechnia refused to sign Moscow's Federal Treaty and adopted a new constitution, establishing the republic as an independent, secular state called Ichkeria, governed by a president and a parliament. As a self-declared, independent country, in 1993 Chechnia boycotted the Russian Duma elections and the referendum on the RF Constitution. Chechnia was, however, very far from being a stable, united, democratic country. Dudayev increasingly used the language of Chechen nationalism so alienating the ethnic Russians, who constituted about a quarter of the republic's population and many of whom had supported him in 1991. Mafia gangs and warlords were the real rulers of much of the republic. In the face of continuing opposition and armed conflict, Dudayev closed the Chechen parliament.

The first Chechen war and continuing post-war chaos

Moscow did not recognise Chechnia's independence and continued to view the republic as part of the Russian federation. In November 1994 the Kremlin backed a coup against Dudayev and when this failed Russian armed forces invaded Chechnia on 11 December 1994. On 3 January 1995 Moscow backed Doku Zagayev as a puppet president and at the beginning of February Russian forces conquered Grozny, the Chechen capital and held the plains. Inconclusive fighting continued in the mountains above Grozny, with atrocities and human rights abuses by all combatants. The Russian forces set up so-called 'filtration camps' to find Chechen fighters hiding among civilians. Chechen men and boys were held without trial in the camps where, according to Amnesty International (2000, 2007) and the New York-based Human Rights Watch (1995, 2000), they are subjected to physical and torture abuse including, beatings, shock treatment and rape. By the end of the war Chechnia lay in ruins; Russian forces had indiscriminately attacked densely populated residential areas leaving an estimated 30,000 civilians, or 10 per cent of the population of Chechnia, dead. Grozny means terrible in Russian, the city of Grozny was well-named.

In April 1996 Dudayev was killed in a rocket attack and the following month Aleksandr Lebed, Yeltsin's new security adviser, arrived in Chechnia to negotiate a peace settlement. Lebed negotiated with Aslan Maskhadov, a former soviet army colonel and the former chief of staff of the rebel forces. Maskhadov was considered a moderate and was a supporter of a secular state. The war ended in August and the Russian army began to leave Chechnia, a process completed in January 1997. On 27 January 1997 Maskhadov was elected president of Chechnia, and in May Yeltsin and Maskhadov signed a peace treaty. In a secret deal the Chechens received amnesties, humanitarian aid, reconstruction funds, special tax and trading privileges, and – so they believed – recognition of their independence. The Chechens agreed to guarantee the safety of oil and gas supplies passing through Ichkeria.

Maskhadov was not in control of most of Chechnia. The so-called 'field commanders' Arbi Barayev and Ruslan Khaikhoroyev, and the 'terrorists' Salman Raduyev and Shamil Basayev, were directing mounting crime and violence within the republic. This included extortion and violence against the Russian population, kidnapping for ransom and slave labour, and the kidnapping of journalists and foreign aid workers. In 1998 Moscow's envoy to Chechnia, General Gennady Shpigun was kidnapped from Grozny airport; his corpse was eventually found in March 2000. Maskhadov declared a state of emergency in response to the mounting chaos and in January 1999 declared that Islamic Shari'ah law would be phased in over the next three years. In a bid to stem the violence, public executions were broadcast on TV. The violence also spilt over into the neighbouring predominantly Muslim republic of Dagestan, threatening to destabilise the Caucasus. In August 1999 Shamil Basayev and Khattab (he only uses one name), self-styled internationalist warriors for Allah, led what they dubbed the 'August Liberation' of Dagestan. Dagestan fought back and the Chechens were finally driven out by the Russian army.

Putin, the second Chechen war and direct rule

The instability and violence of the Caucasus seemed to arrive in Moscow in September 1999 when bomb blasts in two apartment buildings killed more than 200 people. Chechen rebels were swiftly blamed. Then an apartment building bomb in the city of Ryazan was defused by the bomb squad; the would-be bombers were caught red-handed and were found to be carrying FSB identity cards. Despite official denials the FSB are widely believed to have planted the Moscow bombs to justify a new war against Chechnia. The war also boosted support for the then little-known prime minister and former FSB member Vladimir Putin, and catapulted him to victory in the presidential elections in March 2000.

The Russian army invaded Chechnia on 20 September 1999 so beginning the second Chechen war. The Russian army closed the border between Chechnia and Ingushetia trapping thousands of civilians trying to flee the war zone and also set up filtration camps again. In October 1999 former members of the Chechen legislature set up the State Council of the Republic of Chechnia in Moscow; Yeltsin recognised it as the legitimate government of Chechnia and refused to negotiate with his former ally, Maskhadov. In February 2000 Grozny was once again captured by Russian forces, and in May Putin declared direct rule from Moscow and in June appointed Akhmat Kadyrov as the head of the administration. In 2001 Putin appointed Stanislav Ilyasov as the Chechen prime minister. The war continued and on 23 October 2002 Chechen rebels, demanding the end of the war, seized the Dubrovka theatre in Moscow and held approximately 800 people hostage. Russian forces released gas into the theatre and then stormed it, leaving all the rebels and over 100 of the hostages dead.

Putin, Chechnisation and normalisation

Putin wanted Chechnia to remain part of the Russian Federation and for Chechens to run the republic on behalf of the Kremlin. In March 2003 Chechnia held a referendum which approved a new Kremlin-backed constitution for the republic, which recognised Chechnia as an inseparable part of the Russian Federation. It was very important for the Kremlin that the referendum showed overwhelming support for the constitution. According to the official election statistics, 80 per cent of the 537,000 eligible voters cast their vote and 96 per cent approved the constitution; the electorate included 65,000 refugees in neighbouring Ingushetia and the 38,000 Russian armed forces personnel serving in Chechnia (Feifer, 2003). The referendum was conducted against a background of continuing violence and instability and the OSCE (2003) expressed concerns about the lack of consultation in the drafting of the constitution and the conduct of the referendum.

The election of the president of Chechnia was the next important step in the stabilisation and Chechenisation of the republic. In October 2003 the Kremlin-backed candidate Akhmad Kadyrov, who had narrowly escaped assassination by a suicide bomber in May, was elected president in elections with 80 per cent of the vote. Kadyrov deployed his personal militias against his opponents and no

President of the Chechen Republic Alu Alkhanov, Russian President Vladimir Putin, First Vice Premier of Chechnya Ramzan Kadyrov (foreground L–R) attend the first sitting of the re-elected Chechen Parliament, December 2005.

separatist candidate appeared on the ballot paper. The election did not bring peace; in May 2004 Kadyrov was killed in a bombing for which Basayev claimed responsibility and in July 2004 the acting president Sergei Abramov, a Russian, survived an explosion. Chechen separatists engaged in large-scale military action against Grozny and attacked polling stations in the run up to the August 2004 presidential elections. In a 'managed' election the Kremlin-backed candidate Alu Alkhanov was duly elected president. The November 2005 Chechen parliament elections were also 'managed': all the candidates were from Moscow-based parties, there were no separatist candidates and the pro-Kremlin United Russia party dominated the Chechen parliament after the elections.

The elections created a framework for Moscow's control of Chechnia and the normalisation of the situation in the republic, but violence and instability continued. In August 2004 Chechen separatists were suspected of downing two planes and an attack on a Moscow metro station killing 10 people. Then in September 2004 children, teachers and parents were taken hostage at a school in Beslan in North Ossetia (see Chapter 9). In March 2005 Makhadov the president of the separatist Chechen government was killed by Russian troops and was succeeded by Abdul-Khalim Sadullayev who appointed Doku Umarov as vice president and Basayev as first deputy chair. In May Sadullayev ended the policy of seeking peace talks with Russia and vowed to spread the war beyond Chechnia. October saw Basayev launch an attack on Nalchik, the capital of the republic of Kabardino-Balkaria. In June 2006 Sadullayev was killed by government forces and succeeded by Doku Umarov and in July Moscow announced it had finally killed Basayev.

In March 2006, with prompting from Putin, Sergei Abramov resigned as prime minister and was succeeded by Ramzan Kadyrov (the son of Ahmad Kadyrov), who was being positioned by the Kremlin to take control of Chechnia. Kadyrov is a flamboyant character, he has a pet lion, claims to be a friend of the former boxer Mike Tyson, supports polygamy and a ban on gambling and alcohol, and wants to build the largest mosque in Europe. Kadyrov was Putin's choice to lead Chechnia and when in February 2007 Kadyrov reached 30 years of age, the minimum age to be president, Putin sacked Alu Alkhanov as president and replaced him with Ramzan Kadyrov. The Kremlin likes to depict Kadyrov as a good Muslim who respects Chechen traditions but this is an image that is not always easy to sustain in the face of Kadyrov's behaviour and public statements. Kadyrov leads a private militia known as *Kadyrovtsy*, which has taken over much of the military campaign against Chechen separatists from the Russian armed forces. Human Rights Watch (2006) has accused the *Kadyrovtsy* of human rights abuses, but from Moscow's perspective he is a Chechen leader who is containing separatism and maintaining Chechnia as part of the Russian Federation.

District and local government

The complexity of government in the subjects of the federation

In the 1990s most federal subjects had directly elected executives, except the republics of Dagestan and Karachaevo-Cherkessia. The executives were called the governor,

---

Box 7.10 The levels of government in the RF pre-Putin's reforms

Federal government in Moscow

Federal subjects

21 republics	6 *krais*	49 *oblasts*	1 autonomous oblast	10 autonomous okrugs	2 cities: Moscow St Petersburg

District level

2,000 (approx.) *raions*	400 (approx.) cities and towns with district status

Local government

624 smaller towns and cities	2,000 (approx.) urban settlements	2,400 (approx.) rural settlements

president or chair of the government. St Petersburg and Moscow originally had mayors, but now refer to their governor. The legislatures (parliaments) are variously called Duma, Legislative Assembly, City Assembly or State Council and are usually elected. Following the same pattern of a strong president and a weak parliament that exists at the centre, the local legislatures tended to be weaker than the executives. Again mirroring the pattern of federal government, the executives and legislatures have their own committees and administrations. The republican and regional parliaments now have the potentially important role of confirming the Kremlin's choice of governor. However, as the RF president now has more control over the governor this will further reduce the power of the parliaments, both in their relations with the governor and with the federal government.

District and local government in the 1990s

In the 1990s district and local government was not a priority and lacked a coherent approach or structure. The district level was subordinated to the subjects of federation and the local level was subordinate to the district level. The town and city mayors at the district and lowest levels headed the local administrations and were usually, but not always, appointed by the regional governor. The mayors worked jointly with the municipal councils or dumas, which ratified local budgets and oversaw municipal services. It is not possible to provide a clear-cut statement of the jurisdiction and competencies of local government, as this was decided by a complex range of federal agreements and negotiations – and quite simply by what different bodies could get away with. The 1995 federal law 'On the Basic Principles of Local Self-Government in the RF', was essentially a compromise between competing ideas and interests and little attention was paid to quite how it would be implemented. The creation of a single system of local government was also complicated by disputes between the regional leaders on the one hand and the heads of the local government on the other. These disputes typically centred on the same kinds of jurisdictional and ownership issues that plagued Moscow's relations with the regions.

There were disputes with presidents and governors pitted against the mayor of the republic's capital city, or against the leaders of *krais* and *oblasts*, over the budget and/or regional and municipal property. Such disputes took place in the republics of Buryatia and Udmurtia, Primorskii and Krasnodar *krais*, and Arkhangelsk, Omsk and Sverdlovsk *oblasts* (Mironov, 1998). In the case of Tatarstan, Bashkortostan and North Ossetia the presidents and governors responded to such disputes by trying to abolish local government. In Udmurtia the republican parliament did not abolish local government as such but instead in 1996 abolished the territorial subjects that had a right to local self-government (see Blankengael, 1997). Other tactics employed included simply not holding elections to local government bodies or, as in the case of Kursk and Novosibirsk *oblasts*, reducing the status of local government bodies to regional councils and abolishing elected administrations. The result of these developments was that in the second half of the 1990s the number of local government bodies actually decreased threefold (ibid.) leaving 20 per cent of Russia without local government (Petrov, 2006).

District and local self-government under Putin

The Kozak Commission paid considerable attention to 'local self-government', and the resulting 'Law on the General Principles of Local Self-Government in the RF' adopted in 2003 was a concerted attempt to address the deficiencies of the 1995 law of the same name. The 2003 law was also part of Putin's strengthening of the power vertical, as it formally subordinated local government into the government hierarchy below the federal and republican-regional levels. This despite the fact that Article 12 of the RF Constitution states that, 'Local self-government shall be recognised and guaranteed in the Russian Federation. Local self-government shall operate independently within the bounds of its authority.' The 2003 law did, however, also set the very basic democratic requirement that all local officials should be elected, setting a deadline of 1 November 2005 for elections to be held. Since 2006, the line of the power vertical running down from the president to the regional governors has been extended to city mayors, who are now appointed by the governors rather than elected.

Before 2003 a major problem for local self-government was that it was mandated to provide a range of services but did not always have the necessary funding; this phenomenon is known as under-funded mandates. For example, some villages were expected to deliver the same range of services as a city. One way of dealing with this could have been for the federal or regional level government to take on the responsibility for delivering services, but the Kozak Commission decided against this centralisation. Instead it opted for local government to continue to deliver services and so Russia now has a mandatory two-tier structure of local government composed of municipalities, with specific responsibilities (see Martinez-Vasquez and Timofeev, 2003).

Box 7.11 The two tiers of local government since 2003

Top tier municipalities

Rural districts	Urban districts

Bottom tier municipalities

Rural settlements	Urban settlements
A rural area with a population over 1,000 in one or more settlements.	Includes small towns

---

The reforms set out in the 2003 law have yet to be introduced in all regions and the deadline for implementation has had to be pushed back to 1 January 2009. The establishment of the 27,000 new municipalities has encountered a number of practical problems. First, the establishment of the municipalities' boundaries has proved very contentious (see Blandy, 2007). Kozak, while the presidential envoy to the Southern Federal District, even allowed municipalities in the republic of Karachaevo-Cherkessia to be set up along ethnic lines, so setting a potentially dangerous precedent. Each municipality also needs a charter, which has to be written and approved; this too has been a slow process. They also need new municipal government agencies and according to Vladimir Yakovlev, the former regional development minister, an additional 200,000 civil servants (Lankina, 2005). The transfer of housing, clinics, schools and cultural institutions to municipal control is a major logistical undertaking which needs sensitive handling if it is not to frustrate the implementation of Putin's National Programmes in health, education and welfare reforms. Despite changes to the funding of local government aimed at increasing budgetary autonomy, under-funded mandates have not disappeared.

Chapter summary

Yeltsin succeeded in maintaining the RF's territorial integrity, but in the process created an unconstitutional and unbalanced form of federalism. Putin wanted to strengthen the power vertical and to ensure the implementation of presidential decrees and federal law throughout Russia. This has entailed ending many of Yeltsin's innovations such as bilateral treaties, presidential representatives and the election of regional governors. Instead Putin created new federal districts and presidential representatives, replaced election of regional governors with presidential appointment and is gradually merging federal subjects. Putin also used his networks such as the *siloviki* and the presidential party of power United Russia to help push through these reforms. Putin also wanted to create a dictatorship of law and so appointed Dmitry Kozak, a St Petersburg lawyer, to head the Commission drafting the necessary legislation to delineate the competence and jurisdiction of regional and local government and to ensure their adequate funding. Putin used the armed forces to keep Chechnia within the federation, but it remains highly volatile and federal rule does not run throughout the republic.

Discussion points

- Did Yeltsin have to allow the regions to take power at the expense of Moscow in order to stop the Russian Federation from pulling apart?
- Is strengthening the power vertical really an attempt to create a unitary state?
- What is the optimum number of federal subjects for Russia?
- Is centralism always bad for democracy?

Further reading

Comprehensive overviews of federalism are provided by Cameron Ross (2002) *Federalism and Democratisation in Russia*, Manchester: Manchester University Press and Jeffrey Kahn (2002) *Federalism, Democratization, and the Rule of Law in Russia*, Oxford: Oxford University Press. On Putin's reforms, go to Gordon M. Hahn (2003) 'The Impact of Putin's Federative Reforms on Democratization in Russia', *Post-Soviet Affairs*, 19 (2), 114–53; Peter Reddaway and Peter W. Orttung (eds) (2003, vol. 1 and 2005, vol. 2) *The Dynamics of Russian Politics: Putin's reforms of Federal-Regional Relations*, Lanham, MD: Rowman and Littlefield; and Andrew Konitzer and Stephen K. Wegren (2006) 'Federalism and Political Recentralization in the Russian Federation: United Russia as the Party of Power', *The Journal of Federalism*, 36 (4), 503–22.

There is a wide range of literature on Chechnia including the late Anna Politkovskaya's (2001) *A Dirty War. A Russian Reporter in Chechnia*, London: Harvill Press, and her (2007) *A small corner of Hell. Dispatches from Chechnya*, Chicago: University of Chicago Press (trans: Alexander Burry and Tatiana Tulchinsky); Andrew Meier (2004) *Chechnya: To the Heart of a Conflict*, New York, London: W. W. Norton; A. V. Malashenko and Dmitrii Trenin (2004) *Russia's Restless Frontier: The Chechnya Factor in Post-Soviet Russia*, Washington, Carnegie Endowment for International Peace; Matthew Evangelista (2002) *The Chechen Wars. Will Russia Go the Way of the Soviet Union?*, Washington DC: Brookings Institution Press; Anatol Lieven (1998) *Chechyna: Tombstone of Russian Power*, New Haven, CT: Yale University Press; Carlotta Gall and Thomas de Waal (1997) *Chechnya. A small victorious war*, London: Pan; and a useful introduction is provided by Johanna Nichols (1995) 'Who are the Chechens?', *Central Asian Survey*, 14 (4), 573–7.

For an incisive analysis of local government go to Adrian Campbell (2006) 'State versus Society? Local Government and Reconstruction of the Russian State', *Local Government Studies*, November, 32 (5), 659–76.

Useful websites

Many of Russia's regions have their own websites; some useful links are provided below.

Republic of Tatarstan official website: http://www.tatar.ru/?lang=ENG

Moscow city mayor's website: http://www.mos.ru/

Local Government and Public Service Reform Initiative (Open Society Institute): http://lgi.osi.hu/sitemap.php

Russian Regional Reports available from the Russian and Eurasian Security site: http://www.res.ethz.ch/

Unicore, International Conflict Research at the University of Ulster, guide to Internet sources on the conflict in Chechnya: http://www.incore.ulst.ac.uk/services/cds/countries/Chechnya.html

World News website; Chechnia (articles from the world's press): http://www.chechnyanews.com/

Human Rights Watch – reports on Chechnya: http://www.hrw.org/doc?t=chechnya

Chechnya Advocacy Network: http://www.chechnyaadvocacy.org/

Chechnya Weekly **on the Jamestown Foundation website**: http://www.jamestown.org/

Conflict Studies Research Centre, Defence Academy, UK, regularly carries articles on Chechnya in their Caucasus Series: http://www.defac.ac.uk

References

Amnesty International (2000) 'Chechnya: Russian government should open doors of filtration camps to international scrutiny', *Amnesty International*, EUR 46/009/2000, 17 February, http://www.amnesty.org/

Amnesty International (2007) 'Russian Federation: What justification for Chechnya's disappeared?', *Amnesty International*, EUR 46/026/2007, 1 July, http://www.amnesty.org/

Blandy, C. W. (2007) 'Municipal Reform in the North Caucasus: A Time Bomb in the Making', *Conflict Studies Research Centre, Caucasus Series*, 07/7, March, http://www.defac.ac.uk

Blankengael, A. (1997) 'Local Self-Government vs. State Administration: The Udmurtia Decision', *East European Constitutional Review*, 6 (1), Winter, 50–4

EIU (the Economist Intelligence Unit) (2007) 'Surprise, another Kremlin win', *The Economist Intelligence Unit*, 13 March, http://economist.com/

Feifer, Gregory (2003) 'Russian officials say Chechen Referendum broadly approves Constitution', RFE/RL website: http://www.rferl.org/

Fuller, L. (2006) 'Analysis: Are Ingushetia, North Ossetia On the Verge of New Hostilities?', *Radio Free Europe/Radio Liberty* feature article, http://www.rferl.org/

Hafeez, Malik (1994) 'Tatarstan's Treaty with Russia: Autonomy or Independence', *Journal of South Asian and Middle Eastern Studies*, 18 (2), Winter, 1–36

Hanson, Philip (1996) 'Russia's 89 Federal Subjects', *Post Soviet Prospects*, 4 (8), August, http://www.csis.org/html/pspiv8.html

Human Rights Watch (1995) 'Mistreatment and abuse of detainees by Russian Forces', *Human Rights Watch*, February, http://www.hrw.org/

Human Rights Watch (2000) 'Hundreds of Chechens Detainees in "Filtration Camps"', *Human Rights Watch*, 18 February, http://www.hrw.org/

Human Rights Watch (2006) 'Widespread Torture in the Chechen Republic. Human Rights Watch Briefing Paper for the 37th Session UN Committee against Torture', 13 November, Human Rights Watch website: http://www.hrw.org/

Human Rights Watch/Helsinki Organization (1996) *Russia: The Ingush-Ossetian Conflict in the Prigorodnyi Region*, New York: Human Rights Watch

Lankina, T. (2005) 'Local Governmnet at the Crossroads', *The Moscow Times*, 3 October. Available on the Russia Profile website: http://www.russiaprofile.org/

Levin, A. (1993) 'Provozglashena Ural'kaia respublika', *Gubernatorskie Novosti* (27) July

Makrushin, A. and Yudayeva, K. (2005) 'Funding Federalism in the Power Vertical Age', *The Moscow Times*, 14 June. Available on the *Russia Profile* website, http://www.russiaprofile.org/

Martinez-Vasquez, J. and Timofeev, A. (2003) 'An Assessment of the Proposed Sub-Federal Fiscal Reforms in the Russian Federation (The Kozak Commission)', Andrew Young School of Policy Studies, Georgia State University. Available online at: http://www1.worldbank.org/wbiep/decentralization/ecalib/MartinezV.pdf

Mironov, V. (1998) 'Regional Differences in Systems of Local Government: Why Do They Occur?', *Prism*, 4 (4), 20 February, http://www.jamestown.org/

OECD (2000) *OECD Economic Surveys 1999–2000. Russian Federation*, Paris: OECD

Orttung, Robert (1996) 'Russian Regional Report', 1/16, 11 December. Available on the *Open Media Research Institute* (Zurich) website: http://www.isn.ethz.ch/

OSCE (2003) 'Russian Federation. Chechen Republic Referendum of 23 March 2003. Joint assessment Mission, Preliminary Statement', OSCE website: http://www.osce.org/

Petrov, N. (1998) 'The President's Representatives: "Moscow's Men" in the Regions', *Prism*, 4 (7), 3 April, http://www.jamestown.org/

Petrov, N. (2006) 'Local Self-Rule on the Line', *The Moscow Times*, 24 January. Available on the Russia Profile website: http://www.russiaprofile.org/

Project on Ethnic Relations (1992) 'Nationality policy in the Russian Federation', Project on Ethnic Relations website: http://www.per-usa.org/1997-2007/natio_po.htm

Reuters (2007) 'Pro-Kremlin party wins in 13 of 14 regional polls', *The Guardian*, 13 March, 21

Russia Profile (2006) 'The Russia Federation', Russia Profile website: http://www.russiaprofile.org/resources/territory/index.wbp

Smirnov, A. (2006) 'Kremlin signs Power-Sharing Treaty with Tatarstan', 21 November, *Eurasia Daily Monitor*, 3 (216), Jamestown Foundation website: http://www.jamestown.org

Smirnov, A. (2007) 'Putin awards Shamiev a Medal Instead of a treaty', 1 February, *Eurasia Daily Monitor*, 4 (23), Jamestown Foundation website: http://www.jamestown.org

Solnick, S. L. (1995) 'Federal Bargaining in Russia', *East European Constitutional Review*, 4 (4), Fall, 52–8

Szajkowski, B. (1993) 'Will Russia disintegrate into Bantustans?', *The World Today*, 49 (8–9), August–September, 172–6

Tatarstan's Treaty with Russia (1994) 'Tatarstan's Treaty with Russia, February 1994', *Journal of South Asian and Middle Eastern Studies*, 18 (1), Fall, 61–7

Tatarstan (2007) 'Treaty on Delimitation of Jurisdictional Subjects and Powers between Bodies of Public Authority of the Russian Federation and Bodies of Public Authority of the Republic of Tatarstan', 26 June, Republic of Tatarstan Official website: http://www.tatar.ru/english/append20.html

Teague, E. (1994) 'Centre-Periphery Relations in the Russian Federation' in R. Szporluk (ed.) *National Identity and Ethnicity in Russia and the New States of Eurasia*, Chapter 2, Armonk: M.E. Sharpe, Inc.

Traynor, I. (2000) 'Putin redraws the map of Russia', *The Guardian*, 15 May, 13

Unger, A. L. (1981) *Constitutional Development in the USSR. A Guide to the Soviet Constitutions*, London: Methuen

Yasmann, V. (2006) 'Analysis: the Future of Russia's "Ethnic republics" ', *RFE/RL Feature Article*, 21 April, RFE/RL website: http://www.rferl.org/

Zlotnik, M. (1996) 'Russia's governors and the Presidential elections', *Post Soviet Prospects*, 4 (4), April, Center for Strategic and International Studies website: http://www.csis.org/

Chapter 8

The judiciary

Learning objectives

- To explain the importance of judicial reform to Russia's democratisation.
- To outline the court system.
- To examine what happens to an individual from arrest to imprisonment.
- To introduce Russia's commitment to human rights and the role of the ombudsman.

Introduction

The judiciary is the third branch of government and is composed of the courts and the judges who administer justice. In democracies the three branches of government (judiciary, executive and legislature) ideally act as checks and balances on each other and an independent judiciary, free from political or ideological bias, is a basic requirement of a separation of these powers. Democracies need the rule of law to function. The RF Constitution (1993) is the fundamental law and all other laws should be framed in accordance with its basic principles, not least with its commitment to individual, civil and human rights. In the 1990s Russia needed to rewrite its laws, institutions needed to be reformed, and lawyers, judges and law enforcement operatives needed to be retrained. All of these tasks are time consuming and costly and, as with all Russia's reforms, they were conducted against a backdrop of escalating crime and in a context of limited state revenues to fund reform.

In the 1990s the Russian judiciary slowly reformed and began to assert its independence; but just as Putin strengthened the executive's domination over the legislature (see Chapters 5 and 6) he also brought the judiciary increasingly under executive control. Under Putin there were a number of high profile cases against oligarchs, and environmental and human rights activists among others, in which criminal charges were clearly brought for political motives and were part of a concerted campaign to control civil society. In a democracy law enforcement should conform to constitutional norms; it must be fair, transparent, predictable and timely. The judiciary should provide justice for ordinary citizens, social and political organisations and businesses in their dealings with each other and with those in authority. For the individual, how they are treated by government and state officials is a crucial part of their experience of a country's justice system; this might include their experience of the investigation of a crime, arrest, detention, court procedures or even imprisonment. Unfortunately in the opinion of its citizens the Russian judiciary and law enforcement agencies fall far below desired standards. In November 2006 the Public Opinion Foundation asked which government and public organisations and agencies were the most corrupt. The police, customs and law enforcement agencies were rated the most corrupt by 52 per cent of respondents, the traffic police came second cited by 45 per cent of respondents, and the courts and prosecutors' offices came fourth cited by 25 per cent of respondents (FOM, 2006).

The executive and the judiciary

The Imperial Russian and Soviet tradition

The pre-revolutionary Russian and the Soviet tradition was that the judiciary served the interests of the state, rather than acting as the protector of the individual and his/her human and civil rights and freedoms. The Soviet tradition refused to countenance the existence of an autonomous civil society and also believed that the executive, legislature and judiciary should be fused in a system of monopolistic party control. Imperial Russia and the USSR lacked a strong legal tradition and the ruler, whether a tsar or a CPSU secretary, was always above the law. The law was not designed to protect the individual from the arbitrary actions of the state; it was quite simply an instrument of tsarist or CPSU rule. In the USSR the phenomenon known as 'telephone law' meant that local party bosses might decide to take an interest in a case and phone the relevant judge with an instruction about the required verdict. Judges were not expected to be neutral arbiters, they were expected to obey. Soviet people were used to the CPSU's instrumental use of the law to get the results it wanted. The important thing for a soviet citizen was not so much to obey the law as to have a protector. This was an important feature of the patron–client relationships that were such a feature of soviet life. In return for loyalty a patron (protector) would use their official position to protect their client from the consequences of their actions. So, just as a party boss could ensure that a political dissident was found guilty of a trumped-up charge, they could also ensure that a loyal underling's (client's) drunken teenager did not end up in prison.

Perestroika and the soviet judiciary

Under Gorbachev legal reform was part of democratisation. It began in 1986 with a declaration that everything that was not expressly forbidden was legal. This seems like a modest innovation, especially in a country where copies of the legal code were not readily available to the average citizen. It did, however, entail recognition of the importance of the rule of law for all people and institutions, including the CPSU. Legal reform began in earnest in 1988 with the stated aim of turning the USSR into what soviet legal scholars called a 'law-based state' (*pravovoye gosudarstvo*) and what western Europeans and North Americans call the commitment to the 'rule of law'. This emphasis on the law-based state was also part of Gorbachev's endeavours to base the legitimacy of the soviet state on legal-rationality, rather than on the rather discredited claims of the CPSU and its ideology of Marxism-Leninism. This legal-rationality entailed ending the arbitrariness of CPSU rule and creating democratic, transparent, routinised and accountable decision-making procedures. An independent judiciary was the logical corollary of this changing basis of legitimation. The establishment of a Constitutional Court in 1991 was one of the great innovations of the *perestroika* period. For the first time in Russian or Soviet history the country's leaders were no longer above the law and their actions could be declared unconstitutional. It was the tentative beginning of a separation of powers and an independent judiciary.

From Yeltsin to Putin's 'dictatorship of law'

A legal career was not a prestigious career in the USSR and so Russia entered the 1990s with only a small legal profession, trained in the soviet ways of thinking. Nonetheless in the 1990s the Russian judiciary slowly began to assert its independence. Putin wanted Russia to be a stable and secure country and an integral part of the global economy; on becoming president he announced that judicial reform was a top priority and that he would introduce a 'dictatorship of law'. Yeltsin's legacy of a weak state that was unable to collect taxes or control criminal gangs meant that life for most citizens was one of insecurity, economic deprivation, turmoil and corruption rather than democracy and civil rights. Establishing a dictatorship of law was part of the strengthening of the state, another of Putin's stated aims. A 'dictatorship of law' should have meant that citizens would be able to rely on a new stable legal system with fair courts, rather than the arbitrary decisions of state prosecutors and corrupt judges. However, while in most cases this was Putin's ideal, his concept of a dictatorship of law had more in common with traditional Russian-Soviet thinking than with western concepts of the rule of law. Under Putin's dictatorship of law attaining desired results, such as strengthening the state or a particular legal decision, had priority over maintaining particular legal processes and concepts. For example, when Putin announced that he was going to create seven new federal districts headed by presidential representatives, he also stated that he would dismiss any of the existing governors who had acted illegally. According to the Constitution only a court can order such a dismissal, not the president. However, the law could be ignored when it did not fit Putin's goal of strengthening the state.

Just as the CPSU was not interested in every case that came before the soviet courts, the Putin leadership was highly selective about when it intervened and the vast majority of cases proceeded without attention from the executive, although there would be pressure from the Procuracy and law enforcement agencies to secure convictions. The courts are still used for political ends and soviet-style 'telephone justice' enjoyed a renaissance under Putin. For example, the courts have been used to removing election candidates who were unacceptable to the Kremlin. Yury Lodkin, the governor of Bryansk, had his candidature removed in December 2004; the mayors of Pskov and Volgograd who had tried to compete against their governors were also barred from the elections. Putin has also exempted selected government officials and business people from prosecution, even for serious offences.

Box 8.1 RF Human Rights Ombudsman Vladimir Lukin on the merger of the executive and the courts

> The situation with the independence of courts in Russia is very bad. Everywhere I have been in the Russian regions there are very serious complaints about the actions of judges and the courts. In some regions they are clearly merging with the executive branch of power and they practically form the only mechanism for implementing the will of the executive branch and those who stand behind it.

Source: Jeremy Bransten (2005) 'East: Postcommunist Ombudsmen Persevere Despite Obstacles', 29 November, *RFE/RL* website: http://www.rferl.org/

The manipulation of Moscow City Courts

The Kremlin and its allies are able to exert pressure on the courts through the chief judges or chairs of the courts. The chairs are appointed for six years and reappointment depends on a positive review by the presidential administration, making the chairs vulnerable to executive pressure. The chairs in turn allocate cases to judges they believe will deliver the desired verdict, liaise with the prosecution and generally make life difficult for independent-minded judges. Olga Yegorova, whose husband is an FSB general, was appointed chair of the Moscow City Court by the combined efforts of the Kremlin and the FSB, contrary to appointment procedures (Roxburgh, 2005). Between 2000 and March 2005, she removed 80 judges from Moscow City Court and other Moscow city and district court judges resigned because they were placed under direct pressure by the Prosecutors and/or Yegorova to bring in particular verdicts (Page, 2005). In one high profile case Judge Olga Kudeshkina was ordered to find Pavel Zaitsev, a police investigator who had been looking into customs fraud involving people from the security services, guilty of abusing his office. Kudeshkina acquitted Zaitsev and was then called in to see Yegorova, who proceeded to shout at and question Kudeshkina about her decision. In a blatant example of prosecution interference in the courts, Yegorova even phoned the prosecutor general in Kudeshkina's presence and said she would find out what was going on. Kudeshkina was removed from the case and from the court in 2004, officially for being too lenient but really for going public about the lack of court independence. According to another former Moscow city judge Aleksandr Melikov, who was also officially dismissed for being too lenient, it was fairer in soviet times because people knew what to expect, rather than the current

Mikhail Khodorkovsky (L) and his business partner Platon Lebedev (R) listen during the hearing of their case in district court in Moscow, August 2004.

situation when 'they say in public that we are independent when in fact we are not' (ibid.). Melikov continues, 'They needed a judicial system that would guarantee the necessary decisions in cases like Khodorkovsky's' (ibid.) and that Russia has the same conviction rate in criminal cases heard by judges as was seen in Stalin's last years – 99 per cent.

Mikhail Khodorkovsky and the Yukos Affair

In October 2003 the oligarch Mikhail Khodorkovsky was arrested for tax evasion and fraud. His trial was marred by procedural irregularities and the prosecution failed to produce any documents linking Khodorkovsky and Yukos executive Platon Lebedev to the alleged crime. Khodorkovsky and Lebedev did not qualify for a jury trial and so they were tried by three judges, who in 2005 sentenced them each to nine years in prison. The trial was clearly politically motivated as Khodorkovsky opposed Putin and the Kremlin who wanted to gain access to his huge Yukos energy company. The trial sent out the message that oligarchs should not oppose Putin and also that property rights were not always secure. Putin used his network in the security services, law enforcement agencies and the tax police, to provide the 'information' he needed against the oligarchs. The tax records and business activities of the oligarchs who supported Putin were not so rigorously scrutinised. The Yukos affair is not unique and similar smaller scale trials have taken place in the regions. Putin's first oligarch-target was Vladimir Gusinsky who was arrested in June 1999 and charged with defrauding the state of an estimated US$10 million during his acquisition of the Russian Video-Channel 11. Gusinsky also opposed Putin's election and government policy in Chechnia and was one of the few Russian public figures to support NATO's actions in Yugoslavia in 1999.

The RF Constitution (1993) and the Constitutional Court

The Constitutional Court 1991–1993

Following the collapse of the USSR the Constitutional Court was in the rather bizarre situation of being a would-be pillar of Russia's new democracy which nonetheless had to apply the discredited 1978 RSFSR Constitution and its many, somewhat contradictory amendments. However, it moved quickly to assert itself at a time when Yeltsin was making full use of his power to rule by decree. The Constitutional Court's first ruling in January 1992 declared the presidential decree merging the old Soviet Secret Police (KGB) and the Ministry of the Interior unconstitutional. In November 1992 the Constitutional Court, while upholding the president's ban on the Communist Party in the aftermath of the August 1991 coup, ruled that the president could not ban its grassroots organisations. Under its first chair Valery Zorkin, the Constitutional Court was embroiled in the drafting of the new RF Constitution, which necessarily meant that the Constitutional Court was involved in the power struggle between the president and the parliament. In the power struggle both sides could find support for their arguments in the 1978 Constitution and/or its amendments. So, for example, while the 1978 Constitution did provide some support for a separation of powers the amended Article 104 stressed the omnipotence of the Congress of People's Deputies (Nikitinsky, 1997: 84).

During the December 1992 constitutional crisis the Constitutional Court mediated a compromise solution between president and parliament, but as 1993 progressed Zorkin seemed to favour the Congress of People's Deputies over the president. In 1993 the Constitutional Court ruled that Yeltsin had acted illegally when he ordered the dissolution of the parliament. On 21 September 1993 Yeltsin responded to the escalating constitutional crisis by suspending the Constitution. Ten of the Constitutional Court's 14 judges voted against this suspension and in October 1993 Yeltsin responded by suspending the Constitutional Court.

The RF Constitution

The 1993 RF Constitution replaced the 1978 RSFSR Constitution with one appropriate to a democratic country with a market economy. It contains some important statements about the nature of the Russian state. In contrast to its soviet forebears the 1993 Constitution expressly forbids the creation of a state ideology and guarantees freedom of conscience, religion, thought and speech (Arts 28 and 29). Article 1 describes Russia as 'a democratic federative rule of law state', it is multinational (see Preamble), individual rights and freedoms are of supreme value (Art. 2) and the people are sovereign (Art. 3). Subsequent articles guarantee freedom of movement, conscience, belief, expression, association, and assembly. Article 46 guarantees judicial protection and affirms the individual's right, 'if all available means of legal protection inside the state have been exhausted', to appeal to international bodies. Article 15 states that generally recognised principles and norms of international law, and the international treaties to which Russia is

Box 8.2 The Constitutional Court

Location: From 1991–2008 in Kitai-gorod central Moscow. On 12 May 2008 completed its relocation to St Petersburg.

First Constitutional Court October 1991 to October 1993

Created after the adoption of the Constitutional Court of the RSFSR Act (July 1991). In October 1991 the RSFSR Congress of Soviets elected the court's 13 judges (maximum age 65) for unlimited terms.

Valery Zorkin – Chair   1 November 1991 to 5 October 1993

Second Constitutional Court (resumed work February 1995)

The court's legal basis: including its composition, functions and jurisdiction of Constitutional Court are set out in Art. 125 of the 1993 RF Constitution and the 1994 Law on the Constitutional Court.

The judges: must be at least 40, a Russian citizen, have a legal education, have been a lawyer for at least 15 years and have a recognised higher qualification; the maximum age is 70. There are 19 judges who serve for 12-year terms. Judges are nominated by the president subject to ratification by Federation Council.

Structure: two chambers, one presided over by the chair and the other by the deputy chair.

Jurisdiction: consideration of the constitutionality of International treaties before they are ratified by the Duma, the actions of the president, the parliament and lower levels of government. It rules on the impeachment of the president, relations between the two chambers of the Federal Assembly and between central and republican, regional and local governments, and other government agencies. It also rules on the compliance of federal laws with the Constitution.

Other aspects of its operation: the Constitutional Court is not permitted to judge the constitutionality of a law on its own initiative. Laws may be submitted to the Constitutional Court by the president, government, 20 per cent of Federation Council members or Duma deputies and the Supreme Court (Art. 125.2). Any federal court may also ask for a Constitutional Court ruling if they suspect a law is unconstitutional; a private citizen may also ask the Constitutional Court to rule if a particular law violates their rights. All the judges (unless ill or if they have an interest in a case) meet together in the chambers or in plenaries. They decide by a vote and are not allowed to abstain.

Republican Constitutional and Regional Charter Courts: have been set up since the mid-1990s and are subordinate to the RF Constitutional Court.

Nikolai Vitruk – Acting Chair   6 October 1993 to 13 February 1995
Vladimir Tumanov – Chair   13 February 1995 to 20 February 1997
Marat Baglai – Chair   20 February 1997 to 21 February 2003
Valery Zorkin – Chair   21 February 2003–

Source: Constitutional Court website: http://www.ksrf.ru/ (Russian only)

a party, are constituent parts of its legal system and take precedence over domestic laws.

Robert Sharlet a specialist on Soviet and Russian constitutions and law, describes the 1993 Constitution as designed to achieve four objectives for the new Russian political system. First, it establishes the citizen 'as an autonomous person and prime actor of the political universe who is beholden to neither ruler nor ideology'. Secondly, it buffers 'the citizen from the state in the criminal justice process by creating a durable process of law'. Thirdly, it empowers 'the citizen for participation in the political life of the society'. Finally, 'the new civil/political rights are designed to equip the citizen for involvement in the emerging market economy' (Sharlet, 1997: 135). It also continues the soviet practice of providing a variety of social provisions such as a right to housing (Art. 40), healthcare (Art. 41), education (Art. 43), and even to a decent environment (Art. 42). The RF Constitution is Russia's fundamental or basic law, so all the constitutions of Russia's republics and the charters of the regions, as well as all other federal laws and republican and regional laws should conform to it. As the 1990s progressed this principle was violated to varying degrees in most republics and regions. After 1993 Russian federal laws also needed to be reformed, soviet-era laws that were unconstitutional, no longer appropriate or which did not meet the needs of the new Russia's changing society and economy had to be removed or replaced.

The Constitutional Court after 1993

Yeltsin and his allies believed that under Valery Zorkin the first Constitutional Court had favoured the parliamentary cause and had been too partisan in its judgments. Therefore, when the new Constitutional Court finally began to operate in 1995 it did so with a much narrower brief than its predecessor. It could no longer rule on the constitutionality of the actions of top state officials nor initiate its own cases. It was also made more difficult for other bodies to ask the Constitutional Court for judgments, a right that previously could be exercised by individual deputies. The Constitutional Court is also hampered by the lack of mechanisms to ensure compliance with its decisions. For example, Moscow mayor Yury Luzhkov has ignored numerous rulings saying that his administration is violating constitutional guarantees of freedom of movement by retaining the soviet-era system of residence permits (*propiski*). In 1995 the term *propiska* (residence permit) was officially replaced by *registratsiya* (registration), but most people still refer to a *propiska*. Luzhkov argues that Moscow needs to limit its population to prevent overcrowding, ensure security and to prevent terrorism. Registration has not prevented terrorism but has resulted in the violation of constitutional rights, major corruption as individuals bribe officials to be allowed to stay in Moscow, and discrimination, particularly against people from the Northern Caucasus.

Under Vladimir Tumanov, the Constitutional Court was careful not to become involved in what might be considered political matters. So, for example, before the 1995 State Duma elections the Constitutional Court refused the request of a group of deputies to rule on the constitutionality of the 5 per cent threshold for representation on the party list system. The result was that 'political cases' such as complaints about election results or the refusal to register candidates for elections were taken to the courts of general jurisdiction, including the Supreme Court (Nikitinsky, 1997: 85). In 2003 Valery Zorkin, who has a reputation as a liberal and an upholder of judicial independence, became chair once again. In 2005 the Constitutional Court examined the constitutionality of Putin's decision to appoint rather than elect governors. Before considering the case Zorkin had said that he believed the ending of gubernatorial elections contradicted the Constitution (Gessen, 2005: 7), but the court nonetheless ruled that governors could be appointed rather than elected, so putting in place an important component of Putin's strengthening of the power vertical and sealing his domination of the Federation Council (see Chapters 5–7). Just one week before the Constitutional Court was due to hear the case Putin replaced Mikhail Mityukov with Mikhail Krotov as the Plenipotentiary representative of the President in the Constitutional Court. Krotov was a member of Putin's Petersburger network and a Kremlin insider whose role was to ensure the Constitutional Court brought in the 'right' decision. Zorkin remains chair of the Constitutional Court and in an interview with Reuters entitled 'Russian Courts Must Check Kremlin Power Says Judge' published in 2006, argued that while Russia needs a strong and capable executive, a strong presidential power, this is not an aim in itself and that Russia also needs independent courts to protect citizens' rights and to provide checks and to rein in the executive (Lowe, 2006: 3).

The judicial system

Judges

The 1993 Constitution (Art. 119) states that judges must be Russian citizens, at least 25 years old, have a law degree and have worked in the legal profession for at least five years. The 1992 federal law 'On the Status of Judges in the RF' and the Constitution also established that judges should be independent, obey the Constitution, have permanent tenure and enjoy immunity from prosecution except in cases provided by federal law (Arts 120–122). These provisions are supposed to stop judges from being susceptible to political influences and pressures. The Constitution (Art. 128.1) does, however, give the president the right to appoint judges to the Constitutional Court, Supreme Court and Higher Arbitration Court, subject to confirmation by the Federation Council. This infringes the principle of the separation of executive and judicial powers and, as Putin ensured that the president is able to dominate the Federation Council, this also means that presidential nominations will be accepted. Putin began the practice of holding regular meetings with the chairs of the Constitutional Court, Supreme Court and Supreme Arbitration Court; in order to keep them 'on message' and to ensure that they implement the Kremlin's policies. According to the Constitution the president also has the right to appoint judges to other federal courts in accordance with federal law (Art. 128.2) as well as the judges and chairs in most superior and district courts. Once a term is completed the Kremlin decides whether to reappoint a chair or a

Box 8.3 Russia's judiciary

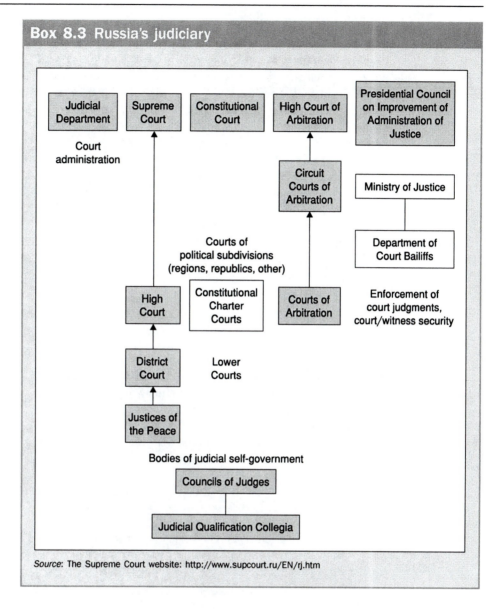

Source: The Supreme Court website: http://www.supcourt.ru/EN/rj.htm

judge following a performance review. This should root out the incompetent and corrupt, but also means that judges feel under pressure to toe the Kremlin line (Mereu, 2004).

The independence of judges may also be compromised by financial inducements. The 1992 federal law 'On the Status of Judges in the RF' guaranteed judges a range of benefits including apartments and access to healthcare; unfortunately judges, particularly at the sub-federal level, are not adequately remunerated, which leaves them open to corruption and bribery. Judges are also vulnerable to physical attacks, threats against their families and even assassination. Poor pay and working conditions together with threats have led to judges leaving their posts, resulting in vacancies. In 2005 judges' salaries were substantially increased, but bribery remains a problem and there are still vacancies. The law 'On the Status of Judges' (2002) sought to reduce corruption in the appointment of judges and to make them more accountable by introducing disciplinary procedures and a compulsory retirement age of 65, rather than 70 as before. In the wake of the Beslan attack Putin took another step that eroded the independence of the judiciary by taking control of the Supreme Court office that supervises the appointment and dismissal of judges.

Since 1996 the OSCE has worked with the Supreme Court and the Russian Academy of Law on professional training programmes for judges and since 1998 the Russian Academy of Jurisprudence has also provided specialised training for judges. Unfortunately judges still tend to be assessed according to how many cases they try – in particular how many guilty verdicts they pass – rather than on the soundness of their verdicts. In 2006 Valery Zorkin argued that the belief that Mikhail Khodorkovsky's trial was stage-managed by the Kremlin to ensure a guilty verdict had deepened the perception that the Russian judiciary is weak and incompetent, and that judges tailor their verdicts to what officials want (Lowe, 2006: 3).

TV and the law

Although public opinion surveys routinely report popular dissatisfaction with the Russian judiciary, nonetheless there is growing popular interest in the judiciary. The reality TV programme *Chas Suda* (Court Hour) seeks to educate people about the judicial system by explaining to its viewers how courts are supposed to function and about their rights. Viewers write in their thousands to have their cases 'tried' on TV by a real judge and lawyers.

Box 8.4　President Putin on the independence of the judiciary

. . . the judicial branch's independence is not an honourable privilege but the necessary condition that it will perform its constitutional duty in the system of divided powers.

Source: 'President Putin Speaks Out on Judicial Branch's Independence', *RIA Novosti*, 30 November, 2004

Courts of general jurisdiction

The structure of the courts of general jurisdiction

Civil, criminal and administrative cases are heard by the courts of general jurisdiction. They form a four-tier court system beginning with the municipal level, then the district and regional levels and finally the Supreme Court. Justices of the Peace (JPs) were re-established in 2000 and their jurisdiction was then broadened in the new Criminal Procedure Code (2002). JPs judge minor criminal cases and may give a maximum three-year sentence in all but two republics and regions. A three-tier system of military courts also forms part of the system of the courts of general jurisdiction.

The Supreme Court

Decisions taken by the lower courts of general jurisdiction can be appealed to the Supreme Court by either the prosecutors or the defence. Double jeopardy, being tried twice for the same crime, is not prohibited. Prosecutors tend to appeal most jury acquittals and between 2000 and 2005, 25–50 per cent of not-guilty verdicts returned by juries were reversed by the Supreme Court (Finn, 2005). One high-profile example is the case of the physicist Valentin Danilov who was acquitted of espionage, specifically of selling secret satellite technology to China, by a jury. The Supreme Court reinstated the espionage case and in November 2004 he was sentenced to 14 years in prison. According to Sergei Nasonov, a professor of criminal law at Moscow State Law Academy, although in theory there are only limited grounds upon which a jury verdict may be overturned on appeal, such as the discovery of new evidence, in practice the Supreme Court has interpreted the law very broadly so that, 'A jury verdict is hardly the final word' (ibid.).

Box 8.5 The RF Supreme Court

The 23 judges: are nominated by the president and appointed by the Federation Council. A judge must be a Russian citizen, aged 35 or over, have a legal education and have been a lawyer for at least 10 years.

Jurisdiction: the Supreme Court is the highest judicial authority on civil, criminal, administrative and other matters, according to Article 126 of the RF Constitution.

Composition: a chair, first deputy and deputy chairs, justices of the court and people's assessor.

Structure: Plenum, Presidium of the Court and Judicial Chambers (Civil Cases, Criminal Cases and the Military Chamber). For those cases when the Supreme Court has the original jurisdiction they are heard in Colleges. Appeals on their decisions are brought to the Cassation College. Colleges review the decisions of the lower courts, but appeals are heard by the Presidium.

Plenary sessions: are held at least once in four months and must be attended by all the Supreme Court judges and the RF Prosecutor General. The sessions study the decisions of the lower courts and adopt resolutions, which are recommendations on how to interpret law.

Vyacheslav Lebedev – Chair   26 July 1989–

Supreme Court website: http://www.supcourt.ru/ (Russian only)

The arbitration courts

The structure of the arbitration courts

The arbitration court system was set up in 1992 to deal with commercial disputes that now arise following Russia's transition to a market economy. It includes the arbitration courts of Russia's federal subjects used elsewhere, regional, city and appellate circuit arbitration courts as well as the RF Supreme Arbitration Court. Anton Ivanov, the current chair of the Higher Arbitration Court is a close friend of Dmitry Medvedev from St Petersburg.

Box 8.6 The RF Supreme Arbitration Court

Composition and appointment: its 53 judges are nominated by the president and appointed by the Federation Council.

Jurisdiction: the highest judicial body resolving economic disputes, according to Article 127 of the RF Constitution.

Structure: a Plenum, Presidium, Judicial Collegium for civil and other legal relations disputes, Judicial Collegium for administrative legal disputes, and eight judicial panels.

Composition of the Plenum: a chair, deputy chair and the Supreme Arbitration Court judges. Representatives of other branches of the judiciary, legislative and executive bodies, scientific institutions and ordinary citizens may also attend.

Veniamin Yakovlev – Chair	23 January 1992 to 26 January 2005
Anton Ivanov – Chair	26 January 2005–

Higher Arbitration Court website: http://www.arbitr.ru/eng/index.htm

---

The Russian justice system

The rights of the accused

Russia today has two seemingly irreconcilable aims: to combat rising crime and to create a democratic law-governed state. According to Chapter 2 'Human and civil rights and freedoms' of the RF Constitution no one can be held for more than 48 hours without being charged (habeas corpus) (Art. 22.2), there is a presumption of innocence (Art. 49), the onus is on the prosecution to prove guilt (Art. 49.2), and the accused has a right to defence counsel (Art. 48). The right to legal counsel is complicated by a continuing shortage of affordable lawyers especially outside the big cities. In June 1994 Yeltsin issued a presidential decree 'On Urgent Measures for the Defence of the Population against Banditry and Other Manifestations of Organised Crime', which contradicted the Constitution's habeas corpus provision. The decree gave prosecutors rather than the courts the right to empower the police to search, confiscate their documents and hold for up to 30 days anybody they suspected of involvement in organised crime. The decree was extended in 1996 to facilitate the work of the Moscow police in their campaign against the so-called 'ethnic mafias', the criminal gangs from the Caucasus and especially Chechnia. A very basic problem was that simply being a Chechen was evidence enough of criminal activity, and justification for the loss of human and civil rights and freedoms. Moscow police used the decree, which also gave them to right to expel people form Moscow, to round up the city's homeless. Although the decree was repealed in 1997 the practice of ignoring the rights of the accused continues.

Box 8.7 The Procuracy

The Procuracy (*Prokuratura*): is the state agency responsible for criminal investigation and prosecution, and the protection of human rights.

Structure: it has a single, centralised, hierarchical structure.

The RF prosecutor general: is Russia's top law enforcement official. A list of holders of the office follows.

Valentine Stepankov	28 February 1991 to 5 October 1993
Aleksei Kazannik	5 October 1993 to 26 April 1994 (suspended from 26 February 1994)
Aleksei Ilyushenko	26 February 1994 to 8 October 1995 (acting)
Oleg Gaidanov	8 October 1995 to 24 October 1995 (acting)
Yury Skuratov	24 October 1995 to 17 May 2000 (suspended from 2 April 1999)
Yury Chaika	2 April 1999 to 6 August 1999 (acting for Skuratov)
Vladimir Ustinov	6 August 1999 (acting for Skuratov from 17 May 2000) to 2 June 2006
Yury Chaika	23 June 2006–

General Procuracy website: http://www.genproc.gov.ru/ (Russian only)

The Procuracy

The Procuracy was the pre-eminent institution of the soviet criminal justice system, combining police and prosecution functions, including investigating cases, signing arrest warrants and presenting the prosecution case in court. A prosecutor's combination of roles was supposed to ensure adherence to the due process of the law. Once a prosecutor presented their evidence a guilty verdict was a foregone conclusion. In this way the Procuracy in the person of the prosecutor acquired its de facto third function as the judge of guilt or innocence before a case even came to court. Therefore, the role of the soviet courts, judges and defence lawyers was reduced to questions of sentencing rather than establishing guilt or innocence. The result was that the prosecutor was part of the soviet state's control system rather than part of a justice system.

In 1992 the Procuracy lost the right to supervise the legality of court proceedings (Mikhailovskaya, 1999: 101) but the 1993 Constitution (Art. 129) and the 1995 'Law on the Prosecutor' maintained the Procuracy's investigative and prosecuting functions, and its role as the supreme supervisor of legality in the RF. The Procuracy also retained its soviet-era role of investigating citizens' complaints against state bodies, a function which since 1992 it has shared with the courts. There remains a built-in conflict between the Procuracy's supervisory and oversight function on the one hand and its investigatory/police function on the other. A prosecutor works very closely with the police and shares the police's primary concern with securing a conviction (Roxburgh, 2005).

The courts and the Procuracy

Since the early 1990s the courts of general jurisdiction (hereafter courts) have been in competition with the Procuracy over jurisdiction. Russian legal reformers generally see the transfer of functions from the Procuracy to the courts as essential to the creation of an independent judiciary and a law-governed state. The 1993 RF Constitution, therefore, transferred the authority to approve pre-trial detention (Art. 22.2), telephone bugging, the interception of correspondence (Art. 23.2) and house searches (Art. 25) from the Procuracy to the courts. Even so in 1996 the Supreme Court, under its chair Vyacheslav Lebedev, ruled that the Procuracy had an automatic right to challenge a court's decision to release someone from custody. The Procuracy had argued for this right on the grounds that mafia gangs were either intimidating or bribing lower court judges to release criminals. According to Karinna Moskalenko, a leading human rights lawyer, although judges are supposed to be impartial in practice they side with the prosecutors, for example by denying appeals to defence lawyers without valid reasons (ibid.). The new Criminal Procedure Code which was phased in during 2002–2004 was supposed to strengthen the role of the judiciary in relation to the Procuracy, for example by ending the then current practice of judges giving prosecutors additional time to improve their cases; however, this practice continues. The new Code also requires judicial approval of arrest warrants, searches, seizures and detention. However, according to the independently-minded Sergei Pashin, a former Moscow City judge who was sacked in 2000, the situation has not improved. Judges now issue even more arrest warrants than the prosecutors did (ibid.). According to Pashin one-third of judges begin their careers in the police or prosecution services and have retained a prosecution mindset. He also points out that the practice of secret trials is spreading, allowing prosecutors to fudge cases by introducing irrelevant secret materials.

The courts

According to Article 124 of the Constitution all courts are financed from the federal budget but during the 1990s the Ministry of Justice did not always have enough funds to pay judges' salaries and benefits, the courts' winter heating bills, electricity and telephone bills, or provide adequate security and hotel accommodation for juries. The lack of funding was so bad that in 1996 there was widespread talk of a crisis in the courts. At this time in Moscow alone, 95 of its 450 judges' posts were vacant, severely compromising the capital's judicial system. The problem is only slowly being addressed, particularly at the local court level where there are difficulties in paying wages, maintaining buildings, buying equipment and paying telephone bills. The result is that just as in soviet times courts and judges are dependent upon republican, regional, municipal and local government to fund their activities, which makes them vulnerable to political pressure and corruption. In January 2003 Prime Minister Mikhail Kasyanov announced that funding for the judicial system would be increased by one-third and additional courts were built under Putin. In August 2005 Putin signed a bill providing state protection for victims and witnesses, including funding for new homes, jobs and identities if necessary.

Trials

Article 123 of the Constitution establishes that trials shall be open and that criminal trials may not be held in absentia, except in cases specified by federal law. Trials must also be conducted on an adversarial and equal basis. Jury trials had been introduced into Russia in 1864 but were abandoned after the Bolshevik Revolution. Soviet trial practice was for a judge to sit with two people's assessors, who were supposed to be independent but who always agreed with the judge. The reintroduction of the jury system in the 1993 Constitution (Art. 47.2) requires not just a change in procedures but also in legal thinking. In a jury system a clear distinction has to be drawn between 'law' and 'fact', as the jurors decide the true facts of a case and the judge decides the law. In the soviet system no such distinction was made. The judge was an inquisitor who had both to ascertain the facts and to apply the law. Jury trials are based on an adversarial rather than this inquisitorial principle of judicial proceedings. The prosecution and the defence have to compete to persuade the jury that their version of the facts is correct and this is supposed to ensure that the accused gets a fair trial.

Jury trials are not without their opponents. For the police and the prosecutors the requirement to prove a case means that they have to put more effort and resources into putting a case together at a time of rising crime and, in the pre-Putin period, decreasing resources. There are also fears that jurors will be bribed by criminals, especially as the courts do not have the funds to keep juries isolated during a trial or to reimburse them for loss of income. Juries are also generally intolerant of sloppy prosecution cases and have been alert to illegally gathered evidence and so their role is an important guarantee of due process. In the 1990s Russia only experimented with jury trials and tended to use them just for the most serious cases. In July 2002 a new criminal procedural code came into effect, which stressed the importance of moving to jury trials; by 2003 jury trials had been adopted for serious crimes in all republics and regions except the Republic of Chechnia. Not guilty verdicts are now given in about 15 per cent of jury trials (ibid.) which is a major improvement on the soviet-era near hundred per cent conviction rate.

Problems remain, however: judges still tend to give the prosecution extra time to prepare cases, jury selection is not always impartial and, amazingly, it is illegal to tell juries if torture has been used to extract a confession.

Box 8.8 The Ministry of Justice

Is responsible for the administration of the judicial system, naming judges and establishing courts below the federal level. The minister is directly responsible to the president.

The ministers

Nikolai Fyodorov	14 July 1990 to 24 March 1993
Yury Kalmykov	13 April 1993 (acting to 5 August 1993) to 7 December 1994
Valentin Kovalyov	5 January 1995 (suspended from 25 June 1995) to 2 July 1995
Georgy Kulikov	28 June 1997 to 2 July 1997
Sergei Stepashin	2 July 1997 to 30 March 1998
Pavel Krashennikov	30 March 1998 (acting to 30 April 1998) to 17 August 1999
Yury Chaika	17 August 1999 to 23 June 2006
Vladimir Ustinov	23 June 2006 to 12 May 2008
Aleksandr Konovalov	12 May 2008–

The law enforcement bodies

Law enforcement is the responsibility of the Ministry of Interior, the Federal Security Service (FSB) and the Procuracy. While the FSB's primary responsibilities are security, counter-terrorism and counter-intelligence, they have a broader remit including the fight against organised crime and corruption. The FSB is directly responsible to the president and their activities have very limited oversight from the courts and the prosecutor general. The police are called the militia (*militsiia*) and fall under the jurisdiction of the Ministry of the Interior. The police are subdivided into public security units responsible for the routine maintenance of public order and criminal units which are subdivided into specialised units, such as the Main Directorate for Organised Crime and the Federal Tax Police Service, which is now independent. Although there have been attempts to reform law enforcement bodies since 1992, they remain a bastion of authoritarian thinking and action. They are also under-funded, lack up-to-date equipment, and suffer from low prestige and unsurprisingly low morale. Their work necessarily brings them into contact with criminals, which gives them ample opportunities to become involved in crime and corruption themselves.

Perversely as the courts since 1992 have increasingly required the police to prove a defendant's guilt, a defendant is now more likely to be subjected to police ill-treatment and even torture. An individual police officer is evaluated by their conviction rate and a confession is the easiest and cheapest way to put a case together and secure a conviction. The methods used include: psychological pressure involving threats of violence against the detainee or their family, sustained beatings and electroshock treatment, various asphyxiation techniques, or tying the prisoner into painful positions. There is also what the NGO Human Rights Watch calls 'torture by proxy', in which detainees in pre-trial detention centres are used by the police to beat, rape and intimidate other detainees into confessions (Human Rights Watch, 1999; Amnesty International, 2006).

In 2005 Yury Levada's Analytical Centre conducted a poll entitled 'The Arbitrariness Index of the Law Enforcement Bodies', which found that only 4 per cent of Russians trust the law enforcement bodies, while 73 per cent fear that they might become victims of police arbitrariness and 46 per cent believe that the authorities used law enforcement to repress political opponents (*Mosnews*, 2005a). When the Moscow radio station *Ekho Moskvy*'s 'Ricochet' programme asked people who had had dealings with the police to phone in, 99 per cent of the 3,935 callers were 'unimpressed' by the police. In response to these figures the human rights ombudsman, Vladimir Lukin, acknowledged that the police make widespread use of torture and ill-treatment to extract confessions and that 'most people are unhappy with the police' (Lukin, 2005). He said that he had reported to Putin that about a third of the complaints he receives are about abuses by the police, and that he (Lukin) was working with the Minister of the Interior Rashid Nurgaliev (a former FSB operative) to rectify this. On 10 November, the annual 'Police Day' holiday in 2005, Nurgaliev criticised police inefficiency and said officers need to do more to win the trust of the people (Medetsky, 2005). Nurgaliev has also criticised police corruption, collusion with criminals, and their callousness and rudeness when dealing with members of the public. Reforming the police is proving an intractable problem not least because the ethos of the Putin presidency, which stressed strengthening the state, frustrated attempts to bring the security services and law enforcement agencies under greater scrutiny and democratic control.

Pre-trial Detention Centres

On arrest prisoners are first held in a police Temporary Detention Centre. They are then moved to a Pre-trial Detention Centre or *Sizo* (*sledstvennyi izoliator*) where they are held until their case is heard and judgment passed. This means that no one in these centres has been found guilty of any crime and yet they are held in conditions that are so appalling that they constitute torture. *Sizos* are grossly overcrowded; sometimes there is not enough space for all prisoners even to lie down. Poor food, sanitation and ventilation, added to prisoner-on-prisoner violence, have resulted in deaths and act as an incentive to confess to get out to the 'better' conditions of a penal colony. During the soviet period the assumption that everybody arrested was guilty and the summary justice dispensed by the courts meant that prisoners spent only very short periods in these centres. In post-communist Russia the crime explosion, the lengthening of the legal and court processes, and the back-log of cases to be heard has meant that the time spent in *Sizos* has lengthened considerably, with periods of over a year not uncommon. Another factor adding to the gross overcrowding is that judges very rarely grant bail. The possibility of bail was introduced in the 1990s and is also permitted in the 2002 Criminal Code, which also limited, in theory at least, the maximum time in a *Sizo* to six months. The police prefer defendants to be held in *Sizos* because it involves less paperwork for them and pressure can be applied, so increasing the possibility of a confession. The result is that even those arrested for quite minor offences will be sent to a *Sizo* rather than given bail.

Lukin (2005) has also criticised the use of OMOM riot police rather than *Sizo* personnel to put down the disturbances caused by the *Sizo* authorities' poor work practices. In July 2005 Putin transferred control of *Sizos* from the FSB to the Ministry of Justice, which satisfied a requirement of Russia's membership of the Council of Europe. However, Lukin points out that while the Ministry of the Interior documents relating to the use of riot police in *Sizos* were available to him, the Ministry of Justice documents are not. This indicates that the Ministry of Justice is concerned with state control rather than justice and rights.

Prisons

There are three types of prisons: correctional labour colonies (ITKs) where the majority of prisoners are held; institutions called prisons for those who have violated ITK rules; and educational labour colonies (VTKs) for juveniles aged 14–20 years. In 1998 the penal system passed from the jurisdiction of the Ministry of the Interior to the Ministry of Justice. This was another one of the commitments that Russia made, together with the abolition of the death penalty, on joining the Council of Europe. The transfer was supposed to signal that Russia's penal institutions are now part of the justice system rather than part of the state's coercive apparatus, but so far this transfer has had little practical impact. The whole of the Russian penal system remains grossly under-funded, prison staff are poorly paid and poorly trained. Their primary function is to isolate and contain prisoners rather than rehabilitation; even ITKs lack education and vocational training opportunities. Another major problem for staff and prisoners alike is that the unsanitary conditions, the overcrowding and the lack of basic medical supplies has led to a rapid rise of HIV-Aids, scabies and tuberculosis. Overcrowding means that it is impossible to isolate infected prisoners and there are no funds for basic items such as syringes or aspirin, let alone more sophisticated drugs to treat diseases. Violence by both guards and prisoners is not uncommon. During the spring of 2002 there was a wave of hunger strikes in protest at the extortion of food, money and valuables from prisoners and their families by their guards. Inmates also enforce their own intricate hierarchies according to which homosexuals, the victims of prison rape, rapists, child molesters and informers are 'untouchables' and so subject to abuse and violence, with no protection from prison authorities.

Russia's penal population peaked at over one million in the late 1990s and had the highest incarceration rate of any developed country. When Putin came to power, those serving sentences for minor crimes were freed, lowering the prison population to between 700,000 and 800,000. Since 2003 tentative steps have been taken to introduce alternative sentences to incarceration and in January 2007 it was announced that to reduce prison numbers and to allow prisoners to do useful work, electronic tagging would be tried. According to Lev Ponomaryov (*Mosnews*, 2005b) of the NGO 'For Human Rights', under Putin new heads were appointed to prison and detention facilities with instructions to use all means available to keep order. Also, while there was no civilian oversight of the prisons under Yeltsin, civil and human rights groups were able to gain access to prisons and talk to prisoners; under Putin such access was denied. Just as with the *Sizos*, Ministry of Justice supervision of the prisons is no guarantee of democratic control or a commitment to human rights.

Human rights and the ombudsman

From the Helsinki Final Act to the 'Year of Human Rights'

In 1975 the USSR signed the Helsinki Final Act, the final document of the Helsinki Conference on Security and Co-operation in Europe (CSCE). The signatories which included the USA and western and eastern European countries, agreed to a range of issues including a commitment to respect human rights. Within the USSR an unofficial Helsinki Monitoring Group was founded by Andrei Sakharov, Anatoly Sharansky and Yury Orlov to monitor the USSR's adherence to the Final Act. By 1982 the group was all but disbanded following the imprisonment or exile of its leading members. A commitment to human rights was an integral part of the RSFSR's political liberalisation and Russia's democratisation. In November 1991 the RSFSR parliament adopted 'The Declaration of the Rights and Freedoms of Man and Citizen', which was modelled on international human rights documents. Russia remained a member of the CSCE and its successor organisation 'The Organization for Security and Co-operation in Europe' (OSCE). During the process of drafting the new RF Constitution, Chapter 2 on 'Human and civil rights and freedoms' was the least controversial chapter (Sharlet, 1997: 129).

In 1994 Yeltsin created the post of human rights ombudsman, then designated 1998 the 'Year of Human Rights' and ratified the European Convention on Human Rights and the European Convention for the Prevention of Torture and Inhuman or Degrading Treatment. In 1996 Russia joined the Council of Europe, which involved various commitments including abandonment of the death penalty. The death penalty retains legal standing in Russia but it has not been applied since 1996. The Council of Europe now monitors Russia's human rights record and Russians can also take cases of human rights violations to the European Court of Human Rights, whose decisions are binding. According to Professor Bill Bowering there have been 10,000 appeals from Russia to the European Court. Although 99 per cent of the cases have not been upheld, this is often because they do not concern human rights abuses and so do not fall within the jurisdiction of the court (Roxburgh, 2005). The Kremlin has increasingly viewed the European Court of Human Rights as anti-Russian. It has, for example, persistently condemned Russian human right abuses in Chechnia and in a ruling in 2002 upheld an appeal against extradition by a group of Chechens who had fled to Georgia. It has also ruled against complaints of discrimination brought by ethnic Russians living in the Baltic states (Harding, 2007: 1). In 2004 the court also upheld the anti-Putin oligarch Vladimir Gusinsky's claim that the Russian authorities had used imprisonment to force him to sell his media assets. The court ordered Russia to pay Gusinsky 88,000 euros (US$105,698) in damages (Bigg, 2006).

Despite these institutional changes and commitments progress has been slow in practice. The failure to establish a law-governed state, the wars in Chechnia, the routine denial of their constitutional rights to conscientious objectors to military service, and the treatment of asylum seekers are a few of many examples of continuing failures to respect human rights by the Russian state.

Beslan – Russia's 9/11

In September 2004 a school in Beslan in North Ossetia was taken over by separatists from Chechnia, leaving 300 children and adults dead. In the wake of Beslan Putin introduced a raft of measures designed to strengthen presidential control over Russia (see Chapters 5–7). Russian human rights and pro-democracy activists argue that psychologically Beslan had a similar impact on Russia as 9/11 had on America (Corwin, 2005). Both countries see themselves as vulnerable to attack, especially by terrorists, leading to a belief that the country must unite and the state must be strengthened. In September 1999 bomb blasts in two Moscow apartment buildings that killed more than 200 people were blamed on Chechen rebels. The bombings led directly to Putin's launch of the second war against Chechnia and a wave of human rights abuses against Chechens: many Chechens in Moscow were detained and subjected to physical abuse to extract confessions of complicity in the bombings and over 800 Chechens were expelled from Moscow on trumped-up charges. The government's hardline response to the bombings also helped to boost support for Putin, the then little-known prime minister, and catapulted him to victory in the March 2000 presidential elections. The Beslan tragedy has been used to provide additional evidence of the need to strengthen the Russian state; opposition or criticism of Putin and government policies was increasingly treated as weakening Russia and traitorous. The Beslan attack was used to justify restrictions on civil society (see Chapter 10) and the media (see Chapter 11) and was also used to link Islam and terrorism. The mass media increasingly trumpet patriotic themes and use xenophobic stereotypes. Muslim citizens are targeted by the police and subjected to humiliating treatment, in the name of cracking down on Islamic extremism and terrorism (Bigg, 2005).

Blagoveshchensk and filtration camps

In December 2004 police and masked OMOM troops literally went on the rampage in the city of Blagoveshchensk in the republic of Bashkortostan. They illegally detained and beat approximately one thousand men in a city of around 30,000 then attempted to block attempts by human rights groups to investigate what had happened. Although six deputy interior ministers were eventually sacked for this, in the course of their investigations human rights activists found a secret Ministry of the Interior document giving the police the right to use extreme force and to set up detention centres in the event of large-scale protests. There had been no such protest in Blagoveshchensk. The document gave the police the right to set up what are in effect 'filtration camps', like those that have been used in Chechnia. In Chechnia filtration camps are supposedly used to find Chechen fighters hiding among civilians. Those held in filtration camps are isolated from the outside world, denied legal advice and subjected to interrogation, including physical and psychological torture. Blagoveshchensk is not an isolated event and so the techniques of control and repression pioneered in Chechnia, are now being used in other parts of Russia. Human rights NGOs which have attempted to raise these issues are also literally under attack from the security services (see Chapter 15).

The human rights ombudsman (or commissioner)

The ombudsman investigates appeals from the public, currently about 20,000 a year (Lukin, 2005), writes reports, keeps the president informed about developments and concerns, and may attend the European Court and Council of Europe. The ombudsman may also suggest changes to legislation, but has no power to implement these recommendations. In an interview broadcast on Moscow's *Ekho Moskvy* radio station in 2005 the current ombudsman Vladimir Lukin described the human rights situation in Russia as 'far from ideal' and stated, 'Of course, the clauses in the Constitution, in the very good, short and clear section of the Constitution on human rights, are observed by no means in full, by no means everywhere, and by no means properly' (ibid.). There is a sense of frustration permeating the ombudmen's accounts of their work and the inability to have human rights taken seriously.

Box 8.9 RF human rights ombudsman*

Appointment: the president proposes a candidate for ombudsman to the State Duma for approval.

Sergei Kovalyov: 17 January 1995 to 10 March 1995

Born 1930. A biologist and mathematician who was a dissident during the soviet period, when he edited the illegal *Samizdat* newspaper, the Chronicle of Current Events. He was arrested in 1974 and only returned to Moscow in 1987. In 1989 he was elected to the Russian Supreme Soviet and was asked by Yeltsin to chair the RSFSR's new Human Rights Committee. He contributed to the writing of Chapter 2 of the RF Constitution. From 1990 to 1993 he was a member of parliament, in 1993 he co-founded Russia's Choice and from 1993 to 2003 was a

Box 8.9 (Continued)

Duma deputy. In January 1995 the State Duma appointed Kovalyov to the post of human rights ombudsman but soon sacked him due to his opposition to the Chechen war. In 1992 he was appointed chair of the president's Human Rights Commission but resigned in January 1996 accusing the president of backtracking on human rights. Between 1996 and 2003 he was a member of the Russian delegation to the Parliamentary Assembly of the Council of Europe and served as a member of the Assembly's Committee on Legal Affairs and Human Rights. Kovalyov remains a vocal critic of Russia's military involvement in Chechnia and of Putin's human rights record. In 2002 he set up the independent Kovalyov Commission to investigate the 1999 Moscow bombings that led to the second Chechen war. One member of the Commission was assassinated, another poisoned with thalium, and its lawyer and investigator were arrested.

Oleg Mironov: 22 May 1998 to 13 February 2004

Born 1939. A law professor and a Communist Party member at the time of his appointment. Human rights activists were initially sceptical about Mironov, but he formed alliances with human rights organisations and became increasingly critical of Russia's human rights record notably on human rights violations in Chechnia, police torture, attacks on freedom of conscience and failure to provide alternatives to military service. On 2 December 2000 the government newspaper *Rossiiskaia Gazeta* carried a Kremlin-inspired letter from members of his staff accusing him of pro-western sympathies.

Vladimir Lukin: 13 February 2004–

Born 1937. An historian and academic. In 1990 he was elected to the RSFSR Parliament for the Democratic Russia party; a member of Yeltsin's Constitutional Commission. From 1992–93 he was the Russian ambassador to the USA. In 1993 he joined the liberal *Yabloko* party and in 1999 was elected to the State Duma. Information about Lukin and some of his writings are available on the *Yabloko* website: http://www.eng.yabloko.ru/People/Luk/lukin1.html

Regional ombudsmen

Regional ombudsmen are not mentioned in the 1993 RF Constitution, but Article 5 of the 1997 Federal law 'On Ombudsmen', allows federal subjects to appoint ombudsmen from their own budgets. Their powers vary according to the regional legislation that set up their office. By the end of Mironov's tenure there were 22 regional ombudsmen. In 2004 Lukin suggested that Chechnia should have a republican ombudsman, but so far one has not been established.

* The term ombudsman is Swedish in origin, it is the name given to a government official who is supposed impartially to investigate citizens' complaints against the government and its functionaries.

Chapter summary

In the late 1980s and during the 1990s Russia made particular commitments to democratisation, the rule of law and the observation of human rights. The 1993 RF Constitution potentially marked a major departure from Russia's authoritarian past. Further legislation has been passed, including new Civil and Criminal Codes, and in speeches Putin stresses the importance of judicial independence. However, the soviet mindset and authoritarian habits have proved difficult to shake off, leaving a huge gulf between reality and the reforms that are supposed to have taken place. Putin's belief in the importance of strengthening the state led to increased control over key judicial appointments and the courts. Putin and his *siloviki* routinely resorted to extralegal means to secure the results they want. 'Telephone justice', bringing pressure to bear on judges, the courts and lawyers, the denial of the rights of suspects, and the physical and psychological abuse of those under arrest are all symptomatic of a disregard for the rule of law. The development of an independent judiciary has also been frustrated by Putin's prevention of democratic, civil society or media scrutiny of the judiciary and the law enforcement agencies. Corruption thrives in this environment and so remains a major problem, despite Putin's declaration that he would root it out.

Discussion points

- What factors inhibit the development of an independent judiciary?
- Has the average citizen's experience of the judicial system improved since 1991?
- Is the 'dictatorship of law' a contradictory expression or a realistic commitment to the rule of law?
- Why does Russia have a human rights ombudsman?

Further reading

Donald D. Barry (ed.) (1992) *Toward the 'Rule of Law' in Russia? Political and Legal Reform in the Transition Period*, Armonk, NY: M.E. Sharpe, Inc and William E. Butler (ed.) (1991) *Perestroika and the Rule of Law. Anglo-American and Soviet Perspectives*, London and New York: I.B. Tauris, provide useful introductions to judicial reform under Gorbachev. For a concise discussion of judicial and legal developments see Robert Sharlet (2005) 'The Search for the Rule of Law', Chapter 8 in Stephen White (ed.) *Developments in Russian Politics 6*, Basingstoke: Palgrave. For assessments of judicial reforms under Putin go to the website of the Foreign Policy Centre, a think-tank launched by Tony Blair at http://fpc.org.uk. It is a valuable source of articles by leading Russian and western specialists including Mary McAuley, Alena Ledeneva and Hugh Barnes (2006) 'Dictatorship or Reform? The Rule of Law in Russia'; Jennifer Moll and Richard Gowan (2005) 'Losing Ground? Russia's

European Commitments to Human Rights'. Also available on the website is Jennifer Moll (ed.) (2005) *Blueprint for Russia*, which includes contributions from William Butler, 'Law and the Abuse of Power: Some Reflections on Policy for the Putin Administration', 35–8 and Karinna Moskalenko, 'The Judicial System in Practice', 39–43. For judicial reforms under Putin there is a series of articles introduced by Stephen Holmes (2002) 'Reforming Russia's Courts', *East European Constitutional Review*, 11 (1/2), Winter/Spring, 90–129. Peter H. Solomon, Jr is a leading specialist on Russian law and his (2005) 'Threats of Judicial Counterreform in Putin's Russia', a paper delivered at the International Conference on 'Commercial Law Reform in Russia and Eurasia' held at the Russian, East European, and Eurasian Center, University of Illinois at Urbana-Champaign, 8–9 April is available online at: http://www.reec.uiuc.edu/events/Conference/ACConf/lawconf_papers.htm.

William E. Butler is also a leading specialist in Russian law: see his (2003) (2nd edn) *Russian law*, Oxford: Oxford University Press; his (2003) *Civil Code of the Russian Federation, Parts I, II, III*, Oxford: Oxford University Press; and his (2003) *Russian Company and Commercial Legislation*, Oxford: Oxford University Press. Kathryn Hendley has written extensively on the arbitration courts: see her (2005) 'Accelerated Process in the Russian Arbitrazh Courts', *Problems of Post-Communism*, 52 (6), 21–31 and her (2003) 'Reforming the Procedural Rules for Business Litigation in Russia: To What End?', *Demokratizatsiya*, 11 (3), 363–80. The journalist James Meek provides a useful analysis of the victims of the dirty war in Chechnia's recourse to the European Court of Human Rights in his (2006) 'Can the victims of the war in Chechnya get justice?', *The Guardian – G2*, 12 June, 7–11.

Useful websites

The journal *East European Constitutional Review* is a particularly good source of articles on legal reform throughout the former soviet block. It is available online at http://www.law.nyu.edu/eecr/

The International Commission of Jurists carries news about the judiciary and human rights in Russia: http://www.icj.org/sommaire.php3?lang=en

The Russian American Rule of Law Consortium is a group of legal communities, its website includes resources about the law in Russia and links to other relevant websites: http://www.rarolc.net

The websites of the human rights organisations Amnesty International http://www.amnesty.org/ and the New York based Human Rights Watch http://www.hrw.org/ regularly carry articles about the RF. As does the Council of Europe website: http://www.coe.int.

There are also websites dedicated to Mikhail Khodorkovsky http://www.mbktrial.com/, to all the defendants in the Yukos case http://www.sovest.org/gb/ and the Platon Lebedev Press Centre http://www.lebedevtrial.com/. The Human Rights Watch website has a case study of Igor Sutiagin, http://www.hrw.org/backgrounder/eca/russia/4.htm

Anne Preis-Heijke (2002) 'Legal Structure of Russia and Electronic Sources of Russian Law', Institute of Advanced Legal Studies, London. Available on the Institute's website (which also provides an extensive list of links): http://www.ials.sas.ac.uk/events/docs/IALS_Russia_Pries_handout.pdf

References

Amnesty International (2006) 'Russian Federation: Beating out "confessions" in police detention', *Amnesty International*, Index: EUR 46/060/2006, 22 November, http://www.amnesty.org/

Bigg, C. (2005) 'Russia: Rights Groups Say Country Intolerant to Minority Religions', *RFE/RL Feature Article*, 19 May, *RFE/RL* website: http://rferl.org/

Bigg, C. (2006) 'Russia: Russians Increasingly Seek Redress in European Court', *RFE/RL Feature Article*, 3 February, *RFE/RL* website: http://rferl.org/

Bransten, J. (2005) 'East: Postcommunist Ombudsmen Persevere Despite Obstacles', 29 November, *RFE/RL* website: http://www.rferl.org/

Corwin, J. A. (2005) 'Russia: Police Brutality shows Traces of Chechnya', *RFE/RL Feature Article*, 20 June, *RFE/RL* website: http://rferl/org/

Finn, P. (2005) 'In Russia, trying Times for Trial by Jury', *Washington Post*, 31 October, A/2

FOM (2006) 'Corruption in Russia Today', 30 November, *Public Opinion Foundation* website: http://bd.english.fom.ru/

Gessen, M. (2005) 'The Dear Departed Judiciary', *The Moscow Times*, 29 December, 7, http://www.themoscowtimes.com/stories/2005/12/29/006.html

Harding, L. (2007) 'I was poisoned by Russians, human rights judge says', *The Guardian*, 1 February, 17

Human Rights Watch (1999) 'Confessions at Any Cost – Police Torture in Russia', *HRW Report*, November, http://www.hrw.org/

Lowe, C. (2006) 'Russian Courts Must Check Kremlin Power Says Judge', *The Moscow Times*, 24 January, 3

Lukin, V. (2005) '"Far from ideal" human rights in Russia', *Ekho Moskvy*, 2 March. BBC Monitoring International Reports, Gateway Russia website, http://www.gateway2russia.com/st/art_270721.php

Medetsky, A. (2005) 'Police criticized on their Day', *The Moscow Times*, 11 November, http://www.themoscowtimes.com/stories/2005/11/11/011.html

Mereu, F. (2004) 'Judges Who Lost Their Jobs Speak Out', *The Moscow Times*, 6 October, http://www.cdi.org/russia/johnson/default.cfm

Mikhailovskaya, I. (1999) 'The Procuracy and its Problems. Russia', *East European Constitutional Review*, 8 (1–2), Winter/Spring, 101

Mosnews (2005a) 'Rights Group Blasts Russian Prison System, Compares It to Gulag', 26 August, http://www.mosnews.com/news/2005/08/26/gulag.shtml

Mosnews (2005b) 'Most Russian's Don't Trust, Fear Law Enforcers – Poll', 3 October, http://mosnews.com/news.2005/10/03/levadapoll.shtml

Nikitinsky, L. (1997) 'Russia Interview with Boris Ebseev, Justice of the Constitutional Court of the Russian Federation', *East European Constitutional Review*, 6 (1), Winter, 83–8

Page, J. (2005) 'Judges take stand against Putin', *The Times*, 19 March, http://www.timesonline.co.uk/

RIA Novosti (2004) 'President Putin Speaks Out on Judicial Branch's Independence', *RIA Novosti*, 30 November

Roxburgh, A. (2005) 'Reforming the Bear 1. Brave New World', *BBC World Service*, October, http://news.bbc.uk./1/hi/programmes/documentary_archive/4363970.stm

Sharlet, Robert (1997) 'The Progress of Human Rights', in Stephen White, Alex Pravda and Zvi Gitelman (eds) *Developments in Russian Politics 4*, Basingstoke: Macmillan

Chapter 9

The state in uniform: the armed and security forces

Learning objectives

▪ To examine the relationship between the armed and security forces and civilians.

▪ To analyse the reforms introduced by Yeltsin and Putin.

▪ To introduce and explain the concept of 'parallel power-wielding structures'.

▪ To examine the development of the security services.

Introduction

On 7 May 1992 President Yeltsin issued a decree establishing the Russian armed forces. The decree was issued just two days before the Victory Day celebrations on 9 May so underlining the continuity between the Red Army that had defeated the Nazi invaders in 1945 and the new Russian Army. The Red Army had been the great pride of the USSR, but Russia inherited under-funded and demoralised armed forces replenished by regular conscription and in dire need of technological modernisation. This raised important questions about the kind of armed forces Russia needed, with most military specialists arguing in favour of smaller, better educated and rewarded, professional forces capable of using the new weapons technologies. Yeltsin also needed to establish clear civilian oversight and control of the armed and security forces. In part he used his usual technique of institutional improvisation and encouraged the armed and security forces to compete with each other for the president's largesse in terms of budgets and missions, to try to control them. Putin is a former KGB agent and the *siloviki* or people from the armed and security forces were one of the main networks that helped him to become president (see Chapter 5). As part of his agenda of strengthening the Russian state, Putin pushed forward with the reform and modernisation of armed forces.

Russian soldiers march in a Victory Day Parade on Red Square in Moscow on 9 May 2008. The show of strength on the 63rd anniversary of victory against Nazi Germany symbolised Moscow's growing boldness following eight years of rule by Putin.

Civil–military relations

Articles 83 and 87 of the 1993 RF Constitution enshrined the president's domination over the armed forces. The president is the commander-in-chief, heads the Security Council, and appoints and dismisses defence ministers and the armed forces' high command. It is the president who has the right to declare states of emergency or war, and to approve the country's Military Doctrine. In Russia's super-presidential system the Constitution established military subordination to the president rather than to a broader system of civilian control. The result is that military–civil relations risk being focused on loyalty to the president rather than a broad loyalty to the Russian political system.

Putin appointed *siloviki*, that is people with an armed or security forces background, into government. In contrast the practice in western democracies is to keep the armed and security services removed from government. Putin also stressed the continuity between Russia's and the USSR's secret police. Within his first two weeks in office a plaque honouring Yury Andropov, a former chair of the KGB, was hung in the Lubyanka – the KGB's and the FSB's headquarters. As if to reassure people of his democratic credentials Putin also placed flowers at the grave of one of the KGB's dissident targets, the liberal Andrei Sakharov. In 2004, the 127th anniversary of the birth of Felix Dzerzhynsky, the founder of the Cheka (secret police), a statue of him was unveiled in Dzerzhynsky a town near Moscow. In

1991 the statue of Dzerzhynsky outside the Lubyanka had been pulled down; President Putin had the statue put back. These developments do not mean that the armed and security forces now run Russia. While the *siloviki* no doubt share the belief that Russia needs to be strengthened, even if this means sacrificing some of the democratic freedoms gained during the 1990s, they do not speak with one voice. Just as under Yeltsin, the various armed and security services compete for missions, influence and above all budgets and it is the president who is the focus of this competition.

Box 9.1 Defence Council (July 1996 to March 1998)

The Defence Council was set up by presidential decree in July 1996 as part of the Presidential Apparatus. The RF president was the Defence Council's chair, appointed its secretary and approved its membership, which was almost identical to the Security Council's membership. According to its statutes it was a standing consultative organ that advised the president on military organisational development and on the implementation of the Security Council's decisions on the strategic aspects of defence policy. This duplicated some of the Defence Ministry's functions. The Defence Council should be understood as part of Yeltsin's attempt to subordinate the Defence Ministry to civilian control. It was also a counterbalance to the Security Council, which was then headed by retired General Aleksandr Lebed, who had stood against Yeltsin in the 1996 presidential elections. The Defence Council's first secretary was Yury Baturin who in August 1997 was replaced by Andrei Kokoshin, the deputy minister of defence.

Defence ministers: from generals to bean counters?

Yeltsin continued the soviet practice of appointing generals as defence ministers. His first defence minister Gen. Pavel Grachev, had demonstrated his loyalty to Yeltsin during the August 1991 coup attempt. He also had a high public profile, being respected for his role as an airborne commander in Afghanistan. Grachev was sacked in 1996 amid allegations of planning a military coup. Yeltsin then appointed another general, Igor Rodionov, as minister of defence. However, Yeltsin asked Rodionov to resign his army commission so he became Russia's first 'civilian' minister of defence since Leon Trotsky's resignation as Commissar of War in 1925. Rodionov soon came into conflict with Yury Baturin over the funding necessary for military reform. Rodionov claimed that reform was not possible within the allocated budget and was sacked in 1997, accused of obstructing military reform. Rodionov was replaced by another serving general, Igor Sergeyev. Yeltsin seems to have believed that by appointing military figures he could co-opt them and so control them, although there is little evidence that this was the case. Sergeyev ignored Yeltsin's instruction to reform and modernise conventional forces and instead concentrated on the preparedness of Russia's nuclear Intercontinental Ballistic Missiles (ICBMs). Sergeyev came into conflict with the General Staff who were keen to see him removed. In

August 2000 the submarine *Kursk* sank in the Barents Sea killing the 118-strong crew, Sergeev accepted responsibility and was dismissed by Putin in March 2001.

In contrast to Yeltsin's appointment of army generals, Putin has appointed non-military men. Sergei Ivanov is a St Petersburg Chekist (see Chapter 5) who, from the late 1970s to 1990s, worked in Soviet and Russian foreign intelligence. Then from July 1998 to August 1999 Ivanov was Putin's deputy director of the Federal Security Service (FSB) and in November 1999 was appointed secretary of the Security Council before being appointed defence minister. The Russian military clearly viewed Ivanov as an unwanted outsider. He had been appointed to push through the military reforms that previous ministers had proved unable to do. This involved confronting, not always successfully, powerful vested interests and tackling endemic corruption. Under Ivanov the military budget almost quadrupled, from 214 billion to 822 billion roubles (Butrin et al., 2007). He was replaced as defence minister by Anatoly Serdyukov, a St Petersburg lawyer and economist who prior to this appointment had spent three years as head of the Federal Tax Police (RIA Novosti, 2007c). Serdyukov was appointed to improve accounting and the supervision of spending within the military and by the Defence Ministry, which both suffered from large-scale misappropriation of funds. At the time of Serdyukov's appointment Putin stated, 'I certainly hope that the ministry, at least that part of it that deals with development, will pay close attention to the economic and financial components [of defence activities]' (RIA Novosti, 2007b).

Box 9.2 The Ministry of Defence (MO)

Developments: In 2004 the Federal Railway Troops (FSZhV) and the Federal Service for Special Construction (*Spetsstroi*), which had been separate force structures, became part of the MO.

Estimated strength of armed forces personnel: 960,000 plus 50,000 railway troops and 14,000 special construction troops (Renz, 2007: 5).

The ministers

Boris Yeltsin	16 March 1992 to 18 March 1992 (acting)
Pavel Grachev	18 May 1992 to 18 June 1996
Mikhail Kolesnikov	18 June 1996 to 17 July 1996 (acting)
Igor Rodionov	17 July 1996 to 23 May 1997
Igor Sergeyev	23 May 1996 to 28 March 2001
Sergei Ivanov	28 March 2001 to 15 February 2007
Anatoly Serdyukov*	15 February 2007–

Defence Ministry website: http://www.mil.ru/eng/

* Serdyukov offered to resign when his father-in-law Viktor Zubkov became prime minister in September 2007, but Putin declined the offer.

The General Staff versus the Ministry of Defence

In November 2001 the newspaper *Nezavisimaia Gazeta* carried an article entitled, 'The Generals are going into opposition to the Kremlin' (Solov'ev, 2001), warning that Defence Minister Sergei Ivanov had lost control of the armed forces. The General Staff did not want Ivanov who, despite his FSB background, they viewed as a civilian; they were also angered by the direction of policy under Putin. Following the bombing of the Twin Towers in New York on 9/11 2001, Russia formed an alliance with the USA in the war against terror. The General Staff, schooled in the soviet era to see the USA as Russia's prime enemy found this alliance and its consequences difficult to stomach, not least Putin's agreement to the presence of American forces in neighbouring Tajikistan, Uzbekistan and Afghanistan. They were also astounded by Ivanov's description of the 1972 ABM Treaty – which President George W. Bush's revival of Reagan's Star Wars programme threatened to abandon – as a 'relic of the past' (ibid.). The military also opposed the closure of Russian bases in Cuba and Vietnam, the reduction of Russian peacekeeping contingents in Bosnia and Kosovo, and their forces in the Transcaucasus and Dniestr region. They also found Ivanov slow to re-equip the armed forces and raise service personnel's pay. Kvashnin tried to use his reports to the president on combat operations in the Caucasus to shift the balance of power from the Defence Ministry to the General Staff, but he was unable to oust Ivanov.

Amendments to the Russian Defence law in June 2004 consolidated the subordination of the General Staff to the Ministry of Defence. The General Staff's role was reduced to long-term planning and overall strategy. Until 2004 the Defence Ministry and General Staff had had joint responsibility for supervising the armed forces, but the Defence Ministry was now given the sole right to supervise the armed forces. The Ministry of Defence also acquired the right to approve the General Staff's statutes; a right it had held until 1998 when it had been transferred to the president. The amendment also transferred operational command of the armed forces to the Defence Ministry. During June 2004 the failure of the General Staff's operational command, and especially its poor coordination, were revealed by major security failures in Ingushetia. In July 2004 Kvashnin and other high ranking military commanders were dismissed and Kvashnin was replaced by the former first deputy director of the Chief of Staff Col.-Gen. Yury Baluyevsky, who was also appointed the first deputy minister of defence.

In February 2007 Putin announced that the General Staff's role would steadily grow (ibid.), but Baluyevsky has been unable to deal with corruption within the armed forces and tensions between the Ministry of Defence and the General Staff have continued. Baluyevsky has repeatedly offered his resignation and opposes Defence Minister Anatoly Serdyukov's plans to reform the armed forces, reduce the staff at the General Staff HQ and the Ministry of Defence by 40 per cent, and the transfer of the Navy Chief Command from Moscow to St Petersburg.

Box 9.3 Chiefs of the armed forces – the General Staff

Viktor Dubynin	June 1992 to 22 November 1992
Mikhail Kolesnikov	23 December 1992 to 18 October 1996
Viktor Samsonov	18 October 1996 to 22 May 1997
Anatoly Kvashnin	22 May 1997 to 19 July 2004
Yury Baluyevsky	19 July 2004–

The Beslan tragedy and civilian oversight

The war on terror, security failures and Putin's response

The Beslan tragedy in 2004 was just one of many major security failures: the Dubrovka or Nord-Ost Theatre siege in Moscow in October 2002; the football stadium bombing in May 2004 that killed President Akhmad Kadyrov of Chechnia; the killing of more than 90 people in Ingushetia in June 2004 by Chechen guerillas; a suicide bombing at a Moscow metro station in August 2004; and the downing of two passenger planes in September 2004. In 2002 in response to 9/11 a new counter-terrorism law, 'On Countering Extremist Activities' was passed. The law allows a prosecutor to ban extremist organisations but gives only a vague definition of what constitutes extremism. The law has been used to silence human rights groups; particularly those working in Chechnia and the North Caucasus (see

Emma Taghaeva, who lost her family in the Beslan school tragedy, holds their picture and a placard asking 'Who is responsible for the death of our children?' in front of the prosecutor general's office. She was accompanied by a group of other women determined to demonstrate their distrust of the government's investigation into the situation.

Pyati, 2005; IHF, 2005). For example, in August 2004 the prosecutor's office in Ingushetia accused the Chechen Committee of National Salvation (CCNS) of disseminating extremist literature. CCNS, which is based in Nazran Ingushetia, had distributed literature alleging human rights abuses by the Russian armed forces.

Between 1 and 3 September 2004 children, teachers and parents were held hostage at School No. 1 in Beslan in the republic of North Ossetia, by people supporting Chechen independence. The hostage-takers' demands included: talks with Aleksandr Dzasokhov the president of North Ossetia, Murat Zyazikov the president of Ingushetia and a prominent paediatrician, Leonid Rochal; the release of jailed fighters; and the withdrawal of Russian troops from Chechnia. Shamil Basayev, a separatist Chechen leader, claimed responsibility for the Beslan siege, the Moscow theatre siege, the downing of the passenger planes and the Moscow metro bomb; he was finally killed by the FSB in July 2006. The siege ended when Russian forces attacked the school leaving hundreds dead. Beslan provided Putin with an additional rationale for the further strengthening of presidential control over all levels of government (see Chapter 7), and a new law 'On Countering Terrorism', which he signed in March 2006. The law allows various counter-terrorist procedures including the shooting down of hijacked planes and operations outside Russian territory. Putin also ordered the creation of a new counter-terrorism committee within the FSB, to coordinate security efforts. Russia's security failings are partially the result of poor coordination between the responsible forces; however, a seeming lack of concern for the innocent, incompetence, corruption and even collusion with terrorists have all played a part to varying degrees. The counter-terrorism law also permits the interception of email and telephone communications and, like the law on countering extremism, it can also be used against civil society organisations trying to reveal abuses and corruption by the armed and security forces.

Box 9.4 The Caucasus

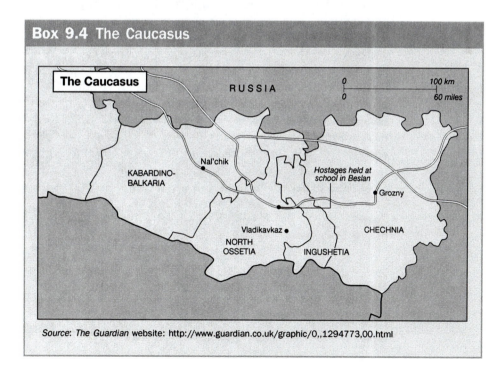

Source: The Guardian website: http://www.guardian.co.uk/graphic/0,,1294773,00.html

Parliamentary oversight: the Beslan Commission

Exactly what happened at Beslan and how it was possible remains unclear, despite a parliamentary commission headed by Aleksandr Torshin, an investigation by Russia's deputy prosecutor general, Nikolai Sheppel who led the criminal investigation into the response to the siege and the trial of the only captured hostage-taker Nur-Pashi Kulayev. The much delayed report by the parliamentary commission finally appeared in December 2005. It found that the siege could have been averted if the local authorities had heeded warnings from the interior minister to improve school security, although the local authorities deny they received any such instructions. It also found that security and law enforcement agencies made a series of errors in their handling of the crisis and criticised the poor coordination between the different branches of the security services (*Moscow News*, 2005). Ella Kesayeva of Mothers of Beslan, an organisation of mothers who lost children in the siege, criticised Torshin for failing to name those responsible. Sheppel's report simply cleared the authorities of any wrongdoing. In contrast the Mothers of Beslan and the Beslan Truth website accuse the security services of incompetence and claim that their tactics caused as many deaths as the hostage-takers; they want the responsible generals to be held to account.

An unofficial report by parliamentarian Yury Savelyev, an explosives expert and a member of the official parliamentary commission, presents a much more critical assessment of the Russian authorities and security forces using witness statements, expert opinion, photographs and video footage. It is available in full on the Russian language version of the Beslan Truth website (Savel'eva, 2005) and parts of it were quoted in the opposition newspaper *Novaia Gazeta*. According to Savelyev the 11-hour gun battle that killed most of the victims was not precipitated by the hostage-takers detonating a bomb, as the authorities claim, but by a Russian incendiary grenade. He also claims that Russian forces attacked the school with flame throwers, rocket grenades, tank cannons and machine guns, killing hostages; and he rejects the official claim that all was done to safeguard the hostages as far as possible. According to Savelyev it was Russian fire that brought the roof down on the hostages, not Chechen bombs. According to the official version of events all the hostage-takers were killed except Nur-Pashi Kulayev who was taken alive. However, Savelyev believes that there were more hostage-takers who managed to escape. More damning for the military are claims by the Beslan Mothers and eye witnesses of collusion between corrupt officials and security personnel and the hostage-takers. For example, they claim that some of the terrorists had been released from Russian prisons in order to take part in the attack, that they were allowed to store weapons and explosives in the school in the weeks running up to the siege, that they were able to build a sniper's post on the roof and also that they were helped to escape at the end of the siege (Dunlop, 2006).

Public opinion of the Beslan tragedy and the official response

Even before the official reports were released surveys conducted by 'The Public Opinion Foundation' revealed both widespread public concerns about the actions of the political authorities and the armed forces, and the belief that the people would never know the truth about what happened at Beslan. The survey 'The Beslan Hostage Crisis' (FOM, 2005a) revealed that 36 per cent of respondents did not believe that the Prosecutor General could not uncover the truth, while only 19 per cent believed that the Prosecutor General would be able to uncover the truth and would also inform the public of the findings. The survey 'Beslan: One Year later' (FOM, 2005b) revealed that while 32 per cent believed that the Russian authorities behaved effectively during the siege, 42 per cent believed they had not. Forty-one per cent believed that the special services had acted professionally but 31 per cent believed that they had not. Worst of all 44 per cent believed that everything had not been done to minimise the number of victims among the hostages compared to 27 per cent who believed that it had.

The Russian armed forces

From Red Army to RF forces

By 1992 changing geopolitical realities – the loss of former allies in east-central Europe and the demise of the Warsaw Pact; the loss of super-power status; the end of soviet socialism and its global alliance system; the collapse of the USSR and arrival of independent and sometimes unstable states around Russia's borders; and instability within Russia itself – all necessitated a profound reappraisal of the type of forces Russia needed. The new Military Doctrine (1993) stated that Russia no longer viewed any country as its enemy, did not intend to use military force unless attacked, and recognised that it is more likely to be involved in local conflicts along its borders than major warfare. However, the soviet Red Army, inherited by Russia, was a classic mass army and the military academies still taught that victory could be achieved by concentrated mass tank attacks, such as in the great tank battles of the Great Patriotic War (1941–45). However, during the Afghan war (1979–89) the Red Army had fought in terrain that was unsuitable for tanks and had been unable to defeat a highly motivated, American-backed guerrilla force. The Afghan war also revealed the USSR's loss of air superiority and that it could not match the mobile American Stinger surface-to-air missiles (SAMs). During the two wars in Chechnia 1994–96 and 1999–2000, RF forces faced similar problems. Another soviet legacy was that while NATO forces in the 1980s had made the technological leap into the new generation of 'smart' weapons, the USSR did not do so.

Russia under Putin was still endeavouring to catch up on decades of under-investment in the technological modernisation of its armed forces. Under Yeltsin a lack of state funding during a time of economic constraint, and the loss of funding and resources due to corruption, meant that this issue remained unaddressed. There were also more basic issues to be dealt with than the move to high-tech weapons. In 1995, so bad was the funding situation that the garrisons in Moscow, Tambov, Kostroma, Ivanovo and Tver *oblasts* and the Kaliningrad garrison had their electricity supplies cut off because they had not paid their bills. Lack of funding also meant that the armed forces could not conduct training exercises and fighter pilots were typically logging no more than 25 flying hours a year, compared to a western training norm of 180–220 hours (Lambeth, 1995: 89). Russian forces were sent into Chechnia not just without adequate training, but without appropriate clothing, rations and shelter. President Yeltsin designated 1995 as the 'Year of Military Reform', but little was achieved so that Serdyuk's modernisation agenda in 2007 identifies a similar range of priority issues.

Box 9.5 Anatoly Serdyuk on the modernisation agenda

Stressing continuity with the course followed during the previous six years, Serdyuk announced on national TV that: 'Our aim is a deep comprehensive modernisation of the Armed Forces, making them look fully in line with the 21st century demands.'

He identified the priority tasks as: 'First of all, this applies to the social sphere – the provision of servicemen with housing, combat training, modernization of the Armed Forces, the increase of the number of troops serving on contract and the transition to a 12-month draft from January 1, 2008.'

Source: RIA Novosti (2007c), 23 February 2007, http://en.rian.org/

What sort of army does Russia need?

An important focus of the military reform debate involved the question of the appropriate size of Russia's army as it entered the twenty-first century and the related question of whether it should be a conscript or a volunteer (contract or professional) force. There were still those in the military who believed that a large standing army was vital to Russia's military prowess and that conscription should be part of the patriotic education of all young men. Article 59.3 of the RF Constitution recognises the right of conscientious and religious objection to military service and provides for the substitution of an alternative civilian service. Yeltsin failed to provide an alternative civilian service, however, so in contravention of their constitutional rights young men were still conscripted into the armed forces. In 2004 Putin finally introduced an alternative civilian service of 36 months, or 18 months for those with a higher education, but the service is within military establishments. Conscription also supplies a steady stream of free labour that officers and sergeants sell to make a personal profit. As recently as November 2006 the then defence minister Ivanov announced that he had sacked three generals for assigning soldiers to tasks 'unrelated to service' (*Moscow News*, 2006c). Although during the 1990s Yeltsin talked about ending conscription, he kept delaying the decision, so young men aged 18–27 were subject to two years of conscript service and could be allocated to any of Russia's uniformed services.

There are military reasons for moving to a professional army, not least the poor performances in Afghanistan and Chechnia. The increasing complexity of military technology requires highly skilled personnel; conscripts, even if able enough, are not in the forces long enough to become proficient in the use of the new technologies. In the early 1990s so many possible exemptions and grounds for deferment were introduced that the lowest rate of conscription was among better-educated, urban men. According to the land forces commander Alexei Maslov, 'In 2006, recruits showed lower education levels, poorer health, both physical and mental, than before. Every fifth conscript was brought up in a single-parent family, every fourth had neither studied nor worked before recruitment and every tenth had police records for different offences' (RIA Novosti, 2007d). Conscription is also failing to deliver enough troops and this has worsened since 2006 when Russia had to confront a gigantic demographic shortfall in young men of the appropriate age (Giles, 2006). During the 1990s conscription had also become increasingly unpopular with the Russian public, particularly as revelations about the abuse of conscripts grew and young men were killed in the Chechen wars. Groups of soldiers' mothers went down to Chechnia in convoys of buses, simply to take their sons home.

In 1991 contract service was introduced in the Air Force, Air Defence Force, Strategic Nuclear Forces Command and the Navy and then extended to other forces. The contract personnel (*kontraktniki*) were supposed to be well-trained, professionals, but they tended to be the misfits and socially disadvantaged who could not fit back into civilian life. More than a third of contract personnel were the wives of officers or warrant officers who could not be used in combat roles. Contract soldiers were also more expensive than conscripts. These early experiments with contract service tended to discourage the abandonment of conscription. In January 2007 the then defence minister, Ivanov, said that conscripts would still make up a large part of the armed forces but that units on constant combat readiness would be fully manned by contract service personnel (RIA Novosti, 2007e). Conscripts are no longer deployed in Chechnia. Finally in March 2007 Putin signed a decree reducing the period of conscription from two years to one, so that from 1 January 2008 45 per cent of Russia's soldiers and NCOs would be serving on a contract basis (ibid.). In early 2007 the Defence Ministry announced that the armed forces would be gradually downsized from the current level of 1,134,000 personnel to 1,000,000 by 2010 (ibid.).

The torture of soldiers: *dedovshchina*

The phenomenon of *dedovshchina*, hazing or bullying, was an integral part of army life in the USSR (see Chapter 1); with the decline of service discipline and morale during the 1990s it became even worse. The media now carry accounts of *dedovshchina* almost daily and the Defence Ministry carries official data on *dedovshchina* each month on its website. The Russian Army has no professional, non-commissioned officers and so nineteen-year-old conscripts in their second year of service act as non-commissioned officers. *Dedovshchina* takes its name from these young servicemen who are known as *dedushki* or grandfathers. While a good deal of the bullying of young servicemen is conducted by the *dedushki*, officers are also either directly involved or fail to maintain the discipline, so making *dedovshchina* possible.

Since the late 1980s the Human Rights NGO, 'The Committee for Soldiers' Mothers', has monitored and publicised the treatment of Russian soldiers and campaigned to bring an end to the abuse of service personnel's human rights (see Chapter 10). The Mothers have consistently fought a wall of military and state indifference and secrecy. In 2006 a scandal hit the headlines that caused public outcry throughout Russia and led to an attempt to clamp down on the violence in the armed forces. The scandal concerned Private Andrei Sychkov, who had both legs and his genitals amputated after being tortured during the New Year holidays at the tank academy in Cheliabinsk (RIA Novosti, 2007a). During 2006, according to the Defence Ministry, 554 servicemen died, a decrease of 50 per cent on the 2005 figure; of these 210 committed suicide and 27 died in *dedovshchina* incidents (ibid.). According to Maslov, violence is the main cause of suicides and desertions in the Russian military (RIA Novosti, 2007d). Maslov blamed the poor morale and education of recruits for an increase in military offences.

Conscripts are not solely to blame for the violence, however. In October 2006 a former captain Vyacheslav Nikiforov was sentenced to 12 years in prison by a court martial in the Ryazan military garrison. A drunken Nikiforov had beaten up two soldiers who had returned to barracks late and one of them had subsequently died (RIA Novosti, 2006b). Then in January 2007 the commander of the 55th marine division, part of the Pacific Fleet in the Far East, was sacked after a number of officers were convicted of violence against servicemen and given sentences ranging from suspended terms to up to five years in prison (RIA Novosti, 2007a). In an article on the Sychkov case the RIA Novosti commentator Viktor Yuzbachev (2006) argued that officers lack the relevant legal knowledge, are poorly trained in human relations, and suffer from poverty and poor morale, and so lack the skills and motivation to conduct the personnel work necessary to eradicate *dedovshchina*. The army's construction battalions, which have a particularly bad reputation for bullying and the misuse of conscripts' labour, were disbanded in 2007.

Pay and housing

Towards the end of the 1980s the USSR began withdrawing its troops from east-central Europe and in 1992 Russia began to withdraw its troops for the Near Abroad (the 14 other former soviet republics). This presented major logistical problems and there was neither the time nor the funds to build new bases or housing. The result was that army officers and their families ended up living in tents or sharing single rooms in barrack blocks; naval families were living on rusting ships or even in submarines. The situation was made worse when funds were diverted from providing housing and social services to fund the first Chechen war (Lambeth, 1995: 90–1). A shortfall in conscripts meant that officers had to perform the menial jobs usually reserved for recruits, not surprisingly morale fell. Salaries also did not keep pace with inflation and, under Yeltsin, this was compounded by protracted delays in paying all service personnel. Although Putin has ensured that the salaries and pensions of all state employees are now paid regularly, the housing shortage and poor salary levels have yet to be addressed. A company commander earns 8,000 roubles (US$300) compared to a Moscow trolleybus driver who earns 22,000 roubles (US$820). Between 30–50 per cent of Russia's 150,000 officers have no housing, and they struggle to feed and clothe their families (Yuzbachev, 2006).

Corruption and the armed and security forces

Although the armed forces and their assets were not subject to privatisation in the same way as the country's economic assets, just as many soviet economic managers appropriated state assets during the privatisation process and treated them as their own (see Chapter 3), army officers similarly saw military assets as a way to make money for themselves. Even as soviet forces were preparing to leave Germany, officers began selling or bartering weaponry, tanks and artillery for money, Mercedes cars and electronics. The armed and security forces and the civilian police quickly became involved with criminal gangs, by selling them weapons, security and protection, labour and the use of buildings. Troops in Chechnia even sold their weapons to the insurgents. In the 1990s Major Rodionov, the commander of a long range aviation base in the Far East, used the base, bomber pilots and crews, to transport commercial goods to China without going through customs. Similarly the customs services are known to aid smugglers. In 1998 a retired general, Lev Rokhlin, was murdered to frustrate any further investigations into army corruption that had already implicated associates of Grachev, the former defence minister. The terrorists who took over the Moscow Theatre in 2002 are thought to have paid police to transport their grenades and assault rifles from Chechnia to Moscow. Bribes to airline security personnel helped Chechen terrorists to bring down two planes in August 2004 and the Beslan tragedy was facilitated by the help sold to the hostage-takers by high-ranking federal police and army officers. In order to combat terrorism and to ensure that the funds allocated to modernise the armed and security forces are used effectively, Putin still needs to address corruption in these institutions.

Box 9.6 The Russian armed forces

Terminology: in Russia all the armed forces are collectively called the 'Army', although the navy is sometimes referred to separately.

The three services

Air Force

Developments: from 1 January 1999 the Air Force and the Air Defence Troops (VPVO) were merged into a single service called the Air Force. The Air Force needs to replace its MiG-29s, Su-24s, Su-27s and the Tu-95 Bears and although there are plans for new subsonic stealth bombers, intermediate-range joint continental bombers and a new multi-role fighter fitted with a new generation of smart weapons, these remain as yet only plans and the Air Force has had to make do with upgrades to the existing planes. Since the early 1980s work has been under way on the development

---

Box 9.6 (*Continued*)

of a new fifth-generation fighter jet called the PAK-FA, which will replace Su-27s and MiG-29s sometime between 2012 and 2015 (*Moscow News*, 2006a).

In September 2006 the Air Force conducted a large-scale exercise, involving dozens of long-range bombers, test firing of cruise missiles and over 50 Tu-160, Tu-95 and Tu-22M aircraft flying missions over the Arctic, Pacific and Atlantic Oceans and the Black and Caspian Seas.

Commander: Vladimir Mikhailov since 21 January 2002.

Ground Force

Organisation: the domestic defence forces are divided into six military districts – Moscow, Leningrad, Northern Caucasus, Privolzh-Urals, Siberian and the Far Eastern.

Commander: Alexei Maslov, since 5 November 2004.

Navy

Composition: four fleets – the Baltic, Northern, Pacific and the Black Sea Fleets, and the Caspian Sea Flotilla.

Developments: in 2006 the Caspian Flotilla took delivery of the new Astrakhan stealth gunboat.

Commander: Vladimir Masorin since September 2005.

Three independent arms

Strategic Rocket Force (SRF)

Developments: on 1 June 2001 the SRF was reduced from a branch of the services to a separate command.

Russian Space Forces

Developments: set up on 1 June 2001 by the integration of the Missile and the Military Space Troops, which since 1997 had been part of the Strategic Rocket Forces. The Space Forces control Russia's missile early warning, missile defence, space object tracking, and military satellite launch and flight control systems.

Airborne Troops (VDV)

Composition and role: a mobile assault force, composed of four divisions based in Novorossiysk, Pskov, Ivanovo and Tula, and one brigade in Ulyanovsk.

Modernisation

During a meeting with senior military men in November 2006 Putin announced that 'The period of patching holes and elementary survival is over . . . The Army and the Navy are again acquiring power and self-confidence' (*Moscow News*, 2006c). Putin has put his personnel in place, specifically Ivanov and Serdyukov, and created new companies in a bid to ensure the development, production and deployment of the latest weapons and equipment. In contrast to the dire financial shortages of the 1990s, Putin has been able steadily to increase the military budget, thanks to windfall oil revenues (petrodollars). Ivanov announced that 300 billion roubles of the 820 billion roubles (US$30.7 billion) military budget for 2007 would be spent on new weapons, including 17 new intercontinental ballistic missiles. Ivanov also announced that the state weapons programme for 2007–2015 planned to spend five trillion roubles (US$188 billion) on the development and production of new weapons (ibid.). At the same time Putin emphasised that Russia's nuclear forces must be capable of guaranteeing the destruction of any potential aggressor, and stressed the importance he attached to the development and deployment of new strategic weapons systems.

Putin, state corporations and weapons procurement

The misappropriation of funds has been one of the major impediments to armed forces modernisation. When Ivanov was replaced as minister of defence he was promoted to deputy prime minister with responsibility for the defence industries, which are vital to the future modernisation of the armed forces. In early February 2007 Putin had instructed Ivanov, then still the defence minister, to create a new civilian agency to preside over weapons systems procurement. This means, in effect, that the new defence minister Serdyuk is in charge of providing the money and Ivanov is in charge of spending it. In February 2006 Putin issued a decree creating the United Aircraft Building Corporation (UABC), through the merger of private companies (Ilyushin, Irkut, Mikoyan, Sukhoi and Yakovlev) with state bodies involved in all stages of the design, manufacture and construction of military and civilian aircraft. Putin appointed Ivanov chair of UABC, which was at first 90 per cent state-owned, but plans were announced to reduce state ownership to 75 per cent (RIA Novosti, 2006a). As well as supplying the Russian air force, the UABC has rapidly become an important player in the lucrative export business.

Rosoboronexport – the Russian arms export state corporation

In the USSR the Ministry of Domestic and Foreign Trade was the main inter-mediary agency for armaments exports from 1953 onwards. In 1993 Yeltsin set up a new state corporation, *Rosvooruzhenie*, to oversee armaments exports. Its progress was typical of the cronyism that characterised Yeltsin's rule. Viktor Samoilov an ally of the defence minister Pavel Grachev was appointed chair and Yeltsin's bodyguard Aleksandr Korzhakov was put in charge of overseeing exports. Within a year it was already clear that while *Rosvooruzhenie* was making exports, not all the transactions were properly recorded and the profits were being stolen. Then in 1997 Yeltsin set up *Promexport* (industrial exports) to break *Rosvooruzhenie*'s near monopoly and deal with the export of the army's surplus weapons, spares and ammunition. The two companies competed for markets and succeeded in driving down the price of Russian exports. In 2000 Putin merged *Rosvooruzhenie* and *Promexport* to form a new state corporation, *Rosoboronexport*; while its predecessors reported to the Ministry of Industry, Science and Technology, *Rosoboronexport* reports to the Defence Ministry. *Rosoboronexport* has successfully restored Russia's arms exports, which fell after 1991. In 2005 Russia's weapons exports to 82 countries were worth US$ 7 billion, that is more than the USA's. China takes 45 per cent of Russia's exports, India 35 per cent and Vietnam 10 per cent (*Moscow News*, 2006b).

Reform and modernisation: new technologies

On 28 March 2007 Army General Alexei Maslov the commander of land forces, announced that Russia's land forces would be rearmed by 2011 and that the next state armament programme would focus on modernising the existing types of armaments (tanks, multiple rocket launch systems [MLRS] and field artillery) and that attention would also be paid to 'creating the scientific basis for a later switch to modern combat methods' (RIA Novosti, 2007f). Maslov pointed out that during 2006 Russian land forces participated in about 500 command and staff exercises, and that of these all the international exercises focused on anti-terrorism or peacekeeping scenarios. Citing instability along the southern borders of the former-USSR, he also stated that land forces would continue to play a dominant role in local and regional conflicts as they might escalate into full-scale war (RIA Novosti, 2007g).

Cossack forces: back safeguarding the borders and the state

In the early 1990s Cossacks in the Far East, Amur and the Primorie (Maritime) border areas re-established their *voyska* or forces and the Transbaikal Cossacks, with the agreement of the local Military District Command, formed their own regiment. In 1994 Yeltsin took the formal decision to restore Cossack units to the Russian armed forces and by 1995 there were more than 20 such Cossack units and combined units, 12 border troop subunits and two detachments on Sakhalin, which is claimed by Japan. Nikolai Yegorov, the head of Yeltsin's Council on Cossack Affairs, stressed that the *voyska* are subordinate to RF armed forces commanders or federal agencies rather than their own Hetmen (leaders). During the 1990s, however, the Cossacks often pursued their own agendas serving in the Dniestr Republic, a Russian populated area that had broken away from the Moldovan republic, in Bosnia, the Abkhazia region of Georgia and in Chechnia. Putin introduced the 'Law on Cossack service' (2005), which sets out the legal and organisational basis for their state service in civilian, military, police capacities and also on behalf of municipalities. It specifies that the Cossacks will serve in units with traditional Cossack names and also gives them a role in civil defence and in combating terrorism. Human rights organisations accuse Cossack paramilitaries of harassing and beating ethnic minorities (Evans, 2005).

Box 9.7 Ministry of the Interior (MVD)

Development: from December 1991 called the Ministry of Security and Interior and since January 1992 the Ministry of the Interior.

Role: policing carried out by the *militsiia* (see Chapter 7) and the State Road Inspection Service (GAI). Supplies troops for deployment within Russia, for example MVD troops fought in Chechnia alongside FSB special units and regular army troops. The troops are also used to guard state institutions, nuclear facilities and military bases; and for the maintenance of public order and crowd control. It also includes a number of special forces (*Spetsnaz*), which conduct anti-terrorism operations and put down prison riots and the OMOM, the Special Purpose Detachment of Militia which is a paramilitary police unit – organised and employed throughout Russia but especially in the Northern Caucasus to control public unrest, demonstrations, anti-terrorism operations, hostage situations and for high-risk arrests. In September 2004 OMOM was used during the Beslan School siege and in October 2005 they were involved in repulsing the attack on Nalchik in Kabardino-Balkaria. Since 2001 when the Federal Migration Service was subordinate to the MVD, it has also dealt with refugee and migration related issues.

Subordinate to: RF president.

Estimated numerical strength: 649,000 uniformed personnel, including 151,100–183,300 internal troops (Renz, 2007: 5).

Ministers:

Viktor Barannikov	19 December 1991 to 15 January 1992
Viktor Yerin	15 January 1992 to 30 June 1995
Yevgeny Abramov	30 June 1995 to 6 July 1995 (acting)
Anatoly Kulikov	6 July 1995 to 23 March 1998
Pavel Maslov	23 March 1998 to 30 March 1998 (acting)
Sergei Stepashin	30 March 1998 to 21 May 1999
Vladimir Rushailo	21 May 1999 to 28 March 2001
Boris Gryzlov	28 March 2001 to 24 December 2003
Rashid Nurgaliyev	24 December 2003– (acting until 9 March 2004)

Website: http://eng.mvdrf.ru

Box 9.8 The Ministry of Justice (Miniust)

Developments: the Federal Service for the Execution of Sentences (FSIN) which oversees Russia's penal system was transferred to Miniust in 1998; FSIN prison guards and militarised special assignment units, which have been used in Chechnia.

Estimated strength: 251,600 uniformed employees, size of special units unknown (Renz, 2007: 5).

See: Chapter 8

> **Box 9.9 Ministry of Civil Defence Matters, Emergencies and the Liquidation of the Consequences of Natural Disasters (MChS)**
>
> **Developments:** originally a State Committee of the same name, it was upgraded to a ministry in January 1994.
>
> **Role:** civil defence, fire safety, protection from natural and manmade disasters, rapid humanitarian response to disasters, search and rescue. Participates in similar missions outside Russia.
>
> **Estimated numerical strength:** 70,000 plus about 300,000 personnel from the State Fire Service (GPS). Its military personnel numbers (civil defence troops) are estimated at 23,000 (Renz, 2007: 5).
>
> **Subordinate to:** the RF President.
>
> **Minister:**
>
> Sergei Shoigu   November 1991–
>
> **Website:** http://www.mchs.gov.ru (Russian only)

Russia's other 'power-wielding' structures

Yeltsin and the proliferation of parallel power-wielding structures

In the 1990s although the total number in the army, navy and air force had been reduced to 1.2 million (Drummond, 1999), according to Chernomyrdin 5.3 per cent of the able-bodied youth were in the armed services and, if private security guards were included, this figure became more like 10 per cent – compared to 1.8 per cent in the UK (Giles to Hosking, 1997). This astonishing figure is explained by the proliferation and expansion of what the Russians call 'power-wielding structures'. In addition to the Defence Ministry's forces, the Interior Ministry and the Security and Emergency Situations Ministry, Federal Border Service, and Federal Agency for Government Communications and Information (FAPSI), Federal Tax Police, Federal Security Service (FSB) and the Foreign Intelligence Agency (SVR) all had troops. There were around 14 'power-wielding structures'. The proliferation of these bodies reflected Yeltsin's tendency towards 'institutional improvisation' and the use of patronage to buy support (see Chapter 5). Yeltsin was particularly keen to create new power-wielding structures during his mid-1990s conflicts with Defence Minister Grachev and the 'War Party' (see Chapter 5). This resulted in bodies with duplicate or overlapping functions and which competed for missions, budgets and personnel. In the mid-1990s the regular armed forces received less than 50 per cent of Russia's conscripts and the remainder went to the other power-wielding structures. In addition to their official duties, all these power-wielding structures have their private businesses, which may involve selling their professional services out for private use, typically as bodyguards, and intelligence and protection services. They also have other commercial enterprises which require labour and this is where the conscripts are a valuable source of free labour.

Box 9.10 Federal Security Service (FSB)

Development: from January 1992 the Ministry of Security (MB) united the functions of internal and foreign intelligence, security and the Federal Border Guard Service. The MB made little inroads into soaring crime and its border troops were not effective in fighting on the Tajik-Afghan border, leading to Barranikov's dismissal. Golushkov was sacked after only three months in October 1993 for failing to warn about the 'parliamentary coup'. The MB was deemed unreformable and abolished in December 1993. It was renamed the Federal Counter-intelligence Service (FSK) and then in April 1995 the Federal Security Service (FSB). During 2003 parts of the disbanded FAPSI were integrated into the FSB, as was the Federal Border Service.

Role: domestic intelligence and counter-intelligence duties, counter-terrorism, the prevention of the export of controlled materials, and the fight against organised crime. The FSB director heads the National Anti-terrorism Commission created in 2006, which coordinates anti-terrorism activities. It has its own special forces such as the Alpha Group and Vympel, which were involved in the Moscow theatre siege in October 2002 and the Beslan school hostage crisis in September 2004. The FSN is empowered to enter homes or businesses without a search warrant and is exempted from oversight by the public prosecutor.

Estimated strength: 66,200 uniformed personnel, including 4,000 armed special forces and 160,000–200,000 border troops (Renz, 2007: 6).

Subordinate to: the Ministry of Justice since March 2004.

Minister of Security:

Viktor Barranikov	24 January 1992 to 28 July 1993

FSK/FSB Directors:

Nikolai Golushko	21 December 1993 to 3 March 1994
Sergei Stepashin	3 March 1994 to 30 June 1995
Anatoly Safonov	30 June 1995 to 24 July 1995 (acting)
Mikhail Barsukov	24 July 1995 to 9 July 1996
Nikolai Kovalyov	9 July 1996 to 25 July 1998
Vladimir Putin	25 July 1998 to 9 August 1998
Nikolai Patrushev	9 August 1999 to 12 May 2008
Aleksandr Bortnikov	12 May 2008–

Website: http://www.fsb.ru (Russian only)

Box 9.11 Foreign Intelligence Service (SVR)

Development: in 1992 the functions of the KGB were divided between new RF organisations. The KGB's First Chief Directorate's spying and counter-espionage role together with its network of foreign agents, electronic monitoring, communications networks and the Space Intelligence Centre were taken over by the Foreign Intelligence Agency (SVR). In 2003 it incorporated part of the disbanded FAPSI.

Role: foreign Intelligence and counter-intelligence, the protection of the state and its personnel from external danger. It is also involved in the prevention of the illegal export of controlled materials and works with its counterparts in other countries to curb the illegal trade in nuclear materials.

Estimated strength: 10,000–15,000, including 300–500 special forces (Renz, 2007: 6).

Subordinate to: the Ministry of Justice, since March 2004.

Directors of Foreign Intelligence Service:

Yevgeny Primakov	26 December 1991 to 9 January 1996
Vyacheslav Trubnikov	10 January 1996 to 21 May 2000
Sergei Lebedev	21 May 2000 to 6 October 2007
Mikhail Fradkov	6 October 2007–

Website: http://svr.gov.ru (Russian only)

Putin and the reduction and streamlining of the power-wielding structures

Putin's reduction and streamlining of the power-wielding structures is part of his overall strategy of cutting costs, increasing efficiency, improving accountability and eliminating corruption. In a series of reforms in 2003–4 Putin reassigned the functions of various power structures to other structures, reducing the number of power-wielding structures to 10 and also reducing the number of deputies to the heads of the remaining power structures. In March 2003 the MVD took on the functions of the Federal Tax Police (FNPS), which was abolished and its staff and resources were directed to a new State Committee for Combatting the Illegal Trade in Drugs and Psychotropic Substances. Russia has a growing drugs problem and is a major smuggling route from Afghanistan and Central Asia into Europe; Putin has identified the battle against narcotics as a priority task. In March 2003 the Federal Border Guards and FAPSI, which had been part of the USSR's KGB, lost their independent status and became part of the FSB. This helped to fuel rumours that Putin intended to reunite Russia's internal and external security services and create a Ministry of State Security (MGB), which had been the name of the soviet secret police from 1946–53. In the event Putin's decree on FSB reform in July 2004 did not reform the MGB or its successor body the KGB, it reduced the number of FSB directors and made FSB directors and deputy directors equal in status, salary, social and medical benefits to ministers and deputy ministers. The FSB formerly had three first deputies and nine deputies; it now has two deputy directors one of whom heads the FSB border service. In July 2004 Putin also issued a decree on the MChS limiting it to three deputy directors and also limiting the number of its central ministry staff.

The other power-wielding structures

The remaining structures are outlined in Box 9.12.

Box 9.12 The other power-wielding structures

The Presidential Security Service (SBP)

Development: a presidential security service was created as part of the KGB's Ninth Directorate after Gorbachev was elected President of the USSR in 1990. In December 1991 it became part of the Main Administration for the Protection of the Russian Federation (GUO) but from 1993–96 the Presidential Security Service was an independent federal body. In July 1996 after Yeltsin sacked Korzhakov (see Chapter 5) it was subordinated to the newly created Federal Protection Service (FSO).

Heads:

Aleksandr Korzhakov	3 September 1991 to 20 June 1996
Yury Kapivin	20 June 1996 to August 1996 (acting)
Anatoly Kuznetsov	August 1996 to January 2000
Viktor Zolotov	April 2000–

Federal Protection (or Guards) Service (FSO)

Developments: until 1990 government security was conducted by the KGB's Ninth Directorate. In December 1991 state security organs, including until 1993 the Presidential Security Service, became part of the Main Administration for the Protection of the Russian Federation (GUO). In 1996 the Federal Protection Service (FSO) was created by a merger with the Presidential Security Service (SBP).

Role: protects high-ranking government personnel, foreign delegations and provides bodyguard services. It also protects strategically important infrastructure and important buildings such as the Kremlin, State Duma and Federation Council. Since 2003 it also operates the government's secure communications service previously run by FAPSI.

Estimated numerical strength: 10,000–30,000, including about 3,000 military personnel in the presidential guards regiment. The majority of FAPSI's estimated 38,000–55,000 personnel are thought to have been transferred to the FSO (Renz, 2007: 5).

Box 9.12 *(Continued)*

Subordinate to: the Ministry of Justice since March 2004.

Heads of GUO:

Vladimir Redkorborody	December 1991 to June 1992
Mikhail Barsukov	12 June 1992 to 24 July 1995
Yury Krapivin	24 July 1995 to 18 May 2000

Head of FSO:

Yevgeny Murov   18 May 2000–

Website: http://www.fso.gov.ru/ (Russian only)

The Federal Service for Control over the Circulation of Narcotics and Psychotropic Drugs (FSKN)

Development: originally created in March 2003 as a State Committee for the Control of Narcotic and Psychotropic Substances (GKPN), taking on the staff and funding of the disbanded Federal Tax Police. It became a Federal Service on 9 March 2004.

Role: fighting drug cartels, coordinating all drug-related investigations, enforcing drugs laws within Russia and controlling the trade in pharmaceutical products. It also has liaison officers in other countries.

Answers directly to: the RF president.

Estimated strength: 36,000–40,000, including an unknown number of special forces (Renz, 2007: 6).

Director:

Gen. Viktor Cherkesov   11 March 2003–

Website: http://www.gnk.gov.ru/

State Courier Service (GFS)

Development: formerly part of the Ministry of Communications but in 1997 it became a federal service.

Role: couriering sensitive and official documents and goods on behalf of federal state bodies.

Estimated strength: 4,570 including about 3,500 uniformed personnel (Renz, 2007: 6).

Directors:

Valery Andreyev	1991–1999
Andrei Chernenko	1999–2002
Gennady Kornienko	2002–

Website: http://www.gfs.ru/ (Russian only)

Box 9.12 (*Continued*)

Main Directorate for Special Programmes under the President (GUSP)

Development: formerly part of the presidential administration, GUSP became a federal agency in 1998.

Role: plans the building and maintenance of an emergency infrastructure such as underground bunkers and transport routes. The organisation of federal bodies in the event of an attack on Russia.

Estimated numerical strength: 8,000–20,000 (Renz, 2007: 6).

Directors:

Vasily Frolov	December 1991 to May 1998
Viktor Zorin	May 1998 to June 2000
Aleksandr Tsarenko	June 2000–

Chapter summary

Russia sees itself as a global power and believes that it needs military might to back this aspiration and to challenge the USA's increasingly unilateral global behaviour (see Chapter 13). Putin used some of Russia's increased oil revenues to begin the reform and modernisation of its forces. He drew on his *siloviki* network to push forward with his reforms and to provide civilian oversight of the armed forces. Continuing tensions between the Defence Ministry and the General Staff are, in part, due to disagreements about reform and modernisation, but also about the broader issue of bringing the armed forces under civilian control. Other difficulties also remain, not least the major security failures during 2002–4 that revealed official incompetence and corruption. These deep-seated problems will not be resolved solely by increased spending and technological innovation as they also need political and judicial solutions. However, the armed and security forces have not welcomed scrutiny by the mass media or civil society and Putin's establishment of a managed democracy means that investigations by journalists and NGOs have been increasingly suppressed.

In an interview with the *Financial Times* (2008) President-elect Medvedev was asked to respond to Viktor Cherkesov's claim that, 'members of the security forces were fighting each other for wealth and influence in Russia'. That the Russian authorities approved this question suggests that dealing with these issues is part of Medvedev's presidential agenda. Medvedev responded that he had no evidence that the security services were competing for wealth, but if he received such information, those involved would be fired immediately and charged with crimes. He stated clearly that violations or crimes by individuals must be investigated and punished appropriately. He noted that the security services' role is to, 'follow their constitutional task to defend the social order. At the same time in any state the security services do compete against each other. This is a guarantee that multi-sided information on the situation in the country will be put on the leader's table' (ibid.). The image Medvedev has created is one of the armed and security services feeding information and ideas to their civilian commander-in-chief, the president.

Discussion points

- Should we be concerned by Putin's appointment of *siloviki* to elite civilian posts?
- Why has military reform been so slow?
- Does Russia need to maintain conscription to keep its armed forces at an appropriate size?
- Why is *dedovshchina* such a widespread practice and how can it be stopped?

Further reading

The Journal of Slavic Military Studies published by Taylor and Francis, as its title suggests, regularly carries up-to-date articles on the armed forces.

An analysis of the development of the relationship between the president and the military is provided by David M. Glantz and Dale Herspring (2006) *The Kremlin and the High Command: Presidential Impact on the Russian Military from Gorbachev to Putin*, Lawrence, KS: University of Kansas Press.

Differing interpretations of the role of the *siloviki* are offered by Olga Kryshtanovskaya and Stephen White (2003) '"Putin's Militocracy"', *Post-Soviet Affairs*, 19 (4), 289–306; Bettina Renz et al. (2007) '"Siloviki" in Politics. Russian Military Reform', *Russian Analytical Digest* (17) March, 1–10, available on the Russian-Eurasian Security Network website, http://www.res.ethz.ch/; and Sharon Werning Rivera, and David W. Rivera (2006) 'The Russian Elite under Putin: Militocratic or Bourgeois?', *Post-Soviet Affairs*, 22 (2), 125–44.

Analyses of the development and modernisation of the armed forces are provided by Rod Thornton (2007) 'Russian Military Reform', *Russian Analytical Digest*, (17) March, 10–12, available on the Russian-Eurasian Security Network website http://www.res.ethz.ch/; Stephen Blank (ed.) (2005) *Potemkin's Treadmill: Russian Military Modernization. Strategic Asia 2005–06: Military Modernization in an Era of Uncertainty*, September, on National Bureau of Asian Research website, http://www.nbr.org/; and Isabelle Facon (2005) 'The Modernisation of the Russian Military: The Ambitions and Ambiguities of Vladimir Putin', *Conflict Studies Research Centre, Russian Series*, August, 05/19(E), http://www.defac.ac.uk/.

Analyses of the Russian security services are provided by the Russian journalist Yevgenia Albats in her (1995) *KGB: State within a State*, London: I.B. Tauris; J. M. Waller (1994) *Secret Empire: The KGB in Russia Today*, Boulder, CO: Westview Press; Jonathan Littell (2006) 'The Security Organs of the Russian Federation. A Brief History 1991–2004', *Post-*

Soviet Armies Newsletter (PSAN), online at http://www.psan.org/sommaire307.html; and Gordon Bennett (2000), 'The Federal Security Service of the Russian Federation', C102, *Conflict Studies Research Centre*, Defence Academy UK, http://www.defac.ac.uk/.

Pavel Felgenhauer is one of Russia's leading commentators on military and defence issues. He is the defence correspondent of the newspaper *Novaia Gazeta* and a regular contributor to other publications and websites, including the Jamestown Foundation website: http://www.jamestown.org/.

Useful websites

Conflict Studies Research Centre, Defence Academy UK – Caucasus Series, Russian Chronologies and Russian Series: http://www.defac.ac.uk/

Center for Defense Information website carries *Russia Weekly*, a weekly newsletter on defence related news about Russia: http://www.cdi.org/russia

Center for Strategic and International Studies, Washington, DC. This website includes the Russia and Eurasia Program, Caucasus Initiative and the Program on New Approaches to Russian Security (PONARS): http://www.csis.org/researchfocus/RussiaEurasia/

Military Parade – News on the Russian defence industry: http://www.milparade.com/

National Security Council: http://www.scrf.gov.ru/ (Russian language only)

Russian and Eurasian Security (RES), for Security Watch reports: http://www.res.ethz.ch/

Post-Soviet Armies Newsletter is an online database devoted to the armed forces and power ministries: http://www.psan.org/

Pavel Felgenhauer is a Moscow-based defence analyst who writes for the English language *The Moscow Times*, which is available online at: http://www.themoscowtimes.com/

***Rosoboronexport* (Russian Defence Export) State Corporation**: http://www.roe.ru/roe_eng/en_news/roe_en_news.html

Beslan Mothers website: http://www.materibeslana.com/rus/index.php (Russian only)

The Beslan Truth website: http://www.pravdabeslana.ru/english.htm

References

Butrin, D. et al. (2007) 'Civilian Economist Heads Defense Ministry', *Kommersant*, 16 February, http://www.kommersant.com/

Drummond, F. (1999) 'Russian Navy Listing up Afloat', *Perspective*, 9 (4), March–April, http://www.bu.edu/iscip/vol9/Drummond.html

Dunlop, J. B. (2006) *The 2002 Dubrovka and 2004 Beslan Hostage Crises: A Critique of Russian Counter-Terrorism*, Stuttgart: Ibidem-Verlag

Evans, J. (2005) 'Putin sends Cossacks in fight against Terrorism', *The Times*, 2 July, http://www.timesonline.co.uk/

Financial Times (2008) 'Interview Transcript: Dmitry Medvedev', *Financial Times*, 24 March, http://www.ft.com/

FOM (2005a) 'The Beslan Hostage Crisis', *The Public Opinion Foundation Database*, 14 July, http://bd.english.fom.ru/

FOM (2005b) 'Beslan: One Year Later', *The Public Opinion Foundation Database*, 30 August, http://bd.english.fom.ru/

Giles, K. (2006) 'Where have all the Soldiers Gone? Russia's Military Plans versus Demographic Reality', *Conflict Studies Research Centre, Russian Series*, October, 06/47, http://www.defac.ac.uk/

Hosking, G. (1997) 'Russia Five Years On: Dialogue with (retd.) Col. Roy Giles', broadcast on BBC Radio 3, 9 January

IHF (2005) 'The Silencing of Human Rights Defenders in Chechnya and Ingushetia', *International Helsinki Fund Report*, http://www.ihf-hr.org/

Lambeth, B. S. (1995) 'Russia's Wounded Military', *Foreign Affairs*, 74 (2), March–April, 86–98

Moscow News (2005) 'Beslan Commission Refutes Reports of Authorities Incompetence in School Siege Actions', *Moscow News*, 27 December, http://mosnews.com/

Moscow News (2006a) 'Genealogy of Fifth Generation Fighters', *Moscow News*, 22 June, http://mosnews.com/

Moscow News (2006b) 'Russian Defense Sector Unable to Meet $17 Bn Demand – Official', *Moscow News*, 20 July, http://mosnews.com/

Moscow News (2006c) 'Putin Says Russia Needs High End Nuclear Forces', *Moscow News*, 17 November, http://mosnews.com/

Pyati, A. (2005) 'The New Dissidents. Human Rights Defenders and Counterterrorism in Russia', *Human Rights Defenders and Counterrorism Series*, No. 1. Available on the Human Rights First website, http://www.humanrightsfirst.org/

Renz, B. (2007) 'The Russian Force Structures', *Russian Analytical Digest*, (17), March, 5–6, http://www.res.ethz.ch/

RIA Novosti (2006a) 'Anti-monopoly watchdog approves Russian aircraft corp', 25 August, *RIA Novosti* website, http://en.rian.ru/

RIA Novosti (2006b) 'Russian ex-officer gets 12-year term in beating death of soldier', 12 October, *RIA Novosti* website, http://en.rian.ru/

RIA Novosti (2007a) 'Crime in Russian Army drops 2% in 2006 – military prosecutors', 25 January, *RIA Novosti* website, http://en.rian.ru/

RIA Novosti (2007b) 'Putin Pledges greater role for General Staff', 15 February, *RIA Novosti* website, http://en.rian.ru/

RIA Novosti (2007c) 'Russia's Defence Ministry to keep upgrading Armed Forces – DM', 23 February, *RIA Novosti* website, http://en.rian.ru/

RIA Novosti (2007d) 'Violence in the military main cause of suicides, desertions – brass', 28 March, *RIA Novosti* website, http://en.rian.ru/

RIA Novosti (2007e) 'Contract soldiers to fill 45 per cent of slots in Russian military by 2008', 28 March, *RIA Novosti* website, http://en.rian.ru/

RIA, Novosti (2007f) 'Russian Land Forces formations to be rearmed by 2011 – commander', 28 March, *RIA Novosti* website, http://en.rian.ru/

RIA, Novosti (2007g) 'Land Forces are core of Russian Armed Forces', 28 March, *RIA Novosti* website, http://en.rian.ru/

Savel'eva, I. (2005) *'Doklad – Beslan: pravda zalozhnikov'*, *Pravda Beslana* website: http://www.pravdabeslana.ru/

Solov'ev, V. (2001) *'Generaly ukhodiat v oppozitsiiu Kremliu'*, *Nezavisimaia Gazeta*, 13 November, http://www.ng.ru

Yuzbachev, V. (2006) 'Sychyov's hazing case: Aftermath for the Russian army', *RIA Novosti* website, 28 September, http://en.rian.ru/

Part 3

POLITICAL IDEAS, PARTIES AND
THE REPRESENTATIVE PROCESS

Chapter 10

Civil society

Learning objectives

- To introduce the concepts of civil society and social capital.
- To examine the legal basis of Russian civil society.
- To explain Putin's attempts to co-opt and control civil society.
- To examine extremism, racism and xenophobia.

Introduction

Civil society is a necessary, but not sufficient, precondition for democratisation and the transition from a procedural to a substantive democracy. Support for democratic values such as human rights and the rule of law helps to create the conditions in which civil society can form and thrive. The development and role of civil society must be understood within the broader context of the changing relations between state and society in the USSR and the Russian Federation. Gorbachev permitted the development of independent, grassroots organisations as part of his democratisation of soviet socialism. During the 1990s under Yeltsin civil society organisations mushroomed, although many quickly folded or just ceased operation. Nonetheless by the end of the 1990s Russia had thousands of non-governmental organisations (NGOs) organised around a wide range of issues. The prospects for the further development and role of civil society under Putin must be understood within the context of his advocacy of managed democracy and his commitment to strengthening the power vertical (see Chapters 5–8). Putin's bid to concentrate power in the presidency and to strengthen the state creates conditions in which it is more difficult for civil society to function. Instead of developing points of access and procedures for interaction and genuine dialogue between state and society, Putin instead set up bodies such as the Civic Forum, the Public Chamber and the Presidential Council for Facilitating the Development of Civil Society Institutions and Human Rights, to which selected representatives of the public and civil society organisations are invited. Such bodies present a dilemma for civil society organisations as they represent the best chance to have any influence, no matter how limited and controlled, on the current leadership; but they are also part of Putin's bid to manage civil society. By its very nature civil society must be independent of the state; however, Putin is seeking to co-opt and incorporate civil society organisations within state structures. This is also part of Putin's broader agenda of strengthening the Russian state which he sees as being under threat from a 'Coloured Revolution' fomented by western influence and money, terrorism, extremism and a lack of patriotism.

Civil society and democratisation

Defining civil society

The modern usage of the term civil society was developed by the Scottish Enlightenment thinker Adam Ferguson (1723–1816) in his *An Essay on the History of Civil Society* (1767). He linked civil society with the emergence of a market economy and used civil society and commercial society almost interchangeably. Ferguson saw civil society as a distinct domain characterised by a sense of public-spiritedness, moral and cultural accomplishments, a complex division of labour and the subjection of government to the rule of law. Drawing on Ferguson's ideas the German philosopher Georg Hegel (1770–1831) also linked the development of civil society with the advent of a market economy. In his *Elements of the Philosophy of Right* (1821), Hegel described civil society (*burgerliche gesellschaft*) as separate and quite distinct from the political state (*der staat*), an idea which remains at the core of the modern understanding of civil society. The term civil society fell out of use but underwent a tremendous revival in the 1980s, particularly among eastern European dissident intellectuals. It is easy to see the appeal of the idea of civil society as the domain where individual rights and liberties are championed and protected from the encroachment of the state, and in the face of seemingly all-powerful authoritarian regimes that sought to suppress autonomous ideas, organisations and activities. Civil society is the arena where relations between the individual and the state are mediated by a range of autonomous bodies, groupings and organisations. Families, charities and philanthropic organisations, voluntary bodies, non-government organisations (NGOs), professional associations, academia, clubs, community foundations, trade unions, religious and cultural groups and the mass media (see Chapter 12) are all part of civil society. Hegel was also aware that at the very heart of civil society there is a tension between individualism and community. The pursuit of individual rights, liberties and ideas may easily shade into self-interest and self-aggrandisement, which could ultimately destroy the community, the free associational life, that forms the basis of collective action. For liberal democrats, therefore, civil society as much as the state must be governed by the rule of law.

Box 10.1 Definitions of civil society

Definition 1: The London School of Economics, Centre for Civil Society

Civil society refers to the arena of un-coerced collective action around shared interests, purposes and values. In theory, its institutional forms are distinct from those of the state, family and market, though in practice, the boundaries between state, civil society, family and market are often complex, blurred and negotiated. Civil society commonly embraces a diversity of spaces, actors and institutional forms, varying in their degree of formality, autonomy and power. Civil societies are often populated by organisations such as registered charities, non-governmental organisations, community groups, women's organisations, faith-based organisations, professional associations, trades unions, self-help groups, social movements, business associations, coalitions and advocacy groups.

Source: http://www.lse.ac.uk/collections/CCS/introduction.htm

Definition 2: Carnegie UK Trust, Democracy and Civil Society Programme

The working definition of civil society used to inform the work of the Inquiry has three dimensions:

- **Civil Society as associational life.** Civil society is the 'space' of organised activity not undertaken by either the government or for-private-profit business. It includes formal and informal associations such as: voluntary and community organisations, trade unions, faith-based organisations, co-operatives and mutuals, political parties, professional and business associations, philanthropic organisations, informal citizen groups and social movements. Participation in or membership of such organisations is voluntary in nature.

- **Civil Society as the 'good' society.** The term civil society is often used as a short-hand for the type of society we want to live in and can therefore be viewed in normative terms. It is often assumed that civil society is a good thing, but this is not necessarily true. For example, civil society associations can help strengthen democracy and improve the well-being of deprived communities as can they undermine human rights and preach intolerance and violence. . . . A 'good' civil society needs to have constructive relationships with government, statutory agencies, the business sector and media. The actions of civil society associations alone cannot achieve a 'good' civil society.

- **Civil Society as an arena for public deliberation.** Civil society is an arena for public deliberation and the exercise of active citizenship in pursuit of common interests. It is the public space in which societal differences, social problems, public policy, government action and matters of community and cultural identity are developed and debated. These public spaces might be physical in nature, such as community centres, or virtual, such as blogs. We may never share a common vision about what a 'good' society might look like and how it might be achieved, but can be committed to a process that allows people of all ages and backgrounds to share in defining how the different visions are reconciled.

Source: http://democracy.carnegieuktrust.org.uk/civil_society/what_is_civil_society (abbreviated)

Civil society and democracy

Previous chapters have examined different aspects of democratisation such as its social prerequisites (Chapter 3) and the creation of new institutions, specifically the legislature, executive and judiciary as well as regional and local bodies (Chapters 5–8). The development of a civil society is an important aspect of democratisation and the transformation of procedural democracies into substantive democracies (see Chapter 3). Ernest Gellner (1994), for example, argues that democracy is simply not possible without a civil society. The groups that mediate between the individual and the state help to limit the state's power to control the individual and to infringe their rights and liberties. Civil society groups and networks help to aggregate interests and articulate demands, which are then fed into policy making and also help to promote government accountability. Francis Fukuyama (1999) argues that in liberal democracies the state is constrained from interfering in a 'protected sphere of individual liberty', it is in this protected sphere that civil society organises itself and counterbalances state power, so protecting the individual. In democracies civil society organisations may support or criticise the state and/or the government, but provided they exercise their rights peacefully and lawfully and do not infringe the rights of others, such organisations and their activities should not be banned just for saying things that state bodies and the government do not want to hear. If civil society organisations break the law by inciting violence or hatred, or by employing terrorist actions, then they are subject to legal penalties.

Social capital and trust

Civil society also contributes to democratic stability and the development of market economies, by both reflecting and encouraging trust and cooperation. In the 1990s the concept of 'social capital' was popularised by the American political scientist Robert Putnam (1993, 2000) and is now widely used to analyse the strength of democracies. Putnam argues that social capital is vital to the creation and maintenance of civil society and, therefore, of democracy. At its simplest social capital is the ability of citizens to trust one another and also their country's institutions. Trust encourages associational activities such as joining groups or working with others, civic engagement and community building, and underpins the economic exchanges of a market economy (see Fukuyama, 1995; Putnam, 2000). Trust, therefore, helps to sustain existing democracies and facilitates the transition process from authoritarianism to democracy. Fukuyama uses the concept of social capital to explain why the transition to democracy and a market economy has proved more difficult in some former communist countries than in others. He argues that 'in the former Soviet Union after the Bolshevik Revolution, . . . the Communist Party consciously sought to undermine all forms of horizontal association in favor of vertical ties between Party-State and individual. This has left post-Soviet society bereft of both trust and a durable civil society' (1995). So the CPSU ensured that the USSR did not develop social capital, which meant that Russia and other former Soviet Union (FSU) states began democratisation with poorly developed, proto-civil societies at best. The result was that in the early 1990s Russia acquired the trappings of democracy, such as a new Constitution and political institutions, but this was not balanced by the recognition that the state's powers should be limited and by the existence of a vibrant civil society to ensure that this happened. In contrast in Poland and Czechoslovakia, the communist regimes did not destroy civil society and so they have experienced smoother transitions to democracy. Fukuyama believes that over time human nature will ensure that social capital and civil society develop, but that this will mean a prolonged transitional period.

Trust in Russian institutions

The Levada Centre, one of Russia's leading public opinion polling organisations, has conducted surveys of Russians' trust in their country's institutions over the period 2001–2007. The latest survey of 2,107 Russians over sixteen years of age was conducted in March 2007 (see Table 10.1). Only the Russian president, Vladimir Putin has been consistently trusted by the majority of Russians.

A more positive picture of the trend in levels of trust in institutions has been identified by surveys conducted by the World Economic Forum (WEF) based in Geneva. Surveys in 20 countries conducted by GlobeScan on behalf of the WEF since 2001 have found that, while public confidence in governments is falling around the world, Russia is the only country where confidence has been steadily growing (Sindelar, 2005). According to Vladimir Andreenkov, the director of the CESSI institute for comparative social research which provided the Russian data, public trust in the Russian government is relatively low, lower than in India, Indonesia or the United States,

Table 10.1 Trust in Russia's institutions 2001–2007

To what extent do you trust . . . ?	Completely			Not completely			Not at all		
	2001	2006	2007	2001	2006	2007	2001	2006	2007
President of Russia	52	56	64	31	30	23	7	7	7
Church, religious organisations	41	38	42	21	21	17	12	11	12
Army	33	20	31	31	35	30	18	28	20
Press, radio, television	28	22	27	43	42	35	18	20	14
State security organs	22	23	24	32	29	27	19	18	18
Government of Russia	21	14	19	41	39	40	22	30	26
Regional (*krai* and republican) organs of power	21	19	18	36	39	35	27	28	33
Courts	13	15	17	34	33	28	26	27	27
Procuracy	11	14	16	32	31	28	30	26	26
Local (city and *raion*) organs of power	20	16	16	36	35	31	31	38	41
State Duma	10	11	13	41	42	41	35	35	33
Federation Council	12	11	12	36	38	37	21	24	22
Police (*militsiia*)	12	11	12	36	34	35	38	42	38
Trade unions	14	9	9	25	20	21	31	33	28
Political parties	7	4	7	28	28	27	36	41	36

Source: Levada-Tsentr (2007) '*Doverie institutam vlasti*', 9 April, *Levada Centre* website, http://www.levada.ru/

Note: Responses in percentages. The 'don't knows' ('difficult to say') are not cited.

but the government has been working very hard to persuade people it is working for them. The government is using the media, especially the television, to publicise its social programmes. GlobeScan's president Douglas Miller believes that Putin's strategy of strengthening the power vertical, standing up to the oligarchs and taking back control of the energy sector have played 'very, very positively with average Russia citizens' (ibid.). This also helps to explain why a higher percentage of Russians have a positive attitude towards the presidential administration than to any other government body. Trust grew as the Putin administration projected itself as successfully tackling Russia's problems, but trust in Russian institutions overall remains extremely low. This also reflects and reinforces a widespread Russian cultural preference for a strong, capable leader who gets things done (see Chapter 3).

Trust and civil society

Networks of trusted friends and colleagues or alliances based on patron–client relationships were an important part of the way in which individuals survived and prospered in the USSR and such networks remain important in Russia today. The trust-based networks are a good basis for the development of civil society. Other aspects of the soviet legacy and by-products of the transition process are not conducive to trust. In the USSR people tended to be very guarded about what they said in front of strangers and such behaviour, born of self-protection, is difficult to change. The growth in crime and corruption and the general insecurity of life in the 1990s contributed to a continuing wariness and suspicion of others, rather than openness and a willingness to trust strangers. Russians are engaged in 'associational behaviour', which may reflect some degree of existing trust or that people are driven to cooperation. One of the most geographically widespread, active and trusted NGOs is the Union of Soldiers' Mothers Committees of Russia (USMCR). It is a human rights NGO composed of mothers working on behalf of their sons. Mothers whose sons are about to be, or have been, conscripted approach the committees out of desperation (Danks, 2006). Generally Russians are suspicious of the motivation of civil society activists and there is a widespread belief that they 'are more concerned with getting western funding than actually changing things' (Malyakin and Konnova, 1999). According to the WEF survey Russia follows the global trend of a drop in trust in NGOs. According to Andreenko, 'Before [the measures to restrict NGOs], generally speaking, very few people had any concept of what an NGO was – for the vast majority of people it just wasn't a relevant issue' (Sindelar, 2005).

The development of civil society in the 1990s

Civil society: the soviet legacy

The relationship between the soviet party-state and civil society has had a major impact on the course of Russia's post-communist transition. During *perestroika* the CPSU allowed informal groups and organisations to be established without its direction or participation (see Chapter 1), which was an important step in the creation of a civil society independent of the party-state. There was a proliferation of groups at this time but, as Gill and Markwick (2000: 70) argue, these groups did not represent a 'mature civil society', they were weak and 'fragmented and were not part of a web of interactions and relations which constituted an arena of activity which the party-state acknowledged as theirs by right' (ibid.). Instead these groups were able to 'carve out niches' in soviet society against a hostile party apparatus. So although the new Russian Federation had a civil society it was 'stunted' or 'immature'. Another soviet legacy is for political elites to set up civil society groups, political parties and think-tanks in a style reminiscent of the soviet practice of setting up what they called 'transmission belts' – such as the trade unions or women's soviets – between the CPSU and the people to serve the party's needs. During the late 1980s and through the 1990s there was a burgeoning of independent groups, including cultural, professional, nationality-based, charities, ecological

---

Box 10.2 The legal framework for 'freedom of association'

The RF Constitution (1993)

Article 30

(1) Everyone shall have the right to association, including the right to create trade unions in order to protect one's interests. The freedom of public associations' activities shall be guaranteed.

(2) No one may be coerced into joining any association or into membership thereof.

Article 56 allows for the limitation of the right of association during a state of emergency.

Federal laws

On Non-Governmental Organisations, 19 May 1995

On Freedom of Conscience and Religious Unions, 26 September 1997

On Trade Unions, their Rights and Guarantees of their Activities, 12 January 1996

On Political Parties, 11 July 2001

On General Principles of Organising of Communities of Indigenous and Minority Nationalities of North, Siberia and Far East of the Russian Federation, 20 July 2000

On Employers' Unions, 27 November 2002

On State Support of Youth and Child Non Governmental Organisations, 28 June 1995

Charitable Activities and Charity Organisations, 11 August 1995

Counteraction to Extremist Activities, 25 July 2002

On State Registration of Legal Entities and Individual Entrepreneurs, 8 August 2001

Source: OSCE Office for Democratic Institutions and Human Rights, http://www.legislationonline.org/

or women's groups, but these groups had limited access to federal and regional political elites. The phenomenon of elite-sponsored groups and the lack of contact between independent civil society groups and political elites has led Richard Rose (1995) to characterise Russia today as an 'hour glass society'. At the top of the hour glass there is a rich political and social life and the elites compete for power, wealth and prestige; at the base of the hour glass there is a rich social life consisting of strong, informal networks relying on trust between friends, relatives and friends of friends, and other face-to-face groups. For Rose, 'Such a society resembles a civil society insofar as a number of informal and even formal institutions are tolerated and now legally recognized by the state. Yet the result is not a civic community but an hour glass society, because the links between top and bottom are limited' (Rose, 1995: 35).

Foreign support for Russian civil society

In the 1990s the number of NGOs grew rapidly, although not all sustained their initial enthusiasm or could finance their activities. Western governments and the European Union were active in providing know-how and finance to Russian NGOs as part of their programmes to support Russian democratisation. The European Union, for example, provided funding to the Union of Committees of Soldiers' Mothers of Russia (UCSMR), to NGOs engaged in retraining women for jobs in the market economy and for women's refuges. International NGOs, such as Amnesty International and Greenpeace set up branches in Russia. The US-based Carnegie Foundation and The Open Society Institute, which is part of the George Soros Foundation Network, also provided funding to support civil society. The lack of domestic sources of funding for NGOs, either from ordinary citizens or from the Russian rich, meant that in the 1990s foreign sources of funding were a lifeline for many NGOs. Russian NGOs also benefited from training in lobbying, information and communications technology, and management; they were also usually required to adopt the administrative and financial accounting practices of western NGOs.

Putin and the control of civil society

Putin, patriotism and civil society

Putin's approach to civil society reflects his security background and a fear that NGOs might seek to subvert the state either on their own behalf or at the behest of a foreign paymaster. Putin's approach to civil society is also in part a response to the 'Colour Revolutions' in other FSU states (see Chapter 3) and to the development of terrorism within Russia. In effect Putin categorised civil society into acceptable patriotic and unacceptable unpatriotic elements. In his 2004 Annual Address to Federal Assembly Putin stressed: 'We want a mature democracy and a developed civil society' (Putin, 2004) but later warned that while thousands of Russia's public organisations worked 'constructively', not all stood 'for the people's real interests' (ibid.). He charged that, 'For some the priority is to receive financing from influential foreign foundations. Others serve dubious groups and commercial interests' (ibid.). Putin has no problem with NGOs undertaking charitable, welfare, educational and training and some commercial activities, or with foreign funding being used to support such work. However, his use of the term 'traitors' to describe not just Chechen rebels but also journalists and environmentalists, implies a concept of patriotism that does not sit well with democratic pluralism and the rule of law. Russia's environmentalists, anti-nuclear campaigners and human rights activists are condemned as western spies and subjected to harassment. In March 2000, for example, the Moscow offices of Greenpeace were ordered to close because a partition wall supposedly infringed planning regulations, the closure order originating in the Anti-terrorism Commission. Soon after Putin's 2004 Annual Address the equipment of the Tatarstan Human Rights Centre in Kazan was smashed by unidentified, armed men. The Centre was funded by the anti-Putin oligarch Mikhail Khodorkovsky, a 'dubious commercial interest', and had previously complained that the local police had been pressurising them because they are critical of Putin (Glasser, 2004: A17).

Civil society, Colour Revolutions and spies

The Kremlin watched developments in Ukraine and Kyrgyzstan in 2005 and feared that similar revolutions might happen in Russia. From the Kremlin's perspective foreign-funded NGOs played a major role in these Colour Revolutions and so must be controlled. In July 2005 Putin said he would not allow foreign countries to use NGOs to fund 'political activities' (The Civil Society Institutions etc., 2005). In 2006 Vladislav Surkov, a close Putin ally, argued that while a military attack on Russia was highly unlikely the principal threats to Russia's national sovereignty came from the possibility of a 'colour revolution' alongside international terrorism and economic non-competitiveness (RIA Novosti, 2006a). Surkov is a presidential aide who also heads a state oil company and has played a major role in the creation of managed democracy, including the organisation of the pro-Kremlin United Russia party. Foreign ties and especially foreign funding of NGOs have been identified by the Kremlin as posing a threat to Russian sovereignty. This idea was highlighted on 22 January 2006 when state-owned television aired a programme called 'Spies', which carried allegations that British spies were funding NGOs and communicating with them using hollowed out rocks. Two days later the Duma called on the FSB to report on political parties and organisations that receive foreign funding and for the legality of the foreign-funding of NGOs to be investigated. Lyudmila Alekseeva, who was a founder member of the Moscow Helsinki Group in 1976, responded by accusing the FSB and the Russian media of violating the rights of NGOs and particularly of human rights advocates by linking them to foreign spies in order to discredit them. One of the claims in 'Spies' was that one of the alleged British spies, worked with the human rights and pro-democracy Moscow Helsinki Group and the Eurasia Fund (Kozenko, 2006).

Box 10.3 Putin on NGOs and foreign finance

In response to a question from the BBC journalist Steven Rosenberg about whether the spy scandal would lead to a tightening of control over NGOs, Putin replied:

> . . . Non-governmental organizations are a necessary part of society because they control the activity of the state and the agencies of power. They are an important part of the social organism. And the Russian government shall support these non-governmental organizations. We want them to be financed in a transparent way, we want these organizations to be independent, and not to be controlled by some puppet master from abroad because such incidents like the one we just saw only compromise the activities of non-governmental organizations. But we cannot fail to address such incidents because non-governmental organizations cannot be used as foreign policy instruments by one state on the territory of another. . . .

Source: 'Transcript of the Press Conference for the Russian and Foreign Media', 31 January 2006, Kremlin website, http://www.kremlin.ru/eng/

Russian foundations: funding civil society

It is very difficult for Russian civil society organisations to fund themselves without support from abroad or the Russian state. During the 1990s most philanthropic work and grants to civil society groups were made by foreign governments, foundations and charities. In the late 1990s the 'Donors Forum', a non-profit making partnership of grant-making organisations was formed in Russia. In 2000 the V. Potanin Charity Fund became the Donors Forum's first Russian member. Russia's rich have been slow to get involved in philanthropic work and with the notable exception of Mikhail Khodorkovsky (see Chapter 16), the Yukos Fund and more recently Dmitry Zimin, they avoid the controversial areas of human rights, social justice and pro-democracy activities that might bring then into conflict with the Kremlin. In 2002 the Yukos Foundation contributed funds to the US-based Eurasia Foundation to promote community and private sector development in rural Russia. The Eurasia Foundation had operated in Russia since 1993 and in 2004 was a co-founder of The New Eurasia Foundation, together with the Brussels-based Madariaga Foundation and Dmitry Zimin's Dynasty Foundation. According to the New Eurasia Foundation website, it supports:

- Citizen participation in the local decision-making process.
- Increasing the transparency and responsiveness of government decision making and administrative reform.
- Local self-governance by assisting in the planning and implementation of regional, social and economic development.
- Reform of the educational system and its institutions.
- The development of entrepreneurship.

- A supportive environment for independent mass media to play a tangible and constructive role in society.

- International cooperation in the development of civil society, local self-governance, education, science and small business, in particular among Russia, the US and European states.

The areas that the Russian foundations are prepared to fund do contribute to the development of civil society, by developing participants' organisational, administrative and financial accounting skills.

Box 10.4 Russia's rich and charitable foundations

Founder and business	Foundation	Supports
Vladimir Potanin, nickel and banking	Vladimir Potanin Charity Fund created in 1999	Arts, culture and education, including individual student grants. Spends about $10 million annually.
Mikhail Khodorkovsky, Yukos oil company, but now in prison for tax evasion.	Open Russia	Democracy oriented projects.
Dmitry Zimin, who built Russia's second-largest cellular phone company, *VympelCom*.	Dynasty Foundation	Originally only funded fundamental science, especially physics. Concern about Russia's political direction led Zimin, in 2006, to devote 25 per cent of Dynasty's US$4 million annual disbursement to fund a liberal think-tank, journalism training and other civil projects.
Mikhail Prokhorov, nickel.	Fund for Cultural Initiatives	Focuses on developing the intellectual and cultural environment of the Norilsk region.
Oleg Deripaska, aluminum	Free Deed Foundation	The Orthodox Church and education. Underwrites the social and educational programmes of Orthodox Churches and funds Orthodox schools and seminaries. Spent US$36 million in 2006.
Dmitry Zelenin, governor of the Tver *oblast*, a former industrialist.	Good Beginnings	Medical and educational.
Viktor Vekselberg, oil and metals	Kind Century	Improvement of mental health treatment.
Nikolai Tsvetkov, *UralSib* financial corporation	Victoria Fund	Orphanages.

Sources: Peter Finn (2006) 'In Russia, Cautious Generosity. Tycoons Pour Money into Causes but Steer Clear of Democracy Issues', *Washington Post Foreign Service*, 22 September, A10, http://www.washingtonpost.com/; and Jamey Gambrell (2004) 'Philanthropy in Russia: New Money under Pressure', *Carnegie Report*, 3 (1), Fall, http://www.carnegie.org/

Government 'non-governmental organisation' and civil society activities

The organisation of civil society under Putin extends to organising demonstrations and setting up pro-Kremlin NGOs. At the beginning of Putin's first administration this was in part an attempt to counter NGOs funded by oligarchs such as Berezovsky and to counter the influence of environmental groups. During the summer of 2000, independent environmental groups collected 2.5 million signatures in a bid to have a referendum called on the import of spent nuclear fuel. In response the government formed *Zeleny Krest* (Green Cross) and *KEDR* (Constructive Ecological Movement of Russia), loyal 'NGOs' designed to show the unity of civil society and government policy. A new law on Referenda in 2004 also made it virtually impossible for a grassroots' initiative to lead a referendum, by setting the requirement of two million signatures to be gathered by groups with at least 100 members, registered in 45 regions. Since 2000 the organisation of civil society has continued. In the wake of Beslan there were nationwide demonstrations and commemorations, which no doubt expressed genuine grief and outrage. However, although these events were ostensibly led by civil society groups including trade unions and youth groups, the particular groups involved in organising the demonstrations have close links to government. There are two youth groups that are especially closely linked to the Kremlin. The first called Walking Together (*Idushchiye Vmeste*) was founded in May 2000 by Vasily Yakimenko, whose previous role was overseeing state-run charities. Vladislav Surkov is also closely involved with Walking Together and the group is financed by pro-Kremlin businesses. It is

Members of the pro-Putin youth movement Nashi *shout 'Putin forever' and express support for the United Russia party, on Putin's 55th birthday, 7 October 2007.*

endorsed by Putin and in November 2000 the group organised a pro-Putin rally in front of the Kremlin. The second pro-Kremlin youth group called *Nashi* (Ours) was founded in March 2005, again by Vasily Yakimenko with Surkov's support. *Nashi* describes itself as an anti-fascist youth movement, although Russian liberals find *Nashi*'s nationalism and proclivity to engage in direct action as more reminiscent of a fascist youth group. *Nashi*'s other stated goal is to prevent pro-western mass movements like the ones that led the Colour Revolutions in the Ukraine and Georgia.

As relations between the Kremlin and Britain deteriorated during 2006 following the spying allegations and the poisoning in London of Alexander Litvinenko, a former KGB agent and ally of the anti-Putin oligarch Boris Berezovsly, *Nashi* subjected Anthony Brenton the British Ambassador to a campaign of harassment (BBC, 2006). *Nashi* explained its campaign as a response to the ambassador's attendance at the 'Another Russia' opposition conference held in Moscow 11–12 July 2006, as an alternative to the G8 summit in St Petersburg. 'Another Russia' is an umbrella organisation for Russian opposition groups and parties ranging from liberals to fascists (see Chapter 16). *Nashi* focused on the attendance of Eduard Limonov, the leader of the National Bolsheviks, to justify their actions. They staked out the ambassador's residence and the embassy, blocked his car, disrupted his meetings and at one lunch members started rocking his chair, leading to fears they would assault him (Blomfield, 2006). On 25 March 2007 15,000 *Nashi* supporters demonstrated in Moscow in celebration of seven years of Putin's presidency; in line with Putin's nationalist agenda they condemned traitors who were trying to help foreigners steal Russia's natural resources (APF/Reuters, 2007). Liberals feared that in the run up to the 2008 presidential elections *Nashi* would be used to intimidate opposition groups and to disrupt their rallies.

Co-opting civil society, joining the two halves of the hour glass?

A problem for civil society organisations has been gaining access to decision makers. Putin has responded to this by creating a series of bodies that create areas of contact between civil society and decision makers. His first initiative was a Civic Forum held in the Kremlin first in June and then in November 2001. Surkov was actively involved in the organisation of the Forum together with Gleb Pavlovsky, another close Putin adviser. The sight of carefully selected 'representatives of the people' walking into the Kremlin was all-too-reminiscent of the CPSU stage-managed Congresses and did not represent a commitment to opening a free dialogue between civil society and the Kremlin. Another 'governmental NGO' called Civil Society (*Grazhdanskoe Obshchestvo*) was involved in selecting participants for the June Civic Forum; invitations were not extended to the Kremlin's most stalwart critics, such as the human rights groups Memorial and the UCSMR. Despite these attempts to stage manage the Civic Forum, it did demonstrate that in Russia today there are a growing number of vocal, experienced and well-organised NGOs, capable of seizing the slightest opportunity to push forward their pro-democracy agenda (see Nikitin and Buchanan, 2002). The human rights NGOs Memorial and the Moscow Helsinki Group and the environmental NGO the Socio-Ecological Union formed a coalition group called the People's Assembly, in a successful bid to stop the Kremlin from controlling the agenda, format and invitations to the November Civic Forum. Lyudmila Alekseeva of the Moscow Helsinki Group and a fierce Kremlin critic was a key speaker at the November Civic Forum. One result of the Civic Forum was the establishment of public relations offices in each Federal Ministry, which are supposed to respond to citizens' questions.

Presidential Council for Facilitating the Development of Civil Society Institutions and Human Rights

In a further post-Beslan initiative, Putin set up the Presidential Council for Facilitating the Development of Civil Society Institutions and Human Rights in November 2004, chaired by Ella Pamfilova. Its council includes Kremlin critics such as Lyudmila Alekseeva and Ida Kuklina who is also a member of the Coordinating Committee of the UCSMR. The Council is described on the Kremlin website as part of the president's executive office, whose role includes advising the president on how to improve the protection of human rights and civil liberties and inform- ing him about their observance. It also helps to coordinate the activities of human rights NGOs and their relations with state power at federal and regional levels. The Presidential Council has been critical of draft federal legislation such as the new Law on Public Associations (see below). In a meeting with Putin in January 2007 Pamfilova also criticised restrictions on rallies and marches during the Social Forum in St Petersburg during the G8 Summit. Putin is, of course, free to reject or ignore the advice of his Presidential Council.

The Public Chamber

In 2005 Putin established the Public Chamber (see Chapter 6) – a consultative com- mittee, a third of whose membership are proposed by civil society organisations. The Public Chamber has been criticised by civil society organisations and by opposi- tion deputies. Aleksei Simonov head of the Glasnost Defence Foundation argues that the Public Chamber is not an independent body as it has no real powers and gets its budget and premises from the government (Brantsen, 2005). Independent State Duma deputy Oksana Dmitrieva who voted against the Public Chamber opposes what she calls an 'alternative parliament' staffed by pro-Kremlin non-politicians. She describes it as 'a smokescreen' to distract the public's attention from the real diminution in democracy that is taking place in Russia under Putin (ibid.). Supporters of the Public Chamber depict it as evidence of Russia's commitment to democracy; Boris Gryzlov argues, 'we are creating an additional opportunity for the development of civil society in the country, . . . It is a completely public organization that will receive broad rights, according to the law. It will have the right to analyze Duma bills, especially bills that deal with constitutional issues. And it will have the right to check the work of the executive. I think our voters, the citizens of Russia, can only welcome the passage of this law' (ibid.: 1).

Financial pressures on civil society organisations

Russia's tax codes have been used to facilitate the work of some NGOs and to make the operation of others more difficult. Changes introduced in July 2002 required funding donors and recipients to register on government-approved lists; it also limited eligibility for tax-free status to groups working in the areas of science, culture, sports and environmental protection, and for specific scientific projects. The same year Valued Added Tax was applied retrospectively and illegally on the services provided by some NGOs. In July 2004 the Tax Code was amended again and extended tax-free status to healthcare, social services and human rights activities for approved groups. However, it also prevented foreign citizens and organisations from making tax-free grants, and required Russian NGOs including charitable foundations, be on a government-approved list of grant makers to be eligible to make tax-exempt grants to other NGOs. Until this change in 2004 only foreign and international organisations had had to be on a government-approved list of grant makers in order to make their grants tax-free for the recipient. The July 2004 Tax Code also set stricter requirements for foreign and international donors to qualify for tax exemption. These measures involve NGOs in time-consuming paperwork and give the authorities considerable discretion and opportunities to facilitate the work of some donors and NGOs and to frustrate the work of others. Any process that involves registration or inclusion on an approved list provides opportunities for bureaucratic foot dragging and/or rejection for 'unacceptable' NGOs or the speedy acceptance of others, challenging such decisions is time consuming and costly.

The Federal Law on Public Associations (2006) also made the work of international NGOs more difficult as they can only have branches in Russia if those branches are financially independent. Such branches are subject to the same requirements as Russian NGOs and the application of the 2004 Tax Code means that they are unlikely to enjoy tax exemption. The shortlist of foreign foundations that are permitted to give tax-free grants in Russia is dependent on state approval. The 2006 law also requires 'transparency' in NGOs' financing, which gives state bodies access to NGOs' financial records. At the end of February 2007 the Tver prosecutor's office wanted to check all the cash receipts, bills and documents relating to a textbook produced by the Memorial Human Rights Centre, called 'Applying to the European Court of Human Rights'. Oleg Orlov the head of Memorial condemned the investigation as politically motivated and as part of an ongoing anti-NGO campaign, in which the NGOs now have to prove that they are not criminals (Voronov and Dudareva, 2007). The European Commission had given Memorial US$80,000 for their work on bringing complaints to the European Court, US$11,000 of which had been spent on the book (ibid.).

Tightening controls on civil society: the re-registration of NGOs

The 1995 Law on Non-Governmental Associations (hereafter NGO law) required all NGOs to register with the state. In 2005 Putin began the process of revising the NGO law with the clear aim of tightening control over civil society organisations

Box 10.5 Comments on the NGO law before the Duma

They will now most likely start cracking down on foundations, there's no doubt about that. It is a rather stupid, awkward, attempt to once more tighten control over what is happening inside the country. . . . I am worried for sciences, for social sciences, for scholars, for people who hold views different to those that prevail in the Duma. It is an assault against all of us, a restriction of our rights.

Viktor Kremenyuk, deputy head of the USA-Canada Institute, a Moscow-based foreign policy think-tank

Nongovernmental organizations – after political parties, state structures, and mass media – are the last structures untouched by state control. If they want to pass it, if they want to build civil society according to a Belarusian scenario, then everything is clear, . . . But then this system should not be called modern – we are going back to Stalin's Soviet Union, and we shouldn't delude ourselves on this account.

Aleksandr Cherkasov, Russian Human Rights Group Memorial

Source: Bigg, C. (2005) 'Russia: NGOs denounce Proposed Status Changes As Move to Curb Their Activities', 11 November, Feature Article, *RFE/RL*, Radio Liberty/Radio Free Europe website, http://www.rferl.org

and especially those with foreign connections. The draft law raised alarm among civil society organisations and political analysts (see Box 10.5), prompting the Public Chamber to make its first attempt to exercise its role of providing societal oversight of state organs and the legislature. Twenty-one of the Public Chamber's 126 members wrote to the Duma asking for the bill to be delayed to give them time to review it. Ella Pamfilova, the head of the Council for Facilitating the Development of Civil Society Institutions and Human Rights met with Putin in November 2005 to express her concern that the bill violated the Constitution and Russia's obligations under international law (Kremlin website, 2005). Pamfilova complained that if the law went through in its draft form it would severely hamper civil society organisations carrying out cultural, educational, health and welfare work; that the re-registration requirements were more onerous than those faced by commercial organisations; and that it could result in the closure of many NGOs. She also questioned the need for the Ministry of Justice to take on the task of closely monitoring NGO finances. Putin's response to Pamfilova foreshadowed his response to a BBC journalist's question about the January 2006 spies scandal (see Box 10.3), namely that he wanted NGOs to continue working in Russia, but that there must be transparency in their finances and that NGOs must not be used as instruments of other countries' foreign policy goals (ibid.)

The Law on Public Associations, 2006

The draft law on Public Associations was slightly revised, signed by Putin in January 2006 and came into effect in April 2006. The new NGO law required all the existing civil society organisations to re-register within one year. Registration and re-registration entails completing registration forms, writing foundation documents stating current and planned programmes plus the submission of a financial statement, in a process overseen by the Ministry of Justice. The law also requires the submission of regular financial statements and gives government officials the right to attend any NGO event or meeting to verify compliance with their foundation documents. The re-registration process quickly revealed which NGOs were favoured and which were not. NGOs – especially those with foreign connections and/or those involved in human rights, pro-democracy or work with refugees – encountered major problems in the re-registration process. At a Democracy Forum held by the Council of Europe in Moscow in October 2006, Vladimir Lukin (2006) Russia's human rights ombudsman, announced that over the previous 15 years Russia had had several hundreds of thousands of regional and national NGOs and that about sixty thousand were concerned with the protection of human, political, social or cultural rights. Lukin denied that re-registration problems were part of a concerted campaign against certain NGOs and instead gave two primary reasons for re-registration problems. The first was that the whole registration procedure is too cumbersome and this had already been raised with Lukin by activists in the Presidential Council on Human Rights. Lukin criticised the Ministry of Justice for failing to recognise this as a genuine issue. The second problem, according to Lukin, was that international NGOs 'are not in the habit of maintaining good paperwork' (ibid.). The registration problems arose he argued, when these two problems collide.

On 27 January 2006 the Ministry of Justice announced that the registration of the Russian Human Rights Centre, an umbrella organisation for various human rights groups including the Union of Soldiers' Mothers Committees of Russia (USMCR), the Moscow Helsinki Group and the Independent Psychiatric Association of Russia, was being revoked due to failure to provide the correct documentation. In 2006 the activities of Human Rights Watch, Amnesty International, the International Republican Institute and National Democratic Institute (both of which are funded by the US Congress), two branches of Doctors Without Borders, the Danish Refugee Council, the Netherlands-based Russian Justice Initiative which helps Russians to bring cases to the European Court of Human Rights, American adoption agencies (*MosNews*, 2006) and more than ninety other foreign NGOs also had to suspend activities for failing to meet re-registration requirements. Human Rights Watch (HRW) failed the registration process because it called itself the 'Representative Office of the Non-Governmental Organization Human Rights Watch in the Russian Federation'. Registration staff rejected this name and said that the group should call itself the 'Representative Office of the Corporation Human Rights Watch Inc. (USA) in the Russian Federation'. This change meant they had to send their documentation back to HRW headquarters in New York for revision, re-notarisation and retranslation into Russian; it then it had to be re-notarised in Russia before resubmission (Finn, 2006). However, for some foreign NGOs the registration process was much smoother and quicker. The American Chamber of Commerce, for example, reported that Russian officials pointed out the errors in their documentation before they submitted it so that they could be corrected in advance to expedite registration (ibid.) Over ninety-nine foreign NGOs were registered including the Carnegie Moscow Centre and the Ford Foundation (ibid.).

Extremism, racism and xenophobia

The negative side of civil society

Civil society must be subject to the rule of law and not infringe the constitutional and legal rights of others. Within Russia today as in many other countries there are problems of racism, xenophobia, hate-speech and violence. The main targets are non-Slavs, particularly Chechens and other people from the North Caucasus and Central Asia. Since 1999 there has been rising Islamophobia and the desecration of mosques. Russia's Roma population is officially put at around 155,000 but Roma organisations claim it is more than 10 times higher (Diaconu, 2003a). The disparity is in part explained because many Roma do not have passports and are not registered, and so they lead a marginalised existence and are also subject to attacks. Anti-Semitism is also on the rise, with attacks on people and synagogues. Incitement and violence is conducted by various far-right groups: neo-Nazis, skinheads, football 'fans' and, in Krasnodar and Stavropol *krais*, Rostov and Volgograd *oblasts* by Cossack groups – often with the collusion of local law enforcement agencies. Meskhetian Turks, who were deported by Stalin from Southern Georgia to Central Asia in 1944, have been a particular Cossack target. In 1989–90 thousands fled from ethnic clashes in Uzbekistan to Krasnodar *krai*, many have been denied Russian citizenship to which they are entitled under Russian citizenship laws and subjected to physical attacks by the Cossacks. In Voronezh, Moscow, St Petersburg and Saratov foreign students have been attacked and killed. In 2006 a nine-year-old girl of mixed African-Russian parentage survived being stabbed nine times by neo-Nazis in St Petersburg, while in March 2005 eight people were found guilty of hooliganism – not murder – in connection with the racially-motivated stabbing to death of a nine-year-old Tajik girl in St Petersburg. The vast majority of Russians are shocked by such violence. In March 2006 the Public Opinion Foundation conducted a survey on fascism, a term which in Russia is frequently used as a catch-all for extremist behaviour. It found that while 12 per cent of respondents thought there were positive aspects to fascism, 76 per cent thought there were not (FOM, 2006).

Legislation to combat extremism or to attack pro-democracy groups?

Russia has introduced a range of laws to deal with extremism, racism, hate-speech and terrorism. However, there is increasing concern that existing legislation and new legislation passed under Putin, is being used to discredit and attack cultural, human rights and pro-democracy groups that are critical of the Kremlin (see Box 10.6).

Box 10.6 Legislation to combat extremism, racism and xenophobia

The RF Constitution (1993)

Article 13 (5) of the RF Constitution forbids the establishment of public associations which aim to incite social, racial, national and religious strife and

Article 19 (2) prohibits the restrictions of rights of citizens on the grounds of 'social, racial, national, linguistic or religious affiliation'.

Article 29 (2) prohibits propaganda or campaigns aimed at inciting social, racial or religious hatred and strife.

The Law on Public Associations (1995)

Article 16 prohibited the registration of public associations, whose goals, activities or statutes involve racial or national intolerance. A problem is that it has been applied sporadically and inconsistently; although the Ministry of Justice did refuse Russian National Unity registration other extremist organisations were registered.

Criminal Code (1996)

Article 74 penalises acts intended to stir up racial, national or religious hatred with a maximum of 10 years' imprisonment. This was replaced in 1997 by articles 136 and 282. Article 136 penalises violation of citizen equality on the basis of gender, race, nationality, language, place of residence, attitude to religion, convictions, and membership of Public Associations. Article 282 penalises actions directed at fomenting national, racial or religious hatred; belittling national dignity; as well as the propagation of exclusiveness, superiority or deficiency of citizens on the basis of their religious, national or racial affiliation, in public or in the mass media. Article 63.1 provides for the imposition of more severe penalties if a crime is nationally, racially or religiously motivated. However, it has been used against the Russian–Chechen Friendship Society, which is trying to development understanding and friendship. After a series of attempts to frustrate the society's work, its executive director Stanislav Dmitrievshy was given a two-year suspended sentence and four years' probation for publishing statements by Chechen separatist leaders.

Law on Mass Media (1991)

Article 4 prohibits the dissemination of information aimed at 'fomenting national or racial intolerance' but it is rarely used. In 2000, three ultra-right newspapers *Sturmovik*, *Vitiaz* and *Slavianin* were closed using this law.

Presidential decree 310, 1995, 'On measures to Coordinate Activities of the State Authorities in Order to Counter Manifestations of Fascism and Other Forms of Political Extremism in the Russian Federation'

Russian National Unity groups were disbanded in Ekaterinburg, Orenburg and St Petersburg following this decree.

Box 10.6 (*Continued*)

Federal Law on Extremism (2002)

This banned the establishment of extremist organisations and activities; however, its definition of extremism is so broad and vague that it is open to official abuse. According to the Human Rights Expert-Analytic Centre on Interethnic and Interfaith issues founded by the Moscow Helsinki Group, 90 per cent of cases alleging extremism and terrorism are fabricated (Khasanova, 2005) and target innocent civil society organisations. However, the Omsk and Khabarovsk branches of the Russian National Unity movement have been ordered to disband for engaging in extremist activities (RFE/RL Newsline, 2002).

Law on Countering Terrorism (2006)

It provides a very broad definition of terrorism and terrorist activity. It also gives law enforcement and security agencies wide discretion in counter-terrorist operations, which present a serious threat to human rights.

Law enforcement agencies

The law enforcement agencies are often guilty of the harassment and ill-treatment of non-Slavs and the Procuracy are unwilling to investigate hate crimes; even if cases are brought they rarely lead to conviction. In the period 1997–2001, 165 cases of hate crimes were initiated but only 30 cases went to court. In 2002, 66 cases were initiated and 17 went to court. The cases that went to court included racist propaganda, desecration of cemeteries, assault, battery and murder (Diaconu, 2003b: 4). Law enforcement agencies often downgrade hate crimes to hooliganism. For example in April 2005 Zaur Tutov the culture minister of Kabardino-Balkaria was attacked by a gang of skinheads. It was only after intervention by the RF Prosecutor General that the Moscow prosecutors categorised the attack as a hate crime rather than just hooliganism. The same month the RF human rights ombudsman condemned law enforcement agencies and individual regional leaders of covering up and condoning racially motivated murders. In a survey conducted by the Public Opinion Foundation in March 2006, only 36 per cent of respondents believed that the authorities were fighting fascism while 42 per cent believed that they turned a blind eye to such activities (FOM, 2006).

Nurgaliyev and Putin on the need to fight extremism

In February 2007 Rashid Nurgaliyev, the minister of the interior, revealed that during 2006 his ministry had identified 220 extremist groups with around 10,000 members in Russia (RIA Novosti, 2007). He also pointed out that, 'Some youth groups have shown a tendency to switch from protests and acts of hooliganism to terrorist activities, murders and robberies', and claimed that in 2006 the police had solved 169 race-hate crimes, which was 27 per cent more than in 2005 (ibid.). Most extremist group members are under 30 and based in Moscow, St Petersburg and the Samara and Voronezh *oblasts* (RIA Novosti, 2006b). Putin has also declared that, 'It is important not only to enforce law and order, but also to protect society against attempts to impose ideologies of extremism, nationalism or religious hatred', and has ordered the FSB to protect Russian citizens against exposure to such ideas (RIA Novosti, 2007). Recognition of the scale and seriousness of this growing problem is very welcome and long overdue. However, the treatment of two different types of civil society activities in April 2007 seems to indicate that extremist, neo-Nazi activities continue to be tolerated, while anti-Putin human rights protesters are clamped down upon.

The time around Hitler's birthday on 20 April, is a peak time for hate-crime and neo-Nazi demonstrations in Russia's cities. During the fortnight either side of Hitler's birthday in 2007 there were 7 murders and 20 attacks in Russian cities and foreign students were advised to stay in their hostels (Sova, 2007). Moscow's city authorities permitted two demonstrations by well-known far-right groups on 21 April. A demonstration in Slavyanskaia Square was organised by the self-styled Party for the Defence of the Constitution (*Rus*) and was attended by about 250 people from Dmitry Rumyantsev's National Socialist Society (NSO) and Maxim Martsinkevich's violent neo-Nazi Format 18, and other neo-Nazi groups including Russian Nationwide Unity (RONS) and Russian Will. The rally culminated with a speech by Rumyantsev claiming racial superiority and inciting violence. Although the speech clearly contravened Russian law, the OMOM police troops did not intervene, nor did they intervene to stop Nazi salutes and slogans. The other rally, held in Pushkinskaia Square, was attended by around three hundred people from the Slavic Union (SS), the National State Party of Russia (NDPR), Russian Nationwide Unity (RONS), the Movement Against Illegal Immigration (DPNI), the Russian Order, supporters of the LDPR Duma deputy Nikolai Kuryanovich and the Union of Orthodox Gonfaloniers. Speakers made anti-Caucasus slogans and incited violence. Although no one was arrested for the hate speeches or Nazi salutes, Alexander Belov the DPNI leader was arrested for making an anti-police speech laden with obscenities. In contrast a peaceful visit by only 20 human rights activists to the scenes of police violence against anti-Putin protests on 14 April were dispersed by several hundred police and 5 activists were detained (Sova, 2007).

Law on Freedom of Conscience and Religious Associations (1997)

The 1997 Law on Freedom of Conscience and Religious Associations (see Chapter 4) has also been used against civil society organisations with foreign contacts and funding, which are often characterised as totalitarian sects or religious cults. The law established 31 December 1999 as the deadline for registration of religious organisations, although the deadline was later pushed back a year. By 31 December 2000 570 religious organisations had either registered or re-registered themselves at the federal level, that is 170 more than were registered in 1997 (ECRI, 2001: 20). But non-traditional religious communities, those which either had not existed for 15 years before 1997 or whose claims to have existed were not accepted, have been denied registration. Under the new NGO law (2006) religious groups that are non-Russian in origin are subjected to especially rigorous reviews of their activities and finance when they seek to register.

The Salvation Army worked in Russia from 1913 until it was banned as an anti-Soviet organisation in 1923. In 1992 it resumed its work in Russia registering as the Moscow branch of the Salvation Army. The Salvation Army conducted evangelical and charitable work, including delivering meals to the elderly and housebound. In 1997 it was required to re-register and to bring its articles of association (foundation documents) into conformity with the 1997 Act. It was unsuccessful in its attempts to re-register by the 31 December 2000 deadline and ordered to disband. In September 2001 the Salvation Army lodged a complaint with the Constitutional Court, which dismissed the dissolution order but it was still refused registration (Rutzen, 2006). The Salvation Army eventually took their case to the European Court of Human Rights which, on 5 October 2006, issued its judgment on the 'Case of the Moscow Branch of The Salvation Army v. Russia'. The Court reiterated that the right to form an association was an inherent part of freedom of association under Article 11 of the European Convention on Human Rights, to which Russia is a signatory; that Russia had interfered with this freedom through the re-registration process and stressed that associations are important to the proper functioning of a democracy. Russian authorities had justified their actions on the basis of the 'foreign origin of the applicant branch', but the Court found foreign nationals could not be treated differently to Russians (European Court of Human Rights, 2006).

Chapter summary

Putin's pursuit of the strengthening of managed democracy has severely hampered the further development of civil society. Putin has consistently sought to concentrate power in the presidency through strengthening the power vertical. This means that he wants to manage democracy and to direct democracy from the Kremlin. He has, therefore, attempted to co-opt civil society through the Civic Forum, the Public Chamber and the Presidential Council for Human Rights; and through the setting up of 'civil society' groups such as Walking Together and *Nashi*. This is reminiscent of the CPSU's bid to destroy the spontaneous and autonomous horizontal links between people and to substitute the top-down organisation and mobilisation of 'the masses' towards CPSU-defined goals. In another echo of the soviet past, foreign links and criticism of the Kremlin and the government are condemned as unpatriotic and hostile to the state. Putin has not, so far, destroyed civil society but he is certainly seeking to destroy opposition.

Discussion points

- What is the relationship between civil society and either democratisation or democracy?

- How and why has the political role of civil society changed under Yeltsin and Putin?
- Why is Putin attempting to control and co-opt civil society?
- What is the evidence for and against the existence of a vibrant civil society in Russia today?

Further reading

For two of the classic statements about civil society see Adam Ferguson (1767) *An Essay on the History of Civil Society*, which is available online on the Faculty of Social Sciences, McMaster University website at http://socserv.mcmaster.ca/~econ/ugcm/3ll3/ferguson/civil.html and on the Constitution Society website, http://www.constitution.org/af/civil.htm. It is also available edited by Fania Oz-Salzberger (1995) and published by Cambridge University Press in their Texts in the History of Political Thought series. Georg Hegel (1820) *The Philosophy of Right*, is also available in the same Cambridge series in a 1991 edition, edited by Allen W. Wood and online in the Hegel archive on the Marxist Organisation website, http://www.marxists.org/. John Ehrenberg (1999) *Civil Society: The Critical History of an Idea*, New York: New York University Press provides a lively discussion of the concept of civil society, while Bob Edwards, W. Foley and Mario Diani (eds) (2001) *Beyond Tocqueville: Civil Society and Social Capital Debate in Comparative Perspective*, Medford, MA: Tufts University Press provides a useful introduction to civil society and social capital.

For analyses of social capital, trust and networks in Russia try Y. Levada, V. Shubkin, G. Kertan, G. Ivanova, V. Yadov and E. Shiraeva (2002) 'Russia anxiously surviving', in V. Shlapentokh and E. Shiraeva (eds) *Fears in Post-Communist Societies: A Comparative Perspective*, New York: Palgrave; William Mischler and Richard Rose (2005) 'What are the political consequences of trust? A test of Cultural and Institutional Theories in Russia', *Comparative Political Studies*, 38 (9), 1050–78; Nicolai N. Petro (2001) 'Creating Social Capital In Russia: The Novgorod Model', *World Development*, 29 (2), February, 229–44; James L. Gibson (2001) 'Social Networks, Civil Society, and the Prospects for Consolidating Russia's Democratic Transition', *American Journal of Political Science*, 45 (1), 55–69. Alena V. Ledeneva provides an extremely stimulating analysis of the importance of networks in her (2006) *How Russia Really Works: The Informal Practices That Shaped Post-Soviet Politics and Business*, Ithaca, NY: Cornell University Press.

Alfred B. Evans Jr., Laura A. Henry and Lisa McIntosh Sundstrom are the editors of (2005) *Russian Civil Society: A Critical Assessment*, Armonk, NY: M.E. Sharpe, Inc. which is the best single publication on Russian civil society currently available. See also Glenn, John K. (2001) *Framing Democracy: Civil Society and Civil Movements in Eastern Europe*, Stanford, CA: Stanford University Press.

Useful websites

Public Chamber (Russian only): http://www.oprf.ru/rus/about
Sova (Human Rights) Centre: http://xeno.sova-center.ru/6BA2468/
Memorial Society: http://www.memo.ru/eng/index.htm

Gay Russia: http://www.gayrussia.ru/en/actions/detail.php?ID=4740

The Consortium of Women's NGOs: http://www.wcons.org.ru/eng/main.php

Open Society Institute: http://www.soros.org/initiatives/regions/Russia

Eurasian Foundation: http://www.eurasia.org

Donors Forum: http://www.donorsforum.ru/eng/who/

Human Rights First: http://www.humanrightsfirst.org/

International Center for Not-for-Profit Law: http://www.icnl.org/

Internet Centre Anti-Racism Europe (Icare): http://www.icare.to/main.php?en

References

APF/Reuters (2007) 'Pro-Kremlin Youth Vow to Defend "Holy Russia"', *RFE/RL Feature Article*, 26 March, http://www.rferl.org/

BBC (2006) 'Russian youths "hound UK envoy"', *BBC News*, 8 December, http://www.bbc.co.uk

Bigg, C. (2005) 'Russia: NGOs denounce Proposed Status Changes As Move to Curb Their Activities', 11 November, *RFE/RL* Feature Article, Radio Liberty/Radio Free Europe website, http://www.rferl/org

Blomfield, A. (2006) 'Envoy demands Kremlin calls off its youth gang', *The Telegraph*, 13 December, http://www.telegraph.co.uk

Brantsen, J. (2005) 'Russia: New Public Chamber Criticized As Smokescreen', *CDI Russian Weekly* #5, 18 March, http://www.cdi.org/russia/

Civil Society Institutions and Human Rights Council under the President of the Russian Federation (2005) '20 July, 2005, President of the Russian Federation Vladimir Putin met with the Council in the Kremlin', *The Civil Society Institutions and Human Rights Council under the President of the Russian Federation* website, http://en.sovetpamfilova.ru/release/6.php

Danks, C. J. (2006) 'Committees of Soldiers' Mothers: Mothers challenging the Russian state', in S. Buckingham and G. Lievesley (eds) *In the hands of women. Paradigms of citizenship*, Manchester: Manchester University Press

Diaconu, I. (Chair) (2003a) 'Fifteenth to seventeenth periodic reports of the Russian Federation', Committee on the Elimination of Racial Discrimination, Sixty-second session, *United Nations*, CERD/C/SR.1564, 14 March, http://www.ohchr.org/EN/Pages/WelcomePage.aspx

Diaconu, I. (chair) (2003b) 'Summary Report of the 1564th meeting', Committee on the Elimination of Racial Discrimination, 62nd session, 10 March 2003, *United Nations*, CERD/C/SR 1564, 14 March 2003, http://www.ohchr.org/EN/Pages/WelcomePage.aspx

European Court of Human Rights (2006) 'Case of the Moscow Branch of the Salvation Army v. Russia', 5 October, *European Court of Human Rights* website: http://www.echr.coe.int/echr

ECRI (2001) 'Second Report on the Russian Federation', *European Commission against Racism and Intolerance*, 16 March, *European Court of Human Rights* website: http://www.echr.coe.int/echr

Finn, P. (2006) 'In Russia, Cautious Generosity. Tycoons Pour Money Into Causes but Steer Clear of Democracy Issues', *Washington Post Foreign Service*, 22 September, A10, http://www.washingtonpost.com/

FOM (2006) 'Fascism', *The Public Opinion Foundation database*, 30 March, http://bd.english.fom.ru/

Fukuyama, F. (1995) *Trust: The Social Virtues and the Creation of Prosperity*, New York: The Free Press

Fukuyama, F. (1999) 'Social Capital and Civil Society', *International Monetary Fund Conference on Second Generation Reforms*; available on the International Monetary Fund website, http://www.imf.org/external/pubs/ft/seminar/1999/reforms/fukuyama.htm#13

Gambrell, J. (2004) 'Philanthropy in Russia: New Money under Pressure', *Carnegie Report*, 3 (1), Fall, http://www.carnegie.org/

Gellner, E. (1994) *Conditions of Liberty: Civil Society and Its Rivals*, London: Hamish Hamilton

Gill, G. and Markwick, R. D. (2000) *Russia's Stillborn Democracy? From Gorbachev to Yeltsin*, Oxford: Oxford University Press

Glasser, S. B. (2004) 'Putin Talk Worries Independent Groups', *The Washington Post*, 1 June, A17, http://www.washingtonpost.com

Khasanova, G. (2005) 'Human Rights Activists Say 90 per cent of Cases against Muslims Fabricated', *Tatar-Bashkir Daily Report*, 1 July, RFE/RL website, http://www.rferl.org/

Kozenko, A. (2006) '*Khel'sinskaia gruppa poshla s kamem v sud'*, *Kommersant*, 31 January, http://www.kommersant.ru/

Kremlin website (2005) 'Beginning of meeting with Chairwoman of the Council for Facilitating the Development of Civil Society Institutions and Human Rights Ellla Pamfilova', 24 November, Kremlin website, http://www.kremlin.ru/eng/

Levada-Tsentr (2007) '*Doverie institutam vlasti*', 9 April, *Levada Centre* website, http://www.levada.ru/

Lukin, V. (2006) 'Statement by Mr Vladimir Lukin. Commissioner for Human Rights of the Russian Federation', Forum for the Future of Democracy, Moscow, 18–19 October, *Council of Europe*, http://www.coe.int/

Malyakin, I. and Konnova, M. (1999) 'Voluntary organizations in Russia: Three Obstacle Courses', *Prism*, 5 (8), 23 April, http://www.jamestown.org/

MosNews (2006) 'Leading Rights Watchdog Resumes Operations in Russia', 7 November, *MosNews*, http://www.mosnews.com/

Nikitin, A. and Buchanan, J. (2002) 'The Kremlin's Civic Forum: Co-operation or Co-optation for Civil Society in Russia?', *Demokratizatsiya*, 10 (2), Spring, 147–65

Putin, V. (2004) 'Annual Address to the Federal Assembly', 26 May, Kremlin website, http://www.kremlin.ru/eng

Putnam, R. (1993) *Making Democracy Work: Civic Traditions in Modern Italy*, Princeton, NJ: Princeton University Press

Putnam, R. (2000) *Bowling Alone: The Collapse and Revival of American Community*, New York: Simon & Schuster

RFE/RL Newsline (2002) 'Another RNE Branch Liquidated', 11 October, *RFERL* website, http://www.rferl.org/

RIA Novosti (2006a) 'Kremlin aide on threats to Russian sovereignty – threat of colour revolution', 3 March, *RIA Novosti* website, http://en.rian.ru/

RIA Novosti (2006b) '150 extremist groups with 10,000 members active in Russia', 15 November, *RIA Novosti* website, http://en.rian.ru/

RIA Novosti (2007) 'Extremism, drug trafficking on the rise in Russia – interior minister', 9 February, *RIA Novosti* website, http://en.rian.ru/

Rose, R. (1995) 'Russia as an Hour-Glass Society: A Constitution without Citizens', *East European Constitutional Review*, 4 (3), Summer, 35–42

Rutzen, D. (2006) 'Salvation in Court: The Salvation Army v. Russia', *International Journal of Not-for-Profit Law*, 9 (1), December, 12–14, http://www.icnl.org/

Sindelar, D. (2005) 'Russia: Trust in Government Up, In Contrast to Global Trend', 15 December, *RFE/RL* Feature Article, 15 December, *RFE/RL* website, http://www.rferl.org/

Sova (2007) 'Hitler's birthday in Russia: neo-nazi demonstrations and attacks', *Sova Center* website, 24 April, http://xeno.sova-center.ru/

Voronov, A. and Dudareva, E. (2007) '*Genprokuratura nagnala Strasburga*', *Kommersant*, 27 February, http://www.kommersant.ru/

Chapter 11

The mass media

Learning objectives

- To introduce the changes to the mass media since the 1980s.
- To examine the changing face of censorship.
- To examine Putin's approach to the mass media.
- To introduce the development of electronic sources of information.

Introduction

The end of soviet socialism heralded a different political and economic environment for the mass media. The late 1980s and early 1990s were heady days, while censorship had not entirely disappeared, a freewheeling pluralism developed as all shades of opinion were published and, to a lesser extent, broadcast. The new freedoms and media privatisation also brought new, harsher economic realities, including the loss or reduction of state subsidies and falling subscriptions. The oligarchs bought media outlets in the mid-1990s to ensure Yeltsin's re-election in 1996 and, while this money was a financial lifeline for some publications, the new proprietors' intervention in editorial policies led to clashes with journalists. Media freedom, subject to the usual restrictions found in most democracies against, for example, inciting hatred or revealing state secrets, is guaranteed by the RF Constitution. There are also NGOs such as the *Glasnost* Defence Fund and the Russian Union of Journalists and its Centre for Journalists in Extreme Situations, which champion media freedom. Although formal government censorship is much less restrictive than in the USSR, informal means to control information or to encourage self-censorship have grown. The state, corrupt politicians, business and criminals all, at times, want to prevent the investigation and reporting of their activities. Putin's commitment to a 'managed democracy' included channelling public debate within tightly defined parameters and managing information flows. Putin sought to achieve this through a combination of support from pro-Kremlin media proprietors and more decisively by bringing Russia's national media into the ownership of government-controlled energy companies. Putin also responded to the development of the new information technologies by targeting cyberspace for state control.

The changing political-ideological and economic environment

The mass media: from soviet ideological workers to *perestroika*

Under soviet socialism the mass media played an important role in promoting Marxism-Leninism as the official state ideology and were part of the Communist Party's (CPSU) ideological and propaganda work. They were not expected to be impartial reporters and interpreters of the news, but to promote the CPSU's world-view, stress the unity of party and people, and to mobilise the people to fulfil the party's goals and plans. Strict censorship was enforced, which not only stifled debate but also enabled inept and corrupt party-state officials to hide their activities safe from the prying eyes of investigative journalists. The communist state enjoyed a near monopoly of the printed and broadcast word; however, despite jamming, this mono-poly was breached by foreign stations such as the BBC's World Service, *Deutsche Welle*, the Voice of America, Radio Free Europe and Radio Liberty. Within the USSR illegal *samizdat* (self-published) books and newspapers provided alternatives to the official propaganda. The soviet media, foreign broadcasters and to a lesser extent *samizdat* were all engaged in an ideological war, each determined to show the supe-riority of either Marxism-Leninism, Russian and other forms of nationalism, or liberal-democracy. During *perestroika* the policy of *glasnost* (openness) enabled the mass media, particularly the print media, to become one of the great battlegrounds for contending ideas. As *perestroika* progressed the mass media became increasingly pluralistic reflecting a wide range of forces and opinions, from anti-reformers through to those who wanted an end to soviet socialism, and all shades of opinion between. The reformers wanted an end to CPSU censorship but they did not want impartial media, they wanted media that would support and advocate their particular views.

In June 1990 the USSR adopted a new 'Law in the Press and Other Media', which did not entirely end censorship, but which did proclaim press and media freedom and so signalled the formal end of the CPSU's already failing attempts to maintain its monopolistic control over the media. Supervision of the media and their activities shifted from the CPSU to the judiciary. As anti-reform opposition to Gorbachev mounted in 1990, Ostankino, the All-Union State Television and Radio Company (*Gostelradio*), whose programmes reached the farthest corners of the country, dropped its previously pro-*perestroika* stance. Yeltsin persuaded the RSFSR parliament to approve and fund an All-Russia Television and Radio Broadcasting Company (RTV) which was launched in May 1991, under the direc-torship of Yeltsin's ally Oleg Poptsov. Reform-minded journalists left Ostankino to work for RTV or Leningrad-TV which was controlled by Leningrad's reformist mayor Anatoly Sobchak. Ostankino on the one side and RTV and Leningrad-TV on the other saw themselves as engaged in a battle for the fate of the USSR and did not aspire to be impartial or to present a range of opinions. Oleg Poptsov played a crucial role in supporting Yeltsin through the August 1991 coup attempt and later during the October 1993 crisis.

The mass media and democratisation

Yeltsin moved quickly to deprive the CPSU of its own media by issuing a presidential decree banning the six CPSU newspapers which had supported the coup; the ban was annulled on 10 September 1991. Between November 1991 and February 1992 the RF discussed new media legislation and passed legislation similar to the 1990 soviet mass media law. The new law guaranteed media freedom but this could, however, be restricted during a state of emergency. Yeltsin suspended media freedom during the October 1993 crisis. Further restrictions were also placed on media freedoms, for example outlawing incitement to racial hatred or the violation of national security. The law was used to prosecute the newspaper *Den'* (Day) for anti-Semitism and incitement to civil disorder. These restrictions were later enshrined in Article 29.2 of the RF Constitution (1993), which states that, 'Propaganda or agitation exciting social, racial, national or religious hatred and enmity is not permitted. Propaganda of social, racial, national, religious or linguistic supremacy is prohibited.' Article 29.5 of the Constitution states that, 'The freedom of mass information is guaranteed. Censorship is prohibited.' Unlike the USSR, Russia does not have an official state ideology to be promoted and defended; however, both Yeltsin and Putin have been keen to control the mass media, particularly those that reached throughout Russia.

Yeltsin and parliament 1993: the battle for the mass media

Yeltsin faced repeated challenges to his rule, most graphically from opposition within the parliament in 1993 and Chechen rebels, but also during elections. Yeltsin realised the importance of controlling the flow of information and while the print media in the 1990s became increasingly pluralistic, he brought the broadcast media under state control. Following the August 1991 coup attempt Yeltsin issued a decree transferring All-Union (the USSR's) assets such as Ostankino to Russia. Yeltsin replaced the hardline chair of Ostankino, Leonid Kravchenko, with Yegor Yakovlev, the editor of the reformist newspaper *Moskovskie Novosti*. However, Yakovlev resisted Yeltsin's attempts to turn Ostankino into a state broadcasting service rather than an independent, public broadcasting service and was dismissed in 1992, to be replaced by the more amenable Vyacheslav Bragin. With his supporters in charge at Ostankino and RTV, Yeltsin was able to ensure a generally positive, if not always entirely uncritical, presentation of his administration. Perhaps more importantly, the opposition to Yeltsin was generally denied positive coverage. The scale of presidential interference and direction at Ostankino led Igor Malashenko, Bragin's deputy, to resign at the beginning of 1993. Yeltsin's opponents also wanted their own media outlets. Ruslan Khasbulatov argued that *Izvestia*, which had been the soviet government newspaper, should become the parliament's newspaper. The editorial and journalistic staff at *Izvestia* resisted this loss of independence and so in October 1992 Khasbulatov sent parliamentary police to *Izvestia*'s Moscow headquarters, to force the newspaper to support the parliamentary cause; but Yeltsin was able to countermand Khasbulatov's order.

Then in January 1993 Yeltsin announced the establishment of the Federal Information Centre (FIC) under the former media minister and close Yeltsin ally,

Mikhail Poltoranin. FIC's stated role was to provide journalists with information about the government, in effect to be a presidential propaganda agency. Parliament appealed against the FIC and in May that year the Constitutional Court ruled the FIC illegal. At the height of the October 1993 crisis parliamentary forces occupied Ostankino, which became the scene of vicious fighting. Following the defeat of the parliamentary rebels in October 1993, Ostankino became an increasingly uncritical mouthpiece of the Yeltsin administration. So although Ostankino had film showing Yeltsin clearly drunk at a press conference in London, the film was never shown and the tape was wiped. This and other incidents of censorship and state intervention led a group of journalists to leave Ostankino and to set up the Independent TV station (NTV). Despite the media's grave concerns at Yeltsin's attempts to censor their activities, the pro-reform media were even more concerned at the prospect of a Communist victory in the 1995 State Duma and the 1996 presidential elections. An NTV spokesman explained that if the media were 'impartial' this would result in a Communist victory that would put back the clock on reform and end media freedom (BBC, 1997). The fragility of Russia's democracy encouraged Russia's beleaguered would-be democrats to behave in anti-democratic ways to preserve the gains of the early 1990s.

NTV, RTV, the Chechen war and censorship

NTV rapidly developed a reputation for tough reporting during the first Chechen war when its chief correspondent, Andrei Cherkasov, presented his first report from an underground Russian field hospital. These were certainly not the kinds of pictures that the Yeltsin administration wanted the Russian people to see. Russian troops imposed censorship on media coverage of the war by denying journalists access, taking their cameras, and confiscating and exposing film. The government also made coverage difficult by not allowing satellite links to be set up in Grozny, so that journalists had to get their videotape out of Chechnia using slow and tortuous routes. NTV journalists persevered and were able to show Russian military aircraft bombing Grozny when the Government Information Centre said that no such bombing was taking place. They also showed the coffins of Russian troops coming home, so helping to develop anti-war sentiments among the Russian people. In contrast the Chechen side positively courted the Russian media and did everything they could to ease their work, including setting up satellite facilities. The journalist Elena Masyuk later won awards for her interviews with the Chechen leaders such as Shamil Basayev.

The more independent coverage provided by RTV's *Vesti* news programme and especially NTV's *Sevodnia* (Today) led to increased viewing figures, while the audiences for Ostankino's *Novosti* (News) and *Vremia* (Time) fell substantially. While there was no reversion to soviet-style censorship, the Yeltsin administration attempted to control the news using the traditional technique of controlling appointments, plus a new device – the revocation of licences. As NTV was independent the government could not sack its head to bring it into line; it did, however, receive a phone call in 1995 from Oleg Soskovets, Yeltsin's Presidential Special Representative to the Chechen republic, who warned that if they continued this type of coverage they would have their licence removed and so be closed down. NTV went on the offensive by giving interviews to foreign journalists revealing the government's attempts to censor their coverage and they were left alone – for a while at least. As RTV was state-owned Oleg Poptsov was simply sacked in February 1995, amid accusations of only presenting the Chechen viewpoint. Poptsov (1996: 65) also believes that Boris Berezovsky wanted him fired, so that he could take over RTV.

Privatisation

The privatisation of the media began in 1990 when most of Russia's central print media were transferred to the ownership of their employees. This was a process similar to the *nomenklatura* privatisation which saw state directors of economic enterprises transformed into the new owners. The new proprietors had to confront a rapidly changing economic and political situation. For some titles this new world necessitated a change of name and content; *Agitator* (The Agitator) the journal of the CPSU's propagandists became *Dialog* (Dialogue) and more tellingly *Party Life* became *Business Life*. At this time most newspapers and journals still received government subsidies, but for some the spiralling inflation of the early 1990s led to bankruptcy. Newspaper subscriptions fell, while the costs of production and, crucially for such a large country, of distribution rose dramatically. In January 1992 alone, 20 newspapers announced that they would cease publication for financial reasons (Korotich, 1997). The 1995 State Budget drastically cut newspaper subsidies and only the pro-Yeltsin press continued to receive any state support. The human rights newspaper *Ekspress-Khronika* (Express Chronicle) ceased production in February 1995 after seven years, as grants from foreign foundations had dried up and its readership fell. For other publications Russia's entry into the global media world provided new opportunities. The newspaper *Izvestia* formed a joint venture with the *Financial Times* of London to produce *Finansovoe Izvestia* (*Financial News*), a weekly business news and analysis supplement.

The regional media

Another consequence of Russia's market reforms in the early 1990s was that the national press virtually disappeared from the regions due to prohibitively high transportation costs. In 1994 subscriptions to the regional press for the first time exceeded subscriptions to the national press (Yasmann, 1995). Between the end of communist rule and October 1993 most of the former republican and regional communist party newspapers were taken over by the soviets (councils) which either did not speak with one voice and/or were in conflict with the republican-regional executive (Slider, 1997: 262). For a brief time the media had considerable room for manoeuvre, but once the October 1993 crisis was settled in Moscow and the regional-republican soviets were dissolved pending elections, the media came under the control of the regional governors and republican presidents. The appointment of regional and republican station directors was formally made by the Russian Federal TV and Radio Service but with the approval of regional governors or republican presidents (ibid.). So a situation developed in which, in contrast to the national media, most of the regional-republican media were either owned or heavily subsidised by the regional-republican authorities. As the central television pays little attention to regional issues, local elites have considerable influence over the information published or broadcast within and about their region or republic. In November 1995 Yeltsin signed a new law on subsidies to smaller district and city newspapers, but as allocation of these subsidies was left to the discretion of the regional legislatures and governors, political loyalty was an important criterion when allocating funding (ibid.).

The oligarchs, the media and elections

As the 1995 Duma and 1996 presidential elections approached, the oligarchs feared that communist victories would lead to the reversal of the privatisations of the early 1990s. In order to preserve their economic gains the oligarchs bought newspapers and used them to support Yeltsin and Chernomyrdin. Sergei Smirnov, the head of Gazprom's news media department told journalists that, 'The most important thing is to get this whole system to work for our main idea: We are acting in the interests of the state, and the state needs us' (Savateyeva, 1996: 10–11). For those newspapers bought by the oligarchs the financial difficulties of the early 1990s were gone but they were replaced by growing oligarch-proprietor intervention in editorial decisions. While the press and broadcast media reported and discussed most issues openly, as ownership became increasingly concentrated in the hands of the oligarchs, reporting became more partisan (see Box 11.2).

Despite Putin's verbal attacks on the oligarchs, they nonetheless used their media outlets to support pro-Putin parties in the 1999 Duma elections and Putin in the 2000 presidential election. The two All-Russia television stations, which at that time were both partly owned by Boris Berezovsky, shamelessly broadcast so-called compromising materials (*kompromat*) or black PR to discredit possible rival candidates. Boris Berezovsky is reported to have said, 'I was extremely pleased [with ORT's work], . . . I believe they helped Russia with a historic task' (Gentleman, 2000a: 22).

Putin, managed democracy and the mass media

Putin's approach to the mass media

Putin described freedom of speech as one of the unshakable values of Russian democracy and essential to the development of civil society; however, his understanding of freedom of speech is one which does not challenge the state in any way. The new Doctrine of Information Security introduced in 2000 emphasised the importance of press freedom but also the need to support the state. As early as 2000 Mikhail Berger, the editor of the Media-Most daily newspaper *Sevodnia*, claimed that 'Putin has divided the media into two categories – those organisations that give him total, utter, unquestioning support and those organisations that don't. He views the latter not simply as papers or television companies, but as enemy units which he has to fight, . . . Under the Soviet Union, everything was categorised either as Soviet or anti-Soviet. Now under Putin, everything is either state or anti-state. Media-Most had been repeatedly accused by the Kremlin of having an "anti-state" position. In terms of press freedoms, I think we could see a swift return to the Soviet Union, not just to the 70s, but the 40s under Stalin' (cited by Gentleman, 2000b: 2). In order to manage Russia's democracy Putin has taken an increasingly interventionist approach to the mass media to ensure that they are 'on message'. Dmitry Medvedev, the then head of the presidential administration, held weekly meetings with the heads of state-owned broadcasters to establish how the news would be covered. Putin also continued and extended the various censorship devices developed in the 1990s to encourage self-censorship. These involved administrative pressures such as specious audits or tying publications and journalists up in costly and time-consuming legal cases. Journalism is also a physically dangerous career as criminals, corporate and political elites may all have reasons to want – literally – to stop investigative journalists. While attempts to silence journalists did not begin when Putin took office, according to Oleg Panfilov he is responsible for creating an atmosphere of impunity for harassment and attacks on journalists. Panfilov argues that, 'Putin takes pleasure is launching verbal attacks on journalists,' and 'It is he who defines the atmosphere in which we work' (Osborn, 2007).

Box 11.1 Censorship devices employed in Russia since 1991

1 **Administrative methods**   Officials suddenly take an interest in a publication. The Fire Brigade find violations of fire regulations, tax collectors give accounts a thorough investigation, and there are constant audits and inspections. This attention can lead to (temporary) closures, takes up staff time, and can prove costly through attempts to conform to the latest regulations or fighting matters in court.

2 **Malicious duplication of titles**   The authorities undermine a publication by telling the head of the registering body to register another publication with an identical name and logo, but with a different editorial staff and journalists. In the 1990s this happened to *Lyuberetskaia Pravda* and *Sovetskaia Kalmykia*, which successfully challenged the duplicate registrations in the courts but could not enforce the judgments.

3 **Economic measures**   State subsidies are used to enforce political obedience. A new law on advertising means that the media can be fined for dishonest advertising. Threats to use this law can be used by the authorities to influence the content of a newspaper or programme or the threat of its use can be used as a way get bribes.

4 **Legal action – libel**   Libel is an offence under the Law on the Mass Media (1992) and the Law on the Protection of Citizens' Honour, Dignity and Business Reputation (1991).

In 2002 Yulia Shelamydova the editor of *Simbirskie Izvestia* was sentenced to a year's corrective labour and a large fine for an article she published about the entourage of Vladimir Shamanov, the governor of Ulyanovsk *oblast*.

Box 11.1 *(Continued)*

In October 2004 the Arbitration Court ordered the newspaper *Kommersant* – then owned by the anti-Putin Boris Berezovsky – to pay Alfa Bank, owned by the pro-Kremlin oligarch Roman Fridman, 321 million roubles (US$ 11.7 million) for libel. *Kommersant* had published an article on 7 July during the summer liquidity crisis which the court found to have damaged Alfa Bank's reputation. Boris Reznik, the deputy chair of the Duma Information Policy Committee, described the size of the fine as an attempt to destroy *Kommersant*.

In 2005 the independent journalist Nikolai Goshko was sentenced to five years' hard labour for libelling the governor and deputy governor of Smolensk.

In September 2006 Vladimir Rakhmankov, the editor of the independent news website *Kursiv*, went on trial in Ivanovo charged under Article 319 of the Criminal Code, 'Insulting a Public Official'. In May 2006 *Kursiv* had carried an article called 'Putin as Russia's phallic symbol', which satirised Putin's calls to increase Russia's population. Following the article *Kursiv*'s Internet provider halted their service for six months and Rakhmankov was fined.

5 **Legal action – using anti-espionage, treason and extremism laws** (see also Chapter 10) In January 2003 a civilian court in Ussuriysk ordered the early release of the journalist and former naval officer Grigory Pasko, who had been found guilty of espionage and had served 33 months of a four-year sentence. His conviction had been politically motivated to punish Pasko for reporting on the environmental dangers posed by the Russian navy's nuclear-waste-dumping practices. For information about Pasko go to the Pen website: http://www.englishpen.org/

In April 2006 Airat Dilmukhametov the opposition leader published two articles criticising corruption and human rights violations in Bashkortostan and called on the republic's president Murtaza Rakhimov to resign. Dilmukhametov and Viktor Shmakov, the editor-in-chief of the opposition newspaper *Provintsial'nye Vesti* (Provincial News), were arrested for extremism by the FSB and the Ministry of the Interior. In August 2006 Shmakov was charged with calling for active insubordination of the authorities and went on trial in March 2007. Shmakov had also organised a local branch of Kasyanov's Popular Democratic Union party.

6 **Threats, intimidation, murder** In the period 1994–96 alone 19 journalists were killed in Russia either to prevent publication of material they had collected or in revenge for what they had already published. The perpetrators included criminal gangs and corrupt officials (see Boxes 11.3 and 11.5).

7 **Short-term contracts** Short-term contracts mean that journalists are constantly under pressure to please their proprietor and wayward journalists are easy to dismiss. At Berezovsky's *Ogonek* in the 1990s journalists typically had two-month renewable contracts. Journalists also often had very low official salaries paid in roubles and then received a dollar 'bonus' in a brown envelope at the end of each month. This practice enabled the proprietors to avoid paying pay roll tax and made the journalists vulnerable (Korotich, 1997).

Source: Points 1 to 5 are adapted from Simonov, A. (1996) 'Censorship yesterday, today, tomorrow', *Index on Censorship* (3), 59–64. Aleksei Simonov is the head of the *Glasnost* Defence Foundation

Putin: bringing the mass media back under Kremlin control

Since 2000, parts of the mass media have been taken back into state ownership, in effect, either directly or through Kremlin front-companies. The Kremlin is the majority shareholder in Gazprom-Media, which in its turn owns *Komsomolskaia Pravda*, Russia's most widely read newspaper, as well as the daily *Izvestia* and the NTV TV station (see Box 11.2). Television, the main source of news for most Russians, was the first target of Putin's campaign to assert Kremlin control over the mass media, followed by national newspapers and then radio. In order to achieve this level of control Putin had to wrest ownership from opposition oligarchs and to gain the compliance of others. The first oligarch target was Vladimir Gusinsky whose Media-Most media empire opposed both Chechen wars, supported the opposition Fatherland-All-Russia alliance in the December 1999 Duma elections and had openly questioned Putin's democratic credentials. Gusinsky was subjected to an escalating campaign to silence him using 'administrative methods'. In May 2000, 40 tax police armed with machine guns, wearing balaclavas and camouflage uniforms, raided Media-Most's headquarters supposedly as part of an investigation into corruption in the Ministry of Finance and allegations that Media-Most was illegally obtaining and disseminating information. Gusinsky was arrested in June 2000 and eventually fled Russia. In 2001 Gazprom-Media acquired Gusinky's NTV. In 2004 REN-TV, the last privately-owned TV station first stopped its critical news coverage and in 2005 was bought by a pro-Kremlin company. Russia's two largest TV channels, ORT and *Rossiia* (Russia) are state-owned and have a pro-Kremlin line.

In March 2004 Putin made other important changes to the interface between the mass media and the government. He replaced the Ministry for the Press, Television, Radio Broadcasting and the Mass Media with a new Ministry of Culture and Mass Communications, headed by the St Petersburg musicologist Aleksandr Sokolev. The task of registering new media outlets was transferred to the Federal Registration Service within the Ministry of Justice, which is responsible to the president. Broadcasting licences are now allocated by a new Broadcast Licensing Department within the Ministry of Culture and Mass Communications.

The media and national security

Russia's laws on libel and extremism are being used to restrict media freedom as well as the activities of other civil society organisations (see Chapter 10 and Box 11.1). The Law on Extremism (2004) includes 13 broad definitions of extremism, which the Kremlin and its allies have used to define critical or opposition opinion as extremism; it is all too easy for a media outlet to contravene the prohibition against organising, giving public support to, calling for or helping extremist activities and opinions. In a move that would place further restrictions on the media and websites, in April 2008 the prosecutor general presented proposed amendments to the law to the Duma Security Committee. If adopted these amendments would make it even easier for the Kremlin to silence its critics as, for example, they would require the media to publish denials of any report an official considered inaccurate.

Box 11.2 The mass media

Newspapers

Rossiiskaia Gazeta http://www.rg.ru

The newspaper of the RF government first issued on 11 November 1990, it is the official publisher of government documents. Published in 29 Russian cities. The Editor-in-Chief is Anatoly Yurkov.

Krasnaia Zvezda http://www.redstar.ru/

Defence Ministry newspaper.

Nezavisimaia Gazeta (Independent) http://www.ng.ru

Began publication in 1990 as a challenge to the soviet state, but temporarily stopped publication in May 1995 for financial reasons and was bought by Boris Berezovsky. Berezovsky wanted the paper to support his business interests and Boris Yeltsin which led to tensions with the journalists who wanted to continue the newspaper's independent reporting. Under Putin *Nezavisimaia Gazeta* became increasingly anti-Kremlin, but in 2005 it was bought supposedly by the wife of Konstantin Remchukov, then an assistant to the economic development and trade minister German Gref. It is of note that government employees cannot own newspapers; Remchukov is close to the pro-Kremlin oligarch Oleg Derispaska.

Izvestia http://www.izvestia.ru/

This is the former soviet government newspaper whose journalists tried to maintain the newspaper's good quality writing and impartiality. In March 1997 *Izvestia* reprinted an article from the French newspaper *Le Monde* alleging that Chernomydin had amassed a personal fortune of over US$5 billion while running *Gazprom*. Chernomyrdin's ally the oligarch Vagit Alekperov was president of Lukoil, which had shares in *Izvestia* and became the majority shareholder in April 1997. *Izvestia* had also attacked Anatoly Chubais, the first deputy prime minister and ally of the oligarch Vladimir Potanin. Potanin's Oneximbank also bought shares in *Izvestia* and, together with Lukoil, had the editor Igor Golembiovsky and other members of the editorial staff sacked in 1997. Boris Berezovsky, who was Potanin and Chubais's great rival at the time, set up a new newspaper which was also called *Izvestia* and recruited Golembiovsky, Otto Latsis and Sergei Agafonov. In 2004 *Izvestia* was the first newspaper to dispute the government's claim that there were only 350 hostages in the Beslan school and published pictures of wounded children on the front and back pages of the 4 September edition. The editor Raf Shakirov was sacked, officially for conflict with Potanin but it was widely rumoured that pressure had been brought to bear by the Kremlin. In 2005 *Izvestia* was bought by *Gazprom-Media* and, under its new editor Vlaidimir Mamontov, became a tabloid-style newspaper with limited political coverage. In 2006 Ilya Kissilyov a spokesperson for the pro-Kremlin United Russia was appointed deputy editor.

Kommersant http://www.kommersant.ru/

Founded in 1991 as business-oriented daily by Boris Berezovsky. In 2006 it was bought by Alisher Usmanov, a metals magnate, who said that while he supports Kremlin policies he does not intend to interfere in editorial policy.

Box 11.2 *(Continued)*

Komsomolskaia Pravda http://www.kp.ru/

Originally the newspaper of the Komsomol, the CPSU youth organisation. A national, mass circulation, left-leaning daily. Controlled by tycoon Vladimir Potanin.

Moskovskii Komsomolets http://www.mk.ru/

A popular national daily controlled by Moscow Mayor Yury Luzhkov.

Argumenty i Fakty http://www.aif.ru/

A popular weekly social and political newspaper founded in 1987. Owned by Proms-vyazbank, which is associated with the banker Sergei Pugachyov, who is a Federation Council member with close links to the Kremlin.

Novaia Gazeta http://www.novayagazeta.ru/

Established in 1993 by Mikhail Gorbachev using his 1990 Nobel Prize money. A twice weekly publication specialising in investigative reporting, especially into government corruption and Chechnia. The late Anna Politkovskaya was one of its journalists. Since 2000 *Novaia Gazeta* has lost a number of expensive libel suits leading to financial difficulties. Fifty-one per cent of *Novaia Gazeta*'s shares are owned by its journalists and in June 2006 Gorbachev and his friend the Duma deputy and banking billionaire Aleksandr Lebedev bought a 49 per cent share. Both men are highly critical of Putin; Gorbachev has said that he will not interfere with the paper's editorial independence.

Obshchaia Gazeta http://www.og.ru/

First published in August 1991. Under its founder and editor-in-chief the legendary Yegor Yakovlev, *Obshchaia Gazeta* was a highly respected, investigative, liberal weekly. The oligarch Vladimir Gusinsky's Media-Most group bought into the paper in the mid-1990s. Anna Politkovskaya was reprimanded by Gusinsky for an article published on 6 March 1997 alleging banks used government funds to illegally finance short-term speculation and that speculation by Oneksimbank had resulted in the nonpayment of workers at the Norilsk Nickel combine. In 2002 Yakovlev sold *Obshchaia Gazeta*, but it ceased publication. There is a new newspaper of the same name.

Pravda http://english.pravda.ru/

The successor to the CPSU newspaper originally founded by Lenin in 1912. Now a communist party daily newspaper, its editor-in-chief is Aleksandr Ilyin.

Sovetskaia Rossiia http://www.rednews.ru/

A pro-communist daily newspaper.

Zavtra (Tomorrow) http://www.zavtra.ru

A weekly newspaper founded by its editor-in-chief Aleksandr Prokhanov. A Red–Brown publication carrying articles by Eurasianists, nationalists, 'patriots', Cossacks and members of the Russian Orthodox Church.

Trud (Labour) http://www.trud.ru/

A left-leaning daily owned by Promsvyazbank.

Box 11.2 (*Continued*)

Lenta   http://www.lenta.ru/

A Russian-language web-based daily published by the Foundation for Effective Policies, part of the rambler media group.

Utrennaya Gazeta **(Morning)**   http://utro.ru

A daily online paper launched in 1999.

Smi.Ru   http://www.smi.ru/

Online Russian mass media digest.

Gazeta.ru   http://www.gazeta.ru/

Internet newspaper.

NEWSru.com   http://2003.newsru.com

Internet newspaper.

Polit.RU   http://www.polit.ru

A daily online Russian-language, independent website, covering Russian politics, economics, international news and cultural issues.

The Moscow Times   http://www.themoscowtimes.com/

English-language. CEO Derek Sauer and editor Andrew McChesney.

The Moscow News   http://english.mnweekly.ru

The English-language version of *Moskovskye Novosti*.

St Petersburg Times   http://www.sptimes.ru/

English-language. CEO Derek Sauer and editor Tobin Auber.

News agencies

MosNews   http://www.mosnews.com/

Partner project of *Gazeta.ru*.

Itar-Tass   http://www.itar-tass.com/eng/

State-owned.

RIA-Novosti   http://en.rian.ru/

State-owned.

Interfax   http://www.interfax.com

Privately owned.

Prima   http://www.prima-news.ru/eng/

The Moscow Human Rights News Agency covering human rights in Russia, the FSU and abroad. It was founded in 2000 on the basis of the *Express-Chronicle* Human Rights newspaper, which had been published in Moscow since 1987. Prima's editor-in-chief is Aleksandr Podrabinek, who is a former political prisoner and editor of *Express-Chronicle*. Prima is sponsored by the C. S. Mott Foundation, IDEE, McArthur Foundation, Barbara S. Bryant (USA).

Box 11.2 (*Continued*)

Television

Russian Public Television (ORT)

Originally owned by Boris Berezovsky but he lost control to the state and sold his shares to Roman Abramovich's *Sibneft*. Now state owned, it reaches 99 per cent of Russian territory.

Rossiia **(Russia)**   http://www.rutv.ru/

A national network, reaching 96 per cent of Russian territory. Run by state-owned Russian State Television and Radio Broadcasting Company (RTR).

Channel One   http://www.1tv.ru/

A national network, 51 per cent owned by state and 49 per cent by private shareholders.

NTV

Originally part of Vladimir Gusinsky's *Media-Most* group and the last remaining independent national TV station. Following attacks by the Kremlin Gusinsky fled to Israel and sold NTV, which was acquired in April 2001 by the state-owned gas monopoly Gazprom. Its new Director the Russian-American Boris Jordan's stated aim was to make NTV profitable. Jordan was sacked following criticism by the Russian authorities of NTV's coverage of the October 2002 Dubrovka theatre siege. NTV's coverage of the Beslan school siege in September 2004 simply reported government statements without any further comment. During 2004 pressure was applied to NTV effectively ending the last venue for political debate on Russian TV and criticism of the Kremlin: in June Leonid Parfenov a popular and respected journalist was sacked and his *Namedni* current affairs programme was closed, following his failed attempt in May to broadcast an interview with Malika Yandarbieva, the widow of the former acting Chechen President Zelimkhan Yandarbiev. (In December 2004 Parfenov became the editor of the Russian edition of *Newsweek* magazine.) In July 2004 Savik Shuster's popular information-analytical programme *Svoboda Slova* (Free Speech) was ended and he was sacked less than two weeks after he had criticised politicians for refusing to debate Putin's controversial new social legislation. *Svoboda Slova* had been the only remaining live broadcast, TV political debate programme that allowed criticism of the Kremlin. In July 2004 Tamara Gavrilova, who had studied with Putin and is a loyal Petersburger, became NVT's first deputy general director.

TV-6 and TVS

Some NTV journalists moved to TV-6 when it was taken over by Gazprom. The pension fund of Lukoil owned 14 per cent of TV-6, and proceeded against TV-6 to force it into bankruptcy because of losses of £30–35 million. In January 2002, the Kremlin ordered the closure of TV-6 and its licence was cancelled. TV-6 was replaced by TVS. TVS was Russia's only privately owned national network until it was also closed, officially for financial reasons, in June 2003.

Box 11.2 (*Continued*)

TV Tsentr (Centre TV) http://www.tvc.ru/

President Oleg Poptsov. A Moscow-based commercial station that began broadcasting in 1997. It now broadcasts to 77 regions and can be seen by 66 per cent of the population. Since 2005 Centre-TV International broadcasts in Russian to other countries including Israel, North America and Western Europe.

Ren TV http://www.ren-tv.com/

Ren-TV was launched on 1 January 1997 by Irena Lesnevskaya and her son Dmitry Lesnevsky, and until 1 July 2005 was owned by the Lesnevskys and Anatoly Chubais's Russian Energy Company. In 2005 Bertelsmann's RTL bought a 30 per cent stake in Ren-TV, and the steel maker *Servastal* and the oil and gas company *Surgutneftegaz* each bought a 35 per cent stake. In December 2006 Lyubov Sovershaeva, Putin's former deputy envoy to the North-West federal district, became REN-TV's chair. In 2006 *Surgutneftegaz* sold its holding in Ren-TV to Abros Investments, which is also chaired by Sovershaeva and is a subsidiary of the St Petersburg *Rossiia* (Russia) bank. The pro-Kremlin *Rossiia* Bank now owns 70 per cent of Ren-TV.

Russia Today http://www.russiatoday.ru/

A state-funded, international English-language news channel, broadcasting via satellite.

Radio

Radio Rossiia (Russia) http://www.radiorus.ru/

A national network run by state-owned Russian State Television and Radio Broadcasting Company (RTR).

Ekho Moskvy (Moscow Echo) http://www.echo.msk.ru/

An influential station which recruited news journalists from TV-6 when it closed and developed a reputation for its political discussion programmes. However, it is now owned by Gazprom.

Radio Maiak (Lighthouse) http://www.radiomayak.ru/

A state-run national network.

Russkoye Radio (Russian Radio) http://www.rusradio.ru/

A major private network, music-based programming.

Voice of Russia http://www.vor.ru/index_eng.phtml

A state-run external service, broadcasting in English and other languages.

In the spring of 2008 a draft law on restricting foreign investment in over 40 strategic sectors of the economy was amended to include Internet providers, typesetting and publishing companies. In order for a foreign company to be allowed to acquire a controlling share in a Russian business in one of the strategic sectors, it will be required to go through a stringent authorisation process and if the foreign company is itself partly owned by a foreign government then it must go through the same authorisation process to gain more than 25 per cent of a Russian business. Russian critics of the draft law, such as the opposition The Other Russia (2008) movement, believe that this will be used to tighten the Kremlin's control over the Internet as, unlike the rest of the mass media, online sources have been highly critical of the Putin administration. Pro-Kremlin businesses have also started to acquire online businesses, for example Alisher Usmanov has bought the online newspaper *gazeta.ru*.

Chechnia, Dubrovka, Beslan and controlling the news

Putin made it clear that he would not tolerate the critical reports that had dogged the first Chechen war. Reports of the second Chechen war on the state-run TV channels followed the official line of a war fought nobly against dangerous Islamic rebels and did not include any of the coverage of atrocities or human rights abuses recorded by organisations such as Amnesty International. NTV took an anti-war stance and tried to continue the objective coverage they had pioneered during the first war. NTV was subjected to administrative measures including an unexpected tax audit and then problems with a bank loan, as well as pressure from the FSB to bring its coverage into line. Chechnia rapidly became a very dangerous place for journalists to work; journalists were killed, abducted or simply disappeared. In order to work in Chechnia journalists needed military accreditation and were only allowed to travel with the military in military-designated zones, supposedly for their own safety. These restrictions were designed to stop independent investigations and were part of the government's media management. The Russian military also have their own press centres in Makhachkala in Dagestan and Mozdok in North Ossetia. In July 2004 the task of issuing permits for journalists to travel to Chechnia was taken over by the Ministry of the Interior.

The case of Andrei Babitsky provides a rather bizarre example of the devices that are employed to silence journalists. In January 2000 Andrei Babitsky, a Russian working for the American-funded station Radio Liberty, was seized by Russian armed forces and accused of lacking the appropriate military accreditation to be in the war zone. After apparently being handed over to the Chechens in return for some Russian POWs, when Babitsky finally re-emerged he was also charged with belonging to an illegal armed group. It is not clear whether Babitsky's arrest was on the initiative of local officials or the Kremlin, but it was perfectly in tune with official policy. In October 2002 Putin cancelled the August 1991 decree that had guaranteed the legal and operational status of the Moscow Bureau of Radio Free Europe/Radio Liberty. In November 2002, despite criticising television coverage of the Dubrovka theatre siege, Putin nonetheless vetoed media legislation passed by both houses of the Federal Assembly which would have limited reporting of anti-terrorist operations. The veto enabled Putin to depict himself as having a balanced approach to the contradictory imperatives of media freedom and the need for secrecy in the war on terror. However, Putin did not need the legislation to control information as he was already bringing major media outlets under Kremlin control.

Beslan, censorship and the murder of Anna Politkovskaya

An Organization for Security and Co-operation in Europe (OSCE) Report (2004), based on research by the Russian Union of Journalists' (RUJ) Centre for Journalism in Extreme Situations, expressed serious concern that the authorities concealed the truth of the scale of the Beslan crisis. While the print media and the Internet provided extensive coverage, according to the report the coverage provided by the three main TV stations was neither accurate nor timely. There was also a concerted bid to stop independent-minded journalists from travelling to Beslan. Radio Liberty's Andrei Babitsky was detained at Vnukovo airport in Moscow on 2 September and the following day was sentenced to 15 days' arrest. The Georgian TV journalist Nana Lezhava claims to have been drugged with benzodiazepines while being held and questioned at a remand centre in Vladikavkaz, following her coverage of Beslan. A poll of 1,216 listeners conducted by the *Ekho Moskvy* radio station found that 92 per cent believed that the TV channels concealed information and only 8 per cent thought they had received full information (ibid.: 10).

The newspaper *Novaia Gazeta* was consistently critical of the Putin administration, but it was also highly critical of the Beslan hostage takers. Anna Politkovskaya, its leading investigative journalist, was famous in Russia for her reporting of the wars in Chechnia, including an interview with the anti-Russian Chechen president Aslan Maskhadov during the first Chechen war. Following death threats she spent 2001 in Austria. She was fiercely critical of the Putin administration in general, of its conduct of the second Chechen war and of Ramzan Kadyrov the pro-Russian president of Chechnia. Politkovskaya was poisoned and fell ill on a flight to Rostov-on-Don on her way to Beslan. On 7 October 2006 Anna Politkovskaya was murdered in her Moscow apartment building. The RUJ Secretary General Igor Yakovenko told the business channel RBK TV that whatever the precise motive for her murder there was no doubt that, 'It is a contract killing committed for political motives' (BBC Monitoring, 2006). In 2007 she was posthumously made a laureate of the UNESCO/Guillermo Cano World Press Freedom Prize.

Supporting the media and journalists

The Public Chamber

In January 2006 Pavel Gusev, the editor of *Moskovskii Komsomolets* and head of the Public Chamber's Commission for the Media and Press Freedom, announced that the Public Chamber would stand up for press freedom. Other members include Eduard Sagalayev and Nikolai Svanidze, the news anchor on state-owned *Rossiia* television. Gusev reported that the Chamber had already been receiving complaints from journalists in the regions about local authorities (Pankin, 2006: 10). In May 2007 the Commission announced that together with the VTsIOM public opinion polling centre, it would develop a system of criteria for assessing the level of press freedom in the regions and Russia as a whole (VTsIOM, 2007). According to the Commission's vice-chair, Yelena Zelinskaya, 'The idea is to get an objective picture of the level of media freedom in Russia and to compare it with data provided by various foreign organizations' (ibid.). Foreign Organisations such as Reporters without Borders and the Russian, but largely foreign-funded, Glasnost Defence Foundation certainly present a rather unflattering picture of the state of the Russian media. It remains to be seen if the Commission's index will provide an objective assessment or if it will be part of an attempt to whitewash the true situation.

At the 2006 conference of the World Association of Newspapers, Nikolai Svanidze came into conflict with representatives of the regional press. Svanidze claimed that the range of views in the Russian media was shrinking because the public 'has grown tired of pluralism', and that 'Our guests from the United States and European countries may not understand what I'm talking about, but the classic Soviet viewer is not used to alternatives'. He continued, 'It's tiring to have a choice because you have to think', then adding, Russian audiences 'don't want either-or, they want to know exactly what's going on and what to do about it' (Boykewich, 2006). Svanidze's statement is in effect seeking to justify managed democracy, the need for the elite to take control. Representatives of independent regional publishers present at the conference challenged Svanidze's claims. Yury Purgin the CEO of *Altapress* said, 'Our readers aren't tired by our offering them different opinions – they thank us for it', and Irina Samokhina the director of *Krestianin* (*Peasant*) said that readers' letters demanded investigations after seeing inaccurate information in government-controlled media (ibid.).

Glasnost Defence Fund (or Foundation)

The Glasnost Defence Fund (GDF) is an NGO founded in 1991 to champion press freedom throughout the FSU and defend the rights of journalists. One of its founders

---

Box 11.3 Glasnost Defence Fund statistics on violence and harassment against journalists and media outlets

	2004	2005	2006
Journalists' deaths	14	7	9
Assaults on journalists	68	63	63
Assaults on editorial offices	15	12	12
Lawsuits filed against journalists and media outlets	34	42	48
Unlawful dismissals of journalists/editors	5	11	16
Detentions by police (FSB, etc.)	37	47	75
Threats to journalists/media outlets	28	25	43
Attempts to drive media outlets from leased premises	16	10	7
Printing/distribution service denials	33	38	50
Media outlets switched off/suspended	19	23	18
Confiscation (buy-up, arrest) of circulation	30	28	28
Media outlets terminated	16	23	26
Other forms of pressure/violation of journalists' rights	269	344	300

Source: Glasnost Defence Foundation's Digest (2007), no. 312, 9 January, http://www.gdf.ru/digest/digest/digest312e.shtml

was Yegor Yakovlev and since 1991 the cinematographer Alexei Simon has been the GDF's president and chair. GDF conducts research and large-scale projects and undertakes individual casework for journalists. It works closely with Russian and foreign human rights organisations including UNESCO, Helsinki Watch, Amnesty International, Committee for the Defence of Free Speech, Memorial, Article 19, Reporters without Frontiers and International PEN. It has received funding from various embassies, the Soros Foundation, the Ford Foundation, the Eurasia Foundation, the McArthur Foundation and the National Endowment for Democracy (USA).

Russian Union of Journalists

The Russian Union of Journalists (RUJ) is the main professional body for journalists in Russia. It was formed on November 1990 and is a full member of the International Federation of Journalists. Its statutes describe the RUJ as 'a professional, independent, self-ruled, non-governmental organisation' (RUJ website). Its membership includes over 100,000 individual members and 81 organisations with full membership status. The member organisations include the journalist unions in the republics, regions, Moscow and St Petersburg. The Association of Newspaper Publishers and Chief Editors, the Association of the Russian Press and the Guild of Parliamentary Journalists are among 27 professional associations with associate membership. The RUJ describes its role as promoting freedom of expression and the press; promoting the conditions necessary for the functioning of the mass media; defending journalists' economic and professional interests and helping to raise mass media workers' living and working conditions. The Center for Journalism in Extreme Situations (CJES) is a Moscow-based NGO established in February 2000 within the Russian Journalists Union. CJES's director is Oleg Panfilov. CJES's main activities include monitoring and investigating violations of journalists' and media rights in Russia and the CIS; researching the conditions journalists work under in hot spots such as Chechnia; and offering legal help and training for journalists working in extreme situations (CJES website).

In 2008 the RUJ's secretary general, Igor Yakovenko, described Russia's media as being in crisis and that, 'This crisis manifests itself in a deterioration in quality, declining trust, a reduction of the role of journalists in society, and shrinking media freedom in our country' (RFE/RL, 2008). In addition Panfilov argued that under Putin, 'Everything was done to turn the independent press into propaganda' and that the authorities believe 'obedient propagandists are more useful than independent journalists' (ibid.). The Russian media are now glossier and slicker that the soviet media, but the journalistic content has become increasingly controlled.

Reporters Without Borders

Reporters Without Borders (RWB) is an international NGO, which bases its works on Article 19 of the 1948 Universal Declaration of Human Rights. According to Article 19 everyone has 'the right to freedom of opinion and expression' and 'the right to seek and impart', information and ideas 'regardless of frontiers'. RWB compiles an annual rating of press freedom around the globe (see Box 11.4), using

Box 11.4 Yearly worldwide press freedom ranking of countries (2002–2007)

Country	2007	2006	2005	2004	2003	2002
Iceland	1	1	1	1	1	1
Estonia	3	6	11	11	12	n/a
UK	24	27	24	28	27	21
USA	48	53	44	22	31	17
Russia	148	147	138	140	148	121
North Korea	168	168	167	167	166	139

Source: Reporters Without Borders (2002, 2003, 2004, 2005, 2006 and 2007) 'Worldwide Press Freedom Index', *RWB* website, http://www.rsf.org/

its own indices. Since 2002 Iceland has shared the highest world ranking for media freedom with other Scandinavian countries, Russia is consistently ranked as having a 'poor' record and each year North Korea has been at the bottom of the ranking. RWB receives funding from the US National Endowment for Democracy and western governments and so its findings are contested.

Violence and harassment of journalists

Russian investigative journalists are subjected to violence and even murder in a bid to silence them. Over twenty journalists died violently while Putin was president and in each case no one has been convicted – in most cases not even arrested – in connection with their deaths (Osborn, 2007). These journalists all, with the probable exception of Elena Shestakova, angered some kind of powerful criminal, business or political interest.

Box 11.5 The death toll of Russian journalists since 2000

Gadzhi Abashilov: the head of the republic of Dagestan's state-owned VGTRK media company, he was shot dead on 21 March 2008 in the republic's capital Makhachkala.

Ilyas Shurpayev: had moved to Moscow from his native Dagestan in February 2007, where he had worked as the local correspondent for North Caucasus, South Ossetia and the Georgian secessionist republic of Abkhazia for NTV and Channel One TV. On 21 March 2007 he was found

In a demonstration in Moscow after the murder of Anna Politkovskaya, a demonstrator holds a poster with a portrait of the murdered journalist and the words 'The Kremlin has killed free speech'.

Box 11.5 (*Continued*)

dead in his burning Moscow apartment; he had been stabbed and strangled. Shortly before his death Shurpayev had claimed that his column in the Dagestan newspaper *Nastoyashcheye Vremya* (*Now*) had been banned. Prosecutors believe that the murder happened in the course of a robbery.

Elena Shestakova: had worked for the newspapers *5-corners* and *Gloria*. She was attacked near her home in February 2008 and died the next day. An 18-year-old student was arrested for her murder.

Ivan Safronov: was the military affairs specialist for the daily national newspaper *Kommersant* and was found dead on 2 March 2007 after 'falling' from a window of his Moscow home. Law enforcement agents said he committed suicide but colleagues say he had evidence that the Kremlin was supplying Iran and Syria with arms and that he was killed to stop the story. According to Oleg Panfilov, the Director of CJES, 'Military issues, especially [the] uncontrolled arms trade, are among the most dangerous issues in Russian journalism. We have every reason to believe that the killing is connected to military issues' (CJES/IFEX, 2007).

Anna Politkovskaya: was a crusading investigative reporter specialising in Chechnia, attached to the fortnightly newspaper *Novaia Gazeta*. She was shot dead in a contract killing outside her apartment block in Moscow on 7 October 2006. Prosecutors accuse the exiled oligarch Boris Berezovsky of ordering her assassination. In 2007 arrests of those alleged to be involved in the plot were made, including a former FSB Colonel Pavel Ryaguzov. Prosecutors claim to have identified the murderer who was placed on Russia's 'most wanted' list in March 2008.

Vyacheslav Plotnikov: a reporter for a local TV channel in Voronezh. His body was found in a forest on 15 September 2006, dressed in someone else's clothes. There were no signs of a violent death, but his colleagues are convinced that he was murdered.

Yevgeny Gerasimenko: an investigative reporter on the regional newspaper *Saratovsky Rasklad* who had been looking into shady local business dealings. He was found dead on 25 July 2006 in his flat. He had been tortured and suffocated with a plastic bag.

Alexander Pitersky: a presenter on the St Petersburg radio station *Baltika*, who sometimes covered criminal investigations. His body was found in his flat, where he had been stabbed to death, on 30 August 2005.

Magomedzagid Varisov: a press commentator and critic of local politicians in his native Dagestan, where he also ran a think-tank. He was killed in a machine gun attack in Makhachkala, the capital of Dagestan, on 28 June 2005.

Pavel Makeev: a cameraman for *Puls*, a local TV station in southern Russia. He died on 21 May 2005 while covering illegal street racing in the town of Azov. His car was rammed by an unknown vehicle and his camera and tapes taken.

Paul Klebnikov: a US citizen of Russian extraction. As editor of the Russian edition of *Forbes* magazine, he put together the country's first rich list and specialised in corruption investigations. He was shot dead in a contract killing in Moscow on 9 July 2004.

Box 11.5 (Continued)

Aleksei Sidorov: the second editor of local newspaper the *Togliatti Overview* to be murdered in as many years. He was stabbed in the chest with an ice pick or similar sharp object outside his apartment block on 9 October 2003.

Yuri Shchekochikhin: an investigative journalist, liberal MP and deputy editor of *Novaia Gazeta*. He specialised in investigating corruption in the prosecutor general's office. He died on 3 July 2003 after an unexplained allergic reaction, his colleagues believe he was poisoned.

Dmitry Shvets: a senior executive at a local Murmansk TV station, TV-21 Northwestern Broadcasting, who had been highly critical of local officials. He was shot dead outside the station's offices on 18 April 2003.

Valery Ivanov: the editor of the *Togliatti Overview* and managing editor of the independent channel Lada-TV, specialising in crime and corruption in the local car industry. He was shot dead in his car on 29 April 2002.

Natalya Skryl: a business reporter on *Our Time*, a local newspaper based in Rostov-on-Don, investigating controversial dealings in a local metals plant. She died on her way home after being beaten with a heavy object on 8 March 2002.

Eduard Markevich: the editor of *Novy Reft*, a local newspaper in the town of Reftinsky, Sverdlovsk region, who was critical of regional authorities. After a series of threatening phone calls, he was shot in the back and killed on 19 September 2001.

Adam Tepsurgayev: a TV cameraman for Reuters who filmed exclusive footage of the conflict in Chechnia. He was shot dead in the village of Alkhan-Kala on 23 November 2000 by masked gunmen who burst into his home.

Sergei Ivanov: the director of the Lada-TV station in Togliatti, who had investigated the area's notoriously corrupt car manufacturing business. He was shot five times outside his apartment building on 3 October 2000.

Iskandar Khatloni: a journalist investigating human rights abuses in Chechnia for the Tajik-language service of Radio Free Europe/Radio Liberty. He was killed by an axe-wielding attacker in Moscow on 21 September 2000.

Sergei Novikov: a senior executive at the *Vesna* radio station in Smolensk. He claimed to be able to prove corruption among high-ranking local officials. He was shot dead on 26 July 2000, in the lobby of his apartment building.

Igor Domnikov: an investigative reporter on *Novaia Gazeta*. He died on 16 July 2000 after being attacked with a hammer in the lobby of his Moscow apartment block. His newspaper believes his murder was a case of mistaken identity.

Artyom Borovik: a senior executive at the investigative magazine *Completely Secret* that exposed the misdeeds of the rich and powerful. He died on 3 March 2000 in a plane crash that the authorities believe may not have been accidental.

Sources: Andrew Osborn (2007) 'The 20 journalists who have lost their lives in Putin's Russia', *The Independent*, 11 March, http://news.independent.co.uk; Committee to Protect Journalists 'Journalists Killed: Statistics and background', CPJ website, http://www.cpj.org/deadly/index.html; and the Glasnost Defence Fund website, http://www.gdf.ru/

Electronic Russia, blogging and controlling cyberspace

Electronic Russia

In 2001 Putin launched a state project called Electronic Russia (E-Russia) to run from 2002–2010. E-Russia is designed to develop telecommunications, improve the existing infrastructure, and to promote the use of Information and Communication Technology (ICT) and thus Russia's entry into the global information community. E-Russia also entails greater government use of the Internet to communicate with the public. In June 2002 the government launched a new version of its official portal with a new emphasis on interaction between officials and the public, through regular updates and opportunities for the public to submit questions, suggestions and complaints. On 24 April 2007 the Russian IT and Communication Ministry announced on its website that it will provide broadband Internet access to 95 per cent of Russian schools and licensed software to all schools by the new school year. Dmitry Medvedev was in charge of this national plan to computerise schools. To date computer ownership and use of the Internet is low in Russia compared to other industrial countries; although 26 million Russians over the age of 18 use the Internet, that is only 23 per cent of the population. In comparison, 30 million Britons or 62 per cent of the British population use the Internet (FOM, 2006). Access is also skewed towards educated, city dwellers living in European Russia.

Websites and blogging

While under Putin Russia's main national print and broadcast media came under the control of pro-Kremlin groups, the Internet continued to provide access to other sources of information and opinion, such as NGO websites and foreign newspapers. Blogging has also become increasingly popular among the young. The Internet, including blogs, is monitored by the security services. For example, in February 2004 Andrei Skovorodnikov the leader of the National Bolshevik party was arrested by the FSB on the same day as he posted on his website a collage of Putin's head on top of a naked women's body with the caption 'Putin is a fag' (Gessen, 2005: 115). He was sentenced to six months' corrective labour. Also in 2004, in the wake of the Beslan hostage crisis, the pro-Moscow administration in Ingushetia closed down the republic's last remaining Internet café because it had been used to spread 'knowingly false information' (Uzzell, 2004). In late 2006 the Russian language part of *Live Journal*, Russia's most heavily used blogging platform, was taken over by a Kremlin-friendly company. This led to a significant fall in blogging, especially political blogging (Krastev, 2007). Self-censorship is also an effective means of censorship.

While in Krasnoyarsk in February 2008, Medvedev spoke up for the Internet as a guarantee of media freedoms in Russia, when he told journalists that he went online at the beginning and end of the day to check news and views. He also told journalists that, 'There is news from the main channels, regional channels, there is news from foreign channels and finally there is news produced, so to say, on media sites which hold opposition views against the authorities.' Medvedev pointed out that, 'They can post all their clips and all their speeches there, generally they say unpleasant things about the authorities' and that, 'This guarantees the independence of the mass media, in my opinion' (Dyomkin et al., 2008). Medvedev seems to be valuing the critical material that is available online; however, proposed amendments to the law on extremism in April 2008 would empower prosecutors to block access to any online news and information that they deem 'extremist'. It remains to be seen whether this amendment is adopted under President Medvedev and then, if it is, whether it will be used only against violent extremists or also to silence irritating, critical voices as well.

Controlling cyberspace and going digital

The Federal Service for Media Law Compliance and Cultural Heritage (*Rosookhrankultura*), part of the Culture and Mass Communications Ministry is responsible for issuing and revoking broadcasting licences. In March 2007 Putin issued a decree merging it with the Federal Information Technologies Agency (*Rossvyaznadzor*) to form a new agency. Boris Boyarskov the head of *Rosookhrankultura* was named the head of the new agency. Boyarskov is a Petersburger who has worked in the security services and is a close ally of Igor Sechin, the first deputy head of the presidential administration (Fossato, 2007). The creation of the new agency together with amendments to existing legislation that the Duma is about to begin work on, is a potentially important step towards establishing greater regulation of the Internet. The new agency will also have an important role in Russia's transition from analogue to digital broadcasting. Russia joined the European Digital Video Broadcasting Standard for television in May 2004 and is supposed to be ready to begin the switch to digital in 2008. Dmitry Medvedev was charged with overseeing Russia's switch to digital television. The government has earmarked a budget of US$4 billion (ibid.) to fund the six-year transition period and part of Boyarskov's role is to ensure that the budget is spent appropriately and does not disappear into corrupt pockets. Digital TV could also herald the arrival of hundreds of new stations and so challenge the dominance of the three national channels: *Rossiia*, *Pervy* and NTV. Boyarskov will no doubt also have an important role in ensuring that broadcasting licences are allocated to worthy recipients.

Chapter summary

Information was one of the great battlegrounds of the USSR's political liberalisation and the beginnings of Russia's democratic transition. In this battle little value has been placed on impartiality. Communists, nationalists, fascists, liberals and all shades of opinion in between want their news to dominate and to at least restrict the platforms available to others. Since 1991 there has not been a return to soviet-style censorship and it is still possible to buy opposition newspapers. Putin moved decisively to draw the mass media into his managed democracy and to exert, both directly and indirectly, Kremlin control over Russia's major sources of news and opinion. The result was that the range of news and the diversity of reported opinions were dramatically reduced, so that by the 2007 Duma elections and the 2008 presidential elections, it was very difficult for opposition voices to find a platform; this helped Medvedev's successful election as president in 2008. Before his election Medvedev spoke of the value of critical ideas and it is too soon to know if he will maintain Putin's tight control of the media or encourage a more lenient application of Russia's law.

Discussion points

- Are the Russian media now subject to less or more censorship than during *perestroika*?
- Why was the use of compromising materials so prevalent in the 1990s?
- Do you agree with Igor Yakovenko that the Russian media are in crisis?
- Will growth in the use of the Internet subvert the state's attempts to control information and ideas?

Further reading

For analyses of the relations between democracy, power and the mass media in Russia see Sarah Oates (2006) *Television, Democracy and Elections in Russia*, London: Routledge; Andrei Rybakov (2004) 'The Mass Media', in Michael McFaul, Nikolai Petrov and Andrei Ryabov (eds) *Between Dictatorship and Democracy: Russia Post-Communist Political Reform*, Washington: Carnegie Endowment for International Peace; Michael McFaul and Masha Lipman (2003) 'Putin and the Media', in Dale Herspring (2003) *The Putin Russia: Past Imperfect, Future Uncertain*, Armonk, NY: M.E. Sharpe, Inc.; and I. Zassoursky (2004) *Media and Power in Post-Soviet Russia*, Armonk, NY: M.E. Sharpe, Inc. The American Public Broadcasting Station (PBS) has a section on its website on 'Moscow and the Media' with links to media developments during Putin's first Administration: http://www.pbs.org/newshour/media/russia/index.html. Floriana Fossato is a leading specialist on the Russian media, she gave a briefing on the 'Russian Regional TV' to RFE/RL on 22 March 2006. An audio version of the briefing is available on the *RFE/RL* website, http://www.rferl.org/.

An analysis of the implications of Russia's Defamation Law is provided by Article 19 and The Black Soil Regional Mass Media Center (2003) *The Price of Honour. A Guide to Defamation Law and Practice in Russia*, February, Article 19 website, http://www.article19.org/. *The Current Digest of the Post-Soviet Press*, (Minneapolis, Ill: East View Information Services) is a regularly updated periodical of translations of Russian newspaper articles. It started publication in 1949 as *The Current Digest of the Soviet Press*.

Useful websites

Russian Union of Journalists: http://www.ruj.ru

Reporters Without Borders: has regularly updated reports on media developments and annual reports on individual countries, http://www.rsf.org/

Mondo Times: The worldwide media guide. Russia – includes links to local media organised by city, http://www.mondotimes.com/1/world.ru

Article 19: Global Campaign for Free Expression (Based in London, UK), http://www.article19.org/

Media and Law Policy Institute: http://www.medialaw.ru/

References

Boykewich, S. (2006) 'TV Presenter and Regional Press Square Off', *The Moscow Times*, 5 June, http://www.moscowtimes.ru/article/918/49/204620.htm

BBC (1997) 'Breaking the News', BBC 2, broadcast 6 July

BBC Monitoring (2006) 'Russian media mourn "fearless" reporter', BBC website, 8 October, http://news.bbc.co.uk/1/hi/world/europe/6031741.stm

CJES/IFEX (2007) 'Murdered journalist was about to expose surreptitious weapons supply to Syria and Iran, says CJES', *CJES bulletin*, 11 March. Available on the *CJES* website, http://www.cjes.ru/

CJES website, http://www.cjes.ru/

Dyomkin, D., Kilner, J. and Fletcher, P. (2008) 'Medvedev lauds online media freedom', 15 February, Reuters website, http://uk.reuters.com/

FOM (2006) 'Project "The Internet Russia"', 20 December, *Public Opinion Foundation (FOM)* website, http://english.fom.ru/

Fossato, F. (2007) 'Russia: Media Decree Targets Internet, Digital TV', *RFE/RL* Feature Article, 28 March, *RFE/RL* website, http://www.rferl.org/

Gentleman, A. (2000a) 'The Hard Men Behind Putin', *The Observer*, 26 March, 22

Gentleman, A. (2000b) 'Back to the USSR', *The Guardian*, 29 May, 2

Gessen, M. (2005) 'Fear and Self-Censorship in Putin's Russia', *Nieman Reports*, 59 (2), Summer, 115–17. Available on the Nieman Foundation for Journalism website at Harvard University, http://www.nieman.harvard.edu/

Glasnost Defence Foundation's Digest (2007) no. 312, 9 January, http://www.gdf.ru/digest/digest/digest312e.shtml

Korotich, V. (1997) 'The High Cost of a "Free" Press', *Perspective*, 8 (1), September–October, Institute for the Study of Conflict, *Ideology and Policy* website, http://www.bu.edu/iscip/perspective.html

Krastev, N. (2007) 'CIS: Freedom House Sees Further Democracy Decline', *RFE/RL* Feature Article, 17 January, *RFE/RL* website, http://www.rferl.org/

Osborn, A. (2007) 'The 20 journalists who have lost their lives in Putin's Russia', *The Independent*, 11 March, http://news.independent.co.uk

OSCE (2004) 'Report on Russian media coverage of the Beslan tragedy: Access to information and journalists' working conditions', 16 September, *OSCE* website http://www.osce.org/

Pankin, A. (2006) 'Cowering of your own Free Will', *The Moscow News*, 31 January, 10

Poptsov, O. (1996) 'Capital Television', *Index on Censorship*, (3), 64–6

Reporters Without Borders (2002, 2003, 2004, 2005, 2006 and 2007) 'Worldwide Press Freedom Index', *RWB* website, http://www.rsf.org/

RFE/RL (2008) 'Russia: Journalists Union Meets Amid Media Crisis', *RFE/RL* website, 22 April, http://www.rferl.org/

Russia Union of Journalists, website, http://www.ruj.ru/

Savateyeva, I. (1996) 'The Russian Press: Beyond Economics', *Novaia Gazeta*, 2–8 December, 10–11

Simonov, A. (1996) 'Censorship yesterday, today, tomorrow', *Index on Censorship*, (3), 59–64

Slider, D. (1997) 'Regional and Local Politics', Chapter 13 in S. White, A. Pravda and Z. Gitelman (eds) *Developments in Russian Politics 4*, Basingstoke: Macmillan

The Other Russia (2008) 'Russia Moves to Limit Foreign Investment in Media, Internet', 21 April, *The Other Russia* website, http://www.theotherrussia.org/

Uzzell, L. (2004) 'Internet cafes shut in Ingushetia', *Chechnya Weekly*, 5 (38), 20 October, http://www.jamestown.org/

VTsIOM (2007) 'Freedom of Speech Index', *VTsIOM* website, 7 May, http://wciom.com/archives/

Yasmann, V. (1995) 'The Fate of the Russian Media', *Prism*, 1 (2), 12 May, http://www.jamestownfoundation.org/

Chapter 12

Elections and political parties*

Learning objectives

- To explain the origins and development of the party system.
- To examine the impact of managed democracy on political parties.
- To introduce the parties registered for the 2007 Duma elections.
- To present the results of the Duma and presidential elections.

*Note: All the election data used in this chapter come from the Central Electoral Commission of the Russian Federation website: http://www.cikrf.ru/eng/

Introduction

In 1992 Russia began its democratic transition and soon acquired many of the trappings of a democracy. Citizens possess formal rights such as the right to vote and to compete in elections; political organisations and parties sprang up in the 1990s and Russia became increasingly pluralistic. This was a frustrating time for Yeltsin who, despite his power under the Constitution, faced a Duma that was obstructionist and largely opposed his reforms. There is no real tradition in Russia that opposition is 'a good thing', that it prevents mistakes and corruption, keeps the government on its toes, makes it justify its actions and gives a voice to the people – including those who did vote not for the winning candidate or party. The idea of a loyal opposition that is loyal to the country's democratic system, but opposes a particular leader or government, is alien to Russia. Yeltsin's response to opposition was to ignore the Duma as much as he could, rule by decree and look to the oligarchs for support. In an attempt to create a pro-Yeltsin group within the Duma his supporters organised 'a party of power' and also tried to create an official opposition party. Putin came to office determined to manage democracy so he could push ahead with his reform agenda and so he quickly ensured that his message dominated the mass media (see Chapter 11). Putin also pushed ahead with the plan to turn Russia into a two-party system, with a pro-president party of power and an official, loyal opposition party. He also used the administrative resources at his disposal to manage the whole election process; these included the registration of candidates and parties, controls over campaigning and the conduct of polling. The result was that Putin ensured his own and Medvedev's elections as president, and the domination of the Duma by pro-Kremlin parties.

Democratisation and the development of the party system

The importance of political parties

The existence of a plurality of political parties is a defining feature of representative democracy. Political parties present the electorate with a choice at the ballot box and their differing programmes provide more or less coherent packages of ideas and policies. For the individual voter party names and manifestos simplify the potentially bewildering task of assessing the relative merits of individual candidates. Political parties also serve important functions for government. Political parties, non-government organisations (NGOs), interest groups and associational groups form an intermediate layer between the people and the government. These parties and groups help to aggregate and filter social demands and interests, so that government is not overwhelmed by a multitude of raw, unprocessed demands. The existence of a small number of disciplined political parties in parliament means that it is possible to anticipate the way that parliament will behave. In contrast lax party discipline and/or a great number of political parties, with no one party enjoying an overall majority, can be a recipe for instability, unstable voting coalitions, and political decisions taken through backroom deals rather than through open debate.

The development of Russia's many-party system in the 1990s

The development of Russia's party system has been profoundly affected by the experience of soviet politics. In the early 1990s the Communist Party of the Russian Federation (KPRF) was the only political party that had a programme, organisation, members, activists and printing presses. Although briefly banned after the August 1991 coup, the KPRF was soon back in operation the following year and remains one of the best organised parties in Russia today. Another feature of soviet politics that affected the development of the Russian party system, is that behind the veneer of the soviet one-party state and ideological unanimity, soviet politics was characterised by institutional and functional lobbying, competing networks or clans, and patron–client relationships. These features encouraged loyalty to an individual, rather than to an idea or an institution. This factor combined with the small number of autonomous social organisations and informals in the early 1990s meant that political parties tended to be established by members of the existing economic and political elite to consolidate their position, rather than by grassroots social movements seeking to gain access to the corridors of power. The result is that political parties are organised around an individual or a small group of allies so that the differences between parties often have less to do with ideological and programmatic differences than with personal rivalries. Yabloko is inextricably identified with the economist Grigory Yavlinsky, Our Home is Russia with Viktor Chernomyrdin, Forward Russia with Boris Fyodorov and Russia's Democratic Choice with Yegor Gaidar. The result is that political parties have tended to be unstable, prone to internal rifts and only a handful have survived more than a few years. The two main liberal parties, Yabloko and the Union of Rightist Forces (SPS), did not form an electoral alliance for the 1999 Duma elections even though their programmes were broadly similar. The result was that in the 1990s rather than having the democratically desirable multiparty system, Russia developed a 'many-party system', which led to a fragmented Duma in which the many parties formed temporary, floating alliances on particular issues, which weakened the Duma's ability to counterbalance the powerful presidency. The federal political parties tended not to contest elections at the regional or local levels, leaving these elections to regional parties.

Defining what constitutes a political party, 1995

The definition, organisation and activities of political parties are subject to the pro-visions of the RF Constitution and a series of laws 'On Political Parties' adopted in 1995, 2001 and 2004. Constitutional provisions mean that political parties may not undermine state security, set up their own armed forces, or stir up social, racial or ethnic discord and enmity. Each new law 'On Political Parties' set up progress-ively more restrictive definitions of a political party. The 1995 law enabled as few as 10 people to set up a political party and categorised political parties according to the number of regions in which they were organised. Parties organised in 45 regions were classified as federation-wide, in two or more regions as inter-regional parties and in just one region as regional parties. Political parties were expected to have registered members and, in theory at least, a person could not be a mem-ber of more than one party at the same time. Political movements, social and socio-political associations could also put forward candidates for elections, but they had much more relaxed membership requirements than political parties. Movements and associations did not always have registered members and their members were allowed to be members of a political party or other movements and associations at the same time. They could also have collective members, so a political party could be a collective member of a movement or association. The law made setting up a political party fairly easy and contributed to the large number of political parties that contested elections, particularly at the federal level but also in some of the regions.

Putin and tightening of the definition of a political party, 2001 and 2004

The sheer number of political parties operating at the federal level in the 1990s did not promote democratic consolidation. Parties came and went, they lacked party discipline and many deputies voted in accordance with backroom deals or their own preferences rather than with the programme their party had put forward at the election. The number of political parties also made it difficult for Putin to manage the outcome of elections. The 2001 law 'On Political Parties' set up a more stringent definition of a political party than its predecessor and had the clear aim of reducing the number of political parties. To qualify for registration as a political party an organisation now needed more than 10,000 members, with branches of least 100 members in at least 45 regions and no less than 50 members in the remaining branches. The new law still allowed political associations to contest elections. All existing political parties were now required to re-register in order to demonstrate that they met the new requirements. State funding was also now mandated for parties that had received more than 3 per cent of the vote in the preceding election. At the same time the new law limited contributions to political parties by private individuals to 3,000 roubles (US$ 100) a year. Putin was also concerned about foreign intervention in Russian politics and so the law banned foreigners and international organisations from funding political parties – a particular blow to the liberal, pro-democracy parties which had difficulties raising adequate funding within Russia.

In the wake of Beslan and in accordance with his bid to manage democracy Putin introduced another new law 'On Political Parties and Movements' in 2004. Its aim was to further reduce the number of political parties in a bid to create a party system dominated by just two parties: a centrist party of power and a centre-left party which would be prepared to cooperate with the party of power on important issues. The 2004 law requires political parties to have a membership of at least 50,000 and to have branches with at least 500 members in more than 45 regions and no less than 250 members in the other branches. Parties meeting these criteria did not have to collect the two million signatures or pay the deposit of 37.5 million roubles necessary to appear on the party list. A practical result of the new law is to make it very difficult to set up a new political party unless there is another organisation, structure or network upon which it can be based and to provide financial resources. It is very difficult for a genuine grassroots movement to set up a new political party in so many regions. The 2004 law also regulates other aspects of party organisation and activity. Russia-wide political parties receive election campaign funding from the federal budget, may accept donations, and may engage in economic activities to generate funds. The prohibition against any foreign funding of political parties remained. The impact of these rules was to reduce the number of political parties able to contest the Duma elections in 2007.

Registering political parties and managing democracy

The Federal Registration Service (FRS) of the Justice Ministry is responsible for registering political parties and checking that they fulfil the minimum membership and regional organisation requirements set out in the 2004 law 'On Political Parties and Movements'. The FRS is also responsible for taking cases to the RF Supreme Court to have a political party banned if it does not meet the registration requirements. The registration process is one of the administrative resources that can be used to prevent particular political parties from contesting elections, so clearing the way for the pro-Kremlin parties. The law came into effect on 1 January 2007 and quickly led to the banning of a number of opposition parties. In March 2007 the liberal Republican Party of Russia (RPR) and the leftist Russian Peace Party were banned by the RF Supreme Court and ordered to disband. The RPR was chaired by Vladimir Ryzhkov and Vladimir Lysenko, who are two independent Duma deputies, and Valentina Melnikova who is also chair of the Union of Soldiers' Mothers Committee. Then in April 2007 the Social Democratic Party of Russia (SDPR), which had been set up by Mikhail Gorbachev in 2002, was refused registration and ordered to disband. Vladimir Kishenin (cited in *RIA Novosti*, 2007) the SDPR's leader condemned the decision as 'purely political' and claimed that the party had over 500 members in 47 regions, but the RF Supreme Court upheld the ban in July 2007. It is not just pro-democracy parties that have been refused registration. In April 2008 the RF Supreme Court upheld the April 2007 ban of Eduard Limonov's National Bolshevik Party on the grounds of extremism.

Article 3.9 of the 2004 law 'On Political Parties', prohibits the creation of political parties on the basis of professional, racial, national, or religious affiliation. The FRS refused to register the Russian All-National Union and the Russian Christian-Democratic party (RKhDP) on these grounds. RKhDP challenged this decision arguing that Article 9.3 violates the RF Constitution's principle of the equality of citizens regardless of their race, nationality and religious affiliation, as well as the constitutional right to association. In 2004 the Supreme Court upheld the ban on religious parties and in December 2004 the Constitutional Court found that Article 9.3 does not violate the RF Constitution.

Yeltsin and the 'party of power'

In Russia it is the president not the majority or single largest party in the Duma who chooses the prime minister, subject to confirmation by the Duma. In this way political parties in Russia do not play as important a role in the formation of the government as they do, for example, in Britain. Furthermore, Yeltsin, Putin and Medvedev were all elected president without joining a political party; they did, however, have the support of a party – one which Russians call 'the party of power' or the 'presidential party'. The party of power is not an autonomous organisation but one of a series of parties set up at the Kremlin's behest to help Yeltsin, Putin and Medvedev win presidential elections and then to provide a support base in the Duma for the president and his prime minister. For the Duma elections in 1993 Gaidar's party Russia's Choice was the main party of power, but together with the pro-Yeltsin party of Russian Unity and Accord only gained 89 of the 450 Duma seats. In 1995 the party of power was Prime Minister Chernomyrdin's centrist Our Home is Russia (NDR), which also supported Yeltsin during the 1996 presidential elections. NDR had the financial support of Chernomyrdin's gas industry Gazprom and with government support it was the best-financed political party in the 1995 Duma elections, but still won only 55 seats. In 1999 NDR only won eight seats and did not form its own faction in the Duma and worked with Putin's first party of power, the Unity party.

To complement the party of power 'official' opposition parties were set up, essentially to take votes away from the Communist Party of the Russia Federation (KPRF) and the far-right Liberal Democratic Party of the RF (LDPRF), which in the 1990s posed very real threats to Yeltsin's attempts to dominate the political life of the country. Ivan Rybkin, the Duma speaker and former communist, established the centre-left Ivan Rybkin block which Yeltsin hoped would act as a loyal centre-left opposition, although in 1995 the Ivan Rybkin block failed to unite the moderate centre-left vote and won only three seats. The KPRF emerged as the largest single party in the Duma after the 1995 elections with 157 seats, followed by the LDPRF with 51; so despite his best efforts Yeltsin was confronting a hostile Duma.

Putin and the creation of a party of power

Putin set up his first party of power called the Unity party just three months before the 1999 Duma elections but it went on to win 73 seats, coming second only to the KPRF which won 113 seats. Unity did not have a mass party membership or structures but it did have the support of Yeltsin and Putin, plus money and resources from pro-Kremlin oligarchs. In December 2001 Unity merged with Moscow mayor Yury Luzhkov's Fatherland-All Russia Party (OVR) to form the new party of power called United Russia. United Russia went into the 2003 elections with the 141 Duma seats that Unity and OVR had won in 1999 and emerged from the 2003 elections with 222 seats, not quite a majority in its own right but enough to ensure that Putin was able to dominate the Duma and push through his legislation. United Russia is a collection of powerful, often competing, government officials with presidential control over the party achieved through the president's distribution of state resources. Putin's ally Boris Gryzlov heads United Russia's Supreme Council and the party benefits from Putin's popularity and the support of the pro-Kremlin mass media; it also enjoys a close working relationship with the Presidential Administration.

In order to create a two-party system, a few months before the 2003 Duma elections the Presidential Administration created the Rodina (Motherland) party led by Dmitry Rogozin, to act as the official opposition party. Rodina had a leftist and nationalist orientation, and its purpose was to split the leftist-nationalist vote and to reduce the electoral support for the KPRF. It had some success and in 2003 the KPRF's number of deputies fell from 113 seats to 52 and Rodina came from nowhere to win 37 seats. However, Rogozin was not prepared to play the role of leader of the loyal opposition; he opposed Putin's social welfare reforms (see Chapter 15) and in late 2004, inspired by Ukraine's Orange Revolution, he cut his ties with the Presidential Administration and turned Rodina into a genuine opposition party with a more radical nationalist agenda. In response Rodina was banned from participating in the local elections held in most of the regions in late 2005 and early 2006, charged with promoting anti-Semitism and xenophobia. In October 2006 the Party of Life and the Pensioners' Party together with most *Rodina* members formed a new pro-Kremlin, leftist-nationalist party called the Social Justice Party of Russia. Vladislav Surkov, Putin's deputy chief of staff, played a leading role in the creation of the party and its chair is Sergei Mironov, the speaker of the Federation Council and the former chair of the Russian Party of Life (*Rossiiskaia Partiia Zhizni*). The Social Justice Party's role was again to take votes away from the KPRF and so it campaigns on a similar programme to the KPRF, including strengthening the state in the people's interests, the creation of a fair and united society, and against NATO.

Rogozin tried to form a new, genuine opposition party called Great Russia (VPR) but it was refused registration in 2007. The Social Justice Party and Great Russia had virtually identical charters (RFE/RL, 2007a), but Rogozin was not as amenable to Kremlin direction as Mironov. Banning VPR denied Rogozin a political platform and removed a potential challenge to the Kremlin's preferred centre-left party. The centre-right United Russia and the centre-left Social Justice Party constituted Putin's two-party system for the Duma elections in 2007, and they are headed by Putin's allies, the speakers of the Duma and the Federation Council respectively. These parties represent different factions within the political elite, and while they compete with each other they were loyal to Putin, supported his agenda and want to keep his system intact. For the 2007 Duma elections the genuine, independent opposition to Putin and United Russia was marginalised, short of funds and media exposure, and too fragmented to pose a real threat.

Box 12.1 Central Election Commission (CEC)

Composition and role: the CEC was set up in 1993 and is responsible for the conduct of federal elections and for overseeing regional and local elections. The CEC has 15 members: 5 members are appointed by the RF president, 5 by the Duma and 5 by the Federation Council. CEC members then elect a chair, deputy chair and a secretary. Each commission serves for a four-year term. In March 2007 Putin appointed a close ally, the St Petersbuger Vladimir Churov, as CEC chair.

Chairs of the Central Electoral Commission

Nikolai Ryabov	23 September 1993 to 14 November 1996
Aleksandr Ivanchenko	14 November 1996 to 24 March 1999
Aleksandr Veshnyakov	24 March 1999 to 26 March 2007
Vladimir Churov	26 March 2007–

Source: CEC Commission website: http://www.cikrf.ru/eng/

State Duma election results, 1993–2007

Duma election, 12 December 1993

Under the election law adopted for the 1993 Duma elections, half of the 450 Duma deputies were elected by a party-list system using proportional representation (PR) and the other half were elected as individual representatives for single-member districts (SMD), so each voter had two ballots. For their PR ballot a voter could either vote for a political party, block or movement or opt for the 'against all' option. For their SMD ballot a voter endorsed an individual by name, but any

Table 12.1 Results of the State Duma election, 12 December 1993

	Votes (as a percentage)		Seats		
	List	SMD	List	SMD	Total (as a percentage)
LDRF	21.4	2.7	59	5	14.3
Russia's Choice	14.5	6.3	40	30	15.6
KPRF	11.6	3.2	32	16	10.7
Women of Russia	7.6	0.5	21	2	5.1
Agrarian Party of Russia	7.4	5.0	21	12	7.3
Yabloko	7.3	3.2	20	3	5.1
Russian Unity and Accord	6.3	2.5	18	1	4.2
Democratic Party of Russia	5.1	1.9	14	1	3.3
Movement for Democratic Reforms	3.8	1.9	0	4	0.9
Civic Union	1.8	2.7	0	1	0.2
Future of Russia	1.2	0.7	0	1	0.2
Cedar	0.7	0.5	0	0	0
Dignity and Charity	0.7	0.8	0	2	0.4
Independents	–	45.2	–	146	32.5
Against All	3.9	14.8	–	–	–
Others	0.0	0.7	0	0	0
Invalid ballots	6.8	7.4			
Valid votes	50.6	50.6			
Invalid votes	3.7	4.0			
Total votes (as a percentage of the electorate)	54.3	54.6			
Total	100	100	225	224*	100

*Note: One seat left empty due to the political situation in Chechnia

party affiliation was not given on the ballot paper. The election produced a fragmented Duma, dominated by parties that opposed Yeltsin. Zhirinovsky's LDPRF was the largest single party with 64 deputies, and the KPRF with its close ally the Agrarian Party had a total of 81 deputies. The party of power, Russia's Choice, managed just 70 deputies.

Duma election, 17 December 1995

A new election law was adopted for the 1995 Duma election which was very similar to the 1993 law but had some minor modifications. Under the 1995 law in order for a party to appear on the party list it was now required to register with the Ministry of Justice at least six months before the election and to gather 200,000 supporting signatures rather than the 100,000 signatures required before. Another change was that the invalid votes were now included in the calculation of the 5 per cent threshold for representation, which had the effect of raising the number

Table 12.2 Results of the State Duma election, 17 December 1995

	Votes (as a percentage)		Seats		
	List	SMD	List	SMD	Total (as a percentage)
KPRF	22.3	12.6	99	58	34.9
LDPRF	11.2	5.4	50	1	11.3
Our Home Is Russia	10.1	5.5	45	10	12.2
Yabloko	6.9	3.2	31	14	10.0
Women of Russia	4.6	1.0	0	3	0.7
Communists of the USSR	4.5	1.8	0	1	0.2
Congress of Russian Communities	4.3	2.9	0	5	1.1
Workers' Self-Government	4.0	0.7	0	1	0.2
Russia's Choice	3.9	2.6	0	9	2.0
Agrarian Party of Russia	3.8	5.9	0	20	4.4
Great Power (Derzhava)	2.6	0.6	0	0	0
Forward Russia!	1.9	1.5	0	3	0.7
Union of Labour	1.6	0.9	0	1	0.2
Pamfilova-Gurov-Lysenko Block	1.6	0.7	0	2	0.4
Power to the People!	1.6	1.9	0	9	2.0
Cedar	1.4	0.4	0	0	0
Ivan Rybkin Block	1.1	1.5	0	3	0.7
Stanislav Govorukhin Block	1.0	0.7	0	1	0.2
Russian Unity and Accord	0.4	0.4	0	1	0.2
Independents	–	31.2	–	77	17.1
Against All	2.8	9.6	–	–	–
Others	6.6	6.6	0	6	0
Invalid ballots	1.9	2.3			
Valid votes	64.4	62.9			
Invalid votes	1.3	1.4			
Total votes (as a percentage of the electorate)	65.7	64.3			
Total	100	100	225	225	100

of votes required to reach the threshold. The SMD ballot paper also now included any party endorsement a candidate might enjoy.

Duma election, 19 December 1999

The election law for the 1999 Duma election introduced some further minor amendments to the 1993 and 1995 laws. Under the 1999 law, a party was now required to register with the Ministry of Justice a year before the election in order to appear on the party list. In another innovation, instead of gathering 200,000 signatures a party could opt to pay a deposit of two million roubles, which would be returned if they won at least 3 cent of the party list vote. Candidates for the SMDs also now had the option of paying a deposit of 84,490 roubles, refundable if they won at least 5 per cent of the vote, rather than having to gather signatures. The law also made a rather complicated innovation under which if the parties attaining the 5 per cent threshold all together gained only 50 per cent of the total vote or less, that is not a simple majority, then parties with at least 3 per cent of the vote would also win seats. For the SMDs, if the 'against all' votes were more than votes for each candidate then a second election had to be held within four months. This new requirement led to eight repeat elections in SMDs following the 1999 Duma election.

Table 12.3 Results of the State Duma election, 19 December 1999

	Votes (as a percentage)		Seats		
	List	SMD	List	SMD	Total (as a percentage)
KPRF	24.3	13.4	67	46	25.1
Unity	23.3	2.1	64	9	16.2
Fatherland-All Russia	13.3	8.6	37	31	15.1
Union of Rightist Forces	8.5	3.0	24	5	6.4
LDPRF	6.0	1.5	17	0	3.8
Yabloko	5.9	5.0	16	4	4.4
Communists of the USSR	2.2	0.7	0	0	0
Women of Russia	2.0	0.5	0	0	0
Party of Pensioners	1.9	0.7	0	1	0.2
Our Home is Russia	1.2	2.6	0	7	1.6
Congress of Russian Communities	0.6	0.7	0	1	0.2
Nikolaev-Fedoryov Block	0.6	1.0	0	1	0.2
For Citizens' Dignity	0.6	0.2	0	0	0
Movement in Support of the Army	0.6	0.7	0	2	0.4
Russian People's Union	0.4	1.1	0	2	0.4
Russian Socialist Party	0.2	1.0	0	1	0.2
Spiritual heritage	0.1	0.9	0	1	0.2
Cedar	–	0.2	–	0	0
Independents	–	41.7	–	114	25.3
Against All	3.3	11.6	–	–	–
Others	2.9	0.6	0	0	0
Invalid ballots	1.9	2.2			
Valid votes	60.5	60.3			
Invalid votes	1.2	1.3			
Total votes (as a percentage)	61.7	61.6			
Total	100	100	225	225	100

Duma elections, 7 December 2003

The 2003 Duma elections were conducted following Putin's first restriction on the definition of a political party. SMD candidates now had the option of paying a deposit of 90,000 roubles rather than collecting signatures. United Russia, the party of power won the largest single number of votes, but not an outright majority. Only four parties gained seats from the party lists: United Russia, KPRF, LDPRF and Rodina. The liberal and pro-western parties SPS and Yabloko failed to pass the 5 per cent threshold. Other political parties did gain SMD seats, however, as most of the minor parties and even the independents were either Putin's clients or supporters, after the election Putin was also to control the Duma.

[handwritten margin notes: "Putin's new restriction", "Putin's connections"]

Table 12.4 Results of the State Duma election, 7 December 2003

| | Votes (as a percentage) | | Seats | | |
	List	SMD	List	SMD	Total (as a percentage)
United Russia	37.6	23.2	120	102	49.3
KPRF	12.6	10.8	40	12	11.6
LDPRF	11.5	3.1	36	0	8.0
Motherland (*Rodina*)	9.0	2.9	29	8	8.2
Yabloko	4.3	2.6	0	4	0.9
Union of Rightist Forces	4.0	2.9	0	3	0.7
Agrarian Party of Russia	3.6	1.7	0	2	0.4
RPP-PSS: Pensioners-Fairness	3.1	0.5	0	0	0
PVR-RPZh: Rebirth-Party of Life	1.9	2.6	0	3	0.7
People's Party	1.2	4.4	0	17	3.8
Conceptual Party Unity	1.2	0.0	0	0	0
New Course: Automobile Russia	0.8	0.4	0	1	0
Greens	0.4	0.1	0	0	0
Development of Enterprise	0.4	0.4	0	1	0
Great Russia – Eurasian Union	0.3	0.8	0	1	0
Communist Workers	–	0.1	–	0	0
Independents	–	26.8	0	0	0
Against All	4.7	12.9	–	3	0.7
Others	1.7	2.1	0	0	0
Invalid ballots	1.6	2.1			
Valid votes	54.8	54.3			
Invalid votes	0.9	1.1			
Total votes (as a percentage of the electorate)	55.7	55.4			
Total	100	100	225	225	100

United Russia (*Edinaia* or *Yedinaia Rossia*): Putin's
party of power was founded in April 2001 by the
merger of Fatherland–All Russia Party (OVR) and the
Unity Party (*Edinstvo* or *Yedinstvo*). Party members
include senior government officials and regional
governors. Boris Gryzlov was the party's leader from
November 2000 to April 2008, when he stood
down in favour of Vladimir Putin. United Russia
describes itself as a centrist party; it is also a
nationalist party, which has the Russian bear on
its emblem. Its programme for the 2007 Duma
election was to support the 'Putin Plan', which focused on economic development,
an independent foreign policy, a strong Russian state and the development of
Russia's unique civilisation. United Russia draws its main support from younger
professionals, the educated and aspirational middle classes. Endorsed Medvedev's
candidacy for the 2008 presidential election.

Website address: http://www.er.ru/

Communist Party of Russia (KPRF): the successor
to the CPSU, but it now tends to downplay
Marxism-Leninism in favour of an emphasis on
Russian nationalism and patriotism; in the 1990s
it also had a Eurasianist orientation. Its leader is
Gennady Zyuganov. KPRF is well organised and
claims to have 500,000 members organised in
20,000 local branches. For the 2007 elections its
programme included the nationalisation of strategic
industries and constitutional reform to devolve
power to workers' councils, economic diversification to end Russia's dependence
on oil revenues, comprehensive provision of social welfare and health benefits, and
the end of NATO. Its supporters tend to be industrial workers, pensioners and former collective farm peasants. It has not managed to extend its appeal to younger
voters. In 2002 KPRF split and the Duma speaker
Gennady Selesnyov left and formed the *Rossiia*
movement.

Website address: http://www.kprf.ru/

**Liberal Democratic Party of the Russian Federation
(LDPRF):** was founded in 1990 by Vladimir
Zhirinovsky who is still the party's leader. The party
is very much Zhirinovsky's party and there is a personality cult surrounding him. The party's name is
misleading as it is a far-right party which has been
accused of fascism. It is a nationalist and populist

Box 12.2 (Continued)

party and has an imperialist attitude towards other FSU states. Its programme emphasises nationalism and economic autarky. Its deputies have been involved in fights in the Duma. Its main supporters are marginalised people, especially young, low-income men in the provinces. Its candidate list for the 2007 Duma election included Andrei Lugovoi, the prime suspect in the murder in London of the former KGB officer Aleksandr Litvinenko in 2006. Lugovoi is now a Duma deputy and has immunity from prosecution. The LDPRF is careful not to attack Putin and United Russia.

Website address: http://www.ldpr.ru/

Social Justice Party (*Spravedlivaia Rossiia*): also known as Fair or Just Russia. The words underneath the banner read *Rodina* (motherland), pensioners, life, which are also sometimes added to its name. It was formed in October 2006 by the merger of *Rodina*, the Russian Party of Life and the Russian Pensioners' Party. In April 2007 the People's Party joined the Social Justice Party. Its ideology is a mixture of socialism,  patriotism and populism; for the 2007 Duma election it campaigned against NATO, and for a strong defence and social justice. Its leader is Sergei Mironov, the chair of the Federation Council. In May 2007 the United Socialist Party of Russia, a leftist party, voted to join the Social Justice Party. Endorsed Medvedev's candidacy for the 2008 presidential election.

Website address: http://www.spravedlivo.ru/

Union of Rightist Forces (SPS): was formed by a coalition of smaller parties including Democratic Choice of Russia (DVR), which was led by Yegor Gaidar and Anatoly Chubais. In 1998 DVR formed a coalition with Right Cause and other small parties including Young Russia, Democratic Russia and Common Cause; in 1999 they were also joined by the former prime minister Sergei Kiriyenko's New Force and the Voice of Russia. They adopted the name Union  of Rightist Forces in 1999. The SPS supports the shock therapy reforms of the early 1990s and favours economic liberalism. Under the leadership of the former deputy prime minister Boris Nemtsov the party fiercely opposed Putin's increasing authoritarianism and his bid to manage democracy. Other leading members of SPS are Vladimir V. Kara Murza and Irina Khakamada who was a presidential candidate in 2004. Since 2005 SPS has been led by Nikita Belykh. Although SPS has discussed a merger with the other leading liberal party Yabloko, most recently in 2006, this has not happened. It is a pro-western, centre-right party and its main supporters tend to be metropolitan, young professionals.

Website address: http://www.sps.ru/

Box 12.2 (*Continued*)

Yabloko: is the Russian word for apple and is an acronym of the names of the party's founders Grigory Yavlinsky, Yury Boldyrev and Vladimir Lukin. It was founded in 1993 and is a pro-western, liberal-left party, favouring capitalism with social protection. It is a fierce critic of Putin's authoritarianism. Its main supporters are middle-aged professionals and the urban liberal intelligentsia.

Website address: http://www.yabloko.ru/

Patriots of Russia Political Party: founded in April 2005 by the businessman Gennady Semigin. In 2004 Semigin, a member of the KPRF, had been elected the chair of the People's Patriotic Union of Russia that united the KPRF with other leftist opposition parties. Semigin was expelled from KPRF the same year, accused of trying to make it pro-Putin. In 2006 Patriots of Russia joined the Rodina faction in the Duma, but did not join the new Social Justice Party. Patriots of Russia is a leftist and patriotic party. On 13 September 2007 it formed a coalition with the party of Russian Rebirth.

Website address: http://www.patriot-rus.ru/

The Party of Peace and Unity (or Harmony): a patriotic and leftist party, founded in 1996 and originally registered in 1998. It re-registered in 2006 and has 57,000 members in 65 regions. Its website says that its supporters are war veterans, creative intelligentsia and that the party's base is people under 50-years-old. It stands for a strong Russian state and is a patriotic-leftist party. In September 2000 the party founded the Social Movement 'To support the RF President's policies'. Notionally independent but pro-Putin.

Website address: http://www.patriotparty.ru/

The People's Party of Russia (NPRF): founded by Duma deputies from the People's Deputy Group led by Gennady Raikov. Failed to get any seats in the 2003 elections and some of its members left to join United Russia. A leftist party.

Website address: http://www.narod-party.ru/

The Agrarian Party: was founded in 1993 by Mikhail Lapshin who led the party until 2004. It is a leftist party and has traditionally worked closely with the KPRF. Its current leader is Vladimir Plotnikov. It endorsed Medvedev's candidacy for the 2008 presidential election.

Website address: http://www.apr.org.ru

The Party of Russian Rebirth (or Revival) (PVR): a centrist, social democratic party. Its leader is Gennady Selesnyov the former Duma speaker who left the KPRF in 2002. On 13 September it formed a coalition with the Patriots of Russia political party.

Website address: http://www.seleznev-inform.ru/

Box 12.2 (*Continued*)

The Ecological Party – 'The Greens': based on the ecological movement *Kedr* (Cedar) which was founded in 1992. The Green party has branches in 58 regions and has more than 12,000 members. The Greens were not allowed to contest the 2007 Duma elections because the Central Electoral Commission claimed that 17 per cent of the signatures on its supporters' list were forgeries.

Website address: http://www.greenparty.ru/main_en.php

The Democratic Party of Russia (DPR): the original DPR was founded in 1990 by Nikolai Travkin but it was moribund by 1996. When Mikhail Kasyanov was sacked as prime minister in 2004 he sought to revive DPR and to make it his own political machine. However, in December 2005 an outside donor offered the party US$10,000 if it elected Andrei Bogdanov rather than Kasyanov as its leader,

which it did. In May 2007 Bogdanov announced that the party was back and that its goal was to steer Russia towards EU membership and ultimately accession to NATO. It does not really have its own political agenda and is a Kremlin creation designed to take votes from Yabloko and the SPS.

Website address: http://www.democrats.ru/

Civil Force (*Grazhdanskaia Sila*): (also translated as Citizens' Force or Power) from 2003–4 it was called the Net Party, then became the Free Russia Party, becoming Civil Force in February 2007. It is a liberal party supporting citizens' rights and the state as the defender of the individual. It also supports private property and business. The party enjoyed close links with the Putin administration and endorsed Medvedev's candidacy for the 2008 presidential election.

Website address: http://www.gr-sila.ru

The People's Union: was formerly called the Party of National Revival – The People's Will (*Narodnaia Volia*), which had been founded in 2001 by Sergei Baburin, a leading nationalist. People's Will was formed by the merger of four nationalist parties and in 2003 joined Rodina. In 2006 the People's Will did not join the Social Justice Party along with most of Rodina. In March 2007 the People's Will and 13 other nationalist, conservative and Russian Orthodox Christian groups formed the People's Union (*Narodnyi Soiuz*). Leading members of the People's Union include Aleksandr Rutskoi, Yeltsin's former vice president and Viktor Alksnis.

Website address: http://www.partia-nv.ru/

DUMA

Putin manager democracy

Duma election, 2 December 2007

The Duma elections in 2007 were an important step in the further development of Putin's managed democracy and helped to set the stage for the election of Putin's chosen heir Dmitry Medvedev as president in 2008. The course of the elections and their outcome must be placed within the general context of Russia's Constitution and its limited checks and balances, the super-presidential system and the further strengthening of the executive under Putin, the weakness of Russia's civil society and the Kremlin's domination of the mass media. Campaigning officially began on 3 November 2007 and one of United Russia's posters encapsulated its electoral platform, it read 'Putin's Plan Is Russia's Future'. During the Duma election in 2007 and the presidential election in 2008, democracy was managed to ensure the continuity both of the rule of the networks that had brought Putin to power and of Putin's agenda.

Thirty-five parties originally applied to contest the election but only 11 made it through the registration process and eventually stood for election. In advance of the elections 15 political parties fulfilled Putin's more restrictive definition of a political party and were registered by the RFC. Then the Patriots of Russia and the Party of Russia's Rebirth formed a coalition; the CEC did not allow the Greens to stand alleging that a large number of their supporting signatures were forgeries and the nationalist People's Union decided to endorse the KPRF. In a major departure from the election procedures followed since 1993, the single member districts (SMDs) were scrapped and all 450 deputies were elected from party lists, with seats allocated by proportional representation among the parties receiving at least 7 per cent of the vote, not 5 per cent as before. The 7 per cent threshold helped to reduce the number of parties qualifying for representation in the Duma. Only four political parties surmounted the 7 per cent threshold and now have deputies; these are United Russia, the Social Justice Party, the LDPR and the KPRF. Of these four parties only the KPRF is a genuine opposition party, the Social Justice Party and the LDRF both vote with United Russia. There are no longer any independent deputies or representatives from the small Red-Brown parties. The 2007 elections also witnessed the final disappearance of the liberal parties, Yabloko and the Union of Rightist Forces (SPS) from the Duma; even if they had formed an electoral alliance, they still would not have gained enough votes to surmount the 7 per cent threshold. The ending of SMDs also cut the connection between Duma deputies and the regions. Under the SMD system regional governors were often able to ensure the election of a candidate who was both loyal to them and who would represent regional interests in the Duma; in the absence of the SMDs, the party list system means that a small number of Moscow-based political parties are now responsible for candidate selection.

no more SMDs — now from party list

loyal to united Russia/Putin

Campaigning in 2007: the issues

In the run up to the 2007 election the Kremlin orchestrated a massive propaganda campaign, depicting the election as a vote of confidence in Putin's record. Putin agreed to head United Russia's list of candidates, although he still did not join the party. Rallies were held across the country portraying Putin as a great leader and the pro-Kremlin youth group *Nashi* organised vociferous street demonstrations. *Nashi* distributed leaflets with a caricature of the American Uncle Sam character sitting on money bags bearing the names of opposition leaders. The leaflet declared, 'The USA had another plan. They wanted traitors and thieves to win – the American citizen [Garry] Kasparov, the fascist [Eduard] Limonov, and the traitor [Boris] Nemtsov' (RFE/RL, 2007c). Domestic opposition forces were depicted as being in the pay of the West, which was trying to foment another Orange Revolution as it had in Ukraine during the winter of 2004–5. An anti-Putin coalition called the Other Russia was barred from putting candidates forward by the CEC and in November 2007 its rallies in Moscow and St Petersburg were broken up, the marchers were beaten and its leaders, including Garry Kasparov and Boris Nemtsov, were detained by the militia (RFE/RL, 2007b). Opposition parties were also denied the coverage they should have been allocated in the fully or partly state-owned print and broadcast media.

The conduct of the 2007 Duma elections was widely criticised by Russian and foreign observers. The Organization for Security and Co-operation in Europe Parliamentary Assembly (OSCE PA) declared that the Duma elections 'were not fair' (OSCE PA, 2007a) and that they were 'not held on a level playing field' (OSCE PA, 2007b). The OSCE PA had four particular concerns, which included the merging of the state and the Kremlin's United Russia party; the media's 'strong bias in favour of President Putin and the ruling United Russia Party'; the new election code that made 'it extremely difficult for new and smaller parties to develop and compete effectively' and, finally, the 'harassment of opposition parties' (OSCE PA, 2007a). Garry Kasparov condemned the elections as 'the most unfair and dirtiest in the whole history of modern Russia' (BBC News, 2007). There were incidences

Table 12.5 Results of the State Duma election, 2 December 2007

Party	Votes (as a percentage)	Number of deputies
United Russia	64.1	315
Communist Party of the Russian Federation	11.6	57
Liberal Democratic Party of the Russian Federation	8.2	40
Social Justice Party	7.8	38
Agrarian Party of Russia	2.3	0
Yabloko	1.6	0
Civil Force	1.1	0
Union of Rightist Forces	1.0	0
Patriots of Russia – Party of Russian Revival Coalition	0.9	0
Social Justice	0.2	0
Democratic Party of Russia	0.1	0
Invalid ballot papers	**1.09**	
Valid ballot papers	**98.91**	
Total votes	**68,537,065**	
Total votes (as a percentage of the electorate)	**63.71**	
Total eligible voters	**109,145,517**	

dirty practices

of students and state employers being pressurised to vote for United Russia and even of voters in St Petersburg being entered into a lottery (ibid.). In Chechnia, which is run by Putin's ally and fellow United Russia member President Ramzan Kadyrov, 99 per cent voted for United Russia on a reported 99 per cent turnout. When asked about these unlikely figures by a journalist from the French newspaper *Le Figaro*, Putin described them as 'perfectly objective' (Hardy, 2008). A survey of Russian voters conducted by the Levada Analytical Center on behalf of Radio Free Europe–Radio Liberty before the elections had found that nearly two-thirds of Russian voters did not believe that the elections would be conducted honestly and fewer than one in five believed the results would reflect the true will of the electorate (Whitmore, 2007).

Presidential elections

Presidential elections

In addition to the Constitution the legal basis for presidential elections is provided by the Law on Presidential Elections (1995) and the Law on Presidential Elections (1999), which was the last law Yeltsin signed as president on 31 December 1999. The current legislation set out that a presidential candidate may be nominated by voters or political parties and electoral blocks. Parties or electoral blocks that attract more than 7 per cent of the total vote in the Duma elections immediately preceding a presidential election have the right to put forward a candidate. Other registered political parties may nominate a candidate by collecting two million signatures, no more than 7 per cent of which may be from any one region. Independent candidates must register a Supporters' Group with the Central Electoral Commission and then gather two million signatures. The Central Electoral Commission is responsible for verifying that these requirements have been fulfilled and that these procedures have been followed correctly.

For a presidential election to be valid, a minimum of 50 per cent of the registered electorate is required to vote. To win a candidate needs an absolute majority of the vote and if no candidate secures a majority, then the election proceeds to a second round vote three weeks later. Only the two front-running candidates from the first round stand in the second round and the candidates securing the most votes wins the second round. The 1996 presidential election went to two rounds, but since then Putin won the 2000 and 2004 elections on the first round as did Medvedev in 2008. Until 2004 Russian voters had the 'vote against all the candidates' option on the ballot paper, but this was no longer available for the 2008 presidential election.

Two k of abstention optional on ballot

The presidential election, 1996

The omens for Yeltsin's election as RF president did not look promising. In January 1996 his popular approval ratings stood at only 8 per cent (Willerton, 1997: 55) and he needed the magical figure of '50 per cent plus 1' in order to win. In his

Table 12.6 Results of the presidential election, 1996

Candidates	Party	First round, 16 June		Second round, 3 July	
		Vote	Total (as a percentage)	Vote	Total (as a percentage)
Boris Yeltsin	None	26,665,495	35.8	40,203,948	54.4
Gennady Zyuganov	KPRF	24,211,686	32.5	30,102,288	40.7
Alexander Lebed		10,974,736	14.7		
Gregory Yavlinsky	Yabloko	5,550,752	7.4		
Vladimir Zhirinovsky	LDPRF	4,311,479	5.8		
Six others: Svyatoslav Fedorov, Mikhail Gorbachev, Martin Shakkum, Yury Vlasov, Vladimir Bryntsalov Aman-geldy Tuleyev		1,636,950	2.2		
Against all		1,163,921	1.6	3,604,462	4.9
Invalid votes		1,072,120	1.4	780,592	1.1
Total votes		75,587,139	69.7	74,691,290	68.8

Total number of registered voters 108,495,023 for the first round and 108,600,730 for second round

May 1996 manifesto Yeltsin acknowledged that he had made mistakes but claimed that he had pulled Russia back from the brink of catastrophe, preserved Russia's territorial integrity, oversaw its reintegration into the international community and created a multi-party democracy. Yeltsin promised to complete his economic reforms, specifically to rewrite the tax code, stimulate small businesses, regulate monopolies and to introduce new laws on land ownership. He also promised to reform the armed forces and to strengthen social welfare. That Yeltsin secured 35 per cent of the vote in the first round had more to do with his presidential powers and the support of the oligarchs than his track record in office or his manifesto. Before the election Yeltsin issued presidential decrees on key economic and social issues; Anatoly Chubais organised and Boris Berezovsky and his fellow oligarchs financed Yeltsin's campaign. The oligarchs made sure that Yeltsin's chief rival, the uncharismatic Gennady Zyuganov, received little coverage in their media outlets. The third-placed Aleksandr Lebed was persuaded to endorse Yeltsin to his erstwhile supporters and in return he was appointed to the Security Council in June 1996, a position he held only until October 1996.

The presidential election, 16 March 2000

Putin won the 26 March presidential elections without issuing a manifesto or campaigning. During the run up to the election Putin presented himself as an acting president who was too busy being an effective leader to take time off to campaign. Although supported by the Unity Party he was not a member of any political party and so voters were asked to vote for Putin the man. This personalisation of

Table 12.7 Results of the presidential election, 2000

Candidates	Party	Votes	Total vote (as a percentage)
Vladimir Putin	None	39,740,434	52.94
Gennady Zyuganov	KPRF	21,928,471	29.21
Grigory Yavlinsky	Yabloko	4,351,452	5.8
Aman-geldy Tuleev		2,217,361	2.95
Vladimir Zhirinovsky	LDPRF	2,026,513	2.7
Konstantin Titov	Independent candidate, SPS member	1,107,269	1.47
Ella Pamfilova	For Citizens' Worth	758,966	1.01
Stanislav Govorukhin		328,723	0.44
Yury Skuratov		319,263	0.43
Alexei Podbereskin	Spiritual Heritage	98,175	0.13
Umar Dzhabrailov		78,498	0.10
Against all		1,414,648	1.88
Total valid votes		74,369,773	68.0
Invalid votes		701,003	0.6
Total vote		75,070,776	68.6

Total number of registered voters 109,378,922

politics enabled Putin to appeal to voters across a wide range of party allegiances and ideological orientations, from pro-market liberals through to communists and nationalists. Even members of the KPRF leadership endorsed Putin, despite the fact that their own party leader Gennady Zyuganov was also a candidate. Putin managed to be all things to all people and so his support cut across ages and classes. Although the oligarchs were less enthusiastic about Putin than they had been about Yeltsin, with the exception of Vladimir Gusinsky, they nonetheless put their media empires at his disposal. Putin was shown on TV every night working on behalf of Russia. There were instances of *kompromat* or black propaganda against Grigory Yavlinsky, the Yabloko candidate, who might have taken enough votes to stop Putin winning outright on the first round. Playing on homophobia it was falsely reported that Yavlinsky was being backed by a gay group called Blue Heart. There was also a television report playing on anti-Semitic sentiments claiming that Yavlinsky was being backed by Gusinsky who has dual Russian-Israeli citizenship. As the election approached there was a very real sense that its result was a foregone conclusion and that the only real issue was whether Putin would gain the necessary majority to win on the first round, which he did.

The presidential election, 14 March 2004

The late Russian journalist Anna Politkovskaya (2004: 170–1) was a fierce critic of Putin and wrote about the 2004 presidential elections that, 'Voting day itself was a contemporary remake of the authoritarian, bureaucratic, Soviet-style pantomime of "the people expressing its will" '. There was a sense throughout the election campaign that the opposition had given up before the election. Gennady Zyuganov declined to stand for a third time, so the KPRF backed Nikolai Kharitonov, a member of the Agrarian Party of Russia. Vladimir Zhirinovsky also decided that there was no point in standing and so the head of his bodyguards Oleg Malyshkin stood instead. Sergei Mironov, the speaker of the Federation Council was also a candidate, but backed Putin. Irina Khakamada, a Duma deputy and a member of the SPS, was the only liberal candidate but she stood as an independent. The final challenger was Sergei Glazyev, a former minister of foreign trade under Yeltsin and a communist Duma deputy, who was a member of Rodina. Glazyev's programme attacked Yeltsin's and Putin's economic reforms and argued in favour of social justice and greater welfare spending, which would seem like sure-fired vote winners, but he only garnered 4 per cent of the vote. Ivan Rybkin had declared his intention to stand, but disappeared in mysterious circumstances and when he reappeared claimed to have been drugged and kidnapped. Supported by Boris Berezovsky, the anti-Putin oligarch, Rybkin tried to continue his campaign from London but withdrew his candidacy on 5 March 2004.

International observers, such as the Organisation for Security and Co-operation in Europe (OSCE, 2004) expressed grave concerns about the conduct of the election. Once again Putin did not issue an election manifesto and refused to debate with the other candidates. The OSCE found that the state-controlled media 'displayed clear bias in favour of the incumbent' (ibid.: 1). The OSCE found that the CEC gave strong professional leadership but that at the lower level the picture was more mixed, including local election officials encouraging group voting and open rather than secret voting, isolated cases of unauthorised people running the polling stations, and voter intimidation (ibid.: 2). The OSCE also found that the turnout figures and Putin's margin of victory 'were implausible and suggestive of fraud or manipulation' (ibid.: 26).

Table 12.8 Results of the presidential election, 2004

Candidate	Party	Votes	Total vote (as a percentage)
Vladimir Putin	None	49,565,238	71.3
Nikolai Kharitonov	KPRF	9,513,313	13.7
Sergei Glazyev	Independent, member of Rodina	2,850,063	4.1
Irina Khakamada	Independent, member of SPS	2,671,313	3.8
Oleg Malyshkin	LDPRF	1,405,315	2.0
Sergei Mironov	Russian Party of Life	524,324	0.7
Against all		2,396,219	3.4
Invalid votes		578,824	0.5
Valid votes		68,925,785	63.8
Total		66,504,609	64.3

Total number of registered voters: 108,064,281

The presidential election, 2 March 2008

On 14 December 2007 the CEC announced that the next presidential election would take place on Sunday 9 March 2008; the election date was quickly changed to 2 March, however, as 9 March was the day after the International Women's Day holiday. The new electoral law adopted in 2004 abolished the option of voting 'against all' from the ballot paper, which removed a way of registering a form of protest by those who believe that they are not being offered a genuine choice. Medvedev refused to participate in televised debates with the other candidates and did not issue an election manifesto. His campaign, such as it was, was to be shown on television working for the country together with his mentor, Vladimir Putin. The Kremlin's control of the mass media ensured that the other candidates received scant attention. Yet again there is also evidence that administrative resources were used to secure the desired outcome. The Other Russia opposition movement claims that there was coercion of 'students, hospital patients and soldiers'; 'Military cadets in one St Petersburg academy were instructed who to vote for up to a month in advance,' and that 'during the vote, the cadets were forced to take their ballots and complete them in front of a commanding officer' (The Other Russia, 2008). The OSCE decided not to monitor the vote claiming that the election lacked choice. There have also been claims of electoral fraud, including ballot box stuffing and the falsification of electoral returns. In April 2008 Sergei Shpilkin, an election analyst at the Institute of Applied Economics, published his analysis of the CEC's election data claiming that he had found evidence of mass electoral fraud. According to Shpilkin a disproportionate number of polling stations returned figures ending in a zero or a five, for both the voter turnout and Medvedev's percentage share of the vote (Harding, 2008). This suggests that local election officials had been told what percentages they were expected to return. There

[handwritten margin notes: "Voter abuse", "voter fraud"]

Gennady Zyuganov, the leader of the Communist Party of the Russian Federation.

Vladimir Zhirinovsky, the leader of the Liberal Democratic Party of the Russian Federation, introduces Andrei Lugovoi, a LDPRF candidate for the December 2007 Duma elections.

were instances where this ballot-rigging backfired and the wrong ballot box was stuffed. For example, in the Dagestani town of Kizilyurt although 766 people voted not one voted for Medvedev. Instead 95 per cent of Kizilyurt's electorate voted for Andrei Bogdanov, the pro-Kremlin 'independent' candidate who only polled 1.3 per cent nationally. Shpilkin also claims that the actual voter turnout was 56 per cent not the record 69.7 per cent turnout claimed by the Central Electoral Commission, meaning that Medvedev had the support of just one-third of Russia's 100 million plus electorate (Halpin, 2008).

Box 12.3 The candidates for the presidential elections, 2008

Four candidates made it onto the ballot paper:

- **Andrei Bogdanov:** born in Moscow in 1970, he is the leader of the Democratic Party of Russia and a liberal conservative. A criminal investigation was started amid allegations that there were forgeries among the signatures used to support his candidature. He is rumoured to be a senior member of the United Russia Party and that his candidature had been backed by the Kremlin to split the opposition vote. He said that if elected he would take Russia into the European Union. Bogdanov has his own blog: http://bonych.livejournal.com/

- **Dmitry Medvedev:** a 42-year-old former business lawyer, a member of Putin's St Petersburg clan and Putin's chosen successor. He moved to Moscow and ran Putin's election campaigns in 2000 and 2004. His candidacy was nominated by United Russia, the Social Justice party, the Agrarian Party and Civil Force (see also Box 16.8).

- **Vladimir Zhirinovsky:** aged 61 the founder and leader of the ultra-right wing Liberal Democratic Party of the Russian Federation and a deputy Duma speaker. He was a candidate in the 1991, 1996 and 2000 presidential elections, but he did not stand in 2004 as it was clear Putin would win. He has evolved into a Kremlin loyalist, he does not criticise Putin or Medvedev.

- **Gennady Zyuganov:** the 63-year old leader of the KPRF. He was a candidate in the 1996 and 2000 presidential elections but, in face of Putin's electoral steamroller, did not bother to stand in 2004. The only real opposition candidate to Medvedev on the 2008 ballot.

The would-be candidates who did not make it onto the ballot paper:

- **Vladimir Bukovsky:** a soviet-era dissident and political prisoner, who has lived in the UK since 1976. As he has not lived in Russia for the last 10 years he did not meet the residency requirements to be registered as a candidate.

- **Aleksandr Donskoi:** a businessman who has been the mayor of Arkhangelsk since 2005. In July 2007 he was arrested and dragged out of his home in his underwear while being filmed by the local media; he has been charged with corruption. Donskoi counters that since announcing he wanted to stand in October 2006 he has been the victim of a smear campaign. He is also in dispute with the Kremlin-appointed regional governor Nikolai Kiselyov.

Box 12.3 (*Continued*)

- **Garry Kasparov:** a former world chess champion, aged 44. He gave up his bid to stand citing Kremlin orchestrated pressures that prevented him from submitting his completed registration paperwork by the 17 December deadline. A leading member of the Other Russia opposition movement.

- **Viktor Gerashchenko:** the former head of the RF Central Bank and a Duma deputy for the nationalist *Rodina* party. He has now joined the Other Russia movement.

- **Sergei Gulyayev:** a former member of St Petersburg city Legislative Assembly for the Yabloko party. He was arrested during the 3 March 2007 Dissenters March in St Petersburg and was subsequently beaten by the police and hospitalised.

- **Mikhail Kasyanov:** a former prime minister, who has accused Putin of abandoning democratic values and setting Russia on a course to totalitarianism. He set up the People's Democratic Union Party, after he failed to win the leadership of the Democratic Party. He left the Other Russia movement in July 2007 because it failed to agree on a single candidate for the presidential election in 2008. Kasyanov was banned in January 2008 from standing in the 2008 presidential election by the Central Electoral Commission, which accused him and his team of forging 13 per cent of the signatures used to support his candidacy. Kasyanov claimed that his election team had been subject to intimidation and that Putin ordered that he should not be allowed to stand and wanted to silence him (see also Box 5.11).

- **Gennady Selesnyov:** the former chair (speaker) of the Duma. He was expelled from the KPRF in 2002 for arguing that it needed to adapt to change and become a social democratic party. A centre-left candidate.

- **Oleg Shenin:** a leader of the newly reconstituted Communist Party of the Soviet Union. During the soviet period Shenin was a member of the CPSU's Central Committee and its Politburo from 1990–91. He spent time in prison for taking part in the August 1991 coup against Gorbachev. A hardline communist candidate.

- **Grigory Yavlinsky:** an economist and the leader of the Yabloko party. He was also a candidate in the 1996 and 2000 presidential elections. He favours capitalism but with a social conscience and justice.

Table 12.9 Results of the presidential election, 2008

Candidate	Nominating parties	Votes	Total vote (as a percentage)
Dmitry Medvedev	United Russia	52,530,712	70.28
Gennady Zyuganov	KPRF	13,243,550	17.72
Vladimir Zhirinovsky	LDPRF	6,988,510	9.35
Andrei Bogdanov	Democratic Party of Russia	968,344	1.3
Invalid votes		1,015,533	1.35
Total votes cast		73,731,116	100

Total registered voters: 107,222,016

Turnout: 69.71 per cent

Chapter summary

In Russia elections are held, there are still a large number of political parties, but it is increasingly hard to see these as part of a truly democratic system. Elections are managed to produce the result the Kremlin wants: the state-run media deny the opposition exposure and act as a propaganda machine for the Kremlin, there is the use of *kompromat* (compromising materials) against opposition candidates, and instances of electoral irregularities and outright fraud are seen. The party system is a real weakness in Russia's democratisation, as parties remain poorly developed and leader-centric affairs. The registration process has been used to prevent opposition parties from contesting elections. The post-2007 election Duma has deputies from four parties but only one of these parties, the KPRF, is a true opposition party. Elections are nonetheless important to the Kremlin, the results were and are used to demonstrate popular support and approval of Putin's and Medvedev's presidencies; they are also a rebuttal of foreign and domestic critics who claim that Russia is turning into a dictatorship. United Russia's domination of the Duma means that President Medvedev and Prime Minister Putin are able to claim a popular mandate to maintain their system of rule and to push forward with their agenda.

Discussion points

- Is there an ideal number of political parties in a democracy?
- What has been the impact of the changing party composition of the Duma?
- How did Putin apply his concept of managed democracy to political parties and elections?
- Why have the liberal parties disappeared from the Duma?

Further reading

On elections and voting behaviour go to Timothy Colton (2000) *Transitional Citizens: Voters and What Influences them in the New Russia*, Cambridge, MA: Harvard University Press; Mikhail Myagkov, Peter C. Ordeshook and Dimitry Shakin (2005) 'Fraud or Fairytales: Russia and Ukraine's Electoral Experience', *Post-Soviet Affairs*, 21 (2), 91–131; Robert Moser (2001) *Unexpected Outcomes: Electoral Systems, Political Parties and Representation in Russia*, Pittsburgh: Pittsburgh University Press; Stephen White, Richard Rose and Ian McAllister (1997) *How Russia Votes*, Chatham, NJ: Chatham House Publishers; Richard Rose and Neil Munro (2002) *Elections Without Order*, Cambridge: Cambridge University Press; Vicki Hesli and William Reisinger (eds) (2003) *The 1999–2000 Elections in Russia*, Cambridge: Cambridge University Press.

For the impact of the party system on policy making go to Paul Chaisty (2005) 'Party Cohesion and Policy-Making in Russia', *Party Politics*, 11 (3), 299–318. There is a wide range of literature on political parties, examining their role in democratisation, why and how they are formed: M. Steven Fish (1995) 'The Advent of Multipartism in Russia, 1993–1995', *Post-Soviet Affairs*, 11 (4), October–December, 340–85; Paul G. Lewis (ed.) (2001) *Party Development and Democratic Change in Post-Communist Europe*, London: Frank Cass, 2001; Henry E. Hale (2006) *Why Not Parties in Russia? Democracy, Federalism and the State*, Cambridge: Cambridge University Press; Kenneth Wilson (2006) 'Party-System Development Under Putin', *Post-Soviet Affairs*, 22 (4), 314–48; Kathryn Stoner-Weiss (2001) 'The Limited Reach of Russia's Party System: Under-Institutionalization in Dual Transitions', *Politics & Society*, 29 (3), September, 385–414; Grigorii V. Golosov (2004) *Political Parties in the Regions of Russia: Democracy Unclaimed*, Boulder, CO: Lynne Rienner, and his (2003) 'Electoral Systems and Party Formation in Russia: A Cross-Regional Analysis', *Comparative Political Studies*, 36 (8), 912–35; and Michael McFaul (2001) 'Explaining Party Formation and Nonformation in Russia: Actors, Institutions, and Chance', *Comparative Political Studies*, 34 (10), 1159–87. On the party of power see B. Williams (2006) 'Parties of power and Russian Politics – A victory of the state over civil society?', *Problems of Post-Communism*, 53 (1), 3–14; and Regina Smyth (2002) 'Building State Capacity from the Inside Out: Parties of Power and the Success of the President's Reform Agenda in Russia', *Politics and Society*, 30 (4), 555–78.

Useful websites

Russian Central Electoral Commission: http://www.cikrf.ru/cikrf/eng/

Russia Votes: the centre for the Study of Public Policy, Aberdeen University and the Levada Center, Moscow, http://www.russiavotes.org/

Carnegie Endowment for International Peace: http://www.carnegieendowment.org/

Democracy Rus: provides Russian election laws in English, http://www.democracy.ru/english/library/laws

Organisation for Security and Co-operation in Europe (OSCE): http://www.osce.org/

Russian Election Watch, Davis Center, Harvard University: http://daviscenter.fas.harvard.edu/publications.rew.html

Public Opinion Foundation FOM, Moscow: http://www.fom.ru/ratings

RuElection.com: http://www.ruelections.com/

Russian Registration Service, Ministry of Justice: http://www.rosregistr.ru/ (Russian only)

References

BBC News (2007) 'Monitors denounce Russia elections', *BBC News* website, 3 December, http://news.bbc.co.uk

Halpin, T. (2008) 'Dmitri Medvedev votes were rigged, says computer boffin', *The Times*, 18 April

Harding, L. (2008) 'From Russia with fraud', *The Guardian*, 20 April

OSCE (2004) 'Russian Federation, Presidential Election 14 March 2004', *OSCE/ODIHR Election Observation Mission Report*, 2 June, Warsaw: OSCE, http://www.osce.org/

OSCE PA (2007a) 'Russian Duma Elections "not fair" say parliamentary observers', 2 December, *OSCE Parliamentary* website, http://www.oscepa.org/

OSCE PA (2007b) 'Russian Duma elections "not held on a level playing field", say parliamentary observers', 2 December, *OSCE Parliamentary* website, http://www.oscepa.org/

Politkovskaya, A. (2004) *Putin's Russia*, London: The Harvill Press

RFE/RL (2007a) 'Authorities deny outspoken politician a comeback', *RFE/RL Newsline*, 27 July, 11 (137), *RFE/RL* website, http://www.rferl.org/

RFE/RL (2007b) 'Russian Police Crush another opposition Protest', 25 November *RFE/RL* website, http://www.rferl.org/

RFE/RL (2007c) 'Pro-Putin Youth Group Looks to Preempt Postelection Rallies', *RFE/RL* website, 30 November, http://www.rferl.org/

RIA Novosti (2007) 'Russian Supreme Court ban on Social Democratic Party', *RIA Novosti* website, 13 July, http://en.rian.ru/

The Other Russia (2008) 'Russian Vote Inundated with Violations and Fraud – Observers', *The Other Russia* website, 3 March

Whitmore, B. (2007) 'RFE/RL: Russians Skeptical About Elections, Hopeful For Future', *RFE/RL* website feature article, http://www.rferl.org/

Willerton Jr., J. P. (1997) 'Presidential Power', Chapter 3 in Stephen White, Alex Pravda and Zvi Gitelman (eds) *Developments in Russian Politics 4*, Basingstoke: Macmillan

Part 4

THE POLICY PROCESS AND
REFORMING RUSSIA

Chapter 13

Foreign and defence policy

Learning objectives

- To place Russian foreign and defence policies within the context of the post-cold war world.
- To describe and analyse the role of the institutions and bodies involved in policy making.
- To explain the influences upon foreign and defence policy making.
- To introduce the key foreign and defence policy documents.

Introduction

Before the 1917 Bolshevik Revolution Russia gave its name to the Imperial Russian Empire and then it was at the heart of the USSR, one of the world's two superpowers. Russia is no longer a superpower and since 1991 it has had to come to terms with this diminished status and the increasingly unilateral approach to world affairs adopted by the USA, the remaining superpower. Although in the 1990s Russia had extensive nuclear and conventional forces, budget constraints prevented their modernisation (see Chapter 9). Economic problems also meant that Russia could not sustain the external aid programmes through which the USSR had projected its influence around the globe. While dealing with the practicalities of its diminished status and capabilities, Russia also had to rethink and define its national identity (see Chapter 4) and interests. As the world's largest country, stretching across the Eurasian land mass to the Pacific Ocean and bordering 14 very diverse countries in Europe, Scandinavia, Asia, Central Asia and the Caucasus, Russia also has had to contend with instability and disputes on and around its borders. Under President Yeltsin institutional rivalries and disagreements about the basic trajectory of Russia's reforms further complicated foreign policy making. President Putin came to office with a clear agenda of restoring the status and strength that Russia had lost at the time of the USSR's collapse. Putin was an active and dignified participant in international summits and a forceful champion of Russian interests and great power status; he also stressed the supremacy of the presidency in decision making and strengthened the state. Russia's great energy reserves combined with the increase in world energy prices are currently financing an extensive programme of nuclear and conventional forces modernisation; threats to cut energy supplies have also been used as an instrument of Russian foreign policy. Overall, under Putin Russia reasserted its status as a global power in its own right, not as a junior partner to the West.

Box 13.1 Russia's neighbours and borders

Neighbouring country	Length of border with Russia (in km)
Azerbaijan	284
Belarus	959
China (South Eastern)	3,605
China (South)	40
Democratic People's Republic of Korea	19
Estonia	290
Finland	1,313
Georgia	723
Kazakhstan	6,846
Latvia	217
Lithuania (with Kaliningrad *oblast*)	227
Mongolia	3,441
Norway	167
Poland (with Kaliningrad *oblast*)	206
Ukraine	1,576
Total length of external land borders	19,913
Total length of coastline (with the Arctic, Atlantic and Pacific oceans)	37,653

Source: CIA (1999) *The World Factbook 1999 – Russia* (adapted), https://www.cia.gov/library/publications/the-world-factbook/

Note: Kaliningrad *oblast* on the Baltic is separated from the rest of Russia by Belarus, Lithuania and Latvia.

Foreign policy making

From 1992–1993: the struggle between the President and Parliament

The formulation and implementation of Russian foreign policy was complicated by the political conflicts between the parliament and president which culminated in the October 1993 crisis, and also by the institutional conflicts and rivalries that Yeltsin encouraged as part of his system and style of presidential rule. Russia inherited from the USSR a constitution which gave the Supreme Soviet the right to frame the general direction of its foreign policy; the Supreme Soviet also had the right to approve the appointment of foreign and defence ministers, sanction the commitment of armed forces abroad and ratify international treaties. Through three specialised foreign affairs committees, the Supreme Soviet scrutinised the government's performance in foreign affairs. From the Russian Federation's inception in January 1992 to the adoption of the new Constitution in December 1993, the Supreme Soviet was in conflict with the president and the foreign ministry over the basic direction of the country's foreign policy. At this time Kozyrev, Yeltsin and his influential adviser Gennady Burbulis, advocated and pursued a westernising foreign policy in the face of mounting Supreme Soviet opposition. While Kozyrev favoured diplomacy to resolve disputes with Russia's neighbours, the Supreme Soviet was much more inclined to be confrontational. So, for example, in May 1992 the Supreme Soviet annulled the 1954 transfer of the Crimea from the RSFSR to Ukraine and rejected the then current deal over the division of the Black Sea fleet between Russia and Ukraine.

Post-1993: foreign policy institutions

The 1993 Constitution changed the legal foundation of foreign policy making to one based on presidential authority. According to Article 86 the president exercises leadership of foreign policy, conducts talks and signs international treaties, signs instruments of ratification, and accepts the credentials and letters of recall of foreign diplomats. The president also approves the military doctrine, appoints the Russia's plenipotentiary representatives, and forms and heads the Security Council (Article 83). In formal terms the Federal Assembly's role is to first, provide legislative support for foreign policy and the fulfilment of international obligations and secondly, to scrutinise and ratify treaties signed by the president. According to Article 102.d the Federation Council has jurisdiction over the sending of armed forces abroad. Both chambers of the Federal Assembly have committees specialising in particular aspects of foreign and security policy and issues.

In the early 1990s the Foreign Ministry was weakened by financial problems and institutional rivalries within the government. Drastic budget cuts undermined its ability to fund embassies, conduct research and to compete with the growing business sector to employ Russia's well-educated, foreign language speakers. The Security Council (see Chapter 5), which resembles the US National Security Council is the Foreign Ministry's main institutional rival. The Security Council is staffed by presidential appointees and drafts the president's decisions on defence, foreign and security policy and monitors their implementation. Under Kozyrev the foreign ministry continued to favour the West-First approach but, under the leadership of the more centrist Yury Skokov between April 1992 to May 1993, the Security Council argued for a downgrading of the West-First priority and championed Russia's great power status. Kozyrev and Skokov, therefore, headed competing institutions with competing visions of Russian foreign policy. This conforms to Yeltsin's general proclivity towards 'institutional improvisation' and the creation of rival institutions. Once Yevgeny Primakov had replaced Kozyrev as foreign minister in 1996, the role of the Foreign Ministry underwent a renaissance.

The 1996 presidential decree 'On the Coordinating Role of the Russian Federation Foreign Ministry in the Conducting of an Integrated Russian Federation Foreign Policy' asserted the Foreign Ministry's primacy in the coordination of the foreign policy activities conducted by the various agencies of the executive branch. In reality during Yeltsin's second presidential term (1996–1999) foreign policy lacked central direction with different groups and institutions pursuing different agendas. A major fault line ran between the Presidential Administration on the one hand and the Ministry of Foreign Affairs on the other.

Box 13.2 Ministry of Foreign Affairs

The Ministers

Andrei Kozyrev	11 October 1990 to 9 January 1996
Yevgeny Primakov	9 January 1996 to 11 September 1998
Igor Ivanov	11 September 1998 to 9 March 2004
Sergei Lavrov	9 March 2004–

Source: Russian Foreign Ministry website, http://www.ln.mid.ru/brp_4.nsf/main_eng

---

Foreign policy making under Putin

As with other policy areas Putin reasserted the role of the president in foreign and security policy making, which has become more centralised and coordinated than under Yeltsin. The formal powers ascribed to different institutions and postholders by the Constitution and presidential decrees provide a very limited, formalistic, understanding of foreign policy making. Although Putin stressed the need to create strong institutions, in reality foreign policy was made by Putin and particular individuals. Putin's government and administration included economic liberals who wanted Russia to open up to the world and who also favoured close relations with the West as well as those who while not sharing the liberals' economic agenda also advocated good relations with the West. For example, Putin inherited Aleksandr Voloshin as head of his Presidential Administration and it was Voloshin who was a particular advocate of Russia's pro-Western strategy after the 9/11 attacks on the USA. Putin also filled key positions with personnel from his St Petersburg and *siloviki* networks (see Chapter 5). This does not mean unanimity of opinion, but these individuals do tend to share with Putin certain core beliefs and dispositions namely that Russia must vigorously and, if necessary, aggressively promote its national interests; it is a great, not to say a global power and not a junior partner to the USA; and finally that Russia needs a strong state and modernised nuclear and conventional forces. Sergei Ivanov, the defence minister 2001–2007, was one of Putin's advisers and a close confidant on foreign and security issues.

Putin inherited Igor Ivanov as his first foreign minister from Yeltsin. Ivanov was a career diplomat and a former first deputy foreign minister who in 2004 was also appointed as secretary to the Security Council, a post akin to the US national security advisor. Sergei Lavrov another career diplomat was then appointed foreign minister in 2007. Igor Ivanov and Sergei Lavrov both have considerable expertise and experience in foreign affairs. Under Putin, Ivanov and Lavrov foreign and security policy was essentially based on the state-realist-centrist orientation (see below) introduced in the mid-1990s.

Russia's foreign policy orientations

The westernisers (*zapadniki*)

From 1991–93 Russia's foreign policy, indeed its whole reform process, was based upon the belief that Russia needed to open up to the West as quickly as possible. In the tradition of Russia's nineteenth-century westernisers (*zapadniki*) and Gorbachev's *perestroika*, the westernisers believed that opening to the West would help to secure democratisation and marketisation against domestic inertia and opposition. Initially, President Yeltsin was one of the leading proponents of this approach together with his foreign minister, Andrei Kozyrev, and deputy Prime Minister Yegor Gaidar. In 1991 when asked by the newspaper *Izvestia* who were Russia's priority partners, Kozyrev enthusiastically replied, 'Rich developed countries, mature democracies with mature economies. This means the United States, Western Europe and Japan' (cited by Hearst, 1996: 21). This thinking led to a 'West-First' or 'Atlanticist' approach to foreign policy making and also entailed the dropping of old soviet-era allies like North Korea, Cuba, Vietnam, India, Angola and Ethiopia. The westernisers expected the West-First policy to generate economic dividends by providing Russia with new markets, investment, know-how and humanitarian aid. It was also an ethical or philosophical stance, signifying Russia's acceptance of 'western values' such as democracy, human rights and the rule of law. In January 1996 the Council of Europe voted to admit Russia as its 39th member precisely in order to send positive messages to Moscow and to counter anti-democratic pressures within Russia. The westernisers also believed that Russian security could be secured through active participation in international institutions, particularly the Organization for Security and Co-operation in Europe (OSCE) and the United Nations (UN). Yeltsin's attempts to extend the role of the OSCE were sidestepped by the leading western powers, which instead put more effort into enlarging the membership and extending the role of NATO in European security. Russia, unlike other FSU states and former socialist states in east-central Europe, has not been offered NATO membership. Russia inherited the USSR's permanent seat on the United Nations (UN) Security Council, but the USA has increasingly bypassed the UN and pursued a unilateral approach to foreign policy.

A wide range of political orientations including Eurasianists, communists and nationalists were highly critical of the westernising agenda. They believed that the

West, led by the USA, was not content with the collapse of soviet socialism and the USSR and that it wanted further to weaken Russia. The West's insistence on economic shock therapy (see Chapter 3), which reduced millions of Russians to poverty, seemed to bear this out. Kozyrev was condemned for appeasing the West, failing to defend Russia's national interests, and was mockingly dubbed the Minister of Foreign Affairs in Russia. The West was also ultra-sensitive to any signs of a renaissance of Russian, aka soviet, imperialism; this meant that Russia's understandable concern to stabilise its borders and protect the 25-million strong Russian diaspora living in the other FSU states was not given adequate attention. For example, ethnic Russians living in Estonia and Latvia were denied citizenship and voting rights, and while the West condemned this discrimination and denial of human and civil rights, they did not apply sanctions in support of the ethnic Russians.

Box 13.3 Foreign policy – terms in current usage

Near Abroad (*blizhnee zarubezh'e*): the term used by Russians for the other 14 successor states of the USSR. For these new states this term is evidence of Russian imperialism as it implies that they are not as fully independent of Russia as the countries of the 'Far Abroad'.

FSU: abbreviation for 'Former Soviet Union'. The 15 republics that comprised the USSR are now sometimes referred to as the FSU states.

The New World Order: in 1990 in the aftermath of the collapse of soviet socialism in east-central Europe, American President George H. W. Bush declared the end of the cold war and of East–West rivalry and the advent of a new world order, a term that Gorbachev also adopted in the USSR.

Uni-polarity: the condition in which the international system is dominated by one power (hegemon). It is used to describe the situation after the collapse of the USSR, when the USA became the world's lone superpower.

Bipolarity: the condition in which the international system is dominated by two competing centres of power. It was used to describe the cold war international system when the two superpowers, the USA and the USSR, competed for global dominance.

Multi-polarity: the condition in which the international system is characterised by a multiplicity of power centres (states), rather than global domination by one or two states.

Multilateralism: the strategy of working within institutions (such as the UN, OSCE, NATO, IMF, WTO and the UN) or with allies (other states) collectively to solve problems and threats.

Unilateralism: the strategy of self-reliance or 'go it alone' to deal with problems or threats.

Although Russia's 1993 Foreign Policy Concept reflected Kozyrev's westernising agenda, in reality as early as 1992 the pro-western foreign policy line was gradually weakening. In 1991 Russia had given verbal support to the Americans in the first Gulf War against Saddam Hussein's Iraq. Within a couple of years, however, Yeltsin started to advocate a patriotic Russia-First foreign policy and went against US policy by renewing Russia's relations with Iraq and the Palestinian Liberation Organisation (PLO). In the Balkans Yeltsin also came out in support of Russia's traditional allies, the Serbs, even depicting Radovan Karadžić and Ratko Mladić – who were condemned as war criminals by the West – as the innocent victims of western aggression. In January 1994 Kozyrev also stressed the importance of defending the Russian diaspora, the need for a Russian presence in the Near Abroad, and for priority to be given to relations with the CIS and Asian countries. Russia also began to open relations with China, which had been soured by the Chinese government's support for the August 1991 coup. In 1996 Kozyrev finally resigned as foreign minister at Yeltsin's request.

Eurasianists: Russia and the West and the clash of civilisations

Eurasianism (see Chapter 4) runs across Russia's political spectrum, from democrats through to proponents of various forms of authoritarianism including fascists and Stalinists. Eurasianists believe that Russia, like its crest the two-headed eagle, looks both East and West and is simultaneously part of Europe and Asia. Eurasianism provides a cultural justification for a powerful Russian state and either downgrading the relationship with the West or outright anti-westernism. In the early 1990s Eurasianist ideas were championed by Sergei Stankevich (1992, 1993) who had entered politics as a pro-democracy reformer during *perestroika* and by Gennady Zyuganov's Communist Party of the Russian Federation. Eurasianists rejected the West-First priority in foreign policy and Russia's junior-partner relationship to the West, arguing that Russia needed an independent foreign policy serving Russia's national interests. To Eurasianists the West is culturally alien to Russia and they have found evidence that Americans also think of the world in these terms in the writings of Professor Samuel Huntington, in his (1996) *The Clash of Civilizations and the Remaking of the World Order* and in *The Grand Chessboard* by Zbigniew Brzezinski (1997). Aleksandr Dugin the leading contemporary Eurasianist philosopher and the leader of the Eurasia political party, argues that there is 'an irreconcilable contradiction between the Eurasian meta-civilisation with Russia at its core and the Western, Atlantic community' (Dugin, 2001: 8). According to Dugin, this contradiction means that there are no changes that Russia can make to its political system or ideology that will end Western aggression. Dugin (ibid.) claims that although Russia is a democracy there is still evidence of western aggression towards it such as the expansion of NATO and NATO's actions in the Caucasus. Eurasianists believe that Russia should not have a West-First foreign policy orientation and should instead focus on the Commonwealth of Independent States (CIS), the Near Abroad, the Middle East, Africa and the economically dynamic Pacific Rim area.

Great power (*derzhavniki*) and strong state *gosudarstvenniki* advocates

Russia's great power (*derzhavniki*) and strong state (*gosudarstvenniki*) advocates believe that Russia must be a great power with a strong state in order to maintain its territorial integrity and to prevent anarchy and chaos. The advocates of these views are inspired by a range of ideas including Eurasianism and Russian nationalism. One such advocate is Sergei Karaganov, the deputy head of the Institute of Europe. In 1992 the Institute's Foreign and Defence Policy Council produced a paper entitled 'Strategy for Russia', which argued that Russia needs a form of transitional authoritarianism and a foreign policy focusing on the stability of its neighbours (Lloyd, 1998: 358). Andranik Migranyan, another advocate of transitional authoritarianism (see Chapter 3), similarly argues against the West-First priority and in favour of the adoption of a much more assertive policy in the Near Abroad. Russia's self-styled national patriots all stress Russia's uniqueness, its distinctiveness from the West, the importance of a strong state and Russia's status as a great power. Zhirinovsky, the leader of the fascist Liberal Democratic Party of the RF, in his *Last Thrust to the South* (1993), for example, argues that Russia should be the centre of a great Eurasian empire. The Russian nationalist writer Aleksandr Solzhenitsyn (1995) stressed the alien nature of the West for Russia, bemoaned the weakness of the Russian state and its inability to protect the Russian diaspora, and had advocated a union of the Eastern Slavs, the Russians, Ukrainians and Belarussians. Gennady Zyuganov (1995) inspired by a combination of Marxism and Eurasianism, advocated the reformation of at least part of the USSR. His earlier anti-westernism has been replaced by a more pragmatic approach to the West, but his rhetoric still champions Russia as a powerful state and a great power. Advocates of Russia as a great power and a strong state, while supporting membership of international organisations tend to be sceptical about its usefulness in the promotion of Russia's national interests. They favour robust and, if necessary, confrontational diplomacy.

State-realist centrists

Just as Russia's economic policy moved away from its western-inspired shock therapy towards a centrist economic policy in 1993 (see Chapter 16), so its foreign policy began to move from its West-First priority to the state-realist centrist approach. This approach is based on the realist approach to international relations which sees states, even so-called allies, as always competing with each other. Realists typically stress the pre-eminent importance of military might (hard power) as an instrument of foreign policy, but also see the value of soft power to promote a state's interests. The state-realist centrists are also champions of Russia as a great power and a strong state, which must champion its national interests, even if that means taking part in military ventures in the Near Abroad. International organisations are seen as potentially useful arenas in which to promote Russian interests and while good relations with the West are preferred, this does not preclude tough bargaining to secure Russian interests. Russia began to move towards a more state-realist centrist approach to foreign policy under Kozyrev, although his personal preference remained for a West-First approach. Kozyrev was succeeded as foreign minister by Yevgeny Primakov, an older generation soviet-era functionary, who after 1991 had served as the head of the External Intelligence Service (SVR). Primakov is an Arabic speaker and an expert on the Middle East; on the eve of the 1991 Gulf War, he conducted intensive shuttle diplomacy to Baghdad on Gorbachev's behalf in an attempt to pre-empt military action against Iraq.

In his first press conference as foreign minister Yevgeny Primakov stated that Russia is a great power and that her foreign policy must correspond to this status. He also rejected any return to the cold war and re-stated Russia's wish to have friendly relations with the USA, but that these relations must be based on an equitable, mutually beneficial partnership that respects each others' interests. Primakov and his successors as foreign minister, Igor Ivanov and Sergei Lavrov, all stress the importance of a multi-polar world underpinned by an international security system to put an end to the USA's uni-polar and increasingly unilateral-ist approach to global politics. Russia has remained critical of the enlargement of NATO, the failure to establish a European security alliance, NATO's actions in the former Yugoslavia and the USA's disregard of the UN. Primakov put particular effort into building up Russia's relations with China and India, and also re-invigorated its relations with former soviet client states such as Syria and Iraq. Russia opposed the resumption of US and UK air strikes against Iraq in October 1998 and the 2003 invasion, neither of which had been sanctioned by the UN Security Council. Since the mid-1990s Russia has also become more concerned with regional security threats, the CIS and its near neighbours Turkey, Pakistan, Afghanistan and Iran. After the 9/11 attacks Russia joined the international war on terror and even supported the West's attack on Afghanistan, while for its part the West dropped its earlier strident attacks on Russia's conduct of the second Russian-Chechen war.

Putin's Foreign Policy and National Security Concepts and Military Doctrine

The new Foreign Policy Concept, 2000

The new Foreign Policy Concept in 2000 describes Russia's geopolitical position as the largest Eurasian power with a responsibility to maintain security at global and regional levels. The Concept continues Primakov's advocacy of a multi-polar system of international relations and commits Russia to conduct bilateral foreign policy activities with individual countries and complementary activities within multi-national frameworks, such as the UN, or regional alliances such as the OSCE. The new Foreign Policy Concept states that only by active cooperation with Europe, USA, China, India and other power centres, will it be possible for Russia to uphold its interests. It condemns reliance on specifically western institutions and forums which have limited memberships, for the resolution of fundamental problems of international security. Russia continues to champion the UN which it believes needs to be reformed so that it can respond quickly and effectively to crises around the world. Russia also believes that the UN Security Council should bear the principal responsibility for maintaining international peace and security, and that it needs to be made more representative by introducing new permanent members from among the developing states. Putin and Ivanov believed that peace and security would only be secured through the recognition of international interdependence and respect for the sovereign equality of all countries. They oppose what they see as US attempts to refashion international laws through concepts such as 'limited sovereignty' and 'humanitarian intervention', which were used to justify NATO military operations in the Balkans and to bypass the UN Security Council. While stressing the UN's importance the Concept still advocates the creation of an All-European security and cooperation system based on the OSCE and the European Council. Russia also wants the Conventional Forces in Europe (CFE) Treaty to be transformed into an effective instrument to maintain European security. The Concept also reaffirms Russia's continuing commitment to deepen its integration in the world economy in order to boost Russia's economic potential and to advance its domestic agenda.

National Security Concept, 2000

In 1999 as secretary of the Security Council Putin began work on what would prove to be extensive revisions to the 1997 National Security Concept. Then while acting president in January 2000 he signed the decree introducing these revisions. The National Security Concept, 2000 continued its 1996 and 1997 predecessors' commitment to political liberalism and to the state's duty to uphold the Constitution, maintain the rule of law and ensure a friendly international environment. It also reasserted the 1997 Concept's statement that the main threat to Russia's security is posed by a possible economic crisis, but places more emphasis on the threat posed by social inequality and the lack of law and order than does the 1997 Concept. In accordance with Putin's overall agenda, the need to strengthen the Russian state and protect the domestic economy are also included in the National Security Concept, 2000. It also places greater emphasis on the threat to Russia posed by both domestic and international terrorism. Russia's National Security Concept understands security in the broad sense as all the factors (political, social and economic) that may strengthen or weaken a country, while the Military Doctrines focus on the military aspects of security.

The Military Doctrine, 2000

The Military Doctrine adopted in 2000 replaced the 1993 Military Doctrine, which had been revised in 1997. The Military Doctrine, 2000 contrasts Russia's commitment to multi-polarity with US attempts to establish uni-polar, superpower domination, using armed force to solve the world's problems. It identifies 10 basic features of the military-political situation at the time, which included 'the declining threat of a world war, the appearance and strengthening of regional centers of force, growing national and religious extremism, the escalation of local wars and armed conflicts, the aggravation of propaganda confrontation' (NUPI: 1999). The Military Doctrine, 2000 bemoans the ineffectiveness of the world's existing security mechanisms, specifically the UN and OSCE, to deal with these problems. For example, it notes that NATO went ahead with the bombing of Yugoslavia in 1999, without seeking the approval of the UN Security Council. It also lowers the threshold at which Russia would launch first strike nuclear weapons. Whereas the 1997 version of the Military Doctrine envisaged the use of nuclear weapons, but only if there was a threat to Russia's very existence as a sovereign state; the 2000 Military Doctrine envisages the use of a first strike when all other means to settle a crisis have been exhausted or proven ineffective, but it does not specify that Russia itself must be threatened. The 2000 Military Doctrine is also much cooler in its language towards the West; for example, it talks of the importance of 'cooperation' with the West, whereas the 1997 Military Doctrine spoke of 'partnership' with the West.

Revising the Military Doctrine

In 2005, Putin ordered a revision of Russia's military doctrine, in response to the deterioration of the international situation since 9/11 and in the aftermath of the attack on Beslan. Although there was considerable discussion in 2007 about a revised military doctrine, by August 2008 it had still not appeared. At the 43rd Munich Conference on Security Policy in February 2007 Putin argued that Russia, the USA and Europe need to join together in the fight against the main global threat of international terrorism and asked, 'Why do they have to move their military infrastructure [NATO] closer to our borders?' and added rhetorically 'Is this connected with overcoming global threats today?' (RIA Novosti, 2007a). From the Kremlin's perspective its revised Military Doctrine is a response to a changing security environment in which NATO's enlargement and the West's development and deployment of new military technologies such as the missile shield in Europe, are evidence of the West's commitment to the use of force in their foreign policies (RIA Novosti, 2007b). At a conference at the Russian Military Academy in January 2007, the chief of the general staff, Yury Baluyevsky said that security cooperation with the West had not led to a reduction in the number of military threats and that Washington's global expansionism and 'its desire to get a foothold in regions where Russia traditionally is present' (cited by de Hass, 2007) are the main threat to Russia. He cited the enlargement of NATO and its involvement in conflicts on Russia's borders as the second threat. Baluyevsky also cited hostile information about Russia and its policies as another threat, with terrorism and separatism further down the list of threats (ibid.).

Russia and the Former Soviet Union (FSU)

The Flag of the Commonwealth of Independent States.

The Commonwealth of Independent States (CIS)

Russia is the great power of the former Soviet Union (FSU) region. It is distinguished from its neighbours by its geographical expanse, population size and GDP. With the dissolution of the USSR, republics which had been part of the USSR and often before that part of the Imperial Russia Empire, suddenly became independent sovereign states. Russia's relations with these successor states were transformed from relations with another part of the same country to an aspect of foreign policy. These relations are influenced by two contradictory impulses: the 'nationalities question' and the need for mutual cooperation. The aspiration for national self-determination had played a fundamental role in the dissolution of the USSR and none of the successor states, with the possible exception of Belarus, want to be part of a new Russian empire. At the same time the new states had for decades been part of the same country; their peoples, economies and armed forces were intertwined. There is, therefore, a tension between upholding new, hard-won national sovereignty and recognition of the need for some form of institutionalised cooperation. The CIS Charter states that all members are independent and sovereign. The three Slav states Russia, Ukraine and Belarus founded the Commonwealth of Independent States (CIS) at Belovezha (Minsk) in December 1991. They were soon joined by nine of the other former soviet republics, Azerbaijan and Georgia joined in 1993 and only the Baltic republics of Estonia, Lithuania and Latvia have never joined. Turkmenistan withdrew in 2005 and is now an associate member. It was agreed in 1991 that the CIS's administrative HQ would be in Minsk, the capital of Belarus, to symbolise that this was not to be a Russian-dominated organisation. However, fears that the CIS would lead to the re-creation of the USSR or Russian domination have meant that it has remained a rather weak organisation.

The central institutions of the CIS include a Council of the Heads of State and a Council of the Heads of Government, which each meet at least twice a year

> ### Box 13.4 Ministry of CIS Affairs
>
> **Developments:** The Ministry was abolished by presidential decree in May 2000 and its functions transferred to the Foreign and Economics Ministries.
>
> **Ministers**
>
> | | |
> |---|---|
> | Valery Serov | 1995 to August 1996 |
> | Aman-geldy Tuleyev | August 1996 to July 1997 |
> | Boris Pastukhov | September 1998 to May 1999 |
> | Leonid Drachevsky | May 1999 to May 2000 |

and the chair rotates. The meetings of the Heads of State tend to focus on policy coordination among member states, with most intra-CIS business conducted by groups of members or on a bilateral basis. The CIS also has an Executive Committee, which provides administrative continuity between meetings.

Problem issues in the CIS in the early 1990s

As soon as the CIS was founded issues generated by the soviet integration of the FSU's economies and military capabilities came to the fore. In 1992 the rouble was the currency for all CIS countries (the rouble zone), which placed a tremendous burden upon the Russian economy. The successor states also expected Russia to continue supplying them with cheap oil and gas, when Russia needed to generate as much income as possible to finance its own reforms. In 1991 the CIS agreed to maintain CIS joint forces, but this was immediately undermined by the creation of national armed forces by several of the successor states including Ukraine. Russia responded by creating its own forces and also claimed soviet military assets located outside Russia. Russia and Ukraine quickly became embroiled in an argument over the ownership of the Black Sea fleet. This argument was fuelled by a territorial dispute over the Crimea, which Khrushchev had transferred to Ukraine in 1954 and which Russia now wanted back. In 1993 the Russian Supreme Soviet claimed that Sevastopol in Crimea, the home port of the Black Sea fleet, was in Russia. In May 1997 Prime Ministers Chernomyrdin of Russia and Lazerenko of Ukraine finally agreed that Russia's part of the Black Sea fleet would remain based in Sevastopol for 20 years. The USSR's strategic and tactical nuclear weapons arsenals also had to be divided between the successor states. Ukraine, Belarus and Kazakhstan agreed to transfer these weapons to Russia and to create a somewhat vaguely defined joint command over them under CIS auspices. The transfer of tactical weapons was swiftly completed by mid 1992, but the transfer of strategic weapons proved more difficult and became yet another point of argument between Russia and Ukraine. Although Russia wanted the CIS to have a unified military command one has never been created.

Box 13.5 Russia's hard and soft power

Hard power: the use by a state of military and economic might as either threats or inducements to affect the actions of another state.

- On Russia's military might, see Chapter 9.

- In 2003, Russia's powerful monopoly United Energy Systems (EES) bought 75 per cent of Georgia's energy network and acquired 80 per cent of Armenia's power-generating capacity.

- Many CIS countries depend on Russia for their energy supplies, including Ukraine, Georgia and Moldova.

- Russia has literally turned off the gas to Ukraine, Belarus and Lithuania in order to get them to pay higher prices. Russia is also the EU's main oil and gas supplier, leading to fears that the EU is also vulnerable to this kind of pressure.

- Energy rich countries such as Azerbaijan and Turkmenistan rely on Russian pipelines.

- In 2006 a pipeline was completed between Azerbaijan and Turkey with US support in order to reduce Russia's position as the chief energy supplier in the region. In 2007 Russia countered this move by concluding a deal to build an oil pipeline across Bulgaria and Greece, making it possible for Russian and Caspian oil to be transported directly to the EU, without going through Turkey.

Soft power: the ability of a state to achieve its aims as its institutions, values and/or culture are admired or respected by other states. The term soft power was first coined by the American Professor Joseph Nye in his (1990) book, *Bound to Lead: The Changing Nature of American Power*, and then developed in his (2004) *Soft Power: The Means to Success in World Politics*.

- The Russian language: remains the *lingua franca* for education, employment and commerce for most of the FSU. Recognition of this led to the reintroduction of compulsory Russian language classes in schools in Tajikistan in September 2003. In June 2003 the State Duma began moves to have Russian adopted as the official language of the CIS.

- Russian culture: the 'high culture' of nineteenth-century novels, ballet and music remains widely respected and there is also a growing market for contemporary Russian popular culture, particularly in the FSU, including fiction especially detective fiction and romances, rock music, films and satellite TV.

- Russian consumer products: including food, CDs and DVDs are sold throughout the FSU.

- Employment opportunities: as the Russian economy expanded under Putin, Russia became a migration magnet for people from Central Asia and the southern Caucasus, whose governments are well aware that this employment contributes to the social stability and prosperity of their countries.

Putin, the CIS and the Near Abroad

In January 2000, Putin approved the document, 'The Main Directions of the Development of Russia's Relations with the CIS Member States', which enshrined the high priority Putin and his *siloviki* advisers gave to relations with the CIS and the Near Abroad. The document also calls for a pragmatic approach towards individual CIS members; greater economic cooperation; and also the need to set clear priorities for further integration with an emphasis on bilateral negotiations. Putin abolished the separate Ministry for CIS Affairs on 17 May 2000 and transferred its functions to the more important Ministry of Economic Development and Trade and the Ministry of Foreign Affairs. On 12 May 2008 Medvedev established a Federal Agency for Commonwealth of Independent State Affairs, within the Ministry of Foreign Affairs.

Integration will always be a difficult issue for the CIS member states, given that their independence was so hard won in 1991. However, these countries are to varying degrees interdependent and geographically close; so cooperation achieved through bilateral treaties, promoting individual national interests, remains a way forward. Russia has both hard and soft power, which it has employed to achieve its foreign policy goals in the CIS. Overall under Putin Russia improved its relations with Armenia, Azerbaijan, Kyrgyzstan, Tajikistan and Uzbekistan, but relations with Moldova, Georgia and Ukraine worsened. In 2003 Russia, Ukraine,

Box 13.6 Georgia and the Pankisi Gorge

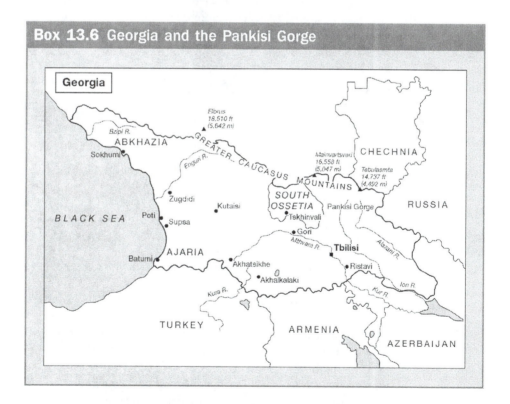

Belarus and Kazakhstan agreed to unite their countries into a 'single economic space', although Ukraine's Orange Revolution frustrated its development. Also in 2003 Russia, Belarus, Armenia, Kazakhstan, Kyrgyzstan and Tajikistan set up the 'Organisation of the Agreement on Collective Security' (ODKB). ODKB's main military base is the Kant airbase in Kyrgyzstan, Central Asia and is clearly meant to balance the US base near Bishek in Kyrgyzstan. Kazakhstan and Russia continue to collaborate over the use of the Baikonur space centre in Kazakhstan and in 2004 signed a mutual defence treaty. So while CIS institutions remain weak, its members are reaching mutually advantageous agreements in pairs or small groups. Four factors have had a particular impact on Russia's relations with the Near Abroad. First, the outbreak of the second war in Chechnia in 1999 had a destabilising effect throughout the Caucasus; secondly Russia's decision to join the USA in the 'war on terror' after 9/11; thirdly the colour revolutions especially in Georgia and Ukraine; and finally, the need to secure routes for Russia's oil and gas through CIS states.

Russia, Georgia and the USA and the war on terror

The war on terror led in 2002 to the arrival of American troops in the Pankisi Gorge in Georgia, at first with Russian support. After fighting resumed in Chechnia in 1999, Chechen refugees sought sanctuary in the Pankisi Gorge, which also became a base for Chechen fighters. The Pankisi Gorge is home to Georgians who are Orthodox Christians and to Kists, a Muslim people who are related to the Chechens (Dalziel, 2002). The Georgians claim that the arrival of Chechens had led to tensions, forcing most of the Christian population to flee. Chechens have also been involved in criminal activity, including the kidnapping of foreign aid workers; and Chechen fighters also conducted raids on Russian troops in Chechnia and then returned to the safe haven provided by the gorge's mountainous terrain. Although Georgia and Russia agreed that they wanted the Chechens out of the gorge, they could not agree joint military action, largely because the Georgians are fearful of Russian ambitions in the Caucasus. The Georgians accused Russia of conducting raids against Chechens in the gorge, which Russia has denied. Eduard Shevardnadze, who had been Gorbachev's foreign minister and was the Georgian president before the Rose revolution, therefore, wanted NATO rather than Russian assistance in clearing the gorge of Chechen fighters. After 9/11 the Americans finally and publicly agreed with Russia's claim that Al Qaeda and Taliban fighters were active in Chechnia. Later they also agreed that there were Afghan fighters in Chechnia and so the Pankisi Gorge became part of their shared war on terror. The US troops who are still in the Pankisi Gorge are officially there to train Georgian troops to clear the gorge of terrorists and insurgents. Initially Putin accepted the American presence and even argued that they contributed to Russia's security. However, Georgia's staunchly pro-American Rose revolution, its final withdrawal from the CIS Defence Council in February 2006, and its decision to seek NATO membership all contributed to Russia's sense that it is becoming isolated and surrounded by members of an anti-Russian security organisation.

Russia and separatists in Georgia and Moldova

An additional cause of Russian–Georgian tension is Moscow's support for separatists in the Georgian regions of Abkhazia and South Ossetia. Moldova, another FSU state, is also in dispute with Russia over its support for the breakaway region of Transdniestria. At the time of the collapse of the USSR these three regions were formed by armed conflict supported directly or indirectly by Russia, which has continued to supply these regions with military and economic aid. It is estimated that 85 per cent of the residents of South Ossetia now have Russian passports and so qualify for Russian social benefits and pensions (Yasmann, 2006). Russia has also made it easier for the residents of Transdniestria to acquire Russian citizenship. Failure to resolve these disputes is an impediment to Georgia's and

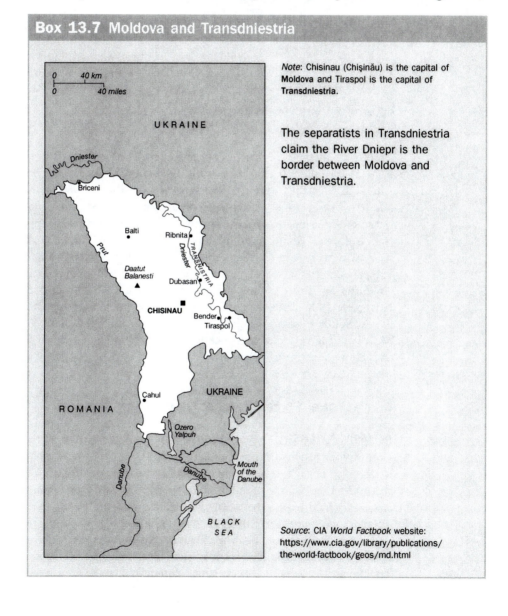

Box 13.7 Moldova and Transdniestria

Note: Chisinau (Chişinău) is the capital of Moldova and Tiraspol is the capital of Transdniestria.

The separatists in Transdniestria claim the River Dniepr is the border between Moldova and Transdniestria.

Source: CIA *World Factbook* website: https://www.cia.gov/library/publications/the-world-factbook/geos/md.html

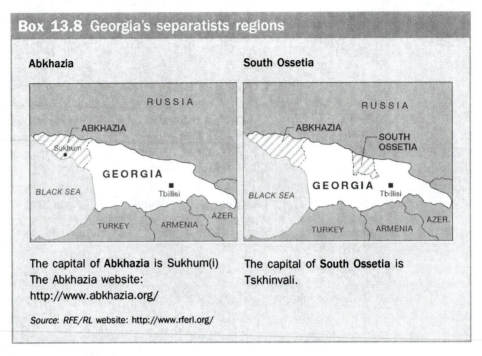

Box 13.8 Georgia's separatists regions

Abkhazia

South Ossetia

The capital of **Abkhazia** is Sukhum(i)
The Abkhazia website:
http://www.abkhazia.org/

The capital of **South Ossetia** is
Tskhinvali.

Source: RFE/RL website: http://www.rferl.org/

Moldova's membership of NATO and the EU, as membership of these organisations is prohibited to states with unresolved border or territorial disputes. Although Moscow supported the separatist regions, it was acutely aware that it had its own separatist movements, notably in Chechnia, and that it had to appear not to condone independence claims. In 2006 Putin changed his approach and argued that if Kosovo could gain its independence from Russia's ally Serbia as the western powers wanted, then Abkhazia and South Ossetia should also be granted independent statehood. The three regions had held referenda on independence: Abkhazia in 1994, Transdniestria in September 2006 and South Ossetia in November 2006. The referenda all showed overwhelming support for independence, but in South Ossetia, ethnic Georgians were not allowed to vote. Georgia and Moldova fear that independence would just be a step towards the incorporation of these regions into Russia.

Conventional Forces Europe: Georgia and Moldova

In 1990 the USSR, USA and other European countries signed the Treaty on Conventional Armed Forces in Europe or CFE. The treaty was originally signed to establish equal levels of conventional forces (tanks, aircraft and other offensive weapons) that the two military blocs – NATO and the Warsaw Treaty Organisation – could deploy between the Atlantic and the Urals. By the time the CFE Treaty entered into force in 1992, the USSR and the Warsaw Treaty Organisation had already ceased to exist; the changing geopolitical situation meant that the signatories already faced new security challenges that had not been foreseen in 1990. The signatories nonetheless remained committed to the CFE as a means to achieve military stability and in 1999 a new version of the treaty established national limits on weapons holdings. Russia has ratified the 1999 revised CFE Treaty, but NATO refuses to do so until Russian forces are withdrawn from their bases in Georgia and from Transdniestria in Moldova.

In 1999 Russia agreed to the unconditional withdrawal of its troops from Georgia and Moldova. In May 2005 Russia and Georgia signed an agreement, on the closure of three Russian bases and the complete withdrawal of Russian garrisons by 2008. Russia began withdrawing troops from Georgia in July 2005, transferring some of these forces to the Russian base at Gyumri in Armenia. The situation was however complicated in August 2008, when Georgia sent troops into the breakaway and largely pro-Russia province of South Ossetia. Russia responded by sending its forces into South Ossetia and claims the right to maintain a peacekeeping, military presence in Georgia in an 'area of responsibility' around South Ossetia (RIA-Novosti, 2008). Russian forces went into the Transdniestria in the early 1990s ostensibly to protect the ethnic Russians of that area and describes its troops there as peacekeepers. The Moldovan government has repeatedly asked Russia to withdraw its troops, however, the stalemate is likely to continue as it has now become embroiled in Russia's dispute with the USA over the creation of a nuclear defence shield in Europe. From Russia's perspective the USA's abandonment of the Anti-Ballistic Missile Treaty provides a rationale for ignoring the CFE Treaty and most western European leaders have made their ratification of the CFE conditional upon Russian troop withdrawals from Moldova. The Moldovan stalemate continues.

Russia, NATO and the EU

NATO and European security after the cold war

In the early 1990s Russia's westernisers had anticipated that as the cold war, the reason for NATO's existence, was now over NATO would quickly be downgraded and that the CSCE (later OSCE) would become the main European security organisation. Russia is a member of the OSCE and, while it is an important forum for discussion of security issues, it has not supplanted NATO. After 1991 the former soviet bloc countries worked with NATO in the North Atlantic Co-operation Council (NACC) and in January 1994 NATO launched a Partnership for Peace (PfP), through bilateral treaties between NATO and individual former Warsaw Pact countries. A PfP is typically a first step to full NATO membership, providing fairly loose political and security ties and access to NATO councils but without decision-making or veto powers. By the end of 1994 23 countries had PfPs with NATO, including 10 CIS countries. In 1994 Russia and NATO even held joint military exercises and in 1995 they also signed a PfP. Since 1997 PfPs have been coordinated through the Euro-Atlantic Partnership Council (EAPC), which replaced the NACC that year. At the June 1996 NATO defence ministers meeting, Pavel Grachev the Russian defence minister agreed to a formal exchange of senior NATO and Russian military personnel, who are now permanently stationed in Moscow and Brussels. They also agreed to work together against terrorism and international crime, to cooperate on joint weapons development and on arms control. Then in May 1997 Russia and NATO signed the 'Founding Act on Mutual Relations, Co-operation and Security between NATO and the Russian Federation' (NATO, 1997). This included commitments to the principles in the UN Charter such as respect for state sovereignty and the right of each country to choose how to ensure its own sovereignty, as well as the creation of a NATO–Russian Permanent Joint Council (PJC) to facilitate joint decision making. The Founding Act also contained commitments to cooperate in conflict resolution, peacekeeping, the prevention of weapons proliferation, and to exchange security and defence information. Crucially, the Foundation Act also reaffirmed NATO's December 1996 commitment not to deploy nuclear weapons on the territory of its new members, which had been a major point of tension in Russian–NATO relations. This commitment facilitated Russia's acceptance of the accession of the Czech Republic, Hungary and Poland to NATO in March 1999, which was NATO's first post-cold war enlargement. In 2002 in the aftermath of 9/11, Russia–NATO relations were upgraded by the formation of a NATO–Russian Council, to take joint decisions on counter-terrorism and other security threats. Then in April 2004 they agreed to establish a Russian military liaison office at NATO HQ. The NATO–Russian Council and the liaison office are not the same as NATO membership, or evidence that NATO and Russia necessarily share common goals and values, but it does suggest that they can work together on issues of shared concern.

Russia, NATO and the Balkans

Russia staunchly opposed NATO's actions in the former Yugoslavia, such as the bombing of Bosnia in 1995. NATO and Russia eventually agreed to Russian participation in the Bosnian peace implementation, when NATO took over from the UN in Bosnia in December 1995. Russia also participated in the joint consultative commission and the contact group or peace implementation force with the USA, United Kingdom, France and Germany. In March 1999 Russian foreign minister Ivanov accused NATO of having violated all the 1997 Founding Act's agreements and to be guilty of genocide in Kosovo. Russia announced a complete cessation of ties with NATO, including the suspension of Russia's participation in the PfP. Yeltsin backed down over Kosovo and in return secured the more valuable prize of a place at the June 1999 G8 conference in Cologne. However, the West's plans for Kosovo, which has been run by the UN, to become an independent state contributed to an escalating war of words during 2007. Russia supports its traditional ally Serbia's claim for the return of their lost region of Kosovo.

NATO enlargement

For FSU and the former soviet socialist states of east-central Europe NATO membership is symbolic of their acceptance into the community of democratic states, recognition that as sovereign states they have the right to decide their own security alliances and also a vital guarantee against possible future Russian imperialist aggression. In July 2001 Putin described Russian membership of NATO as a possibility, and a way of creating a single defence and security space. Russia does not, however, meet the political and military criteria for new members such as democratic institutions, political freedoms and minority rights. There are also lingering doubts as to whether the Russian armed forces are under civilian control and its military budget is not transparent.

From Moscow's perspective NATO's continuing enlargement has brought Europe's only effective security organisation right up to its borders and is interpreted as an attempt to isolate Russia. NATO's 2002 Prague Summit was the first time that a summit was held in a former soviet bloc country; at the summit the USSR's former Baltic republics – Estonia, Latvia and Lithuania – together with Bulgaria, Slovakia, Slovenia and Romania were invited to begin accession talks, which culminated in their accession in March 2004. NATO's summit in 2006 was held for the first time in the FSU, in the Latvian capital of Riga. Then at NATO's Bucharest Summit in 2008 it was agreed that Albania and Croatia should begin accession talks. In 2006 and 2005 respectively Georgia and Ukraine had begun NATO accession discussions and, through their Rose and Orange revolutions, these two FSU states have come much closer to the West. The prospect of two FSU states joining NATO meant that Russia's relations with NATO were badly strained by the time of the Bucharest Summit. At the summit NATO agreed that Georgia and Ukraine should begin to be considered for Membership Action Plans (MAPs), which are usually the first step towards full NATO membership (NATO, 2008). This was a bit of a fudge: on the one hand making it clear that these countries were on track for NATO membership, but without actually giving them a MAP.

Box 13.9 President George W. Bush on Vladimir Putin

In 2001 President George W. Bush told students in Crawford, Texas that:

> . . . the more I get to know President Putin, the more I get to see his heart and soul, and the more I know we can work together in a positive way.

Source: George Bush (2001) 'President Bush and President Putin Talk to Crawford Students', Press Release, 15 November, White House website, http://www.whitehouse.gov/news/

Russia, Western Europe and European Union (EU) under Yeltsin

Europe was a major battleground during the First and Second World Wars and the cold war divide between the soviet East and the West ran through Germany at the heart of Europe. The collapse of communism first in east-central Europe in 1989 and finally in the USSR was greeted with enthusiasm in western European capitals. The countries of east-central Europe were viewed as countries liberated from soviet (Russian) imperialism, which were at last able to find their place in the world. This enthusiasm was tempered by concerns that the collapse of the soviet superpower might lead to geopolitical instability and that the collapse of soviet economies might lead to a poverty line running through the heart of Europe, in turn leading to instability and migration to the West. Following the launch of its TACIS programme in 1991, the EU became Russia's largest provider of economic and technical assistance and also emerged as a major trading partner (Ivanov and Pozdnyakov, 1998). The EU has been particularly concerned with assisting legal and administrative reform – including social reform, fiscal and banking sector reform, and the development of civil society and an independent media. Relations between Russia and the EU are based on the 1994 'Partnership for Co-operation Agreement' (PCA) which came into force on 1 December 1997 and ran until 1 December 2007. The PCA is now subject to automatic, annual extension, although it may be revoked by either partner. The PCA states that a commitment to the values and principles of democracy, human rights, the rule of law and the market economy underpins EU–Russia bilateral relations. It also defined the EU and Russia as strategic partners and led to discussions on general political issues, on trade and economic cooperation, on scientific and technological cooperation, and on justice and home affairs. In 1997 Prime Minister Chernomyrdin even announced that Russia would seek EU membership, although Russia's sheer size and the scale of its economic problems meant that it would not be considered for membership.

Russia pursued good relations with the European Union (EU) and its individual members as desirable goals in their own right, but also to counterbalance the USA. In the 1990s Russia supported EU endeavours to develop a shared EU foreign policy and defence identities, distinct from the USA. In 1996 it seemed briefly as if the WEU would finally be invigorated after decades of inertia, but this did not happen. The meeting of NATO foreign ministers in Berlin in June 1996 agreed to establish a European command structure within NATO, which meant that NATO's European members could organise their own humanitarian and peacekeeping missions. However, the Europeans were reluctant to get involved in Kosovo on their own and instead preferred to work with the Americans in NATO. In December 2004 a new EU-led force (EUFOR) did finally take over peacekeeping duties in Bosnia from NATO. Since the 1990s Russia has also wanted Europe's largest organisation, the OSCE, to be reinvigorated and for it to adopt a European Security Charter. However, again the western Europeans while respecting the OSCE as a forum for discussion view it as too unwieldy to provide a realistic security organisation and continue to prefer to work through NATO.

Box 13.10 Putin on Russia and Europe

I strongly believe the full unity of our continent can never be achieved until Russia, as the largest European state, becomes an integral part of the European process. (. . .) Today, building a sovereign democratic state, we share the values and principles of the vast majority of Europeans. (. . .) A stable, prosperous and united Europe is in our interest. (. . .) The development of multifaceted ties with the EU is Russia's principled choice.

Russian President Vladimir Putin (2007) in a letter to commemorate the 50th anniversary of the European Union, 25 March 2007.

Source: The European Commission's Delegation to Russia website, http://www.delrus.ec.europa.eu/en/index.htm

Russia, Western Europe and the European Union (EU) under Putin

Unlike Yeltsin, Putin does not aspire to EU membership, but is keen to cooperate in areas of shared interest and concern. The EU as a whole remains Russia's largest trading partner and, thanks to its energy exports, Russia exports more to the EU than it imports. In his first term as president, EU–Russia relations expanded to include joint discussions and action on shared security threats such as terrorism, crime, illegal migration, people and drug trafficking and climate change. The EU Security Strategy adopted in December 2003, called for a 'balanced partnership with the USA' (EU, 2003: 14) and said that, 'We [the EU] should continue to work for closer relations with Russia, a major factor in our security and prosperity' (ibid.: 15). The EU and Russia also discuss global issues such as conflict resolution in the Middle East, Sudan and the Balkans, the proliferation of weapons of mass destruction, Iran and North Korea.

On 1 May 2004 the FSU Baltic republics Estonia, Latvia and Lithuania together with Poland joined the EU. This presented particular challenges to the region of Kaliningrad, which is geographically separated from the rest of Russia by Poland and Lithuania. In 2002 the EU, prompted by Poland, decided not to accord Kaliningrad a special visa regime to facilitate travel across EU member states to the rest of Russia, although visa regulations were eased in June 2007. Kaliningrad is also being treated as a pilot area for the way Russia–EU partnership might develop. Since 2004 the EU has funded a 'Support for the Regional Development of Kaliningrad' project, which envisages large infrastructural projects and Special Economic Zone status for Kaliningrad. The EU–Russia PCA also includes Russia, specifically north-west Russia, as a Northern Dimension partner of the European Union. The Northern Dimension, which also includes Iceland and Norway, is concerned with regional development, environmental protection, the promotion of security and stability, and the eventual eradication of uneven levels of regional development between the Northern Dimension countries. Although EU–Russia relations have developed harmoniously, there are two major points of tension. First, the growing dependence of EU member states on Russian energy has led to fears that Russia will use price rises or will cut off or reduce supplies, to exert pressure. Russia has tended to avoid dealing with the EU as an institution and has instead negotiated energy deals with individual countries, so undermining the EU's attempts to reduce its dependence on Russian energy. Secondly, Russia is outraged by EU allegations that under Putin democracy has been rolled back and counter-charge that EU support for Russian civil society organisations is part of a western attempt to destabilise Russia through a 'Colour Revolution', such as occurred in Ukraine or Georgia.

Nuclear proliferation: USA, Russia and Iran

Russia, unlike the USA, has good relations with Iran. Despite domestic pressure to confront Moscow over its treatment of the Chechens, the Iranian government has taken the line that Chechnia is a domestic Russian issue. Iran is an important ally and champion for Russia in the Islamic world and a market for Russian goods,

US President George W. Bush (L) and Russian President Vladimir Putin (R) embrace during their joint press conference at the G8 summit in St Petersburg, 15 July 2006.

especially military hardware and a nuclear power reactor at Bushehr. Russia and Iran are also involved in joint ventures such as the plan to build and launch Iran's first communications satellite and to build power stations in Tajikistan. Russia shares the USA's opposition to nuclear weapons proliferation and concern over its destabilising impact, especially in the Middle East. Russia, however, insists that it must be allowed to act in its political and economic national interests and that the Bushehr reactor is for civilian not military use. Russia has, therefore, resisted American attempts to have political and economic sanctions imposed on Iran. In February 2006 Iran and Russia agreed that the key uranium enrichment part of the nuclear fuel cycle, would take place in Russia not Iran. This agreement was backed by the USA and the EU, as a way to prevent Iran from being able to develop weapons-grade uranium under cover of a civilian fuel programme (Finn, 2006: A09).

The return of Star Wars and a new cold war?

In 2002 the USA unilaterally withdrew from the 1972 Anti-Ballistic Missile (ABM) Treaty, in order to start work on an updated version of Reagan's Star Wars missile defence system, dubbed 'son of star wars'. Construction of the new anti-ballistic missile shield began in the USA the same year, ostensibly to protect it from attacks by terrorists and 'rogue states' such as North Korea and, particularly, Iran. The shield is very much an American rather than a NATO initiative, although Bush and the leaders of some European-NATO countries also want the system to be extended to cover Europe. The Polish and Czech Republic leaderships have agreed to site 10 interceptor missiles and a radar tracking system in their respective countries, with construction being due to begin in 2008. Russia, which was already alarmed by American withdrawal from the ABM treaty, now faces the stationing of US missiles in Europe. Despite a visit to Moscow in April 2007 by the US defense secretary Robert Gates, to reassure Russia that it is not the target of US missiles, Putin did not believe that the system is directed against Iran, which he claimed did not have missiles with a 5–8,000 km range (Sevastopulo, 2007: 11). Both the USA and Russia are now using cold war language; for example, US Secretary of State Condoleeza Rice has contrasted the American desire for 'a 21st-century partnership with Russia' with Russia at times seeming to think and act 'in the zero-sum terms of another [cold war] era' (cited by Kessler, 2007: A12). In the run up to the G8 summit in June 2007 Bush said that the cold war is over, but Putin accused the USA of provoking a return to the cold war and declared that if US missiles were stationed in Europe, Russia would have no choice but to re-target some of its missiles towards Europe (Sevastopulo, 2007: 11). This is not a hollow threat as in the week before the summit Russia successfully tested its short-range Iskander-M cruise missile, which could be deployed in the Kaliningrad area to target the US missiles in Poland and the Czech Republic. At the G8 summit Putin offered to supply the US with information on missile launches near southern Russia, using Russian radar sited in Azerbaijan.

Box 13.11 International institutions

North Atlantic Treaty Organisation (NATO): created on 4 April 1949 by USA, Canada, UK, Belgium, the Netherlands, Luxembourg, France, Portugal, Norway, Denmark and Iceland. In 1952 Greece and Turkey joined. It is a collective defence body, whose members agree to defend each other against external attack. It was founded at the height of the cold war specifically to defend its members against an attack by the USSR. The end of the cold war and the disbanding of the Warsaw Treaty Organisation in 1991, did not lead to the end of NATO. It has enlarged taking in former Warsaw Pact members and has been active beyond Europe, notably in 2003 NATO agreed to take command of the International Security Assistance Force (ISAF) in Afghanistan.

NATO website: http://www.nato.int

Council of Europe: founded in 1949 as a European regional group with the aim to coordinate economic, social, cultural, scientific and judicial legislation. It is a separate organisation to the EU. The Council of Europe established the European Court of Human Rights which considers complaints by citizens against their own governments; member states are supposed to be based on the rule of law and human rights. Since 1989 the Council has been engaged in monitoring democratisation in the former soviet bloc. In 1995 Russia's application for membership was temporarily suspended because of the conflict in Chechnia and human rights abuses. Although Russia was admitted as a member in 1996, the Council was concerned by the renewed conflict in Chechnia and human rights abuses.

Council of Europe website: http://www.coe.int/

Box 13.11 *(Continued)*

Organization for Security and Co-operation in Europe (OSCE): originally founded in Helsinki as the Conference on Security and Co-operation in Europe (CSCE) in 1975, it became the OSCE in 1990. CSCE-OSCE members include East and West European states and the USA. The CSCE-OSCE has held a series of meetings and conference to discuss European security and co-operation, military and trade issues, and human rights. The OSCE provides missions to mediate conflicts and monitors democratisation in Europe. The OSCE has sent missions to Chechnia.

OSCE website: http://osce.org/

Western European Union (WEU): established in 1954 as a European council to co-ordinate regional defence policy, the USA is not a member. It was largely moribund until the 1980s when some European countries, notably France, became interested in activating the WEU as an embryonic military arm of the EEC. The WEU's remit includes peacekeeping and peace enforcement, humanitarian and rescue missions, and collective defence. The WEU currently has 10 full members and 10 associate partners from east-central Europe.

Western European Union website: http://weu.int

European Union: established in 1993 by the Treaty of European Union or Maastricht Treaty, the successor organisation to the European Economic Community, which was established on 1 January 1957. The EU is an organisation for international co-operation formed by democratic states. EU member states delegate some of their sovereignty to make decisions on matters of joint interest to EU institutions. The EU is a single market with freedom of movement for goods, services, people and money. Its members include: Germany, France, Italy, the Netherlands, Belgium, Luxembourg, Denmark, Ireland, UK, Greece, Spain, Portugal, Austria, Finland, Sweden, Cyprus and Malta. Estonia, Latvia and Lithuania joined in 2004 together with former soviet allies the Czech Republic, Slovakia, Hungary, Poland and Slovenia. In 2007 the former soviet allies Bulgaria and Romania joined, while Croatia and the Former Yugoslav Republic of Macedonia are candidate members. The EU is already the world's largest economic and political entity.

European Union website: http://europa.eu/index_en.htm

The Shanghai Co-operation Organisation (SCO): in 1996–7 the 'Shanghai Five' – Russia, China, Kazakhstan, Tajikistan and Kyrgyzia – signed agreements designed to build military confidence and reduce military forces in their border areas. In June 2001 the five were joined by Uzbekistan to form the SCO, which is an intergovernmental organisation. SCO's purpose is to strengthen mutual trust and co-operation across a range of policy areas including security, political affairs, energy, the economy and trade, education and culture.

The Shanghai Co-operation Organisation website: http://www.sectsco.org/

Russia and Asia

Japan

Russia's relations with Japan are complicated by the absence of a peace treaty to bring a close to the Great Patriotic War (World War II) between the two countries and by territorial disputes dating from 1945. Japan claims the Northern Territories and Kurile Islands, a volcanic archipelago between Russian Kamchatka and Japan that the USSR seized at the end of the war. For Russia these have a strategic importance and provide passage to its Pacific ports of Nakhodka and Vladivostock. Under Yeltsin, the islands became a measure of his commitment to stand up for Russia, and local Cossacks swore to fight if there is any attempt to return the islands to Japan. Putin has reaffirmed that Russia has no intention of returning the territory to Japan while Japan will not agree to a peace treaty that does not return its seized territories. Despite this deadlock Japan and Russia have established a pragmatic, working relationship; in the 1990s they concluded fishing agreements and more recently have begun discussing the joint development of the oil and gas fields off Sakhalin Island, projects in the Kovytka and Yakutia gas fields and the construction of a gas pipeline from Russia to Japan.

North and South Korea

During the cold war Korea was divided into the pro-West South Korea and North Korea, which has its own brand of communism and was an ally of the USSR. Gorbachev visited South Korea in May 1991 in order to open relations with this economic powerhouse and Yeltsin continued the policy of courting South Korea and downgrading relations with North Korea. Under Putin trade and economic cooperation continued to grow between Russia and South Korea. In 2012–13 Russia plans to begin supplying South Korea with gas. In the 1990s Russia paid less attention to North Korea than to South Korea, North Korea became increasingly isolated and was condemned by the USA as a rogue state.

In contrast Putin tried to reopen Russia's relations in North Korea. A visit by Russian Foreign Minister Ivanov in February 2000 to the North Korean capital of Pyong Yang resulted in a Russian-Korean Friendship Treaty. The Duma ratified the treaty in July 2000 while Putin was in Pyong Yang, the first Russian leader to visit North Korea since 1956. Putin was also able to take to the G8 meeting in Okinawa, Japan in July 2000, a document signed by the North Korean leader Kim Jong-il stating that he would not launch missiles. Russia is concerned by nuclear proliferation but when in October 2006 North Korea announced that it had exploded a nuclear device, Putin advised the international community not to isolate North Korea. Instead Putin favoured an approach of making it difficult for North Korea to continue its development of atomic weapons. In January 2007 Putin signed a decree setting up a full weapons embargo against North Korea and forbidding entry to Russia of anyone involved in developing North Korea's atomic bomb. Putin also approved a UN Security Council decree imposing economic sanctions on North Korea.

China

Although there are potential points of conflict between Russia and China, such as Russia's belief that China wishes to expand into the Russian Far East, Sino–Russian relations improved considerably during the 1990s. China shares Russia's concern over America's dominance in an increasingly unipolar world, its tendency to unilateral action and its plans to create a nuclear missile shield. Russia and China are permanent members of the UN Security Council and want the UN to be re-invigorated as part of the creation of a multi-polar world and as a mechanism to rein in American ambitions. Under Putin Asia occupied an increasingly important place in Russian foreign policy and he visited China (plus North Korea and Japan) in July 2000. This led to the 'Beijing Declaration' which established a shared commitment to the creation of a multi-polar world, and set out the basic guidelines for future Sino–Russian relations, including strategic cooperation and talks over disputed border areas. In July 2001 Russia and China signed a 20-year friendship treaty. Russia and China also share concerns about security in Asia and central Asia. China has substantial Islamic–Turkic populations in its south eastern regions who are increasingly challenging Beijing's rule. Russia is similarly concerned by instability among the Islamic–Turkic peoples of central Asia. Russia and China work together in the Shanghai Co-operation Organisation on such regional security issues. China's rapidly growing economy is an increasingly important market for Russian goods, especially weapons.

Chapter summary

Russia has travelled a long way from its westernising domestic and foreign agenda of the early 1990s. This does not mean that Russia has reverted to knee-jerk anti-westernism as a result of the lingering soviet legacy or to a resurgent, retrograde Russian nationalism. Yeltsin increasingly employed the language of Russian nationalism in order to define Russian interests, as does Putin, but do not all governments claim to be promoting the best interests of their country? At the annual security conference in Munich in 2007 Putin attacked US unilateralism and specific policies, such as the 2003 invasion of Iraq, the plan to build the anti-missile defence shield and the expansion of NATO to include FSU states, remarks that were interpreted in the western media as signalling the return of the cold war. However, during the cold war the two superpowers were engaged in a global ideological struggle, which is no longer the case. Putin defended Russia's national interests but he has not replaced soviet ideological anti-westernism with an Eurasianist belief in a perpetual East–West conflict of civilisations, for example. Putin was very pragmatic: he consistently stressed the importance of the UN and multilateralism, was active in the NATO–Russia Council, the G8 and the Quartet group which also includes the UN, EU and USA and works for peace in the Middle East; Putin also wanted Russia to join the World Trade Organisation. In the 1990s Russia was an impoverished, debtor-nation with outdated armed forces and reluctantly assumed the role of junior partner to the USA. Even before Putin became president, Russian foreign policy had begun to move away from this subservient position. Now, largely due to the rise in oil and gas prices, Russia is economically and militarily resurgent and this has, literally, fuelled an assertive pursuit of national interests.

Discussion points

- What positive consequences did Yeltsin's Atlanticist approach to foreign policy have for Russia?
- Why do you think Putin placed such an emphasis on the role of the United Nations?
- Is hard or soft power more important to Russia to achieve its foreign policy goals?
- Is there a new cold war between Russia and the West?

Further reading

For overviews of Russian foreign policy see Robert H. Donaldson and Joseph L. Nogee (2005, 3rd edn) *The Foreign Policy of Russia: Changing Systems, Enduring Interests*, Armonk, NY: M. E. Sharpe, Inc; Andrei Melville and Tatiana Shakleina (eds) (2005) *Russian Foreign Policy In Transition: Concepts and Realities*, Budapest-New York: Central European University Press; Peter Duncan (2005) *Russian Foreign Policy from El'tsin to Putin*, London: Routledge. On Putin's foreign policy, try J. L. Black (2004) *Vladimir Putin and the New World Order: Looking East, Looking West?*, Lanham, MD: Rowman and Littlefield; and Bobo Lo (2003) *Vladimir Putin and the Evolution of Russian Foreign Policy*, Oxford: Blackwell/Royal Institute of International Affairs. For analyses arguing that there is a new cold war, see Edward Lucas (2008) *A New Cold War: How the Kremlin Menaces both Russia and the West*, London: Bloomsbury; Mark McKinnon (2007) *The New Cold War. Revolutions, Rigged Elections and Pipeline Politics*, New York: Carroll and Graf, which also looks at Russia and the pro-democracy movements in eastern Europe.

On Russia's energy sector including its political uses, see Fiona Hill (2004) 'Energy Empire: Oil, Gas and Russia's Revival', September, *The Foreign Policy Centre* website, http://fpc.org.uk/. Ida Garibaldi and Andrew Kuchins (2008) debate whether Russia is using energy as a political or an economic weapon in 'Opposing Views: Should NATO Defend Europe Against Russia's Energy Weapon?', 2 April, *RFERL* website, http://www.rferl.org/.

A very useful overview of the relationship between Russia's identity and its foreign policy is offered in Andrei Piontkovsky (2006) 'East or West? Russia's Identity Crisis in Foreign Policy', *The Foreign Policy Centre* website, January, http://fpc.org.uk/. Galina M. Yemelianova provides a far-ranging analysis of Islam both within Russian and the Near Abroad in her (2007) 'The Rise of Islam in Muslim Eurasia: Internal Determinants and Potential Consequences', *The China and Eurasia Forum Quarterly*, 5 (2), May, available on the Russian-Eurasian Security website, http://www.res.ethz.ch.

Useful websites

Commonwealth of Independent States (CIS): http://cis.minsk.by/

European Union (including Russia-EU Summits): http://europa.eu/

The European Commission's Delegation to Russia: http://www.delrus.ec.europa.eu/en/index.htm

The [EU-funded] Kaliningrad Development Agency: http://www.kaliningrad-rda.org/en/

The Conflict Studies Research Centre, Defence Academy of the United Kingdom: carries topical analyses of Russian foreign policy in their Russian Series and Central Asian Series, http://www.defac.ac.uk/

Russian-Eurasian Security: carries topical analyses of foreign policy and security issues, including an online journal called *Russia in Global Affairs*, http://www.res.ethz.ch

Centre for European Reform: is a think-tank whose website carries regularly updated analyses and publications on Russia's relations with Europe, including issues such as energy, Georgia, NATO enlargement, trade and WTO membership, http://www.cer.org.uk

The BBC website has a useful section on the Georgia-Russia conflict: http://news.bbc.co.uk/1/hi/in_depth/europe/2008/georgia_russia_conflict/default.stm

The NATO–Russia Council: http://www.nato-russia-council.info/htm/EN/index.shtml

References

Brzezinski, Z. (1997) *The Grand Chessboard. American Primacy and its Geostrategic Imperatives*, New York: Basic Books

Bush, G. W. (2001) 'President Bush and President Putin Talk to Crawford Students', Press Release, 15 November, White House website, http://www.whitehouse.gov/news/

CIA (1999) *The World Factbook 1999 – Russia* (adapted), http://www.cia.gov/library/publications/the-world-factbook

Dalziel, S. (2002) 'The problem with the Pankisi', *BBC news* website, 5 August, http://news.bbc.co.uk

de Haas, M. (2007) 'Russia's Upcoming Revised Military Doctrine', *PINR* website, 26 February, http://www.pinr.com/

Dugin, A. (2001) '*Yevraziistvo: ot filosofii k politike'*, *Nezavisimaia Gazeta*, 30 May, 8

EU (2003) 'A Secure Europe in a Better World, European Security Strategy, 2003', 12 December, 1–15, The Council of the EU (Brussels) website, http://www.consilium.europa.eu/uedocs/cmsUpload/78367.pdf

Finn, P. (2006) 'Iran, Russia reach Tentative Deal', *Washington Post*, 27 February, A09

Hearst, D. (1996) 'How the East was won – and lost', *The Guardian*, 19 October, 21

Huntington, S. P. (1996) *The Clash of Civilizations and the Remaking of the World Order*, New York: Simon & Schuster

Ivanov, O. and Pozdnyakov, V. (1998) 'Russia and the European Union', *International Affairs* (Moscow), 44 (3), 49–55

Kessler, G. (2007) 'Rice, Putin Trade Cold War Words', *The Washington Post*, 1 June, A 12

Lloyd, J. (1998) *Rebirth of a Nation: An Anatomy of Russia*, London: Michael Joseph

NATO (1997) 'Founding Act on Mutual Relations, Co-operation and Security between NATO and the Russian Federation', 27 May, available on the NATO website, http://www.nato.int/

NATO (2008) 'Bucharest Summit Declaration', 3 April, NATO website, http://www.nato.int/docu/pr/2008/p08-049e.html

NUPI (1999) 'Russia updates military doctrine', 11 October, *NUPI* website, http://www2.nupi.no/cgi-win//Russland/krono.exe?4403

Nye, J. (1990) *Bound to Lead: The Changing Nature of American Power*, New York: Basic Books

Nye, J. (2004) *Soft Power: The Means to Success in World Politics*, New York: Public Affairs

Putin, V. (2007) 'Letter to commemorate 50th anniversary of the EU, 25 March 2007', The European Commission's Delegation to Russia website, http://www.delrus.ec.europa.eu/en/index.htm

RIA Novosti (2007a) 'NATO expansion erodes international trust – Putin', *RIA Novosti* website, 10 February, http://en.rian.ru/

RIA Novosti (2007b) 'Russia revises military doctrine to reflect global changes', *RIA Novosti* website, 5 March, http://en.rian.ru/

RIA Novosti (2008) 'Georgia has lost S. Ossetia peacekeeping rights – Russian military', *RIA Novosti* website, 21 August, http://en.rian.ru/

Sevastopulo, D. (2007) 'Putin threatens to target missiles at Europe', *The Financial Times*, 3 June, 11

Solzhenitsyn, A. (1995) *The Russian Question at the end of the 20th Century*, London: The Harvill Press

Stankevich, S. (1992) 'Russia in Search of Itself', *The National Interest*, 28 Summer, 47–51

Stankevich, S. (1993) '*Rossiia: mezhdu aziatskim molotom i evropeiskoi nakoval'nei*', *Rossiiskoe Obozrenie*, (6), 8 September, 1993, 1–2

Yasmann, V. (2006) 'Russia: Independence Votes popular In the Kremlin', *RFE/RL* Feature Article, 15 September, *RFE/RL* website, http://www.rferl.org/

Zhirinovsky, V. (1993) *Poslednii brosok na iug*, Moscow: LPD

Zyuganov, G. A. and Podberezin, A. I. (eds) (1995) *Rossiia pered vyborom*, Moscow: *Obozrevatel'*

Chapter 14

The economy and economic policy

Learning objectives

- To introduce and explain the liberal and centrist approaches to the economy.
- To explain the main components of shock therapy.
- To explain Putin's economic agenda.
- To analyse the development of state corporatism.

Introduction

In January 1992 Russia embarked upon a programme of 'shock therapy' or 'big bang' designed to transform it from a soviet economy to a capitalist economy as quickly as possible. In the face of mounting economic problems and domestic opposition, shock therapy was quickly abandoned and Russia slowed the pace of its economic transition. In policy making Russia's economic liberals vied for influence with those favouring a more centrist approach. Putin took office determined to push forward economic reform in order to strengthen the economy and bring prosperity to the Russian people. While he wanted to integrate Russia more firmly within the global economy, he wanted to end the exploitation, the vulnerability and 'third worldisation' that had characterised Russia's interaction with the western capitalist economies in the 1990s. In 2006 Russia held the presidency of the G8, the organisation of the world's eight leading industrial nations, and Russia is now recognised as a market economy so its transition seems complete. Problems remain, however, notably the dependence on primary products – particularly oil and gas – and the low number of small and medium size enterprises in comparison to the other G8 countries. The Russian economy is dominated by conglomerates owned by a few oligarchs and under Putin increasingly by state-controlled corporations.

> ## Box 14.1 Economic terms
>
> **Economic structure**: the share of the different sectors (agriculture, industry and services) within an economy.
>
> **Market**: a system of exchange in which buyers' demands interact with the sellers' supply. The existence of a market is a prerequisite of capitalism, but markets may also exist in socialist systems.
>
> **A free market**: exists when the interactions between buyers and sellers are not subject to external interventions such as the government setting minimum or maximum prices or by the operation of cartels or monopolies.
>
> **Inflation**: exists when a sustained rise in the prices of goods and/or services reduces the buying power of a currency.
>
> **Hyperinflation**: an inflation rate of over 50 per cent a month.
>
> **Monetarism**: the advocacy of control of the money supply in order to control inflation.
>
> **Money supply**: the amount of money within an economy.

Forward to capitalism!

Russia's economic liberals: Gaidar's gang

After the August 1991 coup, Yeltsin chose Yegor Gaidar to put together a plan for an independent Russian economy. Gaidar's economics team, dubbed 'Gaidar's gang' after the popular soviet children's book *Timur and his Gang* written by Gaidar's grandfather, were typically only in their early thirties; they were extremely well-educated, spoke foreign languages and were well versed in the theories of the western, liberal economists that they so admired. In contrast to the old men who had dominated the soviet scene, Gaidar's gang represented not only a radically different approach to the economy but also the arrival of a new generation in positions of authority. Gaidar's gang had not worked on the various soviet economic reform programmes designed by Aganbegyan, Shatalin, Petrakov, Abalkin and Yavlinsky. Instead they had spent the 1980s in covert, informal, radical but theoretical discussions about how to transform a centrally planned economy (CPE) into a western style, capitalist economy. They had no practical experience but did have a wealth of self-confidence and an unwavering belief in the correctness of their ideas. In 1990 Gaidar had established an unofficial think-tank called the Institute of Market Reform, which drew on his contacts with like-minded soviet bloc economists such as János Kornai from Hungary, Václav Klaus from Czechoslovakia and Leszek Balcerowicz from Poland. After 1989 Balcerowicz together with Jeffrey Sachs had formulated a programme of economic shock therapy, known as the Balcerowicz Plan, to transform the Polish CPE into a capitalist economy. Gaidar drew on the Balcerowicz Plan when he wrote the economic part of Yeltsin's October 1991 opening speech to parliament, in which he announced that Russia would introduce shock therapy on 1 January 1992.

Box 14.2 The soviet legacy: initial economic conditions

- **Economic disruption and crisis**: by 1992 Russia had already experienced the Brezhnev-era stagnation and the disruption caused by *perestroika*'s half-hearted market reforms. As the USSR hurtled towards disintegration the CPE was teetering on the brink of collapse.

- **The economic structure**: the soviet economy was dominated by technologically outdated, inefficient and ecologically destructive, heavy industry. Agriculture, light industry and the service sector were poorly developed. For decades the soviet state had directed a disproportionate amount of investment into its gigantic military-industrial complexes, heavy industry, machine building, extraction and metallurgical industries, but these were plagued by a growing technology gap with the West. Russia is, however, rich in natural resources such as uranium, gold, oil, gas and diamonds.

- **Changing trade patterns**: in 1989 the former soviet states in Europe took the strategic decision to look to the West for political, military and economic partners. In 1990 this reorientation, together with Russia's economic crisis, led to a fall of around 60 per cent in Russian exports to the Comecon countries (Frydman et al., 1993: 14). Then in 1991 Comecon was formally abolished. As the USSR was disintegrating its constituent republics also began to reorient themselves; the Baltic states towards the West and the central Asian states towards the Middle East, Turkey, Iran and Pakistan. In 1990 70 per cent of Russia's exports worth US$157 billion were to the other soviet republics but in 1991 the value of Russian exports to the other republics had fallen to US$142 billion.

- **Government spending and hidden inflation**: the soviet government provided generous subsidies to industry and funded extensive welfare provisions; while RFSFR president Yeltsin increased demand on the government budget by promising to raise wages and pensions and to reduce taxes. In 1991 Russia had a budget deficit that was equivalent to 31.9 per cent of GDP and there was already considerable hidden inflation (Illarionov cited by Hedlund, 1999: 153). Following the collapse of the USSR, other FSU states (the rouble zone) continued to use the Russian rouble as their currency, which compromised Russia's ability to control its money supply. Russia's money supply grew rapidly during 1991–92 leading to further inflationary pressures.

- **Debt**: Yeltsin believed that following his announcement in October 1991 that Russia would introduce economic shock therapy, his western allies would write-off the soviet-era debts as they had for Poland. However, the debts were not written off and in December 1991 Russia agreed to assume responsibility for 61 per cent or US$37.2 billion of the USSR's external debt. The American economist Jeffrey Sachs criticised the decision not to write-off the debt and in

> **Box 14.2** (*Continued*)
>
> a letter to the *New York Times* on 4 July 1992 revealed that, although in 1990–91 Russia had received US$15.6 billion in western aid, US$13.1 billion of that sum had been used to service Russia's debt. So most of the West's aid to Russia went straight back to the West as debt repayments and so was not available for investment within the Russian economy.
>
> ■ **Lack of a capitalist infrastructure**: in the early 1990s Russia did not have commercial banks, stock exchanges, a labour market, an adequate distribution system, appropriate taxation regulations or an adequate legal framework for a market economy.
>
> ■ **Crime and corruption**: during *perestroika* crime and corruption grew. Then in the early 1990s the weakness of the Russian state and judiciary, the lack of an adequate legal basis for a market economy and the great resources literally up for grabs, all helped to encourage lawless behaviour (see Chapter 3). After decades of soviet condemnation of capitalism and then the lawlessness of the 1990s, entrepreneurial activity had a rather disreputable image.
>
> ■ **Human resources**: the USSR valued education and enjoyed near 100 per cent literacy rates and had world-class universities and colleges. These are tremendous assets. A problem for Russia in the 1990s was that it lacked people with the management, accountancy and marketing skills necessary for a capitalist rather than a socialist economy. Russia's high rates of alcoholism and the falling birthrate also continue to have a negative impact on the economy (see Chapter 15).

Russia's economic liberals and their western advisers

In November 1991 despite opposition from the Russian parliament (see Chapter 3), Yeltsin appointed the leading members of Gaidar's gang to key economic positions within the government. Gaidar was appointed finance minister and a deputy prime minister, Alexander Shokhin a deputy prime minister with responsibility for social affairs, Vladimir Lopukhin became energy minister (a post he lost to Chernomyrdin in 1992), Pyotr Aven became foreign trade minister and Anatoly Chubais became the head of the State Property Committee (GKI), which was established in October 1992 to supervise privatisation. In April 1992 Gaidar also brought in Andrei Illarionov as the first deputy director of the government's Working Centre for Economic Reforms. Then in June 1992 Gaidar became acting prime minister with responsibility for economic affairs and Chubais was promoted to one of the deputy prime minister posts. Yeltsin also acquired a growing number of western economic advisers including: Jeffrey Sachs on behalf of the IMF; Anders Åslund, who is now a senior fellow of the Peterson Institute in Washington; and the British economist Professor Richard Layard of the London School of Economics, who had advised the British Prime Minister Margaret Thatcher. Thatcher took a decade to privatise just 5 per cent of the UK economy – a country that already had well-established capitalist institutions and behaviour. Shock therapy had more ambitious aims in a country largely lacking in capitalist institutions and in which capitalist behaviour had been illegal until *perestroika*.

Shock therapy

Shock therapy was intended to transform Russia from a centrally planned economy (CPE) to capitalism at breakneck speed. Sachs advised that shock therapy should begin with price and trade liberalisation combined with macroeconomic stabilisation focusing on control of the money supply. On 2 January 1992 foreign trade was liberalised together with 80 per cent of domestic prices. Trade was duly liberalised later that month and the streets were immediately full of people selling handicrafts, household possessions, imported goods and reselling goods bought in state stores. After the shortages of the soviet era suddenly everything was for sale, but industrial and agricultural production continued to decline. The future prime minister Chernomyrdin dismissed the economic reforms as having turned Russia into a gigantic bazaar.

Box 14.3 The main components of shock therapy

- **Macroeconomic stabilisation (or adjustment)**: controlling inflation and stabilising the value of the currency, it also entails balancing the budget and the balance of payments.
- **Balance of payments**: the balance between a country's international spending and earnings.
- **Price liberalisation**: abandoning the state setting of prices and allowing market forces (supply and demand) to determine prices.
- **Trade liberalisation**: removing barriers to trade such as trade restrictions, import or export quotas and tariffs.
- **Currency convertibility**: the free exchange of one currency for another.
- **Privatisation**: is a form of institutional reform, ending the state ownership of economic concerns and replacing it with private ownership by individuals, companies, investment groups.
- **Enterprise restructuring**: entails a variety of reforms which include breaking up enterprises into economically viable units, reducing the labour force, retraining workers and management, and bringing in new management techniques.
- **Structural-institutional reforms**: the reforms necessary to establish a market economy, these include legal reforms, anti-monopoly regulations, changes to the taxation system, establishing new accounting systems, the development of new pro-market attitudes.

Voucher privatisation – October 1992 to June 1994

The privatisation of state enterprises was both an important microeconomic reform and an attempt to generate popular support for the economic reforms. Anatoly Chubais the chair of the State Property Committee (GKI) introduced a modified form of the voucher privatisation scheme that had been introduced in Czechoslovakia in 1990. In the autumn of 1992 Russian adults were issued with 10,000 roubles worth of vouchers which were worth the equivalent of US$20. Ninety per cent of adults collected their vouchers which they could then use to buy shares at auction or invest in mutual funds. Many of these funds turned out to be sham financial pyramid schemes that eventually collapsed. Stock exchanges only gradually developed but mostly after, rather than before, privatisation. Nearly 75 per cent of enterprises opted for a worker buy-out model of privatisation, through which workers had special access to 51 per cent of the shares and a minimum of only 29 per cent of shares had to be sold to outsiders for vouchers. In this way most privatisation was conducted as a form of insider (management and worker) privatisation, which kept the existing management in place and maintained the status quo in management–worker relations. By the end of 1993 45 per cent of enterprises had been privatised; by 1996 this figure had risen to 70 per cent. Throughout Russia some 60 per cent of shops and cafés were privatised by August 1992, either through auctions or by direct sale to the retail management and workers.

In this first round of privatisation (1992–94) a lot of the privatised enterprises were so outdated that they had very little real value and the method of privatisation did not bring in new investment for these enterprises. Most industrial enterprises were extremely large by western standards and for them to compete economically, harsh decisions needed to be made about what parts were viable and what were not, about reducing the workforce and changing the management. However, worker and management buy-outs resulted in ownership structures that did not facilitate this kind of decision making. The result was that these enterprises were not broken down into small and medium size enterprises (SMEs) and even by 2000 Russia had very few SMEs when compared to mature market economies.

Voucher privatisation didn't really work

Liberals, centrists and economic reform

At the height of the liberals' influence in 1991–92, they had never managed to completely dominate economic policy. They believed that in the short-term shock therapy would lead to rising prices and unemployment and falling production, but that these problems would ultimately lead to a stronger economy. Throughout 1992 and into 1993 opposition to shock therapy and Yeltsin's leadership began to mount in response to the turmoil and poverty that had been unleashed (see Chapter 3 Box 3.4). Yeltsin responded by sacrificing Gaidar, replaced as prime minister in December 1992 by Chernomyrdin who opposed shock therapy. Then in July 1992 Viktor Gerashchenko, who had headed the Central Bank under Gorbachev, was appointed to head the Russian Central Bank (RCB). Gerashchenko also opposed shock therapy and the IMF's instructions to control the money supply in order to stabilise the rouble and reduce inflation. In the first three months after Gerashchenko's appointment the money supply tripled as he continued to subsidise ailing enterprises and to supply roubles to the rouble zone.

These new appointments did not mean that liberal policies were entirely abandoned in favour of more centrist policies. In July 1992 Boris Fyodorov returned from a senior executive post at the European Bank for Reconstruction and Development in London to become Yeltsin's chief economic strategist, as deputy prime minister for finance and economic policy from March 1993 to October 1994. Fydorov had wanted to head the RCB and throughout 1993 he was in constant conflict with Gerashchenko over the failure to control the money supply. Liberals were not entirely removed from government even after the disastrous showing of the liberal parties in the December 1993 Duma elections. Chubais, for example, remained head of the GKI overseeing privatisation. Rather than liberal economics being abandoned in favour of a centrist approach, it is more accurate to think in terms of the balance of economic policy shifting towards the centrists. Andrei Illarionov later complained that Russia could have been a textbook example of economic liberalism if only the Yeltsin Government had continued the reforms begun on 2 January 1992.

The development of centrism in the 1990s

In the 1990s a centrist approach to the economy was championed by industrial enterprise managers who enjoyed the greater autonomy and control over their enterprises that they had acquired under Gorbachev, but were alarmed by what they perceived as a lack of state support for industry under Yeltsin. In mid-1992 the leading centrist Arkady Volsky brought together his Russian Union of Industrialists and Entrepreneurs (RUIE) and other centrist parties, including the Democratic Party and the Peoples' Party of Free Russia (the heir to Rutskoi's Democratic Communists), to form a new political party called the Civic Union. The centrist approach to the economy includes a belief in the need for a strong, interventionist state in contrast to the economic liberals' support for the Washington consensus belief that states should have only a minimal role and that they should not intervene in the operation of the economic market. Centrists argue that Russia needs a strong state to protect Russian interests in the global arena and to counter the centrifugal forces within Russia itself. In the 1990s the centrists believed that the state should maintain subsidies and provide soft credits to enterprises while also reducing their tax burdens, in order to prevent them from going bankrupt and so to maintain high levels of employment. In what might initially seem a strange alliance, but one that makes perfect sense in the Russian industrial environment, the managers' organisation (the RUIE) worked closely with the new Federation of Independent Trade Unions (FNPR) in order to lobby for the maintenance of real wage levels, state support for industry and extensive welfare provisions. The centrists also believe that Russia should have a strong military and that the defence industries should receive state protection and support. For example, the centrist Yury Skokov, the chair of the Security Council and a close ally of Yeltsin, lobbied hard to maintain defence spending and subsidies for the defence industries. Putin and his allies from the security and military services (the *siloviki*) share these centrist beliefs in the importance of a strong state and adopted policies to support the military and defence industries.

Loans-for-shares privatisation

In a controversial second round of privatisation (1995–96) the GKI auctioned the state's shares in selected enterprises in return for cash loans. This privatisation focused on the gigantic coal, gas and electricity monopolies, and on the oil and mineral industries. The oil industry was already divided into a dozen separate companies in which the government had majority stakes. When the loans were not repaid the firms were auctioned so that huge tranches of the country's most valuable assets were sold to Russia's oligarchs and emerging Financial-Industrial Groups at bargain prices. The auctions were characterised by corruption and a lack of transparency at all stages and at all levels; most of the auctions were won by the bank that was running the auction or by a subsidiary of the company being sold. When *Surgutneftegaz* (Surgut Oil and Gas) in Tyumen, Siberia was auctioned, the whole city was effectively closed for the day to prevent their dreaded rivals *Rosneft* (Russian oil) from bidding. The airport was closed, telephone lines were cut off and – just in case any outsider had managed to slip through – armed guards were put on the doors of the auction building (Lloyd, 1998: 251). In this way Boris Berezovsky acquired Russia's ninth largest oil concern *Sibneft* for just US$100 million. It was during this round of privatisation, conducted in advance of the 1996 presidential elections, that the oligarchs' economic and political power was consolidated and their support for Yeltsin assured.

> ## Box 14.4 Institutional overview of the economics ministries
>
> - In 1997 the Ministry of the Economy absorbed the functions of the former Ministries of Industry and Defence Industry and in 1998 some Ministry of the Economy's functions were transferred to a short-lived Ministry of Industry and Trade.
>
> - In April 1998 the Ministry of Foreign Economic Relations and Trade was abolished by presidential decree and its functions transferred to the new Ministry of Industry and Trade. Then by another presidential decree, in September 1998, its former functions were transferred again to the new Ministry of Trade.
>
> - On 17 May 2000 Putin abolished the Ministry of the Economy and transferred its functions to the new Ministry for Economic Development and Trade and the Ministry for Industry, Science and Technologies. The latter was responsible for devising state science and technology policy, promoting and coordinating R&D efforts with national interests, and armaments exports. It was superseded in March 2004 by the Ministry of Industry and Energy (*Minpromenergo*). German Gref, a leading economic liberal, served as the minister for Economic Development and Trade from 20 May 2004 to 24 September 2007; he was then replaced by his deputy, Elvira Nabiullina.

> **Box 14.4** (*Continued*)
>
> ■ On 12 May 2008 Medvedev reorganised various economic ministries. The Ministry of Economic Development and Trade became the Ministry of Economic Development and is headed by Elvira Nabiullina. Then Viktor Khristenko's Ministry of Industry and Energy became the Ministry of Industry and Trade and a new Ministry of Energy headed by Sergei Shmatko. Alexei Kudrin remained as the Minister of Finance as did Alexei Gordeyev as Minister of Agriculture.
>
> *Useful websites*
>
> Ministry for Economic Development and Trade: http://www.economy.gov.ru/
> Ministry of Industry and Energy: http://www.minprom.gov.ru/eng

Economic liberals and the August 1998 economic crisis

A government reshuffle in March 1997 brought liberal economists to prominence once more. Chubais, who had been sacked in 1996, was brought in as the minister responsible for financial dealings with the IMF, and Boris Nemtsov became the oil and gas minister with Sergei Kiriyenko as his deputy. Mikhail Zadornov was the finance minister and Boris Fyodorov oversaw tax collection. Chernomyrdin was fortuitously sacked as prime minister in March 1998 and replaced by Kiriyenko who became the fall guy for the August 1998 economic crisis. The Asian economic crisis contributed to Russia's economic crisis as it led to a fall in world crude oil prices from US$22 for a barrel in 1997 to US$12 in August 1998. The fall in the price of crude oil meant that the Russian government lost an estimated US$43.5 billion in tax revenues (Crace, 1998: 11), so depleting Russia's gold and hard currency reserves. The economic success story of the previous three years had been the stabilisation of the rouble. On 1 January 1998 the rouble was re-launched and new notes (bills) were issued minus all those embarrassing zeros that testified to the earlier hyperinflation. However, foreign banks began to dump the rouble and its value was only maintained by increasing interest rates to 42 per cent; the Russian Central Bank spent US$ 2 billion to support the rouble. In May 1998 Kiriyenko announced a sweeping 40 billion rouble or 8 per cent reduction in federal spending and regional budgets were also scrutinised for spending cuts.

By July 1998 Chubais had negotiated a new US$22.6 billion IMF rescue package to support the rouble, so averting devaluation and to boost Russia's foreign currency reserves, which were down to less than US$15 billion (Hawkins et al., 1998: 10). The IMF believed that the new loan would also encourage Russian and foreign investors to buy new lower interest state short-term bonds (GKOs) and that Moscow would be able to meet the payments on earlier bonds and have enough funds to cover its budget spending. George Soros (1998), the influential international financier, attacked the IMF's solution arguing instead that the rouble should be devalued. In the first six months of 1998 the value of the Russian stock market fell by 50 per cent and by the end of Black Thursday – 13 August 1998 – the total value of the Russian Stock market had fallen by 84 per cent. The Russian stock market was now worth less on the London Stock Exchange than Sainsbury's the British supermarket (Elliott et al., 1998: 1). On 17 August 1998 Kiriyenko finally ignored IMF advice and announced that the rouble would be allowed to fall by 20 per cent and introduced new currency controls. He also announced a moratorium on the payment of Russia's foreign debts and government bonds (GKOs).

Primakov and the rejection of IMF advice

In the aftermath of the 1998 August economic crisis Yeltsin changed his economics team to include more centrists. Kiriyenko was replaced as prime minister by the centrist Yevgeny Primakov and Gerashchenko was reappointed to the Russian Central Bank to replace the liberal Sergei Dubinin. Primakov rounded on the IMF, on Russia's liberal reformers and particularly on Chubais, accusing them of making a fetish of macroeconomic stability above all other economic goals. Against IMF advice Primakov introduced tighter currency controls, raised government spending on investment in industry and agriculture, and increased duties on imported goods. The devaluation of the rouble made imports more expensive which helped to protect domestic producers and it also made Russian exports cheaper. The trebling of the price of crude oil on world markets in 1999 provided Russia with the opportunity to replenish its hard currency reserves. These factors helped the economy to rebound quickly from the 1998 economic crisis and during 1999–2005 the real annual growth in Gross Domestic Product (GDP) averaged 6.7 per cent (OECD, 2006). However, the competitive advantages enjoyed by Russian producers after 1998, specifically the high price of oil, gas and other commodities, are not enough on their own to sustain continued economic growth. Further economic reforms, including the development of more small and medium size enterprises, the development of the service sector, the modernisation of agricultural production and the wide-scale adoption of new technologies are all still required.

Putin: liberalism and state corporatism?

Putin's economic agenda

In his first presidential Annual Address to the Federal Assembly on 8 July 2000, Putin set out his political and economic agenda. He warned that although the economy was improving, Russia was on the verge of becoming a Third World nation unless its economic problems were urgently addressed and sustainable growth achieved. Although committed to strengthening the state, Putin argued that the state was intervening in areas where it was not needed but not doing things that were needed; therefore, the strategic policy was 'less administration, more free enterprise, more freedom to produce, to trade, and to invest' (Putin, 2000). He argued that problems such as the shadow economy, corruption and the mass flow of capital abroad, were encouraged by the state's vague rules and unjustified restrictions. He identified high taxes, the arbitrariness of state officials and crime as the main obstacles to economic growth and committed his administration to reform the tax system and the state (civil) service.

Box 14.5 Putin's six fundamental principles to deal with Russia's economic crisis in Annual Address to the Federal Assembly, 8 July 2000

- **The protection of property rights**: including guaranteeing shareholders' access to information, the protection of property rights and establishing the legal basis of private property in land and property.

- **Ensuring equality of conditions of competition**: ending the situation in which some enterprises pay lower taxes on energy resources, are allowed not to pay debts and enjoy other privileges. To establish an equal approach to the distribution of state funds, licences, quotas and selective use of bankruptcy procedure.

- **Freeing entrepreneurs from administrative pressure and simplifying procedures**: ending the arbitrary interpretation of legislative norms by central and regional officials, which oppresses entrepreneurs and encourages corruption.

- **Reducing the tax burden**: to avoid tax avoidance and the shadow economy, encourage investment and competitiveness. Simplifying the customs system and unifying tariffs.

- **Developing the financial infrastructure**: including getting rid of inefficient banks and encouraging banking transparency. Using the stock market to direct investment within the economy.

- **Adopting a realistic social policy**: ending the economically impossible and politically inadvisable policy of general state paternalism.

Source: The Kremlin website, http://www.kremlin.ru/eng/

Some progress has been made on these six principles. In 2000–2001 a flat rate of tax and VAT was introduced, which led to better tax collection. A Unified Social Tax was introduced in 2005 as part of a package of pension, healthcare and social benefits reforms (see Chapter 15). A new Customs Code was adopted in April 2003 and in 2004 the State Customs Committee was transformed into the Federal Customs Service. However, problems remain, including ensuring fairness in the way that businesses are treated and reducing their administrative burdens. This is part of the broader problems of Russia's poorly developed judiciary and legal environment, and the lack of corporate and government transparency, none of which were adequately addressed under Putin. Although Putin did not engage in a wholesale reversal of the privatisations of the 1990s, he did attack the property rights of selected oligarchs such as Gusinsky, Berezovsky and Khodorkovsky, which seems to indicate that property rights are subject to a political veto. In 2001 Russia finally adopted its first post-soviet Land Code, which allowed Russian citizens to own, buy and sell land; an additional law adopted in 2002 legalised the buying and selling of agricultural land.

Putin's economics team: liberals and centrists

To plan and carry forward his agenda Putin appointed leading liberals to his economics team in 2000. Andrei Illarionov became Putin's chief economic adviser and until 2005 also served as Russia's envoy to the G8, German Gref was appointed minister of the newly formed Ministry of Economic Development and Trade, Alexei Kudrin became finance minister and then, in 2004, Mikhail Zurabov became minister of health and social development. Gerashchenko stayed as head of the RCB until 2002 and continued to champion a more centrist approach to the economy. Putin's budget for 2001 reflected the economics liberals' belief in the crucial importance of cutting government spending, ending deficits and reducing government subsidies to producers in order to achieve macroeconomic stabilisation.

Putin's emphasis on the need to strengthen the state might seem to put him at odds with the Washington consensus championing of a minimal role for the state. By the end of the 1990s, in the face of the deleterious impact that failed or weak states had on the operation of the market, the IMF and the World Bank started to place greater emphasis on the need for capacity building than they had in the 1980s and early 1990s. In failed states governments have little control over what goes on within their borders; in its most extreme form this could be because there are armed forces (militias, terrorists, warlords) challenging the state. A state may also be weak and in danger of failing if it is ineffective, if it cannot enforce its laws due to factors such as political corruption, high crime rates, and bureaucratic and judicial ineffectiveness. When Putin took office the state was being directly challenged in Chechnia, but was also weakened by the failure to reform the state (civil) service in the 1990s, the lack of an independent judiciary and by corruption and crime. Putin, the IMF and the World Bank share the belief that Russia needs to address these challenges to the state and also needs to create the legal and institutional environment necessary for capitalism to flourish. Putin's emphasis is on the importance of microeconomic reform, the simplification of the tax system and improvement of tax collection, the simplification of the customs system and the improvement of the government's efficiency in framing and implementing legislation; these are all part of capacity building.

A major problem, however, is that in his bid to strengthen the state Putin has become increasingly authoritarian, and his curbs on the media and civil society have helped to create an environment in which crime and corruption flourished. In 2005 Illarionov resigned just before Russia was due to take over the presidency of the G8, complaining that under Putin Russia was no longer free and democratic (BBC, 2005). Illarionov had previously attacked the partial renationalisation of Khodorkovsky's Yukos oil company as the 'scam of the year' (Buckley, 2005). The development of state corporatism and of gigantic state-owned monopolies (see Box 14.9) does not fit with economic liberalism. Putin's stress on strengthening the state goes hand in hand with a reassertion of Russian nationalism, both of which reflect the concerns of the *siloviki*. Putin's nationalism is not about abandoning Russia's integration into the global economy or retreating into a form of isolationism. Whereas in the 1990s Russia went cap in hand to the IMF and the World Bank for loans and aid, it now has a growing economy and its commodities – especially oil and gas – give it considerable clout. Putin is determined to use these assets to strengthen Russia, so he approaches the IMF, World Bank and World Trade Organisation (WTO) from a position of strength.

Support for a market economy

Russians object to crime and corruption, the manner in which the old political and economic elites became the New Russians (see Chapter 3), excess profits and the lack of concern for the ordinary people. It is not capitalism as such that Russians object to, but to what they call their 'wild capitalism'. A survey conducted by Globespan in 2005 (see Box 14.6) found that 43 per cent of Russians supported a free market economy and 34 opposed it, showing less support than in the USA and Great Britain, but more support than in France.

Box 14.6 Support for free enterprise and free market economics

The percentage of respondents who agree or disagree with the statement, 'The free enterprise system and free market economy is the best system on which to base the development of the world' is listed below.

	Agree	Disagree
USA	71	24
Great Britain	66	27
Russia	43	34
France	36	50

Source: adapted from '20 Nation Poll Finds Strong Global Consensus: Support for Free Market System, But also More Regulation of Large Companies', 11 January 2006, *World Opinion* website, http://www.worldpublicopinion.org/

Russia and the world economy

In 2000 Putin asked, 'Will we be able to survive as a nation, as a civilisation, if our wellbeing, again and again, will depend on international loans and favours from leaders of the world economy?' (Putin, 2000). Rather than isolating the Russian economy, Putin instead sought economic development through further engagement within the global economy. In 2000 he improved Russia's standing in the global financial markets by abandoning the government's plan to approach the

> **Box 14.7** Foreign Minister Igor Ivanov on Russia's international economic relations
>
> The chief priority of Russia's foreign policy in the area of international economic relations is to foster the development of its national economy. In the context of globalisation, accomplishing this objective is inconceivable without Russia's broad inclusion in the system of world economic relations. Attaining this goal requires:
>
> ■ achieving favourable external conditions for the establishment of a market-type economy and for readjusting the Russian Federation's foreign-economic specialisation so as to ensure maximum economic benefits from its inclusion in the international division of labour;
>
> ■ minimising the risks entailed in Russia's further integration into the world economy with a view to ensuring our country's economy security;
>
> ■ promoting the creation of an equitable system of international trade in which the Russian Federation's full participation in economic organisations ensures that our country's national interests are defended within them . . .
>
> Source: *Nezavisimaia gazeta* (2000) 'The Foreign Policy Concept of the Russian Federation', *Nezavisimaia gazeta*, 11 July, 1 and 6

Paris Club to negotiate payment deferrals on debt servicing. Russia's growing stabilisation fund, based on oil tax revenues, enabled it to pay all of the soviet-era debts to the IMF and the Paris Club of creditors. Oil earnings also led to increased foreign currency reserves and pushed the balance of payments in Russia's favour and increased its reserves. The RF Ministry of Finance estimated that by 2008, Russia's national debt will reach a record low of 8.5 per cent of GDP. Exports have also grown steadily but are dominated by military hardware (see Chapter 9) and primary products, especially oil, gas, gold, diamonds, furs and timber products.

The inflow of capital into Russia increased from US$40 billion in 2006 to US$41 billion at the beginning of 2007 (Khmelev, 2007). Six countries account for 75 per cent of Russia's Foreign Direct Investment (FDI): Japan, Germany, UK, the Netherlands, USA and Cyprus (OECD, 2006). Russians do not need a visa to visit Cyprus so it is a favourite holiday destination and a good deal of the capital flight from Russia in the 1990s ended up in Cyprus; the FDI from Cyprus largely represents the return of this capital. FDI has mainly gone into the oil and gas sectors, but it has also been invested in the poorly developed goods and services sectors, including hotels, restaurants and telecommunications. McDonald's first arrived in Russia during *perestroika* and now has an extensive network of outlets as does Pizza Hut; IKEA now has shops in Moscow, St Petersburg and Kazan. The company UK Scottish and Newcastle invested heavily in Baltika beer, which is now Russia's leading brand. Russian first applied to join the WTO in the early 1990s but progress was very slow; however, Gref's economic agenda in 2000 placed renewed emphasis on WTO accession. Within Russia, however, there are powerful sector-based lobbies for steel and aluminium, banking and finance, agriculture, aircraft production and cars that want continued protection from outside competition. Continued protectionism is proving a barrier to Russian admission to the WTO.

Putin and the oligarchs

Putin came to office with a broad agenda of re-establishing the authority of the state and strengthening the presidency. He understood that the oligarchs' ownership of the most profitable parts of the economy gave them political power and that they had come to dominate economic policy making. Before the 2000 presidential election Putin announced that he intended to destroy the oligarchs as a class. His language was curiously reminiscent of Stalin's declaration that he intended to liquidate the Kulaks (rich peasants) as a class, in order to bring farms into collective ownership and state control. Putin, like Stalin before him, had identified a group blocking economic progress; however, unlike Stalin he has redefined the Kremlin's relations with the oligarchs rather than physically destroying them. In July 2000 after his election as president, Putin told a meeting of leading businesspeople that he did not intend to modify the outcome of the privatisations of the 1990s in the near future. This meant that although some of these privatisations had taken place in extremely dubious circumstances, their legality and, therefore, the private property rights that they established, would not be reversed. The recognition of private property rights is an important element of a market economy.

Putin adopted a policy of the 'equal proximity' of the elite business groups to the presidency and its administration, which significantly reduced the influence of particular oligarchs on decision making. In 2000 Putin appointed economic liberals such as Andrei Illarionov, German Greff, Aleksei Kudrin and Dmitry Kozak to his economics team. The economic liberals saw the oligarchs' giant corporations and monopolies as impediments to the operation of a market economy. Within the Putin administration the balance quickly tipped away from the economic liberals towards to a more centrist, corporatist approach to the economy. In 2004 Mikhail Kasyanov was droppped as prime minister and Kozak was transferred to deal with the Caucasus. Then in December 2005 Illarionov resigned in protest at growing state corporatism. Illarionov is an advocate of not only economic liberalism but also democratic reforms, which puts him at odds with the statist impulses of Putin and the *siloviki*. Illarionov complained that, 'I had come to the job to pursue an economic policy of broadening economic freedoms . . . We essentially ceased pursing that policy a minimum of two and a half years ago. . . . At the very least, the interests of some corporations, which one may call state corporations, have a disproportionate influence on decision-making' (cited by Cavan, 2006). Other leading liberals Mikhail Zubarov and Gref were finally dismissed as, respectively, the minister of health and social development and the minister for economics and trade in a cabinet reshuffle in September 2007. This left Kudrin, who was promoted to a deputy prime minister in the reshuffle, as the sole remaining liberal in Putin's government.

Box 14.8 Russia's 10 richest oligarchs

Oleg Deripaska

Forbes world ranking – 9 Fortune: US$28 bn
In the late 1990s gained control of Russian Aluminium (UC Rusal), Russia's largest producer. His Basic Element holding company owns Rusal (Russian Aluminium), car manufacturer GAZ, aircraft manufacturer Aviacor and insurance company Ingosstrakh. In 2005 he bought the Razvitie (Development) building firm from Kerimov. In 2007 merged Rusal with SUAL and Glencore International of Switzerland to create the world's largest aluminium producer. Deripaska holds 66 per cent of its shares. He is married to Polina, the daughter of Yeltsin's former chief of staff Valentin Yumashev. He is currently trying to gain a stake in Norilsk Nickel.

Roman Abramovich

Forbes world ranking – 15 Fortune: US$23.5 bn
In the early 1990s became rich through controversial oil-export. In 1995 with Boris Berezovsky acquired Sibneft oil for a fraction of its true value. When Berezovsky fled Russia in 2000, Abramovich bought his shares. In 2000 bought most of Russia's aluminium industry and merged them with Deripaska's Russian aluminium to create UC Rusal (Russian Aluminium). In 2003 he bought over half the shares of Chelsea Football Club, he is thought to have raised the money by selling his shares in Aeroflot. In 2003–2004, he sold his stake in Russian Aluminum to Oleg Deripaska. In 2005 sold his 72.6 per cent share in Sibneft to Gazprom for $13 billion, so liquidating his largest asset. In 2006, although he tried to resign, he was re-appointed governor of Chukotka by Putin. Also in 2006 he bought a stake in Russia's largest steelmaker the Evraz Group. Lives in London.

Alexei Mordashov

Forbes world ranking – 18 Fortune: US$21.2 bn
In the 1990s bought most of the shares in the steel mill where he was finance director and became its general director. Turned it into a conglomerate with interests in coal, ports, transportation and car building. Heads Severstal, Russia's third largest steel company, and in 2007 sold Severstal-Auto to its managers.

Mikhail Fridman

Forbes world ranking – 20 Fortune: US$20.8 bn
In 1989 with German Khan and Alexei Kuzmichov founded Alpha Group, which has interests in oil, retail, telecom (Vimpelcom and Megafon) and banking. In 2003 merged oil company TNK (Tyumen Oil Company) with BP. Has good connections with Kremlin.

Vladimir Lisin

Forbes world ranking – 21 Fortune: US$20.3 bn
In 1992 joined the 'Trans-World' group of traders who came to dominate Russia's aluminium and steel exports. In 2000 he gained a majority stake in the Novolipetsk steel mill. Expanded interests into a seaport, energy company, iron-ore, coal and timber.

Box 14.8 (*Continued*)

Mikhail Prokhorov

Forbes world ranking – 24   Fortune: US$19.5 bn
Built up Interros holding company, which has interests in metals, engineering, agriculture and media with Potanin. In 2002 he became chair of Norilsk Nickel. In 2007 it was agreed Prokhorov would buy Potanin's stake in Polyus Gold and Potanin would buy Prokhorov's stake in Norilsk Nickel.

Vladimir Potanin

Forbes world ranking – 25   Fortune: US$19.3 bn
Built up Interros holding company, which has interests in metals, engineering, agriculture and media with Prokhorov. Together they took over the giant Norilsk Nickel and the oil company Sidanco in the controversial loans for shares auctions. Partner with George Soros in telecom monopoly Sviazinvest. He has served as a deputy prime minister for the economy. In 2007 it was agreed Prokhorov would buy Potanin's stake in Polyus Gold and Potanin would buy Prokhorov's stake in Norilsk Nickel.

Suleiman Kerimov

Forbes world ranking – 36   Fortune: US$17.5 bn
In the early 1990s began buying companies cheaply and selling them for a profit: Vnukovo airline, Murmansk Airport, Avtobank, Nosta metal plant and Ingosstrakh insurance. Also bought a stake in Transneft oil-transportation monopoly. Since 2004 he has been buying shares in Gazprom, the state-run and world's largest gas producer, and Sberbank, Russia's largest retail bank.

German Khan

Forbes world ranking – 54   Fortune: US$13.9 bn
In 1989 with Mikhail Fridman co-founded Alfa-Eco, a commodities trading company, which became the Alpha Group. Heads Alpha Group's oil business, executive director of TNK-BP.

Vagit Alekperov

Forbes world ranking – 56   Fortune: US$13 bn
In 1991 as the soviet deputy minister of fuel and energy he set up Lukoil from the Langepas, Urai and Kogalym oil fields. Lukoil was then bought by its management headed by Alekperov, who is Lukoil's largest shareholder. Currently buying petrol stations in Europe and USA. He has close connections to the Kremlin.

Source: adapted from Luisa Kroll (ed.) (2008) 'The World's Billionaires', *Forbes* website, http://www.forbes.com/

Putin, re-nationalisation and the development of state corporatism

Under Putin state-controlled corporations, whose boards are dominated by government representatives, took control of the most important sectors of the economy. The attack on the oligarchs who owned most of Russia's natural monopolies was a vital aspect of creating these state corporations. Many of the oligarchs were not diligent tax payers and their corporations were not models of transparent accountancy practices and corporate good governance. This meant that although Russia is the world's largest energy exporter the state nonetheless lacked funds. Far from destroying the oligarchs as a class, Putin only sought to destroy those who presented a political challenge, principally Vladimir Gusinsky and Boris Berezovsky, both of whom now live abroad, and Mikhail Khodorkovsky who is now in prison (see Chapter 8). The irony is that Khodorkovsky's Yukos, which in 2004 was Russia's largest oil company, was also one of its better run companies. In December 2004 Yukos's most valuable oil and gas asset Yugankneftegaz was auctioned by the Kremlin in a move that transferred ownership to the state-owned Rosneft. Putin exercised control over these companies and their assets by placing his allies on their boards (see Box 14.9). Once either directly or indirectly under state control,

Box 14.9 Russia's state-controlled companies

Gazprom was founded in 1989 and is the world's largest natural gas extractor and Russia's largest company. In July 2007 the Duma agreed that Gazprom should form its own special armed units to protect its facilities. Its CEO is Alexei Miller and since 2000 Dmitry Medvedev was first the chair, then deputy chair, and then the chair again. After his election as president, Medvedev had to stand down as Gazprom chair and was replaced by the former prime minister Viktor Zubkov. German Gref joined the board in 1999 but in 2008 he was replaced by Elvira Nabiullina who had replaced him as the minister for trade and economic development in September 2007. The board also includes Viktor Khristenko the minister for industry and energy.

Website: http://www.gazprom.com/

Rosneft (Russian oil) is an oil and gas company, which was founded in 1993 as a state enterprise. In 1995 it became a joint stock company, but is effectively owned and controlled by the state. Rosneft's president since 1998 is Sergei Bogdanchikov whose career has been in the oil industry. Igor Sechin, Rosneft's chair since 2004, oversees Rosneft on behalf of the Kremlin. Sechin became a presidential aide in 2000 and rose to be deputy head of Putin's presidential administration. Other important board members include the Petersburger Gleb

Box 14.9 *(Continued)*

Nikitin who currently heads the Federal Property Management Agency; Kirill Androsov who is the deputy minister of economic development and trade; Sergei Naryshkin who is a deputy prime minister and Andrei Reus the deputy minister of industry and energy.

Website: http://www.rosneft.com/

Unified Energy Systems is Russia's largest power holding company, generating electricity for Russia and for export. The government is the majority shareholder. RAO UES's chair is Anatoly Chubais and its board includes Aleksandr Voloshin the head of Putin's presidential administration; German Gref the former minister of economic development and trade; Viktor Khristenko minister of industry, power and energy and Yury Medvedev the deputy head of the Federal Property Management Agency.

Website: http://www.rao-ees.ru/en/

Transneftprodukt was established in 1993 and is responsible for the coordination and management of the transportation of oil products, including the development of oil product pipelines. It is a wholly government-owned monopoly. From 2004–2006 the president of Transneftprodukt was Vladislav Surkov, the deputy head of the presidential administration. When he resigned he was replaced as president by Sergei Maslov who formerly worked for Lukoil. Transneftprodukt's board includes Dmitry Petrov of the president's administration and Andrei Reus the deputy minister of energy.

Website: http://eng.transnefteprodukt.ru/

Transneft (literally oil transportation) was established in 1992 as the successor to the USSR Ministry of Oil Industry's Glavtransneft. Transneft is entirely government-owned and runs Russia's oil pipelines. In July 2007 the Duma agreed that Transneft should form its own special armed units to protect its facilities. Simon Vainshtock has been the president of Transneft since 1999 and before that he was the vice-president of Lukoil from 1995 to 1999. Transneft's board includes Viktor Khristenko the minister of industry and energy; Arkady Dvokovich the head of the President's Expert Department; Andrei Dementiev the deputy minister for industry and energy; Yury Medvedev the deputy head of the Federal Property Management Agency; Sergei Oganesyan the head of the Federal Energy Agency; Dmitry Petrov an adviser of the President's Expert Department; Dmitry Ryzhkov the deputy head of government staff and Andrei Sharonov the deputy minister for trade and economic development.

Website: http://www.transneft.ru/Default.asp?LANG=EN

Box 14.9 (Continued)

Tvel is a joint stock company founded in 1996 and is entirely state-owned. Tvel has a controlling interest in Russia's nuclear fuel-manufacturing enterprises and is Russia's primary nuclear fuel exporter. Tvel is chaired by Sergei Sobyanin who is the former presidential plenipotentiary to the Urals 2000–2001 and from 2001–2005 was the governor of Tyumen region. From 2001–2005 he was chief of the presidential staff.

Website: http://www.tvel.ru/en/

Alrosa Co. Ltd. was established in 1992 and is engaged in exploration, mining and manufacture. It accounts for almost all of Russia's diamond production and for between 20–25 per cent of global diamond production. Aleksandr Nichiporuk has been Alrosa's president since 2004 and Alexei Kudrin, the former finance minister, is a member of the board.

Website: http://eng.alrosa.ru/

Svyazinvest (or Sviaizinvest) is Russia's largest telecommunications company. It was founded in 1994 and since 1995 it has been entirely government-owned. Aleksandr Kiselev (or Kiselyov) has been Svyazinvest's director general since June 2006. He is a Petersburger and a former deputy minister of communications. Svyazinvest's chair is Leonid Reiman who worked in telecommunications in St Petersburg 1988–99 and has been minister of communications (now information technologies and communications) since 1999. Other board members include: Boris Antonyuk the deputy minister for information technologies and communications; Kirill Androsov deputy minister for economic development and trade; and Vadim Stepanov the deputy director of the FSB.

Website: http://eng.svyazinvest.ru/

Sberbank is Russia's largest bank and its majority shareholder is the Central Bank of the Russian Federation. Andrei Kazmin has been the CEO and chair of Sberbank since 1996. He is an economist and was the deputy minister of finance 1993–96.

Website: http://www.sbrf.ru/eng/

Aeroflot is Russia's national airline. It became a joint stock company in 1993 and the government owns 51

per cent of the shares. Since 1997 its general director has been Valery Okulov, Aeroflot's former chief navigation instructor. Aeroflot's chair is Viktor Ivanov who is a former KGB member, who then worked in the St Petersburg mayor's office. He is a close Putin ally and a member of the presidential administration since 2000.

Website: http://www.aeroflot.ru/eng/company.asp

Box 14.9 (*Continued*)

Russian Railways is a government-owned rail monopoly, run by Igor Levitan who was appointed minister of transport in 2004.

Website: http://www.eng.rzd.ru/

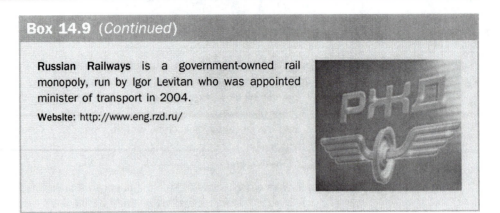

the line between the state and these corporations was blurred and they now function according to both market and statist criteria. For example, Gazprom subsidises its domestic energy prices, which serves the Kremlin's broader economic and social agenda of keeping energy prices down for domestic consumers, rather than reflecting the market-driven imperative of selling for the highest sustainable price. Gazprom usually exports energy according to market criteria, but when under Putin Russia came into conflict with Ukraine and Belarus, threats to reduce supplies and price increases, clearly served the Russian government's priorities.

Chapter summary

In 1992 Russia adopted shock therapy to transform its economy rapidly from a centrally planned economy with state or collective ownership of industry and agriculture into a capitalist economy. The next few years brought enormous hardships for the people and Russia seemed like a economic basket case, with some great assets such as oil, gas, diamonds, gold as well a highly educated and skilled population. In 1998 Russia defaulted on debt payments and devalued its curency, but the economy soon rebounded. When Russia joined the war on terror in 2001, the USA and EU said that in the event of trade disputes they would treat Russia as a normal market economy instead of as a non-market or state trading economy (OECD, 2006). In other words Russia had arrived; it was no longer in transition to a market economy, it is a market economy. In 2007 John Lipsky, First Deputy Managing Director of the International Monetary Fund reported after a visit to St Petersburg that, 'Russia's position is enviable, considering its rich resource base and well-educated population. With the right economic policies in place, the economic outlook will be exceptional' (IMF, 2007). Productivity is rising, the economy is growing at a rate of 6–7 per cent a year, real wages, domestic consumption and FDI are increasing and the rouble is fairly stable. On the debit side Russia's infrastructure is still in dire need of modernisation, there is an over-dependence on the export of commodities, too few SMEs and too many gigantic plants; corruption and crime and the lack of an independent judiciary still bedevil economic activities. The slow pace of agricultural modernisation and Russia's dependence on imported food, also makes it particularly vulnerable as world food prices started to rise rapidly in 2007.

Discussion points

- Do you agree with Grigory Yavlinsky that the Russian economy experienced too much shock and not enough therapy in the early 1990s?
- Is state corporatism a help or a hindrance to further economic development and modernisation?
- Why did Putin not destroy the oligarchs?
- Would you invest in Russia today? If so, what would you invest in?

Further reading

The Financial Times and *The Economist* both carry in-depth analyses of the Russian economy. The journal *Russian Economic Trends* published by Blackwell publishers (Oxford) for the European Commission on behalf of SITE (Stockholm Institute of Transition Economics and East European Economies) provides up-to-date analyses of the Russian economy. Critical analyses of shock therapy are provided by Marshall I. Goldman in his (1996) (new edn) *Lost Opportunity. What has made Economic Reform in Russia so Difficult*, New York, London: W. W. Norton; Igor Birman (1996) 'Gloomy Prospects for the Russian Economy', *Europe-Asia Studies*, 48 (5), 735–50; and by the leader of the Yabloko party Grigory Yavlinsky (1998) 'Russia's phony capitalism', *Foreign Affairs*, 77 (3), 67–79; Peter Reddaway and Dmitri Glinski (2001) *The Tragedy of Russia's Reforms. Market Bolshevism against Democracy*, Washington, DC: United States Institute of Peace Research. More positive assessments of Russia's economic reforms in the 1990s are provided by Richard Layard and John Parker (1996) *The Coming Russian Boom. A Guide to New Markets and Politics*, New York: Free Press; and by Anders Åslund (1995) *How Russia Became a Market Economy*, Washington, DC: Brookings Institute and in his (2001) *Building Capitalism: The Transformation of the Former Soviet Bloc*, Cambridge: Cambridge University Press. Anders Åslund (2007) *Russia's Capitalist Revolution. Why Market Reform Succeeded and Democracy Failed*, Washington, DC: Institute for International Economics; and Anders Åslund (2007) *How Capitalism was built. The Transformation of Central and Eastern Europe, Russia and Central Asia*, Cambridge: Cambridge University Press. Other useful analyses are provided by Yegor Gaidar (ed.) (2003) *The Economics of Russian Transition*, Cambridge, MA: MIT Press; Erik Berglöf, Andrei Kunov, Julia Shvets and Ksenia Yudaeva (2003) *The New Political Economy of Russia*, Cambridge, MA: MIT Press; Joseph R. Blasi, Maya Kroumova and Douglas Kruse (1997) *Kremlin Capitalism: Privatizing the Russian Economy*, Ithaca, NY: Cornell University Press; Vadim Volkov (2002) *Violent Entrepreneurs: The Use of Force in the Making of Russian Capitalism*, Ithaca, NY: Cornell University Press; and Stephen Kotkin and András Sajó (2002) *Political Corruption in Transition*, Budapest: Central European University Press.

An accessible overview of Russia's post-soviet economic development is provided by Rudiger Ahrend and William Tompson (2005) 'Fifteen Years of Economic Reform in Russia: What has been Achieved? What Remains to be Done?', *OECD Economics Department Working Papers*, May (430), OECD website, http://www.oecd.org/

Useful websites

RF Central Bank: http://www.cbr.ru/eng/main.asp

Federal Customs Service: http://www.customs.ru/en/

Norilsk Nickel: http://www.nornik.ru/en/

Lukoil: http://www.lukoil.com/

Yukos: http://www.yukos.com/

Surgutneftegas: http://www.surgutneftegas.ru/eng/index.xpml

International Monetary Fund: http://www.imf.org/

World Bank: http://www.worldbank.org.ru/

OECD: http://www.oecd.org/

G8, St Petersburg, Russia, 2006: http://en.g8russia.ru/

Peterson Institute for International Economics: http://www.petersoninstitute.org/

References

BBC (2005) 'Putin aide resigns over policies', *BBC News*, 27 December, http://news.bbc.co.uk/1/hi/world/europe/4562718.stm

Buckley, N. (2005) 'Putin's chief economic adviser quits', *The Financial Times*, 27 December, http://www.ft.com/

Cavan, S. J. (2006) 'Illarionov takes his leave', *The ISCIP Analyst*, XII (1), 27 January, *ISCIP*, Boston University website, http://www.bu.edu/iscip/

Crace, J. (1998) 'Rouble trouble', *Guardian Education*, 16 June, 10–11

Frydman, R., Rapaczynski, A. and Earle, J. S. (et al.) (1993) *The Privatization Process in Russia, Ukraine and the Baltic States*, Budapest, London, New York: Central European University Press (CEU Privatization Reports, 2)

Hawkins, P., Wright, R. and Krushelnycky, A. (1998) 'Rouble on the run', *The European*, 9–15 February, 9–12

Hedlund, S. (1999) *Russia's 'Market' Economy. A bad case of predatory capitalism*, London: UCL Press

IMF (2007) 'Statement by John Lipsky, First Deputy Managing Director of the International Monetary Fund', *IMF Press Release*, 07/126, 11 June, *IMF* website, http://www.imf.org/

Khmelev, M. (2007) 'The IMF give Russian economy a clean bill of health', *RIA Novosti*, 1 June, *RIA Novosti* website, http://en.rian.ru/

Kroll, L. (ed.) (2008) 'The World's Billionaires', *Forbes* website, http://www.forbes.com/

Lloyd J. (1998) *The Rebirth of a Nation. An Anatomy of Russia*, London: Michael Joseph

Nezavisimaia gazeta (2000) 'The Foreign Policy Concept of the Russian Federation', *Nezavisimaia gazeta*, 11 July, 1 and 6

OECD (2006) 'Economic Survey of the Russian Federation 2006: Sustaining growth in the Russian Federation; Key challenges', 27 November, *OECD* website, http://www. oecd.org/

Putin, V. (2000) 'Annual Address to the Federal Assembly of the Russian Federation', 8 July, Kremlin website, http://www.kremlin.ru/eng/

Soros, G. (1998) 'Letter to the Editor', *Financial Times*, 13 August, 18

Chapter 15

Society and social policies

Learning objectives

- To place these policies within the context of the end of soviet socialism.
- To identify the main ideas, institutions and actors involved in policy making.
- To describe and analyse the policies adopted by the government.
- To assess the changes in health, social and welfare policies.

Introduction

In the 1990s Russians routinely described themselves as 'degraded and insulted' (*unizhennye i oskorblennye*). The word degradation (*degradatsiia*) was employed to describe Russia's diminished international status and the domestic crisis confronting its people. Talk of a Russian genocide became common as, through a combination of a falling birthrate and declining life expectancy, the total population continued to fall. In the 1990s Russia fell down the United Nation's Human Development Index from the top to the medium tier of countries. Poverty levels rose in the face of economic crisis and benefits did not keep pace with rising prices. The economic crisis and poor tax collection in the 1990s led to steadily decreasing federal and regional budgetary resources for the social and health sectors. This situation was further exacerbated by disputes between federal and regional levels over the funding of services. The Russian people, who were accustomed to the state providing for them and who had not been able to make private provisions during the soviet period, were suddenly confronted by a major crisis in state provision. Article 7 of the 1993 Constitution continued the paternalistic role for the state established during the soviet period, but the Russian state was less able than before to meet these constitutional obligations.

The Yeltsin administration struggled and ultimately failed to frame, implement and adequately fund appropriate social policies. Putin asserted the primacy of the president in policy making and of Moscow over the regions, factors which together with Russia's growing economy and improved tax collection meant that his policy making and implementation was more purposeful than Yeltsin's. Putin's

Box 15.1 UNDP, Human Development Index (HDI), 2006

Country	Ranking	HDI value	Life expectancy at birth	Adult literacy rate % ages 15 and above	Combined gross enrolment ratio for primary, secondary, tertiary schools	GDP per capita (ppp US $)	Life expectancy index	Education index	GDP index	GDP per capita (ppp US$ rank minus HDI rank)
USA	8	0.0948	77.5	N/A	93	39.676	0.88	0.97	1.00	−6
Russia	65	0.797	65.2	99.4	88	9,902	0.67	0.95	77	−6
Kazakhstan	79	0.774	71.6	99.5	91	7,440	0.64	0.96	0.72	−5

Source: Data taken from the UNDP, *Human Development Report, 2006*, Human Development Index, Table 1, UNDP website, http://www.undp.org/ Also available on the same website is the UNDP's *National Human Development Report Russian Federation 2006/7. Russia's Regions: Goals, Challenges and Achievements.*

Note: The UN Development Programme's Human Development Index provides a comparative analysis of 177 countries, using indicators such as life expectancy, literacy, education and income. Russia is the second country, after Libya, in the medium level category. The 2006 Report was based on 2004 data.

reform agenda was set out in the 2000–2001 'General Principles of Socio-Economic Development of Russia in the Long-term', which is known as the 'Gref Plan' after its author German Gref, then the economics minister. The Gref Plan set out various goals including a stable increase in the population's living standard through high economic growth rates and a reduction in social inequality. Putin wanted to improve government performance and efficiency in meeting the state's social commitments. He simplified the overall social security system, through the introduction of a Unified Social Tax, and by targeting and means testing benefits. In September 2005 Putin announced the existence of national projects to deal with problem areas, including demography, health and housing. Dmitry Medvedev, who was then Putin's first deputy prime minister, was put in charge of the projects.

Box 15.2 The 1993 Constitution and Russia's social state

Article 7

1 The Russian Federation is a social state whose policy is aimed at creating conditions for a worthy life and a free development of man.

2 In the Russian Federation the labour and health of people shall be protected, guaranteed minimum wages and salaries shall be established, state support ensured to the family, maternity, paternity and childhood, to disabled persons

Box 15.2 (*Continued*)

and the elderly, the system of social services developed, state pensions, allowances and other social security guarantees shall be established.

Article 38

1 Motherhood and childhood, and the family, are under state protection.

2 Care for children and their upbringing are the equal right and duty of the parents.

3 Employable children who have reached 18 years of age must take care of their non-employable parents.

Article 39

1 Everyone is guaranteed social security in old age, in case of disease, invalidity, loss of breadwinner, to bring up children and in other cases established by law.

2 State pensions and social benefits are established by laws.

3 Voluntary social insurance, development of additional forms of social security and charity are encouraged.

Article 40

1 Everyone has the right to a home. No one may be arbitrarily deprived of a home.

2 State bodies and organs of local self-government encourage home construction and create conditions for the realisation of the right to a home.

3 Low-income citizens and other citizens, defined by the law, who are in need of housing are housed free of charge or for affordable pay from government, municipal and other housing funds in conformity with the norms stipulated by the law.

Article 41

1 Everyone has the right to health care and medical assistance. Medical assistance is made available by state and municipal health care institutions to citizens free of charge, with the money from the relevant budget, insurance payments and other revenues.

2 The Russian Federation finances federal health care and health-building programs, takes measures to develop state, municipal and private health care systems, encourages activities contributing to the strengthening of the man's health, to the development of physical culture and sport, and to ecological, sanitary and epidemiologic welfare.

3 Concealment by officials of facts and circumstances posing hazards to human life and health result in their liability in accordance with federal law.

Source: extracted from The Constitution of the Russian Federation, http://www.constitution.ru/en/10003000-01.htm

Social reform: from Yeltsin to Putin

Funding social benefits in the 1990s

In the USSR social spending was funded by the state budget and benefits were largely distributed by trade unions, via the workplace. Reforms in the early 1990s resulted in social benefits being funded by a payroll surcharge of 39.5 per cent, with employers responsible for 38.5 per cent and employees for 1 per cent of this figure. The funds were then transferred to new social funds, which were set up in 1991 and until 1993 were accountable to parliament. The Employment Fund, Pension Fund, Social Insurance Fund and Health Insurance Fund were independent of the state budget and so are described as 'off-budget' funds. The state's role was to ensure that employers made the required transfers. Each of these funds had their own federal and regional structures and there were different models of financial relations between these levels (*Trud*, 1999). The funding and delivery of health-care, social services and housing were complicated by disputes over the division of responsibility between federal and regional government and by the vast disparities in wealth between the regions (see Chapter 7). The richer cities and regions, which often had the most beneficial bilateral treaties with the federal government, were better placed to fund services than the poorer regions. The poorer regions, by their very nature, also tended to have greater demands made upon their budgets due to the poverty and poor health of their people. As with all revenue gathering in the 1990s, the social security system was bedevilled by non-payment or avoidance and administrative inefficiencies. There were also frequent complaints from the regions that the federal government was slow to transfer funds from the state budget to the regional and local levels. The federal government countered with accusations that funds sent to regional and local authorities were being misappropriated. The result was that in some regions, benefits and pensions were simply not paid, sometimes for months at a time.

Box 15.3 The four elements of the social security system in the 1990s

1. Employment-related social insurance benefits provided for employees and their dependents: pensions, employment injury benefits, unemployment benefits, health insurance benefits and short-term cash benefits such as sickness and maternity.

2. Universal benefits: public healthcare system, family benefits and social pensions.

3. Social assistance benefit provisions, benefits of last resort to poor without other or insufficient income: provision of clothing, free meals, cash income support. Administered by regional or local government.

4. Supplementary schemes: voluntary pension schemes, private health insurance, private pension provision, help provided by NGOs such as charities.

The Unified Social Tax, 2000

The Unified Social Tax (UST) was adopted in response to the problems of funding social benefits and as part of Putin's broader tax reforms. The UST was introduced in Part II of the Tax Code adopted in 2000 and implemented on 1 January 2001. The UST consolidated several payroll taxes and replaced the complex system of mandatory deductions and transfers to the various social funds. The Tax Office rather than the social funds is now responsible for collecting a single (unified) payment for each employee from employers. The UST is a regressive income tax up to a maximum of 36.5 per cent, which the employer calculates individually for each employee on the basis of their total annual income. Overall, the UST means that employers now pay less total tax than they were paying to the off-budget social funds. Under the old system recipients received their benefits from the relevant social fund; pensions for example were distributed by the Pension Fund. Under the new system benefits are channelled through the federal budget and then passed on to the social funds. This new system in effect brings the social funds back into the general budget, takes away the opportunities for the regions to misuse these funds, and overall enables the federal government to keep a closer overview of finances and payments.

Reforming social policy: from entitlements to cash payments

The USSR prided itself on providing for its people and established a wide range of social benefits or entitlements (*l'goty*). The entitlements system remained unchanged during the 1990s, even though it did not meet the social needs of the new economic system. In 2000 there were 256 categories with some kind of benefit entitlement, claimed by one million Russians or 70 per cent of the population (Komaravsky cited by Nies and Walcher, 2002: 6). In his first Annual Address to the Federal Assembly in 2000, Putin announced that the 'policy of general state paternalism is economically impossible and politically inadvisable . . . this is dictated by the need for the most effective use of financial resources, and to create stimuli for development, to liberate human potential, and make people responsible for themselves and for the welfare of their families' (Putin, 2000). He, therefore, rejected the system of non-specific entitlements for all within a particular social category in favour of a means-tested system targeting those truly in need. These reforms have the clear imprint of the economic liberals within Putin's administration: Illarionov, Gref, Kudrin and Mikhail Zurabov, the minister of health and social development.

The reforms entailed confronting popular expectations of state paternalism and provoked the first major opposition to Putin and his policies. In 2004 pensioners backed by human rights groups demonstrated in the major cities against the proposed reforms. Nevertheless on 1 January 2005 entitlements such as free public transportation passes, subsidised housing, electricity, gas and telephones, free or heavily subsidised healthcare, medicines and spa treatments were replaced by cash payments, affecting about 32 million people (Mite, 2005). Critics of the new

Communists demonstrate in 2004 against the government's plans to change social and welfare payments

system complained that the cash payments are inadequate and do not cover the full cost of paying for services that were previously received for free or were highly subsidised. The change had an immediate deleterious impact on the lives of Russia's most vulnerable people including war veterans, pensioners and the disabled. This situation was made worse as utility bills for all were also set to rise in 2005. In January 2005 there were further mass demonstrations and even talk of a general strike. The sight of protesting veterans of the Great Patriotic, Afghan and Chechen wars wearing their medals, babushki (grandmothers) and the disabled was a propaganda disaster for Putin. In some instances police and soldiers sent to control the demonstrations even joined the demonstrators. In St Petersburg 10,000 demonstrators blocked traffic and there were smaller demonstrations in Khabarovsk, Stavropol, Moscow *oblast*, Tatarstan and Samara. The Moscow city authorities decided to restore free transportation and subsidised medicines for the city's inhabitants. Putin's economic liberals came under attack from the protestors, oppositionists within the Duma called for a vote of no confidence in Prime Minister Fradkov's government, but Fradkov survived. Putin criticised his finance minister Alexei Kudrin on national TV and also gave the typical response of Russian leaders: he blamed federal and regional officials for implementing the reforms badly. The reforms were not, however, abandoned in the face of the opposition; Putin promised a small increase in pensions and spoke of the need to spend more on social services. Improved tax gathering and the rising price of oil and gas on world markets meant that the government had more funds, but the government's economic liberals feared that increased spending on health and welfare issues would fuel inflation and wanted instead to increase the government's stabilisation fund (see Chapter 14).

The unemployed

In the USSR everyone had the constitutional right to employment and, officially at least, unemployment did not exist. Unemployment was a by-product of the economic transition of the 1990s and the creation of a flexible labour market. During the 1990s underemployment was also a major problem. As welfare benefits were very small, thousands of people carried on going to work even if there was no work for them to do, as many enterprises continued the soviet practice of providing benefits, including healthcare, housing, subsidised canteens and shops. These 'workers' did not appear in the official unemployment statistics but they were not economically active. The unemployment rate for 2006 was 6.9 per cent (Central Bank of the RF, 2006). In 1991 the government set up an Employment Fund as a department of the Labour Ministry and also an independent Institute for Labour Market Research. The Employment Fund was abolished in 2001 as part of the UST reforms and the Institute for Labour Market Research was also abolished in 2001. Since 1 January 2001 the federal budget has financed the State Employment Service at federal and regional levels.

Pension reform

The pensions problem

Pensioners constitute about 20 per cent of the Russian population and in some cities 25–30 per cent of the population are pensioners (Mite, 2005). Russia has an ageing population and soon there will be more pensioners than people in employment. Russia still has the same retirement ages as during the soviet period – 55 for women and 60 for men – which are lower than in most developed economies. In the 1990s the value of pensions did not keep pace with rising living costs and in reality many people continued to work far beyond the official retirement ages. So far Russia has not dealt with its pensions problem by raising the official age of retirement, this would be a politically sensitive step, especially as life expectancy is already low. In the 1990s Russia had a pay-as-you-go pension system, in which pensions were paid out of current tax revenues, that is, from the contributions made by the current working population. Russia's demographic problem, of a falling working age population and a rising pensioner population, meant that to continue funding pensions in this way would require increasing taxes levied from the working people. In the 1990s the Yeltsin administration worked on a draft pension reform, but its adoption was abandoned in the face of the 1998 economic crisis.

Reforming Russia's pension system

In February 2001 Putin set up the National Council for Pension Reform, headed by the prime minister, Mikhail Kasyanov. Its membership included Mikhail Zubarov the head of the State Pension Fund, government ministers, some of the

heads of the 89 regions, representatives of the Duma's party factions, social organisations including the independent trade unions and representatives of business. The
Council's role was to discuss draft pension laws and to encourage public debate.
Pension reform was part of the Gref Plan and it is clear that the direction the
pension reforms should take was very strongly steered by the economic liberals
within Putin's team. Gref's close ally Mikhail Dmitriev, the deputy economics
minister and a specialist in labour and pensions systems, played a leading role within
the Council's deliberations. The introduction of the UST already meant that the
State Pension Fund had lost its former responsibility for collecting pension contributions and Zubarov tried to protect the role of his gigantic bureaucracy by
opposing the liberals' radical reform proposals. In April 2001 Andrei Illarionov,
the liberal senior economic adviser within the presidential administration, invited
José Piñera, a fellow freemarketer and advocate of pension system privatisation,
to Moscow. Piñera was responsible for Chile's pension reform in the 1980s, which
had replaced a pay-as-you-go system similar to Russia's with one based on personal retirement accounts (Piñera, 2000).

The pension reforms 2000–2001

On 30 November 2001 the Duma passed a package of three pension reform laws,
which came into effect on 1 January 2002. These replaced the pay-as-you-go system with a Chilean-inspired system including a fully-funded mandatory contribution scheme and voluntary, private-funded schemes. The new three-tier system of
pension provision, is based on:

- **A basic state pension**, whose amount is determined by law and contributions
  are paid directly to the federal budget, which transfers funds to the State Budget
  Fund that distributes payments to pensioners.

- **A state earnings-related pension**, which is mandatory for all new entrants into
  the labour force, for men born in 1950 or after, and for women born in 1955
  or after. Older workers may opt to make voluntary contributions. Pension payments depend on the amount of contributions.

- **A supplementary pension** financed by voluntary contributions to private pension
  funds. Some of Russia's largest corporations such as Surgutneftegaz, Lukoil and
  Gazprom have used their own company pension funds to buy shares in their
  own companies.

In his Annual Address to the Federal Assembly in May 2006 Putin said that
everything must be done to ensure that pensioners have a decent life. Whereas in
the 1990s pensions in some regions went unpaid for months on end, Putin has
ensured that pensions are paid regularly. Since pension reform was introduced in
2001, pensions have been increased a number of times, including an increase of
nearly 20 per cent in 2007.

The demographic crisis

Box 15.4 Aleksandr Solzhenitsyn, Russia's catastrophe and 'saving the state'

Following his return to Russia in 1994 Solzhenitsyn was greatly concerned by the catastrophe facing Russia. He wrote:

> The Catastrophe entails above all – our dying out. These losses will only increase: how many women will risk giving birth in today's abject penury? Handicapped and sick children also will augment the Catastrophe, and their numbers are multiplying from the miserable living conditions and the boundless drunkenness of their fathers. And the utter collapse of our schools, incapable today of rearing a moral and learned generation. And a meagerness of housing conditions long forgotten by the civilised world. And the teeming grafters in government – some of whom even cheaply sell off our oil fields and rare metals in foreign concessions. (Solzhenitsyn, 1995: 104)

In an interview with Vitaly Tretyakov the editor-in-chief of *Moskovskiye Novosti*, Solzhenitsyn argues that in order to 'save the nation' Russia needs a demographic project among other priorities and that,

> Indeed, 'saving the nation' – numerically, physically, and morally – is the utmost task for the state. (Consider the 25 million compatriots who were cut off from Russia as a result of the crazy conspiracy in the Belovezhskaya Forest: Our lawmakers were in a state of chaos, hysterically and irresponsibly going from one extreme to another and contradicting themselves.) All measures to raise living standards – housing, diet, healthcare, education, morality, etc. – are in effect designed to save the nation. This is an overriding priority. (Tretyakov, 2006)

Note: Solzhenitsyn was a Russian nationalist, author and Nobel Prize winner. He was a dissident during the soviet period and was exiled in 1974. He returned to Russia in 1994 but was highly critical of the Yeltsin administration. The Belovezhskaya Forest conspiracy referred to in the second quotation is Yeltsin's agreement with Belarus and Ukraine to dismember the USSR (see Chapter 1). Solzhenitsyn shared Putin's vision of a restored and strengthened Russian state. Following his death in August 2008, Solzhenitsyn's Moscow funeral at the Donskoi Monastery was attended by President Medvedev and Prime Minister Putin among other dignitaries.

Medvedev has announced that a street in Moscow will be renamed after Solzhenitsyn.

Russia's demographic crisis: the 2002 Census findings

Throughout the 1990s there were angry articles in the mass media arguing that Russia was experiencing nothing less than a national genocide, characterised by a falling population, plummeting life expectancy and an ageing population. There is a popular and elite consensus that Russia has a problem, but there is no domestic consensus on why this is happening. Nationalists and communists typically blame the disruption and traumas of first *perestroika* and then the transition to capitalism and specifically the deterioration in health services, mass poverty, growing unemployment, anxiety and uncertainty about the future, plus rising alcohol abuse. While these factors have played a part in the population decline, the population structure is distorted by the tremendous losses of the 1920s, 1930s and 1940s in the Great Patriotic War (1941–45). Put simply, the millions who died then means that there were fewer potential parents and so Russia does not have their children, grandchildren and great grandchildren today. The 2002 census seemed to confirm the gloomy predictions, finding that since the last census in 1989 Russia's population had fallen by 1.8 million to 145.2 million people (*Pravda*, 2003). Life expectancy started to fall in the mid-1960s and is now down to just 59.9 years for men and 73.3 for women compared to 73 and 79 in the USA, 74 and 82 in France and 72 and 80 in Germany (Titova, 2003). Fertility levels started to fall below the replacement level in the 1960s and most Russian families only have one child. The result is that not only is the total population falling, it is also ageing.

Not a demographic crisis, a demographic transition

There is an alternative interpretation of Russia's demographic changes which replaces the language of 'genocide' with one of evolution and transition from one demographic phase to another. According to this interpretation Russia began its transition to the second demographic phase at the end of the nineteenth century and beginning of the twentieth century; around the 1960s to 1970s beginning the transition to the third, post-industrial phase. Some of the features of contemporary life in Russia are typical of this third phase and are already to be found throughout Europe. These include: a lower birth rate, a rise in women's child-bearing age, the emergence of alternative families, serial monogamy and cohabitation, an increase in divorce, an increase in the number of illegitimate children, and a family model of one or two children (Sokolov, 2005). Improvements in the status and education of women and in their ability to control their fertility are also part of the transition to the third phase. However, in Russia this transition has been accompanied by other developments, such as decreasing life expectancy and increasing mortality, which are not typical of the third phase.

Box 15.5 Demographic phases

- **First phase, pre-industrial, agricultural economies:** characterised by high birthrates, but also high levels of infant and maternal mortality, and high population losses due to famine, disease and wars.

- **Second phase, industrialisation:** characterised by high birthrates but falling mortality rates, especially for infants and children, due to better medicine, hygiene and sanitation.

- **Third phase, post-industrial era:** characterised by a reduction in population growth, a further lowering of infant mortality rate, further improvements in combating diseases and improvements in life expectancy.

Putin's demographic policy

In his Annual Address to the Federal Assembly in 2006 Putin said that Russia's population was now 143 million and that it was falling by 700,000 people a year, on average. He described the demographic problem as 'the most acute problem facing our country today' and said that to resolve it Russia needed to lower the death rate, to adopt an effective migration policy and to increase the birthrate (Putin, 2006). In 2004 he had already asked the ministries to look into Russia's demographic problems and to draft new federal policies, which ultimately resulted in the 'Conception of the Demographic Policy of Russia until 2015' in 2005 and changes to migration policy in 2006.

Box 15.6 The Russian population: findings of the 2002 Census

- Russia is overwhelmingly urban – 27 per cent live in rural areas and 73 per cent in cities and towns with 20 per cent living in cities of more than one million inhabitants.

- The population is ageing. The average age is 37.7 which is three years older than in 1989.

- Women outnumber men – there are 67.6 million men and 77.6 million women. This continues a trend begun 30 years ago for an increase in the ratio of women to men.

- 89 million people or 61 per cent of the population are of working age.

- About one million Russian residents are citizens of other countries.

Source: Pravda (2003) 'First Results of 2002 census published', *Pravda*, 29 October

---

Lowering the death rate

Addressing Russia's low life expectancy and lowering the death rate entails identifying why Russians are dying young. According to official data the two leading causes of death are heart disease which accounts for 60 per cent of deaths and accidents, half of which are due to alcohol. The other leading causes of death are cancer, drug abuse and suicide (Titova, 2003). Demographic and healthcare experts blame alcohol abuse, the psychological stress generated by economic uncertainty, widespread smoking, poor personal safety practices, an unhealthy diet and a general lack of exercise (ibid.). In the 1990s there was rising unemployment; salaries, pensions and welfare benefits often went unpaid for months, food prices rose dramatically and some people had several jobs just to get by. Healthcare and access to prescription pharmaceuticals became more erratic and expensive; none of these factors help to promote a healthy, stress-free life with a good diet. Poverty is clearly part of the problem and so the upswing in the economy should help; however, there are marked regional differences both in the economy and in life expectancy. According to Yevgeny Andreyev, a demography expert at the Institute of National Economic Forecasting in Moscow, Russians pay less attention to regular safety measures than people in Europe so that, 'They are more likely to fall from buildings; drown in rivers; get run over by cars; or die in car accidents because they weren't wearing seatbelts' (cited by Titova, 2003). Andreyev also says that half of all accidents involve alcohol in some way (ibid.).

The suicide rate began to rise dramatically in the 1990s and Russia now has one of the world's highest suicide rates. According to figures released by the World Health Organization (WHO) and the Russian Ministry of Health: in 1990 the suicide rate was 26.4 per 100,000 people; in 1994 it had risen to 42.1; in 1998 it dropped to 35.4; in 2001 it stood at 39.7 (Webster, 2003); and in 2003 it had fallen slightly to 38 (Interfax, 2003). The WHO considers a rate of more than 20 suicides per 100,000 people as high. According to the demographer Irina Orlova (1998: 69) social and socio-psychological reasons such as the loss of social ties, depression, frustration, alcoholism, family disruptions, unemployment, and the loss of prospects explain this dramatic rise in suicide in the 1990s. In 2003, 60,000 Russians committed suicide, giving an overall rate of 38 per 100,000; but the rate for men is six times higher than for women (Interfax, 2003). The 'typical' suicide is a working age man living in one of Russia's depressed economic areas.

Putin and the encouragement of childbirth

Putin's demographic policy plans to raise Russia's current birthrate of 1.3 children per family, which is not enough to replace the population, to 1.7 children by the end of 2025 (*Pravda*, 2007). In his Annual Address to the Federal Assembly in 2006 Putin (2006) cited Solzhenitsyn's phrase about saving the nation and proposed a programme to encourage childbirth, to encourage parents to have two children and to support mothers who stay at home to raise their families. According to Putin the factors that stop families from having a second or third child are, 'low incomes, inadequate housing conditions, doubts as to their own ability to ensure the child a decent level of healthcare and education, and – let's be honest – sometimes doubts as to whether they will even be able to feed the child' (ibid.). The programme to encourage childbirth includes administrative, financial and social support for young families and was introduced on 1 January 2007.

A major problem with the benefits that are supposed to encourage childbirth is that they come nowhere near covering the costs of having and raising children. In 2005 the existing child benefit of 500 roubles for children under 18 months was increased to 700 roubles and in 2007 it was increased to 1,500 roubles a month and 3,000 roubles for a second child. To put this into context, two packets of disposable nappies cost around 1,500 roubles. The government also now provides a one-off second-child bonus, which must be used for children's education or healthcare, but there is no first-child bonus. The government has also increased the one-off childbirth certificate to 7,000 roubles to help with medical costs, but this is not enough to cover maternity hospital charges, which are around 25,000 (*Pravda*, 2007). Improvements in medical services led to a 27 per cent fall in the infant mortality rate between 1995 and 2003 (WHO, 2005). There is another 8,000 rouble one-off maternity benefit, which is supposed to cover the costs of raising a child. Mikhail Zubarov, the healthcare and social development minister at the time of these reforms, believed that this payment would also encourage families to adopt the country's 600,000 orphans.

Immigration, emigration and Russia's migration policy in the 1990s

In the 1990s Russia experienced an unprecedented rise in immigration, with the arrival of 6.9 million people mostly from the CIS and Baltic states (Mukomel, 2004). The peak of immigration by people fleeing ethnic conflicts and the dire economic conditions of some FSU states to Russia was reached by the mid-1990s, but the estimated 20–25 million members of the Russian diaspora did not flock to 'return' to Russia. Although in the 1990s soviet passport holders of any nationality had the right to claim Russian citizenship and live in the Russian Federation, Russia's economic problems and the government's attempts to settle immigrants in underpopulated rural areas did not make it an ideal destination. Russia was also experiencing an unprecedented wave of emigration during the 1990s, which resulted in a net migration figure of 3.8 million people (ibid.). This was not enough to reverse the overall population decline and to stabilise the population. During the 1990s Russia's emigrants included Jews leaving for the USA and Israel and ethnic Germans moving to Germany. Russia also experienced a brain drain (*utechka mozgov*) of some of its best educated and skilled people prompted by the funding crisis in education, science and technology. The FSB accused the USA of organising a brain drain that was threatening Russia's national interests and the army's combat readiness.

Migration policy under Putin

Russia's falling birthrate and ageing population has both economic and security implications. The economic revival since 1998 means that Russian now has a labour shortage and also a diminishing pool of young men of military conscription age (see Main, 2006). In his Annual Address to the Federal Assembly in 2006, Putin stated that Russia's migration policy should give priority to attracting compatriots, that Russia needed to encourage skilled migration by educated and law abiding people and that, 'People coming to our country must treat our culture and national traditions with respect' (Putin, 2006). There are several tangled issues here. First, even if all ethnic Russians living outside the country moved to Russia it would still not be enough to stabilise the population. Secondly, it is estimated that since 1992 between 7 and 14 million illegal immigrants have arrived in Russia, 80 per cent of whom are from CIS states and China. The illegal immigrants are typically unskilled, working in markets, street kiosks and on construction sites. Professional demographers argue that Russia had no choice but to legalise the status of these illegal immigrants (Yasmann, 2005) and in November 2006 Vyacheslav Postavnin, the deputy head of the Federal Migration Service announced an amnesty for illegal migrants affecting about one million people. Russia has begun to issue more work permits: 800,000 in the first four months of 2007 compared to 600,000 for the whole of 2006; 90 per cent of the migrants come from CIS states (Workpermit.com, 2007b). However, this raises a third issue; Postavnin says that Russia favours a model of 'return migration', meaning that migrants should return home rather than settle permanently in Russia. In order to stop Russians from feeling outnumbered Postavnin argues that immigrants must not be allowed to form 'ethnic enclaves' and so they should not form more than 17–20 per cent of the population in particular towns and cities. Since January 2007 foreigners have been barred from selling alcohol and pharmaceuticals. By the end of 2007 the overall number of foreign-born workers in retail outlets is scheduled to fall to 40 per cent of the total workforce and down to zero in 2008 (Workpermit.com, 2007a). These new regulations are enforced by police raids on markets, opening up increased opportunities for the police to seek corrupt payments to turn a blind eye to infringements.

Reforming healthcare and improving the nation's health

Healthcare reforms in the 1990s

In the USSR the state provided a universal system of free healthcare. Plans to reform healthcare funding were initiated in a 1991 law 'On Health Insurance in Russia', which aimed to fund healthcare by compulsory and voluntary insurance contributions rather than from the state budget. This twin approach to funding was continued by the Yeltsin and Putin administrations. In the 1990s most people were insured through a compulsory medical insurance system. For private sector employees this was levied by the employer and the revenues were then divided in the proportion 1:8 between the federal and local Health Funds (Yudaeva and Gorban, 1999: 5). For government employees and the non-working population the federal government transferred funds to the republican and regional budgets (ibid.). The delineation of responsibilities between the different levels of government set up in the 1990s remained largely unchanged under Putin. The federal government is responsible for the Russia's health policy, provides a regulatory framework for the pharmaceutical and medical industries, and monitors the quality of medical care (Green, 1998: 2.79). The regions are supposed to provide environmental health protection and control infectious diseases in addition to administering their own health systems including hospitals, polyclinics, sanatoria and the clinics of scientific centres (ibid.). Local government finances and administers a range of primary services provided by polyclinics, hospices and nursing homes (ibid.). In the 1990s all levels of the Russian healthcare system were severely under-funded and increasingly under-staffed, which both compromised healthcare and frustrated any attempts at modernisation. Healthcare was also embroiled in disputes between Moscow and the regions, with the regions and local government complaining that they did not always receive the appropriate allocations from the federal budget. Although healthcare was in principle free, in practice hospitals began to ask for payment to cover the costs of a hospital stay, medicines and treatment. A legacy of the soviet period is that nurses expect 'presents' such as money, food, alcohol or sweets from patients in return for performing their nursing functions. Doctors, who like other public employees suffered from low or unpaid salaries, also increasingly asked for personal payments. The 1990s also saw a growth in private healthcare. Putin's reforms to the funding of regional and local government (see Chapter 7) are supposed to ensure that these levels have funds to fulfil their health-care responsibilities.

Box 15.7 Ministry of Healthcare and Social Development

From 1992 to 2004 it was the Ministry of Health and in 2004 became the Ministry of Health Care and Social Development

Ministers	Time as minister
Andrei Nechayev	1992 to 28 November 1995
Aleksandr Tsaregorodtsev	5 December 1995 to 17 August 1996
Tatyana Dmitriyeva	17 August 1996 to 5 May 1998
Oleg Rutkovsky	5 May 1998 to 30 September 1998
Vladimir Starodubov	30 September 1998 to 12 May 1999
Yury Shevchenko	5 July 1999 to 9 March 2004
Mikhail Zurabov	9 March 2004 to 24 September 2007
Tatyana Golikova	24 September 2007–

Putin's national healthcare project

Improving the nation's health and healthcare service was one of the national projects announced in 2005. Putin had already introduced reforms to improve primary healthcare and access to high-technology medical services. In his 2006 Annual Address to the Federal Assembly Putin (2006) announced that the National Healthcare project would focus on the detection, prevention and treatment of cardiovascular disease and other illnesses that are the leading causes of death among Russians and would develop effective campaigns to tackle premature deaths. The project plans to provide extra financial support to primary care medical staff who have fewer opportunities to earn extra money than specialists. The salaries of primary care doctors, general practitioners and paediatricians were increased by at least 10,000 roubles a month and nurses' salaries by at least 5,000 roubles a month at the beginning of 2006. Staff shortages are also being addressed by plans to train a further 10,000 primary care doctors and general practitioners. The project also stresses modernisation, re-equipment and includes ambitious plans to replace all ambulances with new vehicles equipped with emergency medical equipment and new communications systems. Municipal and rural polyclinics, regional hospitals and paramedic stations are to be re-equipped with new diagnostic equipment, and new high-tech medical centres are to be built in the regions. Overall, there will be at least a fourfold growth in the number of people whose medical care is funded from the federal budget. These initiatives are all long overdue and

Table 15.1 The ten leading risk factors for Russians' health, 2002

Rank	Males		Females	
	Risk factors	Total DALYS (%)	Risk factors	Total DALYS (%)
1	Alcohol	22.8	High blood pressure	19.6
2	Tobacco	20.5	High cholesterol	12.7
3	High blood pressure	14.1	High BMI	10.7
4	High cholesterol	12.0	Low fruit and vegetable intake	7.0
5	High BMI	7.1	Alcohol	6.8
6	Low fruit and vegetable intake	7.0	Physical inactivity	5.2
7	Physical inactivity	4.3	Tobacco	2.5
8	Illicit drugs	2.7	Unsafe sex	1.8
9	Occupational risk factors for injuries	1.3	Illicit drugs	1.3
10	Lead	1.2	Lead	0.9

Source: World Health Organization website, http://www.euro.who.int/eprise/main/WHO/Progs/CHHRUS/burden/20050606_2

Note: The disability-adjusted life-year (DALY) is a summary measure that combines the impact of illness, disability and mortality on population health.

Table 15.2 Ten leading disability groups, 2002

Rank	Males		Females	
	Disability groups	Total DALYs (%)	Disability groups	Total DALYs (%)
1	Cardiovascular diseases	26.1	Cardiovascular diseases	31.2
2	Unintentional injuries	20.6	Neuropsychiatric conditions	16.5
3	Neuropsychiatric conditions	11.6	Unintentional injuries	9.3
4	Intentional injuries	11.5	Malignant neoplasms	9.3
5	Malignant neoplasms	6.9	Digestive diseases	5.1
6	Infectious and parasitic diseases	6.5	Sense organ diseases	4.9
7	Digestive diseases	4.3	Musculoskelatal diseases	4.9
8	Sense organ diseases	2.4	Intentional injuries	3.7
9	Respiratory diseases	1.8	Infectious and parasitic diseases	3.2
10	Musculoskelatal diseases	1.8	Respiratory diseases	2.3

Source: World Health Organization website, http://www.euro.who.int/eprise/main/WHO/Progs/CHHRUS/burden/20050606_1

Note: The disability-adjusted life-year (DALY) is a summary measure that combines the impact of illness, disability and mortality on population health.

very costly; during 2006 the projected costs of the project rose to 88.4 billion roubles (Simonov, 2007: 119). Konstantin Simonov (ibid.: 120–1) points out that contracts associated with the project have been awarded to companies with close connections to Mikhail Zubarov, the minister of health care and social development. ZAO Medstor, which is associated with the minister's wife Yulia Zubarova, has been awarded one-fifth of the contracts for medical equipment and the GAZ motor plant owned by the pro-Kremlin oligarch Oleg Deripaska's *Russkiye Mashiny* has been another major beneficiary.

Chapter summary

The transition to democracy and capitalism is supposed to lead to the regeneration of Russia, to provide opportunities for material prosperity, political and social participation and inclusion. For the majority of Russians, however, the reform process begun under Gorbachev and accelerated by Yeltsin brought only increasing despair and poverty. Putin's concept of a strong Russian state included a belief in the importance of a prosperous, healthy and growing population. However, Putin also believed that soviet-era paternalism could not be economically sustained, despite growing oil revenues. Putin believed that state provision must be reduced and targeted through means testing to give those truly in need better benefits. He also wanted individuals to make more provision for themselves rather than to rely entirely on the state. This meant challenging peoples' expectations and put Putin at odds with large and vocal sectors of the population. In response Putin did not retreat over the basic trajectory of his reforms, but he did increase benefits.

Discussion points

- Were the pension and benefit reforms a financial necessity?
- What factors do you think will influence whether Putin's national healthcare programme will bring about the desired changes?
- Is talk of a Russian genocide just a lot of nationalist and communist hysteria or are there real causes for concern?
- Are Russians still degraded and insulted?

Further reading

The UN Development Programme commissions regular Human Development Reports on individual countries. The reports on Russia are typically written by large teams of Russian experts. Recent reports include: Sergei N. Bobylev, Anastassia I. Alexandrova and Natalia V. Zubarevich (2006–7) *Russia's regions: Goals, Challenges, Achievements*; and Bobylev and Alexandrova (2005) *Russian in 2015. Development Goals and Policy Priorities. Human Development Report 2005. Russian Federation*, which covers topics such as healthcare, poverty, the environment, women's issues and education. Earlier reports cover issues such as women and development and human trafficking. The reports are available on the UNDP website, http://hdr.undp.org/. The U.S. Social Security Administration, Office of Policy 'Social Security Programs Throughout the World: Europe, 2006', provides a very useful overview of Russia's legislation and benefit payments on its website, http://www.ssa.gov/policy/docs/progdesc/ssptw/2006–2007/europe/russia.html. An accessible analysis of the Unified Social Tax is provided by Susanne Nies and Gesa Walcher (2002) 'The Unified Social Tax and its impact on Social Policy in Putin's Russia', No. 34, February, *Working paper of the Research Centre for Eastern European Studies*, Bremen.

Useful analyses of Russia's demographic situation are provided by Nicholas Eberstadt (2004) 'The Russian Federation at the Dawn of the 21st Century: Trapped in a Demographic Straitjacket', *NBR Analysis*, 15 (2), September, The National Bureau of Asian Research website, http://www.nbr.org/; and Leszek Szerepka (2006) 'Demographic Situation in Russia', which places Russia's demographic problems within their historical context, provides a lot of easily accessible data and examines responses to the situation. It is available in English (and Polish) on the Global Development Network website, http://www.gdnet.org/. The argument against the need for immigration is provided by Alexander Gorianin (2006) 'Russia Does Not Need a Pro Immigration Policy', *Moscow Defense Brief* website, http://mdb.cast.ru/mdb/2-2006/item1/item4/. Information and commentaries on RF legislation relating to various aspects of migration are available on the Legislation online website, http://www.legislationline.org/.

Useful websites

The official site of the 2002 Russian census: http://www.perepis2002.ru/index.html?id=11 (Russian language)

International Organization on Migration: http://www.iom.int/

OSCE (Anti-trafficking): http://www.osce.org/activities/13029.html

United Nations Population Fund is an international development agency. Its website includes information about the agency's work in individual countries and country profiles: http://www.unfpa.org/

World Health Organization on Russia: http://www.who.int/countries/rus/en/

RF Pension Fund: http://www.pfrf.ru/ (Russian only)

References

Central Bank of the Russian Federation (2006 and 2007) 'Key Economic Indicators', *Central Bank of the Russian Federation* website, http://www.cbr.ru/eng/

Green, G. (1998) *Health and Governance in European Cities*, London: European Hospital Management Journal Limited for the WHO

Interfax (2003) 'Russian suicide figures exceed WHO critical threshold – expert', 11 August. Available on the *Johnson's Russia List* website, 12 August #2 7285, http://www.cdi.org/russia/johnson/7285-2.cfm

Kosmarsky, V. (2002) 'Social Policy. First Steps Towards Reform', *Russian Economic Trends Monthly*, The Centre for Economic Reforms, 9.1.2001, cited by Susanne Nies and Gesa Walcher (2002) 'The Unified Social Tax and its impact on Social Policy in Putin's Russia', (34), February, *Working Papers of the Research Centre for Eastern European Studies*, Bremen

Main, S. J. (2006) 'Russia's "Golden Bridge" is Crumbling: Demographic Crisis in the Russian Federation', *Conflict Studies Research Centre. Russian Series*, August, 06/39, http://www.defac.ac.uk/

Mite, V. (2005) 'Russia: Pensioners' Mount Growing Challenge to Putin', *RFE/RL* Feature Article, 17 January, *RFE/RL* website, http://www.rferl.org/

Mukomel, V. (2004) 'Immigration from the near abroad: what is to be expected?', *Center for Strategic Research* (CSR North-West), RF, http://www.eldis.org/

Orlova, I. B. (1998) '*Samoubiistvo – iavlenie sotsial'noe*', *Sotsiologicheskie Issledovaniia*, (8), 69–73

Piñera, J. (2000) 'A Chilean Model for Russia', *Foreign Affairs*, 79 (5), September–October, 62–73

Pravda (2003) 'First Results of 2002 census published', *Pravda*, 29 October, http://english.pravda.com

Pravda (2007) 'Many Russian women are afraid to bear children', *Pravda*, 7 June, http://english.pravda.ru

Putin, V. (2000) 'Annual Address to the Federal Assembly', 8 July, Kremlin website, http://www.kremlin.ru/eng/

Putin, V. (2006) 'Annual Address to the Federal Assembly', 10 May, Kremlin website, http://www.kremlin.ru/eng/

Simonov, K. (ed.) (2007) 'Russia 2006. Report on transformation', III Europe-Russia Economic Forum, Vienna, 23–24 April, http://www.forum-ekonomiczne.pl/docs/Report_Russia_2006.pdf

Sokolov, D. (2005) 'The Third Demographic Transition', *New Times*, September, http://www.newtimes.ru/eng (downloaded 7 October 2005, appears to no longer be available online)

Solzhenitsyn, A. (1995) *The Russian Question at the end of the 20th Century*, London: The Harvill Press

Titova, I. (2003) 'Russian Life Expectancy on Downward Trend', *Johnson's Russia List* website, 17 January, #14 7023, http://www.cdi.org/russia/johnson/7023-14.cfm

Tretyakov, V. (2006) 'Aleksandr Solzhenitsyn: "Saving the Nation Is the Utmost Priority for the State"', *The Moscow News Weekly*, 2 May, http://www.mnweekly.ru/

UNDP (2006) *Human Development Report, 2006*, Human Development Index, Table 1, UNDP website, http://www.undp.org/

Webster, P. (2003) 'Suicide rates in Russia on the increase', *The Lancet*, 362 (9379), 19 July, available from *Johnson's Russia List* website, 20 July, #3 9379, http://www.cdi.org/russia/johnson/

World Health Organization (2005) 'Highlights on health, Russian Federation 2005, Maternal Mortality', World Health Organization website, http://www.who.org/

Work Permit.Com (2007a) 'Immigration limits come into effect in Russia', 15 January, *Work Permit.Com* website, http://www.workpermit.com/

Work Permit.Com (2007b) 'Number of work permits issued in Russia quadruples', 24 May, *Work Permit.Com* website, http://www.workpermit.com/

Yasmann, V. (2005) 'Russia: Immigration likely to increase, mitigating population deficit', 10 November, *RFE/RL* website, http://www.rferl.org/

Yudaeva, K. and Gorban, M. (1999) 'Health & Health Care', *Russian Economic Trends*, Monthly Update, 14 July, 3–10

Part 5

CONCLUSION

Chapter 16

From Yeltsin and Putin to Medvedev

Learning objectives

- To introduce how Russians view Yeltsin, Putin and democracy.
- To examine the lack of effective political opposition.
- To introduce Dmitry Medvedev.
- To examine the possible restructuring of the political system post 2008.

Introduction

The 1990s began with a great deal of hope and perhaps rather unrealistic expectations about how quickly Russia could be transformed into a prosperous democracy. Under Yeltsin Russia developed a rather freewheeling and chaotic pluralism and vital elements of Russia's democratic transition were begun. Russia acquired a new Constitution in 1993, civil society organisations and political parties sprang up, multi-candidate elections were held, and the mass media expressed a wide range of opinions. Economically, culturally and politically Russia was more open to the rest of the world than ever before. However, it was hard for many ordinary Russians, struggling with the day-to-day realities of life to feel empowered by Russia's first decade of democracy, or for the concept of democracy to acquire substantive value. It should also not be forgotten that Yeltsin bombarded the parliament in 1993 to bring it into line, introduced a Constitution that set up a super-presidency and tried to ignore the parliament, launched a war against Chechnia that killed 50,000 people and repaid the oligarchs with state assets for their help in ensuring that he won the 1996 presidential election.

This was hardly a glittering record, but Russia's starting point in 1992 and the legacy of decades of CPSU rule were an unenviable starting point. Democratic transition should not be thought of as a simple linear process without deviations or setbacks, neither is democracy inevitable. In the 1990s Russia was also grappling with the complexities and difficulties thrown up by its economic transition; for many Russians the 1990s were a time of very real economic hardship. A survey

Box 16.1 Russians on Boris Yeltsin

	Answers *(in percentages)*
Question 1: How do you now evaluate Yeltsin?	
Overall positively	8
Neutrally	39
Overall negatively	48
Difficult to say	5
Question 2: Do you think that . . .	
Yeltsin should retain his immunity and security as Russia's first president	32
Yeltsin should be held responsible for the illegal acts and abuses allowed by him during his time in power	44
Difficult to say	24
Question 3: From an historical perspective, do you think that Yeltsin made Russia better or worse?	
Better	15
Worse	64
Difficult to say	21

Source: Levada-Tsentr (2007a) '*Rol' B. El'tsina v otsenkakh rossiian*', *Levada-Centre* website, 1 February, http://www.levada.ru/

Note: The data is based on a survey of 16,000 Russians aged over 18 years conducted in December 2006.

conducted by the Levada Centre in 2006 found that 64 per cent of Russians believed that Russia had got worse under Yeltsin and only 15 per cent believed that it got better (see Box 16.1).

By the end of the 1990s Yeltsin was in failing health and after two presidential terms he had to stand down. The various networks and clans that dominated politics behind the scenes decided that Vladimir Putin should succeed Yeltsin as president. Putin is a great admirer of the Russian Tsar Peter the Great (1682–1725) who created a strong Russian state, modernised the country and would brook no opposition to his rule. Putin set out with a similar agenda, which entailed strengthening the state, strengthening the power vertical and managing democracy to achieve his goals. After two terms he too had to stand down and his chosen successor, Dmitry Medvedev was duly elected. Russia now has its third post-soviet president, but whereas it was clear that Yeltsin was retiring from politics when he stood down as president, Putin stated his intention to continue to have a leading role in the political life of the country. President Medvedev and Prime Minister Putin now talk about working in tandem, but what this means in practice at present remains unclear.

Russia under Putin

Russians on Vladimir Putin

In January 2007 the Levada Centre conducted a survey of Putin's positive and negative characteristics (see Box 16.2). By this time Putin had been running Russia for six years and so there had been time for any earlier enthusiasm to fade in the face of the reality of Putin's Russia, but the survey showed that the respondents were hard-pressed to cite any negative characteristics. Quite the opposite, Putin was valued for his business-like manner and his energy, which were cited by 64 per cent of respondents.

The western media made a great deal of the arrival of a KGB man in the Kremlin, but within Russia Putin's career background does not necessarily elicit the same knee-jerk negative reaction as in the West. The KGB motto was the 'Sword and Shield'; they protected the USSR from external as well as internal threats. For many Russians the Yeltsin era was a time when Russia was devastatingly weakened by the loss of the socialist states in east-central Europe; the break up of the USSR; the advance of NATO towards Russia's borders; too close an alliance with the USA; the disastrous advice of western economic advisers and the predations of global capitalism. In this light a patriotic president who acts as 'the sword and shield' of his country, by representing Russia abroad with both great dignity and determination, is a positive asset. Domestically, it was hard for Russians to feel much sympathy when Putin quickly began to rein in the oligarchs, who had indulged in an orgy of self-enrichment, literally at the expense of their fellow-countrymen. Similarly, for many Russians strengthening the power vertical would have been a more ominous move if all the regional bosses had been democrats, but too many were not.

Box 16.2 Vladimir Putin's positive and negative characteristics

Positive characteristics	Cited by (in percentages)
Business-like, active, energetic	64
Educated, a good professional	46
Intellectual, cultured	43
Intelligent, capable, talented	38
Serious, responsible	38
Experience of political, state activities	32
Pleasant, likeable, charming	32
Leadership qualities, ability to inspire others	31
Strong, resolute, courageous	26
Ability to compromise, have constructive dialogue	25
Consistency of political line	23
Honest, decent, incorruptible	22
Mature, experienced	21

Box 16.2 (*Continued*)

Negative characteristics	Cited by (in percentages)
Difficult to say	65
Talks a lot – does little	12
Being guided, dependent	9
Lack of a clear political line	7
Weak, weak-willed	3
Lack of experience of state activities	2
Mafia links and corruption	2
Ambitious and conceited	2
Grey, insignificant, inexpressive	2
Nothing to recommend him, has not done anything serious	2
Unable to compromise or have a constructive dialogue	2
Passive, lacks initiative	1
Perfidious, vindictive	1
Scandalous, behaves aggressively	0
Irresponsible, not serious	0

Source: Levada-Tsentr (2007b) '*Sil'nye i slabye storony: V Putin, D. Medvedev, S. Ivanov*', Tables 1 and 2, 20 February, *Levada-Centre* website, http://www.levada.ru/

Putin and the economy

Putin first became prime minister in 1999 in the wake of the economic crisis in 1998. In contrast by the time he stepped down as president, Russia had a booming economy. In his last major press conference at the Kremlin as president in February 2008 Putin noted that the domestic growth rate was 8.1 per cent and the windfall fund from high oil prices stood at US$ 158 billion, wages rose by 16.9 per cent in 2007, Russia has the world's seventh largest economy with rising prosperity and living standards and a 3.4 trillion rouble stabilisation fund (Putin, 2008). Unemployment is also falling, from 6.5 per cent in 2006 to 5.7 per cent in 2007, according to official figures (Putin, 2007). There are problems, however, as increasing prosperity has contributed to booming imports which when combined with stagnant exports have led to a rapidly shrinking trade surplus, which could soon be in the red. Economic growth is still largely dependent on favourable external conditions, specifically rising oil prices and cheap foreign borrowing, which cannot be relied upon. Domestic economic reconstruction, such as the development of new industries and services, proceeds slowly. The rise in wages and pensions before the 2007 Duma elections has fuelled inflation, which Putin (2008) noted now stands at 11.9 per cent; he also noted that there is a rising gap between rich and poor. Improving living standards were a major factor in Putin's continuing popularity, but it may not be possible to sustain these improvements. Reforms in the key areas of healthcare, education and housing have also stalled and so the Putin–Medvedev partnership will have to address these issues together with further economic reform in order to maintain their popularity.

Putin and managed democracy

Putin describes Russia as a 'managed democracy', a rather strange expression that seems a contradiction in terms. Management is exercised by or on behalf of the Kremlin, whereas in a democracy it is the people (*demos*) and or their representatives who exercise power (*kratos*). Managed democracy means that elections are held but the results are manipulated with administrative methods used to bar certain political parties or candidates from standing (see Chapter 12). The conduct of elections under Putin has been widely criticised by western observers and Russia's beleaguered liberals. The manner in which the elections were conducted, the Kremlin's domination of the media, the use of administrative measures, the ballot box stuffing and the pressurisation of voters, means that the elections in 2007 and 2008 did not conform to the basic requirements of procedural democracy (see Chapter 3). Managed democracy has ensured that the Duma is dominated by pro-Kremlin parties and it has dutifully passed Putin's legislation. Although Putin stressed the importance of a strong civil society, his aim was to co-opt and control civil society rather than to allow it to play a genuinely independent role (see Chapter 10). The strengthening of the power vertical led to even more power being concentrated in the executive branch of the federal government and changed the composition and behaviour of the Federation Council. Thinking and organising along vertical lines means that little attention has been paid to building up horizontal links between institutions and bodies at the same level or to developing links between such institutions and bodies on the one side and society on the other. This was also one of the major flaws of the soviet system, which left it out of touch, unresponsive and increasingly prone to corruption.

Russians on democracy

Although the Duma elections in 2003 and 2007 and the presidential elections in 2004 and 2008 were increasingly manipulated to ensure Putin's desired result, in a curious way they reflected public opinion. Putin's strong leadership was increasingly viewed as the best kind of governance for Russia (see Box 16.3) and he delivered stability and rising standards of living. In 1991 Russians favoured democratic government over strong leadership by 51 to 39 per cent; by 2005 the pendulum had swung in favour of strong leadership by 66 to 28 per cent (see Box 16.3). Even among the revolutionary generation, those aged 18–34 during the tumultuous days of 1991, democracy has lost adherents (see Box 16.4). In 1991 58 per cent of the revolutionary generation favoured democracy over strong leadership, now only 29 per cent do so. When asked whether a good democracy was more important than a strong economy, only 14 per cent favoured democracy and 81 per cent

Box 16.3 The best kind of governance for Russia

Respondents were asked whether Russia should rely on a democratic form of government to solve the country's problems or a leader with a strong hand. Their responses are given in percentages.

	Democratic Government	Strong leader	Don't Know
Spring 2005	28	66	6
Summer 2002	21	70	9
1991	51	39	10

Source: Pew Research Center (2006) 'Russia's Weakened Democratic Embrace', *Pew Global Attitudes Project*, 1 May, http://pewglobal.org/

Box 16.4 Whose confidence fell the most?

Percentages favouring democracy over a strong leader:

	1991	2002	2005
Total	51	21	28
Men	58	21	30
Women	46	20	27
Revolutionary Generation			
Aged 18–34	58		
Aged 29–45		23	
Aged 32–48			29

Source: Pew Research Center (2006) 'Russia's Weakened Democratic Embrace', *Pew Global Attitudes Project*, 1 May, http://pewglobal.org/

a strong economy (Pew Global Research Project, 2006). Support for democracy falls together with income levels, so while 34 per cent of those earning over 8,000 roubles a month favour democracy, the figure drops to 27 per cent for those earning 4,000–8,000 roubles and 21 per cent for those with an income of less than 4,000 roubles (ibid.). It seems that democracy is a luxury item that the poor cannot afford. These results help to explain Putin's appeal as his presidency coincided with a period of steady economic growth and he ensured that pensions and salaries were paid. For their part, the liberals and communists proved unable to transform and mobilise the very real economic and social deprivation that still exists, or to capitalise on the widespread opposition to the replacement of welfare benefits by cash payments in 2005, into an effective political challenge to Putin.

Box 16.5 Assessments of Putin

Time Magazine **names Putin 'Person of the Year 2007'**

Noting that when Putin became president in 2000, Russia was 'on the verge of becoming a failed state' but that Putin had a vision of what Russia should become and showed the persistence and leadership to carry this out and that:

> Putin is not a boy scout. He is not a democrat in any way that the West would define it. He is not a paragon of free speech. He stands, above all, for stability – stability before freedom, stability before choice, stability in a country that has hardly seen it for a hundred years. Whether he becomes more like the man [Stalin] for whom his grandfather prepared blinis – who himself was twice TIME's Person of the Year – or like Peter the Great, the historical figure he most admires; whether he proves to be a reformer or an autocrat who takes Russia back to an era of repression – this we will know only over the next decade. At significant cost to the principles and ideas that free nations prize, he has performed an extraordinary feat of leadership in imposing stability on a nation that has rarely known it and brought Russia back to the table of world power. For that reason, Vladimir Putin is TIME's 2007 Person of the Year.

Source: Richard Stengel (2007) 'Person of the Year 2007. Choosing Order Before Freedom', *Time Magazine*, 19 December, website http://www.time.com/

Anna Politkovskaya on Putin as a KGB man returning Russia to its soviet past:

> His outlook is the narrow, provincial one his rank would suggest; he has the unprepossessing personality of a lieutenant-colonel who never made it to colonel, the manner of a Soviet policeman who habitually snoops on his own colleagues. And he is vindictive: not a single political opponent has been invited to the inauguration ceremony, not a single political party that is in any way out of step . . . The return of the Soviet system with the consolidation of Putin's power is obvious.

Source: Anna Politkovskaya (2004) *Putin's Russia*, London: The Harvill Press, 269–71 (trans: Arch Tait)

Boris Kagarlitsky on Putin as a president without real opposition:

> The very concept of a political alternative has disappeared during the past three years. The opposition at least made a show of battling with Yeltsin. Today the opposition doesn't hide the fact that the battle is only for second place. It makes no claim to an independent political role. Putin stands above the fray. It's pointless to compare Putin to other politicians in the absence of political competition. Whatever you might think of Putin as president, he's the only show in town. Even if he does absolutely nothing.

Source: Boris Kagarlitsky (2002) 'The Man Without a Face', *The Moscow Times*, 27 August

Putin's failures: security and corruption

Putin's emphasis on strengthening the state, managing democracy and strengthening the power vertical, have not been a total success. Not only have they not dealt with certain issues they have instead exacerbated them. The war in Chechnia is supposed to be over and the republic's leadership and government has been Chechenised. However, fighting is still taking place in Chechnia, human right abuses continue and terrorism has spilled over into neighbouring areas and into the heart of Moscow itself. The sieges at Beslan and in Moscow in 2004 were major intelligence failures, the tactics employed by the armed and security forces displayed a cavalier disregard for human life and there is evidence that corruption by state employees facilitated both sieges.

Putin has acknowledged that corruption is still a major problem and although he has pledged to tackle it, he conspicuously failed to enact an effective anti-corruption policy. In 1999 Russia signed the Council of Europe's Criminal Law Convention on Corruption and then in 2003 signed the UN Convention against Corruption; but neither convention has been ratified and Russia's legislation has not been brought into compliance with either of them. In 2004 Putin raised the salaries of high ranking officials in a bid to make corruption less attractive, but there is no evidence that this has had the desired effect. In 2004 the powers of the Duma Commission on Counteracting Corruption were even drastically reduced as it lost the right to carry out its own investigations. Official anti-corruption campaigns have continued largely to target low-level officials, leaving higher-level officials who are adept at covering their tracks, free. Such campaigns have been a useful device to discredit particular targets and to promote other political goals. For example, during 2004 there was a wave of arrests of regional officials, coinciding with Putin's overall drive to strengthen the power vertical. The result is that corruption remains an endemic problem, not just in the interface between business and the various levels of government, but also for the average Russian citizen in their dealings with government, or even with the education and healthcare systems.

Russia's virtual politics

Andrew Wilson (2005) describes the political systems in FSU states such as Russia and Ukraine as 'virtual democracies'. Virtual democracies have the appearance of democratic systems, but political technologists are able to manipulate their political processes. These political technologists are not just super-spin doctors as they actually create a whole system of virtual political institutions, such as political parties and civil society organisations, that imitate their genuine democratic equivalents. In this way the political technologists effectively construct the political world; they function as combined political meta-programmers, system designers, decision makers and political controllers.

As the Duma elections of 2007 and the presidential elections of 2008 approached, Putin's political technologists devoted considerable energy to 'operation successor'. They wanted to ensure that Dmitry Medvedev would be elected president and that the Duma would be a pliant, pro-Kremlin tool. The creation of

> ## Box 16.6 Andrew Wilson's five elements of 'Virtual Politics'
>
> - The extensive use of compromising materials (*kompromat*) to blackmail opponents.
>
> - The use of 'administrative resources' to aid pro-government and hinder opposition candidates.
>
> - The use of KGB tactics known as 'active measures', such as sponsoring a 'double' candidate with a similar name and platform to an opposition candidate.
>
> - The creation of 'virtual objects' such as a political party to split the vote of an opposition party.
>
> - The creation of a dramaturgy (*dramaturgiia*) or a meta-narrative around an election or an event to communicate the Kremlin's message.
>
> *Source*: Andrew Wilson (2005) *Virtual Democracy: Faking Democracy in the Post-Soviet World*, New Haven, CT: Yale University Press

a dramaturgy was a vital part of the creation and maintenance of support for Putin and of ensuring the continuity of Putin's agenda after he had to step down from the presidency. According to Wilson, Putin's declaration in 1999 that he would destroy the oligarchs as a class was about resetting the narrative of Putin's presidency. It sent a message to the people and the political and economic elites that Putin's presidency marked a sharp rejection of the 1990s. It showed Putin rejecting crony capitalism and also sent a clear message to Yeltsin's clan that even though they had promoted him, Putin was now in charge. Understood in this way the arrest of the oligarch and Yukos CEO Mikhail Khodorkovsky, in October 2003, was a vital element of the anti-oligarch dramaturgy in the run up to the Duma elections in 2003 and presidential elections in 2004.

Wilson also suggests that another suitable dramaturgy could be the threat of nationalism or Islamic terrorism to Russia, with United Russia and the Kremlin-backed presidential candidate depicted as the guarantors of stability and security in the face of the threat. Putin used the threat of terrorism and of vaguely defined extremism to justify the strengthening of the state, the clamping down on civil society and the need for managed democracy. An increasingly important part of the dramaturgy is the West's bid to foment an orange revolution in Russia, as they had in Ukraine over the winter of 2004–5. The Kremlin has used foreign funding and support as grounds for attacking and disparaging the motivation of civil society organisations and political parties that have challenged Putin. According to this narrative those who challenge or even question Putin are attacking the Russian people and state and are probably in the pay of a foreign power. Throughout 2006 and through to the presidential elections in 2008, tension between Russia and the West grew. Russia withdrew from the CFE, objected to President Bush's plans to site missiles in Poland and the Czech Republic and the enlargement of NATO. Russia and Britain are also in dispute on a number of issues, including Britain's alleged spying. For its part Moscow objects to Boris Berezovsky and to the Chechen separatist Akhmed Zakayev being granted asylum in Britain, while Britain wants to extradite Andrei Lugovoi from Russia for the murder in London of Aleksandr Litvinenko, a former KGB man and an ally of Berezovsky.

Russia's relations with the countries of the former soviet empire in Europe and the former Soviet Union (FSU) have also been added to the dramaturgy. After the humiliations of the 1990s Putin wanted to project Russia as a global and regional power. Russia has warned the West against trying to promote more colour revolutions and warned its former allies in Europe and the FSU that actual or proposed membership of the European Union and/or NATO does not mean that Russia is no longer interested in them. In April 2007 the Estonian government removed the Red Army war memorial, which they viewed as a symbol of their lost independence and soviet domination, from the centre of Tallinn. The Kremlin viewed the statue's removal as an insult and a rejection of the great sacrifices that Russians had made to defeat Nazi Germany during the Great Patriotic war (1941–45). The Kremlin orchestrated the reaction of outraged, ordinary Russians to the statue's removal. Ethnic Russians living in Estonia rioted and demonstrated and there were demonstrations by pro-Kremlin youth groups outside the Estonian embassy in Moscow as well as a cyber attack on Estonian government websites (Mite, 2007).

Opposing Putin, Medvedev and United Russia

The disappearing opposition

Following the 2007 elections the KPRF is the only real opposition party with representation in the Duma. In the presidential election in 2008, the KPRF candidate Gennady Zyuganov once again came second. The KPRF's vote is falling, its supporters tend to be older people and it has not been able to broaden its support to include young people. Russia's liberal parties, Yabloko and the Union of Rightist Forces (SPS) have no deputies and did not contest the 2008 presidential election. It is too simplistic to explain the opposition's failure just in terms of managed democracy, including the abolition of the SMDs and the raising of the threshold for representation from 5 to 7 per cent (see Chapter 12) and the Kremlin's control of the media. The KPRF, Yabloko and the SPS have existed long enough for most voters to know who they are and to have a general idea of their agenda. The simple truth is the opposition parties do not appeal to enough voters and United Russia does. The KPRF is associated with the soviet past and Yabloko and SPS with the market reforms of the 1990s that plummeted many Russians into poverty. In contrast Putin and United Russia are able to appeal to all Russians for a variety of reasons, not least Russia's growing prosperity and restored international status.

The Other Russia and Marches of the Discontented

The Other Russia is an umbrella organisation formed in July 2006 to unite the opposition to Putin from across the political spectrum. It was boycotted by the liberal parties Yabloko and the SPS because of the participation of ultranational-ists such as the Marxist-Leninist Vanguard of Red Youth and Viktor Anpilov's far left Russian Communist Workers' Party–Revolutionary Party of Communists. The participation of Eduard Limonov's National Bolshevik Party (NBP), which was banned in April 2007 and whose members favour violent street action and Nazi-style salutes, helped to alienate the liberals' natural constituency. The Other Russia does include some liberals such as Lyudmila Alekseeva of the Moscow Helsinki Human Rights Group, Andrei Illarionov Putin's former economics adviser, Mikhail Kasyanov the former prime minister and Garry Kasparov the former world chess champion. Since December 2006 the Other Russia has organised a series of demonstrations each dubbed a March of the Discontented or Dissenters (*Marsh Nesoglasnykh*) in Moscow, St Petersburg, Nizhnii Novgorod, Samara and Cheliabinsk. Kasparov and Kasyanov were both arrested during the march in Moscow on 14 April 2007, but were later released. For a time Garry Kasparov seemed to be the rallying point for the liberal opposition, but he is a divisive figure; his fam-ily do not live in Russia and he also has close links to two American think-tanks, the Center for Security Policy and the Hoover Institution, which have close links to the Bush administration and US neo-conservatives. Such links provide the Kremlin with evidence that Kasparov and his allies are in the pay of a foreign gov-ernment and that their marches are part of a bid to foment a colour revolution.

Committee 2008 and a Russia without Putin

The Committee 2008 was formed in January 2004 as an umbrella organisation of the democratic opposition to Putin's increasing authoritarianism. Its members wanted to ensure that the 2008 presidential election would be free and fair and to prevent the election from turning into the formalisation of the appointment of whomever would emerge as the Kremlin's chosen successor. They wanted a Russia without Putin after 2008. Committee 2008 is chaired by Garry Kasparov, who also formed and leads the United Civil Front social movement, which is part of the Other Russia movement. Other members of Committee 2008 are well-known liberals such as Boris Nemtsov a former deputy prime minister and co-founder of SPS, Irina Khakamada a SPS member who stood in the 2004 presidential elections, Vladimir Ryzhkov an independent Duma deputy and a member of Other Russia, Yevgeny Kiselyov a political analyst for the English-language *Moscow Times*, Vladimir V. Kara-Murza a journalist and SPS member, and the soviet-era dissident Vladimir Bukovsky.

The democratic opposition did not unite and choose one candidate for the presi-dential elections. For a time it seemed possible that the former prime minister, Mikhail Kasyanov might emerge as a candidate. He was tainted by his association with the Yeltsin era, when he was rumoured to have been 'Misha Two Percent', after the alleged personal cut he demanded for all the business deals he oversaw while prime minister. In June 2007 a wide range of people including Garry Kasparaov, Boris Nemtsov and Eduard Limonov spoke in support of Kasyanov, who promised better apartments for half the population and free healthcare for all (Krainova, 2007). Given the range of political forces in the Other Russia Movement and represented in Committee 2008, it is not surprising that they did not unite behind one candidate. Nemtsov withdrew his candidacy and urged his supporters to back Kasyanov; Yavlinsky similarly withdrew, but urged Yabloko to support Bukovsky. However, the CEC refused to register Kasyanov, Bukovsky and Kasparov as candidates, which meant that there were no liberal candidates for the 2008 presidential elections.

Mikhail Khodorkovsky and the mistakes of the 1990s

Khodorkovsky is an oligarch, the former CEO of Yukos, a self-styled democrat and liberal former, who is now in a Siberian prison colony (see Chapter 8). Khodorkovsky acknowledges that he personally benefited tremendously from the education that he received in the soviet era and then from the privatisations of the 1990s, but believes that fundamental mistakes were made under Yeltsin and that their legacy still needs to be addressed in Russia today. Before his arrest Khodorkovsky gave funds to a wide range of opposition groups across the political spectrum. Khodorkovsky uses the term liberal as a shorthand for the radical reformers in Yeltsin's team and argues that liberals, such as Chubais and Gaidar, made fundamental mistakes. They failed to see that 90 per cent of Russians were unprepared for the sweeping changes ahead; they disingenuously claimed that everyone would benefit from privatisation; failed to address the loss in value of peoples' savings; and failed to reform the areas that were and remain critical to the average Russian, specifically: education, healthcare, the housing sector and support for the poor. The liberals were also dishonest and greedy and indifferent to ordinary people. They were also inconsistent, on the one hand talking of freedom but striving for ever greater financial and administrative control (Khodorkovsky, 2004).

According to Khodorkovsky (2005a) Russia's slide into authoritarianism began not with Putin, but with Yeltsin and the liberals. As opposition to their reforms grew and they lost electoral support, they simply would not listen to genuine and understandable concerns. According to Khodorkovsky the oligarchs and business people did not want a liberal democracy, they wanted stability and to make money and an active civil society could have interfered with their aims by standing up for workers' rights, environmental protection, transparency of business projects and acting as a counterweight to corruption. For Russia's business people it was easier to deal with greedy officials than with civil society organisations (Khodorkovsky, 2004). In 1996 Khodorkovsky was one of the signatories to a letter called 'Breaking the Deadlock', arguing that it was important for Yeltsin to stay in power as the guarantor of fundamental freedoms and human rights, but that the KPRF leader should be made prime minister with broad powers. They also argued that economic and social policies had to become more 'leftist' in order to reconcile freedom with justice for both the winners and the losers in the 1990s privatisations and liberalisations. Neither Yeltsin nor Zyuganov would compromise and form a partnership. Instead, for the liberals, everything was justified on the basis of the ends justifying the means and the need to counter any threat of a communist revival (Khodorkovsky, 2004). For Khodorkovsky Russia needs to change from a presidential to a parliamentary republic, with the president taking on the role of a moral leader. He also argues that the Duma should form the government which would then be responsible to the Duma. There also needs to be true federalism, the election of regional heads and the Federation Council, and real, local self-government (Khodorkovsky, 2005b).

Restructuring the political system?

Back to the USSR: Russia's system of uncontested power

The historian Dmitry Furman who is member of the Russian Academy of Sciences describes Russia today as having a system of uncontested power. He argues that while Russia has nominally broken with its soviet past and adopted democratic values, it is unable to live in accordance with these democratic values (Furman, 2006). Putin's managed democracy is 'a soft variant of the Soviet system' (ibid.), which like the USSR lacks a free struggle between political forces but also does not have anything akin to the soviet system's ideological underpinnings. In this system of uncontested power there is a profound contradiction between the formal and the informal political arrangement. So Russia has elections that seem democratic and contested, but their outcomes are generally known in advance; the courts seem independent, but make decisions that serve the interests of the authorities. For Furman this contradiction between form and reality makes Russia today even

---

Box 16.7 Back to the USSR – the party rules?

Boris Nadezhdin of the Union of Rightist Forces told Radio Free Europe/Radio Liberty that after the 2007 Duma elections:

> There is no doubt this is a different country now, . . . We have returned to the Soviet Union. It is not parliament or the next president that will have real power, but the Unified [United] Russia party.

Source: Robert Coalson (2007) 'Russia: Moscow Shifts From "Managed Democracy" To "Manual Control" ', *RFE/RL* website, 3 December, http://www.rferl.org/

For **Lev Gudkov**, the Director of the Levada Analytical Centre, survey findings that two-thirds of Russians did not expect the 2007 Duma elections to be conducted honestly, but nevertheless expected their lives to improve after the election indicated that Russia was heading towards authoritarianism, that:

> Authoritarianism is growing, as is hope in the great national leader, . . . This is a very dangerous tendency. Every political party has been discredited. Unified Russia is only influential as a result of its connection to the president. We are heading toward a one-party system.

Source: Brian Whitmore (2007) 'RFE/RL: Russians Skeptical About Elections, Hopeful For Future', *RFE/RL* website feature article, http://www.rferl/org/

more fragile and unstable than was the USSR. The system of uncontested power means that power is not rotated, that the same people or forces remain in power, which hinders adaptation and change. However, society is developing even faster than under soviet socialism and so the contemporary system of uncontested power will be corroded even faster than soviet socialism was corroded. According to Furman the managed democracies of Russia, Belarus, Ukraine and Kazakhstan are subject to degradation, manifested by corruption, loss of contact between those in power and society, the use of overt reprisals and assassinations of opponents, and a general loss of legitimacy. For this reason Furman believes that Putin's managed democracy is a transitional entity on the way to Russia becoming a real democracy.

United Russia – the party back in control?

The United Russia party had its origins in the Unity party which was created in the dying days of Yeltsin's presidency to ensure the Kremlin's control of the Duma. For the Duma elections in 2007 Putin headed the list of United Russia's candidates and then in April 2008, while still declining to join the party as a member, he agreed to take on the new post of party chair that was created especially for him. This means that Putin is the party leader with overall strategic control, but he is not responsible for its routine management. This move has provoked speculation that Putin is seeking to restructure Russia's political system, concentrating

Russian President Vladimir Putin (C) delivers his speech to the delegates of pro-Kremlin United Russia party at the party congress in Moscow, April 2005.

power in the United Russia party leadership and that he will continue to rule Russia through United Russia's party apparatus, stretching from Moscow out into the regions, in the manner of a soviet-era CPSU general secretary. As neither Putin nor Medvedev are party members United Russia is not the ruling party or a political entity in its own right. United Russia was created as the Kremlin's tool and Putin has used it to make important announcements, for example it was at its conference in December 2007 that he announced he would be prime minister if United Russia won that month's Duma elections and an 'efficient person' was elected president in 2008. In this scenario the party leadership is more important than the posts of president and prime minister. If the Medvedev–Putin partnership were to split, for example, then President Medvedev could sack Prime Minister Putin, but Medvedev would then need the Duma's support to appoint a new prime minister – and the Duma is controlled by United Russia. There are other similarities with the CPSU; United Russia's youth group *Nashi* is used to mobilise young people in support of the Kremlin in a manner similar to the Komsomol. Members of *Nashi* have recently set up a children's movement called the Teddy Bears (*Mishki*), which is reminiscent of the soviet-era Octobrists and Pioneers (Arnold, 2008).

Putin's popularity

According to the Constitution a Russian president may only serve two consecutive terms. As 2008 (the year Putin had to stand down) approached, speculation was rife both in Russia and abroad that Putin might seek a third term. Putin repeatedly said that he would not seek to amend the Constitution to enable him to stand for office for a third time, although public opinion surveys consistently showed that a majority of Russians favoured such an amendment. For example the newspaper *Kommersant* (2007) carried a report of the findings of a survey conducted in 46 regions by the All-Russia Public Opinion Centre on 7–8 April 2007. The survey found that 65 per cent of the 16,000 respondents supported Sergei Mironov's proposal to extend the presidential term from four to seven years and to allow the president to serve three consecutive terms. A third term for Putin was supported by 69 per cent of the respondents, who also favoured the introduction of the necessary constitutional amendments. In contrast 24 per cent opposed allowing a third term and 23 per cent opposed amending the Constitution. Mironov made this proposal at the end of March 2007 just after he had been elected Federation Council chair (speaker) for a third term. Had Putin wanted to stand for election for a third time, given the popular support he enjoyed throughout the country and United Russia's domination of the Duma, the necessary constitutional amendment could have been made.

Operation successor: networks and Kremlinology

Government reshuffles in 2005 and 2007 stimulated considerable speculation about who might succeed Putin in 2008. It was all very reminiscent of the Kremlinology (see Chapter 2) practised in the soviet era to try to identify the likely outcome of the power struggles going on within the Kremlin. Putin said that he would support the candidacy of a single successor (*Mosnews*, 2006) and help to ensure a smooth handover of power to the new president. Putin needed to identify a candidate who, with the Kremlin's considerable media and administrative backing, could be assured of election in March 2008. The candidate also had to be acceptable to the various institutions and networks that had brought Putin to power in 2000 and who would provide stability and continuity for the policies initiated under Putin. Two possible candidates emerged from Putin's St Petersburg networks: Dmitry Medvedev and Sergei Ivanov. Medvedev is a lawyer with a liberal reputation and no personal security or military (*siloviki*) connections. In contrast Ivanov shares Putin's background in foreign intelligence and is his former defence minister.

In November 2005 Medvedev was appointed to the revived post of first deputy prime minister. While this meant that Medvedev moved from the Kremlin to an office in the White House, the parliament building, he was assigned the task of boosting stalled government reforms, especially in the important areas of construction, agriculture, health and education. At the time it seemed possible that he was being positioned to replace Fradkov as prime minister and so follow Putin's pre-presidential career path. Fradkov remained prime minister but he is a politically unambitious technocrat with a surprisingly low public profile and was never a likely candidate for the presidency. In November 2005 Ivanov became a deputy prime minister, a level down from Medvedev's position as first deputy prime minister. However, Putin also entrusted Ivanov with the vital role of overseeing and coordinating the activities of not just the Defence Ministry, but also of the Interior Ministry and the FSB. It was not until February 2007 that Ivanov was also made a first deputy prime minister. In addition, while he was no longer defence minister, he had been entrusted with another key role: the oversight of civilian and defence industries.

Operation successor: choosing Medvedev

Based on the results of their January 2007 survey of the strengths and weaknesses of Putin, Medvedev and Ivanov, the Levada Centre believed that if their survey had been a presidential election 33 per cent would have voted for Medvedev and 21 per cent for Ivanov (Levada-Tsentr, 2007). Despite their vital roles in Putin's government both men lacked high public profiles. This is in part an effect of Russia's super-presidential system, which focuses power and attention on the person of the president. It also points to a major problem with Russia's elite recruitment. In democracies political leaders usually serve some kind of political apprenticeship, during which they are tested, gain experience and public recognition. The apprenticeship usually starts with some kind of civic or political activism and party membership, which may eventually lead to selection to contest an election. To this may also be added experience in local or regional politics, or in government in junior roles at regional or federal levels. By the time a candidate stands for election as president they have a decade or two of political experience during which their profile has gradually risen. It would be naïve to suggest that patronage plays no role in elite recruitment in democracies, but in Russia it *is* the form of elite recruitment.

On 10 December 2007 Putin announced his support for Medvedev in the 2008 presidential elections. Boris Gryzlov the leader of United Russia and Duma speaker, Sergei Mironov the leader of the Social Justice Party and Federation Council speaker, and the leaders of two other pro-Kremlin parties, were all present at the Kremlin for the announcement. True to his service background Putin has always been very careful about the people he has promoted and expects loyalty. Whereas during the Yeltsin era sacked officials took revenge by publishing their memoirs, this was not a feature of the Putin era. Medvedev was carefully chosen for his loyalty to Putin and was only able to stand because he was backed by Putin. The presidential elections in March 2008 were the first time that Medvedev had ever stood for election to a public office.

Box 16.8 Dmitry Medvedev

Born 14 September 1965 in Leningrad (now called St Petersburg). His parents were both university professors and he was brought up in modest circumstances in a small (40 sq m) flat in the suburb of Kupchino. He became a fan of 70s western rock music, which was only available in illegal *samizdat* at that time. Deep Purple played at the Kremlin in February 2008 to celebrate the 15th anniversary of the founding of Gazprom. As a student Medvedev supplemented his income by working as a street cleaner and on construction sites. He met his wife Svetlana at school and they have a son Ilya, who was born in 1996. His hobbies include rock and classical music, swimming, jogging and yoga.

Between 1982 and 1987 Medvedev studied law at Leningrad State University and was taught by Professor Anatoly Sobchak. (Sobchak had taught Putin more than a decade before and other key political figures including German Gref, Dmitry Kozak and Anton Ivanov the current chair of the Supreme Arbitration Court.) Medvedev worked on Sobchak's campaign for the 1989 elections to the new Congress of People's Deputies. Sobchak was a leading democrat and played a major role in framing Russia's post-Soviet legislation, including the 1993 RF Constitution.

During the 1990s Medvedev combined academic teaching and writing, a private law practice specialising in business and working for the St Petersburg City Administration. He became the legal consultant for the Committee for External Affairs, which was headed by Vladimir Putin. In 1996 Sobchak lost the mayoral election to Vladimir Yakovlev and Medvedev stopped working for the city administration.

In 1999 Putin appointed Medvedev as the head of the government administration and then as deputy head of the presidential administration (Kremlin staff). Medvedev headed Putin's presidential election campaign in 2000. In 2000 he became chair of the state energy company Gazprom then was briefly its deputy chair 2001 to 2002, before resuming the chair in 2002 (a post he only relinquished on becoming RF President). In November 2005 Medvedev was appointed to the revived post of first deputy prime minister and was put in charge of the five stalled national projects on education, health, agriculture, construction and social development.

The 2 March 2008 saw Medvedev elected President of the Russian Federation and on 9 May 2008 he was sworn in – Russia's third post-soviet president. At 42 he is the youngest Russian leader since Tsar Nicholas II ascended the throne in 1894.

President and prime minister: two centres or in tandem?

In his last Annual News Conference in February 2008, Putin stressed that he and Medvedev have a long and successful track record of working together but also said that he intended to retain an important role in the political life of the country. Putin's decision to become prime minister led to speculation that this would involve a redistribution of authority between the executive and the legislature and that there might be changes to the structure of government. Putin has rejected the idea that Russia will develop two centres of power, the prime minister and the government as one centre and the president as the other (see Box 16.9); rather Medvedev and Putin talk about working in tandem. Putin argues that the post of prime minister has ample authority for him and that, 'The president is the guarantor of the constitution', 'he sets the main direction for internal and external policy. But the highest executive power in the country is the Russian government, headed by the prime minister. So there is enough power for Dmitry and me to share' (Putin, 2008). He also said that he did not intend to dictate orders to his successor.

In formal terms the prime minister is the junior role to the president; the prime minister is appointed by the president and, in the past, incumbents of that office have tended to be held responsible for policy failings. Putin appointed a series of low-profile, very able technocrats without any obvious personal political ambitions as his prime ministers. Putin did appoint Mikhail Kasyanov as prime minister and he has since emerged as a leading opposition figure, but Kasyanov was inherited from Yeltsin. Putin clearly does not see himself as a subservient prime minister, suggesting that Medvedev will be Russia's head of state but that this will be largely

Putin and Medvedev share the stage at a victory concert in Red Square, Moscow on election day 2 March 2008. Medvedev repeated his promise 'to preserve the course set by President Vladimir Putin'.

> ## Box 16.9 Putin and Medvedev on Russia's political system
>
> ### Putin rejects the idea of two power centres
>
> We don't have two centres, we have one decision-making centre – the president, and the parliament, of course. As for the government, under the provisions of the Constitution it is the executive branch's main body. I do not think it would be right to either take any of the government's rights, prerogatives and obligations from it, or to burden it with new ones. We certainly do not need to create two centres of power within the executive branch. I am not in favour of curtailing the president's powers. We simply need to ensure more effective interaction between the executive, judicial and legislative branches of power.
>
> *Source*: Vladimir Putin (2007) 'Replies to Journalists' Questions following the Hot Line', Kremlin website, 18 October, http://www.kremlin.ru/eng/
>
> ### Medvedev rejects the idea of a parliamentary republic
>
> In an interview with the newsweekly *Itogi* on 18 February 2008 Medvedev warned that:
>
> Should Russia become a parliamentary republic it will disappear . . . This is my profound conviction . . . Russia was always built around a rigid executive vertical line.
>
> This means that the legislature should follow the orders of the executive.
>
> Source: Medvedev (2008) Medvedev website, http://www.medvedev2008.ru/english_2008_02_18.htm

a ceremonial role and that power will shift to the government headed by Prime Minister Putin. It could be argued that in Medvedev Putin has another technocrat without his own political ambitions. It is clear that Medvedev was only elected because he had Putin's endorsement; if he had stood as an independent without Kremlin support he would not have been elected. For the electorate Medvedev was the candidate who stood for continuity with the Putin era. Putin is Medvedev's patron and mentor and Medvedev does not have his own power base or any independent links to the powerful *siloviki* network, which makes his personal position precarious should he decide to strike an independent course. Even with all the administrative resources and Kremlin control of the media, according to Sergei Shpilkin Medvedev has the support of only about one-third of the electorate (Harding, 2008), which is hardly an overwhelming mandate. He does not have his own mandate and powerbase, so is unlikely to emerge from Putin's shadow.

Medvedev and the evolution of the Putin agenda

Putin and Medvedev appeared on stage together at the post-election victory celebrations in Red Square. Medvedev pledged to continue Putin's policies and there is no evidence so far that Medvedev has his own vision for Russia. Medvedev tends to be described as a liberal, but in Russian terms this could mean as little as not having links to the *siloviki*. Medvedev (2007) did make a very strong pro-democracy statement at the World Economic Forum in 2007, arguing that, 'Today we are building new institutions based on the fundamental principles of full democracy,' and that 'This democracy requires no additional definition. This democracy is effective and is based on the principles of the market economy, supremacy of the law, and government that is accountable to the rest of society. We are fully aware that no undemocratic country has ever been truly prosperous, and this for the simple reason that it is better to have freedom than not to have it.' Also in 2007 in an interview with *Vedomosti* he specifically rejected the concept of sovereign democracy, which was developed by Vladislav Surkov, a deputy head of Putin's presidential administration. Medvedev argued, 'In my opinion as a lawyer, playing up one feature of a full-fledged democracy – namely the supremacy of state authorities within the country and their independence [from influences] outside the country – is excessive and even harmful because it is disorienting' (cited by Abdullaev, 2007). It should be remembered that Putin also emphasises the importance of democracy and of civil society while at the same time talking of the importance of sovereign democracy and managed democracy.

As Medvedev did not formally campaign in 2008 or produce a programme, the speeches included on his 'campaign' website provide a sense of his priorities, which are essentially the same as Putin's. In a major speech at Krasnoyarsk on 15 February 2008 Medvedev talked about the importance of diversifying the economy away from its overdependence on energy revenues, reducing VAT, raising living standards and improving education and healthcare. Putin has also said all these things, although Medvedev's comment about appointing independent directors rather than government officials to the boards of state-owned companies is new, but it could indicate that now the Kremlin has firm control over these industries it no longer needs to have its people on the boards. Medvedev also talked about the importance of freedom, both economic and of expression; he condemned the courts as 'riddled with corruption and the state bureaucracy as weighted with indifference, predatory officials and bloat, and Russia's business climate has been smothered' (Medvedev, 2008). Putin has also attacked corruption and started to reform the state bureaucracy (civil service).

In terms of foreign policy again there is no evidence as yet that Medvedev will push for any major departures. Putin's approach to the West has been fairly pragmatic, joining the war on terror when it suited Russia's national interest but stridently condemning the enlargement of NATO and the deployment of missiles in east-central Europe. The election of the new American president in 2008 will have a profound effect on Russian foreign policy. If America elects a hawkish president with unilateral tendencies then Russia will respond aggressively. If the Americans elect a more conciliatory president with a multilateral approach to foreign affairs, then Russia will be happy to talk, provided they are not lectured. Medvedev shares Putin's pragmatism. As chair of Gazprom, Medvedev implemented Putin's foreign policy agenda of raising prices and reducing supplies to Russia's neighbours, rather than pursuing a strictly business agenda.

Chapter summary

When the Russian Federation came into existence on 1 January 1992 it was committed to becoming a democracy and a market economy. In the following years it was described as being in transition, as if there were a clear trajectory towards its stated goals and it was just a matter of time before they were reached. Russia is now classified as a market economy by the EU and the USA, but its democratic credentials are increasingly in doubt. Russia has the trappings of a democracy: a constitution establishing the necessary principles and rights, political parties, NGOs and elections. On the debit side Putin's commitment to the creation of a managed democracy saw the previous gradual development of an independent judiciary reversed, the dominance of the executive over the legislature, the increasing dominance of Moscow over the regions, the mass media becoming much less pluralistic than in the 1990s together with physical attacks on investigative journalists, and opposition political parties and NGOs being harassed and closed down. At the same time Putin presided over a growing economy, a period of rising standards of living for many Russians and a country that is taken seriously in the world's capitals and international organisations. This is strikingly different to the 1990s when Russia was an economic basket case: in debt and seemingly in permanent economic crisis. Following the elections in 2007 and 2008 Putin and Medvedev, working in tandem, will be able to push ahead with the policies that have brought Russia stability and prosperity; however, they need to address the growing gap between rich and poor, the country's endemic corruption, and also to diversify the economy if Russia is to remain stable and prosperous.

Discussion points

- Has Putin introduced a form of transitional authoritarianism?
- What are the positive and negative aspects of Putin's legacy to the next president?
- Why has liberalism failed in Russia?
- How do you think Russia will change in the next 10 years?

Further reading

Useful analyses of Russia's post-soviet development are provided by Peter Baker and Susan Glasser (2005) *Kremlin Rising: Vladimir Putin's Russia and the End of Revolution*, New York: Simon & Schuster; Michael McFaul, Nikolai Petrov and Andrei Ryabov (2004) *Between Dictatorship and Democracy: Russia Post-Communist Political Reforms*, Washington, DC: Carnegie Endowment for International Peace; Dale R. Herspring (ed.) (2003) *Putin's Russia: Past Imperfect, Future Uncertain*, Lanham, MD: Rowman and Littlefield; Archie Brown and Lilia Shevtsova (2001) *Gorbachev, Yeltsin and Putin*, Washington, DC: Carnegie

Endowment for International Peace; Lilia Shevtsova (2007) *Russia. Lost in Transition: The Yeltsin and Putin Legacies*, Washington, DC: Carnegie Endowment for International Peace (trans: Arch Tait); Dmitri V. Trenin (2007) *Getting Russia Right*, Washington, DC: Carnegie Endowment for International Peace; Richard Sakwa (2004) *Putin: Russia's Choice*, London: Routledge; and finally Anna Politkovskaya (2007) *A Russian Diary*, New York: Random House (trans: Arch Tait).

Useful websites

Dmitry Medvedev's website: http://www.medvedev2008.ru/english_2008_02_18.htm

The Other Russia: http://www.theotherrussia.org/

March of the Discontented: http://www.namarsh.ru/ (Russian only)

Official Garry Kasparov website: http://www.kasparov.com/

Center for Security Policy: http://www.centerforsecuritypolicy.org/

Mikhail Khodorkovsky Press Center website: http://www.khodorkovsky.info/
On the site, see also Mikhail Khodorkovsky (2006) 'Letter from Siberia', *The Economist*, 20 November, 98

Hoover Institution: http://www.hoover.org/

National Bolsheviks: http://www.nbp-info.ru/ (Russian only)

Kompromat.ru: http://www.compromat.ru/ (Russian only)

A website that collects Russia's compromising materials

References

Abdullaev, N. (2007) 'Medvedev, A Soft-Spoken, "Smart Kid" Lawyer', *The St Petersburg Times*, 6 November, http://www.sptimes.ru/

Arnold, C. (2008) 'Russia: New "Teddy Bears" Have Overtones of Soviet-Era Youth Groups', *RFE/RL* feature article *RFE/RL* website, 15 February, http://www.rfel.org/

Coalson, R. (2007) 'Russia: Moscow Shifts From "Managed Democracy" To "Manual Control"', *RFE/RL* website, 3 December, http://www.rferl.org/

Furman, D. (2006) 'A Silent Cold War', *Russian in Global Affairs* (online journal), 8 May, http://eng.globalaffairs.ru/ (article originally published in *Nezavisimaia Gazeta*, March 2006)

Harding, L. (2008) 'From Russia with fraud', *The Guardian*, 20 April

Kagarlitsky, B. (2002) 'The Man Without a Face', *The Moscow Times*, 27 August

Khodorkovsky, M. (2004) 'Liberalism in Crisis: What Is to Be Done?', *The Moscow Times*, 1 April

Khodorkovsky, M. (2005a) 'Left Turn', *Vedomosti*, 1 August

Khodorkovsky, M. (2005b) 'Left Turn-2', *Kommersant*, 11 November

Kommersant (2007) '2/3 Russians Back Up the Third Term Idea', *Kommersant*, 18 April. Available on the *Kommersant* website, http://www.kommersant.com/

Krainova, N. (2007) 'Kasyanov Promises Homes and Health Care', *The Moscow Times*, 4 June

Levada-Tsentr (2007a) '*Rol' B. El'tsina v otsenkakh rossiian*', *Levada-Centre* website, 1 February, http://www.levada.ru/

Levada-Tsentr (2007b) '*Sil'nye i slabye storony: V. Putin, D. Medvedev, S. Ivanov*', *Levada-Centre* website, 20 February, http://www.levada.ru/

Medvedev, D. (2007) 'Speech at the World Economic Forum', 27 January

Medvedev, D. (2008) 'Speech at the V Krasnoyarsk Economic Forum', Medvedev website, 15 February, http://www.medvedev2008.ru/

Mite, V. (2007) 'Estonia: Attacks Seen As First Case Of "Cyberwar"', 20 May, *RFERL* website, http://www.rferl.org/

Mosnews (2006) 'Russian Leader Vows to Ensure Smooth handover of Power in 2008', 13 May, *Mosnews.com* website, http://www.mosnews.com

Pew Global Attitudes Project (2006) 'Russia's Weakened Democratic Embrace. Prosperity Tops Political Reform', 1 May, *Pew Research Center* website, http://pewglobal.org/

Pew Research Center (2006) 'Russia's Weakened Democratic Embrace', *Pew Global Attitudes Project*, 1 May, http://pewglobal.org/

Politkovskaya, A. (2004) *Putin's Russia*, London: The Harvill Press, 269–71 (trans: Arch Tait)

Putin, V. (2007) 'Live with President Vladimir Putin – Hot line (excerpts)', 18 October, Kremlin website, http://www.kremlin.ru/

Putin, V. (2008) 'Transcript of annual Big Press Conference', Kremlin website, 14 February, http://www.kremlin.ru/

Stengel, R. (2007) 'Person of the Year 2007. Choosing Order Before Freedom', *Time Magazine*, 19 December, http://www.time.com/

Whitmore, B. (2007) 'RFE/RL: Russians Skeptical About Elections, Hopeful For Future', *RFE/RL* website feature article, http://www.rferl/org/

Wilson, A. (2005) *Virtual Democracy: Faking Democracy in the Post-Soviet World*, New Haven, CT: Yale University Press

Index

Page numbers in **bold** denote a major section/chapter devoted to subject
Page numbers in *italics* denote a major box section